BPP Professional Education
Law
Library & Information Servic

ADVOCACY AND HUMAN RIGHTS: USING THE CONVENTION IN COURTS AND TRIBUNALS

Cavendish

BPP Law School

015462

ADVOCACY AND HUMAN RIGHTS: USING THE CONVENTION IN COURTS AND TRIBUNALS

Philip Plowden, BA, LLM
Barrister, Solicitor, Principal Lecturer, School of Law,
University of Northumbria
and
Kevin Kerrigan, LLB
Solicitor, Principal Lecturer, School of Law,
University of Northumbria

Cavendish
Publishing
Limited

London • Sydney • Portland, Oregon

First published in Great Britain 2002 by
Cavendish Publishing Limited, The Glass House,
Wharton Street, London WC1X 9PX, United Kingdom
Telephone: + 44 (0)20 7278 8000   Facsimile: + 44 (0)20 7278 8080
Email: info@cavendishpublishing.com
Website: www.cavendishpublishing.com

Published in the United States by Cavendish Publishing
c/o International Specialized Book Services,
5824 NE Hassalo Street, Portland,
Oregon 97213-3644, USA

Published in Australia by Cavendish Publishing (Australia) Pty Ltd
45 Beach Street, Coogee, NSW 2034, Australia
Telephone: + 61 (2)9664 0909   Facsimile: + 61 (2)9664 5420
Email: info@cavendishpublishing.com.au
Website: www.cavendishpublishing.com.au

© Plowden, P and Kerrigan, K   2002
Reprinted   2004

All rights reserved. No part of this publication may be reproduced, stored in a
retrieval system, or transmitted, in any form or by any means, electronic, mechanical,
photocopying, recording, scanning or otherwise, without the prior permission in
writing of Cavendish Publishing Limited, or as expressly permitted by law, or under
the terms agreed with the appropriate reprographics rights organisation. Enquiries
concerning reproduction outside the scope of the above should be sent to the
Rights Department, Cavendish Publishing Limited, at the address above.

You must not circulate this book in any other binding or cover
and you must impose the same condition on any acquirer.

British Library Cataloguing in Publication Data
Plowden, Philip
Advocacy and human rights: using the Convention in courts and tribunals
1 Great Britain – Human Rights Act 1998 2 Human Rights – Great Britain
I Title II Kerrigan, Kevin
342.4'1'085

ISBN 185941 690 X

Library of Congress Cataloguing in Publication Data
Data available

3 5 7 9 10 8 6 4 2

Printed and bound in Great Britain

For Caroline, Mollie and Conor, whose patience knows no bounds.
Kevin

For Penny and Benet, and for my colleagues at Milburn House Chambers,
for putting up with this.
Philip

FOREWORD

When the Judicial Studies Board, in parallel with its counterparts in Scotland and Northern Ireland, set about preparing the judiciary of England and Wales for the coming into force of the Human Rights Act in October 2000, it was acutely aware that the new system of rights was going to be only as good as the courts that administered it. The seminars, some of which involved judges of the European Court of Human Rights and all of which were packed with information and case studies, were rated a success. But at all of them – and I chaired over 30 – the discussion turned to the help that the judiciary were going to need from the practising profession.

At that stage we did not know what to expect. Courses were being run for barristers and solicitors. They were optional, but the DPP made it known that he would not brief chambers that had not had full training in the Act and Convention, and the Bar Mutual then made it known that it would not insure barristers who had not been trained. At the same time, counsel were testing out the courts with proleptic human rights submissions and, perhaps too often for comfort, getting a dusty answer.

Since 2 October 2000, the floodgates have not opened, but we have very clearly entered a new era. Human rights are no longer a discrete academic topic but a set of values which infuse every corner of the law. That, however, is not to say that they change everything. Not only is unambiguous primary legislation impervious to them; there is much which common law or statutory provision already handles compatibly with – and sometimes ahead of – the standards of the Convention.

For solicitors and barristers, the new system therefore poses a mass of problems. The overarching one is whether an apparently viable human rights point is going to bring the case home or get it shot down in flames. What is new is not the problem itself but its scale and implications. To the age-old problem of whether to back up a good point with weaker points or whether to take a point that may backfire, the Human Rights Act adds one of a different dimension: is it practical or wise to take the court down a Convention path to a destination to which, at least on a good day, domestic law also leads?

There is no simple answer to this. Something must depend on the disposition of your court. But much more depends on a complex exercise, on which the courts equally are embarked, of dovetailing domestic and Convention law into a structure of which the final form is not known. For advocates and those preparing the cases they present, there are going as always to be some bad days in court and, by way of compensation, some triumphant ones. But what matters above all is that there should not be, and should not appear to be, try-ons. Once a court gets the message that human rights points are being dropped in as make-weights or fallen back on for want of a decent case, not only the unwise advocate but the development of human rights law is going to be the loser.

That is the reason, among many others, why this book is an important and welcome arrival in an already large field. It goes to the heartlands of human rights jurisprudence: the courts where issues are thrashed out. If that process is not handled well, both by lawyers and by judges, the whole human rights enterprise begins to falter. Here are chapters which do not simply track the Convention article by article but which plot the intellectual and forensic processes by which issues are debated and decided. Here are sources of law disposed not according to some theoretical pattern but in relation to a jobbing lawyer's needs and tasks. It is a book which needed to be written and for which judges as well as practitioners are going to be grateful. Its authors deserve our thanks.

Stephen Sedley
Royal Courts of Justice
December 2001

PREFACE

The Human Rights Act came into force, with a great fanfare of publicity, on 2 October 2000. In England at least, it was clearly one of the most significant pieces of constitutional change since the accession of the European Communities Act 1972, and possibly since the Parliament Acts. The Act introduces a new rights-based culture into the traditional framework of British constitutional law, and in turn it presents advocates, who must now couch arguments in terms of that new framework, with huge challenges in ensuring that they are able to present material to the court in an effective and persuasive way.

Of course, along with the Human Rights Act came a plethora of publications. Many of them were extremely thorough. Often the books were thought-provoking. All of them, however, were necessarily speculative. The books could outline the framework of the Human Rights Act, but they could only guess at how the courts would interpret that legislation. Thus, the Human Rights Act required domestic courts to apply the European Convention to statutory interpretation. The Act created a new tortious act, namely that a public authority or a body exercising functions of a public nature, had acted in such a way as to breach an individual's human rights. But how should a document of international law, which imposed obligations and responsibilities upon the State, be applied in a domestic law context? What were the full implications of the definition of the courts themselves as public authorities for the purposes of the Act under s 6(3)? Would the Act have, in the jargon of the day, 'horizontal' effect so that it would apply as between private individuals, just as it would between public authorities and the individual? Would declarations of incompatibility be as rare as the Lord Chancellor had predicted during the passage of the Bill through Parliament, or would the courts take a conservative approach to the apparently wide-ranging power to 'read down' legislation so as to ensure its Convention-compliance?

While the authors of past books have been able to indicate the potential approaches of the courts, they were understandably unable to predict how the Human Rights Act would develop. Clearly, they were not in a position to give clear guidance to those who would be advancing human rights arguments in the domestic courts and tribunals as to how best to present the material so as to ensure that this new strand of domestic law was applied appropriately and effectively by the courts concerned.

In this book, with an increasing mass of domestic human rights case law to hand, we have the huge advantage of being able to start to assess the approaches of the domestic courts and tribunals, and to suggest to advocates at all levels of court how best to develop Human Rights Act arguments. It is our hope that this book, drawing as it does on the important early case law on the Human Rights Act, will be able to provide advocates with guidance drawn from the *dicta* in the English (and in many cases, the Scottish) courts.

However, this is not simply a book based on hindsight. The past two years have given rise to a number of surprising decisions. Few advocates would have anticipated that the Consumer Credit Act would give rise to one of the first declarations of incompatibility under the Act. Few would have anticipated the sheer range of challenges that have been brought – from prisoners' rights to vote, to the right to an exhumation from a cemetery, from liability for chancel repairs to access to vocational training. Some challenges have been well trailed; it comes as no surprise to find that case law has developed in the criminal context on compelled questioning, on so called 'reverse onus' provisions, and on entrapment (among many other areas), or that the courts have revisited both Mental Health Act and Children Act provisions to ensure Convention-compliance. Nor has it come as a surprise to find the courts developing a right to privacy, although no doubt extensive further litigation will follow to test the limits of that new right.

However, in all these cases, in addition to assessing whether a breach of the Convention is made out in its new domestic law context, the courts have been developing the underlying jurisprudence which indicates to lawyers how the Human Rights Act is to be approached. This is not simply the familiar shot across the bows of those lawyers who are seen to be in some way jumping on a human rights bandwagon – although there have been enough of those judicial warnings, and they are noted and discussed in Chapter 1, since advocates clearly cannot ignore these indications of judicial concern – but it includes the developing domestic case law on how the interpretative obligation under s 3 of the Human Rights Act should be applied, on the meaning of the s 2 duty to 'take account' of the existing Strasbourg jurisprudence, on the appropriate appellate route to be taken where a declaration of incompatibility is sought, and on the vexed issue of the extent to which the Human Rights Act has full or partial retrospectivity.

All of these are clearly key issues for advocates, and we are able therefore to take advantage of the growing body of case law to suggest ways in which advocates can build on this case law to develop human rights arguments in an effective way before domestic courts and tribunals.

Our focus throughout this book is on the effective use of the Human Rights Act. We respect the many judicial comments that deprecate a casual reference to 'my client's human rights' as a throw-away point, but we suggest that where human rights points are identified clearly to the court, where their relevance is clearly explained, and where the court is then provided with a structured argument which indicates how the Human Rights Act should be applied by the court, the courts will understandably be more ready to recognise the novel duty to develop existing legal principles and practices in a manner that protects the human rights of clients.

The focus of the initial chapters of the book is on the core principles of the Human Rights Act and the Convention itself. In Chapter 1 we consider briefly the judicial context of the Human Rights Act, along with the contents of the Convention itself, and the principles of law that arise from the Convention.

Chapter 2 addresses how advocates can best identify human rights issues for the courts. In particular, we consider the issue of who is a public authority for the purposes of the Act, and the implications of the 'public functions' test in s 6(3). The chapter also considers the complex issue of the circumstances in which the Act has retrospective effect, as well as briefly considering the implications of s 7 of the Act and the issue of victim status. Finally, the chapter provides practical guidance as to when and how human rights arguments should be advanced in courts and tribunals, looking in particular at pleadings, skeleton arguments and speeches.

Chapter 3 looks in detail at the crucial – and related – issues of the margin of appreciation doctrine and of proportionality. We suggest that, notwithstanding a slightly confusing tendency in the domestic courts to refer to the margin of appreciation, this doctrine is an international law doctrine, and comments in the House of Lords and Court of Appeal have made clear that it is not applicable in the domestic law context of the Human Rights Act. However, we also identify and discuss the developing case law which indicates that there will be a discretionary area of judgment accorded to elected bodies by the domestic courts, and we go on to consider how this discretion relates to the issue of proportionality. Finally, the chapter looks at the doctrine of proportionality, and at how advocates can properly apply and develop this principle in arguments in the courts, and in particular when relying upon proportionality as a ground for judicial review of the decisions of public authorities.

Chapter 4 deals with two key interpretation issues. First, it examines the obligation under s 2 of the Act to take into account Strasbourg case law, and considers the effect on the domestic doctrine of precedent. Secondly, it addresses the new interpretative obligation under s 3 of the Act and the extent of this duty for courts and tribunals. Detailed guidance is provided as to different approaches to statutory interpretation and what aids to interpretation can be used by advocates.

Chapters 5 and 6 look briefly and in turn at incompatible legislation and at the powers and duties of courts. In the first of the chapters, we focus on how advocates can best address arguments which concern the alleged incompatibility of legislation and the effect of incompatibility on the enforcements of legislation. We suggest a structured approach to arguments on these issues. The chapter then turns to consider declarations of incompatibility and their effect, as well as the issues for advocates in drafting proposed declarations for the court. In Chapter 6 we address the duties and powers of the court itself, and consider both the issues of 'horizontal effect' (the applicability of the Act as between private individuals) and the extent of the positive obligation on the court as a public authority to provide protection for Convention rights. The chapter considers the extent of the remedies that the court can offer and the issues of costs arising from Human Rights Act-based arguments.

In all of these chapters our focus is on how the developing principles that underlie the application of the Human Rights Act can be developed effectively by advocates in legal argument. In Chapters 7 and 8 we look specifically at the criminal context, and at the particular challenges for advocates in developing human rights arguments in this area. We note the significant decisions of the higher courts – and in particular the further development of the principles first elucidated by the House of Lords in *Kebilene* in the later judgments in *R v A* (on the prohibition on cross-examination in rape cases as to prior sexual contact) and *Lambert* (on the 'reverse onus' provisions of the Misuse of Drugs Act and the issue of retrospectivity in criminal appeals) – but also the apparent underlying divergence between Strasbourg approaches (particularly in relation to the Art 6(2) presumption of innocence) and the developing case law of the domestic courts, in cases such as *Brown v Stott*. Chapter 7 covers pre-trial issues, such as legal aid, bail and disclosure, and also considers the developing domestic application of the Strasbourg principle that 'criminal charge' must be given an 'autonomous' meaning. Chapter 8 looks in detail at arguments arising from the national and international case law on points of evidence, on the trial process, on sentencing and on appeals.

Chapter 9 turns to consider the application of the general Human Rights Act principles in the context of civil proceedings generally, and looks in particular at mechanisms for introducing human rights arguments in civil cases. We consider the issue of when a civil right is in issue for the purposes of Art 6, and at what stage there can be said to be a determination of that right. We also address the difficult issue of the curative powers of review by courts of 'full jurisdiction' over lower tribunals that may themselves breach the requirements of Art 6.

In all chapters of the book, our focus is on the practical use of the Human Rights Act. Our aim is to provide guidance and application as to how the Act can and should be used. This book seeks to assist all advocates, whether making or resisting human rights applications, to use the Act creatively, intelligently and responsibly. We have tried to avoid a book which is simply a series of 'How to ...' lists. At times the book is highly detailed, as we try to identify coherent principles from both the national and international courts. But throughout we have tried to ensure that the material is accessible and accurate.

We write conscious of the fact that there are a large number of significant cases that have yet to be argued. The House of Lords decision in *Lambert* will not, we can safely predict, be the final word on the issue of the retrospectivity of the Human Rights Act. The sudden, and surprising, series of decisions that take a narrow view of the meaning of the term 'public authority', and in particular, the meaning of 'functions of a public nature' awaits explication from the House of Lords. The apparent head on conflict between domestic courts and Strasbourg on issues such as compelled questioning and entrapment will no doubt need to be explored before the Strasbourg court. However, our purpose is draw on the clear guidance that we have from the domestic courts in relation to the majority of the areas of the Human Rights Act and to enable all advocates to use the Human Rights Act with confidence in front of all courts and tribunals so that the domestic law can be developed in a coherent and creative manner which recognises the full potential of the Human Rights Act to meet the original aspirations of its supporters.

In the words of Lord Steyn in *Brown v Stott*:

[A]s a European nation [the Convention] represents our Bill of Rights. We must be guided by it.

We hope that this book will assist all lawyers in helping the courts to develop our Bill of Rights so that it becomes an integral and respected element of our domestic law.

We should record our debt of thanks to Cavendish Publishing, but in particular to our editor Jon Lloyd for his work on this book and for his patience in the face of our constant requests to add new material to reflect new and interesting human rights case law. Our hope is that the book is up to date as of the beginning of November 2001.

Philip Plowden
Kevin Kerrigan
November 2001

CONTENTS

TABLE OF CASES

TABLE OF STATUTES

TABLE OF STATUTORY INSTRUMENTS

TABLE OF INTERNATIONAL INSTRUMENTS

International legislation

CHAPTER 1

THE BASICS

1.1 INTRODUCTION

This chapter fulfils two functions. Its main purpose is to remind the reader of the different approach towards human rights within the European Convention on Human Rights, compared with the traditional liberty-based approach English advocates have been used to. It highlights the different language and principles inherent in Convention jurisprudence and the consequential adjustments that have to be made to the structure of decision-making in courts and tribunals since the implementation of the Human Rights Act 1998. First, however, we outline some of the early judicial comments regarding the Act and the Convention that have emerged during the first year of its operation. This provides an insight into how amenable the courts will be to creative use of the new legislation and, just as important, assists advocates to ascertain the limits of what is considered reasonable use of Convention rights arguments. As with all new laws touching on fundamental relationships such as that between the citizen and the state, and particularly with the Human Rights Act, it is important to grasp the developing judicial consciousness in respect of it. This enables the advocate to make the difficult choices about which arguments are worthwhile running and which should be left in the seminar room.

1.2 THE IMPORTANCE OF THE CONVENTION IN DOMESTIC LAW

All members of the judiciary have been trained as to the implications of the Human Rights Act for their decision-making and have been left under no illusions as to its potential to change the status quo in terms of the way the legal system operates and state power is exercised. It is clear that the Act represents, at least in theory, a significant expansion of judicial power and a shift in emphasis from a liberty-based to a rights-based system. This book does not intend to provide a general survey of the impact of the Act[1] but it is

---

1   There are a number of excellent books available. See any of the following: Grosz, Beatson and Duffy, *Human Rights, the 1998 Act and the European Convention* (London: Sweet & Maxwell, 2000); Lester and Pannick, *Human Rights Law and Practice* (London: Butterworths, 1999), hereafter 'Lester and Pannick'; Clayton and Tomlinson, *The Law of Human Rights* (Oxford: Oxford University Press, 2000), hereafter 'Clayton'. There are also some excellent practitioner texts available such as Emmerson and [cont]

clear that the new rules for interpreting legislation and the new duties on public authorities, including the courts, amount to a milestone for the constitution that will have a major impact on the way the legal system operates over a long period.[2]

The importance placed on the Human Rights Act by the government in the White Paper 'Rights Brought Home'[3] would suggest that the Act is intended to have a far-reaching effect. The radical nature of the reform has not gone unnoticed by the leading judicial minds:

> The Convention fulfils the function of a Bill of Rights in our legal system. There is general agreement that the Human Rights Act 1998 is a constitutional measure. [*Per* Lord Steyn in *Turkington v Times Newspapers*.][4]

This general statement is valuable for advocates seeking to persuade courts and tribunals that they should accept the Human Rights Act is a radical measure and use it creatively to provide remedies where none previously existed.

This is reinforced by the following important statement in the first House of Lords decision to consider the Human Rights Act in detail:

> It is now plain that the incorporation of the European Convention on Human Rights into our domestic law will subject the entire legal system to a fundamental process of review and, where necessary, reform by the judiciary. [*Per* Lord Hope of Craighead, *R v DPP ex p Kebilene*.][5]

The focus on review and reform indicates that the judiciary may use the Act as a springboard for active manipulation of the legal process in ways that have not been anticipated.

Extra-judicially there have been numerous statements of the significance of the Act such as the following from Sir Stephen Sedley:

> ... I am concerned that human rights should be regarded not as a fifth wheel on the wagon, but as – what Parliament clearly intends – a new dimension of our legal system. If they are to achieve this status they have to become part of family law, an aspect of tort law, an integral element of property and taxation

---

1 [cont] Simor, *Human Rights Practice* (London: Sweet & Maxwell, 2000, loose-leaf); Starmer, *European Human Rights Law* (London: Legal Action Group, 1999), hereafter 'Starmer'; and Wadham and Mounfield, *Guide to the Human Rights Act* (London: Blackstones, 2000), hereafter 'Wadham'.

2 For a discussion of the constitutional implications of the Act see Feldman, D: 'The Human Rights Act 1998 and constitutional principles' (1999) 19 Legal Studies 165.

3 London HMSO, Cmnd 3782, 1997. See in particular the preface by the Prime Minister: 'We are committed to a comprehensive programme of constitutional reform. We believe it is right to increase individual rights, to decentralise power, to open up government and to reform Parliament ... The Bill marks a major step forward in the achievement of our programme of reform.'

4 *McCartan Turkington Breen (A Firm) v Times Newspapers Ltd* [2000] 4 All ER 913, p 928.

5 [2000] 2 AC 326.

law, a new way of seeing much of criminal law, a fulcrum for the law of evidence, a filter through which the whole law of procedure passes – a new mode, in short, of thinking about law and practising it.[6]

This holistic view of the Human Rights Act underlines the pervasive nature of the Convention and appears to encourage advocates to be pro-active in seeking to mould the legal system in a Convention-compliant manner. This is reinforced as follows:

> So I don't believe that on or after 2nd October it's going to be business as usual in our courts. Whether instead we enter a new world or simply rearrange the furniture in the one we now inhabit is going to be up to us – us the judges and you the lawyers – in roughly equal proportions.[7]

This does not mean that the courts should or will ignore the common law. One of the effects of the Human Rights Act might be a greater focus on the protection for human rights offered by the common law. This is perhaps inevitable given that the courts will be obliged to measure the common law protection against that offered by the Convention. There is already an indication that the common law will be moulded so as to ensure protection for Convention rights.[8] Moreover, some judges are intent on ensuring that the importance of the common law as a source of fundamental rights is not overshadowed by the incorporation of the Convention:

> First, while this case has arisen in a jurisdiction where the European Convention for the Protection of Human Rights and Fundamental Freedoms applies, and while the case is one in which the Convention and the common law produce the same result, it is of great importance, in my opinion, that the common law by itself is being recognised as a sufficient source of the fundamental right to confidential communication with a legal adviser for the purpose of obtaining legal advice. Thus the decision may prove to be in point in common law jurisdictions not affected by the Convention. Rights similar to those in the Convention are of course to be found in constitutional documents and other formal affirmations of rights elsewhere. The truth is, I think, that some rights are inherent and fundamental to democratic civilised society. Conventions, constitutions, bills of rights and the like respond by recognising rather than creating them.
>
> To essay any list of these fundamental, perhaps ultimately universal, rights is far beyond anything required for the purpose of deciding the present case. It is enough to take the three identified by Lord Bingham: in his words, access to a court; access to legal advice; and the right to communicate confidentially with a legal adviser under the seal of legal professional privilege. As he says authoritatively from the woolsack, such rights may be curtailed only by clear and express words, and then only to the extent reasonably necessary to meet

---

6 'Human rights – a new world or business as usual?' (2000) Northumbria Law Press, p 16.

7 *Ibid.*

8 *Douglas v Hello!* [2001] 2 WLR 992.

the ends which justify the curtailment. The point that I am emphasising is that the common law goes so deep.[9]

Issues for advocates: the importance of the Convention

Advocates attempting to utilise the Human Rights Act may encounter some reluctance from judges and tribunal chairs. The following principles seem to us to show that no decision-maker can afford to ignore the Act or the Convention it introduces:

- The Human Rights Act is a constitutional measure – the equivalent of a United Kingdom Bill of Rights

- The government intended the Act to lead to a radical shift from previous practice

- It authorises fundamental review and reform of the legal system by the judiciary

- It pervades all areas of law and procedure

1.2.1 The need to identify human rights issues for the court

There is nothing in the Human Rights Act to suggest that there is a presumption that human rights points arise. Advocates will need to identify human rights issues if they wish to trigger consideration of Convention rights. The courts have made clear that the responsibility lies with the parties to decide when it is appropriate to raise human rights arguments. As we will see, courts and tribunals are themselves bound to act compatibly with the Convention rights, although if they are not aware of the potential arguments they will be unable to address them and the appeal courts may be reluctant to permit parties to raise such issues for the first time on appeal when they could have been raised at first instance.

1.2.2 Approach with caution

The main purpose of this book is to assist those who appear in courts and tribunals in identifying and presenting coherent arguments as to the Human Rights Act and the Convention it incorporates. It is hoped that it will encourage effective submissions regarding human rights issues where appropriate. However, it is important to recognise at this early stage that if the Human Rights Act is misused it will unnecessarily confuse the issues in the

---

9   Lord Cooke in *R (on the Application of Daly) v Secretary of State for the Home Department* [2001] UKHL 26, [2001] 2 WLR 1622 at paras 30–31. For a thorough analysis of the role of the common law in the protection of fundamental rights see TRS Allan, *Law, Liberty and Justice* (Oxford: Clarendon, 1993), especially Chapters 2, 3 and 4.

case, harm the case being advanced and cultivate an attitude of scepticism or worse, hostility, among the judiciary, which could damage the development of domestic human rights jurisprudence.

One of the skills of the advocate is knowing when human rights submissions will assist the case and when they will hinder. This section is not intended in any way to inhibit the advocate from making properly formulated submissions. Our view is that it is only by advocates being creative enough and bold enough to push the boundaries that our courts will come to explore the full potential of European Convention values. However, as a matter of practical reality advocates must recognise the responsibility they have and exercise a degree of caution when advancing their case. The first broadside came from Lord Woolf when he was Master of the Rolls in *Daniels v Walker*:[10]

> With the greatest respect to the submissions contained in that skeleton argument ... I consider that the initial approach of ... not relying on Art 6 was the correct approach. Article 6 has no possible relevance to this appeal. Quite apart from the fact that the Act is not in force, if the court is not going to be taken down blind alleys it is essential that counsel, and those who instruct counsel, take a responsible attitude as to when it is right to raise a Human Rights Act point. ... It would be unfortunate if case management decisions in this jurisdiction involved the need to refer to the learning of the European Court on Human Rights in order for them to be resolved. In my judgment, cases such as this, do not require any consideration of human rights issues, certainly issues under Art 6. It would be highly undesirable if the consideration of those issues were made more complex by the injection into them of Art 6 style arguments. I hope that judges will be robust in resisting any attempt to introduce those arguments ... When the 1998 Act becomes law, counsel will need to show self-restraint if it is not to be discredited.

Counsel had argued that the refusal of a second expert in a personal injury case prevented the appellant from securing a fair trial under Article 6 of the Convention by barring the whole or a fundamental part of the defendant's case. The arguments and case law were set out in an additional skeleton argument, which led to a supplementary skeleton on behalf of the respondent. The court criticised the unnecessary time and expense that the arguments had caused, given that they added nothing to the existing CPR framework in light of the overriding objective to deal with cases justly.[11]

The sentiments of the then Master of the Rolls were echoed in the context of the family courts in *Re L (A Child) (Contact: Domestic Violence) and Other Appeals*:[12]

---

10   [2000] 1 WLR 1382, *per* Lord Woolf, p 1386.

11   Counsel was perhaps optimistic in thinking that Lord Woolf, the architect of the CPR, might be amenable to arguments that their operation breached his client's Convention rights.

12   [2000] 4 All ER 609, *per* Thorpe LJ, p 633.

The addition of European Court of Human Rights' arguments to bolster an almost impossible appeal on the facts may foreshadow a fashion. The judgment of Lord Woolf MR in *Daniels v Walker* [2000] 1 WLR 1382 emphasises the need for counsel to exercise responsibility in this area. That stricture must be of equal if not extra application in family cases.

Further criticism of counsel raising unnecessary Convention points emerged in the Commercial Court in the case of *Alliance and Leicester plc v Slayford and Another*:[13]

Again [counsel] has recourse to Art 6 of the Convention and *Darnell's* case. Again I have to say that I find them of no assistance whatever. Indeed it seems to me that the points taken under the 1998 Act and the Convention fall within the vice to which Lord Woolf MR drew attention in *Daniels v Walker* [2000] 1 WLR 1382 at 1386. Where the CPR, and in particular the overriding objective, cover the point which a litigant wishes to take, it adds nothing to try to dress up the point as one invoking a right under the Convention. The court's obligation to deal with cases justly includes an obligation so far as practicable to deal with cases expeditiously and fairly.

It is perhaps somewhat excessive to describe advocates' endeavours to raise human rights points on behalf of clients as a 'vice'. Even if it is accepted that the overriding objective of the CPR includes the obligation to deal with cases fairly surely Art 6 decisions can, in appropriate cases, assist the court in determining what is and is not 'fair'. The negative sentiments expressed by some of the higher judiciary can be seen as an understandable attempt to prevent the courts from being swamped by human rights arguments following the implementation of the Act but advocates ought not to be intimidated into not making strong submissions where this is thought to be appropriate. It would be worthwhile to have a response, though, to the judge who enquires why such points are necessary in light of *Daniels v Walker*.

The Court of Appeal (Criminal Division) was perhaps more likely than any other court to have to deal with Convention rights arguments following 2 October 2000. The decision in *R v Perry*[14] was an early attempt to clamp down on the indiscriminate use of the Convention in criminal cases. The appellant relied on clear breaches of the PACE Code of Practice on identification procedures and went on to assert that there had been breaches of Arts 5 (liberty), 6 (fair trial) and 8 (privacy) of the Convention. In upholding the conviction the Court of Appeal criticised the fact that it was 'inundated with material and a number of authorities to a completely unnecessary degree in what we regard as a comparatively straightforward case'. The court then cited the alleged breaches of the Convention and went on:

The European Convention on Human Rights was promulgated ... following the horrors and the deprivations of human rights which had occurred in the war in various parts of Europe between 1939 and 1945 ... The purpose

---

13 [2001] 1 All ER (Comm) 1, *per* Peter Gibson LJ, pp 11–12.
14 (2000) *The Times*, 28 April.

underlying the Act is to protect citizens from a true abuse of human rights. If, as it seems to us has happened in this case, it is utilised by lawyers to jump on a bandwagon and to attempt to suggest that there has been a breach of the Act or of the Convention when either it is quite plain that there has not or alternatively the matter is amply covered by domestic law, then not only will the lawyers, but the Act itself (which is capable of doing a great deal of good to the citizens of this country) will be brought into disrepute ... This case is a case, which can be and was properly dealt with under s 78 of the Police and Criminal Evidence Act ... In our judgment questions of breaches of the European Convention on Human Rights or the Act should not have formed any part of this appeal ... It is devoutly to be hoped that the court's time will not be utilised in the future in this way.[15]

Much of the commentary and training that preceded the Act sought to encourage human rights 'activism' in the legal profession and the courts. Comments like those set out above are clearly an attempt to inject a dose of judicial common sense and perspective. However, the idea that just because something can be dealt with under domestic law the Convention must be irrelevant, is contrary to the whole spirit of the Human Rights Act. The Court of Appeal in *Perry* comes close to this proposition. Even before the Human Rights Act came into force it was firmly established that the Convention could be relevant in determining the exercise of judicial discretion under s 78 of PACE[16] and that continues to be the case.

A common theme running through the negative sentiments we have mentioned is the desire not to bring the Convention into disrepute. This is a laudable aim and one that is consistent with its new status as a constitutional instrument. However, we very much doubt that mere submissions by lawyers, certainly in the early days of the operation of the Act, can be held responsible for colouring the perception of the Convention. The judiciary can choose which arguments to accept and which to reject. Lawyers will soon learn to recognise which arguments are going to have chances of success and which are doomed to failure. General assertions of the need to be responsible are not particularly helpful in that process. Much better are reasoned judgments which show why a particular submission was flawed.

The caution that has been urged by the senior judiciary should thus be respected but should not be seen as a red light for human rights arguments by advocates. In fact, as will be seen, failure to raise human rights arguments, which can properly be taken, can have bad consequences for the client and for those representing him or her.

Before leaving the cautionary note, it should be emphasised that the Convention is not a panacea for all of society's ills. Some clients will no doubt believe their human rights have been breached through a variety of hardships,

---

15 *Per* Swinton Thomas LJ at paras 47–48.
16 *R v Khan* [1997] AC 558.

which accompany today's sophisticated world. The Convention will often not hold the answer. Lord Bingham put it as follows, although clients may have to be advised in slightly less expressive terms:

> The Convention is concerned with rights and freedoms, which are of real importance in a modern democracy governed by the rule of law. It does not, as is sometimes mistakenly thought, offer relief from 'The heartache and the thousand natural shocks that flesh is heir to'.[17]

1.2.3 Failure to raise human rights arguments – waiver

If there is a valid human rights argument that could have been raised at first instance, what will be the attitude of the appeal courts if the point is taken for the first time on appeal? It could be argued that the alleged victim had waived his or her rights by not insisting on them on the earlier occasion. Waiver arises most often in the context of Art 6 of the Convention, the right to a fair trial. In *Millar v Procurator Fiscal, Elgin*[18] Lord Bingham described waiver as follows:

> In most litigious situations the expression 'waiver' is used to describe a voluntary, informed and unequivocal election by a party not to claim a right or raise an objection which it is open to that party to claim or raise. In the context of entitlement to a fair hearing by an independent and impartial tribunal, such is in my opinion the meaning to be given to the expression.

At first instance the High Court in *Millar*[19] decided that where appellants had been convicted before temporary sheriffs who were subsequently found to be lacking the requisite independence and impartiality for the purposes of Art 6 of the Convention,[20] they had tacitly waived their rights under that Article:

> [25]... Before the Scotland Act 1998 came into force, the position of temporary sheriffs could perhaps be seen as settled and established ... But ... the enactment of the Scotland Act 1998 had radically altered the rights of accused persons, by providing in s 57(2) that the Lord Advocate had no power to do any act ... so far as it was incompatible with any of the Convention rights. They must be deemed in my opinion to have known that ... there were thus entirely new provisions giving accused persons a right to an independent and impartial tribunal ... They must be deemed, in my opinion, to know that there was a new legal landscape, and that there were new, unsettled, issues to be resolved.
>
> [28][T]he deemed knowledge of the new legislation excludes any contention that the law could be assumed to be as it previously was ... There was

---

17 Per Lord Bingham in *Brown v Stott* (also known as *Brown v Procurator Fiscal (Dunfermline)*) [2001] 2 WLR 817 (PC).

18 [2001] UKPC D4 (PC); (2001) *The Times*, 27 July.

19 [2000] UKHRR 776, High Court of Justiciary.

20 *Starrs v Ruxton* 2000 SLT 42. See further Chapter 7.

nothing which made it 'reasonable' to refrain from taking the point, other than waiver: a decision that it would not be in the clients' interest to take any point in relation to Article 6(1) which the new legislation might make arguable. Simply upon the basis of deemed knowledge of the law, I consider that such a decision was implicit in the agents' silence when these cases came before the temporary sheriffs, and that there was tacit waiver.[21]

Lord Bingham in the Privy Council disagreed:

It was of course for the agents of the accused to decide what points to make on behalf of their clients (proposition (11)) and they could have seen advantages in proceeding before temporary sheriffs (proposition (12)). But the point is whether the agents on behalf of the accused made a voluntary, informed and unequivocal election not to claim trial before an independent and impartial tribunal and not to object to the respective temporary sheriffs as a tribunal not meeting the requirements of Article 6(1). They could only have done this if they appreciated, or must be taken to have appreciated, the effect of the eventual decision in *Starrs* or the real possibility of a decision to that or similar effect. In my regretful conclusion there is no evidence, and nothing in the judicial decisions before the Board, which would entitle us to find that the accused or their agents appreciated this, nor is the Board entitled to infer that they must have done. A finding or inference to the opposite effect is in my view very much more compelling. I conclude, without enthusiasm, that the finding of tacit waiver cannot be supported.[22]

Despite the overturning of the High Court decision, it is still clear that if an advocate fails to take a point that s/he knows is arguable, there is a real risk of the failure amounting to tacit waiver of the right in question. Although advocates will not be fixed with deemed knowledge, they will be at risk if they fail to act on actual knowledge.[23] It provides a strong counterbalance to the restraining words of Lord Woolf in *Daniels v Walker*.

1.2.3.1 Waiver and the court

It might be thought that if it is not reasonable for an advocate to fail to take a point regarding human rights, then the same would apply to the court, particularly given its status as a public authority under the Human Rights Act. This would be particularly the case in respect of lack of independence or

---

21 *Per* Lord Prosser. Similar comments were made in the case of *Clancy v Caird* 2000 SLT 546.

22 *Brown v Stott* (also known as *Brown v Procurator Fiscal (Dunfermline)*) [2001] 2 WLR 817 (PC), para 36.

23 The English courts are already alive to the limitations that may be imposed by the waiver concept. See *Austin Hall Building Ltd v Buckland Securities Ltd* [2001] BLR 272 (Technology and Construction Court) at paras 52–55 (regarding access to a court). See also *Secretary of State for Trade and Industry v Eastaway and Others (No 2)* [2001] 1 BCLC 653 (regarding delay).

impartiality. However, the judicial approach so far is that the courts have no duty to point out Convention arguments that could be raised:

> [26] This deemed knowledge must also be attributed to temporary sheriffs and the prosecution. But I see no obligation upon them to inform defence agents of these known changes in the law, as if they were possibly unknown facts ...[24]

It should be noted that the Privy Council departed from the 'deemed knowledge' approach in the appeal. It is interesting that the High Court of Justiciary made no reference to the duty under s 6 of the Human Rights Act on the court itself to act compatibly with the Convention. If a judge continued to sit after s/he knew that his or her position was likely to fall foul of the Art 6 fairness provisions, it is difficult to see that the court is acting compatibly with the Convention rights of those who appear before it, whether or not any particular objection is raised by the parties.

1.2.4 Helping the court

There is a more general point to be made about the respective roles of advocates and the courts. Although courts and tribunals have a duty as public authorities to act compatibly with the Convention, they are much more likely to give considered rulings relating to Convention rights if they are fully addressed by the advocates that appear before them. This is particularly important in the early years of the operation of the Act as courts and tribunals are often not sufficiently familiar with Convention law to be able to spot issues for themselves. Early identification of Convention issues will assist the court and enable a full and informed discussion to take place at the hearing.

This point is emphasised by the case of *Barclays Bank v Ellis*[25] where Schiemann LJ voiced the following legitimate concerns:

> At the last minute and without any warning, either to his opponent or to the court, [counsel] thought it appropriate to make reference to Art 6 of the European Convention on Human Rights. He was asked by the court whether he wished to develop his submissions by reference to any case law. He declined. Neither he nor his opponent, who had been caught entirely by surprise by this particular line of argument, furnished any material to the court ... If counsel wish to rely on provisions of the Human Rights Act then it is their duty to have available for the information of the court any material in terms of decisions of the European Court of Human Rights upon which they wish to rely or which will help the court in its adjudication. A mere reference in a case to an article does not help the court or enable the court in any way to do justice to a possible argument. To do an argument justice it needs to be formulated and advanced in a plausible way.

---

24 *Millar* [2000] UKHRR 776.
25 [2000] All ER(D) 1164.

The advocate had obviously thrown in the human rights point as an afterthought and is unlikely to do so again. The lesson offered by Schiemann LJ is that advocates should always have Convention case law to back up any human rights assertions. The throwaway line 'And of course my client's human rights are at stake' is to be avoided at all costs. Although his Lordship referred to decisions of the European Court of Human Rights, it may not always be necessary to refer separately to such decisions as the body of domestic human rights precedent grows. Nevertheless, it should be recognised that, despite the Convention law permeating all aspects of domestic law, it is not routine law. Judges will remain wary of submissions based on Convention rights for some time to come and will understandably require submissions to justify them, spending time and effort considering the arguments and weighing the authorities in the domestic context.

1.2.5 Negligence

Finally, advocates will no doubt be aware of the recent loss of immunity from liability in negligence in respect of advocacy in *Arthur JS Hall v Simons*:

> My Lords, I have now considered all the arguments advanced in *Rondel v Worsley*. In the conditions of today they no longer carry the degree of conviction, which would in my opinion be necessary to sustain the immunity.[26]

A seven member House of Lords unanimously agreed that immunity in civil actions should be removed. They also concluded (4:3) that immunity in criminal cases should also be removed. This affects advocacy in all areas and the Human Rights Act is no exception, although advocates are likely to be afforded some latitude as to what is reasonable conduct of a case, particularly in the early development of the case law.

Issues for advocates: identifying human rights issues for the courts

- Courts have a duty to act compatibly with Convention rights whether the issues are raised by the parties or not, but the first responsibility lies with the advocates to ensure that the court is fully informed of relevant matters.

- Advocates need to adopt a measured, realistic approach towards Convention submissions, respecting and dealing with the legitimate fears the courts have about matters being over-complicated by Convention arguments. Convention submissions ought to elucidate not obfuscate the court's reasoning.

- Advocates should nevertheless be willing to advance argument even in the face of judicial opposition if it promotes a way of looking at the

---

26 [2000] 3 WLR 543, *per* Lord Hoffman.

> dispute which assists their client's case. This is true of advocates seeking to prove a breach of Convention rights and also those seeking to show that Convention rights have been respected.
>
> - Advocates should have case law authorities ready (Strasbourg or domestic) to back up any claims made about the implications of Convention law (see also skeleton arguments, later in this chapter).
> - Advocates should avoid being seen to use claims of a breach of Convention rights merely as an afterthought or in order to bolster an inherently weak case.
> - If an area is already covered by domestic law, advocates should use Convention law in order to reinforce propositions about its interpretation or in order to challenge its compatibility. The best submissions are those which seek to marry a domestic and a Convention law approach to produce an outcome favourable to the client.
> - Advocates should be ready to answer the question, 'What does this all add to the existing domestic approach?'.
> - There is a need to be aware of the risk of waiver if arguable Convention points are not taken. This is a spur to making the point even if it is not well received so as to preserve the point for appeal. It might not be necessary to fully argue the point but simply to bring it to the attention of the court.

1.3 THE CONCEPT OF BALANCE IN THE CONVENTION

The Convention is sometimes seen as a charter for undesirables and an unwarranted rein on the discretion of public bodies to act in the public interest. The judiciary are alive to this perception and have strived to explain that the Convention contains an important element of balance between individuals and between individual rights and collective interests:

> The inspirers of the European Convention ... realised that from time to time the fundamental right of one individual may conflict with the human right of another. Thus the principles of free speech and privacy may collide. They also realised only too well that a single-minded concentration on the pursuit of fundamental rights of individuals to the exclusion of the interests of the wider public might be subversive of the ideal of tolerant European liberal democracies. The fundamental rights of individuals are of supreme importance but those rights are not unlimited: we live in communities of individuals who also have rights ... Subject to a limited number of absolute guarantees, the scheme and structure of the Convention reflects this balanced approach. It differs in material respects from other constitutional systems but

as a European nation it represents our Bill of Rights. We must be guided by it.[27]

This approach is a useful reminder for advocates and courts that merely identifying an interference with a Convention right is insufficient. The court must be satisfied that the interference is unjustified before it finds a breach. Those representing public authorities will utilise the principle to focus the court's attention on the alleged public interest exceptions to the right in question.

1.4 IDENTIFYING CATEGORIES OF RIGHT

The above quotation from Lord Steyn also indicates that there is a form of hierarchy of rights within the Convention. Some rights are absolute whereas others are qualified by public interest exceptions. Some texts also refer to limited rights such as Art 5 (right to liberty) in that there are specific limitations set out in the article itself, but no general public interest exception clause. We prefer to focus only on the absolute/qualified distinction, as interference with limited rights requires similar considerations as for qualified rights.

The consequence of the distinction can be important in that it affects the way the parties to a case must pursue the issues. An absolute right cannot be balanced against the public interest whereas a qualified right can be balanced if certain conditions are met, albeit that the justification must be proved to the satisfaction of the court in each case.

The following categorisation serves as a guide, although there is little consensus as to exact groupings. We have attempted to identify below the major areas of contention in respect of alleged violations.

1.4.1 Absolute rights

1.4.1.1 Article 2 (life)

The right to life is said to be absolute, although there are situations in which force which results in death can be an unwanted by-product of action that is 'absolutely necessary' to protect from unlawful violence, effect an arrest or quell a riot or insurrection. In addition, the death penalty is an express exception to the rule against taking life.[28] There can be no derogation from this right under Art 15 except for lawful acts of war. The focus of dispute

---

27 *Per* Lord Steyn: *Brown v Stott* [2001] 2 WLR 817 (PC), para 49.
28 Article 2(1). However, note that Art 1 of Protocol 6 prohibits the death sentence and its execution except in time of war.

tends to be first, whether the public authority is responsible for the death either through the action of a state agent, such as a police marksman, or through the failure to take steps to avert a risk from a third party.[29]

The more likely area of dispute is whether one of the exceptions is made out and this will include questions such as the absolute necessity test and the control of the operation leading to the use of lethal force.[30] An emerging area is the procedural aspect of Art 2, which requires the state to carry out an effective investigation into deaths.[31]

1.4.1.2 Article 3 (torture, etc)

Once treatment or punishment reaches a minimum threshold, depending on the circumstances of the alleged victim, it engages the article and it cannot be justified. The disputes in respect of these cases tend to be on whether the public authority is responsible for the treatment (either committed by a state agent or through its failure to satisfy its positive obligation to prevent it) and whether it passes the minimum threshold. For a recent example, see *Price v United Kingdom* (2001), where the European Court found a breach of Art 3 due to inadequate care of a disabled prisoner by police and prison authorities despite the absence of any improper intent on the part of the state agents. There is sometimes a further issue as to whether treatment is so severe as to amount to torture. Article 3 cases will not focus on excuses of the public authority such as lack of resources or other public interest issues as they are not relevant to the question of whether there has been a breach. There can be no derogation from this article under Art 15 even in times of war or other public emergency.

1.4.1.3 Article 4 (slavery, etc)

The first part of this article – the prohibition on slavery – has no qualifications and may not be derogated from. The second part – the prohibition on compulsory work – contains four narrow exceptions. Thus prison work, military service or equivalent, emergency service and normal civic obligations are expressly excluded from the definition of forced labour.

1.4.1.4 Article 7 (retrospective crime)

This is absolute in the sense that there is no justification for imposing retrospective criminality and no derogation is permissible. However, the

---

29 As was unsuccessfully argued in *Osman v United Kingdom* (2000) 29 EHRR 245.

30 See, for example, *McCann v United Kingdom* (1996) 21 EHRR 97, where a violation of Art 2 was found due to inadequate command and control mechanisms in respect of the fatal shooting of three IRA suspects by the SAS in Gibraltar.

31 See *R (on the Application of Wright) v Secretary of State for the Home Department* [2001] EWHC Admin 520; (2001) *Daily Telegraph*, 26 June and *Jordan v United Kingdom* (2001) *The Times*, 18 May.

prohibition does not prevent the punishment of a person whose conduct was criminal according to general principles of law. This is the exception for crimes against civilised norms such as war crimes. Nor does the article prevent developments in the common law.

1.4.1.5 Article 6 (fair trial)

It may seem to be curious to include this article in the absolute rights list. However, the Privy Council has recently stated that the overall right to a fair trial cannot (unless derogated from) be compromised at all even in the public interest and is in this sense absolute.[32] However, this is a good illustration of the difficulty involved in trying to pigeon-hole some of the rights. Although the overall right to a fair trial cannot be compromised, the question of what amounts to a fair trial most certainly can be affected by the court's judgment of what is in the public interest. There are express and implied limitations on the constituent elements of what makes up a fair trial. Thus, for example, according to the Privy Council, the right not to incriminate oneself is an implied right in Art 6 but is subject to implied limitations where the measure adopted is proportionate to a legitimate public interest. It might be thought that this is just another way of saying that the right to a fair trial is a qualified right, but the two approaches are conceptually different. The Privy Council's approach argues that if the limitation applies there is no question of receiving an unfair trial. Rather than saying it is acceptable to take away someone's fair hearing guarantee in certain circumstances, the approach of Art 6 is that the demands of fairness can themselves vary dependent on the circumstances of the case.

1.4.1.6 Article 9 (religion, etc)

This right is absolute in one respect and qualified in another. The absolute aspect is the freedom of thought, conscience and religion, including the right to change one's religion or belief. The idea is that the individual is sovereign over what is inside his or her own mind. The public interest can never be utilised in order to seek to compel people to change their beliefs, punish them for their beliefs or to reveal them to the authorities. Note, though, that this right in its absolute form does not extend to any conduct on the part of the right-holder. It is limited to his or her internal convictions.

1.4.1.7 Article 12 (marry and found a family)

This right is expressed to be in absolute terms in the sense that so long as the right-holder meets the minimum age requirements for marriage, s/he can marry in accordance with the rules of national law. There is no implied right

---

32 See *Brown v Stott* [2001] 2 WLR 817 (PC).

to divorce. However, the European Commission has ruled that it is possible for right-holders to effectively deprive themselves of access to the right by the situation they create for themselves:

> Although the right to found a family is an absolute right in the sense that no restrictions similar to those in para (2) of Art 8 of the Convention are expressly provided for, it does not mean that a person must at all times be given the actual possibility to procreate his descendants. It would seem that the situation of a lawfully convicted person detained in prison in which the applicant finds himself falls under his own responsibility, and that his right to found a family has not otherwise been infringed.[33]

This has been taken further in subsequent cases so that in a recent ruling on a challenge to the unavailability of artificial insemination facilities for a prisoner and his wife the Court of Appeal said that Art 12 was qualified in the same way as Art 8 is qualified. It refused the claim saying that there was no right to artificial insemination for prisoners albeit that in an exceptional case it might be necessary to relax the restrictions imposed by detention in order to ensure a disproportionate interference with the right did not occur.[34]

Whether the right is seen as absolute but self-limiting or as a qualified right, its scope is not extensive. For a start the right to marry is limited to biological men and women and the right to found a family applies only to couples, not single people. It is not even clear if the right to found a family exists independently of the right to marry.

1.4.1.8 Article 1, Protocol 6 (death penalty)

This is an absolute right that cannot be derogated from under Art 15 of the Convention.[35] It prevents a sentence of death being passed or such a sentence being executed. However, there is a saving so that states may pass laws allowing for the death penalty for acts committed during war or when war is imminent. The United Kingdom ratified the Protocol in January 1999 and it forms one of the Convention rights under s 1 and Sched 1 of the Human Rights Act. Despite the long term abolition of the death penalty in the United Kingdom,[36] the article could have some impact in respect of removals to other countries. It goes further than the Convention, which only prevents removal if conditions on death row would be a breach of Art 3. Protocol 6 will prevent removal to any country where the applicant faces the risk of the death penalty or execution.

---

33 *X v United Kingdom* (1975) 2 DR 105.
34 *R (on the Application of Mellor) v Secretary of State for the Home Department* [2001] EWCA Civ 472; [2001] HRLR 38.
35 Article 3, Protocol 6.
36 Murder (Abolition of the Death Penalty) Act 1965.

1.4.2 Qualified rights

All qualified rights may be derogated from under Art 15 in times of war or other public emergency. The main features of the rights and the areas of dispute are as follows.

1.4.2.1 Article 5 (liberty)

Again this is a difficult right to categorise. It does not have any general public interest exceptions but it does have an exhaustive list of situations where it is permissible to detain a person.[37] Initial arguments about this right tend to focus on whether the claimant was indeed detained[38] and, if so, whether the case falls within one of the reasons justifying detention.[39]

There is no explicit requirement for detention to be necessary in a democratic society so the question of proportionality might appear at first sight to be irrelevant. However, the requirement for detention to be in accordance with a 'procedure prescribed by law' and 'lawful' invokes many of the criteria relevant to assessing necessity in the 'proper' qualified rights such as Art 8. In particular it is clear that the law must be adequately accessible and precise[40] and there is also a suggestion that an arrest must be proportionate to the reason for the arrest.[41] It follows that the second major area of dispute tends to focus on the rules leading to the detention and the decision to enforce those rules against the claimant.

There is another facet to Art 5 – that of providing procedural protection for those who have been arrested under the article. This encompasses the right to reasons (Art 5(2)), to bail in criminal proceedings (Art 5(3)), to have the legality of the detention tested speedily by a court including certain due process rights (Art 5(4)) and to a remedy where there has been detention in breach of Art 5 (Art 5(5)).

---

37 See Art 5(1)(a)–(f): following conviction; for compliance with court order or other specific legal obligation; arrest on reasonable suspicion of offending; educational supervision of children; health reasons, including mental disorder; and preventing illegal entry into the country.

38 See *R v Bournewood Community and Mental Health NHS Trust ex p L* [1999] 1 AC 458 for different approaches towards the concept of detention. The case is currently before the European Court of Human Rights.

39 See, for example, the case of *Re K (A Child) (Secure Accommodation Order: Right to Liberty)* [2001] 2 WLR 1141 (also known as *W BC v AK* and *W BC v DK*) where the dispute was about whether the detention fell within Art 5(1)(d) which justifies the detention of minors for educational supervision.

40 *Steel v United Kingdom* (1999) 28 EHRR 603.

41 See Harris, O'Boyle and Warbrick, *Law of the European Convention on Human Rights*, 1995, Butterworths, p 106 and the authority cited therein.

1.4.2.2 Article 8 (private life, etc)

This is the first of the 'proper' qualified rights in that this right is explicitly made subject to competing public interests and it is in principle permissible to abrogate the right of the individual in order to promote the interests of the democratic society. It protects a bundle of interests by requiring respect for private life, family life, home and correspondence. It is clear that the right is very wide in its scope. The court is asked to ascertain first whether or not the measure complained of amounts to an interference with the right. If it does not then the claimant has not surmounted the initial hurdle and there is no need for further inquiry. Thus, for example, if a court finds that a claimant's family is able to travel with him to the country to which he will be removed, then the actions of the immigration authorities will not interfere with the right to family life.[42]

If an interference is established it must be justified on its own facts. This will involve the court analysing whether it is 'in accordance with law' (that is, does it arise from a law that is sufficiently precise and accessible?),[43] whether it is for a potentially legitimate reason (the list is in Art 8(2) and includes national security, economic well being, prevention of disorder or crime, protection of health or morals and the broad 'protection of the rights and freedoms of others')[44] and last but not least whether it is necessary in a democratic society. This may seem to be a strange concept for an unelected court to be determining but, as we will see below, a number of legal principles have emerged from the phrase including the requirement for the interference to be proportionate so that the ends (the achievement of the public interest exception) properly justifies the means (the measure of interference). Cases will vary enormously. In some cases, all issues from whether there is an interference to whether it is necessary will be in dispute. In others it will be possible to reach agreement on some propositions in order to focus attention on the real issue. Thus, the public authority might concede that there was an interference and the claimant might concede that the interference was in accordance with law. This will leave the two issues of legitimate aim and necessity to be resolved.

1.4.2.3 Article 9 (religion, etc)

We have noted above the absolute limb of this article. The qualified limb is the freedom to manifest one's religion or belief in worship, teaching, practice and

---

42 This does not mean that other aspects of Art 8 will not be engaged such as the right to respect for private life such as disruption of relationships.

43 See *Malone v United Kingdom* (1984) 7 EHRR 14 where the tapping of telephones was not in accordance with law as it lacked clear, accessible domestic law authorising the measure and providing safeguards against abuse.

44 The rights and freedoms referred to need not be Convention rights and freedoms. They have included a wide variety of interests including the protection of contractual rights.

observance. This is subject to similar criteria for limiting its exercise as Art 8 except that the categories of legitimate exceptions are narrower: public safety, protection of public order, health or morals and the protection of the rights and freedoms of others. Disputes tend to focus on whether the conduct concerned is a true manifestation of the religion or belief or is merely motivated by the religion or belief. This is not always an easy distinction to draw. For example, preaching one's faith to non-believers is protected,[45] whereas distributing leaflets about one's pacifist beliefs is not.[46] If the conduct is protected by the right, the focus shifts to the state's justification for limiting the manifestation in the particular circumstances of the case.

Note that s 13 of the Human Rights Act requires courts to have particular regard to the importance of this right whenever they determine questions that affect the exercise by a religious organisation of its rights under Art 9. The section was included following concerns expressed by the church about the potential for other rights in the Convention to undermine traditional religious practice. The section is a triumph of imprecision and has not yet, so far as we are aware, made a difference to the outcome of any case.

1.4.2.4 Article 10 (expression)

The first question for the court is whether there has been an interference with the freedom of expression. Note that the article includes the right to receive information and ideas and to impart those information and ideas. It thus protects the audience and the speaker. Public authorities will not have much success in seeking to persuade a court that certain types of speech or expression fall outside the protected categories. It applies to information or ideas that offend, shock or disturb the state or any sector of the population.[47] It includes, for example, material thought to be pornographic,[48] obscene[49] and direct action campaigns such as lying in front of road building machines.[50] However, extreme racist speech or revisionist views such as holocaust denial has little, if any, protection under the article.[51] The 'offensive' nature of the expression will obviously be relevant when it comes to assessing whether any interference is justified. Public authorities thus often concede that there has been an interference and focus on the reasons for restricting the expression. It

---

45 *Kokkinakis v Greece* (1994) 17 EHRR 126.
46 *Arrowsmith v United Kingdom* (1980 19 DR 5. Note, however, that such conduct will often fall within the protection offered by Art 10 in any event.
47 *Handyside v United Kingdom* (1978–79) 1 EHRR 737.
48 *Scherer v Switzerland* (1994) 18 EHRR 276.
49 *Handyside v United Kingdom* (1978–79) 1 EHRR 737.
50 *Steel v United Kingdom* (1999) 28 EHRR 603.
51 See *Lehideux and Isorni v France* (2000) 30 EHRR 665. Note that this is said to be due to the operation of Art 17, the prohibition on abuse of rights.

should also be noted that there seems to be a hierarchy of importance for different types of speech. Political speech will secure the greatest protection followed by journalistic, and artistic/commercial speech.

Once the article is engaged, a similar exercise is performed as for Art 8 to ascertain whether the restriction is justified. Note that there is a specific reference to duties and responsibilities on the right-holder but this will not be relevant unless his or her particular circumstances point to a duty or responsibility in respect of the expression.[52] Again the list of legitimate exceptions is slightly different to Art 8: national security, territorial integrity, public safety, prevention of disorder or crime, protection of health or morals, protection of the rights or others, preventing the disclosure of information received in confidence and maintaining the authority and impartiality of the judiciary. The categories are exhaustive and are narrowly construed. The restriction must also be 'prescribed by law'. This means the same as 'in accordance with law' in Art 8 and in 'accordance with a procedure prescribed by law' in Art 5 that there must be domestic law justifying the interference that is adequately precise and accessible.[53] Finally, the court must be satisfied that the restriction is necessary in a democratic society.

Note that s 12 of the Human Rights Act applies whenever a civil court[54] is considering whether to grant any relief that may affect freedom of expression. This section introduces a requirement to have particular regard to the importance of the right. Moreover, when the material appears, or is claimed to be journalistic, literary or artistic the court must also have particular regard to the extent of: prior publication, public interest in publishing and any relevant privacy code. This section arose following press fears of a privacy law interfering with press freedom. On one view it creates a hierarchy of rights in that the courts must pay particular regard to the importance of Art 10 (and Art 9, see above) but not to the other articles of the Convention. However, it has not so far been construed in such terms.

In *Douglas v Hello!*,[55] Sedley LJ considered whether s 12 created a trump right for the press in comparison with other Convention rights. He concluded that it did not:

> [Free expression] when one turns to it, is qualified in favour of the reputation and rights of others and the protection of information received in confidence. In other words, you cannot have particular regard to Article 10 without having equally particular regard at the very least to Article 8 ... The European Court of Human Rights has always recognised the high importance of free media of

---

52 See *Vereinigung Demokratischer Soldaten v Austria* (1994) 20 EHRR 56 where soldiers' duties and responsibilities were not relevant to the question of whether a satirical magazine could be distributed.

53 *Sunday Times v United Kingdom* (1978–79) 2 EHRR 245.

54 Orders made by criminal courts are excluded from the section: s 12(5).

55 *Douglas v Hello!* [2001] 2 WLR 992.

communication in a democracy, but its jurisprudence does not – and could not consistently with the Convention itself – give Article 10(1) the presumptive priority ... It will be necessary for the court, in applying the test set out in s 12(3), to bear in mind that by virtue of s 12(1) and (4) the qualifications set out in Article 10(2) are as relevant as the right set out in Article 10(1). This means that, for example, the reputations and rights of others – not only but not least their Convention rights – are as material as the defendant's right of free expression. So is the prohibition on the use of one party's Convention rights to injure the Convention rights of others. Any other approach to s 12 would in my judgment violate s 3 of the Act.[56]

It was never sensible to view s 12 as creating a hierarchy of rights. Surely the courts must have particular regard to any Convention rights that are presented in argument. Sedley LJ confirms that if the right is to have increased relevance then so must the exceptions to it. This view is supported by the Court of Appeal in *Ashdown v Telegraph Group Ltd*[57] where s 12 was effectively sidelined as an issue:

It seems to us that s 12 does no more than underline the need to have regard to contexts in which that jurisprudence has given particular weight to freedom of expression, while at the same time drawing attention to considerations which may nonetheless justify restricting that right.[58]

1.4.2.5 Article 11 (assembly and association)

This right protects three related interests: peaceful assembly, association with others and the right to form and join trade unions. There is also an implied right not to join an association.[59] As with Art 10 the scope of the right is wide so that the disputes tend to be about whether the restriction on the right is justified. Thus, although the right relates to 'peaceful' assembly, a gathering which blocks a road will still fall within its scope[60] and violence itself will not take the assembly outside the scope of the protection if it arose from a counter demonstration or extremist hangers-on. The focus is on the intention of the organisers.[61] A similarly broad view of the scope of association has seen it defined so as to include the coming together of people[62] to further their mutual interests.

---

56   *Douglas v Hello!* [2001] 2 WLR 992, at paras 133–36.
57   [2001] EWCA Civ 1142; (2001) *The Times*, 1 August.
58   *Ibid*, para 27, *per* Lord Phillips MR.
59   *Young, James and Webster v United Kingdom* (1982) 4 EHRR 462.
60   *G v Germany* (1989) 60 DR 256.
61   *Christians Against Racists and Fascists v United Kingdom* (1980) 21 DR 138.
62   There is no right to associate with animals even if it can be shown to be therapeutic: *Artingstoll v United Kingdom* (1995) 19 EHRR CD 92.

Once a restriction has been established it is for the public authority to justify it on one of the grounds set out in Art 11(2). The restriction must be prescribed by law and necessary in a democratic society in the interests of: national security, public safety, prevention of disorder or crime, protection of health or morals, or for the protection of the rights of others. There is an additional provision allowing the state to impose lawful restrictions on these rights by the armed forces, police and civil servants. It seems that such restrictions do not have to satisfy the necessity test, but must not be arbitrary.[63]

1.4.2.6 Article 1, Protocol 1 (property)

This article is one of the most openly qualified rights in that it entitles persons to peaceful protection of their possessions but permits lawful state deprivation of possessions in the 'public interest' and the article in no way impairs the right of a state to enforce such laws it deems necessary to control the use of property in accordance with the general interest. 'Possessions' is widely defined and includes most tangible and intangible economic interests including a range of benefits including social security benefits.

As might be expected, greater justification is required for deprivation of property as opposed to mere control. This can lead to disputes about whether steps taken or proposed amount to deprivation or control. Despite the lack of any explicit requirement for necessity, if a measure amounts to deprivation then it must be for a legitimate purpose and must strike a fair balance between the demands of the community and the need to protect the individual.[64] In addition, there is an implicit right to compensation in most cases of deprivation but not necessarily the full market value. Similar considerations arise in relation to control of property, although it will obviously be easier to justify this lesser interference with rights on the fair balance equation. Compensation will not normally be appropriate for control of possessions.

---

63 See *Council for Civil Service Unions v United Kingdom* (1987) 50 DR 228 which was an unsuccessful challenge to the ban on trade unions at GCHQ, the intelligence headquarters.

64 *James v United Kingdom* (1986) 8 EHRR 123.

1.4.2.7 Article 2, Protocol 1 (education)

This article is expressed in negative terms: 'No person shall be denied the right to an education.' It therefore does not impose any duty on the state to provide schooling. However, it has been interpreted by the European Court to include the right of access to such facilities as have been provided. Moreover, given that the right must be effective, there is an associated right to gain benefit from education through official recognition of studies.[65] The essential question in respect of Art 2 is whether the right to an education has been denied by the steps taken by the public authority.[66]

Although there is no explicit qualification on the right to education, 'its very nature calls for regulation by the state'.[67] Thus regulation through, for example, curriculum and quality control is acceptable and may vary in time and place according to the needs of the community and or individuals so long as the substance of the right is preserved.

Another area of potential dispute is the second limb of the right. This requires the state to respect the right of parents to ensure schooling in accordance with their own religious and philosophical aims such as views about the acceptability of physical discipline.[68]

1.4.2.8 Article 3, Protocol 1 (elections)

This article contains no explicit guarantee of individual rights but looks more like a general democratic obligation on the state. However, it has been interpreted as including the individual right to vote and to stand as a candidate. These rights, being implied, are also subject to implied limitations but must not impair the very essence of the right:

> The rights in question are not absolute. Since Article 3 recognises them without setting them forth in express terms, let alone defining them, there is room for implied limitations. In their internal legal orders the Contracting States make the rights to vote and to stand for election subject to conditions, which are not in principle precluded under Article 3. They have a wide margin of appreciation in this sphere, but it is for the court to determine in the last resort whether the requirements of Protocol No 1 have been complied with; it has to satisfy itself that the conditions do not curtail the rights in question to such an extent as to impair their very essence and deprive them of their effectiveness; that they are imposed in pursuit of a legitimate aim; and that the means employed are not disproportionate. In particular, such conditions must not

---

65 *Belgian Linguistics* case (1979–80) 1 EHRR 241.
66 *R (on the Application of B (A Child)) v Head Teacher and Governing Body of Alperton Community School* [2001] EWHC Admin 229; (2001) *The Times*, 8 June.
67 *Ibid.*
68 See *Campbell and Cosans v United Kingdom* (1982) 4 EHRR 293.

thwart 'the free expression of the opinion of the people in the choice of the legislature'.[69]

This has been considered in relation to a challenge by prisoners against their inability to vote:

> Of course as far as an individual prisoner is concerned disenfranchisement does impair the very essence of his right to vote, but that is too simplistic an approach, because what Article 3 of the First Protocol is really concerned with is the wider question of universal franchise, and 'the free expression of the opinion of the people in the choice of the legislature'. If an individual is to be disenfranchised that must be in pursuit of a legitimate aim. In the case of a convicted prisoner serving his sentence the aim may not be easy to articulate.[70]

This suggests that the 'very essence' of the right in Art 3 is the collective interest in free elections as opposed to the individual right to vote.

1.4.2.9 Article 14 (discrimination)

As is well known, this article is not a stand-alone right to be free from discrimination.[71] Any claim under Art 14 must be pegged to one of the substantive rights. There is no requirement to establish a breach of the substantive right in order to succeed under Art 14 but the treatment must fall within the 'ambit' of the substantive right.

It is sensible to deal with Art 14 with the qualified rights in order to emphasise that it is not every difference of treatment that will amount to a violation of the Convention. If a person is treated in a different way to another in a similar situation on the basis of a status listed in the article[72] then there is *prima facie* discrimination. However, it is permissible to differentiate so long as there is a legitimate aim and the difference of treatment is a proportionate way of achieving the aim. There must be reasonable and objective justification for the difference. Without this it will amount to unlawful discrimination. Sedley LJ recently put it as follows:

> Because the article is framed in such catholic terms, the jurisprudence of the European Court of Human Rights makes the necessary distinction between discrimination which is justified and which is not. Article 14 strikes at discrimination, which has 'no reasonable and objective justification'. This in

---

69 *Mathieu-Mohin and Another v Belgium* (1988) 10 EHRR 1, para 4. A recent example of a challenge under the Human Rights Act in this area was *R (on the Application of Pearson) v Secretary of State for the Home Department* [2001] EWHC Admin 239; [2001] HRLR 39, discussed in Chapter 3, below.

70 *R (on the Application of Pearson) v Secretary of State for the Home Department* [2001] EWHC Admin 239; [2001] HRLR 39.

71 Compare Protocol 12, which is a free standing non-discrimination right. The United Kingdom has not signed up to this and it does not form part of the Human Rights Act.

72 The list is not exhaustive.

turn depends upon (a) the aim and effect of the impugned measure, and (b) whether there is a reasonable relationship of proportionality between the means employed and the end sought to be realised ...[73]

1.5   CONVENTION PRINCIPLES

1.5.1   New thinking – challenging traditional decision-making

Few commentators believe that domestic law and practice is wholly incompatible with the Convention. The United Kingdom has been bound by the Convention since 1953 and individuals have been able to bring cases against it since 1966. British lawyers were influential in ensuring that the Convention respected the common law approach. It was not realistic to expect therefore that the courts would take the opportunity of the Act to attempt root and branch reform of the legal system. However, two qualifications need to be made. First, we are in the very early days of the operation of this legislation. As a constitutional instrument it will have long-term influence over the courts. Lawyers have only just begun the process of systematically measuring domestic law against Convention standards and challenging the status quo where they perceive inadequacies. Secondly, even if there is nothing intrinsically incompatible with the domestic arrangements, they will increasingly be influenced by Convention values. Thus challenges to the conduct and decisions of public authorities will be advanced using Convention reasoning. It follows that justification for such conduct must embrace Convention thinking. We can say with some confidence that decision-making processes of the courts and therefore of all other public authorities has to change significantly to accommodate Convention thinking.

Part of this change is an understanding and application of the various Convention principles that have been developed by the European Court of Human Rights in its case law. Our courts have a duty under s 2 of the Human Rights Act to take these principles into account when deciding Convention rights issues. The principles will, in time, become highly influential in shaping the content of Convention rights in the courts. However, at least in the early development of a body of domestic human rights authority, advocates must recognise that the principles will often be unfamiliar to clients, other lawyers and judges and must be careful to give clear guidance about how their application ought to influence decision-making. This section provides an overview of the principles and some indication of how advocates should utilise them when arguing Convention points in domestic courts.

---

73   *Aston Cantlow and Wilmcote with Billesley Parochial Church Council v Wallbank and Another* [2001] EWCA Civ 713; [2001] 3 All ER 393 at para 49.

1.5.2 Living instrument doctrine

In *Tyrer v United Kingdom*,[74] the European Court noted that the Convention was a:

> ... living instrument, which must be interpreted in the light of present-day conditions.

Similarly in *Cossey v United Kingdom*,[75] the Court stated that it had a duty to:

> ... ensure that the interpretation of the Convention reflects societal changes and remains in line with present day conditions.

This has an impact on interpretation of Convention rights, as our courts will adopt this living instrument approach under s 2 of the Act when deciding the content of the Convention rights. It means that the scope and content of the rights is not cast in stone but will effectively move with the times. For example, in *Selmouni v France*,[76] the European Court considered the distinction between torture on the one hand and inhuman or degrading treatment on the other in Art 3 of the Convention:

> ... having regard to the fact that the Convention is a living instrument which must be interpreted in the light of present-day conditions ... the Court considers that certain acts which were classified in the past as inhuman and degrading treatment as opposed to torture could be classified differently in future. It takes the view that the increasingly high standard being required in the area of the protection of human rights and fundamental liberties correspondingly and inevitably requires greater firmness in assessing breaches of the fundamental values of democratic societies.[77]

A logical extension of this reasoning is that treatment that in the past was not deemed to fall within the ambit of Art 3 at all could now be found to be inhuman or degrading. Certainly advocates seeking to push the boundaries of what is acceptable in terms of treatment of, say, prisoners, the mentally disordered, or hospital patients, will rely on such an approach to try to expand the boundaries of the article.[78]

An important feature of the doctrine is that there is no strict doctrine of *stare decisis* in Convention law. Previous decisions will not be followed if they do not reflect current values. Under the Human Rights Act it will therefore impact on the precedent value of earlier decisions. Whether it in fact adds anything to the flexibility inherent in the domestic approach towards

---

74   (1978) 2 EHRR 1 at para 31.
75   (1990) 13 EHRR 622.
76   (2000) 29 EHRR 403.
77   *Ibid*, at para 101.
78   See *Napier v Scottish Ministers*, Court of Sessions 26 June 2000, where a prisoner obtained an interim order requiring his transfer due to allegations that the practice of slopping out constituted a breach of his rights under Art 3. See also *Peers v Greece*, European Court of Human Rights, judgment of 19 April 2001 (Application No 28524/95).

precedent is doubtful. Our courts have always recognised the need to interpret the common law in light of changes in society. See, for example, the approach in *Fitzpatrick v Sterling Housing Association*[79] where the majority of the House of Lords were able to interpret 'family' in the Rent Acts to include a stable gay relationship because, although not contemplated when the legislation was first passed, such a relationship had all of the hallmarks of a family in modern society. See also *R v R*,[80] where the House of Lords held that the common law could develop in light of changing social economic and cultural conditions. Their Lordships removed the rule preventing a husband from being convicted of raping his wife as the status of women had changed out of all recognition from when the rule was originally developed. Marriage was now viewed as a partnership of equals rather than the wife being seen as the property of the husband.[81]

As with a number of other Convention principles, the living instrument doctrine leaves several questions unanswered:

- What is meant by present-day conditions?
- What sorts of societal changes can lead to the evolution of the Convention?
- How long must elapse before the doctrine will permit the revisiting of earlier decisions?
- What sort of evidence of changing attitudes is required or admissible?

Advocates should be wary of reverting to the doctrine too freely. It would be foolish, for example, to seek to persuade a court that a House of Lords decision from last year could now safely be ignored because things have 'moved on'. Advocates should look for significant milestones that might reflect a changing attitude. Examples could be:

- Policy and legal developments in other countries of the Council of Europe.
- Reports of eminent bodies, particularly those with an international purview.
- Areas of the law that have been relatively dormant for many years.
- Significant *obiter* comments about the need to alter the existing position.
- Situations where there have been parallel developments in related areas of law.

1.5.3 Positive obligations

The Convention rights are primarily about what public authorities cannot do, that is, their negative obligations. Thus they cannot take life, torture, enslave,

---

79 [1999] 3 WLR 1113.

80 [1991] 4 All ER 481.

81 A challenge to the conviction under Art 7 failed, the European Court recognising the ability of the common law to develop in the way it did: *SW v United Kingdom* (1995) 21 EHRR 363.

detain, censor, etc, either at all or without some good justification. It follows that the bulk of cases brought under the Human Rights Act are about challenges to interference by the state. Nevertheless, the European Court has recognised that in order to secure effective protection for the rights it may sometimes be necessary to impose a duty on the state to take steps to facilitate individuals' rights or to protect individuals from violation by non-state agents. In other words the Convention can impose positive obligations on public authorities. This was explained in the recent case of *Z v United Kingdom*[82] concerning the failure of social services to take steps to prevent abuse and neglect of the applicants by their parents:

> The court reiterates that Article 3 enshrines one of the most fundamental values of democratic society. It prohibits in absolute terms torture or inhuman or degrading treatment or punishment. The obligation on High Contracting Parties under Article 1 of the Convention to secure to everyone within their jurisdiction the rights and freedoms defined in the Convention, taken together with Article 3, requires States to take measures designed to ensure that individuals within their jurisdiction are not subjected to torture or inhuman or degrading treatment, including such ill-treatment administered by private individuals ... These measures should provide effective protection, in particular, of children and other vulnerable persons and include reasonable steps to prevent ill-treatment of which the authorities had or ought to have had knowledge ...[83]

This extract also shows the role of Art 1 of the Convention in persuading the Court to impose positive obligations. Article 1 is not one of the rights included in s 1 of the Human Rights Act. This raises a question mark over the applicability of positive obligations under the Act. Elsewhere though, the Act seems to recognise the possibility of positive obligations by stating that a public authority can breach Convention rights by omission as well as by conduct.[84] Moreover, the duty to take into account decisions of the European Court gives a mechanism by which positive obligations can be recognised by domestic courts.[85] Further evidence of the intention to give effect to positive obligations through the Human Rights Act comes from the fact that courts and tribunals are themselves public authorities with a duty to make decisions compatibly with Convention rights even where no public authority has directly interfered with a right. In a famous parliamentary statement during the passage of the Bill the Lord Chancellor said as follows regarding the role of the courts:

---

82 [2001] 2 FCR 246.
83 *Ibid*, at para 73.
84 Section 6(6).
85 Section 2.

... it is right as a matter of principle for the courts to have the duty of acting compatibly with the Convention not only in cases involving other public authorities, but also in developing the common law in deciding cases between individuals. Why should they not? ... It is the other course, that of excluding Convention considerations altogether from cases between individuals, which would have to be justified. We do not think that that would be justifiable; nor, indeed, do we think it would be practicable.[86]

1.5.3.1 Using positive obligations in court

There are two main ways in which positive obligations can be utilised by advocates as follows:

- Seeking to persuade a court that a public authority acts unlawfully where it fails to act to protect the claimant from a third party or fails to provide a service to the claimant.

- Seeking to persuade a court that a public authority is justified in interfering with a Convention right in order to satisfy its positive obligation to others. In this way the positive obligation becomes the legitimate aim for interfering with qualified rights, typically the 'rights and freedoms of others'.

There is clearly scope for creative use of positive obligations by advocates for claimed victims and also advocates for public authorities. However, the latter ought to be cautious about over-zealous claims regarding positive obligations lest they come back to haunt them in future cases with litigants claiming breach of these very positive obligations.

The courts have already given at least an indication that they will not allow the absence of Art 1 from the Human Rights Act to get in the way of the development of positive rights in domestic law:

... Where parliament in this country has been so obviously content to leave the development of the law to the judges, it might seem strange if the absence of Article 1 from our national statute relieved the judges from taking into account the positive duties identified by the court at Strasbourg when they develop the common law. In this judgment, however, I have the luxury of identifying difficult issues: I am not obliged to solve them.[87]

---

86 *Hansard* HL Debs, 24 November 1997, col 783. For a discussion of positive obligations and horizontality, see Chapter 6.

87 *Douglas v Hello!* [2001] 2 WLR 992, *per* Brooke LJ, at para 91.

Issues for advocates: positive obligations

The mechanism for advocates relying on positive obligations under the Human Rights Act can be explained as follows:

- The rights set out in Sched 1 are, by virtue of s 1, 'to have effect' in United Kingdom courts.
- The court is obliged to take into account the decisions of the Strasbourg institutions by virtue of s 2, including rulings about the scope and effect of positive obligations.
- The government intended the Human Rights Act to give effect to its obligation under Art 1 of the Convention to secure to everyone within the United Kingdom the rights and freedoms set out in the Convention.
- It follows that the absence of Art 1 in the Sched 1 rights does not mean that the positive obligations within those rights can be ignored. The Human Rights Act was intended to give effect to the Convention rights in full.
- Failure to recognise positive obligations in the Human Rights Act would lead to a breach of the United Kingdom's obligations under the Convention.
- The Human Rights Act explicitly recognises that omissions to act by public authorities can be unlawful in exactly the same way as actual conduct.
- The courts as public authorities are obliged to act compatibly with the Convention rights even in litigation between private parties.

Issues for advocates: post-Human Rights Act authority on positive obligations

Advocates should be aware of the fact that the courts have already addressed the scope of positive obligations under the Human Rights Act in a number of cases. The following decisions should be built upon, distinguished or challenged, as appropriate by advocates seeking to establish or deny the existence of positive obligations.

Positive obligations have been recognised under the Human Rights Act in the following situations:

- Protection of offenders' rights under Arts 2 and 3 from third parties.[88]

---

88   *Venables and Thompson v News Group Newspapers* [2001] 2 WLR 1038 (positive obligation to protect the lives of two convicted murderers by granting injunctions preventing the revelation of their identities or whereabouts following their release from local authority secure accommodation).

- Investigation of the treatment and death of a prisoner under Arts 2 and 3.[89]
- Protection of private life through expansion of breach of confidence/early development of tort of privacy under Art 8.[90]
- Protection of the rights of children and parents to family life under Art 8.[91]
- Legal safeguards that render possible the child's integration in its family.[92]
- Protection of children from abuse under Art 8.[93]
- A duty for the criminal courts to respect victims' rights under Art 3 in summing up to the jury in assault cases.[94]
- A duty to give life-sustaining treatment where such treatment is in the best interests of a patient under Art 2.[95]
- Protection of the welfare of a mentally incapacitated adult under Art 8.[96]

The courts have also found that no positive obligation arises in the following situations:

- Subsidising of vocational education under Art 2 of Protocol 1.[97]
- Providing gender reassignment surgery under Arts 8 and 3.[98]
- Giving financial assistance for the provision of housing or the protection of family life under Art 8.[99]

---

89 *R (on the Application of Wright) v Secretary of State for the Home Department* [2001] EWHC Admin 520; (2001) *Daily Telegraph*, 26 June (positive obligation to conduct a proper investigation into deaths of those in custody).

90 *Douglas v Hello!* [2001] 2 WLR 992, *per* Sedley LJ.

91 *W and B (Children: Care Plan)* [2001] EWCA Civ 757, [2001] FCR 450 (duty on court to monitor operation of care order).

92 *Re R (A Child) (Adoption: Disclosure)* [2001] 1 FLR 365 (general duty to facilitate relationship between child and its wider family).

93 *R v S Borough Council ex p S* (2001) *The Independent*, 18 June; *R v Governor of HMP Dartmoor ex p N* (2001) *The Times*, 19 March (rights of child justify interfering with the rights of others).

94 *R v H (Reasonable Chastisement)* [2001] EWCA Crim 1024, [2001] 2 FLR 431 (trial judge was right to propose to reflect the decision of *A v United Kingdom* (1999) 27 EHRR 611 in his summing up to the jury regarding the defence of lawful chastisement of the defendant's child).

95 *NHS Trust A v Mrs M; NHS Trust B v Mrs H* [2001] 1 All ER 801 at para 37 (positive duty did not extend to continuing life prolonging treatment where it was not in the best interests of the patient).

96 *Re F (Adult Patient)* [2000] 2 FLR 512 (duty of court and local authority to protect vulnerable adult from damaging influence of her family).

97 *R (on the Application of Youngson) v Birmingham City Council* [2001] EWCA Civ 287; [2000] All ER(D) 2231 (no duty to pay for ballet school fees).

98 *North West Lancashire Health Authority v A, D and G* [2000] 1 WLR 977 (the authority's policy was unlawful for other reasons).

99 *R v Carmarthenshire County Council Housing Benefit Review Board ex p Painter* [2001] EWHC Admin 308; (2001) *The Times*, 16 May (no duty to provide housing benefit).

Some articles plainly give rise to positive obligations as the right itself entails some state assistance. Examples include the right to legal aid in criminal cases under Art 6(3)(c) and the duty on the state to hold elections under Art 3 of Protocol 1. Other articles give rise to positive obligations by necessary implication. Implicit in the Art 6 guarantee of a fair hearing is the right of access to a court in respect of civil disputes. The need for such access to be effective gives rise in turn to an obligation to provide state funding of legal representation if it is the only way of securing the right.[100] Article 2 of Protocol 1 embodies the right to an education in what appears to be a negative manner: 'no one shall be denied the right an education.' However, the court has gone further and recognised that it may nevertheless impose duties on the state:

> In spite of its negative formulation, this provision uses the term 'right' and speaks of a 'right to education'. Likewise the preamble to the Protocol specifies that the object of the Protocol lies in the collective enforcement of 'rights and freedoms'. There is, therefore no doubt that Art 2 (P1–2) does enshrine a right. It remains however, to determine the content of this right and the scope of the obligation, which is thereby placed upon States.[101]

Some articles are of such a nature that public authorities must take steps to prevent third parties from breaching the right in question. As we saw in the above extract from *Z v United Kingdom*, this arises by having a legal framework for the protection of the right, including, where appropriate using criminal sanctions.[102]

Of more significance as far as the actions of public authorities are concerned, is the extension of this principle to the obligation on organisations like the police, social services and the courts to take steps to prevent breaches arising in the first place. It follows that one of the main areas of dispute regarding positive obligations is whether there was a duty on the part of the public authority and, if so, whether it has satisfied its duty. Given that the Human Rights Act permits victims to seek remedies for anticipatory breaches of their rights,[103] there is scope for positive obligations to influence the court's approach to imposing mandatory orders on public authorities[104] and granting protective orders itself.[105] As we will see, the concept of positive obligations is

---

100 *Airey v Ireland* (1979) 2 EHRR 305.

101 *Belgian Linguistics* case (#2) (1968) 1 EHRR 252.

102 *X and Y v Netherlands* (1986) 8 EHRR 235.

103 Section 7(1); s 8(1).

104 *R (on the Application of Wright) v Secretary of State for the Home Department* [2001] EWHC Admin 520; (2001) *Daily Telegraph*, 26 June, where the court was willing to order the prison service to carry out an investigation into a prisoner's death from asthma.

105 See *Thompson and Venables v News Group Newspapers* [2001] 2 WLR 1038, where the court was willing to expand the jurisdiction to grant injunctions and to grant an indefinite injunction against the media to protect the claimants' right to life.

one of the main driving forces behind the development of common law remedies for abuse of human rights.[106]

One of the main difficulties for advocates is anticipating when courts will be willing to impose positive obligations under the Human Rights Act and what it means for the resolution of the dispute between the public authority and the individual. There is in fact little firm guidance from the Strasbourg Court, which leaves a fairly wide discretion to Member States as to how they give effect to their positive duties. For example, the positive duty to protect private life has not yet been ruled by the Strasbourg Court as requiring specific legal protection for privacy.[107] The extent of positive obligations is another area where the international concept of margin of appreciation has played a role in limiting the demands made by the Strasbourg Court. This adds to the uncertainty in respect of domestic application under the Human Rights Act.

There may be more than one way in which a positive obligation can arise within an article. Taking Art 10 as an example, the court has ruled that it creates no positive obligation on the state to provide information to citizens:

> The court reiterates that freedom to receive information, referred to in paragraph 2 of Article 10 of the Convention, basically prohibits a government from restricting a person from receiving information that others wish or may be willing to impart to him ... That freedom cannot be construed as imposing on a State, in circumstances such as those of the present case, positive obligations to collect and disseminate information of its own motion.[108]

However, it is submitted that this should in no way prevent advocates from pushing for the recognition of positive obligations in respect of other aspects of Art 10. For example, we submit that there is clearly scope for limited positive obligations to protect a person's freedom of expression from third parties by analogy with the approach of the court to Art 11.[109] There is some indication of recognition of such protection in *Redmond-Bate v DPP*,[110] where Sedley LJ refused to find that a preacher had been guilty of conduct likely to cause a breach of the peace when faced with an angry reaction to her message:

---

106 For example, the expansion of the common law to embrace greater protection for privacy interests. See Chapter 6 for a fuller discussion.

107 See *Spencer v United Kingdom* [1998] EHRLR 348, European Commission of Human Rights.

108 *Guerra v Italy* (1998) 26 EHRR 357 at para 53. The Commission had ruled that Art 10 imposed a duty to collect, process and disseminate certain environmental information, which by its nature could not otherwise come to the knowledge of the public.

109 *Plattform Ärtze für das Leben v Austria* (1991) 14 EHRR 319 regarding state duties to protect demonstrators from violent counter-demonstrations: 'Genuine, effective freedom of peaceful assembly cannot, therefore, be reduced to a mere duty on the part of the state not to interfere ... Article 11 sometimes requires positive measures to be taken, even in the sphere of relations between individuals, if need be.'

110 [2000] HRLR 249.

> If the threat of disorder or violence was coming from passers-by who were taking the opportunity to react so as to cause trouble ... then it was they and not the preachers who should be asked to desist and arrested if they would not ... Free speech includes not only the inoffensive but also the irritating, the contentious, the eccentric, the heretical, the unwelcome and the provocative provided it does not tend to provoke violence. Freedom only to speak inoffensively is not worth having. What Speakers' Corner (where the law applies as fully as anywhere else) demonstrates is the tolerance which is both extended by the law to opinion of every kind and expected by the law in the conduct of those who disagree, even strongly, with what they hear.

Although this does not state in terms that the police have a positive legal duty to protect free speech, it is only a small step to such a proposition. The point is that the limits of positive obligations are not finalised, and advocates may be required to present courts and tribunals with reasoned arguments as to why there is or is not a positive obligation even in cases where none have previously been recognised by the European Court.

1.5.4 The principle of legal certainty

Pervading the Convention is the idea that state conduct should be in accordance with the rule of law and that the law should clearly inform individuals of the parameters on the exercise of their rights. This means that there must be domestic law justifying any interference with human rights and, as we will see, this law must have certain qualities before it can properly be said to authorise the interference. This in essence, is the principle of legal certainty and it is a basic building block of Convention jurisprudence.

The principle is often referred to as the principle of legality. However, as we will see, this phrase is also used to describe a related domestic approach towards the interpretation of legislation, whereby Parliament will be presumed not to have interfered with fundamental human rights unless it clearly expresses an intention to do so in the language of the legislation.[111]

Some Convention articles explicitly require any interference with the right to be lawful. Although various formulations are used, the essential nature of the principle of legal certainty is common to them all:

- Articles 9–11 restrictions must be 'prescribed by law'.[112]
- Article 8 restrictions must be 'in accordance with the law'.[113]

---

111 See Lord Hoffman in *R v Secretary of State for the Home Department ex p Simms* [2000] 2 AC 115 at page 131. This is discussed further in Chapter 4.
112 See, for example, *Sunday Times v United Kingdom* (1978–79) 2 EHRR 245.
113 See *Malone v United Kingdom* (1984) 7 EHRR 14.

- Article 5 deprivations of liberty must be 'in accordance with a procedure prescribed by law' and 'lawful'.[114]

The first requirement is that there must actually be some provision of domestic law authorising the interference. The common law will be a sufficient legal basis but administrative guidance or practice will not, as the European Court noted in *Khan*, a case about secret bugging of private premises:

> At the time of the events in the present case, there existed no statutory system to regulate the use of covert listening devices ... The Home Office Guidelines at the relevant time were neither legally binding nor were they directly publicly accessible. The Court also notes that Lord Nolan in the House of Lords commented that under English law there is, in general, nothing unlawful about a breach of privacy. There was, therefore, no domestic law regulating the use of covert listening devices at the relevant time. It follows that the interference in the present case cannot be considered to be in accordance with the law, as required by Article 8, s 2 of the Convention. Accordingly, there has been a violation of Article 8.[115]

Examples of the sources of law that can authorise interference with Convention rights include:

- Primary legislation. The Human Rights Act itself does not satisfy this requirement. Although the Convention rights permit lawful interference, the articles do not themselves supply the legal basis for such interference.
- Subordinate legislation.
- European Union law.
- Common law. This means that agreements binding at common law such as contracts, tenancy agreements etc would provide the requisite legal authority for the interference.

The existence of a law authorising the conduct of the public authority is a condition precedent to the lawful interference with the right. Without such a law, there is a breach of the Convention. However, the requirement for legal certainty goes further than a mere requirement to have a law covering the interference. The European Court has said on numerous occasions that the law must itself have certain autonomous qualities in order for it to meet the Convention standard:

> In *Malone v United Kingdom*, the court said as follows:
>
> The court would reiterate its opinion that the phrase 'in accordance with the law' does not merely refer back to domestic law but also relates to the quality of the law, requiring it to be compatible with the rule of law, which is expressly

---

114 See *Steel v United Kingdom* (1999) 28 EHRR 603.
115 *Khan v United Kingdom* (2001) 31 EHRR 45 at paras 27–28.

mentioned in the preamble to the Convention ... The phrase thus implies – and this follows from the object and purpose of Article 8 (Art 8) – that there must be a measure of legal protection in domestic law against arbitrary interferences by public authorities with the rights safeguarded by paragraph 1 (Art 8–1) (see the report of the Commission, paragraph 121). Especially where a power of the executive is exercised in secret, the risks of arbitrariness are evident.[116]

In *Sunday Times v United Kingdom*, the Court explained what these qualities were:

In the court's opinion, the following are two of the requirements that flow from the expression 'prescribed by law'. Firstly, the law must be adequately accessible: the citizen must be able to have an indication that is adequate in the circumstances of the legal rules applicable to a given case. Secondly, a norm cannot be regarded as a 'law' unless it is formulated with sufficient precision to enable the citizen to regulate his conduct: he must be able – if need be with appropriate advice – to foresee, to a degree that is reasonable in the circumstances, the consequences which a given action may entail. Those consequences need not be foreseeable with absolute certainty: experience shows this to be unattainable. Again, whilst certainty is highly desirable, it may bring in its train excessive rigidity and the law must be able to keep pace with changing circumstances. Accordingly, many laws are inevitably couched in terms which, to a greater or lesser extent, are vague and whose interpretation and application are questions of practice.[117]

In that case the court found with some reservations that the development by the House of Lords of the 'prejudgment' principle in the law of contempt as an extension of the existing 'pressure' principle, was reasonably foreseeable with appropriate advice and was thus prescribed by law.[118]

Thus whenever there is an interference with any of the qualified rights the public authority must satisfy the court of the following:

- The interference must comply with domestic law (statute or common law).
- The law must be adequately accessible – there is no place for secret restrictions on rights.
- The law must be sufficiently precise so that a person may, with advice if necessary, anticipate the circumstances whereby the law may justify interference with his or her rights.

In *Hashman and Harrup v United Kingdom*[119] the concept of *contra bonos mores* (conduct contrary to the good way of life) was held not to be sufficiently precise to satisfy the requirements of Art 5. It could thus not be used to justify

---

116 *Malone v United Kingdom* (1984) 7 EHRR 14, at para 67.
117 *Sunday Times v United Kingdom* (1978–79) 2 EHRR 245, at para 49.
118 *Ibid*, at paras 50–53.
119 [2000] Crim LR 185.

detention of the applicants. The Court held that it lacked adequate foreseeability in that there was no requirement for a breach of the peace before it could be imposed. It looked not to past misconduct but purely prospectively to future conduct. Moreover, the concept itself was not defined by reference to effects only by reference to the perceived views of the majority of citizens.

In *R v Smethurst*,[120] the Court of Appeal refused an appeal based on the alleged lack of legal certainty in s 1(1)(a) of the Protection of Children Act 1978. The section creates an offence of making an indecent photograph or pseudo-photograph of a child. The appellant argued that the criteria of indecency lacked the requisite certainty to be a lawful interference with the right of freedom of expression in Art 10, particularly in light of the fact that the statute had been interpreted as making the intention of the photographer irrelevant. Lord Woolf said that it was difficult to apply the *Sunday Times* and *Hashman and Harrup* approach to the current offence because 'what is or what is not indecent very much depends upon the judgment of the individual. There can be conduct which some would regard as highly indecent, which others would regard as acceptable. For that reason ... what is or what is not indecent must be objectively assessed'.[121]

Challenges have also failed in relation to the Consultancy Service Index, a non-statutory database maintained by the Department of Health of persons considered to be unsuitable for work with children.[122] The Index was held to be within the powers of the Secretary of State under the Royal Prerogative, although there was little real analysis of whether the Convention would require a firmer legal basis for the records to be held and distributed. One difficulty was that the courts do not seem to have been convinced that the Index in fact interfered with Art 8 interests in any event.

The scope for alleged victims succeeding on the basis of a lack of sufficiently precise and accessible law seems to be rather limited for two reasons. First, the European Court imposes only minimal requirements of precision and clearly permits a developmental approach within common law systems. Secondly, the domestic courts, working within such a system, are adept at discovering a legal basis for state conduct through lengthy analysis of disparate judicial pronouncements and statutory provisions.[122a]

---

120 [2001] EWCA Crim 772; (2001) 165 JPN 408.

121 *Ibid*, at para 21.

122 *R v Secretary of State for Health ex p C* [2000] 1 FLR 627, CA. See also *R v Worcester County Council and Secretary of State for Health ex p SW* [2000] HRLR 702.

122a See *R (on the Application of Matthias Rath BV) v Advertising Standards Authority* [2001] HRLR 22, where the Administrative Court ruled that recognition of a self-regulatory code of practice by the Control of Misleading Advertisements Regulations 1998 was sufficient 'statutory underpinning' for the code, albeit short of direct statutory effect. The ASA's adjudication was therefore 'prescribed by law' despite the lack of any explicit authorisation by the Regulations.

1.5.5 Legitimate aims for interfering with qualified rights

As has been seen in the brief survey of the Convention rights above, the grounds for interfering with Convention rights vary between each of the rights. Some are explicit justifications for restrictions such as in Arts 8–11 and some are implied, such as in Art 1 of Protocol 1. The explicit justifications fall into four categories as follows:

- National security/public safety.
- Prevention of disorder/crime.
- Protection of health/morals.
- Protection of the rights/freedoms of others.

Article 8 is the only right that permits the economic well being of the country to justify interference. It is expected that public authorities will seek to persuade courts that this criteria can be interpreted as applying on a micro-level so as to justify individual decisions of public authorities on the basis of availability of resources.

Article 10 contains further justifications for restricting free speech as follows:

- The reputation of others.
- Protection of confidential information.
- Maintaining the authority and impartiality of the judiciary.

If a measure does not pursue a legitimate aim then, whether or not it is authorised by law, it cannot be a lawful interference in Convention terms. Moreover, if a legitimate aim ostensibly relied upon is in reality an excuse to justify a restriction for an unjustified purpose, it will fall foul of Art 18.[123] For example, if a court were satisfied that prevention of disorder was used as a reason for an arrest, which was in reality a desire to prevent public criticism, there would be a violation of the Convention. In practice, it is difficult to see how Art 18 adds anything to the requirement for a legitimate aim in the articles themselves.

Note that 'rights and freedoms of others' is not limited to protection of Convention rights. See *S v United Kingdom*[123a] (landlord's contractual rights) and *R (on the Application of Craven) v Secretary of State for the Home Department*[123b] (sensibilities of a murder victim's family).

Once interference has been recognised, it is for the public authority to identify the legitimate aim served by the interference. There has rarely been

---

123 'The restrictions permitted under this Convention to the said rights and freedoms shall not be applied for any purpose other than those for which they have been prescribed.'

123a *S v United Kingdom* (1986) 47 DR 274.

123b [2001] EWHC Admin 850. See in particular, para 35.

much difficulty in satisfying the Convention institutions that there is a legitimate aim and there is no evidence thus far of any different approach being taken by the domestic courts. One recent example where doubt was expressed as to the existence of a legitimate aim was in *Smith and Grady v United Kingdom*, where the European Court said it doubted that the intrusive investigations into the private lives of the applicants could be justified on the general ground of the operational effectiveness of the armed services after the point when they had admitted their homosexuality.[124] Obviously, acceptance of a legitimate aim is not the end of the enquiry. By far the larger question is whether the interference was necessary in a democratic society in pursuit of that aim.

1.5.6 Proportionality

The principle of proportionality is a key concept in the Convention. It is discussed in detail in Chapter 3 but here we summarise its essential features.

The principle was first explored in one of the earliest cases where the European Court tested our domestic approach, *Handyside v United Kingdom*.[125] The Court recognised that Member States had a margin of appreciation in deciding how to give effect to the Convention rights but explained that one of the limiting features was that every formality, restriction, condition or penalty upon freedom of expression had to be proportionate to the legitimate aim pursued by the state.

Although the case was about Art 10, the concept of proportionality has now come to pervade much of the Convention. The general rule is that the means used to interfere with Convention rights must have a reasonable relationship of proportionality to the legitimate aim pursued. In common parlance the state cannot use a sledgehammer to crack a nut. If the level of interference by a public authority is disproportionate it will not be lawful under the Convention and will thus amount to an unlawful act under s 6 of the Human Rights Act.

The incorporation through the Human Rights Act of proportionality principles seems to amount to a statutory overruling of *R v Secretary of State for the Home Department ex p Brind*.[126] This case involved the challenge to the Home Secretary's decision to ban the broadcasting of the direct speech of members of proscribed organisations in Northern Ireland and their supporters, including the political party Sinn Fein. The majority of the House of Lords said that the Court could not examine the lawfulness of executive decisions by recourse to the principle of proportionality as to do so would

---

124 (2000) 29 EHRR 548 at para 74.
125 (1978–79) 1 EHRR 737.
126 [1991] 1 AC 696.

involve an unacceptable judicial intervention with the merits of a decision and the incorporation of the Convention through the back door.

The Human Rights Act clearly brings the Convention in through the front door so the courts are no longer reticent about applying a proportionality test. There is no fixed set of relevant criteria for determining proportionality but the courts will look for the following amongst others:

- Has the public authority provided relevant and sufficient reasons for the existence of a pressing social need justifying the interference?
- Was there a less intrusive alternative that could have reasonably been adopted?
- Does the interference destroy the 'very essence' of the right?
- Has the right-holder been afforded procedural fairness and safeguards against abuse during the decision-making process?

Advocates ought to be willing and able to take courts through these criteria and explain how they affect the proportionality question. This will particularly be the case in situations where the alleged victim is challenging a discretionary interference by a public authority with a qualified Convention right.

1.5.7 Structured decision-making regarding qualified rights

Issues for advocates: a structured approach to qualified rights

Whenever there is an alleged infringement of a qualified right, the court or tribunal deciding the matter must adopt a structured approach towards deciding whether or not there has been a violation of the Convention. This approach is useful as a guide for advocates in advising clients, assessing the areas of agreement and dispute between the parties and guiding the court. It can be formulated into the following series of questions:

1   Is a Convention right engaged?
2   What is the nature of the right? Only qualified rights can be dealt with using this approach.
3   Does the (proposed) conduct or omission of a public authority interfere with the right? Note the influence of positive obligations on the question of whether there has been an interference.
4   Does the claimant have victim status?
5   Is there a legal basis for the interference with the right?
6   Is the legal basis sufficiently accessible?

7   Is the legal basis adequately precise?

8   Is there a legitimate public interest aim served by the interference?

9   Is the interference necessary in a democratic society?

10 Are there relevant and sufficient reasons for the interference?

11 Is there a reasonable relationship of proportionality between the legitimate aim and the interference?

12 Is there a less intrusive alternative that could achieve the legitimate aim?

13 Has the right-holder had an opportunity to have some input into the decision-making process?

14 Are there procedural safeguards in place to prevent abuse of the right?

As a rough guide, in respect of questions 1–4 the burden of proof is on the alleged victim. Thereafter the public authority will have to satisfy the court as to questions 5–14 and failure to do so can lead to a finding of a violation. The questions are essentially cumulative so that failure at any point will remove the legal justification and amount to an unlawful act.

1.5.8   Margin of appreciation[127]

The margin of appreciation is the means by which the European Court, as an international tribunal, accommodates the disparate legal, political and cultural traditions of the 40-plus Member States of the Council of Europe. It is relevant to a wide range of Convention rights in Strasbourg decision-making including: Arts 8–12; Arts 5–6; Art 2; and the rights in the first Protocol. It effectively gives a discretion to the national authorities, the width of which depends on a variety of factors, as to the nature of the need for a restriction on rights and the necessity of the means adopted to deal with it. Without the doctrine it would not be possible for the Court to function, as it would be imposing a uniform set of requirements in a treaty that did not create a unitary legal system.

The principle is also allied to the idea that the Convention imposes minimum standards only and that many states provide much greater protection for rights than is in fact required by the Convention. A consequence of the concept is that it tends to dilute the strength of the rights in the Convention at an international level and can serve to make the reasoning of the European Court less transparent. For example, it is often not clear whether the Court is saying that the measure in question was strictly proportionate to

---

127 The margin of appreciation and the related issues of the 'discretionary area of judgment' and proportionality are discussed in detail in Chapter 3.

the legitimate aim concerned or whether the proportionality requirement was lessened because of the state's margin of appreciation. The concept clearly overlaps with proportionality and it has been criticised for introducing too great a level of uncertainty into Convention law. It is difficult to anticipate in advance the effect that the margin will be said to have in individual cases.

The Human Rights Act potentially makes the margin of appreciation relevant through s 2 whereby courts have a duty to 'take into account ...' the decisions of the Strasbourg Court. However, as will be seen, the margin of appreciation is not applicable in the domestic courts under the Human Rights Act. This does not mean that advocates can forget about the margin. An important question we consider in Chapter 3 is the extent to which analysis of European Court decisions that have applied the principle need to be viewed in a different light when argued before the domestic courts.

1.5.9 Autonomous meanings

The European Court has developed the idea of autonomous meaning to describe the fact that words and phrases within the Convention will be accorded a uniform meaning in all cases coming before the court notwithstanding the fact that there may be a different meaning of the word in domestic law. The rationale for such an approach is the desire not to allow the protection afforded by the Convention from being diluted by individual Member States categorising conduct as falling outside a Convention right. For example, the categorisation of 'poll tax' committal proceedings as civil rather than criminal in *Benham v United Kingdom* wrongly deprived the applicant of state-funded legal representation that he should have been entitled to.[128]

There is no exhaustive list of the words and phrases that have autonomous meanings. We would suggest that they include the following:

> 'life', 'torture', 'inhuman', 'degrading', 'punishment', 'slavery', 'servitude', 'compulsory labour', 'liberty', 'security', 'lawful', 'detention', 'arrest', 'offence', 'unsound mind', 'court', 'civil rights',[129] 'criminal charge',[130] 'penalty', 'private', 'family', 'home', 'expression', 'peaceful assembly', 'association', 'in accordance with law', 'prescribed by law', 'discrimination', 'possessions', 'property'.

The consequence of finding that a word or phrase has an autonomous meaning is that the courts will be obliged to take into account the previous approach to the phrase adopted by the European Convention institutions, before deciding the outcome of the case under the Human Rights Act. It is

---

128 (1996) 22 EHRR 293. See paras 56 and 64.
129 See further Chapter 9.
130 See further Chapter 7.

likely that the courts will adopt the same interpretation as has been adopted in Strasbourg. In doing so they will apply the criteria laid down by the European Court for ascertaining whether the matter at issue falls within concept. Evidence that this is happening can be seen in the approach of the courts to phrases like 'criminal charge', where they have begun to review a number of processes using the well established Convention criteria as the yardstick.

However, not all Convention criteria are as clear as those for assessing criminal charges and it may not be possible to discern any consistent Strasbourg approach. In addition, it should be recalled that the courts are not obliged to adopt the Strasbourg definition in domestic law but only to take it into account.[131] Our courts could take a different approach and will be encouraged to do so where this provides greater protection than required by the European Court. For example, the approach towards what constitutes a 'family' for the purpose of Art 8 and Art 12 has evolved in a haphazard manner in Strasbourg with little coherent policy apparent. United Kingdom courts may be asked to develop their own generous approach towards the concept.

1.5.10 Derogations and reservations

The Convention rights in the Human Rights Act have effect subject to any derogation or reservation applying to the United Kingdom and designated by the Secretary of State under the Act.[132]

1.5.10.1 Derogations

Derogation is where the state indicates its intention not to comply with a Convention right in time of war or other public emergency threatening the life of the nation. Derogations are permitted under Art 15 in respect of all of the Convention rights apart from Arts 3, 4(1) and 7. Derogations under Art 2 may only be made in respect of lawful acts of war. The state can derogate from its obligations only so far as is 'strictly required by the exigencies of the situation' and provided that the measures are consistent with its other international law obligations. This confirms that the justification for and the measures taken under derogation remain subject to the scrutiny of the European Court. Presumably, then, the domestic courts have a similar supervisory jurisdiction in respect of the measures taken when there is a derogation in place.

Until recently, the United Kingdom had no derogations in force, the long-standing derogation from Art 5(3) in respect of detention of terrorist

---

131 See Chapter 4.
132 Sections 1(2), 14, 15 and Sched 3.

suspects[133] having been removed following the implementation of a new detention authorisation procedure in Sched 8 of the Terrorism Act 2000.[134] However, on 12 November 2001, the Home Secretary entered a derogation in respect of Art 5 in anticipation of the internment powers contained in the Anti-Terrorism, Crime and Security Bill.

1.5.10.2 Reservations

Article 57 of the Convention provides that a state may 'make a reservation in respect of any particular provision of the Convention to the extent that any law then in force in its territory is not in conformity with the provision'. The reservation must contain a brief statement of the law concerned and reservations of a 'general character' are not permitted. This means that a reservation 'couched in terms that are too vague or broad for it to be possible to determine their exact meaning and scope' is not valid under the article.[135]

The United Kingdom has one reservation, in the field of education, which accepts the right of parents to respect for their religious and philosophical convictions under Art 2 of Protocol 1 'only in so far as it is compatible with the provision of efficient instruction and training, and the avoidance of unreasonable public expenditure'.[136] In light of the prohibition on general reservations mentioned above, and the fact that most education legislation post-dates the date it was entered, the validity of this reservation has been questioned.[137] It might be wondered whether the explicit inclusion of the reservation in the Human Rights Act gives new life to it in that, at least so far as domestic courts are concerned, it applies to all education statutes up to the Human Rights Act coming into force. In any event, whether or not the reservation is valid might not become an issue given the reluctance of the courts to view Art 2 of Protocol 1 as imposing any positive duties to fund particular educational provision.

1.5.11 Just satisfaction

Section 8 of the Human Rights Act permits the courts to award compensation in order to provide 'just satisfaction' after it has considered the effect of any other order made (such as an injunction, quashing order etc). The concept comes from Art 41 of the Convention. Unfortunately the European Court has

---

133 See Human Rights Act, Sched 3.

134 See Human Rights Act (Amendment) Order 2001, SI 2001 No 1216, 27 March 2001, made pursuant to s 16(7) of the Act. As from 1 April 2001, ss 14 and 16 of the Act were amended and Part 1 of Sched 3 was repealed so as to reflect the withdrawal of the derogation on 26 February 2001.

135 *Belilos v Switzerland* (1988) 10 EHRR 466 at para 55.

136 Reservation 20 March 1952. See Sched 3.

137 *SP v United Kingdom*, European Commission of Human Rights, Application No 28915/95, 17 January 1997.

not provided any really consistent or coherent approach towards the granting of just satisfaction. The following points provide the barest outline of the applicable rules:

- Awards are normally made on an 'equitable basis'. This takes into account the conduct and antecedents of the victim and the nature of breach involved.

- It is said that just satisfaction must be claimed in order to be granted: *Sunday Times v United Kingdom*,[138] but see *Djaid v France*[139] where 20,000 Fr for non-pecuniary loss was awarded despite there being no claim in the application.

- Remedies are awarded by the European Court for pecuniary loss – that is, any financial loss consequent on the breach such as loss of earnings.

- Awards are also made for non-pecuniary loss. Examples include *Johnson v United Kingdom*[140] (unlawful detention) = £10,000; *Aydin v Turkey*[141] = £25,000 (breach of Art 3 by a rape); *Halford v United Kingdom*[142] = £10,000 (unlawful interception of telephone conversations); *McCann v United Kingdom*[143] = £Zero (violation of right to life – antecedents of victims affected the court's decision).

- The third category of award is costs and expenses, which can cover the costs of domestic proceedings.

- A finding of violation can be sufficient on its own but it is not possible to predict with any certainty when the European Court will make such a finding.

- The Court will also refuse to speculate on the outcome of cases had there been no breach. It will thus be reluctant to find causation between a breach of the right to a fair trial and the adverse consequences of the verdict: *Saunders v United Kingdom*.[144]

- The Court has awarded compensation for the loss of opportunity to bring proceedings against the police (in violation of Art 6) despite finding no breach by the police of other Convention rights: *Osman v United Kingdom*.[145]

---

138 Decision on just satisfaction, 6 November 1980, unreported, at para 14.

139 European Court of Human Rights Application No 38687/97, 29 September 1999.

140 (1997) 27 EHRR 296.

141 (1997) 25 EHRR 251.

142 (1997) 24 EHRR 523.

143 *McCann v United Kingdom* (1996) 21 EHRR 97.

144 (1997) 23 EHRR 313.

145 (2000) 29 EHRR 245. Note that the Court has subsequently declined to follow the *Osman* decision on the substantive law point following clarification by the United Kingdom courts of the elements of negligence: see *Z v United Kingdom* [2001] 2 FCR 246.

- The Court makes no award for aggravated or exemplary damages. One Law Lord recently expressed doubt as to whether exemplary damages could remain part of domestic law of tort in light of the Convention.[146]
- The Law Commission has published a report[147] analysing over 250 cases from Strasbourg to provide assistance to United Kingdom courts having to make decisions about compensation.[148]

146 See Lord Scott in *Kuddus v Chief Constable of Leicestershire Constabulary* [2001] UKHL 29; [2001] 2 WLR 1789.

147 Damages under the Human Rights Act 1998, LC 266, October 2000, available at www.lawcom.gov.uk. See also *Human Rights Damages* by Scorey and Eicke, 2001, Sweet & Maxwell.

148 See the summary in *The Times Law Supplement* by Robert Carnworth, 3 October 2000.

CHAPTER 2

IDENTIFYING A HUMAN RIGHTS
ISSUE FOR THE COURT

2.1 INTRODUCTION

The Human Rights Act 1998 creates a new framework for relying on Convention rights in the courts and tribunals. Anyone seeking to make Convention points in litigation needs to understand how this framework operates. The first part of this chapter seeks to provide detailed guidance as to the main mechanisms for introducing Convention arguments and the obstacles that need to be overcome. The second part provides more practical advice about when and how advocates can best introduce Human Rights Act submissions.

2.2 IDENTIFYING THE CAUSE OF ACTION

> 6(1) It is unlawful for a public authority to act in a way, which is incompatible with a Convention right ...

One of the main pillars of the Act is the new legal duty on public bodies. This duty is created by s 6 of the Act and is crucial to the way in which the legislation operates. It can be seen that s 6 creates a new statutory cause of action against public bodies. This is sometimes referred to as a 'human rights tort' but this is somewhat misleading as it gives rise to public law in addition to private law obligations. As will be seen, breach of the s 6 duty can lead to challenge by way of judicial review (public law) where it creates a new head of illegality[1] or suit in the High Court/county court (private law) and may be relied upon in any other legal proceedings.

Nothing in the Human Rights Act creates a criminal offence.[2] However, this is not to say that the Act is irrelevant when it comes to the extent of criminal liability. There is certainly scope for the restriction of available defences in line with victims' rights[3] and there is already some indication that this will occur.[4]

---

1   See Chapter 3 for a discussion of the development of Convention-based judicial review.
2   Section 7(8) of the HRA 1998.
3   See for example the difference in the tests for use of lethal force under domestic law (reasonable force on the facts the defendant honestly believed them to be) and Art 2 of the Convention (no more force than is absolutely necessary to avoid a specific risk). See Wadham at p 71.
4   In *R v H (Reasonable Chastisement)* [2001] EWCA Crim 1024; [2001] 2 FLR 431, the direction to the jury regarding the defence of reasonable chastisement was properly adjusted to reflect the complainant's rights under Art 3 of the Convention in light of *A v United Kingdom* (1999) 27 EHRR 611.

2.3 THE RIGHT TO USE CONVENTION RIGHTS IN COURTS AND TRIBUNALS

7(1) A person who claims that a public authority has acted (or proposes to act) in a way which is made unlawful by section 6(1) may–

    (a) bring proceedings against the authority under this Act in the appropriate court or tribunal, or

    (b) rely on the Convention right or rights concerned in any legal proceedings,

but only if he is (or would be) a victim of the unlawful act.

This important provision enables a 'victim' to sue the public authority for breach of Convention rights. There is no requirement that the conduct is unlawful under pre-existing domestic law. Note there is the possibility of pre-emptive action such as an application for an injunction before the alleged breach has taken place.

2.3.1 Free-standing Convention rights proceedings

Paragraph (a) enables a victim to bring free-standing proceedings alleging a breach of human rights. This also includes an appeal against the decision of a court or tribunal that is alleged to have breached Convention rights[5] and counter-claims by defendants in civil proceedings.[6] Free-standing claims must be brought by way of judicial review when the claimant seeks a quashing order, a mandatory order or a prohibiting order and may be so brought when the claimant seeks a declaration or an injunction.[7] Such claims may also be brought in the High Court or county court when normal civil remedies are sought. They are then subject to the same rules for allocation as any other civil case except that a claim regarding a judicial act must be made in the High Court.[8] In addition, it should be remembered that the county court cannot make a declaration of incompatibility so this will affect where the action should be commenced. It should be noted at this stage that there appears to be limited scope for bringing free-standing claims, which are outside the judicial review procedure. This is because any challenge to the 'exercise of a public

---

5   Section 9(1) of the HRA 1998. This provision is curious as an appellant does not really 'bring' proceedings as such but rather pursues an existing case to the next level. It means that s 7(1)(a) is potentially relevant in cases between private parties where an aggrieved party seeks to challenge a judicial act.

6   *Ibid*, s 7(2).

7   See s 7(3) and CPR Part 54, rr 54.2 and 54.3. Note that a claim for damages may be made on a judicial review but it cannot be the only remedy that is sought: CPR, r 54.3(2).

8   See CPR, r 7.11: 'Human Rights – (1) a claim under s 7(1)(a) of the Human Rights Act 1998 in respect of a judicial act may be brought only in the High Court. (2) Any other claim under s 7(1)(a) of that Act may be brought in any court.'

function' falls within the definition of judicial review and is subject to the special procedure for dealing with such claims.[9]

Issues for advocates: bringing free-standing Convention proceedings

Section 7(1)(a) is used when the alleged victim alleges only a breach of Convention rights. It may be relied on in order to:

- Bring judicial review proceedings against a public authority.
- Bring judicial review proceedings against a court or tribunal, where judicial review is available.[10]
- Appeal against a judicial decision, where there is a right of appeal.
- Issue civil proceedings in the High Court against a judicial act.
- Issue civil proceedings against any other public authority in the High Court or county court.
- Issue a counterclaim against a public authority in the High Court or county court.

2.3.2 Reliance on Convention rights in legal proceedings

Paragraph (b) enables a victim to tack human rights arguments on to other legal proceedings either as part of a defence or as an additional aspect of an existing cause of action. 'Legal proceedings' include but are not limited to proceedings brought by or at the instigation of a public authority and an appeal against the decision of a court or tribunal.[11] It is thus very broad in scope in that it permits advocates to argue for the re-interpretation of existing legal remedies in light of human rights principles. For the avoidance of doubt the Act makes clear that a party may rely on Convention rights without impairing his or her right to bring traditional domestic law proceedings.[11a] Thus a false imprisonment action might also include argument about breach of Art 5. Those claiming assault might add arguments about breach of Arts 3 and 8. Even judicial review claimants might tack on Convention rights arguments as part of a wider challenge to decision-making. The Convention does not change fundamentally the nature of the cause of action in question. Rather it requires the justification of the public authority defendant to be measured against the Convention right and permits an incremental development of common law protection. Advocates should be alive to the potential for the Convention to impact upon the interpretation of torts, for

---

9   CPR, r 54.1(2). See further at para 2.6.
10 The Act does not affect any rule of law, such as s 29(3) of the Supreme Court Act 1981, which prevents a court from being subject to judicial review: s 9(2).
11 Section 7(6) of the HRA 1998.
11a Section 11.

example, Art 8 privacy interests can push the boundaries of breach of confidence[12] and also the scope of defences, for example, Art 10 can affect liability for contempt of court.[13]

The right to sue and to rely on Convention rights is limited to challenges against the conduct of public authorities. It is therefore almost exclusively reserved for proceedings involving a public authority. One exception is where there are two private parties to litigation and one seeks to rely under paragraph (b) on the unlawful conduct of a public authority, although in such circumstances it would be safer to join the public authority to the proceedings. In this context, see also the discussion of horizontality in Chapter 6.

Issues for advocates: relying on Convention rights in other proceedings

Section 7(1)(b) is used where the alleged victim is:

- The claimant in civil proceedings against a public authority and is relying on the Convention right as part of that claim.

- The claimant in judicial review proceedings where the Convention right forms only part of the allegation of unlawfulness.

- The defendant in civil proceedings brought by a public authority.

- The defendant in criminal proceedings brought by a public authority.

- The claimant in private law proceedings against a private defendant and is relying on the unlawful act of a public authority as part of the claim.

- The defendant in private law proceedings against a private claimant and is relying on the unlawful act of a public authority as part of the defence.

- The appellant or respondent in an appeal against a decision in any of the above proceedings.

2.4 IDENTIFYING DEFENCES

6(2) Sub-section (1) does not apply to an act if–

    (a) as the result of one or more provisions of primary legislation, the authority could not have acted differently; or

    (b) in the case of one or more provisions of, or made under, primary legislation which cannot be read or given effect in a way which is compatible with the Convention rights, the authority was acting so as to give effect to or enforce those provisions.

---

12 See discussion of *Douglas v Hello!* [2001] 2 WLR 992 and *Venables and Thompson v News Group Newspapers* [2001] 2 WLR 1038 in Chapter 6.

13 *Ashworth Security Hospital v MGN Ltd* [2001] 1 WLR 515; *HM Attorney General v Punch Ltd* [2001] EWCA Civ 403; [2001] 2 WLR 1713.

This might be termed the 'Parliament made me do it' defence. A central theme of the Human Rights Act is that Parliamentary sovereignty is retained. Thus Parliament may, if it wishes, pass laws that are in breach of Convention rights. The aggrieved person will not be able to challenge the lawfulness of the legislation and will be left to seek a remedy in the European Court of Human Rights in Strasbourg. It follows that where Parliament has passed laws that are incompatible with Convention rights, the conduct of public bodies enforcing such laws cannot itself be unlawful. If it were otherwise, the intention of Parliament would be frustrated because, although it could pass incompatible laws, those laws could not be lawfully implemented.[14] Section 6(2) is intended to safeguard the position of public authorities who: (a) have a mandatory duty to act in a particular way; or (b) are merely acting to enforce provisions, which are themselves incompatible with Convention rights.

However, public authorities must act with caution when relying on s 6(2). They must be satisfied that they really do have no choice but to act in the way they have done (if they are relying on (a)). Alternatively, they must be satisfied that the legislation they are enforcing really is incompatible with the Convention right and that there is no compatible way of enforcing it (if they are relying on (b)). A court looking at the matter later might decide that the law was not in fact incompatible with the Convention. It might say that the law could have been interpreted in a way that was different to the public body's interpretation. In such circumstances the public body would not be able to avail itself of the s 6(2) defence as the court would have ruled that the provision was not itself incompatible.

It will be rare indeed that an advocate representing a public authority will commence his or her case by submitting that the law concerned is incompatible with the alleged victim's Convention rights. Much more likely is the public authority arguing that the law is compatible and that it has been implemented in a compatible manner. If it is successful, the public authority can be confident that the law and its practice are Convention-compliant. However, there are two ways in which a court might disagree with such an approach. First, it might say that the law is itself incompatible, in which case the public authority will rely on s 6(2). Secondly, it might decide that the law itself is compatible but that it was implemented in an incompatible manner. In such a situation the authority will lose the case and will learn a lesson about how to act compatibly with the Convention when enforcing legislation.

A further difficulty is the role of the court as a public authority when deciding on appropriate orders to make following proceedings that breach a person's Convention rights but are explicitly authorised by primary

---

14 See discussion of *Re K (A Child) (Secure Accommodation Order: Right to Liberty)* [2001] 2 WLR 1141 in Chapter 5 for a stark illustration of the difficulties that would be caused were this otherwise.

legislation. This could arise when a court is unable to interpret a criminal offence in a way is compatible with the accused's Convention rights. If he or she is convicted what sentence should the court impose? A normal tariff sentence might compound the breach whereas a nominal sentence would frustrate the intention of Parliament. For example, it is clear that convictions for gross indecency where more than two people are present or take part are a breach of the Art 8 right to respect for private life.[15] If a person was charged in such circumstances and the court was unable to interpret the offence compatibly the dilemma we have described would arise for the sentencing judge or magistrates.

2.5 IDENTIFYING A PUBLIC AUTHORITY

Identifying a public authority is essential for claimants seeking to bring proceedings for breach of Convention rights or relying on such rights in other legal proceedings and seeking a remedy for a breach. It is a condition precedent for invoking the protection of the Human Rights Act that there is an act or omission by a public authority that has or would violate a Convention right. As we shall see, the court is also a public authority and that is why the Convention can have relevance in litigation concerning only private parties.

Section 6(3) provides as follows:

6(3) In this section 'public authority' includes–

   (a) a court or tribunal, and

   (b) any person certain of whose functions are functions of a public nature

   ...

This is clearly not an exhaustive definition of public authority. It is generally accepted[16] that the Act creates three broad categories:

* pure (or standard) public authorities;
* hybrid (or functional) public authorities; and
* private persons.

The first are caught by the Act in respect of everything that they do. A police force would fall within this category; as it is a pure public authority there is no aspect of its activity that is immune from the operation of s 6. Thus, its employment and contractual relationships are just as much part of its public persona as are its core policing activities.[17] The second are caught only in

---

15 *ADT v United Kingdom* [2000] 2 FLR 697.

16 See generally, Grosz, Beatson and Duffy, *Human Rights, the 1998 Act and the European Convention*, 2000, London: Sweet & Maxwell, pp 60–71.

17 See *ibid*, paras 4.10–4.14 for a detailed discussion of this category.

respect of their public functions, not their private acts.[18] The example offered by the government during the passage of the Bill was Railtrack, which was said to be a private corporation but with some public functions, for example, in relation to rail safety.[19] Such an organisation is caught by the s 6 duty, in respect of its public functions only but it remains unaffected by the duty in respect of its private relationships.[20] The Act speaks of a 'person' having public functions but it is clear that this phrase includes a 'body of persons corporate or unincorporate'.[21] The latter category is not caught at all so that private bodies or individuals will only be affected by the Human Rights Act to the extent that the courts recognise horizontal effect.[22]

There is thus a distinction between public authorities and public functions. A pure public authority must act compatibly with Convention rights whether or not it performs public functions. A hybrid body must act compatibly with Convention rights when it performs public functions but not otherwise. The Lord Chancellor urged that when considering the status of organisations for the purposes of the Act, 'the focus should be on their functions and not on their nature as an authority'.[23] The phrase 'public functions' is clearly central to identifying a public authority where the body in question is not obviously an emanation of the state. However, the Act does not itself explain what is meant by 'public function' – there is no guidance as to what it is about a function that makes it public. Thus once the courts have focused on the function they must develop their own criteria for deciding whether it is public in nature.

The clearest indication of the type of body the government had in mind was given by Jack Straw, the Home Secretary. He said that the intention was as far as possible to reflect in the definition of public authorities those bodies for which the United Kingdom would be liable in Strasbourg. He said that the test must relate to the substance and nature of the act, not to the form and legal personality of the body in question. He went on to explain:

> The government have a direct responsibility for core bodies, such as central government and the police, but they also have a responsibility for other public authorities, in so far as the actions of such authorities impinge on private individuals. The Bill had to have a definition ... that went at least as wide and took account of the fact that, over the past 20 years, an increasingly large number of private bodies, such as companies or charities, have come to exercise public functions that were previously exercised by public authorities ...[24]

---

18 Section 6(5) of the HRA 1998.
19 Lord Chancellor, *Hansard*, HL, 24 November 1997, col 784.
20 Section 6(5) of the HRA 1998.
21 Section 5 and Sched 1 of the Interpretation Act 1978.
22 See Chapter 6.
23 Lord Irvine of Lairg, Lord Chancellor, HL Comm Stage, 24 November 1997, col 784.
24 Jack Straw, Home Secretary, HC Debs, 16 February 1998, col 775.

It is thus clear that the definition of public authority was intended to go beyond the traditional view of governmental bodies. However, aiming to peg the definition of public authority in the Human Rights Act to the definition of state responsibility in Strasbourg was a somewhat hopeless task. There are two reasons for this. First the Strasbourg Court often declines to identify which particular bodies engage state responsibility.[25] Indeed in two cases against the United Kingdom the Court and Commission have explicitly avoided deciding whether the conduct of the BBC[26] and British Rail[27] engage the responsibility of the United Kingdom. Beyond the most obvious examples like the police,[28] the Strasbourg case law has not up to now explored in detail the different tentacles of the state. It should be recalled that the United Kingdom Government is always the respondent in claims before the Strasbourg Court. This is not always the case under the Human Rights Act.

The second and more substantial reason is that the concept of state responsibility encompasses not just the activity of agents of the state but also the failure of the state to satisfy its positive obligations inherent in many articles of the Convention:

> Under Article 1 of the Convention, each Contracting State 'shall secure to everyone within [its] jurisdiction the rights and freedoms defined in ... [the] Convention'; hence, if a violation of one of those rights and freedoms is the result of non-observance of that obligation in the enactment of domestic legislation, the responsibility of the State for that violation is engaged. Although the proximate cause of the events giving rise to this case was the 1975 agreement between British Rail and the railway unions, it was the domestic law in force at the relevant time that made lawful the treatment of which the applicants complained. The responsibility of the respondent State for any resultant breach of the Convention is thus engaged on this basis.[29]

Examples of the state's responsibility being engaged include its laws being inadequate to prevent a breach of Convention rights by a third party,[30] its failure to have an adequate legal framework for securing a remedy for breach of rights,[31] or by the failure of state agents to act to prevent a risk of a breach of rights arising.[32] It follows that just because the conduct of an individual or body triggers state responsibility cannot, without more, be the test for a

---

25 'There has therefore been a violation of Art 6, s 1 (Art 6(1)). The Court does not have to specify to which national authority this violation is attributable: the sole issue is the international responsibility of the State.' *Zimmermann and Steiner v Switzerland* (1984) 6 EHRR 17.

26 *Hilton v United Kingdom* (1988) 57 DR 108.

27 *Young, James and Webster v United Kingdom* (1982) 4 EHRR 38 at para 49.

28 *Osman v United Kingdom* (2000) 29 EHRR 245.

29 *Young, James and Webster* (1982) 4 EHRR 38, at para 45.

30 *A v United Kingdom* (1999) 27 EHRR 611 (defence of lawful chastisement of child).

31 *Z v United Kingdom* [2001] 2 FCR 246 (immunity for social services departments).

32 *Osman v United Kingdom* (2000) 29 EHRR 245 (duty of police to protect life).

defendant being a public authority. In *A v United Kingdom*[33] state responsibility was engaged following the beating of a child by his step-father and the inadequacy of the domestic law to protect the child. It could not seriously be suggested that the violent father would now amount to a public authority under the Human Rights Act. In such a case the court dealing with the allegation of assault would be the relevant public authority and would have to assess whether it could give effect to the rights of the child in its decision about the ambit of the common law defence of reasonable chastisement.[34]

It follows that decisions of the Strasbourg Court do not really provide much assistance in determining which type of body exercising which type of function ought to be subject to the duties that s 6 imposes. The truth is that the Strasbourg Court has not, thus far, shown any real interest in the distinction between public and non-public functions. Yet the domestic courts are unable to rest on the international concept of state responsibility. They have to decide whether particular individuals and organisations are exercising public functions so as to give rise to obligations under s 6.

2.5.1 Public functions in domestic law

In the first decision to analyse the meaning of public function in any detail the Court of Appeal in *Poplar Housing and Regeneration Community Association Ltd v Donoghue*[35] considered whether Poplar Ltd, a registered social landlord set up by Tower Hamlets local authority, was a public authority for the purposes of s 6 of the Human Rights Act. Lord Woolf, giving the judgment of the court, did agree that the courts should give a generous interpretation to the concept of public function but went on:

> The fact that a body performs an activity which otherwise a public body would be under a duty to perform, cannot mean that such performance is necessarily a public function ... The purpose of section 6(3)(b) ... is not to make a body, which does not have responsibilities to the public, a public body merely because it performs acts on behalf of a public body which would constitute public functions were such acts to be performed by the public body itself.[36]

The first part of this statement might at first seem surprising – a natural reaction is that former state activity must surely remain state activity even if carried out by the private sector. However, this presupposes that the activity

---

33 (1999) 27 EHRR 611.

34 See now *R v H (Reasonable Chastisement)* [2001] EWCA Crim 1024; [2001] 2 FLR 431, where the Court of Appeal held that a trial judge should, pending a change in the law, adjust the direction to the jury to take account of the decision in *A v United Kingdom*.

35 [2001] EWCA Civ 595, [2001] 3 WLR 183.

36 *Ibid*, paras 58–59.

was public in nature in the first place. This is not always the case. Few people would contemplate the making of motor cars or the running of an airline as public functions now, although they were formerly carried out directly by the state. The last phrase is somewhat curious as it postulates the possibility that functions can be public if carried out by a public authority whereas they are private if carried out by an ostensibly private body. The better view is that a function is public or private irrespective of the body which performs it. The key difference is that if a pure public authority performs the function then, whether it is public or private, the performance is caught by the Human Rights Act. By contrast, if a function is performed by a body that is not a pure public authority then it will only be caught by the Human Rights Act if the function is public in nature.

The closest the Court of Appeal came to setting down a test for public function is as follows:

> ... What can make an act, which would otherwise be private, public, is a feature or a combination of features which *impose a public character or stamp* on the act. *Statutory authority* for what is done can at least help to mark the act as being public; so can the extent of *control* over the function exercised by another body which is a public authority. The more closely the acts that could be of a private nature are *enmeshed* in the activities of a public body, the more likely they are to be public. However, the fact that the acts are supervised by a public regulatory body does not necessarily indicate that they are of a public nature.[37]

The court thought that the concept of public authority was 'clearly inspired' by the approach of the courts to identifying bodies amenable to judicial review.[38] The act of providing accommodation to rent was not without more a public function irrespective of the section of society for whom the accommodation was provided. Neither did the charitable or not-for-profit status of the body point towards it being a public authority. However, the court thought that the closeness of the relationship between the local authority and Poplar was important. Poplar was set up by the authority, which retained members on Poplar's board and guided it as to how it should deal with

---

37 *Ibid*, para 65, our emphases. Compare the approach in the chancel repairs case – *Aston Cantlow and Wilmcote with Billesley Parochial Church Council v Wallbank and Another* [2001] EWCA Civ 713; [2001] 3 All ER 393 – where the parish council was held to be a public authority, para 35: 'In our judgment it is inescapable, in these circumstances, that a PCC is a public authority in the sense that it possesses powers, which private individuals do not possess to determine how others should act. Thus, in particular, its notice to repair has statutory force. It is public in the sense that it is created and empowered by law; that it forms part of the church by law established; and that its functions include the enforcement through the courts of a common law liability to maintain its chancels resting upon persons who need not be members of the church. If this were to be incorrect, the PCC would nevertheless, and for the same reasons, be a legal person certain of whose functions, chancel repairs among them, are functions of a public nature.'

38 See, for example, *R v Panel of Takeovers and Mergers ex p Datafin* [1987] QB 815 and *R v Jockey Club ex p Aga Khan* [1991] 2 All ER 853.

tenants and in particular the defendant tenant. It concluded that, for the purposes of that particular case only, Poplar's role was 'so closely assimilated to that of Tower Hamlets that it was performing public and not private functions. Poplar therefore is a functional public authority at least to that extent'.[39]

The use of the word 'assimilated' is a significant limitation on the circumstances in which a private body can be said to be endowed with public functions. Where such a body is carrying out functions that used to be performed by a local authority and (as with housing) those functions are not obviously public in nature there must be an assessment of the extent to which the private body is *absorbed* into the public body's role before it can be said to be performing public functions. In this way privatisation of functions that used to be performed by the state can have a dramatic effect on the availability of remedies under the Human Rights Act. While the function remains in the hands of the state body it does not matter whether it is public or private in nature. Once it is transferred to the private sector, its nature becomes central to assessing whether the Human Rights Act applies to its performance.

Poplar was distinguished in *Heather and Others v Leonard Cheshire Foundation and Another*[40] when the High Court decided that a charitable foundation providing residential and nursing care was not a public authority under s 6. The claimants were all residents at a home run by the defendant charity and claimed that a decision to close the home and move them was a breach of their Art 8 right to respect for their home due to promises that they would have a home for life.[41] They had been placed at the home by a local authority and a health authority pursuant to their statutory duties to provide residential accommodation[42] and nursing services.[43]

The court rejected an argument that funding of the care places by the state meant that the charity must thereby be a public authority in respect of the claimants. Grant funding and particularly contractual arrangements between a public authority and the provider of a service would not be indicative of the provider being a public authority. There would have to be 'true delegation or sharing of functions' for an otherwise private body to be deemed to be a public authority. Moreover, state regulation (in this case under the Registered Homes Act 1984), pointed away from the regulated organisation being a public authority. It was the regulator that exercised a public function.

---

39 [2001] EWCA Civ 595; [2001] 3 WLR 183, para 66.

40 [2001] EWHC Admin 429; [2001] All ER(D) 156 (Jun), Stanley Burnton J.

41 See *R v North East Devon Health Authority ex p Coughlan* [2000] 3 All ER 850 for the first case where this argument was successful against a public authority.

42 Sections 21 and 26 of the National Assistance Act 1948.

43 Section 3(1) of the National Health Service Act 1977.

The court ruled that the Act could not have introduced a purely functional test of public authority, as it would make the nature of the body and the source of its authority irrelevant. As a general proposition this is surely correct and was illustrated by the fact that if residential and nursing care, as functions, were public, the charity would be a public authority even in respect of its private fee-paying residents.[44] The position is that whereas hybrid bodies may be public authorities by reference only to their functions, pure public authorities are just that, whether they perform public or private functions.[45] This confirms the earlier point that a pure public authority may, in contracting with a private organisation, be transferring public or private functions. If it transfers private functions then, when performed by the private organisation, they are immune from Human Rights Act mechanisms.

The court went on to analyse the purpose of the Human Rights Act in establishing the test for public authority. Intriguingly, Burnton J decided that Parliamentary statements were inadmissible as there was no ambiguity in s 6.[46] He therefore refused to consider statements such as the Home Secretary's contribution set out above. Instead His Lordship considered Art 8 of the Convention and said that:

> 71 ... it is not possible easily to fit Article 8(2) with any application of Article 8(1) to a private body. First and most obviously, Article 8(2) is the counterpart to Article 8(1), and its limitation to public authorities indicates that the obligation corresponding to the right conferred by Article 8(1) is an obligation imposed on public authorities. That obligation may include an obligation to secure the right in question generally under domestic law; but such an obligation is quintessentially an obligation of the government, and not of any non-public body. Secondly, the justifications referred to in

---

44 Although it should be noted that the Lord Chancellor assumed that education and health provision would be public functions whatever the form of delivery – see HL Deb Vol 583, col 800, 24 November 1997.

45 Sedley LJ put it as follows in the *Aston Cantlow* case [2001] EWCA Civ 713; [2001] 3 All ER 393, above (para 33): '[Counsel] submits that the test of what is a public authority for the purposes of s 6 is function-based. There is plainly force in this in relation to the "hybrid" class of public authority created by s 6(3)(b), which depends on the performance of "functions of a public nature". But it does not follow that this governs the principal category of "public authority", though it may well have a bearing on it ... Article 34 limits the status of potential victim of a breach of the Convention to "any person, non-governmental organisation or group of individuals". In other words, the Convention assumes the existence of a state, which stands distinct from persons, groups and non-governmental organisations. It is in order to locate that state for the Act's purposes that the concept of a public authority is, used in s 6.'

46 *Pepper v Hart* [1993] AC 593. For a similar view – albeit leaving the issue open for subsequent cases – see the *Aston Cantlow* case, *ibid*, para 29: 'The phrase "public authority" is not a term of art; nor is its application always obvious or easy. This, however, is some distance from Miss Asplin's submission that it is so ambiguous or obscure that resort may be had to *Hansard* for help in interpreting it (see *Pepper v Hart* [1993] AC 593). The words are perfectly intelligible. The fact that there will be cases in which their application is problematical does not begin to bring them within the class of words for which parliamentary debates have been held to be an admissible aid to construction. We accordingly declined Miss Asplin's invitation to look at these.'

> Article 8(2) are all matters relevant to government, but not to non-governmental bodies.[47]

The court went on to consider *Costello-Roberts v United Kingdom*[48] where the ECHR ruled that the United Kingdom Government could not absolve itself of responsibility to secure Convention rights by delegating its obligations to private bodies or individuals. The court refused to accept that, when transmuted into the domestic context, this case was authority for a wide view of public authority:

> The party which would have been liable in *Costello-Roberts* if there had been a violation ... was the UK Government ... The Convention was [not] intended to make non-governmental bodies, acting in accordance with their ... domestic law, directly liable for breach of a right that the government had failed to secure under domestic law.[49]

It followed that the charity, as an ostensibly private body, did not have any duties under the Convention and was not a public authority. It could be distinguished from *Poplar* as it was set up by private individuals, had no statutory duty to co-operate with the funding authorities, was not extensively controlled by those authorities – registration under the Registered Homes Act 1984 did not involve the kind or extent of regulation that applied to a Registered Social Landlord. Finally, there was neither co-membership nor such a closely integrated relationship as Poplar had with its local authority.

What emerges from the two cases discussed above is a relatively narrow view of what might be a public authority. A public authority is limited to:

(i) classic state bodies (pure public authorities);

(ii) bodies that are enmeshed/assimilated with the role of the classic state body; or

(iii) bodies that are private but are performing public functions.

The courts have not so far accepted the government's apparent view that charities and companies assuming former public authority activity will, without more, be said to be exercising public functions. Undoubtedly we will see further clarification in the courts in due course and it is right to say that the decisions under review have not set down any hard and fast rules. There is clearly scope for other considerations[50] to be raised in future cases.[51]

---

47 This seems to be the first judicial approval of Sir Richard Buxton's extra-judicial analysis of the impact of the Convention on private law (see 'The Human Rights Act and private law' (2000) 116 LQR 48) described by Professor Wade as a *'non sequitur'* (see 'Horizons of horizontality' (2000) 116 LQR 217).

48 (1993) 19 EHRR 112, paras 27–28.

49 [2001] EWHC Admin 429; [2001] All ER(D) 156 (Jun), para 78.

50 See, for example, the indicators suggested by Professor Dawn Oliver in *The Frontiers of the State: Public Authorities and Public Functions under the Human Rights Act* [2000] PL 476.

51 At the time of writing the *Leonard Cheshire* case is subject to an expedited appeal to the House of Lords on the issue of whether the charity is a public authority.

2.5.2 Consequences of a narrow test for public authority

First, on a practical level, bodies that have may hitherto have conceded the public authority point and argued the case on its merits might now be inclined to pursue a jurisdiction point from the outset. The courts have already assumed without any real dispute that privately run detention centres[52] and water utility companies[53] are public authorities for the purpose of s 6.[54] However, if we measure their activities against the restrictive approach we have analysed it is not inevitable that they are exercising public functions.

Secondly, the test of amenability to judicial review could, notwithstanding Lord Woolf's comments in *Poplar* that the concept of public authority was inspired by the judicial review criteria, be wider than the test for amenability to claims under s 7 of the Human Rights Act. Thus, although Human Rights Act actions would have wider reach in respect of pure public authorities,[55] they could be unavailable to challenge bodies that are otherwise answerable in public law.[56] It is doubtful that the court would wish to see this occur and we would expect the law to develop at least to the extent that public bodies in judicial review are also public authorities for the purpose of the Human Rights Act.

Thirdly, bodies that are emanations of the state for the purposes of European Union law might nonetheless have no direct responsibilities to respect citizens' human rights. In the leading case of *Foster v British Gas*[57] the European Court of Justice held that a privatised utility was an emanation of the state for the purpose of deciding whether it was bound by an unimplemented directive.[58] The test applied was whether: (i) the body had

---

52   *Quaquah v Group 4 (Total Security) Ltd and Another* [2001] All ER(D) 279 (May).

53   *Marcic v Thames Water Utilities Ltd* [2001] All ER(D) 202 (May).

54   There was no dispute about the status of a university in *R (on the Application of Mitchell) v Coventry University and Another* [2001] EWHC Admin 167, 2 March, although the case focused on alleged fee discrimination under the Education Fees and Awards Act 1983 as opposed to any particular action by the University.

55   The Act recognises no distinction between public and private activities for pure public authorities, unlike judicial review: *R v East Berkshire Health Authority ex p Walsh* [1985] QB 152.

56   One example would be universities. In *Clark v University of Lincolnshire and Humberside* [2000] 3 All ER 752, Sedley LJ said of challenges to 'new' universities, 'That judicial review is available in such a case seems plain on first principles. A number of such applications have been reported – for example *R v Manchester Metropolitan University ex p Nolan* [1994] ELR 380 – in none of which has any challenge been offered to the court's jurisdiction' (at p 756). His Lordship described the relationship as 'a contractual relationship, which happens to possess a public law dimension' (at p 757).

57   [1990] 2 CMLR 833.

58   There is also an interesting parallel with bodies governed by public law for the purposes of Art 1 of Council Directive 93/37/EEC of 14 June 1993 concerning the co-ordination of procedures for the award of public works contracts (OJ 1993 L 199, p 54). Universities fall within this category: see *R (on the Application of University of Cambridge) v HM Treasury* (C380/98) [2000] 1 WLR 2514 (ECJ).

been made responsible for providing a public service; (ii) the service was provided under the control of the state; (iii) it had special powers beyond those resulting from normal rules applicable between individuals. These might be thought to be useful criteria for assessing whether a body is exercising public functions for the purposes of the Human Rights Act, although it is unclear the extent to which British Gas would be a public authority given the views expressed by the courts so far, particularly the comment in the *Leonard Cheshire* case, that state regulation is, if anything, a negative indicator of public authority status. By way of contrast it will be recalled that the Court of Appeal has held that a voluntary aided school was an emanation of the state in that it provided public schooling within the state system notwithstanding the lack of state control. It said that the test in *Foster v British Gas* was not to be applied as though it were a statutory definition of emanation of the state and that a body could be an emanation even though it was not under the control of central government.[59]

Fourthly, the cases throw into sharper focus another consequence of the public/private divide in public law and human rights law. Public authorities are apparently able to divest themselves of liability under the Human Rights Act by contracting with private providers to satisfy statutory duties. In so doing state provision shrinks and the alleged victim is deprived of any remedy under the Human Rights Act they might have been entitled to had the public authority continued to provide the service itself. For example, if the current government keeps its promise to increase the partnership between the National Health Service and the private medical sector then the increasing number of NHS patients treated at private hospitals would have no recourse to arguments about breach of their Convention rights by the new provider. The private hospital would not become a public authority merely because the treatment it gives would be caught by s 6 if carried out by the NHS. The court in *Leonard Cheshire* recognised this 'protection gap' might lead to citizens losing the protection that judicial review offers. However:

> The privatisation of formerly governmental activities has been authorised by Parliament. Privatisation means, in general, that functions formerly exercised by public authorities are now carried out by non-public entities, often for profit. It has inevitable consequences for the applicability of judicial review, which the courts are not free to avoid.[60]

The court agreed with Professor Dawn Oliver[61] that the response to this gap should be for the courts to discharge their functions as public authorities

---

59 *National Union of Teachers v Governing Body of St Mary's Church of England (Aided) Junior School* [1997] ICR 334.

60 Paragraph 104. In *Quaquah v Group 4 (Total Security) Ltd and Another*, the Divisional Court held that a private security firm which ran an immigration detention centre was a public authority under s 6(3), although the security firm was not represented at the hearing.

61 See [2000] PL 476.

under the Human Rights Act by developing private law so as to provide remedies for those whose Convention rights have been interfered with.

This finally, then, gives rise to another related issue – the extent that the Act might apply in litigation between private parties – so called horizontal effect.[62] The courts have already indicated that they will be willing to develop the Common law incrementally in order to give effect to the courts' positive obligations under the Convention to protect the rights of individuals that appear before them. Thus, in *Douglas v Hello!*,[63] Sedley LJ said in respect of whether the law of confidentiality could be expanded in order to protect privacy interests in litigation between private parties:

> [Counsel argues that] whatever the current state of common law and equity, we are obliged now to give some effect to Article 8 ... of the Convention ... If the step from confidentiality to privacy is not simply a modern restatement of the scope of a known protection but a legal innovation — then I would accept his submission ... that this is precisely the kind of incremental change for which the Act is designed: one which without undermining the measure of certainty which is necessary to all law gives substance and effect to s 6 ... Such a process would be consonant with the jurisprudence of the European Court of Human Rights, which s 2 of the Act requires us to take into account and which has pinpointed Article 8 as a locus of the doctrine of positive obligation.[64]

If the courts were able to develop this approach in order to fully protect the Convention rights of citizens that were once in the bosom of the state and are now being dealt with by ostensibly private bodies then the narrow parameters of the concept of public function might not matter too much in terms of securing protection for Convention rights. However, we wonder whether this will be possible. Sedley LJ felt able to discern the development of a right to privacy in the *Douglas* case not simply on the basis of the positive obligations imposed by the Convention, but on the normal development of the common law, and in particular on the fact that the United Kingdom had itself argued at Strasbourg that the common law had developed so as to protect privacy via the remedy for breach of confidence.[65] In other cases, the courts may not feel able to develop the common law or equitable remedies in order to sufficiently protect the citizen. In *Mowan v Wandsworth LBC*,[66] for example, the Court of Appeal was unwilling, despite its clear sympathy for the claimant, to extend the torts of nuisance and negligence to make the local authority landlord liable for breaches of Art 8 caused by one of its tenants. Sir Christopher Staunton put it as follows:

---

62 See further in Chapter 6.
63 [2001] 2 WLR 992.
64 At paras 128–30.
65 *Spencer v United Kingdom* [1998] EHRLR 348, where the United Kingdom successfully argued that the applicants had failed to exhaust domestic remedies.
66 [2001] EGCS 4.

> [The conduct] is certainly a breach of Mrs Mowan's rights, and I would hope of her human rights too. But I fear that we cannot accept the invitation to bend the common law so that it affords a remedy against the Council. The principles are too well established for that. If they are to be altered, that must happen elsewhere.

The Court of Appeal noted that there might be a remedy in judicial review against the council, but obviously this would not be available if the landlord was a private body, which was not amenable to judicial review.

2.5.2.1 Example

Is elementary education a public function? It is not possible to say in the abstract that education is public as it is certainly possible to educate a child privately for profit either in an independent school or through private tuition. What then of private delivery of state education? If an education authority contracts with a private provider to manage its schools it can satisfy its responsibilities under the Education Acts.[67] What happens in such arrangements if there is a human rights dispute between the school management and a pupil or parent? On the shrinking state approach it is at least arguable that the school management no longer qualifies as a public authority. If so, are the courts able to fashion common law remedies under their duty in s 6(3)(a) to provide similar protection for Convention rights as was provided prior to the shift of responsibility? Not all disputes will be like the *Douglas* case where there is at least the peg of an existing cause of action that is itself ripe for development in line with Convention rights. Burnton J in *Leonard Cheshire* recognised that in some areas, 'the scope for development [of the common law] may be limited, and Parliament may have to consider enhanced regulation'. If his test for public authority survives the test of time these questions will be given added significance following the passage of the education and health service Bills announced by the new Labour Government in 2001.[68]

The courts have so far countenanced the idea that the state can shrink through privatisation of former state functions and with it shrinks the ability of the citizen to claim a breach of Convention rights directly under the Human Rights Act. In this sense it challenges the view that there is an 'enduring

---

67 Surrey County Council recently entered into a contract with Nord Anglia, a profit-making plc, to run one of its schools. A seven-year contract was awarded for the company to manage all aspects of the school, effectively supplanting the role of the local education authority. See 'Is this School Privatisation?' M Baker, BBC News Online, 25 May 2001.

68 See the Queen's Speech, 20 June 2001, with its emphasis on reform of education and health provision to increase private sector involvement.

reality' of what amount to public functions.[69] It excludes a raft of bodies carrying out what used to be state activity from the Human Rights Act and instead requires the courts to focus on whether they can fashion the common law to protect human rights in the private sphere. In contrast to the developing clarity of approach based on the broader tests of emanations of the state and of judicial review, this proposed Human Rights Act approach seems necessarily piecemeal and uncertain.

Issues for advocates: public authority checklist

It is difficult at this early stage in the development of the case law to make any firm predictions as to the long-term position. However, the following reflects the current position but should be read in light of the analysis, which precedes it.

- There is no one test for what is a public authority.
- Pure public authorities are not defined and will be decided on a case-by-case basis where there is dispute. They include all of the 'obvious' state bodies such as central and local government, the police, the prison service, the courts, etc.
- A pure public authority is bound by the Human Rights Act whether it performs public or private functions.
- An ostensibly private body may be a public authority either if its role is enmeshed/assimilated with that of a pure public authority or if it carries out public functions.
- The previous decisions on amenability to judicial review remain relevant. Activity that is not amenable to judicial review (for example, employment disputes) will not be immune from claims under the Human Rights Act if the employer is a pure public authority.
- Private bodies may be amenable to judicial review in respect of some of their activity but nonetheless be immune from action under the Human Rights Act if they are deemed not to be carrying out public functions.
- The fact that activity used to be performed by a pure public authority is not determinative of it being a public function.
- The fact that activity would be a public function if carried out by a public authority is not determinative.
- The test of public authority is not purely one of functionality.
- The courts will develop the concept on a case-by-case basis looking at the circumstances of each body and the activity in question.

---

69 See Michael Smith, *Business and the Human Rights Act 1998* (London: Jordans, 2000), para 3.95 *et seq*. He identifies a number of former state owned utilities, for example, BP Amoco, and asks whether such companies can cease to be public authorities as time passes.

Matters suggesting a body has a public function include:

- If there is statutory authority for the act.
- If there is a degree of control over the body exercised by a public authority.
- If the body was established by public authority.
- If the management board of the body includes members of public authority.
- If the body is working in collaboration with public authority in respect of the decision in question.
- If the body's functions are 'enmeshed' with activities of a public authority.
- If it can be said that the body's functions are 'governmental' in nature.
- If there is a 'true delegation or sharing of functions' with a government authority.

Matters not (or not necessarily) suggesting a body has a public function include:

- The status of the body as private legal entity.
- If a public body would have to perform the function if there was no other provision.
- If there is state funding through grants.
- If there is a contractual relationship with public authority.
- If there is regulation by a statutory authority.
- If the body has charitable or not-for-profit status.
- The fact that a substantial number of people are affected.

2.6 DEALING WITH TIME LIMITS

7   (5) Proceedings under sub-subsection (1)(a) must be brought before the end of–

    (a) the period of one year beginning with the date on which the act complained of took place; or

    (b) such longer period as the court or tribunal considers equitable having regard to all the circumstances,

but that is subject to any rule imposing a stricter time limit in relation to the procedure in question.

This creates a shorter limitation period for free-standing human rights claims than exists for other causes of action. Note also that if the challenge is made by judicial review, the limitation period (maximum three months) will still apply.[70] Claimants may be tempted to argue that a Human Rights Act claim against a public authority is a free-standing proceeding rather than an application for review. If successful this would have the effect of removing from the public authority defendant the protections available under that procedure, including the requirement for permission to proceed and the restricted time limits. However, if the reality is that the challenge is a public law challenge the courts will be highly unlikely to permit such an approach, as it would effectively remove from the judicial review procedure all human rights challenges against public authorities. In *Rushbridger v Attorney General*,[71] the *Guardian* newspaper sought a declaration that the Treason Felony Act 1848 had to be read down under s 3 of the Human Rights Act so as not to criminalise peaceful calls by the paper for the establishment of republican government. Secondly it sought to challenge the refusal by the Attorney General to undertake not to prosecute the paper. Alternatively it sought a declaration of incompatibility. It sought to argue that the challenge was freestanding under s 7(1)(a) and was not brought by way of judicial review so that permission to proceed was not required. The court rejected this:

> Each of the claims made by the claimants falls within the definition set out in Part 54 of the CPR of 'judicial review proceedings'. That definition does not *expressly* exclude applications under the Human Rights Act 1998 ('HRA') and I do not believe that there are any reasons why such applications should be impliedly excluded. On the contrary, there is a strong argument for ensuring that all applications falling within Part 54 (whether brought under the HRA or otherwise) are covered by that regime, of which one significant feature is the requirement to obtain permission from the court in order to pursue such a claim so as, in Sedley J's words, 'to prevent abuse' (*R v Somerset CC and ARC Southern Ltd, ex p Dixon* [1990] COD 323). I consider that this threshold should be passed by all applications falling within the Part 54 definition, irrespective of whether or not they are made pursuant to the HRA.[72]

CPR 54.1(2) provides that a claim for judicial review means:

> ... a claim to review the lawfulness of –
>
> (i)   an enactment; or
>
> (ii) a decision, action or failure to act in relation to the exercise of a public function.

It follows that it is difficult to envisage much scope for free-standing human rights challenges to public authorities that will not fall within the Part 54 procedure. As has been seen, the concept of public function is a big part of the definition of public authority. If it is also the essence of a judicial review then most direct human rights challenges to public authorities will be judicial

---

70   CPR Part 54, Rule 54.5.
71   [2001] EWHC Admin 529.
72   *Ibid, per* Silber J at para 53.

review challenges. It seems that the only free-standing challenge under s 7(1)(a) that would fall outside the Part 54 procedure is where a 'pure' public authority is the defendant in respect of its private functions.

As regards the one-year time limit, one possible way around it is to raise the human rights claims as part of an existing cause of action. This would then be raised under s 7(1)(b) and be subject to the same rules regarding limitation as the cause of action concerned.

For example, if a tenant claims that a council landlord breached its duty to maintain his property to such a degree that it harmed his health (it failed to check for asbestos despite his complaints and he later suffered from asbestos related disease). It is at least arguable that the council was in breach of its obligations under Art 8 or even Art 3 of the Convention as the conditions of his property were so poor. However, if more than 12 months have passed since the alleged failure of the council, is the tenant out of time regarding any human rights claim? Not if he can bring his arguments into another cause of action – such as a personal injury negligence action or a breach of landlord's covenant action. This would amount to reliance on a Convention right in other legal proceedings under s 7(1)(b) and would not be subject to the one-year limitation of actions under s 7(1)(a). Public authorities may argue that such an approach is an abuse of process; a mechanism for getting around the strict limitation periods set by Parliament but it appears to be permitted by the Act where there is an existing cause of action covering the harm alleged.

2.7 IDENTIFYING A VICTIM

The concept of victim is important because only a victim may bring proceedings against a public authority or rely on a breach of Convention rights by a public authority in other legal proceedings. In other words, status as a victim is a precondition to having standing in claims of breach of human rights.

The definition of victim is taken directly from the Convention:

6(7) For the purposes of this section, a person is a victim of an unlawful act only if he would be a victim for the purposes of Article 34 of the Convention if proceedings were brought in the European Court of Human Rights in respect of that act.

In determining whether a party is a victim for the purposes of the Act the United Kingdom courts are bound by the decisions of the Strasbourg bodies. This is the only situation where the Human Rights Act requires the courts to follow the Strasbourg approach as opposed to merely taking it into account. It appears that the courts are not able to develop a broader concept of victim even if they are inclined to do so. Strasbourg case law suggests that the person (which includes any legal person)[73] must be personally affected (or at risk of being affected)[74] or be indirectly affected by an alleged violation against a family member.[75] The European Court explained the limitation as follows in the case of *Klass v Germany*:[76]

> [The Convention] requires that an individual applicant should claim to have been actually affected by the violation he alleges ... [It] does not institute for individuals a kind of *actio popularis* for the interpretation of the Convention; it does not permit individuals to complain against a law *in abstracto* simply because they feel that it contravenes the Convention. In principle, it does not suffice for an individual applicant to claim that the mere existence of a law violates his rights under the Convention; it is necessary that the law should have been applied to his detriment. Nevertheless, as both the government and the Commission pointed out, a law may by itself violate the rights of an individual if the individual is directly affected by the law in the absence of any specific measure of implementation.[77]

Importantly, the prohibition on '*actio popularis*' seems to exclude pressure groups from bringing proceedings to challenge the actions of a public authority either for themselves or on behalf of an affected person. It thus seems that we have two tests for standing. In traditional judicial review cases, the courts have taken a fairly liberal view of the types of organisations who may have standing to challenge a decision of a public authority. For example, respected pressure groups are often permitted to bring judicial reviews.[78]

In Human Rights Act challenges, such groups will not be permitted to bring challenges on their own. The most they can hope for is the ability to fund challenges by victims or to intervene in cases brought by victims.[79] This can cause a major problem for such groups in that the public authority will know that it can 'pay off' individual victims in order to avoid a policy being challenged in the courts. Once the victim has obtained their individual

---

73 *Pine Valley Developments Ltd v Ireland* (1991) 14 EHRR 269.

74 In *Dudgeon v United Kingdom* (1981) 4 EHRR 149, the applicant was a gay man in Northern Ireland. He was a victim because he was at risk of being prosecuted for his private sexual activity even though this had not (yet) materialised.

75 *McCann v United Kingdom* (1996) 21 EHRR 97.

76 (1978) 2 EHRR 214.

77 *Ibid*, at para 33.

78 See for example, *R v Secretary of State for Foreign and Commonwealth Affairs ex p World Development Movement* [1995] 1 WLR 386 (standing of respected pressure group to challenge funding of Pergau Dam project in Indonesia).

79 An application might be made to be formally joined as an interested party or to make written submissions. See for example the submissions made by JUSTICE in the House of Lords case of *R v Lambert* [2001] UKHL 37; [2001] All ER(D) 69 (Jul).

remedy the challenge becomes academic and the court is likely to reject it, at least if any party objects to the case going ahead.[80]

Advocates should be alive to the problems and possibilities caused by the victim requirement. Those representing public authorities against public interest or pressure groups will seek to limit the claimant's standing to pre-Human Rights Act public law matters. Conversely, those representing pressure groups will urge as broad an approach towards victim as possible and will emphasise that even non-victims are able to raise human rights arguments in so far as they relate to the interpretation of legislation or even the development of the common law.[81]

In three early cases the courts have examined standing since the implementation of the Human Rights Act. In *R v (1) Secretary of State for the Home Department (2) Lord Chief Justice ex p Bulger*,[82] the father of a murder victim sought leave to judicially review the setting of the sentence tariff by the Lord Chief Justice. The court declined to alter the standing rules:

> ... It is true, that the threshold for standing in judicial review has generally been set by the courts at a low level. This, as it seems to me, is because of the importance in public law that someone should be able to call decision makers to account, lest the rule of law break down and private rights be denied by public bodies ... But in the present matter the traditional and invariable parties to criminal proceedings, namely the Crown and the defendant, are both able to, and do, challenge those judicial decisions which are susceptible to judicial review ...[83]

In *Rushbridger v Attorney General*,[84] discussed above, the court rejected the application for declarations considering that the applicants, the editor and a journalist of the *Guardian*, did not qualify as victims:

> ... first, no prosecution for the Treason Felony Act 1848 has been brought or threatened against either claimant and that second, the wide form of relief sought is in a very general and wide form, being unrelated to any actual publication or any specifically threatened publication. Third, no evidence has been adduced to establish any fear by either claimants that he or she will be prosecuted for publishing articles advocating republicanism. This suggests that

---

80 In the case of *R (on the Application of Johns) v Bracknell Forest BC* [2001] HLR 45 the Divisional Court was reluctant to continue hearing a challenge to introductory tenancies as the tenant had since been awarded a secure tenancy by the council. It was only persuaded to continue by a 'united front' request from all parties for resolution of the Convention issue. However, the court did refuse leave to appeal largely on the basis that the decision was academic: 'if the Court of Appeal is to be encouraged to express a view about this Act, it should really do so in a case that actually matters.' The Court of Appeal did itself grant leave to appeal, although only in respect of the Art 6 challenge, and upheld the first instance decision: *McLellan v Bracknell Forest BC* [2001] EWCA 510.

81 Section 3 and s 6 are not limited in their application to cases brought by victims. In addition, s 11 of the Human Rights Act preserves all existing legal rights.

82 [2001] EWHC Admin 119, [2001] 3 All ER 449.

83 *Ibid*, at para 20.

84 [2001] EWHC Admin 529.

the claimants cannot establish that they have the 'victim' status needed to bring a claim under HRA, s 7.[85]

In *R v Weir*[86] the House of Lords rejected the Director of Public Prosecution's application for an extension of time in which to bring an appeal against a decision of the Court of Appeal quashing the accused's conviction for murder. The Crown submitted that denial of the extension would deny its right to effective access to a court. Their Lordships rejected this argument and offered some insight into the respective interests of the state and the citizen:

> The civil rights of the Director are not here in issue and he is not charged with a criminal offence ... The Convention was conceived in the aftermath of the war as a bulwark to protect private citizens against abuse of power by state and public authorities. This explains why certain important rights are guaranteed to criminal defendants. But it would stand the Convention on its head to interpret it as strengthening the rights of prosecutors against private citizens. In truth the present situation does not engage the human rights of the Director at all.[87]

This reflects a more general issue regarding standing in human rights cases. The Strasbourg decisions suggest that public authorities cannot rely on the Convention themselves. This is based on the idea that public authorities are themselves emanations of the state and it would not make sense for the state to claim a violation of human rights against itself.[88] This has the potential to cause difficulties in the courts. It is certainly possible to envisage a public authority, say a privatised utility, seeking to rely on its own Convention rights against another public authority, like a regulator. If public authorities have no standing under the Human Rights Act it will be prevented from doing so.

This was recently confirmed in the High Court:

> ... the consequence of holding that a body is a public authority is that it has no legal right under the Human Rights Act to the protection of its Convention rights against the Government. The Act confers rights on citizens against the Government and other public authorities, not on public authorities against the Government. Public authorities have no Convention rights.[89]

Quasi-public authorities would appear to have a better case for being able to rely on the Human Rights Act, given that at least some of their activity is private in nature and they cannot therefore be seen as an emanation of the state. Nevertheless, the Strasbourg approach towards public authorities and standing does seem to give rise to another two-tier approach towards

---

85 [2001] EWHC Admin 529, *per* Silber J at para 55.

86 *R v Weir (Michael Clive) (Extension of Time)* [2001] 1 WLR 421.

87 *Per* Lord Bingham.

88 *Ayuntamiento de M v Spain* (1991) 68 DR 209; *Austria Municipalities v Austria* (1974) 17 YB 338.

89 *Heather and Others v Leonard Cheshire Foundation and Another* [2001] EWHC Admin 429; [2001] All ER (D) 156 (Jun), para 105, *per* Stanley Burnton J.

standing. It is firmly established that one arm of the state may judicially review another. It is not yet clear whether Convention rights arguments will be permitted as part of such a challenge.[90]

2.8   ASKING FOR THE RIGHT REMEDY

8(1) In relation to any act (or proposed act) of a public authority, which the court finds is (or would be) unlawful, it may grant such relief or remedy, or make such order, within its powers as it considers just and appropriate.

(2) But damages may be awarded only by a court which has power to award damages, or to order the payment of compensation, in civil proceedings.

This section gives a wide discretion to courts as to the type of remedy that may be granted. It must be within its powers – no new powers are given to courts to deal with breaches of human rights – and it must be considered to be just and equitable. The remedy may range from a simple adjournment (if the allegation is that the party would not have a fair hearing without more time to prepare) to the granting of damages (if the breach of human rights requires some form of monetary compensation). It also confirms that the court must have the power to award compensation in civil proceedings in order for an award of damages to be made for breach of human rights. It follows that not all courts and tribunals are able to award damages, so victims will have to issue separate free-standing proceedings in order to secure compensation for any violation. Note that any award of damages can only be made for the act of a public authority. There can be no damages awarded due to the act or omission of a private person or body.

The requirement for the remedy to be within the powers of the court or tribunal has important consequences for where proceedings are commenced and the appropriate remedy advocates should request.

2.8.1   'Just satisfaction'

(3) No award of damages is to be made unless, taking account of all the circumstances of the case, including –

(a) any other relief or remedy granted, or order made, in relation to the act in question (by that or any other court), and

---

90 See Dawn Oliver in *The Frontiers of the State: Public Authorities and Public Functions under the Human Rights Act* [2000] PL 476 at p 491 for a discussion of the negative consequences that could flow from the inability of public authorities to claim victim status. In *London Regional Transport v Mayor of London* [2001] EWCA 1491, the Court of Appeal assumed that all parties were public authorities, but had no hesitation in utilising the Human Rights Act and the Convention right of freedom of expression when deciding whether it was lawful to prevent publication of a confidential report into public private partnership on the London Underground. If the Mayor of London has rights under the Convention then it is difficult to see why other public authorities would not similarly be able to claim victim status.

(b) the consequences of any decision (of that or any other court) in respect of that act,

the court is satisfied that the award is necessary to afford just satisfaction to the person in whose favour it is made.

This provision makes clear that even if a court does have the power to award compensation it will only do so if it feels that there has been insufficient remedy elsewhere to afford 'just satisfaction'. This is a Convention phrase meaning compensation for breach of Convention rights. The European Court has not been particularly consistent in its approach towards the granting of compensation as just satisfaction.[91] Often it says that the finding of a violation alone is sufficient just satisfaction.

For example, assume that a public authority is being sued by an employee for injuries sustained at work. Evidence of covert video surveillance of the employee is excluded by the judge on the basis that it violates the employees right to private life and home. Is the employee entitled to compensation for the breach? Certainly the claimant's advocate should consider making an application for damages under s 8. This is the case whether the client wins or loses the main cause of action. However, the defendant's advocate will be able to make a strong submission based on the fact that the remedy has already been obtained by the exclusion of the evidence and there is no need to make an additional award of damages to afford just satisfaction.

2.8.2 Recognising the relevance of the 'missing' articles

Article 1 (duty of states to protect human rights) and Art 13 (right to an effective domestic remedy) are not implemented under the Human Rights Act. The government took the view that the Human Rights Act itself fulfilled the obligations under these articles. One potential problem in respect of Art 1 was the fact that this article is the main reason why the European Court has felt able to develop the concept of 'positive obligations' whereby the state not only has to refrain from interfering with rights itself but has to take steps to prevent breaches of certain rights and deter others from breaching such rights. In the absence of Art 1 in the Human Rights Act would our judges rule that there was no positive obligation on United Kingdom public authorities? As we have seen in Chapter 1, the courts have not seen the absence of Art 1 as any impediment to the imposition of positive obligations on public authorities.

As for Art 13, it is doubtful that the Human Rights Act can fulfil this obligation in every instance given that the courts and tribunals are given no additional powers to grant remedies under the Act. The government

---

91 See Chapter 1, para 1.5.11.

suggested that the powers under s 8 were sufficient and that, despite the absence of Art 13 in the Act, the courts 'may have regard to Art 13. In particular they may wish to do so when considering the very ample provisions of Clause 8(1)'.[92] The mechanism for doing so was the s 2 duty to take into account Strasbourg case law. Nevertheless, the Scottish court has already ruled that the absence of the article does make a difference in that any claim that ought properly to be brought under Art 13 cannot be raised under the Human Rights Act.[93] We will also see that the High Court has refused to extend the availability of judicial review to provide a remedy for breach of human rights, as the lack of a remedy is not itself a breach of the Human Rights Act.[94] This could take on added significance given the approach the European Court has recently taken towards public authority immunity, viewing it as an Art 13 issue as opposed to an Art 6 issue.[95]

Most recently the House of Lords in *Lambert*[96] refused to quash a pre-Human Rights Act conviction obtained in breach of the right to a fair trial because it decided the Act did not apply retrospectively in appeals. Lord Hope put it as follows:

> A deliberate choice was made by Parliament as to the extent to which section 7(1)(b) could be given effect to retrospectively in order to provide a person whose Convention rights have been violated with an effective remedy. But Article 13 of the Convention, to which section 7 gives effect, is not one of the Convention rights mentioned in section 1(1). I do not think that it is open to the court to make a different choice than that which was made by Parliament. To do so would not be to construe the enactment in the way which section 3(1) contemplates. It would be to do something which it does not permit, which is to legislate.[97]

Advocates seeking to restrict the remedies offered by the courts should rely on comments like this and point to the explicit inclusion of Arts 16–18 as informing the construction of the other articles in the Convention but the absence of Art 13. They will also point to the fact that s 2 of the Act (the duty to take into account Strasbourg decisions) is limited to questions arising in connection with a 'Convention right', which does not include Art 13 and that the decision of the Strasbourg Court must be 'relevant'. Advocates advancing a more expansive view will point to the words of the Lord Chancellor and will

---

92 *Hansard* HL, 18 November 1997, col 477.

93 *Birse v HM Advocate* (2000) *The Times*, 28 June (the lack of a remedy arising from an *ex parte* application for a search warrant would be an Art 13 claim).

94 See discussion of *R (on the Application of Regentford Ltd) v Crown Court at Canterbury* [2001] HRLR 18 at para 4.2.8.5.

95 See *Z v United Kingdom* [2001] 2 FCR 246, reversing the approach taken in *Osman v United Kingdom* (2000) 29 EHRR 245.

96 [2001] UKHL 37; [2001] All ER(D) 69 (Jul); discussed in detail at 2.9.1.4 below, and in Chapter 8.

97 *Ibid*, para 111.

emphasise that he was consciously making a *Pepper v Hart* statement at the time.[98]

2.9 FROM WHAT DATE IS THE HUMAN RIGHTS ACT APPLICABLE?

This is an important question that has not received a wholly coherent response thus far from the courts. Advocates should be alive to the possibility that the Convention rights may impact upon decisions and conduct occurring before the Human Rights Act was implemented – so called retrospective effect – and devise rational arguments as to whether there is any retrospectivity in the case before them. As will be seen, the answer can have a major effect on the outcome of the case.

The Act came fully into effect on 2 October 2000. Broadly, the Act differentiates between proceedings, which are brought by public authorities, where the Convention rights can be relied upon retrospectively, and proceedings brought by private persons, where the Act is purely prospective.

When considering freestanding actions under s 7(1)(a), the act complained about must have occurred on or after 2 October 2000. However, when considering the ability of a litigant to rely on a Convention right in legal proceedings under s 7(1)(b) the situation is different. This is because of s 22(4), tucked away at the back of the Act and the subject of no debate during the passage of the Bill. It provides as follows:

> Paragraph (b) of sub-section (1) of section 7 applies to proceedings brought by or at the instigation of a public authority whenever the act in question took place; but otherwise that sub-section does not apply to an act taking place before the coming into force of that section.

It follows that s 7(1)(a) can never be retrospective whereas s 7(1)(b) is retrospective if, and only if, the proceedings in which the Convention right is relied upon were brought or instigated by a public authority. In such circumstances the act complained about can take place at any time, even before the Human Rights Act received the Royal Assent. These propositions are not without difficulties, as we will see, but some retrospective effect was clearly intended by the parliamentary draughtsman. An example is where a criminal investigation commenced prior to 2 October 2000 but the trial takes place after that date. Allegations of breach of the accused's Convention rights by the police can be relied on at the trial no matter when the conduct took place. The effect is not limited to criminal proceedings. It applies whenever a public authority brings or initiates the proceedings, for example, public

---

98 The Lord Chancellor was answering a question and he said, 'One always has in mind *Pepper v Hart* when one is asked questions of that kind. I will reply as candidly as I can'.

housing possession cases, local authority Children Act applications and requests for anti-social behaviour orders.

2.9.1 'Proceedings brought by or at the instigation of a public authority'

This phrase is central to the existence of retrospective effect and has caused considerable confusion in the courts. There are two main issues. First, when will a public authority, as opposed to the citizen who has the dispute with the public authority, be said to have brought or instigated the proceedings? Secondly, once it is established that a public authority brought or instigated the proceedings, does the phrase permit retrospective effect to apply to an appeal against the decision of the court of first instance?

2.9.1.1 Who brings the proceedings?

As regards the first question, in many cases there will be no problem as the public authority will be the formal initiator of the proceedings by being the claimant or the prosecutor. Thus, criminal proceedings brought by the police and/or Crown Prosecution Service are clearly subject to retrospective effect. An ingenious attempt was made in a recent case to argue the judicial review proceedings are brought by a public authority – the Crown – and are therefore caught by s 22(4).[99] The Court of Appeal rejected this as the Crown was found to have only nominal involvement in the proceedings, which were in effect a dispute between the individual and the public authority whose conduct was challenged.[100]

However, there are other situations that are not so clear-cut. In numerous cases the public authority will have done something that may affect the rights of the individual and can only be changed if the individual affected challenges the action of the public authority. Examples are where a person is detained by hospital authorities under the Mental Health Act or where the Benefits Agency reviews past benefit decisions and decides that the claimant is not entitled to a benefit that has hitherto been paid. The only way that the affected people can 'defend' themselves against the authority's decision is by issuing tribunal proceedings. These proceedings are clearly brought by the individual. Can they nonetheless be said to be brought 'at the instigation of' the public authority? The inclusion of this phrase clearly indicates that there are situations where the Act will have retrospective effect despite the public authority not itself bringing the proceedings.

---

99 *R (on the Application of Ben-Abdelaziz and Another) v Haringey London Borough* [2001] All ER(D) 274 (May).

100 It followed that damages could not be awarded for an unlawful act of dispersal of the claimant asylum seeker, which occurred prior to the Act coming into force.

In *King v Walden (Inspector of Taxes)*[101] the High Court had to consider whether a taxpayer's appeal in respect of a tax assessment was brought by or at the instigation of the Inland Revenue and ruled as follows:

> Assessments to tax are, in the first instance, made by an inspector (see s 29 of the TMA as it stood before amendment in 1994, now s 30A). If the taxpayer is unhappy, he may appeal within 30 days. If he does not appeal, the assessment stands. So the taxpayer's only method of challenge to an assessment is by way of 'appeal'. Thus an appeal is essentially a defensive step, rather than offensive. ... In these circumstances I think it is artificial to say that proceedings are instigated by the taxpayer. It is the assessments which instigate the proceedings which come before the Commissioners, not the appeal itself.[102]

This gives encouragement to a broad approach towards whether the public authority instigated the proceedings. It looks to the substance rather than the form of the proceedings and seeks to avoid artificial restrictions on the ability to raise human rights points. The court drew an analogy with criminal proceedings whereby an appellant does not by entering a notice of appeal instigate the proceedings. The prosecutor remains the instigator. Similarly it was thought that there was a lot of sense in considering the tax assessment and the appeal as part of the same process. As we will see, the position of criminal appellants is not as secure as the court in *King* assumed and in any event the analogy is not exact as a criminal appeal is against the finding of a lower court. Thus, there have already clearly been legal proceedings commenced by the Crown. The *King* case removes the need for there to have been any legal proceedings actually issued by the public authority. It is sufficient that the public authority can in some way be said to be responsible for the victim's predicament that led to the need for the proceedings. Attractive though this might be for those who seek an expansive approach towards the Act, it is difficult to see where one draws the line. Numerous decisions taken by public authorities affect the rights of citizens and the only way of challenging such decisions is often by recourse to the courts or tribunals. Compulsory purchase orders, refusals of licences, planning enforcement notices, special educational needs assessments, dismissal from employment and a host of other decisions of public authorities appear at least *prima facie* to fall into the same category as tax assessments. In any event it is difficult to discern any clear principles by which to distinguish between them. Advocates may wish to advance arguments based on legal certainty to challenge or limit the applicability of the approach outlined.

---

101 [2001] STC 822.

102 *Ibid, per* Jacobs J at paras 57–58. A similar approach was adopted by the VAT Tribunal in *Murrell v Customs and Excise*, 13/10/2000, in respect of a civil evasion penalty under s 60(1) of the Value Added Tax Act 1994. This was based largely on the view that the proceedings were in fact criminal for the purposes of the Convention, a decision that has been confirmed, albeit reluctantly, by a majority of the Court of Appeal in *Han and Yau v Customs and Excise Commissioners* [2001] EWCA Civ 1048, [2001] STC 1188, discussed further in Chapter 7.

It is sometimes suggested that the Human Rights Act can be used retrospectively as a shield to defend oneself against a public authority but not as a sword to make a claim against a public authority. This is based on the idea that the public authority must have brought or instigated the proceedings. However, as we have seen, the broad view of 'instigated' that has been adopted in the early decisions permits legal challenges against public authority decisions to be made in reliance on acts occurring prior to implementation. If this view survives, there seems to be no reason in principle why such challengers cannot also claim additional remedies such as damages, where available, from the court or tribunal in which a challenge succeeds. This would hardly be in keeping with the shield analogy.

2.9.1.2 Does retrospectivity apply to appeals?

At first sight, it seems to follow that an appellant may rely on breaches of Convention rights retrospectively in an appeal so long as a public authority commenced the original proceedings. The Act provides that legal proceedings includes 'proceedings brought by or at the instigation of a public authority' and 'an appeal against the decision of a court of tribunal'.[103] Indeed, as we will see, a number of decisions have accepted that the appellate court is obliged to consider the Convention rights arguments if it hears an appeal after the commencement of the Human Rights Act even when the original trial occurred prior to the Act coming into force. However, in the recent decision of *Lambert*[104] the majority of the House of Lords rejected this interpretation and drastically restricted the scope of the retrospective effect. The following section examines the basis for retrospectivity in appeals and considers in more detail the most recent House of Lords opinion. It is highly unlikely that this will be the last word in the highest court about this troublesome issue.

2.9.1.3 The basis for retrospective effect in appeals

As we have seen, the argument for retrospective effect in appeals arises principally from the wording of s 7(1)(b) and s 22(4). It also derives support, at least in the criminal context, from the House of Lords decision in *R v DPP ex p Kebilene*,[105] a pre-trial judicial review of anti-terrorism offences on the basis that they violated Art 6. The Divisional Court had found that the defendants would, once the Act came into effect, be able to rely on the retrospective effect of the Human Rights Act in any appeal against conviction. The House of Lords, although reversing the Divisional Court's decision on the judicial review upheld the retrospectivity point. The DPP argued that the backward-

---

103 Section 7(6) of the HRA 1998.
104 [2001] UKHL 37; [2001] All ER(D) 69 (Jul).
105 [2000] AC 326.

looking effect of the Human Rights Act was apt only to extend to the trial but not any appeal the defendants may wish to mount. Lord Steyn expressly rejected the argument:

> ... a construction which treats the trial and the appeal as parts of one process is more in keeping with the purpose of the Convention and the Act of 1998. It is the sensible and just construction. I would reject the argument advanced on behalf of the DPP on this point.[106]

He went on to suggest that the defendants would indeed be able to use their Convention rights in any appeal should the 1998 Act be in force by that time.

2.9.1.4 Early decisions regarding retrospective effect in appeals

Kebilene was followed with some unarticulated reluctance by the Court of Appeal in *R v Lambert, R v Ali, R v Jordan*.[107] The cases involved challenges to offences where the burden of proof was alleged to have been reversed contrary to Art 6. The Court of Appeal agreed that the retrospective effect of the Act did apply at least in respect of Art 6 cases, although Lord Woolf voiced some concern as to whether Parliament could have intended such a result.[108]

The first judicial dissent emerged in *Parker v DPP*[109] when Waller LJ expressed serious reservations about whether the Act could have been intended to have such a wide retrospective effect. This was echoed in *R (on the Application of Fleurose) v Securities and Futures Authority Ltd*[110] where the Administrative Court considered whether the penalties imposed by the SFA were criminal charges for the purposes of Art 6 of the Convention. An issue arose as to whether the Convention was applicable at all. Morrison J ruled as follows:

> Second, [counsel] submitted that the Human Rights Act has retrospective effect by virtue of sections 22(4) and section 7(1)(b). It seems to me that this submission is based on a misreading of the Act. After the Act came into force in October 2000, its provisions applied whenever the act in question took place; that is, both before and after the Act came into effect. The element of retrospectivity on which [counsel] relies can only exist after the Act came into force. There is no retrospectivity before that date, because the retrospective provision itself had no effect until after that date. The acts complained of in this case all occurred, and the proceedings were issued before October 2000, and the Act does not, therefore, apply.[111]

---

106 [2000] AC 326. Lord Slynn agreed with Lord Steyn. Lords Cooke and Hope delivered concurring judgments. Only Lord Hobhouse appeared to disagree on the question of retrospectivity.

107 [2001] 1 All ER 1014.

108 *Ibid*, at p 1024.

109 (2001) 165 JP 213

110 [2001] EWHC Admin 292, [2001] All ER(D) 189 (Apr).

111 *Ibid*, at para 27.

If this view prevailed there would still be retrospective effect as regards proceedings issued by public authorities after 2 October 2000. For example, a person charged with a criminal offence on 3 October 2000 would be able to rely at trial and appeal on alleged breaches of the Convention by the police. However, it would significantly limit the scope of retrospectivity. It would exclude all those cases where the proceedings were issued prior to the Human Rights Act coming into force, including appeals against such decisions. It has the attractiveness of legal certainty but suffers from an artificially narrow view of the language used in the statute.

In two recent decisions the Court of Appeal appeared to have resolved the issue. In *R v Benjafield and Other Appeals*,[112] the Court of Appeal clearly supported the applicability of retrospective effect in criminal appeals in the face of a dogged attempt by counsel for the Crown to persuade it otherwise. Having examined the decision in *Kebilene*, their Lordships ruled as follows:

> ... we feel we should adopt Lord Steyn's approach, so the appellants are entitled to rely on s 7(1)(b) and s 22(4) of the 1998 Act in an appeal which takes place after 2 October 2000. In our judgment, where the original proceedings are brought by, or at the instigation of, a public authority, as is the case with a prosecution, an appeal by the defendant is part of the proceedings to which s 22(4) applies. There cannot be a different position on an appeal from that of the trial so far as the issue of the retrospectivity of the 1998 Act is concerned. Any other construction would mean that in criminal cases, the Court of Appeal could not give the required protection to the individual (who would clearly be a victim of any unlawful act) so that there would be a need for an otherwise unnecessary but time-consuming and expensive trip to Strasbourg.[113]

This was followed in the case of *R v Kansal*[114] where the Court of Appeal vividly illustrated the consequences of such an approach. It was dealing with a reference by the Criminal Cases Review Commission (CCRC) following a 1992 conviction for various dishonesty offences. The appeal was based, *inter alia*, on the change in the law recognised by the House of Lords in *R v Preddy*[115] and the decision of the European Court of Human Rights in *Saunders v United Kingdom*.[116] Rose LJ recognised that there was no time limit for CCRC references and no time limit in the Human Rights Act for retrospective effect. The appeal therefore had to be allowed due to the admission of compelled answers in breach of the appellant's rights under Art 6 of the Convention. His Lordship commented as follows:

---

112 [2001] 2 All ER 609.

113 *Ibid*, at p 625, *per* Lord Woolf CJ. At the time of writing the decision in *Benjafield* is subject to appeal to the House of Lords.

114 [2001] EWCA Crim 1260; [2001] All ER(D) 311 (May).

115 [1996] 3 All ER 481.

116 (1997) 23 EHRR 313.

> We reach this conclusion with no enthusiasm whatever. Leaving aside colourful historical examples such as Sir Thomas More, Guy Fawkes and Charles I, all of whom would have benefited from Convention rights, until the Criminal Evidence Act 1898, no defendant was permitted to give evidence on his own behalf. That is a clear breach of Article 6. Many examples in the 20th century of other rules and procedures which, viewed with the wisdom of hindsight, were in breach of the Convention could be given. But we resist that temptation lest, by succumbing, we exacerbate the problem to which we are drawing attention.[117]

The court urged the CCRC to reconsider the exercise of its discretion to refer 'law change' cases but recognised that Parliament had, consciously or otherwise, hugely expanded the scope for appeals in old cases and hoped Parliament or the House of Lords could review the matter at an early opportunity.

2.9.1.5 Rejection of retrospective effect in appeals

The issue returned to the House of Lords in *Lambert*.[118] It seems fairly clear that policy considerations loomed large in their Lordships' minds. The desire to avoid a flood of appeals from those convicted in less enlightened times or their families, is an inevitable response from the judiciary. It was previously satisfied by the Court of Appeal refusing on policy grounds to extend the time for appealing old convictions. However, as the court in *Kansal* recognised, an aggrieved person could simply turn to the CCRC and if the case were referred, the court would have to deal with the case on its merits.

The first and most obvious difficulty in the way of their Lordships ruling against retrospectivity in appeals was the fact that a majority of the House had already ruled in favour of retrospective effect in the *Kebilene* case. The House there followed the clear reasoning of the Divisional Court and heard extensive and complex argument from senior counsel seeking an alternative approach. Moreover, despite the case being heard before the Act came fully into force, it is not easy to describe the judgments as *obiter*. Given that the principle of retrospectivity formed the basis of the Divisional Court decision, it was incumbent on their Lordships to deal with it. Nonetheless, the fact that the House of Lords decided the case largely on the grounds of reviewability of the DPP's decision to prosecute, there was at least some room for sidelining Lord Steyn's comments. In the event, little attempt was made to marginalise the authoritative status of Lord Steyn's view in *Kebilene*. It was simply rejected as wrong.

The majority of the judicial committee in *Lambert* (Lord Slynn, Lord Clyde and Lord Hutton) rejected outright the proposition that s 22(4) required an

---

117 [2001] EWCA Crim 1260; [2001] All ER(D) 311 (May) at para 24.
118 [2001] UKHL 37; [2001] All ER(D) 69 (Jul).

appeal court to consider breaches of Convention rights retrospectively. The basis of this view was that although the Act defines legal proceedings to include both proceedings brought by or at the instigation of a public authority *and* an appeal against a decision,[119] s 22(4) speaks only of the former. Thus, s 7(1)(b) was only intended to be retrospective in so far as it relates to first instance hearings, not appeals. Lord Hope was willing to accept that the Act applied to appeals but drew a distinction between unlawful acts by the prosecutor, which could be relied on, and unlawful acts by the court, which could not. His reasoning was that the same public authority that brought the proceedings must be the one that committed the alleged unlawful act. In this case the act complained of was the summing up by the trial judge not the conduct of the prosecutor. Lord Steyn did not rest on his earlier view in *Kebilene* but instead developed a wider proposition, which, he said, had nothing to do with retrospectivity at all. Section 6 of the Act required the House of Lords to act compatibly with the Convention rights of the appellant now. For an appellate court to uphold a conviction obtained in breach of a Convention right involved it in acting incompatibly with a Convention right and thus unlawfully.

The majority view is clear and it reduces the scope for retrospective effect dramatically. It restricts reliance on allegations of pre-Human Rights Act breaches to first instance decisions. It thus avoids many of the fears of the Court of Appeal in *Kansal* in so far as they related to Convention rights. Historical cases where there has been a breach of Convention rights will have no remedy at all in domestic law, as once a court has reached a decision the proceedings brought by the public authority cease and an appeal is not covered by the s 22(4) retrospective effect. It means that retrospective effect will be fairly short lived. Once the initial stream of cases coming to trial where the pre-Human Rights Act conduct of public authorities is an issue have been dealt with there will be no right to revisit older decisions. As we get further away from 2 October 2000 retrospective challenges will become less and less until they only arise in the comparatively rare cases where a public authority issues proceedings years after it committed the impugned conduct.

One bizarre consequence is that even if a trial takes place after 2 October 2000 and a defendant properly relies on Convention rights retrospectively, he or she will be prevented from running the same arguments on appeal should the trial court reject the arguments. It is strange to permit a litigant to rely on arguments at one level of the court hierarchy but prohibit him or her from challenging the decision that the lower court makes in respect of those arguments. However, this is the logical consequence of the strict dichotomy between initial proceedings and appeals.

---

119 Section 7(6) of the HRA 1998.

Moreover, it seems that the prohibition will even apply if the public authority brings the appeal. A natural reaction would be to say that such an appeal would be proceedings brought by a public authority. However, *Lambert* draws such sharp distinction between 'proceedings' on the one hand and 'an appeal against the decision of a court or tribunal' on the other that whoever initiates the appeal is irrelevant. The provision itself draws no distinction between appeals brought by the alleged victim and those brought by the public authority. If this is right then whenever a public authority loses a case because of pre-Human Rights Act violations of the Convention all it needs to do is to enter a notice of appeal. The considerations that led the trial court to find for the victim cannot be raised by the respondent on the appeal and the public authority is thus bound to succeed.

Thus, although the *Lambert* decision ostensibly leaves open some scope for retrospective effect of the Human Rights Act the reality is that it is removed almost completely. The only situations where arguments about pre-Human Rights Act violations could assist the victim is where they are accepted by the trial court and the Crown has no right of appeal, for example, decisions of a trial judge during a criminal trial in the Crown Court.

We submit that the majority of their Lordships, in their desire to avoid the perceived ill consequences of full-blown retrospectivity, have fastened on to a linguistic device that makes little sense when read in the context of the Act as a whole. When s 22(4) refers to proceedings brought by or at the instigation of a public authority it is attempting to distinguish between public authority inspired proceedings and private party inspired proceedings. It is not attempting to distinguish between trial proceedings and appeal proceedings. There was no linguistic reason for Parliament to have prefaced 'proceedings' with 'legal' in s 22(4) given that it explicitly refers to s 7(1)(b). The consequences of the decision as explained above show that it removes almost all meaning from s 22(4) and effectively usurps the expressed will of Parliament. The judiciary should not take a restrictive approach towards constitutional instruments such as the Human Rights Act that will deny citizens the right to raise the Convention rights in legal proceedings. Ultimately we feel it is for Parliament to rectify any perceived deficiencies in the legislation. We hope that a future House of Lords will show a similar willingness to interfere with the majority view in *Lambert* as their Lordships did in respect of the decision in *Kebilene*, although early signs are not promising. In *R v Allan*[119a] a differently constituted House of Lords followed the majority decision in *Lambert*.

119a [2001] UKHL 45; (2001) *The Independent*, 26 October.

Issues for advocates: retrospectivity and appeals

Given the current view of the House of Lords the cards are all in the hands of advocates representing public authorities. The following summarises the position:

- Retrospective effect is where a party relies on a breach of a Convention right that allegedly occurred prior to 2 October 2000.

- Retrospectivity can be relied on in any proceedings that are brought by a public authority, for example, criminal proceedings, child-care proceedings, council housing possession proceedings etc.

- It also applies to any proceedings that are brought at the instigation of a public authority so long as the alleged victim is only relying on the Convention rights defensively and the substance if not the form of the proceedings were initiated by the public authority, for example tax assessment appeals.

- There is no retrospective effect in appeals against decisions occurring prior to 2 October 2000.

- Neither is there any retrospective effect in appeals against decisions occurring after 2 October 2000.

- If in any trial after 2 October 2000 a public authority loses a case due to Convention rights arguments being raised retrospectively it should appeal against the decision. The respondent will not be able to rely on the violation in the appeal.

- The inability of an appeal court to consider pre-Human Rights Act violations of the Convention leaves a lacuna in the protection offered by the Act. However, this is a matter to be raised under Art 13 of the Convention, which was not implemented under the Human Rights Act.

- A victim who is refused the chance to raise alleged violations retrospectively has no remedy apart from an application to the European Court of Human Rights.

2.9.1.6 The preferred approach – s 7/22(4)

We submit that the proper approach towards retrospectivity in appeals is to adopt a broad approach towards the s 22(4) provision outlined in *Kebilene* and *Benjafield*. If the public authority commenced the proceedings it is logical to view an appeal against the first instance decision as a continuation of those proceedings so that an alleged victim may rely on a pre-October 2000 breach of a Convention right where relevant. There is no place for the artificial distinction between proceedings and appeals identified in *Lambert*. As for the risk of a flood of old appeals wreaking havoc on the legal system we recall

Lord Steyn's minority view when rejecting the Crown's 'consequentialist arguments of an alarmist nature':

> ... one is reminded of the unfounded predictions that the 1998 Act would cause chaos in our legal system. A healthy scepticism ought to be observed about practised predictions of an avalanche of dire consequences likely to flow from any new development.

In any event, as already indicated, if there is a deficiency in the way the Human Rights Act operates then, so long as it does not create incompatibility with Convention rights, it ought to be left to Parliament to resolve. The previous broad interpretation of s 22(4) enhances victims' remedies under the Human Rights Act. The current narrow view severely restricts such remedies.

2.9.2 Retrospective interpretation of statutes

Section 3 of the Human Rights Act is not explicitly subject to the retrospective approach. It would seem to logically follow that where an appeal court is reviewing a pre-Human Rights Act decision of a lower court or tribunal, the pre-Human Rights Act interpretation should be applied. Support for this approach was found in the Employment Appeal Tribunal[120] where it refused to review a decision of an employment tribunal as to the meaning of 'sex' in the Sex Discrimination Act and Equal Treatment Directive in light of Convention jurisprudence involving discrimination on the grounds of sexuality. The tribunal decision had occurred prior to the 1998 Act coming into force and the challenge would involve a ruling that an act which was lawful at the time it was committed could become unlawful at a later stage and secondly, that a tribunal decision, which properly interpreted a statute at the time, could later be said to have been incorrect. This would be contrary to the general presumption against retrospectivity and was not required by the Human Rights Act.

Nevertheless, despite there being no express reference to s 3 in the retrospective provisions of the Act it would make sense if the s 3 duty applied at least in situations where an alleged victim was able to rely retrospectively on breach of his or her Convention rights under s 7(1)(b). The need for such an approach was explained by the Court of Appeal in *Benjafield*:

> ... s 6(1) does apply to the Court of Appeal, and s 7(1) covers not only a past, but a proposed act ... It would, in those circumstances, be curious if the court were unable to apply s 3(1). Then, if satisfied that there was an incompatibility, the court would be unable to remedy it by applying a compatible construction of the relevant provision. Furthermore, and equally importantly, the court

---

120 *Gibson v British Gas Energy Centres* [2001] All ER(D) 229 (Feb).

would be unable to give the guidance needed for future application of the relevant provisions. This is not the position and s 3(1) has retrospective effect if ss 22(4) and 7(1)(b) of the 1998 Act apply.[121]

This indicated that the courts would review legislation in light of the s 3 duty, if necessary adjusting the (then correct) interpretations of statutes applied pre-Human Rights Act. However, this would only apply where a public authority instigated the proceedings. As a general principle this remains true but as we have seen, the circumstances in which reliance can be placed on acts occurring prior to the Human Rights Act has been substantially eroded by the House of Lords in *Lambert*.

The Court of Appeal (Civil Division) went further in *JA Pye (Oxford) Ltd v Graham*,[122] a dispute about limitation periods in land law, seemingly removing any need for a public authority to be involved in the proceedings. Keene LJ said as follows:

> ... there was an issue between the parties as to whether section 3(1) of that Act ... applies at all to the circumstances of this case. For my part, I regard that sub section as applying to all cases coming before the courts on or after 2 October 2000, irrespective of when the activities, which form the subject matter of those cases took place. Section 3(1) imposes a clear obligation on the courts in respect of its interpretation of legislation. That applies irrespective of the date of the legislation (see section 3(2)(a)) and I can see no reason to adopt one interpretation of a statute from 2 October 2000 onwards in a case involving activities before that date and a different interpretation where the activities took place after that date.

Mummery LJ agreed:

> The principle of the interpretation of primary and secondary legislation contained in section 3 of the 1998 Act can be relied on in an appeal which is heard after that Act came into force, even though the appeal is against an order made by the court below before the Act came into force.

This had the advantage of simplicity in that it adopted a uniform test for the interpretation of all statutes considered after 2 October 2000. It represented another case where the courts took an expansive approach to allowing Convention law to pervade domestic law. It had some curious consequences, however. Thus far we have assumed that s 22(4) explicitly rules out any retrospective application of Convention rights in claims brought by individuals, as opposed to proceedings brought by public authorities. If the impugned conduct occurred prior to the Human Rights Act coming into effect, the Convention is irrelevant in measuring the lawfulness of the conduct. The *Pye* case threw this approach into confusion, at least where the conduct was done pursuant to statute. If the claimant argued that the

---

121 [2001] 2 All ER 609 at p 625, *per* Lord Woolf, CJ.
122 [2001] EWCA Civ 117, [2001] HRLR 27.

defendant's pre-Human Rights Act activity was unlawful because it violated his Convention rights, the court deciding the case would have to decide whether the activity was within the powers granted by the statute. In so doing it would, according to the Court of Appeal, interpret the statute compatibly with the Claimant's Convention rights, if possible. The statute would be interpreted as not giving any power to do anything in breach of a Convention right. Pre-Human Rights Act conduct could thus be retrospectively judged on the basis of Convention rights even in cases brought against public authorities.[123]

For example, let us assume that the courts rule, using the s 3 interpretation test, that the word 'sex' in the Sex Discrimination Act applies to sexuality as well as gender.[124] In any claims brought by gay people alleging pre-Human Rights Act sex discrimination, the lawfulness of the defendant's conduct would be judged, according to *Pye*, on the current understanding of the statute, that is, to prohibit discrimination on the grounds of sexuality. Thus the conduct of the defendant would be judged unlawful even though it was not unlawful at the time it was committed. Arguably this would make a nonsense of the clear attempt by Parliament to distinguish between pre- and post-2nd October conduct. This view is confirmed in *Pearce v Governing Body of Mayfield School*[124a] where the Court of Appeal ruled that 'sex' did not include sexual orientation and that s 3(1) of the Human Rights Act could not be used to give a different construction to statutes from that which bound the lower tribunals at the time of their decisions.

The House of Lords in *Lambert* also considered s 3 and the majority rejected the idea that it could have any retrospective effect independent of that provided in ss 7(1)(b) and 22(4).[125] The position is illustrated by Lord Hope as follows:

> But there is nothing in the 1998 Act to indicate that [s 3] is to be applied retrospectively to acts of courts or tribunals, which took place before the coming into force of section 3(1). The provisions of section 22(4) are to the contrary.

Lord Clyde explained further that:

> In my view section 3 only became obligatory on courts on 2 October 2000. The rule of construction, which it expresses, applies to all legislation whenever enacted. But there is nothing to show that it was intended by section 3 that the meaning given to a statutory provision by a court prior to 2 October 2000

---

123 This would seem to apply only in respect of interpretation of legislation. The High Court has refused to retrospectively re-interpret a pre-Human Rights Act contract so as to make it Convention compliant – see *Biggin Hill Airport Ltd v Bromley LBC* (2001) 98(3) LSG 42. Upheld by the Court of Appeal [2001] EWCA Civ 1089.

124 See *McDonald v Ministry of Defence* [2001] 1 All ER 620.

124a [2001] EWCA Civ 1347; [2001] IRLR 669.

125 *Lambert* [2001] UKHL 37; [2001] All ER(D) 69 (Jul), *per* Lord Slynn at para 11, Lord Hope at para 115, Lord Clyde at para 142 and Lord Hutton at paras 169–70.

should be changed in the event of an appeal against that decision being heard on or after that date.

Although their Lordships do not explicitly refer to the *Pye* approach their views do appear to be inconsistent with the broad view taken by the Court of Appeal in that case. The position now is that s 3 can be used to construe statutes compatibly with the Convention but only where the first instance proceedings arise on or after 2 October 2000. Pre-implementation decisions about the meaning of legislation are not appealable on the basis of alleged incompatibility with Convention rights. There may well be, contrary to the view in *Pye*, two different meanings for the same legislative provision. Where a court examines a statute at first instance after 2 October 2000 it must, pursuant to s 3, adopt a Convention-compliant interpretation where possible. Where an appeal court is considering the same statute it cannot use s 3 to review the interpretation given by a court or tribunal prior to the implementation of the Act. The facts of *Lambert* illustrate the position neatly. Although the House of Lords refused to review the safety of the trial judge's (pre-October 2000) summing-up as regards the reverse burden in the Misuse of Drugs Act, any post-implementation summing up ought to have re-interpreted the defence so as to remove the legal burden on the defendant.

The House of Lords left unresolved the question whether a court of first instance when faced with a claimant's challenge to the lawfulness of a defendant's pre-October 2000 conduct, must adopt a Convention-compliant meaning of any relevant statute or may say that, since the conduct as opposed to the proceedings arose before s 3 came into force, the section is irrelevant. The latter approach would be consistent with the overall thrust of the judgment – s 3 would have no application to pre-October 2000 conduct except in so far as s 22(4) permits retrospective effect, that is, only in first instance proceedings brought by or at the instigation of a public authority.

2.9.3 Retrospectivity and the courts' duties under s 6

In theory there is a simple way around the difficulties caused by the extent of retrospective application in appeals. This lies in the duty on courts and tribunals as public authorities to act in a way that is compatible with the Convention rights.[126] The appellate courts are clearly covered by this duty.[127] They could thus eschew the debate about retrospectivity and simply decide that they are under a duty to decide any appeal in line with the alleged victim's Convention rights, if necessary overturning any previous decision that was not compatible.

This approach was adopted by Lord Steyn in *Lambert*. His Lordship explained as follows:

---

126 Section 6(1), (3) of the HRA 1998.

127 Section 6(4) ensures that although Parliament is not a public authority for the purposes of s 6, the House of Lords in its judicial capacity is.

It will be noted that the effect of section 6(1) is to provide that it is unlawful for the House *to act* in a way, which is incompatible with a Convention right ... Given that it is expressed to limit the way in which a court may act, it is difficult to escape the conclusion that in the relevant sense no appellate court may act incompatibly with a Convention right. Surely, for an appellant court to uphold a conviction obtained in breach of a Convention right, must be *to act* incompatibly with a Convention right. It is unlawful for it to do so. So interpreted no true retrospectivity is involved. Section 6(1) regulates the conduct of appellate courts *de futuro* ... The language of the statute points in one direction only: the House may not act unlawfully by upholding a conviction, which was obtained in breach of a Convention right. It will be observed that this interpretation reads nothing into section 6(1); it implies nothing into the language of section 6(1); it simply gives effect to the obvious meaning of the plain words. It is the contrary view, which needs to find a legitimate basis for restricting the natural meaning of the words. And there is not legitimate basis in the language or purpose for cutting down the natural effect of section 6(1) ... If the contrary view is adopted the stark consequence is that in appeals on and after 2 October 2000 the Court of Appeal and the House will contrary to the wording of section 6(1) have 'to act in a way which is incompatible with a Convention right'. Those matters will then have to go to the European Court of Human Rights. In the recent language of the Court of Appeal (Civil Division): 'The alternative, which will have been apparent to Parliament, is a continuing residue of non-compliant decisions of public authorities kept indefinitely in effect by their own antiquity.'[128] Instead the Court of Appeal and the House in such cases applying and developing Convention principles in the light of our legal system it will be necessary to await the decisions of the court in Strasbourg. In my view such an interpretation is inconsistent with the plain terms of section 6(1) and a purposive approach to the construction of the statute.[129]

The majority of their Lordships rejected this approach. They were unwilling to accept that s 6 could force the appeal courts to quash decisions retrospectively when ss 7(1)(b) and 22(4), the provisions explicitly introducing retrospective effect, did not require such a result. Lord Clyde put it as follows:

... if section 6(1) is to be construed as requiring courts of appeal to apply the Convention to acts which occurred prior to 2 October 2000, that would not seem to me to be consistent with the careful and precise provision which Parliament did make for the extent to which acts prior to 2 October 2000 could be relied upon ... As I have already decided, section 7(1)(b) does not allow a person to rely on a Convention right allegedly breached prior to 2 October 2000 in an appeal heard on or after that date. So the argument reaches the result that under section 6(1) the appeal court is bound to take account of that Convention right, although the appellant may not rely upon it. That does not seem to me to be a likely interpretation of the intention of Parliament in passing section 6(1) and it does not seem to fit comfortably with the express

---

128 *Per* Sedley LJ in *Aston Cantlow and Wilmcote with Billesley Parochial Church Council v Wallbank and Another* [2001] EWCA Civ 713; [2001] 3 All ER 393, at para 7.

129 [2001] UKHL 37; [2001] All ER(D) 69 (Jul), at paras 28–29, Lord Steyn's emphasis.

provision made in section 22(4) ... I accept that section 6(1) imposes an obligation on a court ... to act in conformity with the Convention. But section 6(1) does not provide any remedy ... In my view section 6 is part of the series of sections on public authorities and cannot be isolated so as to be independent of them ... I would hold that the appellant cannot invoke the provisions of the 1998 Act for the purposes of overturning a conviction which was not unlawful for the purposes of section 6(1) at the time it was obtained, being a time prior to the coming into effect of that section.[130]

Lord Hutton made the same point in a slightly different way:

It is a well established principle that no statute should be construed so as to have retrospective operation unless its language is such as plainly to require such a construction. In addition, save as to the proceedings described in the first part of section 22(4), I consider that that subsection supports the view that the 1998 Act is not to have retrospective effect ... In my opinion it is no answer for the appellant to maintain that he is only concerned with the lawfulness of a decision taken by the Appellate Committee on a date after 2 October 2000. I consider that this argument does not alter the reality that if the House were to quash the conviction it would be giving a retrospective effect to section 6.[131]

The upshot is that s 6 can never operate so as to retrospectively measure the lawfulness of pre-October 2000 conduct against the standards of the Convention. We agree that there would be no point in specifying the extent to which the Act was retrospective in s 22(4), if s 6 could effectively oblige an appeal court to apply the Convention retrospectively in any event. The Act should not be read so as to be retrospective beyond that which it expressly provides. However, as has been seen, our concern lies in the highly restrictive view that the House of Lords has taken towards the extent of this express retrospectivity.[132]

2.9.4 Judicial review and the execution of pre-Human Rights Act decisions

In *R (on the Application of Mahmood) v Secretary of State for the Home Department*[133] the applicants challenged by way of judicial review a decision

---

130 [2001] UKHL 37; [2001] All ER(D) 69 (Jul), at paras 144–48.

131 *Ibid*, at para 169. See to similar effect Lord Slynn at paras 11–12 and Lord Hope at paras 115–16.

132 It remains the case, however, that the courts must be alive to their duty to interpret the common law in a manner which is Convention compliant. In *R (on the Application of Carroll) v Secretary of State for the Home Department* [2001] EWCA Civ 1224, Lord Woolf suggests that this long-standing principle will be applicable prior to the commencement of the Human Rights Act:

[I]n relation to the question of fairness at common law it is wrong to ignore the ECHR jurisprudence. That jurisprudence can still inform the common law as to what are the requirements of fairness and on the hearing of this appeal this court applies contemporary standards of fairness. Those standards of fairness today reflect the influence of the ECHR including Article 6 in circumstances where it can apply [para 34].

133 [2001] 1 WLR 840.

regarding asylum status taken prior to the Human Rights Act coming into force. The Court of Appeal held that the Convention rights could not be directly relevant to the determination of the lawfulness of the conduct as there were no extant proceedings brought by a public authority to which the limited retrospective effect of the Act could apply. The court went further and rejected an argument that it should nonetheless consider the Convention rights in light of the fact that the applicant had not yet been removed and so it should consider the legality of the future action of the respondent. It ruled that the court's primary role is historic, to review the legality of decisions already taken, not to police the possible future enforcement of such decisions. Such an approach would submit the court's public law jurisdiction to 'undesirable and possibly insupportable distortions'.

Thus, if pre-Human Rights Act decisions are to be challenged on Convention grounds they must be challenged at the point of execution.[134]

2.10 WHEN TO RAISE CONVENTION ISSUES

It may well be that points relating to Convention law have already been raised in correspondence between the parties, letters before action, notices of appeal etc. From the advocate's point of view it will be important to ensure that, where relevant, Convention issues are highlighted in the following:

* Pleadings and other court documents
* Skeleton arguments
* Oral applications
* Opening speeches
* Examination of witnesses
* Closing speeches

2.10.1 Pleading human rights

CPR Practice Direction 16, para 16.1 provides as follows:

A party who seeks to rely on any provision of or right arising under the Human Rights Act 1998 or seeks a remedy available under that Act –

(1) must state that fact in his statement of case; and

(2) must in his statement of case–

---

134 No consideration seems to have been given to whether the initial exercise of discretion could be subjected to Convention rights retrospectively given that it was statutory in nature. To this extent it is not clear how far it is compatible with the attitude of the Court in *Pye*, although, as we have seen, the authoritative status of *Pye* must be seriously questioned in any event.

(a) give precise details of the Convention right which it is alleged has been infringed and details of the alleged infringement;

(b) specify the relief sought;

(c) state if the relief sought includes–

    (i) a declaration of incompatibility in accordance with section 4 of that Act, or

    (ii) damages in respect of a judicial act to which section 9(3) of that Act applies;

(d) where the relief sought includes a declaration of incompatibility in accordance with section 4 of that Act, give precise details of the legislative provision alleged to be incompatible and details of the alleged incompatibility;

(e) where the claim is founded on a finding of unlawfulness by another court or tribunal, give details of the finding; and

(f) where the claim is founded on a judicial act which is alleged to have infringed a Convention right of the party as provided by section 9 of the Human Rights Act 1998, the judicial act complained of and the court or tribunal which is alleged to have made it.

It is important to bear in mind that this practice direction supplements the general requirements as to statements of case in CPR, r 16.1–16.4. The Human Rights Act may also be relied on in a defence[135] and if so, the factors referred to in the above paragraph should be also be reflected in the defence.[136] We will refer to the claimant throughout this chapter but the comments are equally applicable to a defendant alleging breach of Convention rights. Although the practice direction is applicable only to civil claims under the CPR it is a useful guide for pleadings in any court or tribunal.

The most important aspects of the practice direction are, first, the requirement to give details of the Convention right and the alleged infringement and, secondly, the requirement to specify the relief sought.

2.10.1.1 Specifying the alleged infringement

This part of the statement of case should clearly set out why the claimant's Convention right has been violated. This may be relatively simple where, for example, the public authority has itself allegedly treated the claimant in an inhuman or degrading manner in breach of Art 3. However, it may be complicated where the breach is not directly committed by the public authority or not immediately apparent from the facts. For example, if the claimant considers that a public authority failed in a positive obligation to prevent a third party from violating his/her Convention right, say a factory

---

135 Section 7(1)(b).
136 See also CPR, r 16.5 and CPR 16 PD, paras 11–14.

from polluting the environment, then the statement of case should establish the positive obligation before going on to assert the breach of such obligation. Alternatively, some further explanation may be required where the interference with rights is not immediately obvious. For example, detail may be required to establish that the claimant was detained for the purposes of Art 5 and that detention was attributable to the public authority before asserting the breach.

It is sometimes difficult to know what level of detail to go into in the statement of a case. Should the statement merely allege an interference with a Convention right or go on to explain why the alleged interference is not justifiable? Normally it would be sufficient merely to plead the interference in order to shift the burden on to the public authority to deny the interference and/or to justify it. In other words the justification for any interference is a matter for the defence rather than a matter for the initial claim. For example, if the claimant is alleging breach of the Art 8 right to respect for private life it would be necessary to plead the facts which establish the interference by the public authority with the right (say, a strip search). It would then be incumbent on the public authority defendant, if it wished to do so, to seek to justify the search under one or more of the qualifications in Art 8(2).

The article itself should be specified with 'precision'. This simply means that, where appropriate, the relevant part of an article should be specified as opposed to the whole article. For example, if the claim related to lack of interpretation facilities during criminal proceedings the claim would specify Art 6(1) (the general right to a fair trial) and Art 6(3)(e) (the right to an interpreter).

2.10.1.2 *Specifying the relief sought*

It is unlikely to be sufficient simply to claim 'just satisfaction' under s 8 of the Human Rights Act or Art 41 of the Convention as this is not a remedy in itself, but rather a principle of compensating a breach of a Convention right. The remedy requested should be one of the traditional remedies available under English law. Note that the Human Rights Act does not alter the remedies available from courts or tribunals. Thus the remedy sought must be within the existing powers of the court or tribunal.[137] If damages are claimed they may only be awarded by a court or tribunal with the power to award damages or compensation in civil proceedings. This covers the civil courts but not the criminal courts.[138] Some tribunals such as the employment tribunal clearly qualify as they have the statutory power to award compensation. Others such

---

137 Section 8(1) of the HRA 1998.

138 *Quaere* whether the Court of Appeal (Criminal Division) may award damages for breach of Convention rights given that the Civil Division does have the power to award damages in civil proceedings and the court is a unified court.

as the Mental Health Review Tribunal have no powers to award damages even if a breach is found. In such circumstances separate proceedings will have to be brought under s 7(1)(a) of the Act relying on the finding of the tribunal as evidence of a breach. The claimant's reliance on the earlier proceedings should itself be pleaded.

Issues for advocates: pleading human rights violations

Set out below is a sample extract from a statement of a case alleging breach of Art 10 of the Convention by a police officer removing the Claimant's means of communicating with a crowd at a political rally. It conforms to the rules in CPR Practice Direction 16.1 and provides one model for pleading Convention rights in civil litigation:

1 The Defendant is and was at all material times a police officer purporting to act as such.

2 The Defendant is and was at all material times a public authority for the purposes of s 6(1), (3) of the Human Rights Act.

3 The Defendant committed an unlawful act contrary to s 6(1) of the Human Rights Act.

4 The Claimant is and was at all material times the Chairman of the Northern Pensioners Association (NPA), an unincorporated association representing the interests of older people in the north of England. Between 7 April and 7 May 2001 the Claimant organised a lawful demonstration to take place in Newtown on 7 May 2001 as part of the NPA's general election campaign.

5 The arrangements made by the Claimant included the presence of a camera team from TV North to film the Claimant's speech at the demonstration for the purposes of the 'North Life' news programme. The Claimant's purpose in arranging for the camera team to be present was to ensure that his speech reached as wide an audience as possible and thereby had an increased chance of influencing the General Election debate.

6 On 7 May 2001 the demonstration commenced as arranged in Central Square, Newtown. Approximately 500 people were present, mainly composed of pensioners from in and around Newtown. The Claimant commenced his speech and the camera team arrived to record his speech.

7 The Claimant's speech was lawful and peaceful and related to the particular concerns of pensioners regarding law and order. He used a battery-powered loudhailer belonging to NPA in order to amplify his voice so that the crowd could hear him.

Particulars of unlawful act

8   A short time after the commencement of the Claimant's speech the Defendant approached the Claimant and seized the loudhailer. The Defendant removed the batteries and returned the loudhailer to the Claimant, saying that he was confiscating the batteries. Despite the Claimant's objections, the Defendant refused to return the batteries to the Claimant. The Claimant had no other batteries and it was not possible to obtain more batteries.

9   The Claimant attempted to make himself heard by shouting without the loudhailer but this was unsuccessful.

10 Within a short time of the seizure the camera team packed their equipment away and left. They had not been able to record any of the Claimant's speech and the item planned for the 'North Life' programme was not broadcast.

11 Soon after the camera team left, the crowd of demonstrators began to disperse and left the area.

12 The seizure of the loudhailer and the confiscation of the batteries was a breach of Art 10 of the European Convention on Human Rights (the Convention).

Particulars of breach

13 The Claimant's speech was intended to impart information and ideas within the meaning of Art 10(1) of the Convention and amounted to an exercise of his right to freedom of expression.

14 Seizure of the loudhailer and the confiscation of the batteries amounted to an interference with the Claimant's right to freedom of expression under Art 10(1) of the Convention.

15 The actions of the Defendant prevented the Claimant from being heard by the camera team and the assembled crowd.

16 The departure of the camera team and the dispersal of the crowd were due to the actions of the Defendant in preventing the Claimant from being heard.

17 The actions of the Defendant prevented the Claimant's speech from being broadcast on the 'North Life' television news programme.

18 The interference with the Claimant's right to freedom of expression was not justified under Art 10(2) of the Convention.

Remedy

19 The Claimant seeks damages for the breach of his Convention rights to the extent that the court considers just and appropriate pursuant to s 8(1) of the Human Rights Act.

> 20 The Claimant asserts that damages are necessary in order to afford just satisfaction within the meaning of s 8(3) and 8(4) of the Human Rights Act.

2.10.1.3 Defending claims of a breach of human rights

If a public authority is faced with a statement of case alleging that it has breached a claimant's Convention rights it must deal with the allegations in its defence. Decisions will have to be taken as to how much of the claimant's case is accepted so that admissions may be made in the defence. In cases where there are several layers to establishing liability the defendant may well accept the initial parts of the claimant's case but deny the remainder. Thus, in the sample claim above, the defendant police service might well admit that the claimant's speech amounted to expression under Art 10 and that the actions of Sergeant Todd interfered with that right. It would then assert that the interference was in accordance with the law, was for a legitimate reason and was necessary in a democratic society.

2.10.1.4 Can a public authority counterclaim under the Human Rights Act?

Obviously a public authority faced with a private law action may counterclaim against the claimant. However, what is contemplated here is a different proposition – the public authority alleging that its own human rights have been violated by the claimant. For example, if a public authority employer has dismissed an employee for unauthorised disclosures to the press, the employee might claim breach of Art 10 – freedom of expression. Could the employer enter a defence and counterclaim breach of Art 8 – respect for private life or correspondence? The answer seems to be that a public authority cannot claim to be a victim of a breach of human rights.[139] It may not therefore counterclaim under the Human Rights Act. However, the allegations it wishes to make are not for that reason irrelevant. They may be relied upon to justify the interference that is alleged. In our example, the protection of information disclosed in confidence is one of the permitted reasons for interfering with freedom of expression in Art 10(2) and could be pleaded as such.

2.10.2 Human rights in skeleton arguments

Many courts and tribunals order the parties to produce and exchange skeleton arguments in advance of any hearing where complex areas of fact or law are

---

139 *Ayuntamiento de M v Spain* (1991) 68 DR 209. However, see the discussion at para 2.7 above.

to be raised. The Human Rights Act has seen a dramatic increase in the number of requests for skeleton arguments at all levels of the legal system. Advance notice of the issues ensures that fuller argument can take place between the parties and assists the courts to make better-informed decisions.

The approach under the CPR is as follows:

Practice Direction: (CPR PD 39): (miscellaneous provisions relating to hearings)

...

8.1 If it is necessary for a party to give evidence at a hearing of an authority referred to in section 2 of the Human Rights Act 1998 –

(1) the authority to be cited should be an authoritative and complete report; and

(2) the party must give to the court and any other party a list of the authorities he intends to cite and copies of the reports not less than three days before the hearing.

This is not a requirement to produce a skeleton argument as such but it does require exchange of Strasbourg authorities at least three days prior to any hearing at which they will be referred to.[140] It seems sensible to exchange skeleton arguments at the same time, if practicable.

Issues for advocates: human rights in skeleton arguments

The following matters ought to be raised by the advocate in the skeleton argument, where relevant:

- In respect of each authority cited there should be an explanation of the proposition of law the authority is said to establish. If more than one authority is referred to this must be justified. This applies equally to Strasbourg authorities as it does to domestic authorities.[141]

- An explanation as to why any foreign case law is relevant to the decision. This is particularly relevant in respect of human rights decisions of Scottish courts, the Privy Council and foreign constitutional courts.

- An extract of the relevant Convention right or rights relied upon.

- An explanation of which sections of the Human Rights Act are relevant.

---

140 A similar direction applies in family proceedings but there the requirement is for inclusion as part of the court bundle, which must be lodged with the court two clear days prior to the hearing. See *Practice Direction: (Human Rights Act 1998): (Family Proceedings: Human Rights)* [2000] 4 All ER 288 and *(Practice Direction) (Family Proceedings: Court Bundles)* [2000] 1 WLR 737.

141 See *Practice Direction: (Citation of Authorities)* referred to below.

- Identification of any defence under the Human Rights Act, such as s 6(2) defences (compelled by or enforcing incompatible primary legislation).
- An explanation of whether a declaration of incompatibility is sought.
- Identification of any derogation issues that arise.
- Submissions as to whether the Convention right has been violated. Any areas of agreement should be highlighted in the skeleton. For example, if there is agreement that there has been an interference with Art 10 freedom of expression and that the interference was in accordance with the law and pursued a legitimate aim this should be stated and the interference, law and aim should be specified. The argument can then focus on whether the interference was necessary in a democratic society.

2.10.3 Oral applications

When making applications to the court it is important to have prepared the argument in sufficient detail in order to show the court that a live Convention right issue arises. Note the criticism of the Court of Appeal highlighted in Chapter 1 for those advocates who merely 'throw in' the Convention to bolster an otherwise weak application.

For example in a bail application there may be a temptation to say to the court something like the following:

> You will, of course, be aware that my client has a right to liberty under the Human Rights Act.

This of course adds nothing to the existing right to bail under the Bail Act and the advocate who threw it in might well find him or herself subject to some searching questioning by the court as to what significance this has for the application. This is not to say that advocates should avoid using the Convention in routine applications, merely that there must be some good reason for raising the Convention – it should not be used as window dressing or, even worse, as a smoke screen for a weak submission. The Convention should be utilised in a constructive way:

> The Crown is seeking a remand in custody on the basis of stereotyped assumptions that my client will abscond because of its view of the type of person he is. There is no coherent indication that the risk of absconding will actually materialise. This is just the type of stereotyped reason that has been found by the European Court of Human Rights to amount to a breach of the requirement for reasons under Article 5(3) of the Convention.

2.10.3.1 Opening speeches

An opening speech is the opportunity for the advocate to set out his or her case in summary for the court. It is at this stage that the court should be informed of the prominence that the human rights arguments will play in the case. The level of detail will obviously depend on a variety of factors such as the nature of the proceedings, whether a skeleton argument has been filed, whether the court has heard previous argument during interlocutory applications, the level of expertise of the tribunal of fact and the relative importance of the human rights arguments compared with the other aspects of the case.

2.10.3.2 Examination of witnesses

Obviously the party who alleges a breach of human rights will have to establish in evidence at least a *prima facie* case of a violation. This will often be a relatively simple task given that the dispute in human rights cases is more often over the justification for the interference rather than whether any interference took place at all. It follows that the more fruitful area for the advocate will often be in respect of public authority witnesses. They will have to provide an evidential basis for the public authority's justification of any interference that the court finds proved. The public authority's advocate will need to be alive to the fact that the burden of proving any justification lies with his or her client and will seek to anticipate the points likely to be raised in cross-examination. The public authority witness may face broader questioning in cross-examination in human rights cases. Such questioning might focus on issues like: relevant policies, training methods, procedures, human rights awareness, safeguards, record keeping, consultation with the claimant and balancing exercises conducted by the decision-maker. For example, a local government official might be cross-examined about the extent of his or her awareness and application of 'Core Guidance for Public Authorities',[142] a government handbook of guidance for decision-makers.

2.10.3.3 Closing speeches

More than any other part of a trial, the human rights content of a closing speech will depend on the audience. A speech to an experienced High Court judge, for example, who has shown awareness of the issues throughout the trial, may be little more than a summary of the following:

1   The Human Rights Act issues ('We submit that the defendant is a public authority under s 6 and that the claimant is, in the special circumstances of the case, a victim for the purposes of Art 34. We have tried to persuade

---

142 Home Office, London, 2000.

you that only a broad view of the legislative provision is compatible the claimant's Convention rights ...').

2   The Convention issues ('We confirm that there is agreement that the claimant was detained and that the detention was for a permissible reason under Art 5(1)(c). The principal area of disagreement is the level of information supplied to the claimant when he was detained under Art 5(2)').

3   The remedy sought ('Assuming the court is with us on the broad construction of the statute, the claimant seeks damages for false imprisonment. If the court is against us on the interpretation issue, we seek a declaration under s 4 of the Human Rights Act that the statute is incompatible with the claimant's right to liberty under Art 5 of the Convention').

Speeches to juries are likely to be more expansive and will seek to simplify the human rights issues and make them more relevant to their own experience:

> Ladies and gentlemen, you have heard a lot of talk about 'human rights' today and in particular of the Art 10 right to freedom of expression. In plain terms this means that every person is entitled, within reason, to speak his or her mind and should not be prevented by others or punished for doing so. The right enshrines the basic notion that in democratic countries people should be able to communicate with others, although of course those others cannot be forced to listen. You will no doubt be aware of many examples of where people exercise this right: Speakers' Corner in Hyde Park is a famous example but it can be much more mundane than that. If you have ever asked a question at a meeting, filled in a council questionnaire or even sung a song on the football terraces you have exercised your right to freedom of expression ...

Juries are not experts in human rights law. They might be more likely to be swayed by arguments regarding breach of human rights even if as a matter of law the arguments do not affect the existing legal position. Thus a defendant in a criminal case who has failed to persuade a trial judge to expand the available defences in order to protect his right to freedom of expression[143] might well make similar arguments to the jury in urging an acquittal.

2.11 CITING AUTHORITIES

The *Practice Direction: (Citation of Authorities)*[144] is applicable to all courts other than criminal courts and is intended to limit the number of cases that are cited

---

143 David Shayler, the former MI5 agent, failed in his bid at a pre-trial hearing to have the Official Secrets Act 1989 interpreted so as to include a public interest defence: see BBC Online: 16 May 2001: 'Shayler loses legal battle'.

144 (2001) *The Times*, 1 May.

as authority in courts. It is relevant in all areas of advocacy whether human rights are argued or not. It has special significance though, for advocates raising Convention rights arguments. The relevant extracts are set out below:

Method of citation

8.1 Advocates will in future be required to state, in respect of each authority that they wish to cite, the proposition of law that the authority demonstrates, and the parts of the judgment that support that proposition. If it is sought to cite more than one authority in support of a given proposition, advocates must state the reason for taking that course.

8.2 The demonstration referred to in paragraph 8.1 will be required to be contained in any skeleton argument and in any appellant's or respondent's notice in respect of each authority referred to in that skeleton or notice.

8.3 Any bundle or list of authorities prepared for the use of any court must in future bear a certification by the advocate responsible for arguing the case that the requirements of this paragraph have been complied with in respect of each authority included.

8.4 The statements referred to in paragraph 8.1 should not materially add to the length of submissions or of skeleton arguments, but should be sufficient to demonstrate, in the context of the advocate's argument, the relevance of the authority or authorities to that argument and that the citation is necessary for a proper presentation of the argument.

Authorities decided in other jurisdictions

9.1 Cases decided in other jurisdictions can, if properly used, be a valuable source of law in this jurisdiction. At the same time, however, such authority should not be cited without proper consideration of whether it does indeed add to the existing body of law.

9.2 In future therefore, any advocate who seeks to cite an authority from another jurisdiction must:

(i) comply, in respect of that authority, with the rules set out in paragraph 8 above;

(ii) indicate in respect of each authority what that authority adds that is not to be found in authority in this jurisdiction; or, if there is said to be justification for adding to domestic authority, what that justification is;

(iii) certify that there is no authority in this jurisdiction that precludes the acceptance by the court of the proposition that the foreign authority is said to establish.

9.3 For the avoidance of doubt, paragraphs 9.1 and 9.2 do not apply to cases decided in either the European Court of Justice or the organs of the European Convention of Human Rights. Because of the status in English law of such authority, as provided by, respectively, s 3 of the European Communities Act 1972 and s 2(1) of the Human Rights Act 1998, such cases are covered by the earlier paragraphs of this Direction.

Paragraph 8 of the Practice Direction makes it important not simply to list all of the authorities cited in the Human Rights Act textbooks. The advocate should examine each case relied on and seek to ensure so far as possible that only one case is relied on for each proposition of law. It may be that more than one authority is required, particularly when dealing with the fast developing case law under the Human Rights Act, but the advocate should be ready to justify this approach in the skeleton and also in court. This could arise especially where the advocate wishes to extract *dicta* from a number of different Human Rights Act cases in order to make a general proposition. For example, as we have seen, a number of cases would need to be cited in support of arguments about the definition of public authority. The Direction also emphasises the need to clearly distinguish the separate strands of legal principle making up the Convention right so that separate authorities may safely be cited for each strand.

Paragraph 9 is of particular relevance given the importance of foreign decisions in assisting the courts to interpret Convention law. Although decisions of the Strasbourg authorities are immune from the duties imposed by the paragraph, decisions of the Scottish courts need to be justified in accordance with its terms. Such decisions are often of major importance given that they interpret the same provisions of the Human Rights Act and the Convention as the English courts. In addition, decisions of other international courts and foreign constitutional courts can be of considerable assistance to the domestic courts. For each such decision, the advocate must explain that the proposition of law is not covered by domestic authority, or that domestic authority ought to be added to and that there is no domestic decision preventing the adoption of the proposition of law relied upon. This has the potential to considerably add to the duties on the advocate as in theory the advocate must trawl through domestic and Strasbourg authorities every time a foreign case is cited. However, it is likely that the courts will show some leeway in respect of established foreign constitutional courts given the relevance attached to such decisions by the Strasbourg Court and, increasingly, by the domestic courts under the Human Rights Act.[145]

---

145 See Chapter 4 for a full discussion of the relevance of non-domestic authority under the Human Rights Act.

CHAPTER 3

INTERFERENCE WITH QUALIFIED RIGHTS: PROPORTIONALITY ARGUMENTS IN HRA ADVOCACY

The key requirement for advocates who are presenting Human Rights Act arguments is the adoption of a structured approach, which enables the courts to identify the constituent elements of an application or of a defence. The issue of proportionality is likely to arise in many aspects of Human Rights Act arguments. It will often be clear that there has been an interference with a qualified right (such as Art 8), so that the focus will be whether that interference was for a permitted reason, whether it was prescribed by law and, most contentiously, whether it was necessary in a democratic society. It is this last element that introduces the concept of proportionality – a concept of some antiquity[1] whose exact boundaries remain curiously ill-defined.

Proportionality has been said to be no more than Lord Diplock's principle that 'you must not use a steam hammer to crack a nut'.[2] The challenge, however, for advocates who are seeking to couch arguments in terms of proportionality – whether attacking some interference, or defending it – are twofold: first, how can an argument on proportionality be structured in such a way as to clearly identify the constituent elements of this often vague and confusing principle; secondly, to what extent does proportionality imply a more merits-based challenge to the public body's decision?:

> The need for a clear approach to issue of proportionality can be seen even in factually simple cases. Jim brings an action against his public authority employers under the Disability Discrimination Act for failure to make reasonable adjustments to his work in respect of his chronic back pain. He claims he cannot lift or carry objects, and that he cannot walk without sticks. The employers, who have protected their car park with a CCTV system, have video footage of Jim carrying a heavy desk-top PC one hundred yards across the car park from the building to his car without any sign of difficulty. They wish to adduce this evidence at the Employment Tribunal.
>
> The employers concede that Article 8 is engaged,[3] and Jim concedes that the action is in accordance with law[4] and for a permitted Article 8(2) reason. The

---

1   Clayton and Tomlinson suggest that the principle has its roots in 19th century Prussian law: Clayton, 6.40.
2   *R v Goldstein* [1983] 1 WLR 151.
3   It is clear that a right to privacy can arise in the workplace: see for example, *Halford v United Kingdom* (1997) 24 EHRR 523. More significantly, note the decision in *R v Loveridge* [2001] EWCA Crim 973, (2001) 98(23) LSG 36 (discussed at Chapter 8), where a right to privacy was held to exist even within the magistrates' court. However, there may be initial issues about waiver (especially where there are signs warning that the car park is subject to CCTV surveillance), and indeed whether there is a limited waiver of privacy, which is implied by bringing a legal action.
4   Itself far from clear. It would appear that the use of the CCTV system has not been covert and that arguably there has been no breach of the Regulation of [cont]

tribunal is therefore faced with the issue of whether the interference with Article 8 is necessary in a democratic society – or its proportionality. Among the issues that the tribunal must consider will be: the extent of the interference – its length (was this a one-off incident or part of a lengthy surveillance operation), its extent (was he simply recorded in the car-park or was he recorded elsewhere), and its focus (was he targeted or was he simply caught on a general surveillance system). The tribunal must also consider the purpose of the interference, and whether a less intrusive means could have sufficed. As part of this exercise, the tribunal will inevitably consider the purpose for which this evidence is to be adduced – and the general Article 6 rights of Jim,[5] and the public interest in ensuring that justice is done. Moreover, even if the advocates fail to raise these issues, the tribunal as a public body will need to have regard to them, and will expect advocates to be able to address the issues in a structured way.[6]

The difficulty in presenting proportionality issues in a coherent manner is further complicated by the Strasbourg doctrine of margin of appreciation – a doctrine which is logically distinct from arguments as to proportionality, but which in practice seems to have overlapped with the proportionality principle, making it hard to distinguish which particular elements are being said to be relevant in any particular application. Although the case law, both at Strasbourg and domestic levels is far from clear, with both national and international courts tending to use terms somewhat haphazardly, we suggest a number of principles that accord with the case law but have the advantage to lending clarity to submissions in this area:

1   We suggest that the margin of appreciation in its strict sense is an international law concept and that domestic authorities such as *Kebilene*[7] now make clear that it has no role in domestic law.

2   We suggest that there is a new domestic law principle – the discretionary area of judgment – which amounts to a recognition by the domestic courts that in some areas it will be appropriate to defer to the decisions of the democratically elected legislature.

3   We suggest that the discretionary area of judgment inevitably overlaps to some degree with the principle of proportionality, but will need particular

---

4   [cont] Investigatory Powers Act 2000. However, there may well be issues under the Data Protection Act 1998.

5   Bizarrely, it appears that the public authority employer will not itself have Art 6 rights (*Ayuntamiento de M v Spain* (1991) 68 DR 209), although a general 'natural justice' argument remains applicable.

6   Nor is the issue of whether a breach of Art 8 has arisen the end of the matter; the tribunal will need to go on to consider whether the breach gives rise to a requirement to exclude the evidence. In a number of criminal cases, and in particular *Khan v United Kingdom* 8 BHRC 310, it has been made clear that evidence obtained in breach of Art 8 will not automatically need to be excluded under Art 6: see Chapter 8.

7   *R v DPP ex p Kebilene and Others* [2000] 2 AC 326 (HL).

attention when addressing the issue of whether a policy that has been adopted by the legislature corresponds to a pressing social need.

4   Arguments as to the proportionality of any interference will also overlap with the developing principle of the discretionary area of judgment, and will arise only once the court is satisfied that the public body has shown a pressing social need.

The first section of this chapter considers margin of appreciation issues, and the new domestic formulation of the 'discretionary area of judgment'. Then the chapter looks at whether any interference is necessary in a democratic society, and looks at how best to identify the elements of arguments on specific proportionality issues.

3.1 THE MARGIN OF APPRECIATION

3.1.1 What is the margin of appreciation?

The margin of appreciation is a principle adopted by the European Court of Human Rights, which recognises the court's status as an international court, and permits a degree of latitude to the Contracting Parties in their interpretation of the Convention in a domestic context. Effectively, Strasbourg recognises the disparity of legal and cultural approaches to the protection of the core human rights contained in the Convention and permits the signatory states some leeway in deciding how best to secure those rights within the domestic law context.

The classic statement of the margin of appreciation doctrine is found in *Handyside v United Kingdom*.[8] In *Handyside*, the Strasbourg Court was asked to consider whether the United Kingdom had breached the Art 10 right to freedom of expression in its action against the *Little Red Schoolbook*:

> The Court points out that the machinery of protection established by the Convention is subsidiary to the national system safeguarding human rights. The Convention leaves to each Contracting State, in the first place, the task of securing the rights and liberties it enshrines ...

> By reason of their direct and continuous contact with the vital forces of their countries, State authorities are in principle in a better position than the international judge to give an opinion on the exact content of these requirements as well as on the 'necessity' of a 'restriction' or 'penalty' intended to meet them ... [I]t is for the national authorities to make the initial assessment of the reality of the pressing social need implied by the notion of 'necessity' in this context.

---

8   (1976) 1 EHRR 737.

> Consequently, Article 10 para 2 ... leaves to the Contracting States a margin of appreciation. This margin is given both to the domestic legislator ('prescribed by law') and to the bodies, judicial amongst others, which are called upon to interpret and apply the laws in force ...
>
> Nevertheless, Article 10 para 2 ... does not give the Contracting States an unlimited power of appreciation. The court, which, with the Commission, is responsible for ensuring the observance of those States' engagements (Article 19) ... is empowered to give the final ruling on whether a 'restriction' or 'penalty' is reconcilable with freedom of expression as protected by Article 10 ... The domestic margin of appreciation thus goes hand in hand with a European supervision. Such supervision concerns both the aim of the measure challenged and its 'necessity'; it covers not only the basic legislation but also the decision applying it, even one given by an independent court.[9]

However, for advocates in the domestic courts the difficulty in dealing with Strasbourg decisions that include reference to the margin of appreciation is in assessing the limits of that residual discretion accorded to the state. It requires the drawing of a distinction between domestic variations in the means of implementation of the Convention and the underlying, and non-negotiable, protection of the rights contained in the Convention. Domestic variations – cultural or legal – cannot permit a state to act in breach of a person's Convention rights, notwithstanding the doctrine.

Having said this, however, where there is a clear lack of any common ground across the Contracting Parties, the Strasbourg Court may decline to lay down a common principle on the basis that no such principle can be derived from the shared laws of the Contracting Parties. Thus, there are widely differing approaches between states as to the legality of abortion, and in this context the Commission has declined to lay down specific requirements under any of the Convention Articles (including Art 2) on the basis that there is a lack of common ground:

> [I]t is clear that national laws on abortion differ considerably. In these circumstances, and assuming that the Convention may be considered to have some bearing in this field, the Commission finds that in such a delicate area the Contracting States must have a certain discretion ...
>
> As the present case shows there are different opinions as to whether such an authorisation [for termination of the pregnancy] strikes a fair balance between the legitimate need to protect the foetus and the legitimate interests of the woman in question. However, having regard to what is stated above concerning Norwegian legislation, its requirements for the termination of pregnancy as well as the specific circumstances of the present case, the Commission does not find that the respondent State has gone beyond its discretion, which the Commission considers it has, in this sensitive area of abortion.[10]

---

9   (1976) 1 EHRR 737, paras 47–49.

10   *H v Norway* (1992) 73 DR 155.

In many areas where there has in the past been a lack of common ground between Contracting Parties, societal developments may mean that the Strasbourg Court will at a later date be able to find sufficient commonality of approach on which to found a common standard.[11] In the *Bellinger*[12] case the Court of Appeal carefully reviewed the recent series of Strasbourg decisions on transsexuality, and expressed its 'dismay' that the United Kingdom was failing to respond to the clear warnings from the Strasbourg Court that the changes in societal (and scientific) attitudes to transsexuality required the United Kingdom to keep its refusal to amend the law under review. By a majority, however, the domestic court took the view that this was an area where it was for Parliament to change the law notwithstanding the court's own concern that the government's failure to respond made future applications to Strasbourg likely 'sooner rather than later'.[13]

A more deep-rooted problem for advocates is the potential confusion between the doctrine of margin of appreciation and the issue of proportionality. Where Strasbourg indicates that, notwithstanding an interference with a qualified Convention right (such as Art 8 or Art 10), the state has not breached the Convention, it is not always clear whether the international court is saying that the state has a margin of appreciation in its approach to the article in question, or whether the Court is saying that the interference with the right is within the range of proportionate responses ('necessary in a democratic society') to meet an identified and permitted concern ('the protection of the rights and freedoms of others', for example).

The distinction between the doctrine of margin of appreciation and the principle of proportionality is an important one since it is increasingly clear that the margin of appreciation doctrine will not have any place in arguments under the Human Rights Act, at least in its classic form. The reasons for this are considered in the following section, and in the section after that we consider the re-statement of the margin of appreciation principle as 'the discretionary area of judgment', which is to be accorded the legislature in domestic law.

---

11   According to the *Sheffield and Horsham v United Kingdom* judgment ((1998) 27 EHRR 163) the only legal systems that do not recognise a change of gender are the United Kingdom, Ireland, Andorra and Albania.

12   *Bellinger v Bellinger* [2001] EWCA Civ 1140, Lawtel 17/7/2001.

13   Thorpe LJ in a strong dissenting judgment took the view that the lack of definition of the term 'female' in the Matrimonial Causes Act 1973 left the court free to interpret the term 'in the light of moral, ethical and societal values as they are now rather than as they were at the date of first enactment or subsequent consolidation'. In his judgment it is interesting to note, however, that although he took the view that the clear lack of progress made in introducing a statutory revision of the law meant that the courts were bound to take a lead, there is little suggestion that this is as a result of the interpretative obligation laid down by the Human Rights Act itself.

3.1.2 Margin of appreciation as an international law concept

On its face the margin of appreciation is an international law concept, and makes little sense in the context of domestic law. It is hard to see how an advocate can argue that the domestic court must accord the state a margin of appreciation in its application of the Convention because of the inability of that domestic court to appreciate domestic mores and concerns. This approach, flagged up in the decision of Lord Justice Buxton in the case of *Imbert*,[14] was confirmed by the House of Lords in *Kebilene*,[15] where Lord Hope stated:

> This doctrine is an integral part of the supervisory jurisdiction, which is exercised over state conduct by the international court. By conceding a margin of appreciation to each national system, the court has recognised that the Convention, as a living system, does not need to be applied uniformly by all states but may vary in its application according to local needs and conditions. This technique is not available to the national courts when they are considering Convention issues arising within their own countries.[16]

Thus, for example, it would be wrong for an advocate representing a public authority to argue that his or her client has a margin of appreciation:

> An advocate appearing on behalf of the police in order to justify the policing of a demonstration should refrain from arguing that an especial deference must be given to decisions in this area on the basis that the police are in principle better placed that the court to make such decisions. The issue of whether the police have breached an individual's human rights under s 6(1) is the core concern of the court, and the court as a public authority cannot abrogate its responsibilities by deferring to police judgment about where any balancing of rights should occur. By contrast, however, the issue of the proportionality of any interference by the police will clearly be a matter that the advocate appearing for the police could, and should, raise.

However, the margin of appreciation doctrine will still potentially be of relevance to advocates in two contexts: where the advocate is asking the domestic court to take account of Strasbourg case law as required by s 2 of the Human Rights Act; and where the advocate is dealing with the extent of a positive obligation on the state.

3.1.2.1 *Margin of appreciation arguments and s 2 of the HRA*

Section 2 requires that the court 'takes account' of Strasbourg jurisprudence in determining any question that has arisen in connection with a Convention right. Where the Strasbourg case law – be it at Court or Commission level –

---

14   *R v Stratford Justices ex p Imbert* [1999] 2 Cr App R 276.
15   *R v DPP ex p Kebilene and Others* [2000] 2 AC 326 (HL).
16   *Ibid*, para 380H.

indicates that there has been no breach of a Convention article, advocates will nonetheless need to go further and to look to the rationale of the decision. There will be Strasbourg decisions where the state is permitted a 'margin of appreciation' in its approach to the protection of a designated right. This margin will not *per se* be available to the state in arguments in domestic law.

It is not clear, however, that the domestic courts have fully accepted that the international nature of the Strasbourg's Court's supervisionary jurisdiction may mean that adjustment is needed in domestic cases in any event. Notwithstanding Lord Hope's confirmation in *Kebilene* that the margin of appreciation principle is not applicable in a domestic law context, the House of Lords in that case took the view that the Strasbourg case of *Salabiaku*[17] permitted (at least to some extent) the use of presumptions in criminal law without considering whether this principle might require a more rigorous analysis when seen in a domestic law context, where the national courts are able to assess its applicability within the national legal framework. Indeed, there have now been a plethora of domestic cases which cite Strasbourg's self-denying ordinance in respect of issues of evidential admissibility without any accompanying recognition that this may in turn call for a closer scrutiny of the principles involved by the domestic courts, who effectively have a role of primary supervision.[18]

Thus for an advocate who wishes to argue, for example, that forfeiture of a publication on grounds of obscenity offends against Art 10, the fact that the Strasbourg Court in *Handyside* ruled that there had been no breach of Art 10 will not in any way be conclusive since the Court made clear that it was according to the state a significant margin of appreciation. This can be seen in the Court's conclusion that the fact that the publication in question was freely available in other states was in no way determinative of the issue of whether there had been a breach of the right to freedom of expression within the United Kingdom:

> The applicant and the minority of the Commission laid stress on the further point that, in addition to the original Danish edition, translations of the 'Little Book' appeared and circulated freely in the majority of the Member States of the Council of Europe.

> Here again, the national margin of appreciation and the optional nature of the 'restrictions' and 'penalties' referred to in Article 10 para 2 ... prevent the court from accepting the argument. The Contracting States have each fashioned their approach in the light of the situation obtaining in their respective territories; they have had regard, *inter alia*, to the different views prevailing there about the demands of the protection of morals in a democratic society. The fact that most of them decided to allow the work to be distributed does not mean that

---

17 *Salabiaku v France* (1988) 13 EHRR 379.
18 See Chapter 8, para 8.1.

the contrary decision of the Inner London Quarter Sessions was a breach of Article 10 ...[19]

For the advocates in such a case, whether appearing for a publisher or for a public authority, it is clear that any Strasbourg authority where the state is accorded a margin of appreciation cannot be determinative of an issue in domestic law. The advocate for the public authority can properly argue that the international court's decision in *Handyside* indicates that there is no necessary breach of the Convention right – and that the domestic court should be slow to apply a more stringent level of protection than can be found across the Contracting States. The advocate for the publisher will argue that s 6 of the Human Rights Act imposes a positive obligation on the court as public authority to protect the Art 10 rights of the individual and that since the domestic court is not hampered by lack of knowledge of and contact with the national cultural context, it is for the domestic court to apply a more searching investigation of the public authority's claims that the interference with the right to freedom of expression is justified.[20]

3.1.2.2 The margin of appreciation and positive obligations

The other context in which margin of appreciation arguments may still be of some relevance is in cases where the advocates are seeking to establish whether a positive obligation on the state can be said to exist. This is again an area where in some cases the Strasbourg Court has recognised a diversity of approach within the Contracting States by according a wide margin of appreciation. One example that has been cited[21] is in connection with the right of transsexuals to change their legal status following gender-reassignment, an area where there is a divergence in the approaches of different states. While Art 8 is recognised as creating a positive obligation on states to protect the family life of individuals, in *Rees v United Kingdom*[22] and the cases that have followed it, Strasbourg has been prepared to give the state a wide margin of appreciation in this area, albeit warning that it is an area where societal developments may in due course require a change in the law.[23]

One indication of the approach of the domestic courts to the issue of positive obligations can be found in the judgment of Lord Justice Sedley in *Douglas v Hello!*,[24] where the Court of Appeal was prepared to accept that a

---

19   *Handyside v United Kingdom* (1976) 1 EHRR 737, para 57.
20   For a fuller discussion of this argument, in the context of the Copyright, Designs and Patents Act 1988, see *Ashdown v Telegraph Group* [2001] EWCA Civ 1142 (CA); (2001) *The Times*, 1 August, discussed below at 3.1.3.1.
21   Clayton, 6.39.
22   (1987) 9 EHRR 56.
23   See comments in *Bellinger v Bellinger* [2001] EWCA Civ 1140, Lawtel 17/7/2001, as to the failure of the United Kingdom Government to do this.
24   [2001] 2 WLR 992.

combination of the development of the common law and the positive obligations introduced by the Human Rights Act enabled the recognition of a right to privacy in domestic law:

> Nevertheless, we have reached a point at which it can be said with confidence that the law recognises and will appropriately protect a right of personal privacy.
>
> The reasons are twofold. First, equity and the common law are today in a position to respond to an increasingly invasive social environment by affirming that everybody has a right to some private space. Secondly, and in any event, the Human Rights Act 1998 requires the courts of this country to give appropriate effect to the right to respect for private and family life set out in Article 8 of the European Convention on Human Rights and Fundamental Freedoms. The difficulty with the first proposition resides in the common law's perennial need (for the best of reasons, that of legal certainty) to appear not to be doing anything for the first time. The difficulty with the second lies in the word 'appropriate'. But the two sources of law now run in a single channel because, by virtue of s 2 and s 6 of the Act, the courts of this country must not only take into account jurisprudence of both the Commission and the European Court of Human Rights which points to a positive institutional obligation to respect privacy; they must themselves act compatibly with that and the other Convention rights.[25]

Thus advocates are able not merely to set to one side the international law principle of margin of appreciation, but are able to turn to s 6(3) of the Human Rights Act to argue that the status of the domestic courts as public authorities makes clear that the court may itself be acting unlawfully if it fails to take positive steps to provide protection for the victim of a violation.

Here advocates who appear for public authorities may be able to rely upon the margin of appreciation doctrine in arguing that Strasbourg case law indicates that there is no commonality of approach such as to justify the creation or extension of a positive obligation:

> For example, Richard is divorced from Shona, but continues to occupy the former matrimonial home. He has agreed to pay her rent. He claims Housing Benefit, but is refused benefit under a provision which bars entitlement where a liability to pay rent to a former partner arises.[26] Richard's advocate attempts to argue that this constitutes a breach of Article 8, since the effect is to prevent Richard from living in the same house as his children. It will also deprive him of his home, since he will have to move to another property where he can claim Housing Benefit to meet his housing costs.
>
> The advocate for the public authority will argue that while Article 8 undoubtedly can give rise to positive obligations upon the State,[27] there is no basis in Strasbourg law for imposing a positive obligation on the State to make

---

25   *Ibid*, paras 110–11.
26   Regulation 7(1)(c)(i) of the Housing Benefit (General) Regulations 1987, as amended.
27   See, for example, *Glaser v United Kingdom* [2001] 1 FLR 153.

payments of Housing Benefit. Indeed, the advocate would argue that housing policy and social security are *par excellence* areas where Strasbourg gives a wide margin of appreciation to the individual States. It is therefore legitimate for the domestic court to take account of that margin of appreciation in coming to a conclusion as to whether such a positive obligation could exist.[28]

Issues for advocates: margin of appreciation arguments

1   The margin of appreciation is an international law doctrine relating to the supervisory jurisdiction of the international court. It is not available to the state in a domestic law context.

2   When approaching Strasbourg case law where the state has been accorded a margin of appreciation:

   • the fact of the margin of appreciation is relevant in indicating the range of responses which the Strasbourg Court has found to be acceptable;

   • it is for the domestic courts to decide what response is appropriate in a domestic context, and since the state cannot argue that the domestic court is not competent to judge the particular social and political values of the United Kingdom, the court's assessment can be more stringent in assessing the extent to which interference with, or failure to protect, rights is permissible.

3   Where the advocate is arguing for the existence of a positive obligation, the margin of appreciation will still be relevant in assessing whether the Strasbourg Court has imposed such an obligation upon Contracting Parties.

3.1.3   What is the discretionary area of judgment?

In the previous section we have suggested that the margin of appreciation is a doctrine, which will not normally be applicable in the domestic courts. Is this to say, then, that the issue of national discretion can never be relevant in a domestic law argument?

Clearly the issue of discretion is an integral element of any proportionality-based submission: this is discussed further below. However,

---

28   See the decision of Lightman J in *R v Carmarthenshire County Council Housing Benefit Review Board ex p Painter* [2001] EWHC Admin 308; (2001) *The Times*, 16 May, where the advocate for the claimant conceded that no such positive obligation could exist. Note, however, that the fact that the claim could not succeed under Art 8 did not, of course, prevent the advocate for the claimant from arguing that there had been a breach of Art 14, in that the 'ex spouse' provision meant that there had been discrimination in access to the Art 8 right. The argument on this point failed on the basis that there was objective justification for any discriminatory treatment, and that the measure was proportionate. A similar challenge to reg 7(1)(d) of the Housing Benefit (General) Regulations 1987 also failed in the Court of Appeal: *R v Secretary of State for Social Security ex p Tucker*, Lawtel 8/11/01.

the national courts have also now begun to develop a new doctrine – the discretionary area of judgment – which requires courts to have regard to the rights of the democratically elected organs of the state to decide matters of policy in certain circumstances.

In his judgment in *Kebilene*, cited above, Lord Hope, having ruled that the margin of appreciation was not applicable in a domestic law context, continued:

> [The margin of appreciation] is not available to the national courts when they are considering Convention issues arising within their own countries. But in the hands of the national courts also the Convention should be seen as an expression of fundamental principles rather than as a set of mere rules. The questions, which the courts will have to decide in the application of these principles, will involve questions of balance between competing interests and issues of proportionality.

> In this area difficult choices may have to be made by the executive or the legislature between the rights of the individual and the needs of society. In some circumstances it will be appropriate for the courts to recognise that there is an area of judgment within which the judiciary will defer, on democratic grounds, to the considered opinion of the elected body or person whose act or decision is said to be incompatible with the Convention.[29]

It is clear therefore that it will not be possible for the advocate simply to argue that since no margin of appreciation can properly be imported into domestic law the domestic court can only have regard to its own view of what steps must be taken to provide the protection required by any given Convention article. Through the creation of this 'discretionary area of judgment' the courts can re-delineate the boundaries between the judiciary and domestic legislature in deciding the appropriate response to the requirements of the Convention.

The original formulation of this new principle is to be found, as Lord Hope indicates, in *Human Rights Law and Practice*,[30] although clearly the issue of the proper boundary between the role of courts and the legislature or executive is a long-standing concern in constitutional law. Lester and Pannick suggest that a number of factors will be of relevance in applying this form of domestic margin of appreciation.

1 What is the nature of the right in issue?

As Lord Hope stated in *Kebilene*:

> It will be easier for such an area of judgment to be recognised where the Convention itself requires a balance to be struck, much less so where the right is stated in terms which are unqualified.[31]

---

29 *R v DPP ex p Kebilene and Others* [2000] 2 AC 326 (HL), 380–381E.
30 See Lester and Pannick.
31 *Ibid.*

There are few entirely unqualified Convention rights – even Art 2 (the right to life) has qualifications. Article 3, the right not to be tortured or subjected to inhuman or degrading treatment, is absolute. Similarly, Art 4(1) (the prohibition on slavery) and Art 7 (the prohibition on retrospective criminalisation of conduct) are unqualified. In these absolute contexts there is generally no question of the balancing of rights, and hence there is less role for the democratically elected body to decide where any such balance should lie.[32]

By contrast, the majority of the rights in the Convention are qualified, so that, for example, Art 8(2) permits interference with the right to respect for privacy, home, family life and correspondence, but only for a prescribed reason, and so far as is in accordance with law and is necessary in a democratic society. In the context of Art 3 of Protocol 1, which on its face concerns the holding of free and fair elections, the European Court of Human Rights had inferred an extension of the provision to cover the right to vote itself, but when the High Court was asked to consider this provision in the context of the disenfranchisement of prisoners, the court noted the implied nature of the right, concluding not only that it was not unqualified, but also that it concerned an issue where the courts were 'well placed' to assess the balance:

> Clearly we are dealing with an area where the Convention requires a balance to be struck, and the right is not stated in terms, which are unqualified. It has been inferred. The issues do involve questions of social policy but, as Mr Fitzgerald points out, the right to vote, even if under used, is of high constitutional importance and in so far as disenfranchisement is regarded as a punishment the courts may be said to be as well placed to assess the need for protection as they would be in relation to any other sentence in the armoury which the legislature controls.[33]

Thus an advocate who, for example, wishes to argue that the The Telecommunications (Lawful Business Practice) (Interception of Communications) Regulations 2000, which permit the employer to monitor staff communications, are in breach of Art 8 may face the argument that these regulations have been passed by the democratically elected body, which has itself considered where it is most appropriate to draw the line between the employee's right to privacy and the employer's right to ensure that company resources are not being misused, and that a margin of discretion must be permitted the democratic body in arriving at the conclusion that the regulations provide the appropriate balance.

---

32 For a fuller discussion of qualified and absolute rights, see Chapter 1 above.
33 *R (on the Application of Pearson) v Secretary of State for the Home Department* [2001] EWHC Admin 239; [2001] HRLR 39, at para 21.

2 Does the right in issue require consideration of 'social, economic or political' factors?

Drawing on jurisprudence under the Canadian Charter of Rights and Freedoms, Lester and Pannick argue that the legislature may be uniquely well placed when required to balance different policies in order to reconcile competing interests:

> This is a role properly assigned to the elected representatives of the people, who have at their disposal the necessary institutional resources to enable them to compile and assess social science evidence, to mediate between competing social interests and to reach out and protect vulnerable groups.[34]

Advocates will wish to be cautious, however, in accepting such arguments too readily; public authorities are often ready to claim that the right to allocate resources and to balance competing interests are uniquely within their sphere.[35] If this were an absolute proposition, however, there would often be little real scope for the protection of the rights of the individual. The Strasbourg Court has made clear that the protection to be offered by the Convention must be effective, and the fact that there may be competing interests does not remove the duty of the domestic court to review the balance that has been struck.

As to the traditional argument that national security is an area where the courts will defer to the Executive, advocates should note the decision of Turner J in the *Farrakhan* case,[35a] where the Home Secretary's long-standing exclusion order on the claimant was successfully challenged. The judge noted in particular that:

> In a constitutional democracy there is still an important role for the elected representative, who is answerable to Parliament.

> The Secretary of State often enjoys an expertise which is specific to him as, for example, in assessing risks to public order on the occurrence of certain events.

> Here, the Home Secretary had given his personal attention to the particular problem posed by the application.[35b]

However, the judgment continues:

> The fact that there exists in any member of the Executive branch of Government a discretionary area of judgment is not in issue in the present case. What is in issue is the question whether it can be seen from the terms in

---

34 *Libman v AG of Quebec* (1998) 3 BHRC 269 at 289, cited in Lester and Pannick, 3.26.

35 Indeed, it is interesting that the justification in the *Quebec* case is the greater degree of expertise of the legislature. The other argument that is frequently put forward is that democratically elected bodies are answerable to an electorate, which can then express its own judgment on their judgment. This latter, however, is potentially a dangerous argument if taken too far, since the purpose of the Convention is to protect minorities against the 'tyranny of the majority'.

35a *Farrakhan v Secretary of State for the Home Department* [2001] EWHC Admin 781, Lawtel 1/10/2001.

35b *Ibid*, para 36.

which his decision was cast that the Home Secretary has properly found and identified substantial and objective justification for it. It must, in my judgment, be the case that where, as here, the Home Secretary relies so heavily on his discretionary area of judgment for the purpose of justifying his decision he should make good his claim to have acted for good and sufficient reason. The inference which a court is bound to draw in the absence of a sufficiency of justification (reasons) is that there are none which will support the conclusion reached, or decision made, as being properly within the discretionary area of judgment.[35c]

The discretionary area of judgment does not therefore relieve the state from providing adequate evidence of reasoning for the exercise of that judgment, and it is clear that the courts remain under a duty to give close scrutiny to the basis of the decision.

A similarly robust approach was taken by the Information Tribunal in *Baker v Secretary of State for the Home Department*.[35d] Here the tribunal held that the Minister must have reasonable grounds in order to issue a certificate exempting the Security Service from the provisions of the Data Protection Act. This required responses to be considered individually rather than on a blanket basis. Only in this way could any given exemption be properly justified.

The discretionary area of judgment doctrine, however, makes clear that in the context of that review by the courts, it may be more appropriate for the court to defer to the judgment of the legislature where economic and social policy issues are at stake. Even in these contexts, however, the courts will not automatically defer to the legislature but will wish to consider evidence as to the basis of the policy. Thus, in *Wilson v First County Trust*,[36] where the Court of Appeal made a declaration of the incompatibility of the Consumer Credit Act 1974 with the Article 1, Protocol 1 right to property, the court was unimpressed with the Government's argument as to the discretionary area of judgment, notwithstanding the social policy nature of the right at stake:

> Counsel for the Secretary of State urged, rightly, that the Consumer Credit Act 1974 is concerned with issues of social policy rather than matters of high constitutional importance. The issues fall within an area in which the courts should be ready to defer, on democratic grounds, to 'the considered opinion of the elected body or person'. We recognise the force of those arguments. But, unless deference is to be equated with unquestioning acceptance, the argument that an issue of social policy falls within a discretionary area of judgment which the courts must respect recognises, as it seems to us, the need for the court to identify the particular issue of social policy which the legislature or the executive thought it necessary to address, and the thinking which led to that issue being dealt with in the way that it was. It is one thing to accept the need to defer to an opinion which can be seen to be the product of reasoned

---

35c *Ibid*, para 48.
35d Lawtel, 2/10/2001.
36 *Wilson v First County Trust Ltd (No 2)* [2001] EWCA Civ 633; [2001] 2 WLR 42.

consideration based on policy; it is quite another thing to be required to accept, without question, an opinion for which no reason of policy is advanced.[37]

There are some signs, however, that the rationale of the 'discretionary area of judgment' principle may be being overlooked. In *Ford v Press Complaints Commission*[38] the Administrative Court was prepared to extend the principle to the Press Complaints Commission, apparently ruling that it was a specialist body which had a membership and an expertise in balancing the conflicting rights of privacy and freedom of expression to which the courts should defer. This would be a worrying extension of the principle to an unelected body, and seems to represent an abrogation of responsibility on the part of the court. The decision is of course first instance, and needs to be seen in the context of an application for review, which was ruled to be out of time and which was in any event seen as unmeritorious. However, it is an indication that the new principle has, if not carefully applied, the potential to undermine the courts' own duties of review.

3 Is this an area where the courts have a special expertise?

This proposition is effectively the reverse of the preceding proposition, suggesting that there will be some areas where the courts are particularly well placed to balance competing rights. The related nature of the two propositions is recognised by Lord Hope in *Kebilene*:

> It will be easier for [the discretionary area of judgment] to be recognised where the issues involve questions of social or economic policy, much less so where the rights are of high constitutional importance or are of a kind where the courts are especially well placed to assess the need for protection.[39]

It is interesting that the criminal law is often used as an example of an area where the courts have a high degree of expertise. The vast number of recent pieces of criminal legislation, which have had, and will continue to have, very wide-ranging effects on the criminal trial and sentencing process, might suggest that there is a strong argument that the criminal process and penal reform are both areas where the legislature would lay claim to both social policy expertise and the mandate of the electorate. However this is an area where the courts are clear that they have a particular right to examine the balance that has been struck – perhaps on the basis that criminal cases generally involve the state as prosecutor, and the individual as defendant, or, in the words of a Canadian judge:

> [T]he courts will judge the legislature's choice more harshly in areas where the government plays the role of the 'singular antagonist of the individual' ...[40]

---

37 *Wilson v First County Trust Ltd (No 2)* [2001] EWCA Civ 633; [2001] 2 WLR 42, para 33.
38 Lawtel, 31/7/2001.
39 *R v DPP ex p Kebilene and Others* [2000] 2 AC 326 (HL), para 381C.
40 *Per* McLachlin J in *RJR McDonald Inc v Canada (AG)* (1995) 127 DLR 4th 1.

In the domestic context of the s 41 of the Youth Justice and Criminal Evidence Act 1999 prohibition on the cross-examination of rape victims as to prior sexual contact with the defendant, Lord Hope in the House of Lords took the opportunity to apply the *Kebilene* formulation:

> 58 I would take, as my starting point for examining section 41, the proposition that there are areas of law which lie within the discretionary area of judgment which the court ought to accord to the legislature. As I said in ... *Kebilene* ... it is appropriate in some circumstances for the judiciary to defer, on democratic grounds, to the considered opinion of the elected body as to where the balance is to be struck between the rights of the individual and the needs of society ... I would hold that *prima facie* the circumstances in which section 41 was enacted bring this case into that category ... [T]he right to lead evidence and the right to put questions with which that section deals are not among the rights which are set out in unqualified terms in Article 6 of the Convention. They are open to modification or restriction so long as this is not incompatible with the right to a fair trial. The essential question for your Lordships, as I see it, is whether Parliament acted within its discretionary area of judgment when it was choosing the point of balance that is indicated by the ordinary meaning of the words used in section 41. If it did not, questions will arise as to whether the incompatibility that results can be avoided by making use of the rule of interpretation in section 3 of the Human Rights Act 1998, failing which whether a declaration of incompatibility should be made. But I think that the question, which I have described as the essential question, must be addressed first.[41]

The point is also made with some brevity by Lord Steyn in the same case, responding to an argument from the state that this was a matter where Parliament had a discretion in choosing how to balance the rights of the individual, the victim and society as a whole:

> Counsel for the Secretary of State further relied on the principle that, in certain contexts, the legislature and the executive retain a discretionary area of judgment within which policy choices may legitimately be made: see *Brown v Stott* [2001] 2 WLR 817. Clearly the House must give weight to the decision of Parliament that the mischief encapsulated in the twin myths must be corrected. On the other hand, when the question arises whether in the criminal statute in question Parliament adopted a legislative scheme which makes an excessive inroad into the right to a fair trial the court is qualified to make its own judgment and must do so.[42]

However, it is clear that it is not merely in the context of criminal law – or indeed those cases where the balance to be drawn is solely between the state as 'singular antagonist' of the individual – that the court will claim a special expertise. The supervisory role of the court in family law matters, and

---

41 *R v A* [2001] UKHL 25; [2001] 2 WLR 1546, para 58.
42 *Ibid*, para 36.

particularly in public family law cases, indicates a high degree of accepted expertise. Indeed, in this context, the domestic courts have taken upon themselves to substantially re-interpret the Children Act so as to provide a degree of on-going review, and hence positive protection for the child's rights, notwithstanding a clear statute-based regime that sought to separate the role of the court and the public authorities.[43]

Thus the domestic courts have in some specialised circumstances shown that the discretionary area of judgment will have little role to play.

4 Where the rights claimed are of 'especial importance'

Strasbourg has traditionally accorded a high degree of protection to certain rights that are seen as the bedrock of democratic societies – in particular, plurality in both expression and lifestyle, and the right of access to courts in order to protect rights. Where, therefore, the public body proposes to interfere with, for example, the right to freedom of expression – 'one of the essential foundations of a democratic society'[44] – it is unlikely that the courts will accord a significant discretion to the decision-maker. In this particular regard, it should be recalled that freedom of expression issues are not confined to political speech, but also extend to commercial and artistic speech – with the Strasbourg Court evenly divided on whether commercial speech should merit an identically high level of protection to political speech.[45] There will therefore be comparatively wide areas of the Convention where it is appropriate to argue that in view of the constitutional importance of the right in issue the discretionary area of judgment is either inappropriate or should be narrowly construed.

3.1.3.1 Is the discretionary area of judgment a domestic margin of appreciation test?

The better view is that it is not.[46] The focus of the margin of appreciation is the balance between international and domestic jurisdictions. The doctrine is not simply a recognition that Strasbourg is less directly informed by the evolution

---

43 See the discussion of *W and B (Children: Care Plan)* [2001] EWCA Civ 757; [2001] FCR 450, discussed at 1.5.3.1 above.

44 *Handyside v United Kingdom* (1976) 1 EHRR 737.

45 See *Markt Intern Verlag GmbH v Germany* (1989) 12 EHRR 161: the case was decided against the applicant, but only on the vote of the President of the Court, traditionally exercised in favour of the state.

46 Note, however, the comment of the Court of Appeal in *R v Secretary of State for the Home Department ex p Isiko* [2000] 1 FCR 633 which appears directly to equate the margin of appreciation with the discretionary area of judgment:

> Where the Court reviews a decision which is required to comply with the Convention by the Human Rights Act 1998, it does not substitute its own decision for that of the executive. It reviews the decision of the executive to see if it was permitted by law – in this instance the Human Rights Act. In performing this exercise the Court has to bear in mind that, just as individual States [cont]

of the national cultural and legal environment; it is also recognition of the disparity of approaches across the Contracting States. For advocates, therefore, the margin of appreciation is a matter that requires recognition in domestic law only to the extent that its effect on any relevant Strasbourg jurisprudence is to be discounted. By way of contrast, the discretionary area of judgment doctrine appears to require the domestic court to look at the substantive right that is in play and to interpret its extent in domestic law.

However, this distinction between the international and domestic law contexts does not seem to be being recognised in every case by the domestic courts. Thus in *Ashdown v Telegraph Group*, where Lord (Paddy) Ashdown was arguing that the publication by the *Sunday Telegraph* of a secret memorandum amounted to a breach of copyright to which there was no defence, the newspaper argued that the Art 10 right to freedom of expression required that the Copyright, Designs and Patents Act 1988 be interpreted in the light of each case to see whether the restriction on freedom of expression was justified. Morrit VC, in the first instance decision, rejected this, couching his argument in terms the margin of appreciation accorded to the United Kingdom and ruling that the Act itself provided a determinative balancing mechanism for the classes of right concerned:

> In my view the provisions of the Act alone can and do satisfy the third requirement of Article 10(2) as well. The needs of a democratic society include the recognition and protection of private property ... The terms of s 30 CDPA were evidently intended to implement the latitude afforded by Article 10 of the Berne Convention 1971. Likewise the United Kingdom is entitled to a margin of appreciation in giving effect to the provisions of Article 10 of ECHR in the field of intellectual property ... I can see no reason why the provisions of CDPA should not be sufficient to give effect to the Convention right subject only to such restrictions as are permitted by Article 10(2).[47]

When the matter was considered by the Court of Appeal, however, the court ruled that it could not be said that the Act could conclusively address all potential issues arising in relation to Art 10. Interestingly, the Court of Appeal did not refer either to the margin of appreciation or to the discretionary area

---

46   [cont] enjoy a margin of appreciation which permits them to respond within the law in a manner which is not uniform, so there will often be an area of discretion permitted to the executive of a country which needs to be exceeded before an action must be categorised as unlawful. In this area difficult choices may have to be made by the executive or the legislature between the rights of the individual and the needs of society. In cases involving immigration policies and the rights to family life, it will be appropriate for the courts to recognise that there is an area of judgment within which the judiciary will defer, on democratic grounds, to the considered opinion of the elected body or person whose decision is said to be incompatible – see *Mahmood*, para 38.

Query whether in any event this element of the decision survives the House of Lords 're-writing' of *Mahmood* in *R (on the Application of Daly) v Secretary of State for the Home Department* [2001] UKHL 26; [2001] 2 WLR 1622, discussed below at 3.4.2.

47   *Ashdown v Telegraph Group Ltd* [2001] 2 All ER 370, High Court, para 14.

of judgment, ruling that it would be necessary to proceed on a case by case basis:

> [W]e have reached the conclusion that rare circumstances can arise where the right of freedom of expression will come into conflict with the protection afforded by the Copyright Act, notwithstanding the express exceptions to be found in the Act. In these circumstances, we consider that the court is bound, in so far as it is able, to apply the Act in a manner that accommodates the right of freedom of expression. This will make it necessary for the court to look closely at the facts of individual cases (as indeed it must whenever a fair dealing defence is raised). We do not foresee this leading to a flood of litigation.[48]

Part of the reason, however, that advocates are likely to continue to face an up-hill struggle in trying to persuade courts to distinguish between the international and domestic law doctrines is a fundamental underlying confusion as to the distinction between the margin of appreciation doctrine and the wider principle of proportionality. In the following section we consider the initial hurdle that public bodies will need to be able to show that they have crossed when interfering with a qualified right: the issue of legitimacy. In the section that follows we then consider the issue of how best to present arguments on the issue of whether any lawful interference is necessary in a democratic society.

Issues for advocates: the discretionary area of judgment

1   The House of Lords has made clear that there are areas where it remains appropriate for the courts to defer to decisions taken by bodies, which are answerable to the electorate.

2   Where a body is not directly answerable to an electorate, the duty of the court as a public authority to act in a way which protects an individual's human rights makes it inappropriate to accord a margin of discretion, although clearly courts will take account of the expertise of any body: cf *Ford v Press Complaints Commission.*

3   In deciding whether it is appropriate to permit the elected body a 'discretionary area of judgment', a number of factors have been suggested:

    • Is the right in issue qualified or absolute? Clearly an interference with an absolute right is unlikely to be permissible.

    • Is the area one which concerns social, economic or political policies? If so, it is more likely that the courts will accord the legislature a discretion. Housing policy is often cited as an area of social policy *par excellence.*

---

48   [2001] EWCA Civ 1142; (2001) *The Times*, 1 August.

- Is this an area where the courts can claim special expertise?
- Is the right claimed one of special importance? Thus one might contrast freedom of speech under Art 10 with the right to respect for property (Art 1, Protocol 1). However, all of the rights in the Convention are rights which have been guaranteed by the State, and a hierarchy of rights argument must be treated with some caution.

4   Is this an area where two or more sets of rights are in conflict? The court may be more ready to permit a discretion to the legislature where there are competing rights at stake. Thus it may be appropriate for the elected local authority to set local planning targets which will balance the right of the property developer to develop houses in multiple occupation as against the rights of the local community not to be subjected to over-crowding and inappropriate developments.

5   Inevitably the court will need to have regard to the extent of the interference. Where it is clear that the interference is disproportionate to the express purpose, we would suggest that it is less likely that the courts will accord the elected body a discretion. There is thus an inevitable overlap with issues of proportionality.

3.2   THE NEED FOR LEGITIMACY

The issue of the legitimacy of any interference has been discussed earlier in this book (see Chapter 1). However, it is worth recalling at this point the need for a structured approach to interference with a qualified right. It will be recalled that while the terminology varies slightly from article to article, there is, in relation to most of the qualified rights, a dual requirement for legitimacy of purpose and for lawfulness, in the sense of a matter being 'prescribed by law' (Arts 9–11) or 'in accordance with law' (Art 8) or 'in accordance with a procedure prescribed by law' and 'lawful' (Art 5).

Article 8(2) provides a good example of both elements of the legitimacy test. The provision begins by requiring that any interference is 'in accordance with the law' and then specifies the grounds on which the interference can arise:

> ... such [interference] as is necessary in a democratic society in the interests of national security, public safety or the economic well-being of the country, for the prevention of disorder or crime, for the protection of health or morals, or for the protection of the rights and freedoms of others.

Advocates must be clear about the need to adopt this structured approach to the analysis of any interference, whether they are seeking to attack or to justify the interference. Where an advocate seeking to justify the actions of a local authority employer in using covert CCTV surveillance of the workplace simply asserts that the means adopted are proportionate to the scale of the Internet misuse that has been taking place, there is a danger that the advocate will not be able to respond effectively if challenged as to the lawfulness of the interference (Where is the legal basis for this interference? Have the requirements of the statute or the common law been complied with?) or if challenged as to the basis of the interference (Is this for public safety, or for the prevention of crime, or to protect morals, or for the economic well-being of the country?).

In Chapter 1 we have looked in some detail at the requirement for interference to be prescribed by law, and at the need for any lawful interference to be aimed at a permitted concern, such as the protection of the rights and freedoms of others. Because proportionality appears to involve the simple balancing of competing interests (and in the section that follows, we indicate a wider range of issues that are comprised within proportionality) it is tempting for advocates to focus on this proportionality of an interference without first dealing with these matters. Human Rights Act advocacy requires a recognition of the need to address these legitimacy issues before turning to address proportionality – the issue of whether the public authority can satisfy the court that the interference is necessary in a democratic society.

3.3 NECESSARY IN A DEMOCRATIC SOCIETY: WHAT IS PROPORTIONALITY?

The test for deciding whether the interference is necessary in a democratic society is often approached as a threefold test (based on the decision in *Handyside*):

    (a) Are the reasons given to justify the interference relevant and sufficient?

    (b) Does the interference correspond to a pressing social need?

    (c) Is the interference proportionate to the aim pursued?

Sometimes all three elements are given the label of 'proportionality' and the individual elements are treated as aspects of the requirement for the interference to be proportionate. Proportionality can, however, be used in a narrower sense, focusing on the third element of the test. In either sense proportionality has, of course, traditionally been eschewed as a ground for judicial review in the domestic courts, but has been a necessary consideration in determining matters of EU law. Equally, the principle is a long-established element in Convention case law, and it is therefore clear that proportionality arguments are necessarily of relevance when dealing with Convention points in domestic courts under the Human Rights Act.

The subsidiary issues of whether proportionality is now becoming a ground for judicial review, and whether proportionality amounts to a merits-based review by the courts are dealt with separately below. First however this section considers the constituent elements of the proportionality test, and considers how best advocates can structure arguments that focus on proportionality issues.

3.3.1 Identifying the elements of a proportionality test

For one commentator proportionality is 'the test which is normally used to assess whether there is a violation of Convention rights'.[49] The difficulty is that the test which proportionality requires – that the restriction on the Convention right be 'proportionate to the aim pursued'[50] – will vary depending on its context.

Thus advocates who wish to argue that an interference with an Art 8 right is permissible will need to show that, in the terms of Art 8(2), the interference is in accordance with the law and is necessary in order in order to meet one of the prescribed interests – such as national security or public safety. The test under Art 10(2) is broadly similar. In these contexts, the Strasbourg Court has indicated that it is necessary to apply a three-fold test:

> It must now be decided whether the 'interference' complained of corresponded to a 'pressing social need', whether it was 'proportionate to the legitimate aim pursued', whether the reasons given by the national authorities to justify it are 'relevant and sufficient under Article 10(2) ...'[51]

Interference cannot be necessary unless it is also proportionate:

> [A] restriction on a Convention right cannot be regarded as 'necessary in a democratic society', two hallmarks of which are tolerance and broadmindedness, unless, amongst other things, it is proportionate to the legitimate aims pursued.[52]

By way of contrast, however, there will be no question of whether an interference is necessary in a democratic society where the state is seeking to justify interference with the right to liberty on the basis of one of the permissible grounds in Art 5(1). In the context of Art 5 it is clear that the grounds will be extremely narrowly construed, and less leeway will be available to states in the steps taken to comply with the procedural guarantees in Art 5(3) and 5(4). On the other hand, in the context of Art 1, Protocol 1 – which permits the state 'to enforce such laws as it deems necessary to control the use of property in accordance with the general interest' – the scope of any review of the public interest defence will be limited.

---

49 Clayton, 6.40.
50 *Handyside v United Kingdom* (1976) 1 EHRR 737.
51 *Sunday Times v United Kingdom* (1979) 2 EHRR 245, at para 62, drawing on the earlier *Handyside* decision.
52 *Dudgeon v United Kingdom* (1981) 4 EHRR 149.

Proportionality is a principle of Community law, and has therefore often arisen in connection with state interference with an economic activity. In *R v MAFF and Secretary of State for Health ex p FEDESA*[53] the European Court of Justice stated:

> The court has consistently held that the principle of proportionality is one of the general principles of community law. By virtue of that principle, the lawfulness of the prohibition of an economic activity is subject to the condition that the prohibition measures are appropriate and necessary in order to achieve the objectives legitimately pursued by the legislation in question; when there is a choice between several appropriate measures, recourse must be had to the least onerous, and the disadvantages caused must not be disproportionate to the aims pursued.[54]

A similar formulation was applied by the Privy Council in *de Freitas v Ministry of Agriculture*,[55] an Antiguan case, where Lord Slynn considered both Canadian and Zimbabwean authorities and adopted the analysis of Gubbay CJ:[56]

> [H]e saw the quality of reasonableness in the expression 'reasonably justifiable in a democratic society' as depending upon the question whether the provision which is under challenge 'arbitrarily or excessively invades the enjoyment of a the guaranteed right according to the standards of a society that has a proper respect for the rights and freedoms of the individual'. In determining whether a limitation is arbitrary or excessive he said that the court would ask itself:
>
>> whether: (i) the legislative objective is sufficiently important to justify limiting a fundamental right; (ii) the measures designed to meet the legislative objective are rationally connected to it; and (iii) the means used to impair the right or freedom are no more than is necessary to accomplish the objective.
>
> Their Lordships accept and adopt this three-fold analysis of the relevant criteria.

In *R v Secretary of State for the Home Department (ex p Daly)*[57] the House of Lords reviewed the practice of the examination of legal correspondence by prison staff in the absence of the prisoner during the conduct of searches of living accommodation. Lord Bingham considered the matter both in terms of the infringement of the common law right to legal professional privilege and the Art 8(1) right to respect for correspondence. In this case 'the common law and the convention yield the same result'.[58] The analysis indicates how clearly an argument must be structured:

---

53 [1990] CER 1–4023.

54 *Ibid*, para 13, 1–4063.

55 [1999] 1 AC 69.

56 In *Nyambirai v National Social Security Authority* [1996] 1 LRC 64.

57 [2001] UKHL 26; [2001] 2 WLR 1622.

58 *Ibid*, para 23.

1   Was there an interference with a right? Yes: legal professional privilege attached to the correspondence and '[I]n an imperfect world there will necessarily be occasions when prison officers will do more than merely examine prisoners' legal documents, and apprehension that they may do so is bound to inhibit a prisoner's willingness to communicate freely with his legal adviser'.[59]

2   Was there any ground for interfering with the right? Yes: '[S]ome examination may well be necessary to establish that privileged legal correspondence is what it appears to be and is not a hiding place for illicit materials or information prejudicial to security or good order.'[60]

3   Can the policy therefore be justified as a 'necessary and proper response'? Here each of the reasons put forward by the Secretary of State (namely, the risk of intimidation of officer; the risk that staff may be conditioned by prisoners to relax security; and the need to preserve the secrecy of search methods) was examined in turn. Lord Bingham noted that the policy was a blanket one in a number of respects: it applied to all prisoners, regardless of whether they had been shown to be intimidatory or disruptive; it applied to all searches, regardless of the circumstances (and thus whether conditioning by prisoners was likely); it applied regardless of whether there was some sophisticated search technique that it was undesirable for prisoners to learn of. Lord Bingham's conclusion, still dealing with the matter in terms of the common law, was that:

> The policy cannot be justified in its current blanket form. The infringement of prisoners' rights to maintain the confidentiality of their privileged legal correspondence is greater than is shown to be necessary to serve the legitimate public objectives already identified.[61]

This conclusion was supported by evidence that other less intrusive means were available to the Prison Service: the correspondence could be sealed and then searched in the prisoner's presence after the main search had been conducted, a policy that had already been adopted in one prison; in Scotland searches were conducted in the prisoner's presence, without any issue arising; and only two items had ever been found in legal correspondence, suggesting that '[i]t does not appear that legal files or bundles have been regarded by prisoners as a highly favoured hiding place for materials they are not permitted to hold'.[62]

The blanket approach of the Government, along with the ability of the applicant to show that other, less intrusive steps were available, clearly undermines the argument that the interference is proportionate. Lord Bingham makes clear that the same result arises under Convention law principles:

---

59   *Ibid*, para 16.
60   *Ibid*, para 17.
61   *Ibid*, para 19.
62   *Ibid*, para 20.

I have reached the conclusions so far expressed on an orthodox application of common law principles derived from the authorities and an orthodox domestic approach to judicial review. But the same result is achieved by reliance on the European Convention. Article 8(1) gives Mr Daly a right to respect for his correspondence. While interference with that right by a public authority may be permitted if in accordance with the law and necessary in a democratic society in the interests of national security, public safety, the prevention of disorder or crime or for protection of the rights and freedoms of others, the policy interferes with Mr Daly's exercise of his right under Article 8(1) to an extent much greater than necessity requires. In this instance, therefore, the common law and the convention yield the same result.[63]

The starting point in formulating any argument based upon the proportionality – or disproportionality – of any interference must be to look at the status of the Convention right and its significance in the scale of rights. Having done this, however, it will still be necessary in the majority of cases to identify those factors, which need to be considered by the court in deciding whether the interference was proportionate.

3.3.1.1 Who has the burden of proof in proportionality arguments

Once the court is satisfied that an interference with a Convention right has taken place, it will be for the public body to prove that the interference is in accordance with the Convention. Where the public body cannot show this, the action will be unlawful (s 6(1) of the HRA) unless it falls within the limited defence offered by s 6(2). This principle applies to each element of the interference – whether it was prescribed by law, whether the aim it addresses is a permitted aim, and whether it is necessary in a democratic society.

3.3.1.2 What is the relationship between margin of appreciation arguments and proportionality?

The difficulty with the margin of appreciation is that it seems to be applied at different stages in the process in different cases. Clayton and Tomlinson suggest that the reason for this is that the doctrine of margin of appreciation is used to cover two different situations:

- an interpretative obligation to respect domestic cultural traditions and values when considering the meaning and scope of human rights;

- a standard of judicial review to be used when enforcing human rights protection.[64]

Such a division has the advantage of clarity, but unfortunately it can be hard to find such a tidy divide in both the Strasbourg and domestic jurisprudence.

---

63   *Ibid*, para 23. For further application of *Daly*, and criticism of a blanket policy approach as disproportionate, see *Baker v Secretary of State for the Home Department*.

64   Clayton, 6.32.

Since it is clear that the doctrine cannot be seen as 'an unlimited power of appreciation',[65] if any court proposes to exercise a power of review, it must give attention to the rationale for any interference, its extent and its appropriateness in meeting the specified concern: in short, proportionality. An overlap between the concepts seems to arise.

Thus in *Ahmed v United Kingdom*,[66] a case concerning the prohibition on political activity by certain categories of local government officers, the margin of appreciation is applied at a number of different states in the consideration of whether that restriction is 'necessary in a democratic society': it is applied in relation to the issue of whether the restriction corresponded to a pressing social need; it is applied in relation to the 'duties and responsibilities' element of Art 10(2) (because of the status of the applicants as public officials); and it is applied to the proportionality of the interference. No clear distinction is drawn between the margin of appreciation as 'interpretative obligation' and standard of review:

> The court's task is to ascertain in view of the above-mentioned principles ... whether the restrictions imposed on the applicants corresponded to a 'pressing social need' and whether they were 'proportionate' to the aim of protecting the rights of others to effective political democracy at the local level ... In so doing it must also have regard to the fact that whenever the right to freedom of expression of public servants such as the applicants is in issue the 'duties and responsibilities' referred to in Article 10 s 2 assume a special significance, which justifies leaving to the authorities of the respondent State a certain margin of appreciation in determining whether the impugned interference is proportionate to the aim as stated ...[67]

A similar confusion can arise in the domestic context. In *R (on the Application of Johns) v Bracknell Forest DC*[68] the applicants were challenging the introductory tenancy regime adopted by the local authority. The court took the view that Art 8 – the right to respect for the home – was engaged, since what was at stake was the review process by which introductory tenants could be dispossessed of their homes. There was a clear interference with the right, and that interference was permitted by law. The issue was therefore whether the interference was necessary in a democratic society, and here the court makes clear the overlap between issues of discretionary judgment and proportionality:

> Necessary in a democratic society does not mean indispensable; nor does it mean desirable. Convention jurisprudence has decided that it means:
>
> (a) that the reasons given to justify the interference must be relevant and sufficient;
>
> (b) that the interference must correspond to a pressing social need; and

---

65 *Handyside* (1976) 1 EHRR 737.
66 (2000) 29 EHRR 1.
67 *Ibid*, para 61.
68 (2001) 33 HLR 45.

(c) that the interference must be proportionate to the aim pursued: see *Handyside v United Kingdom* ...

[The reasons for the adoption of the introductory tenancy regime are then set out.]

To my mind, these considerations show that the interference with the respect for one's home, to which everyone is entitled, is indeed relevant, sufficient and corresponds to a pressing social need. This means that neither the enactment of the scheme for introductory tenancies for optional adoption by local housing authorities, nor the actual adoption of such a scheme by this Council is incompatible with the Convention.

41   In this connection it is important to note that the European Court has itself recognised that housing policy is an area where a national legislature must be accorded a wide margin of appreciation. In the context of Article 1 of Protocol No 1, the court has said in *Mellacher v Austria* (1989) 12 EHRR 391 that laws controlling the use of property are especially called for and usual in the field of housing 'which in our modern society is a central concern of social and economic policies'. The court went on to say that the national legislature must have a wide margin of appreciation both with regard to the existence of a problem of public concern warranting measures of control and as to the choice of the detailed rules for the implementation of such measures: see paragraph 45 of that judgment.[69]

It will be noted that the court has regard to the margin of appreciation doctrine without considering whether it can properly be said to apply in a domestic context. It would appear, however, that the approach can be recast in terms of the 'discretionary area of judgment' principle. This approach was taken by the Lord Chief Justice in another housing case, *Poplar Housing and Regeneration Community Association Ltd v Donoghue*,[70] where the 'margin of appreciation' was couched as a principle of deferment to Parliament. In *Poplar Housing* the Court of Appeal considered whether the restricted discretion of the court under s 21(4) of the Housing Act 1988 offended against the right to respect for the home under Art 8 or of the right to a fair hearing under Art 6. Here the discretionary area of judgment is accorded to the legislature in determining how best to ensure the health of the rented sector:

We are satisfied, that notwithstanding its mandatory terms, s 21(4) of the 1988 Act does not conflict with the defendant's right to family life. Section 21(4) is certainly necessary in a democratic society in so far as there must be a procedure for recovering possession of property at the end of a tenancy. The question is whether the restricted power of the court is legitimate and proportionate. This is the area of policy where the court should defer to the decision of Parliament. We have come to the conclusion that there was no contravention of Article 8 or of Article 6.[71]

---

69   (2001) 33 HLR 45, *per* Longmore J, paras 39–41. Decision was upheld by the Court of Appeal, *sub nom McLellan v Bracknell Forest BC*, Lawtel 16/10/2001.

70   [2001] EWCA Civ 595; [2001] 3 WLR 183.

71   [2001] EWCA Civ 595; [2001] 3 WLR 183, para 72.

The difficulty for advocates that arises from the general lack of precision in the application of both the international and domestic principles is that it is not clear whether the discretion should be seen as an overarching principle which lessens the intensity of the review by the court, or amounts to a self-denying ordinance that the court will not substitute its own opinion as to the desirability of the s 21 provision; nor is it clear whether the principle is applied to the issue of 'necessity in a democratic society' in its larger sense, or the specific issue of proportionality. Perhaps the most realistic view for advocates is that if the court takes the view that the 'discretionary area of judgment' is engaged, it will then be harder to persuade the court to substitute its own view as to the existence of the pressing social need, with the inevitable consequence that the specific issue of the proportionality of the state's interference will need to be considered on the basis of that the state's original concerns were justified.

3.3.2 Proportionality under the Human Rights Act: identifying relevant factors

There are a number of questions, which need to be asked in assessing the proportionality of any interference:

- What is the extent of the restriction?
- Is there a less restrictive means of achieving the result?
- Where has the balance been drawn between the impact upon the individual and the aim to be achieved?
- Are there sufficient reasons provided for the restriction?[72]

If these questions are asked in a structured way, Sedley LJ suggests, in his judgment in *London Regional Transport v Mayor of London*,[72a] proportionality can be a 'methodical concept'. Proportionality, he suggests, can offer the courts – and therefore advocates – a clearer and more precise analytical tool than the traditional approaches of the common law:

> 57 ... it replaces an elastic concept with which political scientists are more at home than lawyers with a structured inquiry: Does the measure meet a recognised and pressing social need? Does it negate the primary right or restrict it more than is necessary? Are the reasons given for it logical? ...

> 58 It seems to me, with great respect, that this now well established approach furnishes a more certain guide for people and their lawyers than the test of the reasonable recipient's conscience [in the common law duty of

---

72 For a slightly different formulation, see Jowell, *Beyond the Rule of Law: Towards Constitutional Judicial Review* [2000] Public Law 671, at 679, where Professor Jowell proposes the following four stages: (i) Did the action pursue a legitimate aim?; (ii) Were the means employed suitable to achieve that end?; (iii) Could the aim have been achieved by a less restrictive alternative?; (iv) Is the derogation justified overall in the interests of a democratic society?

72a [2001] EWCA Civ 1491, Lawtel 17/10/2001.

confidentiality]. While the latter has the imprimatur of high authority, I can understand how difficult it is to give useful advice on the basis of it. One recipient may lose sleep a lot more readily than another over whether to make a disclosure, without either of them having to be considered unreasonable. If the test is whether the recipient ought to be losing sleep, the imaginary individual will be for practical purposes a judicial stalking-horse and the judgment more nearly an exercise of discretion and correspondingly less predictable. So for my part I find it more helpful today to postulate a recipient who, being reasonable, runs through the proportionality checklist in order to anticipate what a court is likely to decide, and who adjusts his or her conscience and conduct accordingly.

3.3.2.1 The extent of any restriction

Where an interference goes to the heart of the right which is in issue it will clearly be difficult to show either that the interference is in general terms 'necessary in a democratic society' or, in the narrower sense, that the interference is proportionate to the objective which is sought. Thus, in *Rees v United Kingdom*[73] while Art 12 permitted Contracting States to govern the right to marry by laws '[t]he limitations thereby introduced must not restrict or reduce the right in such a way or to such an extent that the very essence of the right is impaired'. In *Rees*, however, it was held that national laws in relation to transsexuals and marriage did not offend against this principle. By contrast in *F v Switzerland*,[74] where F was the subject of a three year ban of re-marriage following his third divorce, the Strasbourg Court held that while the state's aim in ensuring the stability of the institution of marriage was a legitimate aim, the means employed by the state were disproportionate and went to the essence of the right. It is notable that the Court came to this conclusion notwithstanding its recognition of the particular cultural concerns which may give rise to the domestic law, and hence presumably a significant margin of appreciation to be accorded to the state:

> The Court notes that a waiting period no longer exists under the laws of other Contracting States, the Federal Republic of Germany having abolished it in 1976, and Austria in 1983. In this connection, it recalls its case law according to which the Convention must be interpreted in the light of present-day conditions ... However, the fact that, at the end of a gradual evolution, a country finds itself in an isolated position as regards one aspect of its legislation does not necessarily imply that that aspect offends the Convention, particularly in a field – matrimony – which is so closely bound up with the cultural and historical traditions of each society and its deep-rooted ideas about the family unit.[75]

---

73 (1987) 9 EHRR 56.
74 (1998) 10 EHRR 411.
75 *Ibid*, para 33.

In *Ahmed v United Kingdom*[76] a subsidiary point concerned the right to free and fair elections under Art 3, Protocol 1 – a right which was held to imply 'subjective rights' to vote and to stand for election. However the European Court of Human Rights concluded that the bar did not go to the essence of the Art 3 right:

> As important as those rights are, they are not, however, absolute. Since Article 3 recognises them without setting them forth in express terms, let alone defining them, there is room for implied limitations. In their internal legal orders the Contracting States make the rights to vote and to stand for election subject to conditions, which are not in principle precluded under Article 3. The Court considers that the restrictions imposed on the applicants' right to contest seats at elections must be seen in the context of the aim pursued by the legislature in enacting the Regulations, namely, to secure their political impartiality. That aim must be considered legitimate for the purposes of restricting the exercise of the applicants' subjective right to stand for election under Article 3 of Protocol No 1; nor can it be maintained that the restrictions limit the very essence of their rights under that provision having regard to the fact that they only operate for as long as the applicants occupy politically restricted posts; furthermore, any of the applicants wishing to run for elected office is at liberty to resign from his post.[77]

'The very essence' of a fair trial?

Interference with Art 6 rights in a criminal context is discussed in some detail in Chapter 8. However, it is worth noting at this point the tension between domestic and Strasbourg approaches to issues such as the admissibility of evidence obtained as a result of compelled questioning. In *Brown v Stott*[78] compelled questioning was essentially seen as a proportionate interference with the presumption of innocence, which left undisturbed the fundamental right to a fair trial. The justification for this stance was expressed in terms of the relatively low level of punishment for the road traffic offence at issue, and hence the quasi-regulatory natures of the offence, along with the particular need to combat drink driving.

By way of contrast, in *Heaney v Ireland*[79] the punishment of the applicant for failure to respond to compelled questions was held to be a breach of his Art 6 rights, notwithstanding that he had been in any event acquitted of the substantive terrorist offence. The Strasbourg Court treated the compelled questioning as going to the very essence of the presumption of innocence.

Notwithstanding the current domestic case law, it there seems that the issue of proportionality in the context of Art 6 is highly contentious and that

---

76 (2000) 29 EHRR 1.
77 *Ibid*, para 75.
78 *Brown v Stott* [2001] 2 WLR 817 (PC).
79 [2001] Crim LR 481.

interference with the component elements of Art 6 may be seen the European Court of Human Rights as going to the very essence of the fair trial guarantees.

3.3.2.2 Is there a less intrusive means of achieving the same result?

Clayton and Tomlinson suggest that the principle of the 'least restrictive means' will often be applied in practice by the European Court of Human Rights:

> Convention case law does not explicitly recognise the 'least restrictive means' test as an aspect of proportionality (although this is a well recognised part of the doctrine in, for example, European Community and Canadian law). Nevertheless, the court has often in practice decided the question of proportionality by asking whether a particular measure could be achieved by a less restrictive means.[80]

Where arguments are to be presented to the court on the issue of proportionality, it is inevitable that the court will be influenced where an advocate can show that less intrusive measures are available to achieve the intended result. It will be recalled that Lord Bingham's conclusion in *Daly* that the interference with legal professional privilege was disproportionate was couched in terms of the blanket nature of the policy, but was supported by evidence that less intrusive methods might meet the objectives of the Government.[81]

Where the public body can show that it has taken steps to minimise interference, especially if it can show that it has avoided the imposition of a blanket policy, it will clearly be easier to satisfy the court that the interference is proportionate. In the *Ahmed* case, the Strasbourg Court considered whether less intrusive means could have been employed in order to meet the concerns of the Widdicombe Committee that the political neutrality of senior officers needed to be strengthened:

> As to whether the aim of the legislature in enacting the Regulations was pursued with minimum impairment of the applicants' rights under Article 10 the court notes that the measures were directed at the need to preserve the impartiality of carefully defined categories of officers whose duties involve the provision of advice to a local authority council or to its operational committees or who represent the council in dealings with the media. In the Court's view, the parent legislation has attempted to define the officers affected by the

---

80 Clayton, para 6.47.

81 For a discussion of proportionality in the criminal context, see Chapter 8 and the case of *R v Lambert* [2001] UKHL 37; [2001] All ER(D) 69 (Jul), where the majority of the House of Lords took the view that the legitimate concern of the legislature in dealing with misuse of drugs could be achieved by limiting any inroad into the presumption of innocence to the placing of an evidential burden on the defence rather than a probative burden, and reading down s 28 of the Misuse of Drugs Act under s 3 of the HRA accordingly.

restrictions in as focused a manner as possible and to allow through the exemption procedure optimum opportunity for an officer in either the second or third categories to seek exemption from the restrictions which, by the nature of the duties performed, are presumed to attach to the post-holder ... It is to be observed also that the functions-based approach retained in the Regulations resulted in fewer officers being subject to restrictions than would have been the case had the measures been modelled on the Widdicombe Committee's proposal to apply them to principal officers and above as a general class and irrespective of the duties performed (see paragraph 10 above).[82]

The fact that the public authority has sought to avoid a blanket policy will clearly be persuasive. In a domestic law context under the Human Rights Act a challenge to the random tapping of telephone calls from patients at Ashworth Special Hospital was held not to contravene Art 8. The Divisional Court took account of the distinction drawn between 'high risk' patients and other patients in determining the level of monitoring – and in particular the fact that non-high risk patients had no more than 10% of calls monitored:

> The treatment also reflects the different assessment. No risk that the purpose of a telephone call will be abused is accepted for the former [high risk group], but the risk that the latter [non-high risk group] could abuse up to ninety per cent of their calls has been assessed as acceptable and capable of being met by random monitoring. Manifestly the consequent reduction in actual interference is significant. It can also be said that the measure exemplifies the concept of tailoring the measure to the aim to be achieved. It achieves its aim of meeting the assessed security risk by limited actual interference.[83]

By way of contrast in *R (on the Application of P) v Secretary of State for the Home Department*[84] the Court of Appeal (overturning the decision of the Administrative Court) held that a rigid policy in respect of the provision of facilities for mothers with young babies in prison could not be sustained:

> 100 The only question we have to decide is whether the Prison Service is entitled to operate its policy in a rigid fashion, insisting that all children leave by the age of 18 months at the latest (give or take a few weeks if their mother is about to be released), however catastrophic the separation may be in the case of a particular mother and child, however unsatisfactory the alternative placement available for the child, and however attractive the alternative solution of combining day care outside prison with remaining in prison with the mother.

> 101 In our view the policy must admit of greater flexibility than that. We say so for two inter-related reasons. The first is that the policy's own declared aim, both in general and in individual cases is to promote the welfare of the child ... We accept that this aim has to be set in the context of what prison and the Prison Service is all about. It cannot therefore ... be the only aim. But if the effect of the policy upon an individual child's welfare will

82 *Ahmed v United Kingdom* (2000) 29 EHRR 1, para 63.
83 *R (on the Application of N) v Ashworth Special Hospital Authority and Secretary of State for Health* [2001] EWHC Admin 339; (2001) *The Times*, 26 June, para 15, *per* Newman J.
84 [2001] EWCA Civ 1151; (2001) *The Times*, 1 August.

be catastrophic, the policy is not fulfilling its own objectives. The policy documents themselves contemplate the need for individual consideration.

102 The second reason is that the interference with the child's family life, which the Prison Service has allowed and encouraged to develop, must be justified under Article 8(2).[85]

The court considered how the principle of proportionality should apply. The policy had to balance competing aims including the necessary limitations on the mother's rights and freedoms intrinsic in a custodial sentence, along with any problems that might arise for the Prison Service from a relaxation in policy, but also taking into account the welfare of the *individual* child. The policy did not necessarily offend against the Convention rights (indeed one of the applications was refused, and one upheld); what offended was its blanket nature.

3.3.2.3 Where has the balance been drawn between the impact upon the individual and the aim to be achieved?

Although linked to the issue of whether the public body has minimised the interference with the individual rights, the issue of whether an appropriate balance has been drawn between the impact upon the individual and the aim to be achieved is an additional concern, and lies at the heart of the concept of proportionality. In this context advocates are likely to find that it may be necessary to look at the overall social context of the restriction in broad terms, as well as looking at the related issues of the extent of the interference, and the significance of the right at stake.

In *Lehideux and Isorni v France*[86] the context was Art 10, which as has been noted is an area where the courts are likely to treat the protection of the right as being of particular importance. At the same time, however, the freedom of speech related to the publication of material in support of the collaborationist regime of Marshal Petain. The applicants had been convicted of the criminal offence of publicly defending the crimes of collaboration in respect of a newspaper advertisement defending the actions of Marshal Petain during the Second World War. The European Court of Human Rights considered the proportionality of the interference with the applicants' rights of freedom of expression and concluded that the criminal penalty had been disproportionate, notwithstanding that:

> There is no doubt that, like any other remark directed against the Convention's underlying values ... the justification of a pro-Nazi policy could not be allowed to enjoy the protection afforded by Article 10.

---

85 *Ibid*, paras 100–02.
86 (2000) 30 EHRR 665, at para 53.

Factors that the court took into account included on the one hand the failure of the authors to indicate that Petain had knowingly contributed to the 'Nazi barbarism' to which the authors did refer – 'The gravity of these facts, which constitute crimes against humanity, increases the gravity of any attempt to draw a veil over them,'[87] – but on the other hand the fact that it had been the investigating judge who had proceeded with the case when the prosecution ('whose role it is to represent all the sensibilities which make up the general interest and to assess the rights of others'[88]) had decided not to proceed. Additionally the events were now over 40 years in the past so that they fell within 'part of the efforts that every country must make to debate its own history openly and dispassionately'.[89] The Court reiterated its long-standing principle that Art 10 is applicable:

> not only to information or ideas that are favourably received or regarded as inoffensive or as a matter of indifference, but also to those that offend, shock or disturb; such are the demands of that pluralism, tolerance and broadmindedness without which there is no democratic society ...[90]

The Court took into account that the publication was directly corresponding to the aims of the two associations which had produced it, and that those associations were legally constituted and had not themselves been prosecuted for pursuing their objectives. Finally, the fact that the proceedings were criminal had to be considered in the light of other potential and less serious means of 'intervention and rebuttal'. On balance the criminal conviction was therefore disproportionate.

Equally, in the *Dudgeon* case the Court had regard to the balance between the need to recognise the strong public opinion in Northern Ireland against the decriminalisation of homosexual acts and the rights of Mr Dudgeon under Art 8:

> On the issue of proportionality, the Court considers that such justifications as there are for retaining the law in force unamended are outweighed by the detrimental effects, which the very existence of the legislative provisions in question can have on the life of a person of homosexual orientation like the applicant. Although members of the public who regard homosexuality as immoral may be shocked, offended or disturbed by the commission by others of private homosexual acts, this cannot on its own warrant the application of penal sanctions when it is consenting adults alone who are involved.

> Accordingly, the reasons given by the government, although relevant, are not sufficient to justify the maintenance in force of the impugned legislation in so far as it has the general effect of criminalising private homosexual relations between adult males capable of valid consent. In particular, the moral attitudes towards male homosexuality in Northern Ireland and the concern that any relaxation in the law would tend to erode existing moral standards cannot,

---

87 *Ibid*, para 54.
88 *Ibid*, para 55.
89 (2000) 30 EHRR 665.
90 *Ibid*.

without more, warrant interfering with the applicant's private life to such an extent. 'Decriminalisation' does not imply approval, and a fear that some sectors of the population might draw misguided conclusions in this respect from reform of the legislation does not afford a good ground for maintaining it in force with all its unjustifiable features.

To sum up, the restriction imposed on Mr Dudgeon under Northern Ireland law, by reason of its breadth and absolute character, is, quite apart from the severity of the possible penalties provided for, disproportionate to the aims sought to be achieved.[91]

Balancing the rights of others

In all of the cases cited in this section – *Ahmed, Lehideux* and *Dudgeon* – the balance is to be drawn between the rights of the individual and the more general interests of the state. It will often be the case in the Human Rights Act context, where actions may arise between individuals (because of limited horizontal effect) or where the public body is acting to protect the rights of another individual, that the balancing act required by proportionality becomes less abstract and more focused on the interference that will be caused to each individual. In domestic law, the Court of Appeal took the view that notwithstanding commercial confidentiality issues, there was an overriding public interest in the disclosure of a redacted, but highly critical, report criticising Government proposals for the financing of the London Underground. Proportionaltiy dictated that disclosure should be made: *London Regional Transport v Mayor of London.*

In *Lambeth v Howard*[92] the Court of Appeal considered the proportionality of an immediate possession order, which had been imposed upon Howard, who had been convicted under the Protection from Harassment Act in respect of a long-running but intermittent campaign of harassment against his next-door neighbour, Miss Gabriel. During the criminal proceedings Howard had complied with his bail and had not harassed Miss Gabriel. Following his conviction, when he had been subject to a restraining order, which prevented him from returning to the neighbourhood, he had complied with that order. He argued that the imposition of an immediate possession order for the property was disproportionate; the judge should have imposed a suspended order.

Lord Justice Sedley made clear that the issue of whether the making of the possession order was reasonable meant that proportionality was in issue:

The real question is the one the judge goes on to address: is the interference justified? ... [B]y virtue of section 3 of the Act as a matter of statutory construction, whoever the lessor may be ... the meaning given to the word 'reasonable' in a statute such as the Housing Act 1985 must now, so far as

---

91 *Dudgeon v United Kingdom* (1981) 4 EHRR 149, at paras 60–61.
92 *Mayor and Burgesses of the London Borough of Lambeth v Howard* [2001] EWCA Civ 468.

possible, be Convention-compliant. As this court has said more than once, there is nothing in Article 8, or in the associated jurisprudence of the European Court of Human Rights, which should carry county courts to materially different outcomes from those that they have been arriving at for many years when deciding whether it is reasonable to make an outright or a suspended or no possession order. Nevertheless, as the judge in the present case has demonstrated in the final passage of his judgment, it can do no harm, and may often do a great deal of good, if the exercise is approached for what it is, an application of the principle of proportionality.[93]

The court then identifies the threshold requirement – is the interference necessary in a democratic society?:

Here, the question is whether eviction of the appellant, without suspension, is not only in accordance with the law (plainly it is), but is necessary in a democratic society to prevent disorder or crime or to protect the rights and freedoms of others. On Judge Medawar's clear and compelling findings, not only has the appellant been guilty of the crime of harassment, but Miss Gabriel and her daughter have been denied by him one of the most important freedoms and one of the most important rights in modern urban society, albeit that neither is spelt out in the Convention, freedom from fear and the right to live in peace.[94]

As part of the proportionality test, it is necessary to consider whether a less restrictive interference would have met the concerns. Is an outright possession order proportionate, or could the matter have been more appropriately dealt with by suspending the order? The court commends the structured approach adopted in R (on the Application of Johns) v Bracknell Forest DC[95] and then analyses the facts of the case to identify whether the evidence is sufficient to justify the fundamental interference with Art 8, the immediate deprivation of the appellant's home:

What Miss Gabriel had said in evidence included her evidence-in-chief, contained in a witness statement, which is before this court. In a series of paragraphs she describes (and it is manifest from what I have quoted that the judge accepted in broad terms what she said) the way in which the mere presence of Mr Howard terrified her daughter; indeed, how the mention of him would do so. She says of her daughter that 'her school work has suffered and friendships have suffered because other parents don't like their child visiting a flat where I am powerless to protect them, if need be'. She went on to say that the child finds difficulty in discussing the problem, although her fear is visible, and that she and the child are both continuously anxious about what could happen if Mr Howard were to return as a neighbour. She describes earlier in the witness statement the previous events as 'a living nightmare that both myself and my daughter went through'.

---

93 *Ibid*, para 31.
94 *Mayor and Burgesses of the London Borough of Lambeth v Howard* [2001] EWCA Civ 468, para 32.
95 (2001) 33 HLR 45.

The picture (there is far more of it than I have summarised) is one of real significance to what the judge had to decide and is at least a counterweight (in my judgment more than a counterweight) to the matter relied on by Mr Watkinson of the relatively good conduct in the year in which the appellant was on bail. It illustrates the hard fact that the harassment of neighbours, especially although not only those with children, may reach a point where what has been done cannot be undone. So here it may be that the appellant in 1997 to 1998 had demonstrated a capacity to behave himself more or less properly when the stakes were high enough for him. It may even be that he would probably continue to do so if allowed to return to his flat. But although, as the judgment points out, the harassment in past years had been intermittent and not continuous, what the appellant cannot do – and it is entirely his own fault that he cannot – is dispel the fear and the tension which his return, on the judge's findings, will bring to Miss Gabriel. She holds down a job and is often out at work, and her daughter, now 13 years old, needs all the concentration that she can get on her schooling and all the protection that she can get from fear and stress.

If from these facts one turns to the Convention questions, just as if one asks whether an outright possession order is reasonable rather than a suspended one, there is only one answer. It is the one that the judge reached: an outright possession order against the appellant was necessary to protect Miss Gabriel and her daughter from the continuing consequences of the appellant's obsessive harassment of them in the past. It would be necessary even if he were to return next door and commit no acts of harassment in the future. The shadow of the past is too heavy upon the present. Such an order is within the law. It meets a pressing social need. It is proportionate to that need in the straightforward sense that nothing less will do and that it is an acceptable means of achieving a legitimate aim. The judge so held below, and I agree with him.[96]

It is clear that where an advocate is able to point to the effect of the interference on a clearly identifiable individual, whose Convention rights are thereby themselves being contravened, it will be far easier to show that some form of interference was justified. However, the mere fact that interference is necessary in order to protect the rights and freedoms of others will not of itself ensure that that interference is proportionate. The advocate will still need to be prepared to identify for the court the elements of the interference on the other individual and to show why the judgment that is sought provides an appropriate balance between two sets of competing rights. As Lord Justice Sedley makes clear in *Howard*, the outcome of the hearing may not differ from pre-Human Rights Act hearings, but where an advocate is unprepared to present the material to the court in a way that clearly identifies the factors that the court is required to consider in determining the proportionality of any interference, there will be a risk that these factors may be overlooked and an adverse decision made.

---

96 *Mayor and Burgesses of the London Borough of Lambeth v Howard* [2001] EWCA Civ 468, paras 37–39.

3.3.2.4 Are there sufficient reasons provided for the restriction?

It will be noted that one of the factors to which the Strasbourg Court had regard in assessing the balance between the rights of the individual and the rights of society in the *Dudgeon* case was whether the reasons given were adequate to justify the continuation of the criminalisation of homosexual activity. Where an advocate is required to justify an interference it will generally be necessary to identify why it is necessary in a democratic society. Even in the context of Art 1, Protocol 1, where the state is given a wide discretion in enforcing 'such laws as it deems necessary to control the use of property in accordance with the general interest', it will be necessary to identify what general interest is engaged, and how the interference is proportionate with that interest.

Thus, in the context of Art 1, Protocol 1, Air Canada argued that the failure of the Customs and Excise Commissioners to give reasons for exercising what the Strasbourg Court was to call a strikingly wide power of forfeiture over an aircraft undermined the United Kingdom's case that the forfeiture was a response to a history of complaints about lax security prior to the discovery of drugs which had triggered the forfeiture.[97] The Strasbourg Court accepted that Air Canada could have easily obtained such reasons by commencing a judicial review of the forfeiture, and in any event took the view that the airline was on notice. In other cases, however, it may be harder for public bodies to argue that an interference was justified where reasons have not been made known to the subject at the time.

The burden is clearly on the state to justify any interference, with the effect that where a public authority under the Human Rights Act admits that an interference has occurred it will be for the public authority to show that the interference is permitted and proportionate. In *Vogt v Germany*[98] the applicant was a long-standing member of the DKP (*Deutsche Kommunistische Partei*) and was eventually dismissed from her employment as a teacher (and thus a civil servant) for breaching the duty of 'political loyalty' imposed on all civil servants – that is 'the duty to dissociate themselves unequivocally from groups that attack and cast aspersions on the state and the existing constitutional system'.[99] The duty is a blanket one, and applies to all civil servants of all ranks and in all circumstances, whether public or private. Notwithstanding this blanket policy the Court indicated that it understood that the particular circumstances of Germany history gave rise to a concern that the state should be 'a democracy capable of defending itself'. However, the Court then analysed the impact of this policy upon Mrs Vogt:

- her dismissal was a very severe measure because of its impact upon her reputation, and because she was unlikely to be able to obtain another

---

97   *Air Canada v United Kingdom* (1995) 20 EHRR 150.
98   (1995) 21 EHRR 205.
99   *Ibid*, para 58.

> teaching job since posts outside the civil service were rare; it further noted that this was a job for which she had trained and in which she had skills and experience;

- as a language teacher, Mrs Vogt did not hold a sensitive post with security implications;

- no criticism had ever been levelled at her teaching, and in particular there had never been any suggestion that she had in any way sought to indoctrinate pupils;

- there was no suggestion that even outside the workplace Mrs Vogt had ever made anti-constitutional statements; and

- the DKP itself was a legitimate party and had not been banned by the Federal Constitutional Court.

The Court therefore concluded that there had been a breach of Art 10, notwithstanding that the reasons put forward by the state in justification of the interference were accepted as being relevant:

> [A]lthough the reasons put forward by the Government in order to justify their interference with Mrs Vogt's right to freedom of expression are certainly relevant, they are not sufficient to establish convincingly that it was necessary in a democratic society to dismiss her. Even allowing for a certain margin of appreciation, the conclusion must be that to dismiss Mrs Vogt by way of disciplinary sanction from her post as secondary-school teacher was disproportionate to the legitimate aim pursued.[100]

However, there have been some cases at the Strasbourg level where the international court appears to have accepted over-readily the reasons put forward by states in justification of interferences with rights. Thus in the *Ahmed* case the restrictions on political activity were successfully justified by reference to the findings of the Widdicombe Committee, which had looked into the concern that local government officials were becoming politicised. The court appeared to accept this at face value. A more critical assessment can be found in one of the dissenting judgments:

> According to the Widdicombe Committee there was a need for regulation. The Committee referred to a tradition of a corps of politically neutral officers and to an increased risk of senior officers' abusing their positions for political reasons. At the same time, however, the Committee indicated that no serious problems had arisen in the past and that there had been no cases of disciplinary action being taken. Nor had there been any complaints from citizens or local administrations.

---

100 *Ibid*, para 61. Similarly, in *Hatton v United Kingdom*, judgment of 2 October 2001, the European Court of Human Rights found the UK liable for interference with the applicants' Art 8 rights arising from noise from night flights at Heathrow. The court noted the attempt to argue that the interference was justified on the basis of the economic well being of the country but stated that the onus was on the State to achieve such an aim in the least onerous way as regards human rights. The lack of a 'proper and complete investigation and study' meant that there was a lack of critical assessment to justify the interference.

The mere fact that the Committee noticed a change of atmosphere in recent years in the direction of stronger party affiliation of civil servants, especially at the local government level, does not in itself mean that the same standard of political neutrality in public service could not be maintained without recourse to such restrictive regulations as those in issue. In particular, it has not convincingly been argued by the Government why civil servants would not, as a rule, be responsible enough to decide for themselves the sort of political action their position permits and does not permit, subject to *ex post facto* disciplinary supervision. In that respect, it seems relevant for the assessment of the necessity in a democratic society test that in other Member States of the Council of Europe, which claim to be strong democracies as well, a regulation with similar far-going restrictions to the freedom of expression of civil servants has not been considered necessary. There, the primary responsibility and discretion is placed on the civil servants themselves, with possibilities for corrective but not preventive restraint.

We are inclined to agree with the Canadian Supreme Court, quoted by Liberty in its submission to the court, which held that public servants cannot be silent members of society and that as a general rule all members of society should be permitted to participate in public discussion of public issues.[101]

It may be that in the domestic courts, where no margin of appreciation exists, the courts will be more critical of the rationale put forward for an interference. Certainly the focus of judicial review on the procedural propriety of the actions of public bodies has tended to impose a focus on the reasons put forward in justification for the decision, albeit that the proportionality of the decision taken has historically not been available as a ground for review in domestic law.

Equally, however, there is a danger that domestic courts may be more prepared to accept domestic approaches, especially where they have some long-standing historical basis, and advocates who wish to challenge the rationale for an interference may need to look to other Contracting Parties, and to other jurisdictions, to show that other approaches are possible.

3.3.2.5 What is the quality of the reasoning?

Where the reasons are defective[101a] in the view of the court, it will generally be the case that the interference will be unjustified. Thus in the *Autronic AG*[102] case the Swiss Government sought to justify a refusal of a license to receive programmes from a Russian satellite on the basis that it was required to do so under the terms of an international telecommunication convention, an argument that was undermined by evidence, *inter alia*, that other states

---

101 *Ahmed v United Kingdom* (2000) 29 EHRR 1, dissenting judgment of Judges Spielmann, Pekkanen and Van Dijk, para 5.
101a Or based on inadequate investigation: *Hatton v United Kingdom.*
102 *Autronic AG v Switzerland* (1990) 12 EHRR 485.

allowed reception of uncoded television broadcasts from telecommunications satellites without the consent of the authorities of the transmitting country without protest from international authorities. When the Government then sought to justify the interference on the basis that:

> a total ban on unauthorised reception of transmissions from telecommunications satellites was the only way of ensuring 'the secrecy of international correspondence', because there was no means of distinguishing signals conveying such correspondence from signals intended for the general use of the public.[103]

The Court was dismissive since the had already conceded that there was no risk of obtaining secret information in this way.

Issues for advocates: factors of relevance to proportionality arguments

1   Is the right a qualified right? Proportionality will rarely, if ever, be relevant when dealing with absolute rights.

2   Has there been an interference which is for a prescribed reason and which is in accordance with the law?

3   Is the interference 'necessary in a democratic society': that is, it does not have to be indispensable, nor is it sufficient if it is merely desirable. What is the 'pressing social need' that gives rise to the interference?

The elements of the proportionality test:

4   What is the extent of the interference?

  •   In particular does the interference go to the very essence of the right?

  •   Note the conflict between domestic and Strasbourg approaches to interference with some elements of Art 6 (in particular in relation to compelled questioning).

5   Are less intrusive means available? In particular, consider if this is a blanket policy or one which has been or can be tailored to the individual.

6   Where has the balance been drawn between the rights of the individual and the achievement of the aim of the interference? What is the impact on the individual and how does this compare to the importance of the aim that is at stake?

  •   In particular, is this a case where two sets of rights conflict so that a balance has to be found between two individuals rather than the individual and the state?

7   Have sufficient reasons been given for the interference, and for the means adopted to meet the aim? In particular, what is the quality of the

---

103 *Ibid*, para 63.

reasons: do they stand up to scrutiny? Where it is said that social values require the interference, can this be justified in the overarching context of protecting the individual from the 'tyranny of the majority'? What are the reasons for adopting the particular method of interference, and the extent to which the interference has been permitted?

3.4 PROPORTIONALITY AS A GROUND FOR JUDICIAL REVIEW

Notwithstanding some continuing judicial suggestions to the contrary,[104] it seems to have been accepted that prior to the commencement of the Human Rights Act, proportionality has not been a separate ground for judicial review in the domestic courts. In *Brind*[105] Lord Ackner stated:

> Unless and until Parliament incorporates the Convention into domestic law ... there appears to me to be at present no basis upon which the proportionality doctrine applied by the European Court can be followed by the courts of this country.[106]

Is it therefore the case, now that the Convention has effectively been 'incorporated into domestic law', that proportionality is a basis on which the courts can review the acts of public bodies?

Clearly the tenor of this chapter has been to indicate that where a qualified right is in play, once the individual can show interference with that right, it will be for the public authority to show that the interference is permitted, and that will clearly involve in the majority of cases the court being satisfied that the interference is necessary in a democratic society. Proportionality will therefore be a necessary component in any argument. This however, is different from the proposition that proportionality will now, of itself, become a ground for judicial review. In order to consider the current position it is necessary to review briefly the attitude of the domestic courts when addressing human rights issues prior to October 2000.

3.4.1 'A heightened scrutiny': the super-*Wednesbury* test

The domestic courts had already struggled to reconcile the traditional limitations of *Wednesbury* unreasonableness – of which a proportionality test was undoubtedly an element – with the focus of the Convention on the protection of the right, as opposed to the rationality of the decision-maker.

---

104 See, for example, Sedley J in *R v Manchester Metropolitan University ex p Nolan* [1994] ELR 380.
105 *R v Secretary of State for the Home Department ex p Brind* [1991] 1 AC 696.
106 *Ibid*, p 763A.

This led to the formulation of a 'heightened scrutiny' test, the classic statement of which is to be found in the judgment of the Master of the Rolls in the judicial review in *Smith*, the 'gays in the military' case:[107]

> The court may not interfere with the exercise of an administrative discretion on substantive grounds save where the court is satisfied ... that it is beyond the range of responses open to a reasonable decision-maker. But in judging whether the decision-maker has exceeded this margin of appreciation the human rights context is important. The more substantial the interference with human rights, the more the court will require by way of justification before it is satisfied that the decision is reasonable in the sense outlined above.[108]

This was reformulated into a fractionally more stringent test by Lord Woolf in *R v Lord Saville ex p A*:[109]

> What is important to note is that when a fundamental right such as the right to life is engaged, the options available to the reasonable decision-maker are curtailed. They are curtailed because it is unreasonable to reach a decision that contravenes or could contravene human rights unless there are sufficiently significant countervailing considerations. In other words it is not open to the decision-maker to risk interfering with fundamental rights in the absence of compelling justification. Even the broadest discretion is constrained by the need for there to be countervailing circumstances justifying interference with human rights. The courts will anxiously scrutinise the strength of the countervailing circumstances and the degree of the interference with the human right involved and then apply the test accepted by Bingham MR in *Ex p Smith*, which is not in issue.[110]

It will be noted, however, that notwithstanding the recognition by the courts of the need for 'anxious scrutiny', the test remains based in classic *Wednesbury* principles – namely, has the decision-maker acted in a way that is so beyond the range of responses open to the reasonable decision-maker? The fact that interference with a human right is a consequence of the decision enables the court to reduce the range of reasonable responses; it does not, however, entitle the courts to interfere with a decision simply because it is in contravention of the Convention.

These limitations were effectively recognised by the decision of the Strasbourg Court in *Smith v United Kingdom*[111] where the European Court of Human Rights considered less restrictive alternatives to the blanket bar on homosexuals serving in the military and concluded that less restrictive means (such as a disciplinary code) might have dealt with the concerns of the state, stressing the importance of having regard to the qualities of 'pluralism, tolerance and broadmindedness' in any democracy. But not only did the court

---

107 *R v Ministry of Defence ex p Smith* [1996] QB 517.
108 *Ibid*, p 554.
109 [1999] 2 All ER 860.
110 *Ibid*, p 872.
111 *Smith and Grady v United Kingdom* (2000) 29 EHRR 548.

effectively hold that the 'heightened scrutiny' of the domestic courts had been inadequate to protect the applicants' rights, the court went on to find a breach of Art 13 (the right to an effective remedy) because of the limitations of the judicial review test:

> In such circumstances, the court considers it clear that, even assuming that the essential complaints of the applicants before this court were before and considered by the domestic courts, the threshold at which the High Court and the Court of Appeal could find the Ministry of Defence policy irrational was placed so high that it effectively excluded any consideration by the domestic courts of the question of whether the interference with the applicants' rights answered a pressing social need or was proportionate to the national security and public order aims pursued, principles which lie at the heart of the court's analysis of complaints under Article 8 of the Convention.[112]

At least in the *Smith* context, then, the high test of irrationality under even a super-*Wednesbury* principle was insufficient protection for the applicants' human rights. The court did, however, confirm that this would not be the case in every situation:

> The present applications can be contrasted with the cases of *Soering* and *Vilvarajah* ... In those cases, the Court found that the test applied by the domestic courts in applications for judicial review of decisions by the Secretary of State in extradition and expulsion matters coincided with the Court's own approach under Article 3 of the Convention.[113]

This therefore left to the domestic courts the issue of whether the Human Rights Act – and in particular the Act's recognition of the courts' status as public authorities (s 6(3)) – required the development of a different test.

3.4.2 Judicial review and the Human Rights Act

The leading case on the status of the *Wednesbury* principle post-October 2000 is *R (on the Application of Mahmood) v Secretary of State for Home Department*.[114] The case involved a challenge to the deportation of Mahmood as an illegal entrant. Although the case also considered problematic issues, such as the retrospectivity of the Human Rights Act,[115] the key focus is on the nature of the test to be adopted in determining whether the deportation could be reviewed on the basis of an unlawful interference with Mahmood's Art 8 right to family life, Mahmood having married a British citizen.

---

112 *Smith and Grady v United Kingdom* (2000) 29 EHRR 548, para 138.
113 *Ibid*, para 138.
114 [2001] 1 WLR 840.
115 An attempt was also made to separate the decision to deport, taken prior to October 2000, from the act of deportation itself (which would occur post-October). The court rejected this: its task was normally to review decisions already made: see *ibid*, para 29, *per* Laws LJ.

It is worth setting out the *dicta* of the Master of the Rolls (Lord Phillips) in some detail, since, with one important proviso, these have now been confirmed by the House of Lords. The Master of the Rolls reviews the decisions of the domestic courts in *Smith* and in *Lord Saville* and concludes that '[t]hey support the application of three principles to that situation':

(1) Even where human rights were at stake, the role of the court was supervisory. The court would only intervene where the decision fell outside the range of responses open to a reasonable decision-maker.

(2) In conducting a review of a decision affecting human rights, the court would subject the decision to the most anxious scrutiny.

(3) Where the decision interfered with human rights, the court would require substantial justification for the interference in order to be satisfied that the response fell within the range of responses open to a reasonable decision-maker. The more substantial the interference, the more that was required to justify it.

He then considers the extent to which these principles remain good law in the light of the Human Rights Act:

38 I consider that the first principle remains applicable were the court reviews an executive decision, which is required to comply with the Convention as a matter of law. The court does not substitute its own decision for that of the executive. It reviews the decision of the executive to see whether it was permitted by law – in this instance the Human Rights Act 1998. In performing this exercise the court has to bear in mind that, just as individual States enjoy a margin of appreciation which permits them to respond, within the law, in a manner that is not uniform, so there will often be an area of discretion permitted to the executive of a country before a response can be demonstrated to infringe the Convention ...

39 As to the second principle to be derived from the authorities referred to above, that principle also remains applicable where the Convention is directly in play. The decision must be subjected to the most anxious scrutiny. It is the third principle that requires modification where a decision is reviewed that was required, pursuant to the 1998 Act, to comply with the Convention. In such circumstances the court can no longer uphold the decision on the general ground that there was 'substantial justification' for interference with humans rights. Interference with human rights can only be justified to the extent permitted by the Convention itself. Some articles of the Convention brook no interference with the rights enshrined within them. Other articles qualify the rights, or permit interference with them. Thus Articles 8, 9, 10 and 11 contain second paragraphs which permit interference with rights in accordance with the law and in so far as necessary in a democratic society in the interests of specified legitimate aims.

40 When anxiously scrutinising an executive decision that interferes with human rights, the court will ask the question, applying an objective test, whether the decision-maker could reasonably have concluded that the interference was necessary to achieve one or more of the legitimate aims

> recognised by the Convention. When considering the test of necessity in the relevant context, the court must take into account the European jurisprudence in accordance with section 2 of the 1998 Act.

However, notwithstanding this analysis of the principles to be applied, it is not clear that the test in *Mahmood* represents a fundamental shift from the super-*Wednesbury* approach which was found wanting by the Strasbourg Court in the *Smith* case. It is true that the decision holds that the old 'substantial justification' test is no longer valid, but it is replaced by a test which asks merely whether the decision maker could have reasonably concluded that the interference was necessary to achieve a permitted aim.

It was this latter aspect of the test, which was amended by Lord Steyn (with whose comments on this point the other Law Lords agreed) in *Daly*,[116] where he stated:

> The explanation of the Master of the Rolls in the first sentence of the cited passage requires clarification. It is couched in language reminiscent of the traditional *Wednesbury* ground of review ... and in particular the adaptation of that test in terms of heightened scrutiny in cases involving fundamental rights as formulated in *R v Ministry of Defence ex p Smith* ... There is a material difference between the *Wednesbury* and *Smith* grounds of review and the approach of proportionality applicable in respect of review where convention rights are at stake.[117]

He goes on to cite the *de Freitas* formulation of the elements of proportionality (discussed above) and continues:

> Clearly, these criteria are more precise and more sophisticated than the traditional grounds of review. What is the difference for the disposal of concrete cases? Academic public lawyers have in remarkably similar terms elucidated the difference between the traditional grounds of review and the proportionality approach ... The starting point is that there is an overlap between the traditional grounds of review and the approach of proportionality. Most cases would be decided in the same way whichever approach is adopted. But the intensity of review is somewhat greater under the proportionality approach. Making due allowance for important structural differences between various convention rights, which I do not propose to discuss, a few generalisations are perhaps permissible. I would mention three concrete differences without suggesting that my statement is exhaustive. First, the doctrine of proportionality may require the reviewing court to assess the balance, which the decision maker has struck, not merely whether it is within the range of rational or reasonable decisions. Secondly, the proportionality test may go further than the traditional grounds of review in as much as it may require attention to be directed to the relative weight accorded to interests and considerations. Thirdly, even the heightened scrutiny test developed in *R v*

---

116 *R (on the Application of Daly) v Secretary of State for the Home Department* [2001] UKHL 26; [2001] 2 WLR 1622.
117 *Ibid*, para 26.

Ministry of Defence ex p Smith [1996] QB 517, 554 is not necessarily appropriate to the protection of human rights ...

28 The differences in approach between the traditional grounds of review and the proportionality approach may therefore sometimes yield different results. It is therefore important that cases involving convention rights must be analysed in the correct way. This does not mean that there has been a shift to merits review. On the contrary, as Professor Jowell [2000] PL 671, 681 has pointed out the respective roles of judges and administrators are fundamentally distinct and will remain so. To this extent the general tenor of the observations in *Mahmood* [2001] 1 WLR 840 are correct. And Laws LJ rightly emphasised in *Mahmood*, at p 847, para 18, 'that the intensity of review in a public law case will depend on the subject matter in hand'. That is so even in cases involving Convention rights. In law context is everything.[118]

Thus it appears from *Daly* that there is now judicial recognition at the highest domestic level that proportionality is not simply available as a test of the legality of public authority decision-making where there is a Convention right in play; *Daly* makes clear that the courts *must* adopt a proportionality approach since this is what is required by the Convention itself.

As Lord Steyn suggests, this then requires specific consideration of issues such as balance and the weight given to competing considerations. We would also suggest that the other elements of the proportionality test – such as the 'least intrusive means' approach – will also necessarily be relevant. *Mahmood* therefore sets out the structured approach, which the court will adopt, when dealing with an interference with Convention rights, and which we have suggested will be necessary for advocates to adopt in their analysis of their cases. However, *Daly* effectively recognises the limitations of even a super-*Wednesbury* approach and substitutes proportionality as the appropriate means of review.

3.4.3 How will proportionality develop in future?

Daly makes clear that proportionality is an essential component of the test that must be applied by the court when considering interference with those human rights where an interference is permitted. There are, however, two further matters that should also be noted, indicating how far the domestic courts have now developed the power of judicial review.

The first of these matters is the suggestion from Lord Slynn in the House of Lords decision in *Alconbury* that proportionality should not be confined merely to human rights cases, but should now be recognised as a ground for review in all domestic cases:

---

118 *R (on the Application of Daly) v Secretary of State for the Home Department* [2001] UKHL 26; [2001] 2 WLR 1622, paras 27–28.

> I consider that even without reference to the Human Rights Act the time has
> come to recognise that this principle [of proportionality] is part of English
> administrative laws, not only when judges are dealing with Community acts
> but also when they are dealing with acts subject to domestic law. Trying to
> keep the *Wednesbury* principle and proportionality in separate compartments
> seems to me to be unnecessary and confusing.[119]

Clearly the focus of this book is on the implications of the Human Rights Act
for advocates, but if the principle of proportionality is more widely applicable
across the domestic law, whether or not human rights are in issue, it will
clearly be easier to persuade the lower courts that the proportionality test is
one that they must adopt, and it will become even more important for
advocates to provide the court with a structured approach to proportionality
in order to bring together the disparate elements of this test.

The second matter, which itself suggests that proportionality may
increasingly be given a wider role in domestic law, is an increasingly overt
unhappiness on the part of some senior judges with the very basis of
traditional *Wednesbury* unreasonableness. The most recent and forceful of
these criticisms is provided by Lord Cooke in the *Daly* case:

> ... I think that the day will come when it will be more widely recognised that
> *Associated Provincial Picture Houses Ltd v Wednesbury Corporation* [1948] 1 KB 223
> was an unfortunately retrogressive decision in English administrative law, in
> so far as it suggested that there are degrees of unreasonableness and that only
> a very extreme degree can bring an administrative decision within the
> legitimate scope of judicial invalidation. The depth of judicial review and the
> deference due to administrative discretion vary with the subject matter. It may
> well be, however, that the law can never be satisfied in any administrative field
> merely by a finding that the decision under review is not capricious or
> absurd.[120]

It seems unlikely that this will be the final word on the matter. Advocates may
in due course find not only that proportionality has a wider application as a
ground for judicial review in all aspects of law, but *also* that the traditional
fetters of *Wednesbury* unreasonableness are gradually removed.

3.4.4 Does proportionality introduce a merits-based challenge to decisions?

One final issue remains to be considered in relation to proportionality
arguments: does the adoption of a proportionality test amount to a merits-
based form of review? It was on the basis that such a development would be

---

119 *R v Secretary of State for the Environment, Transport and the Regions ex p Holding and Barnes and Others ('Alconbury')* [2001] EWHL 23; [2001] 2 WLR 1389, at para 51.
120 [2001] UKHL 26; [2001] 2 WLR 1622, para 32.

inevitable were proportionality to be introduced into domestic law that Lord Ackner based his objections in the *Brind* case.[121]

The general consensus is that a clear dividing line remains: the court will now undertake a more stringent review of the decision-making of public authorities, at least where Convention rights are in play; however, while the public authority will need to show that any interference is legitimate (rather than simply that it is reasonable or not unreasonable), the decision remains that of the public authority, the court's power is one of review. In short the court will not ask itself whether the decision is one that it would have made (a merits-based approach); nor will it ask itself whether the decision was so unreasonable that it cannot be sustained (*Wednesbury*). Rather, the court will require the decision-maker to show that a decision which interferes with the human right of any individual, is one that is for a permissible reason and one that is necessary in a democratic society.

Professor Jowell puts it as follows:

Judges are not being set free to second-guess administrators on the merits of their policies. The respective roles of judges and administrators in a democratic society, and their competence, are fundamentally distinct and will remain so. Stricter scrutiny and the abandonment of *Wednesbury* obscurity does not mean that courts will be entitled to ignore the limitations in competence of their own role.

Under the new constitutional litigation the courts ask essentially two questions. First, is there a breach of a fundamental democratic right? If the answer to that question is in the affirmative, the second question asks whether the decision, which appears on its face to subvert democracy, is in fact necessary to preserve it in the interest of a legitimate countervailing democratic value. In assessing these questions the courts will look to the process of justification of the decision and to the inherent qualities of a democratic society. This kind of review is a far cry from review on the basis of the desirability of the decision in abstract terms.[122]

The dividing line between an assessment of merits and a supervisory jurisdiction is nonetheless a fine one and it is likely that courts will maintain an anxious scrutiny where they feel that advocates are inviting them to trespass on matters of merit, which have traditionally been the prerogative of the government. It is important therefore to make clear that the role of the court remains supervisory. Indeed, *per* Lord Steyn, it appears that even the more stringent proportionality-based review is unlikely to give rise to a different result in the majority of cases. However, it is the case that the reasons given by the state for the interference will now come under close scrutiny, as

---

121 *R v Secretary of State for the Home Department ex p Brind* [1991] 1 AC 696.
122 Jowell [2000] PL 671, pp 681–82.

will the initial justification for the need for the interference in the first place. The key is Professor Jowell's point that the Human Rights Act introduces a new constitutional recognition of certain human rights: it is therefore the role of the courts to require a higher level of justification from the state for actions which on their face 'subvert' that constitutional guarantee.

Issues for advocates: proportionality as a ground for judicial review

1   Proportionality has traditionally not been available as a ground for judicial review: *Brind.*

2   However, where human rights are in issue, even a 'heightened scrutiny' or 'super-*Wednesbury*' test will not be sufficient to ensure that those rights are protected: *Smith v United Kingdom.*

3   Where human rights are in issue, courts must consider the proportionality of any interference: *Daly.* This goes beyond a simple consideration of whether the decision was within the range of rational decisions.

4   In the majority of cases this is unlikely to lead to a different result than the application of traditional domestic judicial review principles: *Daly.*

5   This is not merits-based review: the court is not being asked to substitute its own view of the merits of the policy or the actions of the state. The review is limited to a consideration of whether the consequent interference with the rights of the individual can be justified as proportionate.

6   It is the case, however, that as part of this process, the reasons, which are put forward by the state for the interference, will be scrutinised in order to ensure that the policy is 'necessary in a democratic society'.

7   There are some indications that proportionality may be accepted more widely as a ground for judicial review in non-human rights arguments.

3.5 CONCLUSION

Proportionality is a principle, which advocates are likely to encounter in almost every context where a Human Rights Act issue is said to arise. It is an increasingly familiar principle, at least in the context of European Union law. However, many (lower) courts will not have had to address proportionality-based arguments prior to the Human Rights Act. Moreover, in the wider social and political context of the European Convention arguments on the proportionality of interference need to be approached in a structured way in order to avoid a generalised, and non-specific, 'balancing exercise'.

We have argued that the doctrine of 'margin of appreciation' is not applicable in domestic courts, and we suggest that this has been clearly accepted by the higher courts. A new doctrine which accords elected bodies a 'discretionary area of judgment' in certain areas of social and economic policy seems to have been adopted, and advocates will need to take account of this. However, it is necessarily a limited doctrine and cannot of itself justify interference with an individual's rights: it acts to argue that in certain areas of policy no such rights arise in a domestic context.

The most important issues set out in this chapter are the elements of the proportionality test itself. As advocates, and courts, become more familiar with the contours of the principle of proportionality it is likely that courts will expect to be addressed on each of these points, and will require argument from advocates where the evidence is unclear. At least in the immediate future, however, advocates will need to be prepared to assist the courts in order to ensure that the appropriate level of review is undertaken, and that at each stage the court is able to examine the nature, the extent and the effect of any interference with the constitutional rights of the individual.

CHAPTER 4

INTERPRETATION

4.1 INTRODUCTION

This chapter examines two interpretation issues. First, it looks at how the courts go about ascertaining the meaning of Convention law, including the influence of the case law of the European Court of Human Rights. Secondly, it considers the role of the courts when interpreting statutes, including the important new duty to find a Convention-compliant meaning in legislation, where possible.

4.2 DECIDING ON THE MEANING OF CONVENTION LAW

One of the consequences of the Human Rights Act is that domestic courts have to come to terms with Convention law. It is not going to be possible to decide whether legislation can be read consistently with the Convention (s 3) or whether public authorities have acted compatibly with Convention rights (s 6) without forming a view of what Convention law requires in the circumstances of the case. The courts have to become familiar with the Convention rights in Sched 1 to the Human Rights Act and also with the case law emanating from the Strasbourg institutions. The key to understanding the impact of such case law is s 2 of the Human Rights Act, which provides as follows:

> 2(1) A court or tribunal determining a question which has arisen in connection with a Convention right must take into account any [decision of the European Court, Commission or Committee of Ministers] whenever made or given, so far as ... it is relevant to the proceedings in which that question has arisen.

4.2.1 Pre-Human Rights Act attitude to Convention law

The test for whether s 2 has a real impact in the United Kingdom is the extent to which it alters the previous approach towards the relevance of the European Convention on Human Rights. Approaches varied but there was nothing to prevent United Kingdom judges being wilfully ignorant of the Convention rights when interpreting domestic law.[1] The reason was that the

---

1   Curtin J at first instance in *R v Ministry of Defence ex p Smith* [1996] QB 517: 'If it makes no difference, why refer to it?' See Wadham, p 36.

Convention was not seen as part of the domestic law but only binding at an international level on the state as a party to the treaty. The position was consistently that the Convention could be referred to as an aid to the interpretation of ambiguous legislation or common law but not otherwise.[2]

However, even prior to the Human Rights Act there were indications that the judiciary were moving to ensure closer scrutiny of legislative measures in light of human rights values:

> Parliament does not legislate in a vacuum. Parliament legislates for a European liberal democracy based upon the principles of the common law ... and ... unless there is the clearest provision to the contrary, Parliament must be presumed not to legislate contrary to the rule of law.[3]

This section seeks to show how far s 2 has begun to push the courts further along the path towards harmonising domestic reasoning with that in the European Convention. Whenever advocates are considering whether to deploy Convention decisions in argument and what the likely effect of those decisions is they should have regard to the following issues that arise from s 2 and the case law to which it has given rise.

4.2.2 When should advocates use Strasbourg case law?

Reference to Strasbourg case law should be made whenever they are relevant to a 'question that has arisen in connection with a convention right'. It has already been seen how advocates are under a duty to have available to the court any decisions that will enable the court to do justice to arguments about a breach of Convention rights.[4] The purpose of referring to Strasbourg decisions will be to persuade the court of the correct construction of Convention law. It follows that the Strasbourg decisions relied on might not bear any similarities to the facts of the case being tried. Moreover, it may not be possible to find an exact match between the Strasbourg reasoning and the point in issue in the case under consideration. However, this does not mean that the Strasbourg decisions are irrelevant. Convention law focuses much more on general principles as compared to the traditional common law approach. Advocates, and in turn the courts, must accommodate such an approach when dealing with cases under the Human Rights Act. Sedley LJ when considering a case under Art 1 of Protocol 1 (the right to property) helpfully suggested as follows:

---

2   See, for example, *R v Secretary of State for the Home Department ex p Brind* [1991] 1 AC 696. For a more expansive view of human rights law in domestic courts pre-Human Rights Act, see Hunt, *Using Human Rights Law In English Courts* (Oxford: Hart, 1997) especially Chapter 6.

3   Lord Steyn in *R v Secretary of State for the Home Department ex p Pierson* [1998] AC 539, at p 575.

4   *Barclays Bank v Ellis* [2000] All ER(D) 1164.

In interpreting and enforcing this right, we are required by s 2 of the Human Rights Act 1998 to take into account any relevant jurisprudence of the European Court of Human Rights or opinion of the (now defunct) Commission ... Our task is not to cast around in the European Human Rights Reports like black-letter lawyers seeking clues. In the light of s 2(1) of the Human Rights Act 1998 it is to draw out the broad principles, which animate the Convention. These, in our view, include a requirement that the legitimate aim of taxation in the public interest must be pursued by means which are not completely arbitrary or out of all proportion to their purpose.[5]

If the court's task is to 'draw out the broad principles which animate the Convention' then advocates ought to be given some considerable latitude when it comes to advancing Strasbourg authority. As we have seen in Chapter 1, Strasbourg has developed principles regarding the scope and nature of the Convention rights that will be applicable across a range of rights and a variety of factual situations. Of course, where there is a relevant Strasbourg authority from the area of law that is under consideration, then that decision is likely to be preferable to an unrelated decision. It goes without saying that Strasbourg decisions may relate to any of the member states of the Council of Europe. Cases against countries other than the United Kingdom are no less valuable but they have to be read against the background of the laws and procedures of the state in question. For example, in *Daniels v Walker*[6] the Court of Appeal was critical of the reliance on *Mantovanelli v France*[7] as the argument did not recognise the differences between civil jurisdictions and the approach in this country. Decisions against other member states will be of use in so far as they confirm, restrict or extend the general rules regarding Convention rights, but their application in the United Kingdom must recognise the difference in procedures between the foreign and the United Kingdom courts.

4.2.3 Is some Strasbourg case law more important than others?

Section 2 permits reference to Strasbourg decisions 'whenever made or given'. This confirms that there is no temporal restriction on the relevance of cases. However, in deciding on the relevance of decisions, advocates ought to bear in mind the principle that views the Convention as a 'living instrument' whereby older decisions may have to be reviewed in light of changing societal attitudes.[8] In addition, although the Human Rights Act permits reference to decisions of the Commission and the Committee of Ministers, it should be noted that the Commission was abolished when the full-time court was set

---

5   *Aston Cantlow and Wilmcote with Billesley Parochial Church Council v Wallbank and Another* [2001] EWCA Civ 713; [2001] 3 All ER 393 at paras 38, 44.

6   [2000] 1 WLR 1382.

7   (1997) 24 EHRR 370.

8   See discussion of living instrument in Chapter 1.

up[9] and the Committee of Ministers no longer makes decisions on the construction of Convention law. Thus such decisions, albeit relevant, are a fixed body of authority that will not be added to in the future.

Section 2 does not indicate the relative importance of Strasbourg authorities. Thus if there is to be a hierarchy of importance, it must come from the way the court structure operates. The following suggested hierarchy emerges, although domestic courts are likely to take a relatively flexible approach towards Strasbourg authority:

1   European Court Grand Chamber decisions. Since the 11th Protocol came into effect in 1999 there has been a limited right to appeal from a decision of a Chamber of the Court to a Grand Chamber (Art 44(2)). It follows that decisions of the latter have greater importance.

2   European Court decisions. Decisions are now normally taken by Chambers, which have less weight than the Grand Chamber. Prior to Protocol 11 all court decisions as to violations were in theory of equal standing, although domestic courts are likely to have regard to whether the decision came from a Chamber or the Plenary Court.

3   European Commission opinions on merits. Note that the opinion was set out in a report to the European Court. If the court, when subsequently hearing the case, came to a different conclusion, the court's view prevailed. It is possible that domestic courts will use strong Commission opinions to justify departing from court decisions, especially where the court itself was split.

4   Decisions on admissibility by the European Court or European Commission. The thoroughness of such decisions varies enormously and domestic courts will wish to examine such decisions carefully before drawing firm conclusions as to the construction of Convention law. Such decisions are now taken by chambers of seven judges or committees of three judges. This too may affect the relative weight to be attached to the decision by the domestic courts.

5   Committee of Ministers decisions. These are of little, if any, value to domestic courts as no reasons were given and the procedure was not a judicial process.

6   Advisory opinions of the court. Although mentioned in s 2, there have never been any advisory opinions given by the court.

4.2.4   Where can Strasbourg case law be found?

There are a number of sources for finding Strasbourg decisions as follows:

---

9   See European Convention Protocol 11 November 1998

1   The official reports are published by Carl Heymanns, Cologne. They consist of *Series A* (judgments of the European Court and Commission report) and *Series B* (submissions by the parties, etc). Since the end of 1995 this has been superseded the *Report of Judgments and Decisions* (RJD) again published by Heymanns.

2   A more accessible set of reports is the *European Human Rights Reports* (EHRR) published by Sweet & Maxwell, London.

3   There is also number of new series that have emerged since the Human Rights Act was announced. Butterworth's *Human Rights Cases* includes human rights cases from around the world and Sweet & Maxwell's *Human Rights Law Reports* (UK) focuses on decisions of the domestic courts. Although useful, this series cannot hope to be comprehensive, restricted as it is to domestic decisions.

4   The most relevant reports of Commission decisions is *Decisions and Reports* (DR) published by the Council of Europe since 1975.

5   The European Court of Human Rights website www.echr.coe.int hosts a powerful searchable database of cases known as HUDOC. This holds all court decisions and a more limited range of Commission and Committee of Minister decisions.

6   *Blackstone's Human Rights Digest*;[10] is a guide to the Human Rights Act and the Convention but it comes with a useful searchable CD Rom database containing all of the court judgments up to the date of publication and selected Commission decisions. Although this will date quickly, it is useful particularly if the HUDOC server is inaccessible.

4.2.5   How should Strasbourg case law be cited?

See Chapter 2 for a discussion of the rules regarding the citation of Strasbourg case law.

4.2.6   Are other human rights decisions relevant?

Section 2 makes clear that Strasbourg case law is relevant in the United Kingdom Courts. However, it is silent on the relevance of other foreign authority. Nevertheless, decisions made under various other human rights instruments may well be of assistance in determining the scope and substance of the Convention rights. It is fairly clear that decisions of courts such as the Canadian Supreme Court, the South African Constitutional Court, the US Supreme Court etc are of increasing relevance in so far as they grapple with similar provisions in their respective constitutions. Decisions of the Privy

---

10   Starmer, London: Blackstones, 2001.

Council have taken on added significance, especially when it acts as a final court of appeal for human rights devolution points in Scotland, where it will be explicitly determining Convention rights issues.[11] It is also relevant, though, where it interprets the constitutional provisions of commonwealth and ex-commonwealth nations.

The status of these decisions remains persuasive only. What has altered is that the United Kingdom courts now have to interpret similar provisions and so may gain significant assistance from decisions interpreting mature human rights instruments.

However, there is a limit to the relevance of such decisions. Where the right is expressed in different terms to the Convention right under scrutiny, the decisions of international courts is of less assistance. This point was made by Lord Hope in *Brown v Stott* in respect of decisions regarding self-incrimination in Canada:

> ... the Lord Justice general derived support ... from the Canadian case of *R v White* [1999] 2 SCR 417. Reference to Canadian cases was understandable in view of the reference in *Saunders v United Kingdom* to generally recognised international standards ... But care needs to be taken in the context of the European Convention to ensure that the analysis by the Canadian Courts proceeds upon the same principles as those, which have been developed by [Strasbourg] ... The principle against self-incrimination is held in Canadian law ... to be a principle of fundamental justice ... the questions, which the Supreme Court of Canada was asking itself, were not the same and there are some important differences of detail. So I do not think that the balancing of the relevant principles, which was undertaken, in that case can be regarded as a reliable guide as to how the balance ought to be struck in the European context.[12]

4.2.7 Which courts are bound by the s 2 duty?

All courts and tribunals are obliged to take account of Strasbourg decisions. It is not limited to the higher courts. No judge, magistrate or tribunal chairperson should be heard to say that Strasbourg decisions are not relevant in their court/tribunal.

4.2.8 Are courts obliged to follow Strasbourg decisions?

As already noted, the duty is to 'take into account' the Convention case law. Courts cannot refuse to consider Convention jurisprudence but they are not bound to follow its reasoning. This should be distinguished from the s 6 duty

---

11   Scotland Act 1998, s 103 and Sched 6.
12   [2001] 2 WLR 817.

to act compatibly with the Convention rights about which there is no discretion. The court has a choice whether it follows Strasbourg decisions in deciding what Convention law requires but once it has reached a settled view on what Convention law requires it must follow that approach, unless, of course, it is prevented from doing so by primary legislation.

In the normal course of events advocates will expect courts to follow the Strasbourg view of the content of Convention law, although recourse will no doubt be had to traditional methods to avoid following an undesirable approach, such as distinguishing it on the facts of the case. The need to follow the Strasbourg approach is particularly keen when the Strasbourg decisions are clear and consistent. Judges know that if they consciously decline to follow a decision of the European Court of Human Rights, the aggrieved litigant is likely to appeal the decision to the higher courts, which are themselves likely to follow the Strasbourg approach or ultimately pursue a petition against the United Kingdom to the European Court directly under the Convention.[13]

It is often said that the Convention provides a floor and not a ceiling[14] in the sense that United Kingdom Courts should not adopt an approach that provides less protection for human rights than the Convention, but are free to develop more extensive protection than offered by the European Court. As an observation about the United Kingdom legal system as a whole this is a fair point – clearly the courts are not restrained from going further than Strasbourg. In this sense it can be said that the United Kingdom Courts are free to develop their own distinctive body of human rights jurisprudence so that the Human Rights Act will become the United Kingdom's distinct Bill of Rights.[15] However, courts and tribunals should not see this view as giving them an untrammelled ability to develop novel means of pushing the boundaries of rights far beyond that envisaged by the Strasbourg machinery. Public authorities will no doubt appeal if decisions are seen to go too far and the higher courts will decide whether the expansive view of the Convention rights is permissible or not. This is another situation where advocates will have to be responsible and show an appreciation of the way the law may develop in the long run in the higher courts. There is little point in bamboozling lower courts into providing remedies under the Human Rights Act if the public authority is likely to succeed on appeal.

---

13 Strasbourg applications are generally outside the scope of this book. See further, Clements, L, *Taking a Case Under the Convention*, 2nd edn (London: Sweet & Maxwell) and Emerson and Simor, *Human Rights Practice* (London: Sweet & Maxwell, loose-leaf), Chapter 19.

14 See, for example, Nicolas Bratza, *Implications of the Human Rights Act 1998 for Commercial Practice* [2000] EHRLR 1 at p 4.

15 An example sometimes cited is the House of Lords decision in *Fitzpatrick v Sterling Housing* [1999] 3 WLR 1113 that a stable gay relationship amounted to a family for the purposes of the Rent Acts before the European Court had recognised it as a family relationship for the purposes of Art 8.

The desirability of following Convention decisions was confirmed recently by Lord Steyn in the *Alconbury* case:

> Although the Human Rights Act 1998 does not provide that a national court is bound by these decisions it is obliged to take account of them so far as they are relevant. In the absence of some special circumstances it seems to me that the court should follow any clear and constant jurisprudence of the European Court of Human Rights. If it does not do so there is at least a possibility that the case will go to that court which is likely in the ordinary case to follow its own constant jurisprudence.[16]

As a matter of strict law, the fact that the European Court might come to different conclusions than the United Kingdom Courts as to the meaning of Convention law is neither here nor there. The European Court remains only an international court in its relationship to our own courts. It is not a court of appeal or a court of reference in respect of Convention law.[17] However, Lord Steyn is reflecting the understandable desire to ensure that domestic law generally marches in-step with Convention law unless there is a good reason for it taking a different route. As one commentator put it: '... the Strasbourg method of judicial reasoning will gradually enter English legal practice.'[18] Indeed, the overriding purpose of s 2 must be to ensure that domestic decision-making coheres more to the Convention norm.[19]

A further reason is the practical desire not to see United Kingdom Court decisions criticised and found to be lacking by the European Court. Although figures are not yet available, it would not be surprising to find that increased awareness among United Kingdom lawyers about Convention rights leads, at least initially, to an increase in Convention applications when arguments fail in the domestic courts.

However, there are also indications that the courts will not refrain from criticising Strasbourg decisions where necessary. The reasoning of the Strasbourg Court will not be accepted with blind faith:

> With due respect I have to say that the reasoning in *Saunders* is unsatisfactory and less than clear ... It may be that the observations in *Saunders* will have to be clarified in a further case by the European Court. As things stand, however, I consider that the High Court of Justiciary put too great weight on these observations.[20]

In this case the Privy Council surveyed a range of decisions of the European Court on the implied limitations to Art 6 and concluded that the right not to

---

16 *R v Secretary of State for the Environment, Transport and the Regions ex p Holding and Barnes and Others ('Alconbury')* [2001] EWHL 23; [2001] 2 WLR 1389.

17 *Locabail (UK) Ltd v Bayfield Properties Ltd* [2000] QB 451.

18 Wadham, p 34.

19 See the *Rights Brought Home* (Cm 3782, October 1997), hereafter 'the White Paper', para 1.15.

20 *Per* Lord Steyn in *Brown v Stott* [2001] 2 WLR 817.

incriminate oneself could also be limited if the limitation was proportionate to the legitimate public interest of safety on the roads. This was despite apparently clear *dicta* to the contrary in *Saunders*.[21]

In *Attorney General's Reference (No 7 of 2000)*[22] the Court of Appeal was faced with what it thought were apparently conflicting decisions regarding whether the privilege against self-incrimination was breached by the seizure of documents. The court preferred the approach in *Saunders v United Kingdom* to that in *Funke v France* when considering the ambit of Art 6 of the Convention. However, their Lordships went on to find in the alternative that if the Convention case law did not give a clear answer to the question, that was reason to follow earlier House of Lords authorities.[23] The implication is that if the Convention law is clear then it will be preferred to earlier domestic decisions. This last point brings us to another issue – the impact that the Human Rights Act has on earlier domestic authority.

4.2.9   What is the effect of s 2 on precedent?

This is an important question in that courts will wish to be advised by advocates as to the precedent value of previous domestic decisions that appear to have a bearing on the case in hand. Section 2 has a powerful interplay with both s 3 regarding the interpretation of legislation and s 6 regarding the development of the common law. As we will see, s 3 requires all legislation to be interpreted so far as possible consistently with Convention rights. Additionally, s 6 requires all public authorities, including the courts, to act in a way that is compatible with the Convention. The new relevance of Convention decisions is bound to have an impact on the way the courts view existing domestic decisions regarding the meaning of statutes and also the way the courts feel obliged to develop the common law.

This impact works by requiring the courts to reconsider existing authority in light of Convention decisions and the principles developed therein. Given that this is done under statutory authority, no previous decision is immune from such a re-appraisal.

A good example is the way the House of Lords decision in *R v Gough*[24] regarding bias has been re-interpreted in light of the European jurisprudence as to the requirements for an independent and impartial tribunal:

---

21 The case of *Osman v United Kingdom* (2000) 29 EHRR 245 was subject to trenchant criticism and this has led to the European Court of Human Rights adjusting its approach towards public policy immunity cases, see *Z v United Kingdom* [2001] 2 FCR 246 (immunity amounted to a breach of Art 13, not Art 6).

22 [2001] EWCA Crim 888 (2001) 98(22) LSG 35.

23 See now *JB v Switzerland*, European Court of Human Rights, judgment of 3 May 2001, discussed in Chapter 8.

24 *R v Gough* [1993] AC 646.

[The Convention] approach comes close to that in *Gough*. The difference is that when the Strasbourg Court considers whether the material circumstances give rise to a reasonable apprehension of bias, it makes it plain that it is applying an objective test to the circumstances, not passing judgment on the likelihood that the particular tribunal under review was in fact biased.

When the Strasbourg jurisprudence is taken into account, we believe that a modest adjustment of the test in *Gough* is called for, which makes it plain that it is, in effect, no different from the test applied in most of the Commonwealth and in Scotland.[25]

It appears that the position is different when the applicable Convention law was fully considered in the earlier domestic decision that is being reviewed. In *R v Central Criminal Court ex p Bright*[26] the Divisional Court considered production orders made against journalists under the Police and Criminal Evidence Act 1984 requiring them to produce material supplied to a newspaper by the dissident security service officer, David Shayler. One issue was the extent to which the journalists could rely on the privilege against self-incrimination to prevent or restrict the order for production. The journalists sought to rely on Convention case law to explain the scope of the privilege. Judge LJ was not particularly impressed:

105 In *R v Hertfordshire CC ex p Green Environmental Industries Ltd* ... the impact of Art 6(1) and (2) of the convention, and the relevant decisions of the European Court on these provisions, were analysed by Lord Hoffman in the context of domestic legislation. Without implying any disrespect for the decisions of the European Court, sitting in the Divisional Court in England, where such a decision, or group of decisions has been examined by the House of Lords or Court of Appeal, this court is bound by the reasoning of the superior courts in our jurisdiction. We are not permitted to re-examine decisions of the European Court in order to ascertain whether the conclusion of the House of Lords or Court of Appeal may be inconsistent with those decisions, or susceptible to a continuing gloss. The principle of *stare decisis* cannot be circumvented or disapplied in this way, and if it were, the result would be chaos. In my judgment, in this court it is appropriate to consider and apply the principles against self-incrimination as explained in *Ex p Green Environmental Industries Ltd* but we should not now attempt to revisit the decisions in *Saunders v United Kingdom*, *Funke v France*, and *Serves v France*, and attempt to reconcile their apparent contradictions. So far as we are concerned the impact of this group of decisions has been authoritatively decided. We have been told how they should be taken into account.

106 I respectfully venture to suggest that when the 1998 Act comes into force the possible relevance of the decisions of the European Court for the

---

25 *Re Medicaments and Related Classes of Goods (No 2)* [2001] 1 WLR 700, also known as *Director General of Fair Trading v The Proprietary Association of Great Britain and Another*, paras 85–86.

26 [2001] 2 All ER 244.

purposes of s 2(1) should be examined in the light of any available analysis by the House of Lords and the Court of Appeal, and in that way properly but sufficiently taken into account. It would therefore be unnecessary to recite massive passages from the judgments, and inappropriate to seek to undermine the decisions of our superior courts about their true ambit.

Given the very recent nature of the House of Lords decision being considered there, it is perhaps not surprising that his Lordship did not want to be dragged into a full review of the Convention decisions. It is also important to note that the *Green* case was decided following the passing of the Human Rights Act, albeit prior to implementation. We suggest that the position should be different where the courts are considering pre-Human Rights Act decisions. The reason is that, prior to the Human Rights Act, the United Kingdom Courts had no obligation to consider the Convention jurisprudence. Thus, even when Strasbourg decisions were considered it was often a fairly superficial analysis in order to confirm the decision already reached under the domestic law. Moreover, given the then status of the Convention, *dicta* regarding Convention law must normally be viewed as *obiter*. It follows that the lower courts ought not to feel bound by pre-Human Rights Act decisions regarding Convention case law even if made by the higher courts.

There is another reason why domestic courts ought not to become too wedded to existing interpretations of Convention law even those contained in post-Human Rights Act decisions. The 'living instrument' doctrine prevents the Convention from having a fixed meaning and the courts ought always to be open to new arguments based on the changing social norms:

> The court must also recall that the Convention is a living instrument, which ... must be interpreted in the light of present-day conditions. In the case now before it the court cannot but be influenced by the developments and commonly accepted standards in the penal policy of the Member States of the Council of Europe in this field.[27]

It will be more likely that the Convention will be seen to be dynamic in areas of social policy impacting on issues of morality where attitudes can be shown to have changed over the years. Thus some articles, particularly Arts 3 and 8, are more susceptible to living instrument arguments than others. It is also relevant to consider the practice across the Member States of the Council of Europe. It is much more likely to be able to recognise altered values if these are generally recognised throughout European legal systems. It seems that once changes in common values are recognised it can shift the Convention paradigm significantly, giving rise to a re-appraisal of numerous previous decisions. Note in particular the discussion relating to *Selmouni v France* in Chapter 1.

---

27 *Tyrer v United Kingdom* (1978) 2 EHRR 1 at para 31 – examining whether birching was inhuman and degrading punishment.

Issues for advocates: determining the meaning of Convention law

- Courts and tribunals have a mandatory duty to take into account Convention case law. This goes much further than the old approach whereby courts could look at Convention law at their discretion but it had no formal status in domestic law.

- Advocates are able to rely on Convention case law whenever it is relevant to an issue in the case. It will be relevant whenever it assists the court to understand the construction or application of Convention law that has arisen in the case.

- The court should determine what the Convention requires before attempting to decide whether legislation can be read compatibly and whether a public authorities has acted unlawfully.

- Merits decisions of the European Court of Human Rights should be the main source of Strasbourg authority relied on through s 2, although it does permit other decisions to be cited.

- It should be recalled that the European Court does not consider itself bound by its previous decisions. This will lead to advocates suggesting possible developments in Convention case when existing authority is not supportive of their propositions. Note the rapid backtracking between the decision in *Osman v United Kingdom* and *Z v United Kingdom*.

- Older Strasbourg decisions should be considered with caution in light of the living instrument doctrine.

- Other human rights jurisprudence can be relied upon if it displays the attitude towards international standards of fairness etc but the courts will have to be convinced of its applicability in the European context.

- The courts should normally follow any clear and consistent jurisprudence of the European Court but it should never be suggested that a court is bound by Strasbourg decisions.

- The courts are, however, obliged under ss 3 and 6 to give effect to the Convention rights once they have, with or without reliance on Strasbourg decisions, construed its meaning.

- Section 2 should influence the courts as to the precedent value of earlier decisions. However, once post-Human Rights Act authority emerges, it will bind in the same way as previously.

4.3 EXPLAINING THE COURT'S INTERPRETATIVE OBLIGATIONS

Section 3 is one of the key provisions of the Human Rights Act in that it alters the way in which legislation is interpreted and applied.

Issues for advocates: important preliminary points arising from s 3
- It applies to legislation whenever passed, either before or after the Human Rights Act.
- It applies to all legislation – primary and delegated.
- It applies to all courts and tribunals at all levels.
- It is a duty not a discretion.
- All public authorities, not just the courts, must adopt the s 3 way of looking at legislation.
- It does not enable courts to override legislation but does require a more flexible approach towards interpretation.

4.3.1 The interpretative rule

Section 3(1) provides as follows:

> So far as it is possible to do so, primary legislation and subordinate legislation must be read and given effect in a way which is compatible with the Convention rights.

4.3.2 Traditional canons of interpretation

The 'traditional' rules of statutory interpretation can be summarised as follows.

4.3.2.1 Literal rule

The words used in the statute should be given their plain, ordinary or literal meaning. Parliament is assumed to have given effect to its intention by the words used in the drafting of the legislation. The court is obliged to give effect to this intention by gleaning the true meaning of the words used and cannot adjust that meaning in order to achieve what in the court's view might be a more acceptable or just result:

> When Parliament legislates to remedy what the majority of its members at the time perceive to be a defect or a lacuna in the existing law (whether it be the

written law enacted by existing statutes or the unwritten common law as it has been expounded by the judges in decided cases), the role of the judiciary is confined to ascertaining from the words that Parliament has approved as expressing its intention what that intention was, and to giving effect to it. Where the meaning of the statutory words is plain and unambiguous it is not for the judges to invent fancied ambiguities as an excuse for failing to give effect to its plain meaning because they themselves consider that the consequences of doing so would be inexpedient, or even unjust or immoral.[28]

4.3.2.2 Golden rule

This rule can be seen as a modification to the literal rule. If the words used by Parliament are ambiguous the court may adopt an interpretation, which avoids an absurd outcome in the case before it. Even if the words used are not ambiguous but the reading of the statute as a whole reveals that Parliament had intended to give effect to an existing public policy principle, the court may depart from what appears to be a clear, but absurd, meaning:

> ... statutory duties, which are in terms absolute, may nevertheless be subject to implied limitations based on principles of public policy accepted by the courts at the time when the Act is passed.[29]

4.3.2.3 Mischief rule

This permits the court to look at the mischief in the common law or statute law that the legislation was intended to remedy and then give the wording a meaning which will best address the previous defect in the law. The court, which developed this rule, stated that the role of the judiciary was 'always to make such construction as shall suppress the mischief, and advance the remedy'.[30] More recently the rule has been used to assist the court to choose between narrow and wide interpretations of words within statutes. The following case was about the use of the word 'obtained' in the Company Securities (Insider Dealing) Act 1985:

> It is permissible to look at circumstances preceding the legislation in order to see what was considered to be the mischief in need of a remedy ... This tends to show that the mischief consists of dealing in securities while in possession of the confidential information ... The object of the legislation must be partially defeated if the narrow meaning of 'obtained' is adopted ... In this case the choice is between the primary meaning and the secondary but correct and acceptable meaning ... I am ... satisfied that the wider meaning is the meaning which Parliament must have intended the word 'obtained' to have in this Act

---

28 *Per* Lord Diplock in *Duport Steel v Sirs* [1980] 1 All ER 529 at p 541.
29 *Per* Donaldson LJ in *R v Secretary of State for the Home Department ex p Puttick* [1981] 1 All ER 776 at p 780.
30 *Heydon's* case (1584) 3 Co Rep 7a.

and that, accordingly, there is no room for the kind of ambiguity on which the appellant has attempted to rely.[31]

4.3.2.4 Presumptions

The courts have also been able to draw on other tools to aid construction of legislation. Presumptions have been developed which acknowledge Parliament's ability to alter any legal rule but decline to imply such alteration unless such a result is clearly required by the statute. In this way the common law traditionally sought to uphold certain human rights through, for example, the presumption against deprivation of liberty,[32] the presumption against retrospective effect[33] and the presumption protecting private property rights.[34] Following the passing of the Human Rights Act but before its implementation, the courts were forced to focus more acutely on the existing protection offered by the common law approach. This led to Lord Hoffman crystalising the following principle from various strands of authority:

> Parliamentary sovereignty means that Parliament can, if, it chooses, legislate contrary to fundamental principles of human rights. The Human Rights Act 1998 will not detract from this power. The constraints upon its exercise by Parliament are ultimately political, not legal. But the principle of legality means that Parliament must squarely confront what it is doing and accept the political cost. Fundamental rights cannot be overridden by general or ambiguous words. This is because there is too great a risk that the full implications of their unqualified meaning may have passed unnoticed in the democratic process. In the absence of express language or necessary implication to the contrary, the courts therefore presume that even the most general words were intended to be subject to the basic rights of the individual. In this way the courts of the United Kingdom, though acknowledging the sovereignty of Parliament, apply principles of constitutionality little different from those, which exist in countries where the power of the legislature is expressly limited by a constitutional document.[35]

As if to confirm that this was an existing common law principle, His Lordship went on to explain that the Human Rights Act would supplement it by adding the European Convention as an instrument to be read in conjunction with the common law; by providing a specific statutory mechanism (s 3) for reading legislation compatibly; and by allowing declarations of incompatibility in the rare situations where the legislation could not be read compatibly.

---

31 *Per* Lord Lowry in *Attorney General's Reference (No 1 of 1988)* [1989] 2 All ER 1 at pp 6–8.

32 *R v Secretary of State for the Home Department ex p Khawaja* [1983] 2 WLR 321: 'If Parliament intends to exclude effective judicial review of the exercise of a power in restraint of liberty, it must make its meaning crystal clear.' *Per* Lord Scarman at p 344.

33 For example, *Alexander v Mercouris* [1979] 3 All ER 305.

34 For example, *British Airports Authority v Ashton* [1983] 3 All ER 6.

35 *R v Secretary of State for the Home Department ex p Simms* [2000] 2 AC 115 at 131.

4.3.2.5 Aids to construction

Courts also draw upon 'intrinsic' and 'extrinsic' aids to construction. The former permits examination of all textual evidence within the Queen's Printer's copy of the Act. The latter permits a more limited scrutiny of Commission reports, international treaties and, significantly, parliamentary debates.[36]

Advocates may be tempted to seek to make much greater use of the parliamentary history of a statute in order to persuade the court about its meaning before going on to argue about whether or not it is consistent with a Convention right. The extent to which this is permissible, though, is questionable. In *R v Secretary of State for the Environment, Transport and the Regions ex p Spath Holme Ltd*[37] Lord Hope of Craighead explained the restrictive nature of the rule in *Pepper v Hart*.[38] He said that ministerial statements from *Hansard* were strictly speaking only admissible to prevent the executive from placing a different meaning on words used in legislation from that which they attributed to those words when promoting the legislation.[39] In the Human Rights Act context, statements of ministers would thus only be admissible in assessing the intention of the legislation so as to prevent the executive advocating a different meaning for s 3 than was advanced during the passage of the Bill. This was recognised by Lord Steyn in an article[40] and confirmed when sitting judicially:

> In the progress of the Bill through Parliament the Lord Chancellor observed that 'in 99% of the cases that will arise, there will be no need for judicial declarations of incompatibility' ... For reasons which I explained in a recent paper, this is at least relevant as an aid to the interpretation of s 3 against the executive.

Construction of the Human Rights Act itself might benefit from examination of ministerial statements during the parliamentary process.[41] However, in one of the first cases to arise as to the interpretation to place on s 6 of the Human Rights Act the court decided that it was not permissible to examine the parliamentary history, as the provision was not ambiguous.[42]

---

36 *Pepper v Hart* [1993] AC 593.

37 [2001] 2 WLR 15 at p 48C–E.

38 [1993] AC 593.

39 See also *R v A* [2001] UKHL 25; [2001] 2 WLR 1546, para 81, *per* Lord Hope of Craighead.

40 '*Pepper v Hart*: a re-examination' (2001) 21 OJLS 59.

41 The debate over whether the Act has 'horizontal' effect has focused on various statements made by the Lord Chancellor during the passage of the Bill. See, for example, Buxton, R: 'The Human Rights Act and Private Law' (2000) 116 LQR 48; Wade, W: 'Horizons of horizontality' (2000) 116 LQR 217; and Phillipson, G, 'The Human Rights Act, "horizontal effect" and the common law: a bang or a whimper?' (1999) 62 MLR 824. One of the leading practitioner texts contains lengthy extracts from the *Hansard* Debates, anticipating controversy over the meaning of the 1998 Act itself (see Wadham, pp 223–53).

42 See discussion of *Heather and Others v Leonard Cheshire Foundation and Another* [2001] EWHC Admin 429; [2001] All ER(D) 156 (Jun) in Chapter 2.

4.3.3 What additional use may be made of extraneous material under the Human Rights Act?

Despite the fact that the courts may still insist on adherence to the *Pepper v Hart* criteria before resort is made to parliamentary statements for the purpose of construing legislation, it is fairly clear that they will be more prepared to examine the legislative history in order to decide whether a statute breaches a Convention right. The distinction is important. When it is alleged that a statute violates a Convention right the statute must first be interpreted using normal interpretative techniques outlined above and generally without resort to parliamentary statements. The court then needs to determine whether, so interpreted, the provision violates the Convention right before it goes on to apply the s 3 test. As we have seen, the answer to the question of whether there is a violation often depends on whether the measure serves a legitimate aim and is proportionate to that aim. This is where the legislative history becomes relevant in that it helps the court to understand the policy objectives of the legislation. An understanding of these objectives is vital when assessing whether the measure is a proportionate means of achieving them.

A useful lesson in the relevance of the legislative history was offered in *Wilson v First County Finance*[43] as follows:

> It was submitted on behalf of the Secretary of State that an attempt to investigate, through examination of preparatory materials and the content of debates in Parliament, what reason of policy led enacted legislation to take the precise form that it does is, itself, illegitimate ... We reject that submission. We note that the European Court of Human Rights has thought it helpful to look at preparatory material in order to identify the policy aims and justification of social legislation ...[44]

The court then explained that it had examined the history of the Consumer Credit Act 1974 in some detail and went on:

> ... The purpose of that exercise was not to aid construction. There is no difficulty in construing s 127(3) of the Act. The question on which we sought assistance was ... 'what was the reason which led Parliament to enact a provision in those words?' ... The material to which we have been taken provides no answer to that question ... In the absence of extraneous assistance as to the policy aims of the legislation, or as to the justification for the exclusion of any judicial remedy in cases where there is no signed document, which contains all the prescribed terms, we must decide the issue on the basis of the legislation as enacted.[45]

---

43 *Wilson v First County Trust Ltd (No 2)* [2001] EWCA Civ 633; [2001] 2 WLR 42, para 34.
44 See *James v United Kingdom* (1986) 8 EHRR 123, paras 47–48 and 52 and *Mellacher v Austria* (1989) 12 EHRR 391, para 47.
45 Paragraphs 35–38.

The court then set out the policy objectives that could be gleaned from the face of the legislation but decided that the legislative response (an inflexible rule removing judicial discretion in respect of the enforcement of the credit agreement) was disproportionate. If a clear policy had appeared from the legislative history it is perhaps more likely that the court would have deferred to that policy in deciding whether the means adopted to achieve it were proportionate.[46]

4.3.4 The relationship between traditional methods of statutory interpretation and s 3

The rule in s 3 does not replace the existing canons of statutory interpretation. Rather, it overlays the existing rules and will operate only where Convention rights are in issue and, as we shall see, only where on a 'normal' interpretation, the statute is incompatible with the Convention right.

The contrast between traditional methods of interpretation and the s 3 method is illustrated in the case of *R v A*.[47] The House of Lords had to consider s 41 of the Youth Justice and Criminal Evidence Act 1999 which, on its face appeared to prevent an accused from adducing relevant evidence of previous sexual activity between him and the complainant in a rape case. The accused alleged that this would amount to a violation of his right to a fair trial under Art 6 of the Convention.[48] Lord Steyn considered and contrasted the traditional and the s 3 methods of interpretation:

> 39 ... Two processes of interpretation must be distinguished. First, ordinary methods of purposive and contextual interpretation may yield ways of minimising the *prima facie* exorbitant breadth of the section. Secondly, the interpretative obligation in s 3(1) of the 1998 Act may come into play ... It is a key feature of the 1998 Act.

His Lordship then examined the 'ordinary methods of interpretation' in detail asking whether any of the provisions of s 41 could be interpreted as a 'gateway' through which to permit the relevant evidence and questioning to take place. He concluded that they could not:

> 43 ... In my view ordinary methods of purposive construction of s 41(3)(c) cannot cure the problem of the excessive breadth of s 41, read as a whole, so far as it relates to previous sexual experience between a complainant and the accused. Whilst the statute pursued desirable goals, the methods adopted amounted to legislative overkill.

Hitherto, having found the traditional methods inadequate, the courts would have to stop there and accept that injustice would be caused. However, as we

---

46 See, in this respect, the discussion of the discretionary area of judgment in Chapter 3.
47 [2001] UKHL 25; [2001] 2 WLR 1546.
48 Article 6(1) in conjunction with Art 6(3)(d) – the right to call and question witnesses.

shall see, s 3 provides a further and more powerful tool for avoiding the unfairness expressed in the legislation.

Remember that in practice courts should be encouraged to use ordinary purposive methods of interpretation first, as they may obviate the need for recourse to s 3. If having done so, advocates then encounter difficulties in persuading judges to move beyond the traditional methods of statutory interpretation, they should be directed to the judgment of Lord Steyn in this case.

4.3.5 What is the procedure for using s 3?

This may seem a curious question given that s 3 is a rule of statutory interpretation. It might be thought that the courts would have regard to s 3 whenever they examine the meaning of legislation. However, it is implicit in s 3(1) that some view about the non-s 3 meaning of the Act and the requirements of the Convention right will have been formed before any question arises of looking for a possible interpretation which is compatible with that right.

Lord Woolf CJ confirmed this in the housing case of *Poplar Housing and Regeneration Community Association Ltd v Donoghue*:[49]

> ... unless the legislation would otherwise be in breach of the Convention s 3 can be ignored; so courts should always first ascertain whether, absent s 3, there would be any breach of the convention ...[50]

Issues for advocates: explaining the steps to using s 3

It follows that the advocate may helpfully pose the following series of questions to the court:[51]

1   Are you satisfied that a Convention right is engaged?

2   Are you satisfied, taking into account Convention case law, that the Convention right requires X to occur? (X being the act contended for by the claimed victim.)

3   Are you satisfied that on a normal reading of the legislation, it does not allow X to occur?

4   If each of these questions is answered in the affirmative, does the s 3 interpretative duty permit an interpretation which allows X to occur?

---

49   [2001] EWCA Civ 595; [2001] 3 WLR 183.
50   This was approved by Lord Hope in *R v A* [2001] UKHL 25; [2001] 2 WLR 1546, para 58.
51   See also Lord Hope, *ibid*, para 68.

Another procedural issue is the level of detail that is required when arguments about interpretation are advanced. We have already said that the interpretative duty applies to all courts and tribunals at all levels. Submissions about whether statutory provisions are compatible with Convention rights may often seek to include wide ranging material about the policy of the provision, the statutory history of similar provisions, the parliamentary proceedings, the social and economic impact of the policy, the approach in other countries and so on. Do all courts have a duty to consider all of this material?

In the *Poplar* case[52] the defendant tenant (of a periodic assured short-hold tenancy) sought to introduce a range of material to show that s 21(4) of the Housing Act 1998 (which required the court to grant a possession order if the relevant notice had been given) was incompatible with her right to respect for her home under Art 8. The district judge refused an adjournment and decided the case on the basis of the limited material he had in front of him on the day of the hearing (it had not been anticipated that human rights arguments were going to be advanced). He decided that s 21(4) was an acceptable interference with the right to respect for the home in that it seeks to secure the rights and freedoms of others – in this case other people in the housing queue – within the meaning of Art 8(2). One of the questions on appeal was whether the district judge was entitled to dispose of the issue summarily in the way he did.

The Court of Appeal accepted that s 7(1)(b) of the Human Rights Act permitted the tenant to rely on her Convention rights 'in any legal proceedings' which included the possession proceedings. The judge was therefore required to deal with the Art 8 argument 'notwithstanding the language of s 21(4)'. The court thought, however, that he was permitted to deal with the matter in the way he did:

> A district judge is familiar with housing issues and is perfectly entitled to apply his practical experience and common sense to an issue of this sort. It is not necessary at his level to hold a State trial into successive governments' housing policies in order to balance the public and private issues to which Article 8 gives rise. A great deal of expense and delay was avoided in a case which he was aware would be likely to come before this court in any event. (There is no power to make a declaration of incompatibility in the County Court.)[53]

This dose of Court of Appeal pragmatism will appeal to courts and advocates who foresee that the case is likely to end up in the higher courts in any event. It accepts that the scrutiny of human rights issues need not be as detailed at the lower levels of the judiciary than at appeal level.[54] There is a danger,

---

52 [2001] EWCA Civ 595; [2001] 3 WLR 183.

53 *Ibid*, para 28.

54 It should be noted that the Court of Appeal did take a more flexible approach to the evidence that it would consider due to the fact that the hearing in the lower court had not gone into a full fact-finding exercise.

though, that it will encourage superficial consideration of Convention law arguments in lower courts and tribunals. Moreover, if courts are able to limit the amount of material they need to consider, it will be difficult for advocates to ascertain in advance the type and volume of testimony and other material that will be admissible in evidence.

Convention rights are rarely amenable to simple resolution given that they apply complex broad principles such as legality, necessity in a democratic society, balance between individual and societal interests, discretion in decision-making, etc. The Human Rights Act could have limited the consideration of Convention rights to the higher judiciary but it did not.[55] There is no provision for 'fast-tracking' human rights cases into specialist courts.[56] Rather, a decision was taken to adopt a 'path of least resistance' approach, whereby human rights cases will be argued in the context of the specialist area in which they arise by the normal courts and tribunals and that normal appeal and review routes will be available. It is to be hoped that the decision in *Donoghue* is not seen as justifying a simplistic approach. This would defeat the government's stated aim that 'the rights will be brought much more fully into the jurisprudence of the courts throughout the United Kingdom and their interpretation will thus be far more subtly and powerfully woven into our law'.[57]

4.3.6   Is s 3 designed to make a difference?

The government's intention was clearly that the new rule of statutory interpretation would break new ground:

> This goes far beyond the present rule, which enables the courts to take the Convention into account in resolving any ambiguity in a legislative provision. The courts will be required to interpret the legislation so as to uphold the Convention rights unless the legislation itself is so clearly incompatible with the Convention that it is impossible to do so.[58]

If necessary, the White Paper might be used as an extraneous aid to interpretation of the Act in order to illustrate that it does require a more interventionist approach from the judiciary. In any event, emerging authority suggests that the higher judiciary already recognise that s 3 heralds a major reform.

---

55 Section 7(1) enables proceedings to be brought against public authorities in the County Court or High Court and enables reliance to be placed on Convention rights in any legal proceedings ie in any court or tribunal. Moreover, all courts and tribunals have been designated as public authorities under s 6(3).

56 Although the Divisional Court has adopted a policy of fast-tracking Human Rights Act cases – see *Practice Direction: Crown Office List* (2000) *The Times*, 24 March.

57 White Paper, para 1.14.

58 *Ibid*, para 2.7.

4.3.7 The significance of the s 3 rule

In *R v A*[59] the House of Lords provided the first thorough analysis of s 3.

Lord Steyn said as follows:

> On the other hand, the interpretative obligation under s 3 of the 1998 Act is a strong one. It applies even if there is no ambiguity in the language in the sense of the language being capable of two different meanings. It is an emphatic adjuration by the legislature: *R v Director of Public Prosecutions ex p Kebilene* [2000] 2 AC 326, *per* Lord Cooke of Thorndon, at p 373F; and my judgment, at p 366B ... The draftsman of the Act had before him the slightly weaker model in s 6 of the New Zealand Bill of Rights Act 1990 but preferred stronger language. Parliament specifically rejected the legislative model of requiring a reasonable interpretation. Section 3 places a duty on the court to strive to find a possible interpretation compatible with Convention rights. Under ordinary methods of interpretation a court may depart from the language of the statute to avoid absurd consequences: s 3 goes much further. Undoubtedly, a court must always look for a contextual and purposive interpretation: s 3 is more radical in its effect. It is a general principle of the interpretation of legal instruments that the text is the primary source of interpretation: other sources are subordinate to it ... Section 3 qualifies this general principle because it requires a court to find an interpretation compatible with Convention rights if it is possible to do so ... In accordance with the will of Parliament as reflected in s 3 it will sometimes be necessary to adopt an interpretation, which linguistically may appear strained. The techniques to be used will not only involve the reading down of express language in a statute but also the implication of provisions.[60]

Applying this test, Lord Steyn and three of the other Law Lords[61] held that s 41 could be interpreted sufficiently widely to permit questioning and evidence about previous sexual encounters between the defendant and the complainant in the weeks preceding the alleged rape if relevant to the issue of consent:

> In my view s 3 requires the court to subordinate the niceties of the language of s 41(3)(c), and in particular the touchstone of coincidence, to broader considerations of relevance judged by logical and common sense criteria of time and circumstances. After all, it is realistic to proceed on the basis that the legislature would not, if alerted to the problem, have wished to deny the right to an accused to put forward a full and complete defence by advancing truly probative material. It is therefore possible under s 3 to read s 41, and in particular s 41(3)(c), as subject to the implied provision that evidence or questioning which is required to ensure a fair trial under Article 6 of the Convention should not be treated as inadmissible. The result of such a reading

---

59   [2001] UKHL 25; [2001] 2 WLR 1546.

60   *Ibid*, para 44.

61   Lords Slynn, Clyde and Hutton gave speeches consistent with the approach of Lord Steyn.

would be that sometimes logically relevant sexual experiences between a complainant and an accused may be admitted under s 41(3)(c) ... If this approach is adopted, s 41 will have achieved a major part of its objective but its excessive reach will have been attenuated in accordance with the will of Parliament as reflected in s 3 of the 1998 Act. That is the approach which I would adopt.[62]

Advocates may wish to draw a court's attention to the important principles emerging from this careful analysis:

- Section 3 is a strong interpretative obligation – courts are under a duty to find a possible interpretation which is compatible with the Convention rights.
- There is no requirement for ambiguity in the statute being interpreted.
- Courts are not limited to situations where the statute would otherwise lead to absurd results.
- Section 3 is more robust than the New Zealand Bill of Rights Act 1990.
- Courts do not need to seek a 'reasonable interpretation'.
- Express and implied provisions may be 'read down'.
- It is permissible to strain the language of the statute. The 'niceties' of the language may be subordinated to broader considerations of relevance.
- Section 3 goes beyond contextual and purposive interpretation.
- The text of the statute is not necessarily the primary source of interpretation – the Convention-compliant interpretation is what should be strived for.
- The technique does not offend against the will of Parliament. It upholds Parliament's intention as expressed in the 1998 Act.

It should not be thought that there is unanimity as to the scope and effect of s 3. Lord Hope in the same case took a somewhat more restrictive view:

> ... I would find it very difficult to accept that it was permissible under s 3 of the Human Rights Act 1998 to read in to s 41(3)(c) a provision to the effect that evidence or questioning which was required to ensure a fair trial under Article 6 of the Convention should not be treated as inadmissible. The rule of construction which s 3 lays down is quite unlike any previous rule of statutory interpretation. There is no need to identify an ambiguity or absurdity. Compatibility with Convention rights is the sole guiding principle.That is the paramount object, which the rule seeks to achieve. But the rule is only a rule of interpretation. It does not entitle the judges to act as legislators ... The compatibility is to be achieved only so far as this is possible. Plainly this will not be possible if the legislation contains provisions which expressly contradict the meaning which the enactment would have to be given to make it compatible. It seems to me that the same result must follow if they do so by necessary implication, as this too is a means of identifying the plain intention of Parliament.

---

62 [2001] UKHL 25; [2001] 2 WLR 1546, at para 45.

> In the present case it seems to me that the entire structure of s 41 contradicts the idea that it is possible to read into it a new provision which would entitle the court to give leave whenever it was of the opinion that this was required to ensure a fair trial. The whole point of the section, as was made clear during the debates in Parliament, was to address the mischief which was thought to have arisen due to the width of the discretion which had previously been given to the trial judge ... It seems to me that it would not be possible, without contradicting the plain intention of Parliament, to read in a provision which would enable the court to exercise a wider discretion than that permitted by s 41(2).[63]

These comments serve to underline the radical nature of the approach adopted by the majority of the House. It should be recalled that prior to the implementation of s 41, s 2(2) of the Sexual Offences (Amendment) Act 1976 permitted the trial judge to give leave to adduce evidence or ask questions regarding the complainant's previous sexual activity (other than with the accused) only if it would be unfair to the accused to prevent it. In light of the judgment of their Lordships it might be asked whether they have rebuffed Parliament's attempt to restrict the trial judge's discretion. Trial judges may give leave if the evidence is required to secure a fair trial.

Although Lord Hope agrees with much of what has been said about the importance of s 3, he also emphasises the inability of the courts to make law and clearly views the expansion of the admissibility provisions as a step too far for the courts.[64] In doing so he focuses on the structure of the section as a whole, the mischief the Act was designed to avoid and the plain intention of Parliament as expressed in the language of the statute and any necessary implications that must be drawn from it. Note that Lord Hope reverted to the traditional methods of statutory interpretation in order to assert that the s 3 tool was inadequate. It might be retorted that such methods must give way to an interpretation which is Convention-compliant.

This illustrates the difficulty advocates have when faced with statutory provisions which are apparently clear in their intention and effect. To what extent can courts be urged to ignore the apparent meaning and adopt a meaning, which accords with their view of what the Convention would require?[65] How far can they go before they cross the Rubicon between interpreting and inventing the law? Those seeking to show that the statute can be read compatibly will be urging the approach of the majority in *R v A*. Those seeking to show that the law is incompatible will emphasise the limitations on that approach highlighted in the speech of Lord Hope.

---

63 [2001] UKHL 25; [2001] 2 WLR 1546, at paras 108–09. See further Lord Hoffman in *R v Secretary of State for the Home Department ex p Simms* [2000] 2 AC 115, at p 131F–G.

64 His thoughts may have been coloured by his decision (again, a minority view) that the provisions of s 41 were not, in fact, a violation of the accused's right to a fair trial. See para 106.

65 This obviously assumes that the court has been persuaded that on an ordinary construction the provision is incompatible with a Convention right.

In its second major analysis of s 3, in *R v Lambert*,[66] the House of Lords had to consider the interpretation to be applied to the Misuse of Drugs Act 1971 and the apparently reverse burden imposed on an accused in drug possession cases. If the prosecution prove that an accused was actually in possession of a controlled drug an offence is committed under s 5 of the Act. There is a defence only if 'he proves that he neither believed nor suspected nor had reason to suspect that the substance or product in question was a controlled drug ...'.[67] The majority of their Lordships thought that this provision, if read so as to place the legal burden of proving the defence on the accused, violated the right to a fair trial because it reversed the burden of proof in a disproportionate way. Lord Hope took the opportunity to elaborate on what he said in *R v A*. His Lordship re-iterated his cautious approach to s 3 emphasising the inability of the judges to make law. He also added some further points of note for advocates:

> Resort to it will not be possible if the legislation contains provisions, either in the words or phrases which are under scrutiny or elsewhere which expressly contradict the meaning which the enactment would have to be given to make it compatible. The same consequence will follow if legislation contains provisions which have this effect by necessary implication ... It does not give power to the judges to overrule decisions which the language of the statute shows have been taken on the very point at issue by the legislator ... Great care must be taken, in cases where a different meaning has to be given to the legislation from the ordinary meaning of the words used by the legislator, to identify precisely the word or phrase which, if given its ordinary meaning, would otherwise be incompatible. Just as much care must then be taken to say how the word or phrase is to be construed if it is to be made compatible. The justification for this approach to the use of s 3(1) is to be found in the nature of legislation itself. Its primary characteristic, for present purposes, is its ability to achieve certainty by the use of clear and precise language. It provides a set of rules by which, according to the ordinary meaning of the words used, the conduct of affairs may be regulated. So far as possible judges should seek to achieve the same attention to detail in their use of language to express the effect of applying s 3(1) as the parliamentary draftsman would have done if he had been amending the statute. It ought to be possible for any words that need to be substituted to be fitted in to the statute as if they had been inserted there by amendment. If this cannot be done without doing such violence to the statute as to make it unintelligible or unworkable, the use of this technique will not be possible. It will then be necessary to leave it to Parliament to amend the statute and to resort instead to the making of a declaration of incompatibility. ... As to the techniques that may be used, it is clear that the courts are not bound by previous authority as to what the statute means. It has been suggested that a strained or non-literal construction may be adopted, that words may be read in by way of addition to those used by the legislator and

---

66 *R v Lambert* [2001] UKHL 37; [2001] All ER(D) 69 (Jul).
67 Section 28(3)(b)(i) of the Misuse of Drugs Act 1971.

that the words may be 'read down' to give them a narrower construction than their ordinary meaning would bear ... It may be enough simply to say what the effect of the provision is without altering the ordinary meaning of the words used ... In other cases ... the words used will require to be expressed in different language in order to explain how they are to be read in a way that its compatible. The exercise in these cases is one of translation into compatible language from language that is incompatible. In other cases, as in *R v A*, it may be necessary for words to be read in to explain the meaning that must be given to the provision if it is to be compatible. But the interpretation of a statute by reading words in to give effect to the presumed intention must always be distinguished carefully from amendment. Amendment is a legislative act. It is an exercise, which must be reserved to Parliament.[68]

Lord Hope is clearly concerned about the constitutional propriety of taking too broad a view of the power in s 3. If the courts are able to stifle the expressed desires of Parliament by over-zealous use of the interpretative function they will effectively be taking upon themselves a power to strike down legislation, something which Parliament decided not to give them, and was perhaps not even in Parliament's gift given the traditional view of the inalienability of parliamentary sovereignty. He is trying to find some coherent means by which to identify the limits of the s 3 power. He focuses not only on the phrase 'if possible to do so' but also emphasises the side note to the section, 'Interpretation of legislation', as if to remind his fellow judges that they have not been bestowed with a new authority to make law. He also points to the need for certainty in statute law so that the makers of the legislation and those whom it affects can generally be confident that the legislation will mean what is says.

There is also some useful practical advice in that he urges judges who re-interpret (and hence advocates who suggest interpretations) to be clear in their explanations as to (i) precisely which word or phrase in a statute that would be incompatible if not re-read and (ii) precisely how the word or phrase must be re-read in order to make it compatible. Judges should try to achieve the same level of clarity, as the parliamentary draftsman would do when preparing the legislation in the first place. Given that the s 3 duty applies across all tiers of the legal system this is perhaps an optimistic objective. There is a lot to commend Lord Hope's approach in that he is seeking to establish the dichotomy between the proper province of the legislature and that of the judiciary. He uses both textual and principled arguments. Nevertheless, we are still left with doubt as to the true limits of the s 3 function. We doubt that is always going to be possible to distinguish clearly between intensive interpretation to find the 'presumed intention' of Parliament, which is acceptable, and amendment of legislation by judicial fiat, which is not.

---

68 [2001] UKHL 37; [2001] All ER(D) 69 (Jul), at paras 79–81.

For the avoidance of doubt, we should emphasise that the only time that the court will be concerned with using s 3 to interpret legislation is when it has come to the conclusion that the Convention requires an approach which is not permitted on a normal reading of the statute. For example, an issue may arise as to whether a statute contains a power to adjourn a hearing for the preparation of Convention arguments. This is where the focus of disagreement in most cases will lie. The putative victim will be arguing for an interpretation of Convention law and domestic law which requires the adjournment whereas the public authority might argue that Convention law does not require an adjournment or that, if it does, this is adequately catered for on a normal interpretation of the law. Section 3 will only arise if the public authority fails to satisfy the court of this. Of course, situations will arise where there is no public authority as a party in the proceedings. The court must still assess whether the Convention requires any particular approach, as it is a public authority itself and must adopt a convention compliant interpretation of legislation whether or not it affects the actions of a public authority.

It follows that, despite its importance as a constitutional measure, s 3 ought not to be routinely paraded before the courts except in so far as it is the culmination of a submission about the proper construction of Convention law, the result that Convention law requires in the case being argued and whether the legislation, on a normal reading, complies with that result. Most cases alleging breach of Convention rights fall at the first of these obstacles so detailed consideration of s 3 is not required.

4.3.8 Interpretative techniques available using s 3

We have already seen in the case of *R v A* just how far the courts might be willing to go to secure compatibility. The following section is intended to provide some further guidance for advocates as to the extent of, and the limits on, the s 3 technique.

4.3.8.1 *Reading words into legislation*

Perhaps the most dramatic consequence of s 3 is that the courts are able to read words into legislation where to do so ensures that the legislation is compatible. During the parliamentary debates, the Lord Chancellor offered the example of *Litster v Forth Dry Dock*[69] as an example where transfer of undertaking regulations had words read into them to make them compatible with rights in European Community law. There are significant differences

---

69 [1990] 1 AC 21.

between the status of EC law and of the European Convention,[70] but it is likely that some methods will be borrowed from the approach in EC law.

This approach is supported by Ben Emmerson, co-author of *Human Rights Practice*:

> There is a major shift of power from Parliament to judges. They will, in effect, be able to rewrite sections of Acts by reading into them words that are not there and by massaging away any potential conflicts with the Convention.[71]

The best example so far of the courts' willingness to read new provisions into statutes is in *W and B (Children: Care Plan)*.[72] The Court of Appeal had to decide whether the powers of the courts to make care orders were sufficient to protect parents' and children's Convention rights. They decided that the framework as hitherto interpreted did not provide adequate judicial control following a care order to protect against a breakdown in the implementation of the care plan or a fundamental change in the plan leading to an unjustified interference with family life. In order to make the Children Act compatible with the Convention the court introduced new powers to supervise fundamentally important elements of the care plan. Hale LJ put it as follows:

> Where elements of the care plan are so fundamental that there is a risk of a breach of Convention rights if they are not fulfilled, and where there is some reason to fear that they may not be fulfilled, it must be justifiable to read into the Children Act a power in the court to require a report on progress. In effect, such vital elements in the care plan would be 'starred' and the court would require a report, either to the court or to the guardian *ad litem* (in future to CAFCASS), who would then decide whether it was appropriate to return the case to court ... There is nothing in the Children Act to prohibit this. Simply there is nothing to allow it. The courts have so far been true to the division of responsibility underlying the 1989 Act and declined to introduce it. But when making a care order, the court is being asked to interfere in family life. If it perceives that the consequence of doing so will be to put at risk the Convention rights of either the parents or the child, the court should be able to impose this very limited requirement as a condition of its own interference.[73]

The court in *W and B* was at pains to point out that the new powers were not to be seen as a replacement for the structures adopted by Parliament in the Children Act:

> Such a limited process, in such limited circumstances, should not place an undue strain upon resources or drive a coach and horses through the careful division of responsibility established by the 1989 Act. The object is simply to

---

70 The effect of s 2(1) and (4) of the European Community Act 1972 is that EC law prevails over incompatible domestic legislation and s 3(1) affords decisions of the European Court of Justice a greater status than those of the Strasbourg Court.

71 (1998) *The Times*, 26 November. See also *Human Rights Practice*, para 18.037.

72 [2001] EWCA Civ 757; [2001] FCR 450.

73 Paragraphs 79–80.

secure that the care system is operated in such a way as to comply with the Convention rights.

4.3.8.2 The limits to reading words into legislation

The fact that Her Ladyship saw fit to provide this explicit reassurance is perhaps recognition of the radical nature of the reform. The courts may well take a lot of persuading of the need to read words into legislation, which have the effect of causing significant change in the law and procedure anticipated by Parliament. However, the only limitation expressed by the Court of Appeal is to ensure that legislation operates in 'such a way as to comply with Convention rights'. If advocates are able to persuade the courts that a statute contains gaps that must be filled in order to make it compliant with their client's human rights, s 3 clearly provides the power for the court to fill those gaps.

The essential limitation appears to be that words may only be read into legislation if there is nothing in the Act to prevent the implied words. Section 3 effectively gives the courts the power to decide what ought to be in legislation in order for it to be compatible with Convention rights and then, if such content is not inconsistent with the rest of the statute, implement it by judicial decision. As Sedley LJ put it, 'nothing in the Children Act 1989 prevents our giving effect to the European Convention on Human Rights, as required by the Human Rights Act 1998'.[74]

The courts will be rightly cautious about such judicial activism as by its very nature it cannot have been the subject of extensive analysis and democratic debate that we normally expect of our legislation. A crafty 'not' inserted here or there in a statute is capable of turning its meaning on its head. The courts will want to avoid accusations of usurping parliamentary prerogative like this from Lord Kingsland:

> ... we are not so very far away from the world of Humpty Dumpty. What price the democratic will of the people as expressed through a parliamentary statute?[75]

The limits of 'reading in' were recognised in *Poplar v Donoghue*.[76] The Court of Appeal considered whether s 21(4) of the Housing Act 1988 could be construed differently if the court had concluded that the existing interpretation was not compatible with Art 8:

> The most difficult task which courts face is distinguishing between legislation and interpretation. Here practical experience of seeking to apply s 3 will provide the best guide. However, if it is necessary in order to obtain

---

74 *W and B* [2001] EWCA Civ 757; [2001] FCR 450, para 48.
75 (2000) *The Times Law Supplement*, 26 September.
76 [2001] EWCA Civ 595; [2001] 3 WLR 183.

compliance to radically alter the effect of the legislation this will be an indication that more than interpretation is involved ... In this case [counsel] contends that all that is required is to insert the words 'it is reasonable to do so' into the opening words of s 21(4). The amendment may appear modest but its effect would be very wide indeed. It would significantly reduce the ability of landlords to recover possession and would defeat Parliament's original objective of providing certainty. It would involve legislating.[77]

In *Wilson v First County Trust*[78] the Court of Appeal had to consider whether it was necessary to grant a declaration of incompatibility in respect of the Consumer Credit Act. The court first examined the s 3 duty, to see if a compatible meaning could be found:

Where the court finds that what we may describe as a 'non-Convention' interpretation of the words used in legislation would lead to the conclusion that the legislative provision was incompatible with a Convention right, it must consider whether there is some other legitimate interpretation of those words which avoids that conclusion. If there is, then the interpretation, which avoids that conclusion, must be adopted ... In that context, by 'some other legitimate interpretation' we mean some interpretation of the words used which is legally possible. The court is required to go as far as, but not beyond, what is legally possible. The court is not required, or entitled, to give to words a meaning which they cannot bear; although it is required to give to words a meaning which they can bear, if that will avoid incompatibility, notwithstanding that that is not the meaning which they would be given in a 'non-Convention' interpretation.[79]

Lady Justice Hale again in *W and B*:

We must beware the temptation to use the Human Rights Act 1998 and this litigation to find solutions to problems, which raise serious policy issues, which are the province of Parliament. Our role is only to ask ourselves what might be necessary to secure compliance with the Convention rights, and in particular the 'right to respect for family life' protected under Article 8.

However, it might be questioned how simple will be the task of unravelling the 'serious policy issues' from the 'compliance with Convention rights'. It is clear that the Convention entails a more complex interface between law and policy and necessitates a reconsideration of the respective roles of judiciary and Parliament. Advocates should be ready to advance or, as appropriate, resist, calls for more interventionist social policy style judgments.

4.3.8.3 'Reading down' legislation

This technique involves the court applying a narrower meaning to the legislation than it might naturally bear in order to make it compatible with a

---

77   [2001] EWCA Civ 757; [2001] FCR 450, paras 76–77.
78   [2001] EWCA Civ 633; [2001] 2 WLR 42.
79   *Ibid*, paras 41–42.

Convention right. An excellent example of this technique is the approach of the majority of the House of Lords in *R v Lambert*[80] where they narrowed the meaning of the words 'prove' and 'proves' in s 28(2) and (3)(b)(i) respectively of the Misuse of Drugs Act 1971. On their natural meaning the words meant that the defendant would have to prove on the balance of probabilities that he had no reason to suspect a substance was a controlled drug. This would mean that a jury could convict the accused because s/he did not satisfy his/her burden despite the jury having reasonable doubts about the point. Having concluded that such a position would breach an accused's Convention right to a fair trial, the words were read down by their Lordships to mean that the accused was only required to provide an evidential basis for his or her assertion about lack of suspicion, the legal burden remaining on the Crown to prove its case to the criminal standard.

4.3.8.4 Implying new safeguards

In *McCartan Turkington Breen (A Firm) v Times Newspapers Ltd*[81] Lord Cooke of Thoradon considered whether the Defamation Act provided sufficient protection for the Art 10 right of freedom of expression and speculated on whether it was permissible under s 3 to extend the statutory provisions so as to provide a safeguard for free expression:

> If s 7 and para 9 of the Schedule in the 1955 Act were the only relevant rules of law, it might well be necessary to stretch their language beyond its natural and ordinary ambit. They are not; the legislation expressly leaves intact the common law privilege, which complies with the convention; s 3(1) is not needed.[82]

This shows a willingness to expand statutory protection for Convention rights if, but only if, the lack of common law protection requires such a step.

4.3.8.5 Expanding the jurisdiction of the court

In *Lichniak*[83] the court was faced with a jurisdictional problem in respect of a challenge to the mandatory life sentence following conviction for murder. There was no right of appeal because the sentence was fixed by law under s 9(1) of the Criminal Appeal Act 1968 and judicial review was statute barred because the sentence related to a matter on indictment (s 29(3) of the Supreme Court Act 1981). However, the court recognised that the issue was a matter

---

80 [2001] UKHL 37; [2001] All ER(D) 69 (Jul). Lords Slynn, Steyn, Hope and Clyde. Lord Hutton did not address the issue as he dissented on the question of whether the provision violated Art 6.

81 [2000] 4 All ER 913.

82 *Ibid* at p 931.

83 *R (on the Application of Lichniak) v Secretary of State for the Home Department; R v Lichniak and Another* [2001] EWHC Admin 294; [2001] All ER(D) 22 (May).

that ought to be addressed under the Human Rights Act and was determined to find a way round the jurisdictional problem:

> ... For present purposes we are satisfied that the most attractive route to jurisdiction is to have resort to s 3(1) of the 1998 Act which requires us to read and give effect to s 9(1) of the 1968 Act in a way which is compatible with Convention rights. If a statutory provision which requires the imposition of a sentence of life imprisonment is incompatible with the Convention then, at least until Parliament has had the opportunity to consider its response to the court's declaration of incompatibility, the sentence is not for the purposes of s 9(1) of the 1968 Act fixed by law; alternatively the exclusion of sentences fixed by law is itself subject to an implied exception where the statutory provision fixing the sentence is incompatible with the Convention.

Contrast the case of *Regentford*.[84] There an acquitted defendant sought a judicial review of the Crown Court's refusal of a defence costs order alleging that it amounted to a breach of the presumption of innocence. The problem was that s 29(3) of the Supreme Court Act 1981 as hitherto interpreted did not permit a judicial review of any matter relating to trial on indictment, including orders relating to costs.[85] Clearly there was no appeal as the claimant had been acquitted. The court agreed that the lack of an available remedy for Crown Court decisions, even ones that were plainly wrong, could violate the Convention right to a fair trial in certain cases. Nevertheless, this was not sufficient to be able to use s 3 to create a remedy by expanding the previous view of s 29(3). That provision was about the availability of judicial review. The restriction was not itself in breach of any Convention right:

> All that can be said is that in some cases it may be that breach of a Convention right by a trial judge may not be capable of review. That does not bring about a further independent breach of a Convention right. Section 3 does not thus compel the court to place an interpretation on s 29(3) contrary to that already placed on it by previous decisions.[86]

Certainly at first sight the reasoning in the two cases does not appear to be compatible. In *Lichniak* the court seemed to be willing to be much more expansive in its interpretation of jurisdiction in order to address the substantive Convention issue at stake. In *Regentford* the court was content to allow that the lack of a remedy may breach a Convention right and leave it to be resolved at Strasbourg. However, there is a distinction between the two. Arguably in the former case it was s 9 itself, that would breach the Convention because the right claimed was to have the sentence reviewed by the court – the very thing that the provision prevented. In the latter case the alleged breach arose out of the order made by the Crown Court. The inability to challenge it was a step removed from the breach itself. The argument then

---

84   *R (on the Application of Regentford Ltd) v Crown Court at Canterbury* [2001] HRLR 18.
85   In *Re Sampson* [1987] 1 WLR 194.
86   [2001] HRLR 18, at para 22 *per* Waller LJ.

becomes that there is no effective remedy for breach of Convention rights in domestic law, an Art 13 issue that is not within the Human Rights Act. Admittedly the distinction is a fine one, but we maintain that both decisions are supportable.

4.3.9   Is there a distinction between legislation passed before the Human Rights Act and that passed after?

Pre-Human Rights Act and post-Human Rights Act legislation will be subject to the s 3 duty and will therefore be interpreted compatibly if possible. As Lord Woolf put it in *Poplar v Donoghue*:

> It is as though legislation, which predates the Human Rights Act and conflicts with the Convention, has to be treated as being subsequently amended to incorporate the language of s 3.[87]

In both cases recourse may also be had to the general presumption that legislation is intended to conform to international obligations.[88] The only difference is that in respect of pre-Human Rights Act legislation there is no statement of compatibility made under s 19 of the Human Rights Act.[89] Whatever assistance is to be gleaned from s 19 statements (see below) is therefore not available to a court considering pre-Human Rights Act legislation.

Unlike traditional approaches towards legislation, it is not correct to speak of pre-Human Rights Act statutes being impliedly repealed by the Human Rights Act. Indeed it is not correct to speak of statutes being 'incompatible' with the Human Rights Act at all given that it merely applies a new interpretative standard. The test for compatibility relates to the Convention, not the Act. The standard is applied in the same way to pre-Human Rights Act statutes as it is to post-Human Rights Act ones. Thus, the Mental Health Act 1983 (pre-Human Rights Act) was found to be incompatible with the Convention right to liberty[90] but remained valid and this was entirely consistent with the scheme of the Human Rights Act.

---

87   [2001] EWCA Civ 595; [2001] 3 WLR 183, at para 75.

88   This will obviously only be available in respect of legislation passed following ratification by the United Kingdom. The Convention came into operation on 3 September 1953.

89   Section 19 came into effect on 24 November 1998: Human Rights Act 1998 (Commencement) Order 1998 SI 1998 No 2882. It is therefore available only for legislation introduced after this date.

90   *R (on the Application of H) v Mental Health Review Tribunal North and East London Region* [2001] EWCA Civ 415; [2001] HRLR 36, discussed below.

Issues for advocates: examples of judicial approaches towards s 3

The following table sets out examples from recent cases to illustrate some of the ways in which the courts have so far dealt their duty to interpret legislation compatibly with Convention rights.

- In *R v Lambert*[91] the majority of the House of Lords thought that s 28(2) and (3)(b)(i) of the Misuse of Drugs Act 1971 could be read so as not to impose a legal burden on the defendant to prove the defence that s/he was in possession of a controlled drug but rather imposed an evidential burden only.

- In *R v A*, Lord Slynn said that the exception to the prohibition on evidence of complainant's previous sexual behaviour if it was 'at or about the same time'[92] as the alleged sexual offence might be capable of being stretched to cover a few hours or perhaps a few days but even s 3 could not reasonably extend the phrase to cover a few weeks which was what was alleged in that case. However the s 41(3)(c) exception relating to past sexual behaviour 'so similar' to the behaviour at the time of the alleged offence that it 'cannot reasonably be explained as a coincidence' was capable of being expanded to ensure that relevant evidence regarding previous sexual contact with the accused could be adduced if necessary in order to secure a fair trial.

- In *Poplar v Donoghue* it was not permissible to add the phrase, 'if reasonable to do so' at the beginning of s 24(1) of the Housing Act 1988 in order to given the court a discretion as to whether or not to grant possession of an assured short-hold tenancy. It would defeat Parliament's original objective of providing certainty and would thus involve legislating.

- In *W and B (Children) and W (Children)* it was possible to imply into the Children Act a wider ability for the court to make interim care orders and a new power to exercise 'extended supervision' of care orders once made in order to ensure compliance with Convention rights. This was because the Children Act was silent as to whether such powers and procedures were possible.

- In *Ashdown v Telegraph Group Ltd*[93] the Court of Appeal interpreted the Copyright Designs and Patents Act 1988 more widely than previously so as to expand the defence of breaching copyright in the public interest to protect freedom of expression under Art 10 of the Convention. Lord Phillips said as follows: '... the circumstances in which public interest may override copyright are not capable of precise categorisation or definition. Now that the Human Rights Act is in force, there is the

---

91 [2001] UKHL 37; [2001] All ER(D) 69 (Jul).
92 Section 41(3)(b) of the Youth Justice and Criminal Evidence Act 1999.
93 [2001] EWCA Civ 1142; (2001) *The Times*, 1 August.

clearest public interest in giving effect to the right of freedom of expression in those rare cases where this right trumps the rights conferred by the Copyright Act. In such circumstances, we consider that s 171(3) of the Act permits the defence of public interest to be raised.'[94] Their Lordships also held that the Convention could be protected by the court's exercise of its discretion as to whether or not to grant an injunction to prevent publication.

- In *Wilson v First County Trust* it was not possible to construe s 127(3) of the Consumer Credit Act 1974 so as to give the court any discretion to enforce a credit agreement in a case where the document signed by the debtor did not contain all the prescribed terms of the agreement. The court was not permitted to give words a meaning which they could not bear. A declaration of incompatibility was granted.

- In *Cachia v Faluyi*[95] the Court of Appeal interpreted s 2(3) of the Fatal Accidents Act 1976 as not prohibiting a second action being issued and served on behalf of dependent children of a woman who was killed in a road accident. Their Lordships found that traditional views of the legislation would not enable the court to allow their appeal as there had previously been an issued writ that had never been served and the 1976 Act appeared to prevent a second action in such circumstances. However, as Brooke LJ said: 'It is certainly possible to interpret the word "action" as meaning "served process" in order to give effect to the Convention rights of these three children. Until the present writ was served in July 1997, no process had been served which asserted a claim to compensation by these children for their mother's death. Section 2(3) of the Fatal Accidents Act 1976 therefore presents no artificial bar to this claim ... This is a very good example of the way in which the enactment of the Human Rights Act now enables English judges to do justice in a way which was not previously open to us.'[96]

- In *R (H) v Mental Health Review Tribunal* the court could not interpret ss 72 and 73 of the Mental Health Act 1983 so as to place the burden on the state to show that the patient still suffered from a mental disorder warranting detention: 'It is of course the duty of the court to interpret statutes in a manner compatible with the convention and we are aware of instances where this has involved straining the meaning of statutory language. We do not consider however that such an approach enables us to interpret a requirement that a tribunal must act if satisfied that a state of affairs does not exist as meaning that it must act if not satisfied that a state of affairs does exist. The two are patently not the same.' A declaration of incompatibility was granted.

---

94 [2001] EWCA Civ 1142, at para 58.
95 [2001] EWCA Civ 998; [2001] All ER(D) 299 (Jun).
96 *Ibid* at paras 20–21.

- In *R v Offen*[97] the court was able to interpret s 2 of the Crime (Sentences) Act 1997 as requiring a life sentence only where the accused represented an unacceptable risk to the public as to do otherwise could well be arbitrary and disproportionate under Art 5 and could amount to inhuman or degrading punishment under Art 3. It did this by expanding the previous interpretation of 'exceptional circumstances'. This would still give effect to the intention of Parliament but would do so 'in a more just, less arbitrary and more proportionate manner'. The 'objective of the legislature' would still be achieved because it would be mandatory to impose a life sentence in situations where the offender constituted a significant risk to the public. This was said to provide 'a good example of how the 1998 Act can have a beneficial effect on the administration of justice, without defeating the policy which Parliament was seeking to implement'.[98]

- In *Re K (A Child) (Secure Accommodation Order: Right to Liberty)*[99] the Court of Appeal rejected an argument that s 25 of the Children Act 1989, which permitted secure accommodation orders, was incompatible with Art 5 of the Convention because it fell within Art 5(1)(d) exception for educational supervision. It was accepted that theoretically there might be circumstances in which a s 25 order was made in circumstances that were not covered by the exception. However, this did not mean that the whole section was incompatible. A distinction had to be drawn between steps taken by a local authority under the statute and the statute itself, which would be construed compatibly. The implication was that any detention not in accordance with Art 5 would not be authorised by s 25.

- In *R (on the Application of the DPP) v Havering Magistrates Court*[100] the Divisional Court found that provisions of the Bail Act 1976[101] appeared to permit the remand in custody of a person arrested on suspicion of breach of a bail condition without the court being satisfied that he or she is likely to abscond, or has or is likely to breach a bail condition. It decided that the section led to a clear breach of Art 5 if interpreted literally. The court held, *obiter*, that the provisions should be construed under s 3 of the Human Rights Act as providing that such an arrest was capable of being taken into account in determining whether or not any of the grounds for refusing bail arose but could not be a reason on its own.

---

97 *R v Offen, McGilliard, McKeown, Okwuegbunam* [2001] 2 All ER 154.

98 *Ibid*, at p 176.

99 [2001] 2 WLR 1141.

100 *R (on the Application of the DPP) v Havering Magistrates Court, R (on the Application of McKeown) v Wirral Borough Magistrates Court* [2001] 2 Cr App R 2.

101 Paragraph 6 of Part 1 of Sched 1 and para 5 of Part 2 of Sched 1.

- In *Douglas v Hello!*[102] Sedley LJ construed s 12 of the Human Rights Act. He decided that it could not give the press a trump card when asserting its right to freedom of expression over other competing rights. He used s 3 of the Act to assist in this decision: '... a ... bland application of s 12(4), simply prioritising the freedom to publish over other Convention rights (save possibly freedom of religion: see s 13), might give the newspaper the edge even if the claimant's evidence were strong ... This cannot have been Parliament's design. This is not only ... because of the inherent logic of the provision but because of the court's own obligation under s 3 of the Act to construe all legislation so far as possible compatibly with the Convention rights, an obligation which must include the interpretation of the Human Rights Act itself. The European Court of Human Rights has always recognised the high importance of free media of communication in a democracy, but its jurisprudence does not – and could not consistently with the Convention itself – give Article 10(1) the presumptive priority which is given, for example, to the First Amendment in the jurisprudence of the United States' Courts. Everything will ultimately depend on the proper balance between privacy and publicity in the situation facing the court.'[103] This case confirms that the Human Rights Act is in the same category as all other legislation when it comes to the interpretative obligations of the court. Advocates will be relieved to learn that the Human Rights Act must be interpreted so as to be compatible with the Convention rights!

- In *King v Walden (Inspector of Taxes)*[104] the High Court had to consider whether s 7(1)(b) of the Human Rights Act when read with s 22(4) enabled a taxpayer to rely on alleged breaches of Convention rights that occurred prior the Act coming into force. The Act allowed this only in situations where the proceedings were brought by or at the instigation of a public authority. The problem was that the proceedings in question were the taxpayer's appeal against his assessment. The Revenue argued that it had only made the assessment and had not instigated the proceedings. Jacobs J thought that it was artificial to say that the taxpayer had instigated the proceedings and adopted a similar approach to s 3 as we saw in *Douglas* above: 'I am reinforced in that view by s 3(1) of the Human Rights Act itself. This requires that, so far as it is possible, primary legislation (that includes the Human Rights Act by way of self-reference) to be read and given effect in a way which is compatible with the Convention rights. So if one is choosing between two constructions, one of which confers Convention rights and the other not, one chooses the former, as I do here.'[105]

---

102 [2001] 2 WLR 992.
103 *Ibid*, at para 135.
104 [2001] STC 822.
105 *Ibid*, at para 59.

4.4   USE OF STATEMENTS OF COMPATIBILITY

Section 19 of the Human Rights Act requires that the minister in charge of a Bill in either House must, before the Second Reading stage, either make a statement that the Bill is, in his or her view, compatible with the Convention rights, or that despite the Bill being incompatible, the government nevertheless wishes to proceed with the Bill. These statements, often referred to as s 19 statements, must also be produced in writing and published.

The government takes legal advice before making the statement of compatibility and it represents the government's current view of the proposed legislation. It does, of course, take account of the strong interpretative power of the judiciary in s 3 of the Human Rights Act when forming a view about the compatibility of the legislation. This is why the government is willing to make statements in respect of proposed legislation even though it knows that there is significant controversy over its compatibility with the Convention. Ultimately, until the courts have applied the s 3 test to the legislation it is impossible to say whether it is compatible or not.

The statements that have been produced so far are not fully reasoned justifications. In fact the government does not say why the Bill is thought to be compatible with the Convention. Thus, it may be, we do not know, that the government's statement of compatibility on the Youth Justice and Criminal Evidence Bill was based partly on a view that the Convention permitted the extensive restriction on the accused's right to call evidence and so did not undermine his right to a fair trial. The actual decision of the House of Lords found that it was compatible but for different reasons – because the courts could limit the restriction on the accused's right in the interests of fairness. The point is that s 19 statements tell us very little about the purpose of the government.

The question for advocates is what use should or may be made of s 19 statements in court? The Lord Chancellor said extra-judicially that:

> ... it should be clear from the parliamentary history, and in particular from the Ministerial statement of compatibility which will be required by the Act, that Parliament did not intend to cut across a Convention right. Ministerial statements of compatibility will inevitably be a strong spur to the courts to find means of construing statutes compatibly with the Convention.[106]

This might encourage advocates to make widespread use of s 19 statements in order to encourage the court to find a compatible construction. Indeed the fact that the government intended the law to be compatible with the Convention and informed Parliament of this fact before it went about the task of

---

106 Tom Sargant Memorial Lecture, December 1997, see also Lord Irvine of Lairg LC, 'The Development of Human Rights in Britain under an Unincorporated Convention on Human Rights' [1998] PL 221 at p 228.

approving the legislation provides could fortify a court's willingness to adopt a consistent construction. Any apparent inconsistency can be put down to oversight, not intent. However, advocates need to place such statements in the right perspective:

> 69 [Counsel] for the Secretary of State did not seek to rely on this statement in the course of his argument. I consider that he was right not to do so. These statements may serve a useful purpose in Parliament. They may also be seen as part of the parliamentary history, indicating that it was not Parliament's intention to cut across a Convention right ... No doubt they are based on the best advice that is available. But they are no more than expressions of opinion by the minister. They are not binding on the court, nor do they have any persuasive authority.[107]

This supports the thrust of Lord Irvine's argument but the approval of counsel's strategy and the comment that the statements have no persuasive status is an indication that their use should be limited to a general assertion of Parliament's intention.

There is a further reason why such statements ought not to be relied on too heavily by advocates. There is no provision for re-affirmation of the statement after the parliamentary process but prior to Royal Assent. Thus alterations to the Bill during its passage might alter the government's view on compatibility but not be reflected in any official document. Major alterations to legislation during its passage are all too common and the Ministerial statement may no longer be relevant to the final version of the statute.

Issues for advocates: reliance on s 19 statements

- Statements of compatibility can probably be raised before the courts.
- They are not particularly probative beyond the government's desire to, and belief that, they are complying with the Convention rights when introducing new legislation.
- The government's view that the legislation is compatible with the Convention rights can also have regard to the duty on the courts to use the s 3 compatibility test. Thus legislation, which appears on normal reading to be incompatible, may still receive a statement.
- There is no fresh check for compatibility when the legislation has completed its parliamentary rounds culminating in the Royal Assent. Thus care should be taken to check for major changes during the passage that are unaffected by the ministerial statement.

---

107 *R v A* [2001] UKHL 25; [2001] 2 WLR 1546 at para 69.

4.5 SECTION 3 – THE EFFECT ON PRECEDENT

The operation of the Human Rights Act rule of interpretation can give rise to the potential for conflict between the Convention compliant interpretation of legislation and pre-existing authority on the meaning of statutes. This in turn begs the question of the precedent value of pre-Human Rights Act authority. This section should be read in conjunction with the material on precedent and s 2, above at para 4.2.9.

Issues for advocates: persuading courts to depart from precedent

How do advocates deal with the judge or magistrate who says, 'but wasn't this matter was resolved some years ago by the High Court/Court of Appeal/House of Lords?'. Such a situation calls for clear but diplomatic explanation of the change introduced by s 3. The following points may be utilised:

- The earlier court did not have the advantage of argument about the compatibility of the provision with the Convention right.
- The earlier court had no duty to interpret the statute compatibly with the Convention right.
- Parliament has dictated that courts will now interpret statutes differently from earlier decisions where appropriate.
- The earlier decision is not binding on the instant court in so far as a different (and Convention compliant) interpretation is possible.
- Departing from the earlier decision shows no disrespect to the higher court but is merely the implementation of Parliament's intention.
- If there is any doubt about the meaning of s 3 recourse may be had to the statements of ministers during the Bill's passage through Parliament.
- The government's White Paper made clear the intention to significantly alter the status of existing decisions on the interpretation of legislation.
- The higher courts have urged the judiciary at all levels to re-interpret legislation where necessary, ignoring earlier contrary authority as appropriate.

The last point requires elaboration. In *W and B (Children: Care Plan)*[108] the Court of Appeal was faced with a raft of authority concerning the interpretation of the court's powers under the Children Act in care proceedings which were alleged to be incompatible with the parents' and children's rights under Arts 6 and 8 of the Convention.

---

108 [2001] EWCA Civ 757; [2001] FCR 450.

The trial judge in one of the cases said as follows:

> The role of the court of first instance is to follow existing and binding authority until a higher court has reconsidered the position in light of the Human Rights legislation. Accordingly, I have no choice, as I see it, but to follow the existing authority ...

This desire for certainty ignores the explicit requirement in the Human Rights Act to interpret legislation compatibly if possible to do so. The Court of Appeal found no great difficulty in departing from these authorities to create a new framework for dealing with care orders. It did so in order to give effect to the Convention rights and referred to the duties in ss 3 and 6 in order to justify its interventionist approach.

Thorpe LJ commented as follows:

> It was only the authorities that constrained [the judge] to make the full care order. The only possible criticism of the judge is his failure himself to apply the Human Rights Act 1998. It may be that he was mindful of the fact that the power to make a declaration of incompatibility only lies at a higher level in the system. I would therefore set aside the care order and replace it with the interim care order that the judge clearly would have made had he felt free to do so.

Another example of Human Rights Act revision of decided cases came in *Offen*.[109] The Court of Appeal commented as follows regarding the potential for breaching Art 5 and Art 3 due to the imposition of automatic life sentences under the Crime (Sentences) Act 1997:

> The problem arises because of the restrictive approach, which has so far been adopted, to the interpretation of exceptional circumstances in s 2. If exceptional circumstances are construed in a manner which accords with the policy of Parliament in passing s 2, the problem disappears.[110]

It avoided this problem by re-interpreting s 2 of the 1997 Act giving 'exceptional circumstances' a much broader scope despite very recent decisions adopting a narrow interpretation of the phrase.

---

109 [2001] 2 All ER 154.
110 *Ibid*, at p 175, *per* Lord Woolf.

Issues for advocates: interpretation of legislation

- Courts will accept greater reliance on the parliamentary history of legislation. This will not, at least in theory, expand the approach in *Pepper v Hart* vis à vis the interpretation of the legislation. However, it will certainly apply to consideration of the background and policy of the legislation so as to decide whether it presents a proportionate interference with the Convention.

- The s 3 test for construing legislation goes much further than the previous canons of interpretation. Courts cannot remain wedded to the old way of reading legislation.

- The courts must first decide what the Convention requires in a case; they must then go on to interpret the legislation under the traditional approach; only if this fails to achieve a compatible construction should they resort to straining the language of the legislation (see the checklist above, para 4.3.5). The duty applies whatever the legislation – primary or secondary – and no matter when it was passed.

- The s 3 duty permits creative interpretation but does not permit the courts to make law.

- If it is necessary to do so in order to make legislation operate in a way that is compatible with Convention rights, it is permissible for the courts to read new words into legislation and even whole new procedures. This can only be to the extent that it is not inconsistent with the rest of the legislation. It is useful to ask: 'does the Act as a whole prohibit the reading in of the new meaning?' A negative response permits judicial creativity but only to the extent required in order to make the legislation comply with the Convention rights. Moreover, there are limits. Words that reverse or substantially change the meaning of provisions may be seen as unacceptable judicial legislating.

- Examples of judicial approaches to the s 3 duty are set out following para 4.3.9.

CHAPTER 5

DEALING WITH INCOMPATIBLE LEGISLATION

5.1 INTRODUCTION

Assuming that the court has attempted to reconcile the wording of the statutory provision with the Convention right and has been unable to do so, the question then arises as to what to do with the legislation as interpreted. In Human Rights Act jargon the legislation is 'irredeemably incompatible'[1] in that the s 3 tool has not enabled the court to find a compatible interpretation. The court will have come to the conclusion that it is not 'possible' to interpret the legislation compatibly. The answer to the question about what happens to the legislation depends on its status.

5.2 INCOMPATIBLE PRIMARY LEGISLATION

In respect of primary legislation, s 3(2) provides as follows:

> This section ... (b) does not affect the validity, continuing operation or enforcement of any incompatible primary legislation ...

This is why, in *Wilson v First County Trust*,[2] despite finding that the Consumer Credit Act 1974 breached the pawnbroker's right to property, the court refused to enforce the credit agreement and the debtor kept the loan monies and recovered her car.

The same rule applies to delegated legislation if '(disregarding any possibility of revocation) primary legislation prevents the removal of the incompatibility'.[3] In such a situation it is the primary legislation which is the true cause of the incompatibility; the legislation passed pursuant to it is inevitably incompatible and it is thus right that it falls into the same category. It is not possible to compel a minister to revoke the incompatible delegated legislation using the duty in s 6. The reason is that he or she has the defence of 'giving effect' to a provision of primary legislation (the Parent Act) which itself cannot be read or given effect in a compatible manner.[4] This obviously assumes that the rule making power cannot be interpreted in any way that is compatible with the Convention right in issue. In modern statutes, which tend

---

1   *Per* Lord Hobhouse in *R v DPP ex p Kebilene* [2000] 2 AC 326.
2   [2001] EWCA Civ 633; [2001] 2 WLR 42.
3   Section 3(2)(c).
4   Section 6(2).

to delegate in a relatively broad manner it would be rare that the enabling provision cannot be interpreted compatibly.

Thus, Parliament may (i) breach Convention rights itself through primary legislation or (ii) it may pass a Parent Act which delegates law making powers that can only be implemented in an incompatible manner. Both are protected from judicial interference. In a case of irredeemable incompatibility, the court is obliged to give effect to the legislation notwithstanding that it would breach the litigant's Convention rights. The Court might require some persuading of this proposition. It may be reluctant to make any order, which it knows contravenes the Convention, and, bearing in mind that it is a public authority under the Act, may be concerned about being held responsible for breaching Convention rights, particularly if it does not have the power to make a declaration of incompatibility.[5] In this context it is worthwhile recalling that, as a public authority, the court does not act unlawfully if it is only giving effect to or enforcing rules made by or under primary legislation that is itself incompatible with a Convention right.[6] In this sense the Human Rights Act clearly provides protection for parliamentary sovereignty and courts should be reminded of this where appropriate. Secondly, a court may need to be informed of the consequences if it were alleged to have breached a litigant's Convention rights. As a general rule, allegations of a breach by a court must be brought by way of appeal or by way of judicial review. It is not generally possible to issue civil proceedings against a court directly for breach of Convention rights where the court has acted in good faith.[7] Moreover, it is not possible to obtain damages at all unless, taking in to account all the circumstances of the case including any other relief or remedy granted, damages are necessary to afford the victim just satisfaction.[8]

The only domestic remedy available to someone whose Convention rights are breached by the operation of irredeemably incompatible primary legislation or inevitably incompatible secondary legislation is a declaration of incompatibility discussed at para 5.5 below.

5.3 INCOMPATIBLE DELEGATED LEGISLATION

The Act is silent as to what happens to delegated legislation found to be incompatible with a Convention right where primary legislation does not prevent the removal of the incompatibility. It is clear though that delegated legislation cannot be enforced if to do so would breach a Convention right.

---

5   Section 4(5) of the HRA 1998.
6   *Ibid*, s 6(2).
7   The exception is damages for breach of the right to liberty in Art 5(5) – see s 9(3).
8   See Chapter 6, para 6.3.

The express saving for the validity of inevitably incompatible delegated legislation implies that delegated legislation, which is not inevitably incompatible, will not be valid. The constitutional justification is that it would be *ultra vires* the Parent Act, which would be interpreted (using s 3 if necessary) as delegating only such powers as are compatible with Convention rights. Alternatively the making of the legislation by the minister or other public authority concerned would be an unlawful act under s 6 of the Human Rights Act. In any event, the court cannot enforce it as to do so would be to commit an unlawful act that is not protected by the 'Parliament made me do it' defence.[9]

There is the potential for some complication to arise over incompatible delegated legislation passed before the Human Rights Act came into force on 2 October 2000.[10] Although s 3 invalidates any new incompatible delegated legislation being made after that date it is difficult to see how it can invalidate legislation that has already been made and which was within the powers of the Parent Act at the time it was made. To achieve such a result would require mental gymnastics from the courts. They would have to rule that, from 2 October 2000, s 3 could be used to re-read the Parent Act at some earlier date when the delegated legislation was made and that on the new reading of the Parent Act the delegated legislation ought never to have been passed and can somehow be retrospectively invalidated. Although s 3 applies to legislation 'whenever enacted' such an approach would go beyond this and apply to legislation when it was enacted even though the Human Rights Act was not in force. Thankfully such complications can be jettisoned by focusing on the enforcement of the legislation rather than its validity. Even assuming that such legislation is valid, any public authority, including a court, that sought to enforce it would be committing an unlawful act under s 6 and could be challenged under s 7, by way of judicial review or by way of a collateral challenge to proceedings brought under the authority of the incompatible legislation. A range of potential remedies would be available. The administrative court could grant a quashing order in respect of the legislation or a declaration of its status. Alternatively a public authority could be prohibited from enforcing it.

5.3.1 Severance of incompatible provisions

One important issue that arises when delegated legislation is found to offend against Convention rights is the extent to which the legislation can be

---

9   See Chapter 2, para 2.4.

10   See 'The impact of the Human Rights Act 1998 upon subordinate legislation promulgated before 2 October 2000' [2000] PL 358 where the advocates' joint note for the Court of Appeal in the case of *R v Lord Chancellor ex p Lightfoot* [2000] 2 WLR 318 is reproduced.

enforced without the offending sections. Can a court simply ignore the provisions that breach the Convention and enforce the remainder of the regulation or does the whole of the provision fall to be quashed? This raises the prospect of severance.

In *DPP v Hutchinson*[11] Lord Bridge described severance as the 'blue pencil test' and ruled as follows:

> Taking the simplest case of a single legislative instrument containing a number of separate clauses of which one exceeds the law-maker's power, if the remaining clauses enact free-standing provisions ... capable of operating independently of the offending clause, there is no reason why those clauses should not be upheld and enforced ... The invalid clauses may be disregarded as unrelated to, and having no effect upon, the operation of the valid clauses ...[12]

His Lordship identified a double test of (1) textual severability, whereby the offending words may be disregarded leaving text that is still grammatical and coherent and (2) substantial severability, whereby the substance of what remains is essentially unchanged in its legislative purpose, operation and effect, albeit that there has to be some modification in the language to make it cohere. Textual severability would not always be required in order for a law to remain valid but if the court did have to modify the text in order to achieve severance this could only be done when 'the court is satisfied that it is effecting no change in the substantial purpose and effect of the impugned provision'.[13]

The textual severance test was recently applied to r 3(2) of the Crown Court Rules 1982 regarding the composition of licensing appeals in the Crown Court. This rule required that two justices from the same petty sessions area that refused the application must sit on the appeal. The judge, having ruled that such a composition would offend against the Art 6 requirement for an independent and impartial tribunal, deleted the requirement saying that such a step gave legislative effect to the objects of the Rules whilst at the same time being compliant with the Convention.[14]

Advocates should be aware of the possibility of severing non-compliant provisions in delegated legislation and proceeding to enforce the remaining regulations. This will be easier where textual severence can be effected leaving a coherent remainder. However, it may be difficult to persuade courts that substantial severance can be effected where what is left is not grammatically correct. Any modification following removal of the offending provisions might be said to effect a change in the substantial purpose and effect of the regulation.

---

11 [1990] AC 783.
12 *Ibid*, at p 804.
13 *Ibid*, at p 811
14 *Gosling v Preston Licensing Justices* (2001) unreported, 6 April, Preston Crown Court.

5.4 INCOMPATIBLE NON-STATUTORY POLICIES

If the offending rule is found not in legislation but in non-statutory administrative practice or guidance such as government circulars then s 3 does not come into play at all. Rather, the incompatible practice amounts to an unlawful act under s 6 of the Human Rights Act and cannot be enforced by the courts.

Issues for advocates: s 3 and enforceability of legislation

Whenever an issue is raised as to the compatibility of legislation the court's approach should be as follows:

- If the court is dealing with a provision of primary legislation and cannot, despite s 3, find a compatible interpretation it must give effect to the natural meaning notwithstanding the fact it results in a violation.[15]

- If it has the power to do so, it should consider a declaration of incompatibility.

- If the court is dealing with delegated legislation it should first apply the s 3 test to see if it can be interpreted compatibly.

- Failing this, it should examine the Parent Act (using s 3) and ask whether it inevitably requires the delegated legislation to be incompatible.

- If the answer is yes, then the court should enforce the delegated legislation notwithstanding the fact it results in a violation.

- Again, it should consider any power to make a declaration of incompatibility.

- If the answer is no, ie, it is possible to read the enabling power in a compatible manner, then, if it was made after 2 October 2000, the incompatible delegated legislation is *ultra vires*.

- If it was made before 2 October 2000, the incompatible delegated legislation is *intra vires* but cannot lawfully be enforced by a public authority or the court.

- If the incompatibility arises due to non-statutory procedures such as government circulars or practice directions the public authority concerned acts unlawfully in relying upon the measure concerned.

In summary, the impact of s 3 on the enforceability of rules is as follows:

- Primary legislation – court must enforce any rule that is irredeemably incompatible.

---

15   See Chapter 4, para 4.3.5 for discussion of the procedure for using s 3.

- Delegated legislation made under primary legislation that cannot be read compatibly – court must enforce any rule that is irredeemably incompatible
- Delegated legislation – court cannot enforce any rule that is irredeemably incompatible: consider severance
- Administrative practice – court cannot enforce any practice that is irredeemably incompatible

5.5 PROVIDING A REMEDY FOR INCOMPATIBLE LEGISLATION – DECLARATIONS OF INCOMPATIBILITY

We have seen that where incompatibility arises due to the clear meaning of primary legislation and the court has found, using s 3, that it is not possible to interpret the wording compatibly (that is, it is 'irredeemably incompatible'), the legislation must be enforced.

The Human Rights Act does provide a remedy of sorts in the form of a declaration of incompatibility. This section considers the implications of such a remedy for the legislation and examines how advocates ought to approach the procedure in court.

Issues for advocates: declarations of incompatibility preliminary considerations

The following basic matters should be noted at the outset:

- Only the High Court and above can grant a declaration of incompatibility.[16]
- A declaration is a discretionary remedy: the court is not obliged to grant one if it finds a statute to be incompatible.
- A declaration can be made in respect of a provision of primary legislation or subordinate legislation but, in relation to the latter, only where primary legislation prevents the removal of the incompatibility.[17]
- A declaration does not affect the validity, continuing operation or enforcement of the legislation concerned.[18]
- A declaration is not binding on the parties to the proceedings.[19]

---

16 Section 4(5).
17 Section 4(3) and (4).
18 Section 4(6)(a).
19 Section 4(6)(b).

- Notice must be given to the Crown before a declaration is made.[20]
- The Crown is entitled to be joined as a party. [21]

5.5.1 The procedure for making a declaration of incompatibility

Consideration of a declaration of incompatibility will always be the last step of the legal analysis of a statute as Lord Hutton said in *R v A*:

> The first [question] is whether the evidence would be admissible under s 41 on ordinary principles of construction. If the answer to this question is in the negative the second question is whether the exclusion of the evidence infringes the defendant's right to a fair trial ... If the answer to this question is in the affirmative the third question is whether s 41 can be construed pursuant to s 3 of the Human Rights Act 1998 in such a way that it is compatible with Art 6. If the answer to this question is in the negative it would be the duty of the House ... to consider making a declaration that s 41 is incompatible with the Convention right given by Art 6.

It is also clear that the courts will be slow to grant a declaration. They will wish to ensure that all other methods of securing compatibility have been exhausted:

> A declaration of incompatibility is a measure of last resort. It must be avoided unless it is plainly impossible to do so. If a clear limitation on Convention rights is stated in terms, such an impossibility will arise ...[22]

Under s 5(1) the Crown must be given notice where a court is considering whether to make a declaration of incompatibility. If read literally this would appear to require the court to begin its deliberations and only when it decides that it may grant a declaration, serve notice on the Crown and adjourn the proceedings. This has happened on a number of occasions,[23] but the Civil Procedure Rules do provide for notice to be given in advance of the actual hearing if there is a claim for a declaration of incompatibility in the statement of case or there is an issue for the court to decide which may lead to the court considering making a declaration.[24] In the criminal context, the House of Lords has permitted the Crown to be joined under s 5 prior to the actual hearing in order to avoid the need to adjourn where it is necessary to proceed

---

20 Section 5(1) and CPR Part 19, r 19.4A.

21 Section 5(2).

22 *R v A* [2001] UKHL 25; [2001] 2 WLR 1546, *per* Lord Steyn at para 44.

23 For example, *Wilson v First County Finance* [2001] EWCA Civ 633; [2001] 2 WLR 42; *R (on the Application of H) v Mental Health Review Tribunal North and East London Region* [2001] EWCA Civ 415; [2001] HRLR 36 and *S v Principal Reporter, sub nom S v Miller* [2001] UKHRR 514.

24 CPR Part 19 Practice Direction, para 6.1.

with expedition and where, although no party was actively seeking a declaration, it was clear that this remedy would be sought as a last resort.[25]

Issues for advocates: the giving of notice to the Crown

Guidance regarding the giving of notice was offered in *Poplar v Donoghue* in order to avoid unnecessary expense and unnecessary involvement of the Crown while at the same time ensuring that the proceedings are not unduly disrupted by the requirement to give notice at a later stage:

- The formal notice should always be given by the court because it is in the best position to assess whether there is a likelihood of a declaration being made.

- Wherever a party is seeking a declaration or thinks that a declaration may be made it should give as much informal notice as possible.

- Notice should be given to persons named in lists published under s 17 of the Crown Proceedings Act 1947.

- Copies of any informal notice should be sent to the court and to the other parties in the case.

5.5.2 Why seek a declaration?

There will be a variety of reasons for advocates seeking a declaration of incompatibility in legal proceedings. It should be recalled that the CPR require any application for a declaration of incompatibility to be made in the statement of case. Advocates should be alive to the need to apply to amend a statement of case in good time if it subsequently emerges that a direct attack will be made on the compatibility of primary legislation. At the time of writing there have been a fairly small number of decided cases where declarations have been requested, although they offer useful illustrations of the range of reasons why a request might be made.

- In *R v Secretary of State for the Home Department ex p Pearson and Others*[26] the applicants sought a declaration in judicial review proceedings. The Representation of the People Act 1983 prevented them from voting while they were detained in prison. The meaning of the Act was eminently clear so the applicants sought a declaration from the outset knowing that it was the only way that they could effectively raise their Convention rights arguments in the court.

---

25 *R v A (Joinder of Appropriate Minister)* [2001] 1 WLR 789. Whenever a party wishes the House to make, uphold or reverse a declaration it must notify the Principal Clerk by letter when it lodges the petition: House of Lords Practice Direction 1 May 2001.

26 (2001) *The Times*, 17 April.

- In *Lichniak*[27] the conduct that was challenged (a sentence of life imprisonment following a conviction for murder) followed as a matter of law due to clear statutory provisions. As in *Pearson* it was clear that the sentencing judge would have a defence under s 6(2),[28] so the challenge had to be a full frontal attack on the legislation.

- In *Re K (A Child) (Secure Accommodation Order: Right to Liberty)*[29] an application for a declaration was made against s 25 of the Children Act 1989, which had led to a secure accommodation order against the appellant. The Court of Appeal decided that the power to make such an order could be interpreted compatibly with the Convention and declined to make the declaration. It may have been that the child's legal team took the view that the legislation could not be interpreted so as to prevent the making of an order but it seems that the better approach would have been to seek initially to persuade the court that the legislation ought to be re-read in light of s 3 and only if this approach failed to make the declaration. The approach may have been affected by the mistaken view that damages would be available following a declaration (see below under consequences of a declaration).

- In *R (on the Application of H) v Mental Health Review Tribunal North and East London Region*[30] the applicant sought to challenge the decision of a Mental Health Review Tribunal refusing to order his discharge from a hospital order[31] imposed following his conviction for manslaughter. He sought first to argue that the legislative provision applied by the tribunal[32] (which appeared to breach the Convention by placing the burden of proof on the patient) could be interpreted compatibly and in the alternative that a declaration should be granted. The Secretary of State for Health[33] argued that the provision could be read compatibly by straining the natural meaning but also sought a declaration if the court disagreed. The Court of Appeal granted the declaration. Interestingly, the court made no finding about whether the applicant was unlawfully detained. The case focused on where the burden of proof should lie. Indeed Lord Phillips said that it would only rarely be the case that the Mental Health Act would constrain a Tribunal to act in breach of Art 5. There was no immediate advantage to the applicant in securing the declaration apart from the government

---

27 *R (on the Application of Lichniak) v Secretary of State for the Home Department; R v Lichniak and Another* [2001] EWHC Admin 294; [2001] All ER(D) 22 (May).

28 Section 6(2)(a) – the judge could not have acted otherwise. As we have seen, there were also jurisdictional problems in this case.

29 [2001] 2 WLR 1141.

30 [2001] EWCA Civ 415; [2001] HRLR 36.

31 It was a hospital order subject to restrictions pursuant to ss 37 and 41 of the Mental Health Act 1983.

32 Sections 72 and 73 of the Mental Health Act 1983.

33 Who was joined to the proceedings pursuant to s 5 of the Human Rights Act.

having to consider whether to change the law. The Department of Health's initial (and, we submit, correct) reaction was that it had to be 'business as usual' for Tribunals.[34] Consideration would be given though as to whether a Remedial Order was necessary under s 10 of the Human Rights Act.[34a]

- A further example of the government seeking a declaration if it failed to persuade the court of its approach towards Convention law was in *Poplar Housing v Donoghue*: 'We note that if we decided that there was a contravention of Art 8, the Department would prefer us not to interpret s 21(4) 'constructively' but instead to grant a declaration of incompatibility.'[35] The defendant in that case also sought a declaration as a last resort if her submissions as to Convention law and construction of the statute failed.

What emerges from the few cases so far decided is that the most sensible approach for victims is to examine the statute concerned carefully to see whether it can possibly be interpreted compatibly with the Convention rights. Only if it is clear that the statute cannot be interpreted so as to secure what the victim seeks should an application be made for a declaration at the outset. This will also affect the advice to be given regarding appeals from lower tribunals. If it is clear that the statute is incompatible there is little point appealing to an appellate body that itself has no power to grant a declaration. For example, if a man is convicted in the magistrates' court of gross indecency because more than two people were present, it is fairly clear that the statutory offence[36] is incompatible with the right to private life in Art 8.[37] In such circumstances there is little point in appealing to the Crown Court against conviction. Rather, the client ought to be advised to appeal by way of case stated to the High Court. Similarly, if incompatibility arises in civil proceedings, an application should be made for an appeal straight to the Court of Appeal from a district judge on the basis that it raises important points of principle rather than being heard by a circuit judge.[38] The same

---

34 Department of Health, *Guidance to Chairmen of Mental Health Review Tribunals*, 5 April 2001. The Department advised Tribunals that in most situations where it refused applications for discharge it would be able to make positive findings as to the criteria for continued detention, thereby avoiding breaching the patient's Convention rights. We understand that a draft Remedial Order has been produced but if the guidance is seen to work in practice the government may decide to do nothing about the declaration. This illustrates why in some situations it may be in the interests of the government to seek a declaration rather than to seek a reinterpretation of the legislation – in this way the government retains control.

34a See now the Mental Health Act 1983 (Remedial) Order 2001, SI 2001/3712, which came into force on 26 November 2001 and reversed the burden of proof in the Mental Health Act. This was the first Remedial Order made under s 10 of the Human Rights Act.

35 *Poplar Housing and Regeneration Community Association Ltd v Donoghue* [2001] EWCA Civ 595; [2001] 3 WLR 183, at para 73.

36 Section 13 of the Sexual Offences Act 1956.

37 *ADT v United Kingdom* [2000] 2 FLR 697.

38 CPR 52.14. This occurred in *Poplar v Donoghue*.

point applies across a range of tribunal decisions, although there is often not a choice of appeal forums. In cases where a declaration will be sought, the aggrieved party should seek a judicial review of the decision of the tribunal from the administrative court rather than pursuing the case in the appellate tribunal.

One factor for a victim deciding whether to seek a declaration of incompatibility is the power for the government to make a remedial order retrospective.[39] Thus, although the declaration itself provides no immediate remedy for the breach of Convention rights, pressure might be put on the relevant department to backdate a remedial order to enable the victim to seek a remedy in the courts.

A further reason for seeking a declaration is that it will be a highly useful document to include in any application to the European Court of Human Rights. The fact that the domestic courts themselves consider the law in question to have violated the applicant's Convention rights is bound to weigh heavily in the reasoning of the Court.

5.5.3 The exercise of the court's discretion

Section 4 provides that a court 'may' make a declaration if it finds that legislation is incompatible with a Convention right. There is clearly no obligation to do so:

> ... where despite the strong language of section 3 it is not possible to achieve a result which is compatible with the convention, the court is not required to grant a declaration and presumably in exercising its discretion as to whether to grant a declaration or not it will be influenced by the usual considerations which apply to the grant of declarations.[40]

The factors that will determine whether a declaration will be granted were explored further in *Wilson v First County Trust*[41] where the Court of Appeal did grant a declaration:

> The question, therefore, is whether, as a matter of discretion, a declaration of incompatibility should be made in the present case. In our view it is right to do so for three reasons. First, the point has been identified and fully argued at a further hearing appointed for that purpose. Second, in the circumstances that we have held that the order which a non-Convention interpretation of s 127(3) of the 1974 Act requires the court to make on this appeal would be incompatible with Convention rights, we could not lawfully make that order unless satisfied that the section cannot be read or given effect in a way which is compatible with Convention rights; and it is appropriate that that should be formally recorded by a declaration which gives legitimacy to the order. Third,

---

39 Schedule 2, s 1(1)(b).
40 *Poplar v Donoghue* [2001] EWCA Civ 595; [2001] 3 WLR 183, para 75, *per* Lord Woolf.
41 [2001] EWCA Civ 633; [2001] 2 WLR 42.

a declaration serves a legislative purpose under the 1998 Act; in that it provides a basis, under section 10(1)(a) of that Act, for a Minister of the Crown to consider whether there are compelling reasons to make amendments to the legislation by remedial order (under Schedule 2 to the Act) for the purpose of removing the incompatibility which the court has identified.[42]

This does not take us very far in predicting when a court will exercise its discretion in favour of making a declaration in that it largely re-iterates the statutory provisions. The novel idea is that the declaration gives legitimacy to an order contrary to a party's Convention rights. This is a curious statement. Surely the legitimacy for the order is the statute that cannot be read compatibly. Those seeking a declaration will attempt to use the legitimacy argument as a lever with which to persuade a court that a declaration is required, but it is submitted that there is no substance in such an approach.

Issues for advocates: urging and resisting declarations of incompatibility

Advocates ought to consider the following points in their submissions about whether a declaration ought to be made:

- Whether the victim intends to seek to persuade the government to alter the offending provision.
- The fact that the only possible way a remedy will be obtained is by way of a retrospective remedial order, which can only be made following a declaration.
- The intention of the party to make an application to the European Court of Human Rights (this is unlikely to have much influence on the domestic courts).
- Whether a declaration would achieve anything. The court will need to examine the current status of the legislation. It is highly unlikely that the court will countenance a declaration of incompatibility if the legislation under consideration has been superseded after the victim was affected but before the court considers his or her case. In such circumstances there would be no possibility of a remedial order and thus no point in granting the declaration. One difficulty will be when legislation has been replaced but the new provisions replicate the incompatible parts of the repealed statute. Can the court grant a declaration in respect of the old statute in order to bring to the government's attention the incompatible nature of the provision that replaced it? The better view is that it may not, but no doubt the judgment will make the position clear enough.
- What the intention of the government department is regarding the legislation. If, for example, fresh legislation is already proposed, this

---

42 *Ibid*, para 47.

might persuade the court that a declaration is unnecessary. The Court of Appeal declined to make a declaration in *R v Y (Sexual Offence: Complainant's Sexual History)*.[43] Rose LJ said: 'even if a declaration of incompatibility were to be made, it would not, of itself avail this or any other defendant unless, of course, the Home Secretary were to exercise his remedial powers under s 10 to amend the legislation so speedily that this defendant would benefit from such amendment.' This should not be taken as a general rule that a declaration will not be made if the government indicates that it will not do anything about it anyway. The appeal in that case was interlocutory so the matter could clearly be returned to following conviction if necessary and moreover, the government had not even been joined at that stage.

5.5.4 Drafting a declaration of incompatibility

Once a court has decided that it will make a declaration of incompatibility the question of the terms of the declaration will arise and the court will seek the guidance of the advocates as to precise terms of the order. Advocates should be ready with suggested forms of the declaration at the end of the hearing at which the matter was raised so that it may be possible to avoid an adjournment. Obviously it is helpful if the various parties can agree on the terms of the declaration.

One difficulty the court faces is that when it comes to draft the declaration it must move from the specific to the general. Throughout the case the Convention law is applied to the particular circumstances of the victim rather than in the abstract. However, the declaration must by its nature reflect the general deficiency in the law, which has led to the declaration, rather then focus on the particular facts of the case in hand.

Issues for advocates: drafting a declaration of incompatibility

Ideally an advocate should have a draft declaration in writing to be able to present to the court if it accepts that a declaration ought to be made. It is submitted that the declaration should do the following as a minimum:

(1) Identify itself as a s 4 declaration.

(2) Specify the provision(s) that are said to be incompatible.

(3) Specify the Convention right(s) that are violated.

(4) Explain why 2 is incompatible with 3.

---

43 *R v Y (Complainant's Sexual History)* [2001] EWCA Crim 4; [2001] Crim LR 389. This is the case that became *R v A* in the House of Lords.

The latter point may seem to be unnecessary given that the court will have handed down a detailed judgment. However, it should be recalled that the declaration will be used by the government in deciding what, if any, changes to make to the law and may become relevant at any subsequent appeal or application to the European Court. The government and the courts ought not to have to trawl through a number of judgments in order to ascertain why the declaration has been granted. Our view is that the need for certainty normally requires that the declaration should so far as possible be self-contained. Thus the declaration ought to provide a concise but accurate statement of the reasons for the violation.

A useful example of a declaration of incompatibility arose following the case of *R (on the Application of H) v Mental Health Review Tribunal North and East London Region*.[44] Following consultation with counsel, the Court of Appeal on 4 April 2001 granted the following declaration:

> A declaration under section 4 Human Rights Act 1998 that ss 72(1) and 73(1) Mental Health Act 1983 are incompatible with Arts 5(1) and 5(4) of the European Convention on Human Rights in that, for the Mental Health Review Tribunal to be obliged to order a patient's discharge, the burden is placed upon the patient to prove that the criteria justifying his detention in hospital for treatment no longer exists; and that Arts 5(1) and 5(4) require the Tribunal to be positively satisfied that all the criteria justifying the patient's detention in hospital for treatment continue to exist before refusing a patient's discharge.[45]

Clearly each declaration will have to be drafted in light of the particular issues that arise in each case where incompatibly is found but this example provides a useful basic model.

5.5.5 Consequences of a declaration of incompatibility

As previously stated, s 4 provides that a declaration has no effect on the validity of the legislation and is not binding on the parties to the case. In one sense then, a public authority has no difficulty when a declaration is granted as it shows that the existing law ought to be followed. It follows that the public authority has a s 6(2) defence to any existing or new actions based on a breach by the enforcement of the statute.

In *Re K*,[46] the applicant sought a declaration that s 25 of the Children Act 1989, which permitted secure accommodation orders to be made in respect of

---

44 [2001] EWCA Civ 415; [2001] HRLR 36.
45 Department of Health, *Guidance to Chairmen of Mental Health Review Tribunals*, 5 April 2001.
46 [2001] 2 WLR 1141.

young people, was incompatible with Art 5 of the Convention. Counsel attempted to persuade the Court of Appeal that if it granted the declaration, the victim was entitled to damages for deprivation of liberty under Art 5(5) of the Convention and s 8 of the Human Rights Act. Butler-Sloss LJ emphatically ruled that s 4 gave rise to no right in damages and confessed to her astonishment at counsel's proposition:

> If the argument were correct the implementation of the Human Rights Act 1998 on 2 October 2000 would have produced a constitutional earthquake ... The effect of a declaration of incompatibility is that remedial action may be taken by a Minister of the Crown to make whatever amendments to the primary legislation are thought necessary to remove the incompatibility. So, notwithstanding the declaration, the statutory provision continues in force until such time as it is amended, if indeed that ever happens. And until it does, the law, which judges must apply, includes the statutory provision, which has been declared to be incompatible.

Her Ladyship confirmed that the courts would be protected by the s 6(2) defence and went on to ponder the practical consequences if she was wrong:

> ... s 25 would continue in force. Yet the right to damages under Article 5(5) would arise every time such an order was made, while simultaneously, judges up and down the country ... would remain under a continuing obligation to apply s 25. In some court buildings, one judge would be making an award of damages to a minor who had been deprived of his liberty on the basis of a s 25 order: in the court next door, another judge would continue to make s 25 orders in relation to different children ... It would be nonsense for the local authority, or the court, properly fulfilling the duties imposed on it by an unrepealed, unamended statute simultaneously to render itself liable to an order for damages in another domestic court on the basis of this Convention right. The end result would be that the court, and the local authorities, would abdicate their statutory responsibilities and in practice dispense with or fail to apply s 25, while s 25 remained on the statute book ... The result would be, at best a constitutional mess, and at worst something of a constitutional crisis.[47]

These comments are *obiter* but they are undoubtedly correct. The remedy for a person whose rights have been breached by the operation of an incompatible statute is to seek a remedial order from the government whereby the legislation is amended to make it compatible.

In an apparent departure from this clear approach, Collins J in *R (on the Application of C) v Secretary of State for the Home Department*[47a] quashed the decision of the Home Secretary to refer a patient's case back to the Mental Health Tribunal. He did this partly on the basis that the hearing before the tribunal would violate the patient's Art 5 rights following the declaration of incompatibility in the *H* case, above. It is submitted that the Home Secretary ought to have succeeded with a defence under s 6(2) of enforcing incompatible legislation.

---

47   Paragraphs 35–42.
47a [2001] EWCA Admin 501.

5.5.6 Remedial orders

A declaration of incompatibility is one of the triggers enabling the government to amend the offending legislation by way of a remedial order.[48] The other trigger is a decision of the European Court of Human Rights in a case concerning the United Kingdom.[49] It is possible to make a remedial order without either of these triggers but that is only in relation to delegated legislation that has been quashed by a court as incompatible with a Convention right.[50]

The decision whether to make a remedial order is a matter for the discretion of the government and the decision cannot itself be challenged under the Human Rights Act.[51] The government minister can only make a remedial order if he or she considers that there are compelling reasons for making it. Presumably if there is no need for expedition in the matter it may better be dealt with by way of normal legislative techniques. The effect of a remedial order is to amend the offending legislation and may also amend other primary and delegated legislation, including those that do not contain incompatible provisions.[52] This is so that the government can ensure that the body of legislation remains coherent following a remedial order.

An important provision enables the government to make a remedial order retrospective and make different provision for different cases.[53] It follows that a declaration might be made to operate from a date before the declaration was granted. This could enable the court subsequently to award the victim just satisfaction for the breach.

The other remedy is, of course, an application to the European Court of Human Rights.[54] The declaration would be powerful evidence for the European Court that the applicant's rights were breached, although it would not be conclusive and it would still be open to the government to defend the case on the basis that the domestic courts applied the wrong test or a different test than has to be applied in Strasbourg.[55]

---

48 Section 10(1)(a).
49 Section 10(1)(b).
50 Section 10(4).
51 Section 6(6)(b).
52 Schedule 2, para 2.
53 Schedule 2, para 1.
54 It is often incorrectly stated that a person may 'appeal' to the European Court. This is not the position. The Human Rights Act and the European Convention remain separate regimes and the European Court has no direct role to play in domestic law apart from the relevance of its decisions via s 2.
55 See Chapter 3 on the non-applicability of the margin of appreciation doctrine in the domestic context.

CHAPTER 6

GIVING EFFECT TO THE HUMAN RIGHTS ACT IN JUDICIAL DECISIONS

6.1 THE COURT AS A PUBLIC AUTHORITY

The Human Rights Act explicitly denotes that courts and tribunals are themselves public authorities.[1] Important consequences flow from this.

First and most obviously, a court must itself act in a way that is compatible with Convention rights. It must respect the Convention rights of those that appear before it as parties, witnesses, defendants (and even advocates!). Thus, for example, if a court official made an unauthorised disclosure to the press of a litigant's personal information there would arguably be a violation of the right to respect for private life under Art 8. In addition, since the court is a 'pure' public authority it must act compatibly with Convention rights even in areas that would normally be viewed as private relationships such as employment and other contracts.

There are also Convention rights, which specifically engage the obligation of the courts. Article 6 provides that everyone must have a fair and public hearing within a reasonable time by an independent and impartial tribunal in the determination of any civil or criminal case. There are additional due process rights in respect of criminal defendants. Any failure by a court or tribunal to offer the fair hearing guarantees amounts to an unlawful act under s 6.[2] Note that the ability to challenge unlawful acts by courts and tribunals is circumscribed.[3]

Article 5 of the Convention also engages the court/tribunal's direct obligation when it makes decisions concerning an individual's liberty. For example, in applications for discharge by persons detained on a hospital order, the Convention requires that the tribunal order discharge unless the state can satisfy it that the patient still suffers from a mental disorder requiring detention.[4] Primary legislation prevents the tribunal from doing so.

---

1   Section 6(3)(a).

2   For example, in *Scanfuture UK Ltd v Secretary of State for Trade and Industry* [2001] IRLR 416 the Employment Appeal Tribunal held that a tribunal that had members employed by the Secretary of State for Trade and Industry was not independent and impartial when it heard cases in which the Secretary was one of the parties.

3   Section 9(1) provides that free-standing proceedings against judicial acts may only be brought by an appeal, a judicial review or such other forum as may be prescribed by rules. The CPR Rule 7.11(1) prescribes the High Court as the appropriate forum. In addition, damages may not be awarded for a judicial act done in good faith except in so far as required under Art 5(5) of the Convention (remedy for deprivation of liberty).

4   See *R (on the Application of H) v Mental Health Review Tribunal North and East London Region* [2001] EWCA Civ 415; [2001] HRLR 36.

A question of some controversy is whether the court must go beyond the obligations so far identified. Should it go beyond the duty not to breach the human rights of those that appear before it and actively protect the Convention rights of those people? There is no problem with this question when one of the parties is a public authority. The court must clearly protect the Convention rights of private individuals against public authorities and grant any remedy within its power that is just and equitable when a public authority has or will breach a person's Convention rights.

In addition, when an individual applies for any order that is within the court's power to make, the court ought to exercise its power in accordance with the applicant's Convention rights, always assuming that the order does not breach anyone else's rights or conflict with any provision of primary legislation. In *Re Crawley Road Cemetery*[5] the court held that although the applicant would not normally have displaced the presumption against exhumation of her husband's body, the court had a duty to make its order compatibly with her Convention rights and this required respect for her humanist beliefs under Art 9 (freedom of religion).

6.2   HORIZONTAL EFFECT

The more difficult issue is the extent to which the court must intervene to protect the Convention rights of a party when the other party is not a public authority. In other words, does the Human Rights Act have any horizontal effect and if so, what is the extent of that effect? It is apparent from what has been said that the Act was intended, at least primarily, to affect the conduct of public bodies. However, questions have arisen over its applicability to disputes between private litigants. The debate has focused largely on the consequences of the courts themselves being public authorities as Sedley LJ recently recognised:

> [The Human Rights Act] requires every public authority, including the courts, to act consistently with the ECHR. What this means is a subject of sharp division: does it simply require the courts' procedures to be Convention-compliant or does it require the law applied by the courts, save where primary legislation plainly says otherwise, to give effect to Convention principles?[6]

The 'sharp division' his Lordship referred to is the extensive debate in the legal journals over whether the Human Rights Act has 'horizontal' effect.[7] In summary, the possibilities seem to be as follows:

---

5   [2001] 2 WLR 1175.
6   *Douglas v Hello!* [2001] 2 WLR 992.
7   See the articles cited in Chapter 4 at 4.3.2.5.

1   Direct horizontal effect in that a private party may rely on the Convention right as a cause of action against another private party and the courts may grant remedies against private parties for breaching Convention rights.

2   Indirect horizontal effect so that the Convention rights affect private parties in so far as the court applies legislation, interprets the common law and exercises discretion.

3   Vertical effect only so that the courts will enforce Convention rights only in actions against public authorities.

Thus far the courts seem to have rejected the first and the third propositions and accepted the second. Nevertheless, the case law is at an early stage of development and there is still considerable uncertainty as to the extent of the Human Rights Act's application even within the notion of indirect horizontal effect.

6.2.1   Rejection of direct horizontal effect

In *Venables and Thompson v News Group Newspapers and Others*[8] two child murderers sought life-long injunctions preventing the press from publishing details of their identities or whereabouts following their release from custody. These were sought on the basis that their lives would be in danger if the injunction did not restrain the press. Butler-Sloss LJ added judicial weight to those who believe that the Convention does not give rise to direct horizontal effect:

> It is clear that, although operating in the public domain and fulfilling a public service, the defendant newspapers cannot sensibly be said to come within the definition of public authority in section 6(1) of the Human Rights Act. Consequently, Convention rights are not directly enforceable against the defendants, see section 7(1) and section 8 of the Human Rights Act.[9]

When considering the court's duty to apply the Convention, Her Ladyship went on:

> That obligation on the court does not seem to me to encompass the creation of a free standing cause of action based directly upon the Articles of the Convention ... The duty on the court, in my view, is to act compatibly with Convention rights in adjudicating upon existing common law causes of action, and that includes a positive as well as a negative obligation.[10]

---

8   [2001] 2 WLR 1038.
9   *Ibid*, at para 24.
10 *Ibid*, at para 28.

6.2.2 Rejecting vertical effect alone

The idea that the Convention is irrelevant when the courts are considering disputes between private parties has not been favourably received. This view is normally attributed to Buxton LJ following his extra-judicial observations[11] and he has repeated it while sitting as a judge. His approach was rejected by the Court of Appeal in *P v P (Removal of Child to New Zealand)*,[12] a case involving a disputed application to permanently remove a child from the United Kingdom:

> The Human Rights Act 1998 came into force in October last year and all the previous decisions have to be scrutinised in the light of the European Convention on Human Rights. In anticipation of the Convention ... *In Re A (Permission to Remove Child from Jurisdiction: Human Rights)* [2000] 2 FLR 225 ... the Court considered the effect of Article 8 but saw no reason to interfere with the established line of authority followed by the judge and which bound this Court. Buxton LJ doubted whether the difficult balancing exercise performed by the judge came within the purview of the Convention at all. The question whether the Convention applied to private proceedings would appear to me to have been settled by the decision of the European Court in *Glaser v The United Kingdom* [2000] 3 FCR 193.[13]

6.2.3 Accepting indirect horizontality I – satisfying positive obligations[14]

Despite the inability of claimants to bring a Human Rights Act action directly against the press, this does not mean that the Convention is irrelevant in private litigation. As the court in *Venables* made clear:

> That is not, however, the end of the matter, since the court is a public authority, see section 6(3), and must itself act in a way compatible with the Convention, see section 6(1) and have regard to European jurisprudence, see section 2 ... The decisions of the European Court ... seem to dispose of any argument that a court is not to have regard to the Convention in private law cases.

Her Ladyship was satisfied that, despite both parties being private, she had to apply the applicants' rights under Arts 2, 3 and 8 of the Convention and balance these against the newspapers' rights to freedom of expression under Art 10. She recognised that she was being asked to extend the protection that the law of confidence had hitherto granted but she was willing to do so:

---

11 See Buxton, R, 'The Human Rights Act and private law' (2000) 116 LQR 48.

12 *P v P (Removal of Child to New Zealand)* [2001] EWCA Civ 166; [2001] 2 WLR 1826, also known as *Payne v Payne*.

13 *Ibid, per* Butler-Sloss LJ at para 81.

14 For a fuller discussion of positive obligations under the Convention see Chapter 1, para 1.5.3–1.5.3.1.

I am satisfied that, taking into account the effect of the Convention on our law, the law of confidence can extend to cover the injunctions sought in this case and, therefore, the restrictions proposed are in accordance with the law. There is a well-established cause of action in the tort of breach of confidence in respect of which injunctions may be granted. The common law continues to evolve, as it has done for centuries, and it is being given considerable impetus to do so by the implementation of the Convention into our domestic law ... The issue is whether the information leading to disclosure of the claimants' identity and location comes within the confidentiality brackets. In answering that crucial question, I can properly rely upon the European case law and the duty on the court, where necessary, to take appropriate steps to safeguard the physical safety of the claimants, including the adoption of measures even in the sphere of relations of individuals and/or private organisations between themselves. Under the umbrella of confidentiality there will be information, which may require a special quality of protection. In the present case the reason for advancing that special quality is that, if the information was published, the publication would be likely to lead to grave and possibly fatal consequences. In my judgment, the court does have the jurisdiction, in exceptional cases, to extend the protection of confidentiality of information, even to impose restrictions on the Press, where not to do so would be likely to lead to serious physical injury, or to the death, of the person seeking that confidentiality, and there is no other way to protect the applicants other than by seeking relief from the court.[15]

This case seems to suggest a need to find an existing common law or equitable remedy 'peg' upon which to hang a Convention rights argument and then urge the court, by virtue of its positive obligation, to expand the protection offered by the common law.[16] This may well be true in respect of those who actively seek the protection of the court against breach of Convention rights by others. In *Douglas v Hello!*[17] the Court of Appeal had to deal with an application for an injunction against a celebrity magazine that had obtained secretly taken pictures of a Hollywood couple's wedding. The application was brought ostensibly on the basis of breach of confidence but it was clear that it was seeking to expand the notion of the remedy to cover privacy interests. Sedley LJ said as follows:

... [Counsel argues that] whatever the current state of common law and equity, we are obliged now to give some effect to Article 8 ... of the Convention ... If the step from confidentiality to privacy is not simply a modern restatement of the scope of a known protection but a legal innovation – then I would accept his submission ... that this is precisely the kind of incremental change for which the Act is designed: one which without undermining the measure of certainty which is necessary to all law gives substance and effect to s 6 ... Such

---

15 [2001] 2 WLR 1038, pp 1064–65 at paras 80–81. See also *Mills v News Group Newspapers* [2001] All ER(D) 09 (Jun) at para 27 *per* Collins J.
16 See further Chapter 2, para 2.5.2.
17 [2001] 2 WLR 992.

a process would be consonant with the jurisprudence of the European Court of Human Rights, which s 2 of the Act requires us to take into account and which has pinpointed Article 8 as a locus of the doctrine of positive obligation.[18]

The basis for this approach and that in the *Venables* case is that the court as a public authority has a duty to ensure that the common law develops so as to safeguard those rights which the state has a positive obligation to protect. The courts have for some time accepted that the Convention can be used as an aid to the construction of the common law,[19] but the approach we are considering here goes somewhat further. It accepts that the Convention may push the courts further than the normal evolution of the common law would allow. It has significant implications for the traditionally conservative approach of the courts and beckons creative thinking by advocates and judges alike.

It is tempting to go further and say that all common law rules, because they are developed by the judiciary – a public authority – must now give way to Convention law in private law disputes. However, we submit that it would be wrong to think that all common law rules are susceptible to re-reading in light of the Convention. The cases that have arisen so far under the Human Rights Act have been able to identify a positive obligation on the state to act to protect the right in question and have used the application of the common law to give effect to this protection. Even then they have done so in a careful 'incremental' manner. In the absence of a positive obligation on the state (and therefore the courts) to act, it is difficult to see the courts being amenable to large scale adjustment to common law rules.

An example of judicial reluctance in this field is *Biggin Hill Airport Ltd v Bromley LBC*.[20] In that case local residents sought to be joined to an action regarding the interpretation of a lease of an airport. They argued that if it were interpreted as permitting scheduled flights, their rights under Art 8 of the Convention would be violated. It was argued that the court, being a public authority, ought to interpret the lease so as not to permit any interference with the Convention rights. The first instance judge noted that there was no provision in the Human Rights Act affecting the interpretation of contracts and declined to develop the common law so as to create a power to interpret contracts so that they are Convention compliant:

> [Counsel] submitted that I should be prepared to interpret or develop the common law, if necessary radically, to achieve consistency with the Convention and there is indeed pre-Act authority to support this, where the common law is uncertain or ambiguous[21] ... However, the submission in this case is that, whilst it is conceded that the terms of the Convention were of no

18 *Per* Sedley LJ at paras 128–30.
19 See the approach of the Court of Appeal in *Derbyshire County Council v Times Newspapers* [1992] QB 770.
20 (2001) 98(3) LSG 42; upheld by the Court of Appeal [2001] EWCA Civ 1089.
21 *Rantzen v Mirror Group Newspapers (1986) Ltd* [1994] QB 670.

relevance to the construction of the lease at the time it was entered into at any time before 2 October 2000, now they are. To accede to this submission would go beyond the resolution of an uncertainty in the common law; it would require me to disregard a long line of House of Lords authority to the effect that a contract is to be construed in the context of the factual background at the time it was entered into ...[22]

The judge did not appear to consider whether a positive obligation might arise and whether this would affect his decision. The case was complicated by the fact that the fact that the lease was entered into years before the Human Rights Act was passed and the residents were not a party to it.

It has been argued[23] that the judiciary should use the development of the common law to provide protection to citizens in private law, rather than taking a broad view of the type of body classified as a public authority. There is some judicial support for this approach but it is yet to be fully developed.[24]

An interesting example of positive obligations being used to provide novel remedies arose in *R (on the Application of Wright) v Secretary of State of the Home Department*.[25] This was an application for judicial review of the conduct of the prison service following the death of a prisoner from an asthma attack. The court held it was arguable that there had been a breach of the positive duties under Arts 2 and 3 and that the state had a duty to hold an effective investigation into the death of persons in custody.[26] The inquest had been an inadequate inquiry and the court ordered the prison service to carry out an investigation into the death.

Issues for advocates: positive obligations and horizontality

Advocates should be ready to advance and, where appropriate, object to, arguments that positive obligations require the court to protect one party's human rights against a breach by another. Advocates should identify Strasbourg case law showing whether there is a positive obligation in the area under scrutiny or whether there is scope for developing such an obligation. One difficulty, as we have seen, is that the concept of positive obligation is not particularly well developed at Strasbourg level. Moreover,

---

22 (2001) 98(3) LSG 42, at para 172.

23 Oliver, D, 'The frontiers of the State' (2000) PL 476.

24 Burnton J in *Heather and Others v Leonard Cheshire Foundation and Another* [2001] EWHC Admin 429 [2001] All ER(D) 156 (Jun) agreed with Professor Oliver in a preliminary ruling about whether a charity was a public authority. He indicated that he would examine at the hearing itself whether the common law relating to charities could be developed so as to protect Art 8 interests. The preliminary point is being appealed to the House of Lords.

25 [2001] EWHC Admin 520; (2001) *Daily Telegraph*, 26 June.

26 See for example *Selmann v Turkey*, European Court of Human Rights, 27 June 2000 and *Keenan v United Kingdom* 10 BHRC 319; (2001) *The Times*, 18 April.

the Strasbourg Court has taken a fairly *laissez-faire* approach towards positive obligations, seeing the state's duties as primarily a matter for the domestic authorities.

It is insufficient simply to assert that a positive obligation exists. Advocates must go further and explain why the positive obligation translates into a duty on the court to grant the remedy sought. For example, there is clearly a positive obligation on the state to prevent harassment which impinges on the victim's private and family life.[27] However, this does not mean that an injunction must be granted against the defendant even if there is good evidence of harassment. Issues such as the nature and seriousness of the breach, other potential remedies, the conflicting rights of the defendant and the conduct of the claimant will all be relevant in the exercise of the court's discretion and the court will still apply the balance of convenience test when deciding if an injunction is appropriate.

6.2.4 Accepting indirect horizontality II – court orders

If, rather than actively seeking the protection of the court, the individual is seeking to prevent the court making an order which will itself interfere with his or her Convention rights, it seems that the court does not need to find any positive obligation before applying Convention law. This is because the breach, if there is one, arises due to the order of the court (a public authority) not the conduct of another private individual. Thus such a situation, properly analysed, engages the direct vertical effect of the Human Rights Act albeit that it will clearly have an impact on the enforcement of rights in private litigation. If a court does make an order that breaches a Convention right then the aggrieved party may challenge the order on appeal or judicial review.[28]

Looked at another way, the court has a duty under s 6 to act compatibly with Convention rights and this includes making sure that, so far as possible, any order or other remedy is granted or refused in a way that is compatible with the Convention rights of the litigants appearing before it. This is sometimes referred to as 'remedial horizontality'.[29]

For example, where there is a dispute between estranged parents over the care of their child, the court may be asked to make orders which will impact on Convention rights and will have to ensure that the order made properly takes into account the rights which are affected by it. In *P v P*[30] the Court of Appeal dealt with an application by a mother to take the child permanently

---

27 See *Whiteside v United Kingdom* (1994) 76A DR 80.
28 Section 9(1).
29 See Clayton, at para 5.82.
30 *P v P (Removal of Child to New Zealand)* [2001] EWCA Civ 166; [2001] 2 WLR 1826.

out of the jurisdiction to New Zealand. Butler-Sloss LJ reiterated the view that the Convention was relevant in actions between private parties and went on:

> All those immediately affected by the proceedings, that is to say, the mother, the father and the child have rights under Article 8(1). Those rights inevitably in a case such as the present appeal are in conflict and, under Article 8(2), have to be balanced against the rights of the others ... Article 8(2) recognises that a public authority, in this case the court, may interfere with the right to family life where it does so in accordance with the law, and where it is necessary in a democratic society for, *inter alia*, the protection of the rights and freedoms of others and the decision is proportionate to the need demonstrated.[31]

In cases such as this, although no public authority is a party to the proceedings and where the court is not being asked to protect one party's Convention rights from breach by another under its positive obligation, the order must still conform with the Convention rights of those involved. This is because the court is being asked to make an order, which interferes with the family life of one of the parties. As a public authority it can only make such an order if the interference with the rights is justified under Art 8(2). Obviously the interests of one party might be used as part of this justification, but there is no question of such rights being irrelevant to the decision of the court.

Other examples include awards in defamation proceedings,[32] housing possession decisions,[33] orders in probate disputes[34] and the grant of search orders.[35] An interesting application of the latter example occurred in *St Merryn Meat Ltd and Others v Hawkins*.[36] The High Court discharged two freezing and search orders obtained *ex parte* by the claimant. The sole basis for the discharge was material non-disclosure in the application in that the claimant concealed the fact that it had intercepted the defendant's home telephone calls in order to gather evidence against him. Geoffrey Voss QC analysed the position as follows:

> The applications in this case were made after the Human Rights Act 1998 had come into force. It seems to me that the court considering an interim application would have wanted to be satisfied that any order it made did not involve a breach of Article 8. But that is not the allegation here. Here it is suggested that, because the evidence for the application had been obtained by a method, which infringed Article 8(1), the court should have been informed. I have formed the view that the method of obtaining this evidence was relevant

---

31 [2001] EWCA Civ 166; [2001] 2 WLR 1826, at para 82.

32 *Tolstoy Miloslavsky v United Kingdom* (1995) 20 EHRR 442.

33 *Scollo v Italy* (1996) 22 EHRR 514. See also *Mayor and Burgesses of the London Borough of Lambeth v Howard* [2001] EWCA Civ 468, where although the landlord was a public authority there was no indication that the need for proportionality was limited to such cases.

34 *Inze v Austria* (1986) 8 EHRR 498.

35 *Chappell v United Kingdom* (1990) 12 EHRR 1.

36 (2001) *Daily Telegraph*, 10 July.

to the courts' decisions with or without overt unlawfulness. That fact that a right under Article 8 *had been* violated made this disclosure all the more important ... Accordingly, it seems to me that, looked at strictly, the question of the enforceability of Article 8 rights between private citizens is not in issue. What was in issue is whether there was a breach of Article 8 and whether the court would have wanted to be informed of the circumstances giving rise to that breach. I have held that the interception of Mr Hawkins' telephone did infringe Article 8(1), even though it was not undertaken by a public authority, and that the court should have been informed of the facts, which amounted to that breach, namely the manner in which the claimants' evidence had been obtained.[37]

The approach adopted here is that a private individual can indeed violate Convention rights and, although there is no remedial mechanism in the Human Rights Act for such a violation, it can have an impact on the view the court takes of the parties' conduct and on the discretion it exercises when making orders.

Issues for advocates: court orders

Advocates resisting court orders should be ready, where appropriate, to identify the elements of the proposed order which interfere with the Convention right of the client and focus the mind of the court on the importance of the right and whether the grounds for making the order justify the interference. The court should be asked to apply structured decision-making to ensure that the order is not made unless the court is satisfied that the grounds for making it show that it is a proportionate response to a pressing social need. For example, whenever an injunction is sought against a journalist, the advocate should emphasise the particular importance of freedom of the press, the existence of remedies short of an injunction, whether the grounds relied on amount to an Art 10(2) reason, whether the proposed terms are too wide to make the order proportionate, etc.[38]

---

37 *Ibid*, at paras 88–89 of the judgment.

38 See *Ashdown v Telegraph Group Ltd* [2001] EWCA Civ 1142; (2001) *The Times*, 1 August at paras 45–46 (freedom of expression could be protected by the court's refusal to grant the discretionary remedy of an injunction in an action for breach of copyright). The newspaper defendants in the *Venables* case made similar types of submission. Although they were unsuccessful, the court was at pains to point out the unique nature of the circumstances in that case and addressed at length the proportionality of the interference.

6.2.5 Accepting indirect horizontality III – interpreting and enforcing legislation

As has been seen, all legislation must be interpreted and given effect in a way that is compatible with Convention rights, if possible. Courts must also exercise statutory discretions in a way that is compatible with Convention rights. This is not limited to cases where one of the parties is a public authority. Indeed it would be untenable to have different interpretations of the same statute depending on who is a party to the dispute. Thus if a statutory provision is sought to be relied upon by a party either as part of a claim or as part of a defence, it must be interpreted, so far as it is possible to do so, to comply with the Convention rights.

An example is the approach of Lord Cooke in *Turkington v Times Newspapers*[39] where he would have been willing to interpret the Defamation Act 1952 as protecting the newspaper's reporting of a press release had it not been for the common law providing adequate protection in any event. This was an action by a firm of solicitors against a newspaper but there was no question of Convention rights being irrelevant to the decision the court had to make.

The best example so far of the Convention impact on statutes in the private sphere is in *Wilson v First County Trust*.[40] The case illustrates that the duty to interpret statutes compatibly with the Convention rights clearly extends to disputes between private individuals. The case was a financial dispute between a pawnbroker and its debtor. The court strived to interpret the Consumer Credit Act 1974 compatibly with the property rights of the pawnbroker and when it could not do so, it granted a declaration of incompatibility. However, it is important to recognise that the Court of Appeal in that case ruled that the court itself pursuant to the Consumer Credit Act was depriving the creditor of its property by failing to enforce the credit agreement. In *Family Housing Association v Donellan*[41] the High Court refused to accept that the right to protection of property in Art 1 of Protocol 1 was applicable to assess the lawfulness of the adverse possession limitation period in private property disputes. The article was directed at deprivation or control of property by the state or at its direction for public purposes, not the operation of the law in disputes of a private character. The 12 year limitation period, in the court's view, plainly gave the owner of the title a reasonable opportunity to seek possession.

Another good example of statutory provisions being interpreted in light of Convention rights in litigation between private parties is *Cachia v Faluyi*,[42]

---

39 [2000] 4 All ER 913.
40 *Wilson v First County Trust Ltd (No 2)* [2001] EWCA Civ 633; [2001] 2 WLR 42.
41 [2001] All ER(D) 156 (Jul).
42 [2001] EWCA Civ 998; [2001] All ER(D) 299 (Jun). See also Chapter 4, para 4.3.9.

where the Court of Appeal read down the limitation in s 2(3) of the Fatal Accidents Act 1976 so as to permit a second writ to be issued and served on behalf of dependent children of a road traffic accident victim despite the fact that an earlier writ had been issued and never served. To order otherwise would have been to undermine the children's right of access to a court. The Court noted that the Human Rights Act enabled it to provide a remedy in a case where previously it would have been unable to prevent the injustice arising from the natural reading of the statute. It is acknowledged that the risk of a breach of the Convention arose not because of the conduct of the defendant driver but because of the restrictive operation of the limitation provisions in the 1976 Act. Nevertheless, it clearly affected the position of the defendant in that without the Convention argument no claim could have been brought.

6.3 JUDICIAL REMEDIES UNDER THE HUMAN RIGHTS ACT

Chapter 2 outlined the powers of the courts under the Human Rights Act to provide a remedy for breach of Convention rights. Here we explore the remedial framework in more detail. We will not survey the approach of the European Court towards the concept of just satisfaction[43] but rather examine how the powers of the courts under the Human Rights Act fit into the existing legal processes.

Following a finding of actual or anticipated violation of Convention rights the remedies that can be awarded can be summarised as follows:

- Any remedy that is within the powers of the court or tribunal hearing the case.
- This includes damages, although the power to award damages is qualified.
- A declaration of incompatibility. This is only available if the High Court or above is hearing the case and the violation is caused by irredeemably incompatible primary legislation.[44]

The court must, in addition, consider that the remedy is 'just and appropriate'. The phrase is not defined but it clearly establishes that the power under s 8 is discretionary. It enables a court to agree that a Convention right has or would be violated but nonetheless to grant no remedy. The court will probably also consider the state's obligations under Art 13 to provide an effective domestic remedy. We say 'probably' because Art 13 is not included as one of the Convention rights in the Human Rights Act. Nevertheless the requirement to

---

43   See Chapter 1, para 1.5.11 for a summary of these principles.
44   See Chapter 5.

take into account Convention jurisprudence under s 2 of the Act will permit the courts to consider Art 13 decisions.[45] Even so, this will not always lead to the courts being able to fashion a remedy.[46]

6.3.1 The remedy must be within the powers of the court or tribunal

Section 8(1) of the Act provides as follows:

> 8(1) In relation to any act (or proposed act) of a public authority, which the court finds is (or would be) unlawful, it may grant such relief or remedy, or make such order, within its powers as it considers just and appropriate.

This is not intended to add to the existing powers of courts and tribunals. Rather, it permits those powers to be used in new ways in order to protect against and to compensate for breaches of Convention rights. It would be a mistake to think that section does not make much difference to previous practice. So long as the court possesses a power s 8 may lead to it being exercised in novel ways, challenging long-held approaches towards the appropriate use of remedies.

For example, in *Marcic v Thames Water Utilities Ltd (No 2)*[47] the High Court, having found a breach of the claimant's Convention rights due the intermittent flooding of his property by the defendant, went on to consider the appropriate remedy. It found that it was permissible to award substantial damages in lieu of an injunction which extended the previous approach.[48] Secondly, and more significantly, the judge departed from the common law approach, which would not have permitted damages for the future loss suffered by the claimant. He said:

> [Counsel] further submitted that I should follow the common law in not awarding damages for future wrongs. In my judgment, I should not do so. The common law would not afford the claimant just satisfaction. He would have to bring onerous proceedings from time to time to enforce his rights. Nor would he be able to recover any diminution in the value of his property caused by the prospect of future wrongs.[49]

He went on to decide that damages should cover the difference in the value of the property as it was, which included the prospect of future flooding, as

---

45 'The courts must take account of the large body of Convention jurisprudence when considering remedies ... they are bound to take judicial notice of Article 13, without being specifically bound by it.' Jack Straw, Home Secretary, *Hansard*, HC col 981 (20 May 1998).

46 See Chapter 2, para 2.8.2.

47 [2001] All ER(D) 111 (Jul) Technology and Construction Court.

48 *Shelfer v City of London Electric Lighting Co* [1895] 1 Ch 287.

49 [2001] All ER(D) 111 (Jul) Technology and Construction Court, *per* HHJ Richard Havery QC at para 17.

compared with what it would be if the defendant completed the works to remedy the continuing breach. This novel use of damages clearly breaks new ground and the court recognised this but justified it as providing just satisfaction under the Human Rights Act.

In *W and B (Children: Care Plan)*[50] the Court of Appeal used the Human Rights Act to radically expand on the remedies available under the Children Act 1989 so as to safeguard against breaches of Art 8 in care proceedings. In addition to the new procedures the Court recognised that children and their families might need to be able bring proceedings to prevent breaches of their Convention rights and/or seek damages. The proposed solution was for the aggrieved party to bring proceedings under s 7(1)(a) of the Human Rights Act in the court that made the original care order (unless it was a family proceedings court, as that court had insufficient powers). Hale LJ said as follows:

> For my part, I would not require a separate claim to be made under the CPR and then consolidated with the Children Act application. I see no need to read the words 'in the proceedings' after the words 'within its powers' in section 8(1) of the 1998 Act. County courts must now be able to exercise their powers to grant injunctions to prevent a local authority acting unlawfully under the 1998 Act even in a care case.

Thus, because county court judges have the power to award injunctions in their general jurisdiction, s 8 enables them to exercise such a power in care proceedings. The courts are in effect able to 'borrow' powers from other parts of their jurisdiction to protect human rights even though such powers would not normally be exercisable in the case before them. So long as they otherwise possess the power it does not matter that it is not normally exercisable in the proceedings with which they are concerned.

If this is right it has significant implications for courts and tribunals of limited jurisdiction. They may be able to provide a remedy beyond that provided for by the legislation, which gives them jurisdiction over the case. For example, an employment tribunal has a statutory power to make an award of compensation for unfair dismissal but only if it finds that the grounds of the complaint are well founded.[51] What if the tribunal finds that the employer breached the employees Convention rights but that the dismissal itself was not unfair? On the face of it there is no power to provide any remedy for the breach of the Convention right, as the statutory complaint will have failed and the tribunal has no general jurisdiction to award compensation. Nevertheless, given that it does in some circumstances have a power to award compensation, albeit not in the proceedings that it has just determined, can it use s 8 to compensate for the breach of the Convention?

---

50 [2001] EWCA Civ 757; [2001] FCR 450.
51 Section 112(1) of the Employment Rights Act 1996.

The approach in *W and B (Children)* would suggest that it would. It might also enable it in other cases to make awards of compensation above the statutory maximum for the procedure in question.

The government has the power to add to the relief or remedies which tribunals can grant and the grounds upon which they may be granted in order to ensure that appropriate remedies can be provided. Nevertheless, it is clear that there will be situations where a tribunal does not possess a power to remedy a breach of the Convention. For example, a Mental Health Review Tribunal cannot, under the Mental Health Act, order the transfer of a restricted patient even if the refusal of the Home Office to consent to transfer amounts to a breach of the patient's Convention rights. Similarly, a Crown Court has no power to award compensation for any breach that it may find by the police or the Crown Prosecution Service. The best that an advocate representing the victim can do in such circumstances is to persuade the court or tribunal to state in its reasons that there is an unremedied breach. Separate proceedings will then need to be issued in the appropriate court to seek the remedy and reliance might be placed on the earlier finding.

6.3.2 Damages

Section 8(2) of the Act provides as follows:

> 8(2) But damages may be awarded only by a court which has power to award damages, or to order the payment of compensation, in civil proceedings.

The basic test for the ability to award damages is that the court or tribunal must have the power to award damages or compensation in civil proceedings. This extends the previous position in that numerous bodies have the power to award compensation but this would not normally be described as the ability to award damages. Thus the Employment Tribunal, the Land Tribunal and the Criminal Injuries Compensation Appeals Panel all have powers to award compensation in their respective fields. Section 8 thus gives them an additional power to make discrete awards of damages for breach of Convention rights and may enable them to make overall awards that are greater than the maximum that they would normally be permitted to award.

Advocates should check the powers of a court or tribunal before making representations about damages. If the body has no power to award compensation then, no matter how grave the breach, it will not be able to award damages. Compensation is not defined but it is clear that it contemplates an award for loss suffered. Thus tribunals that only have the power to decide over disputed financial assessments by the authorities and have no powers to compensate parties for consequent loss are not able to award damages. Examples include the Social Security and Child Support Commissioners, Special Commissioners of Income Tax and the VAT and Duties Tribunals.

6.3.2.1 Limitation for judicial acts

The power to award damages against a judicial act is limited, in the case of acts done in good faith, to compensation to the extent required by Art 5(5) of the Convention, that is, to compensate for breach by a court or tribunal of the right to liberty.[52] A judicial act is defined as a judicial act of a court or tribunal and includes an act done on the instructions of or on behalf of a judge, which includes tribunal members, magistrates and clerks or other officers entitled to exercise the jurisdiction of a court. Despite the wide definition of judge, the concept of judicial act does not extend to purely administrative matters such as the processing of information and the sending of correspondence.

6.3.2.2 Assessing whether to award damages

Section 8(3) provides as follows:

8(3) No award of damages is to be made unless, taking into account all of the circumstances of the case, including –

(a) any other relief or remedy granted, or order made, in relation to the act in question (by that or any other court); and

(b) the consequences of any decision (of that or of any other court) in respect of that act,

the court is satisfied that the award is necessary to afford just satisfaction to the person in whose favour it is made.

This provision is intended to ensure that a victim does not receive damages unless the violation has not been adequately remedied by previous orders and the consequences of these. The following examples illustrate the types of situation where this provision might be relevant:

- If a county court judge excludes evidence obtained in breach of Art 8 he or she may decide that the victim has received just satisfaction by the protection which the order gives and decline to grant any damages.

- If a breach of Convention rights removes the lawful authority that a public authority would otherwise have for tortious conduct then damages will be awarded for the tort in line with normal damages principles. Obviously this award of damages will have a major bearing on whether further damages are necessary to afford just satisfaction.

- If a prosecution was stayed on the ground that Convention breaches made it an abuse of process, a civil court that subsequently hears a claim for damages by the accused will take account of the effect of the criminal court decision in deciding whether it is still necessary to award damages as just satisfaction.

---

52 Section 9(3).

- If a previous litigant was awarded damages for future breaches of Convention rights by the defendant, a court will take account of this when deciding whether damages are appropriate. In *Marcic (No 2)*, above, the court illustrated one possible use of the provision:

  > [Counsel] submitted that ... in the event of an award of damages to the claimant, the defendant would be under a continuing liability to pay damages to every successive occupier of the claimant's property until the crack of doom. Such damages would be in respect of the same loss and damage as that suffered by the claimant. I reject that submission ... as regards all occupiers, if a person chooses to go into occupation of a property known to be subject to flooding, I do not think that failure to alleviate the flooding could be regarded as an infringement of his human rights. Moreover ... section 8(3) of the Human Rights Act 1998 covers the situation.[53]

- If a public authority has undertaken to reconsider a decision or review a policy in light of a finding that there has been a breach of a Convention right then this will be a consequence that the court will have regard to in deciding if the victim still requires damages.

It seems that there is a fine distinction between situations where a court will find that there is a breach of Convention rights that has been adequately remedied by an earlier decision and situations where the earlier decision means that there is no breach of Convention rights at all. In *Re Medicaments and Related Classes of Goods (No 4)*[54] the Court of Appeal rejected an application for costs against the Lord Chancellor. The application arose out of a successful appeal against the refusal of the Restrictive Practices Court to rescue itself on the ground of apparent bias.[55] This meant that the proceedings had to be commenced again and the applicants estimated that they had wasted over £1 m as a consequence. They sought these costs from the Lord Chancellor as the emanation of the state responsible for providing impartial tribunals. The Court of Appeal took the view that its earlier decision to order a fresh hearing remedied the first instance decision. Moreover, it was trite Convention law that an appeal court could remedy defects in first instance decisions if the appeal was by way of full rehearing or otherwise involved a careful review of the merits. This meant that there had in fact been no breach of Art 6 at all in that the right to a fair hearing cannot be looked at in isolation but across the whole of the proceedings, including the appeal court.

---

53 [2001] All ER(D) 111 (Jul) Technology and Construction Court, at para 12.
54 [2001] EWCA Civ 1217; (2001) *The Times*, 7 August.
55 *Re Medicaments and Related Classes of Goods (No 2)* [2001] 1 WLR 700.

6.3.2.3   Assessing the level of damages

Section 8(4) provides as follows:

> (4) In determining –
>
>   (a) whether to award damages; or
>
>   (b) the amount of an award,
>
>   the court must take into account the principles applied by the European Court of Human Rights in relation to the award of compensation under Article 41 of the Convention.

This makes clear that Art 41 is relevant not only to the level of damages to award but also whether to make an award at all. As we saw in Chapter 1, the European Court often decides that a finding of a violation itself affords the victim just satisfaction. In international law at least the victim has the satisfaction of knowing that the state is obliged to bring its law or practice into compliance with the ruling. For domestic victims, victories resulting in nil awards will seem hollow indeed as unless there has been an order or undertaking as regards the conduct of the public authority there will be no expectation of future change.

Article 41 (formerly Art 50) provides:

> If the Court finds that there has been a violation of the Convention ... and if the internal law of the High Contracting Party allows only partial reparation to be made, the Court shall, if necessary, afford just satisfaction to the injured party.

This is a similar provision to s 2. The domestic courts are thus not bound by the decisions of the Strasbourg Court but advocates are clearly permitted to rely upon it and domestic courts can be expected to follow any clear and constant jurisprudence of that Court. Obviously Art 41 cannot be followed without adjustment as the European Court only grants compensation to the extent that the law of the member states do not provide full reparation for violations. The main difficulty for advocates will be in discerning any clear and constant approach in respect of Art 41.[56]

6.4   COSTS OF HUMAN RIGHTS LITIGATION

The normal rule is that costs follow the event so that the losing party has to pay his or her own costs and the costs of the successful party(ies). There are a number of potential complications in respect of human rights cases.

---

56 A loose-leaf practitioners' text, *Human Rights Damages*, is published by Sweet & Maxwell, 2001. There is also an extensive Law Commission Report, Damages under the Human Rights Act 1998, LC 266, October 2000, available at www.lawcom.gov.uk.

6.4.1   Costs as a disincentive to asserting rights

It is clearly in the public interest that real disputes about Convention rights are litigated in a competent and timely fashion. However, embarking on human rights litigation is a somewhat uncertain task, particularly in the early development of the law. If unsuccessful litigants face the risk of extensive cost orders they will clearly be less likely to press ahead with challenges based on the Convention. This is, of course, the case with any recourse to the courts but given the constitutional importance of Convention rights and the fact that defendants are generally state bodies, the courts might decide that the normal rules regarding costs should be relaxed so as not to discourage reliance on such rights.

Some support for this view comes from the Privy Council in *Gilbert Ahnee v DPP*[57] where, upon dismissing the appeal, Lord Steyn said as follows:

> Given that the real substance of the appeal concerned important matters of constitutional law, and that *bona fide resort to rights under the Constitution ought not to be discouraged*, their Lordships make no order as to costs. (His Lordship's emphasis.)

6.4.2   Costs following a declaration of incompatibility

If a declaration of incompatibility is granted it does not affect the validity, continuing operation or enforcement of the provision in respect of which it is given and neither is it binding on the parties to the proceedings.[58] Thus the normal result of the case is that the public authority will succeed because of its conduct is saved by s 6(2) of the Act, being authorised by an irredeemably incompatible piece of legislation. The individual will be in the unusual position of being the victim of a breach of his or her Convention rights but also the loser of the litigation. If costs are awarded against such a person there would seem to be little point in applying for the remedy and an important part of the Human Rights Act mechanism might not be used.

The better view is that costs should follow the declaration, at least in so far as the proceedings for the declaration itself are concerned. Such proceedings will sometimes be separate from the actual decision on liability but sometimes both issues will be tried and decided together, in which case it will be much more difficult to dissect the costs of the primary issue from the costs of the declaration application.

If this is right and a party is successful in obtaining a declaration, then the other party(ies) would be responsible for paying his or her costs. This could potentially include the Crown if it had been joined as a party, although we

---

57   [1999] 2 AC 294.
58   Section 4(6). As to declarations of incompatibility in general, see Chapter 5.

believe that the Crown ought to be dealt with separately and normally bear only its own costs. In *Wilson v First County Trust*,[59] the defendant was successful in obtaining a declaration of incompatibility but was still ordered to pay the applicant's costs. One important factor in that case was that neither of the principal parties were public authorities, although the Crown was joined as a party pursuant to s 5 of the Act. There was no explanation why no order was made against the Crown. Conversely, in *R (on the Application of H) v Mental Health Review Tribunal North and East London Region*[60] the Court of Appeal granted a declaration of incompatibility to a restricted patient and also granted him his costs. However, an important feature is that this was not a case where the declaration was a by-product of an unsuccessful appeal. The patient was successful in his appeal, which was solely about whether the law was compatible with the Convention and whether a declaration was necessary.

6.4.3 Costs following a failed application for a declaration of incompatibility

Subject to what was said above about the public interest of bringing claims under the Human Rights Act, the failed applicant can expect to be faced with an order for costs in respect of the public authority. However, what of the costs of the Crown if it was joined under s 5 of the Act and represented at the application? On one view its costs should be paid by the unsuccessful party as it was formally joined as a party to the action. However, the better view is that it should bear its own costs. First, it joins the litigation only at its own request. The requirement on the court is only to give notice to the Crown. If, and only if, it gives notice that it wishes to be joined does it play any part in the proceedings? Secondly, it may not always be right to describe the refusal by the court of a declaration as a success for the Crown. It may be that the Crown would be actively seeking a declaration or it may be neutral on the issue. The point is that the involvement of the Crown is designed to ensure input from the government responsible which would be responsible for dealing with a declaration should it be granted. It is not right to describe the Crown as the opponent of any of the parties and it is inappropriate for it to seek its costs from any of them.

---

59 [2001] EWCA Civ 633; [2001] 2 WLR 42.
60 [2001] EWCA Civ 415; [2001] HRLR 36.

CHAPTER 7

THE HRA AND CRIMINAL ADVOCACY

7.1 INTRODUCTION

Criminal law has traditionally been the subject of the highest number of applications from the United Kingdom to Strasbourg. The early application of the Convention rights in Scotland, in the context of the devolved powers of the Scottish Ministers under the Scotland Act 1998,[1] again indicated that challenges to the criminal justice system were likely to predominate in domestic law. It comes as no surprise to find that this has been borne out in English law, although the fact that the initial trickle of successful applications for declarations of incompatibility have come from other areas of legal practice will be treated by some as evidence of the fundamental fairness of the English criminal justice system, and by others as the indication of the conservative approach taken by domestic courts.

This chapter considers the implications of the Human Rights Act for criminal litigation, focusing on the initial issue of what will amount to a criminal matter for Strasbourg purposes, and then considering pre-trial issues, such as arrest, legal aid, bail and disclosure.

In the following chapter, we consider some the implications of the Human Rights Act for advocates raising arguments on points of evidence, as well as considering issues arising from the criminal trial process, from sentencing and in relation to appeals.

7.1.1 A question of finding the balance?

The difficulty that advocates will encounter, in seeking to persuade the court to expose the criminal law to the full scrutiny of human rights principles, is indicated most powerfully by the Privy Council's decision in *Brown v Stott*,[2] and in particularly in the comment of Lord Bingham:

> The jurisprudence of the European Court very clearly establishes that while the overall fairness of a criminal trial cannot be compromised, the constituent rights comprised, whether expressly or implicitly, within Article 6 are not themselves absolute. Limited qualification of these rights is acceptable if reasonably directed by national authorities towards a clear and proper public objective and if representing no greater qualification than the situation calls

---

1   See ss 29 and 57.
2   [2001] 2 WLR 817.

for. The general language of the Convention could have led to the formulation of hard-edged and inflexible statements of principle from which no departure could be sanctioned whatever the background or the circumstances. But this approach has been consistently eschewed by the court throughout its history. The case law shows that the court has paid very close attention to the facts of particular cases coming before it, giving effect to factual differences and recognising differences of degree. *Ex facto oritur jus*. The court has also recognised the need for a fair balance between the general interest of the community and the personal rights of the individual, the search for which balance has been described as inherent in the whole of the Convention ...[3]

The difficulty for advocates is the lack of specificity. To what extent can any interference be limited if it seems to go to the heart of the right to a fair trial? This was arguably the case in *Brown*, where the court was ruling that compelled answers to police questions were admissible in evidence, at least in a road traffic context. If the issue is merely one of finding a proper balance between social interests and the rights of the individual, then in each case it will be open for prosecuting advocates to argue that a provision that restricts an Art 6 right is nonetheless permissible as the 'overall' right to a fair trial is preserved, since the balance between society's rights and the individual's is appropriate. If this is the case, a great deal of time is likely to be spent in the appellate courts arguing about how far the interference has gone, and where the balance has been struck.[4]

However, we would argue that this approach does not sit happily with the approach taken by the European Court of Human Rights. Thus, in *Heaney v Ireland*,[5] a Strasbourg decision which unfortunately arose shortly after the Privy Council decision in *Brown*, the Strasbourg Court had to consider s 52 of the Offences Against the State Act 1939, an Irish law that provided that suspects committed a criminal offence where they failed to account for their own movements, and to provide information regarding the commission of certain specified offences. Heaney and others were questioned in Ireland following the bombing of a checkpoint. They refused to answer questions, and although they were eventually acquitted of the substantive offence of IRA membership, they were convicted of the summary offence of failing to answer questions under s 52. Notwithstanding the strong argument that there could have been no breach of Art 6, since the defendants had been acquitted of the substantive charge, the Strasbourg Court held that the reality of the situation and the importance of safeguarding the rights of the individual required a more critical stance:

---

3   [2001] 2 WLR 817, p 836B.

4   Indeed exactly this type of argument as to the extent of the interference, and its proportionality, seems to have occurred in the House of Lords in *Lambert* [2001] UKHL 37; [2001] All ER(D) 69 (Jul). The decision in *Lambert* is discussed in the following chapter in relation to 'reverse onus' provisions.

5   Judgment of 21 December 2000 [2001] Crim LR 481. To similar effect see also *Quinn v Ireland*, judgment of the same date.

Accordingly, the court finds that the 'degree of compulsion', imposed on the applicants by the application of s 52 of the 1939 Act with a view to compelling them to provide information relating to charges against them under that Act, in effect, destroyed the very essence of their privilege against self-incrimination and their right to remain silent.

...

The court, accordingly, finds that the security and public order concerns of the government cannot justify a provision, which extinguishes the very essence of the applicants' rights to silence and against self-incrimination guaranteed by Article 6 s 1 of the Convention.[6]

The court accordingly found a breach of both Art 6(1) and Art 6(2) – the presumption of innocence.[7]

There is undoubtedly therefore a tension between the more 'pragmatic' approach, which appears to be being adopted by the domestic courts, where the issue is the 'balance' between the competing rights of the defendant and of society, and the focus of Strasbourg on the protection of the rights of the individual. This apparent underlying conflict between the two approaches will inevitably make it difficult for all advocates in domestic courts to be confident that existing Strasbourg cases will be followed in a domestic context. Equally it suggests that an adverse decision in the domestic courts should not be taken to indicate that an application to Strasbourg would be unsuccessful.

7.1.2 Criminal trials and the range of Convention rights

There is a danger in assuming that Art 6 (the right to a fair trial) will be the key focus of attention for advocates in the context of criminal applications. As will be seen in this chapter, criminal advocacy is likely to require consideration of the whole range of Convention rights.

Article 3 (the right to freedom from torture, inhuman and degrading treatment) has been held applicable in the context of sentencing law; it will also be of relevance in the context of applications to exclude evidence obtained in breach of the provision.

Article 5 (the right to freedom of the person) is of primary relevance in the context of pre-trial detention – from stop and search, to bail and custody time limits – but will also potential apply in arguments that the imposition of a given sentence amounts to an arbitrary deprivation of liberty (see below the discussion of the application of these arguments in R v Offen[8] and Lichniak[9]).

---

6 [2001] Crim LR 481, paras 55 and 58.

7 For a further discussion of the *Heaney* judgment, see Chapter 8.

8 *R v Offen, McGilliard, McKeown, Okwuegbunam* [2001] 2 All ER 154, discussed in Chapter 8.

9 *R (on the Application of Lichniak) v Secretary of State for the Home Department; R v Lichniak and Another* [2001] EWHC Admin 294; [2001] All ER(D) 22 (May), discussed in Chapter 8.

Article 8 (the right to respect for private life, etc) has arisen a number of times both in the context of attacks on criminal offences themselves (particularly sexual offences – see, for example, *ADT v United Kingdom*)[10] but also in applications for evidence that has been obtained in breach of this provision to be excluded (see later discussion of *Khan v United Kingdom*).[11]

Articles 10 and 11 will be relevant in the context of public order legislation, although as with many of the rights, advocates will need to ensure that any arguments take account of the qualified nature of these provisions, and the balancing rights of other groups of protesters or of the public in general. It is also worth noting that while the domestic courts are currently classifying such quasi-criminal orders as Anti Social Behaviour Orders as attracting only civil standards of protection (see *R (on the Application of M (A Child)) v Manchester Crown Court*),[12] advocates will still wish to rely upon Arts 10 and 11 arguments in this context.

Finally, Art 1 Protocol 1 arguments have also arisen, in the context of confiscation orders and may well also arise in the context of orders for forfeiture.

However, the key provision with which advocates will need to be familiar in the context of criminal work is undoubtedly Art 6 – the right to a fair trial – and in particular the specific due process rights set out in Art 6(2) and (3) which are applicable to criminal matters only.

At this point it should, however, be noted by advocates undertaking mental health and child care work that domestic courts, treating the Strasbourg jurisprudence as a floor rather than a ceiling, have been prepared to import elements of Art 6(2) and (3) into these contexts. Thus, Thorpe LJ in *Re C (A Child) (Secure Accommodation)* said:

> I therefore reject the submission that C's rights under Article 6 extend beyond the general right enshrined in ss (1). Nor do I think that my conclusion is of much practical significance. Ss (3) guarantees to everyone charged with a criminal offence five specific minimum rights. I am in no doubt that any child facing an application for a secure accommodation order, however it may be categorised, should be afforded those five specific minimum rights.[13]

It is therefore worth starting by noting the constituent elements of Art 6.

---

10   [2000] 2 FLR 697.

11   *Khan v United Kingdom* 8 BHRC 310.

12   [2001] 1 WLR 358; [2001] EWCA Civ 281; [2001] 1 WLR 1085. See the discussion at 7.2.2.1 below.

13   [2001] EWCA Civ 458; [2001] 2 FLR 169. Confusingly, also known as *Re M (A Child) (Secure Accommodation Order: Representation)*.

7.1.2.1 Article 6(1): the right to a fair trial by an independent and impartial tribunal in public within a reasonable time

The rights provided by Art 6(1) are discrete, rather than compendious. Thus there will be a breach of the provision where the tribunal lacks independence, notwithstanding its apparent impartiality (see *Starrs v Ruxton*).[14] The argument in *Starrs* that Scottish temporary sheriffs lacked the requisite security of tenure in order to ensure independence from the executive was successful in the Scottish courts, leading to the immediate confirmation of all such judicial appointments on a longer-term basis. Arguments in relation to the independence – or lack of independence – of the English judiciary, and in particular in relation to lay justices in the magistrates' court, are considered in the following chapter.

Advocates will note the right to a public hearing. In the past challenges have tended to come from the press, who have been excluded – see, for example, *Atkinson v United Kingdom*:[15] exclusion of journalists from a sentencing hearing – but have been unsuccessful. The right is qualified:

> Judgment shall be pronounced publicly but the press and public may be excluded from all or part of the trial in the interests of morals, public order or national security in a democratic society, where the interests of juveniles or the protection of the private life of the parties so require, or to the extent strictly necessary in the opinion of the court in special circumstances where publicity would prejudice the interests of justice.

Where advocates therefore wish to argue that proceedings should more appropriately be held in open court or (perhaps more likely) are applying for the matter to be heard in private, but are facing arguments from other parties that this would amount to a breach of Art 6, arguments will need to be structured so as to identify clearly the basis on which the restriction is said to be justified.

The right to a hearing within a reasonable time is also a separate right. There is now conflicting case law as to whether a breach of this right will necessarily indicate that the accused has not received a fair trial. There is also conflict as to whether this breach will necessarily require that any conviction be quashed. Both issues are explored in Chapter 8.

7.1.2.2 Article 6(2): the presumption of innocence

The presumption has clear application to court proceedings:

> Paragraph 2 embodies the principle of the presumption of innocence. It requires, *inter alia*, that when carrying out their duties, the members of a court should not start with the preconceived idea that the accused has committed the

---

14 2000 SLT 42.
15 (1990) 67 DR 244.

offence charged; the burden of proof is on the prosecution, and any doubt should benefit the accused. It also follows that it is for the prosecution to inform the accused of the case that will be made against him, so that he may prepare and present his defence accordingly, and to adduce evidence sufficient to convict him ...[16]

The right to silence arises from the presumption of innocence and is closely allied to it:

> The court recalls that, although not specifically mentioned in Article 6 of the Convention, the right to silence and the right not to incriminate oneself, are generally recognised international standards, which lie at the heart of the notion of a fair procedure under Article 6. Their rationale lies, *inter alia*, in the protection of the accused against improper compulsion by the authorities thereby contributing to the avoidance of miscarriages of justice and to the fulfilment of the aims of Article 6. The right not to incriminate oneself, in particular, presupposes that the prosecution in a criminal case seek to prove their case against the accused without resort to evidence obtained through methods of coercion or oppression in defiance of the will of the accused. In this sense the right is closely linked to the presumption of innocence contained in Article 6(2) of the Convention.[17]

Strasbourg case law has clearly indicated the fundamental nature of the right to a presumption of innocence in a criminal context, although in practice its application in such contexts as the right to silence and the shifting of evidential burdens to the defence has not been so clear. These matters are considered in more detail in the following chapter.

7.1.2.3 The Art 6(3) due process rights

Article 6(3) sets out a number of specific criminal due process rights:

> Everyone charged with a criminal offence has the following minimum rights:
>
> (a) to be informed promptly, in a language which he understands and in detail, of the nature and cause of the accusation against him;
>
> (b) to have adequate time and facilities for the preparation of his defence;
>
> (c) to defend himself in person or through legal assistance of his own choosing or, if he has not sufficient means to pay for legal assistance, to be given it free when the interests of justice so require;
>
> (d) to examine or have examined witnesses against him and to obtain the attendance and examination of witnesses on his behalf under the same conditions as witnesses against him;
>
> (e) to have the free assistance of an interpreter if he cannot understand or speak the language used in court.

---

16 *Barbera Messegue and Jabardo v Spain* (1988) 11 EHRR 360, para 77.
17 *Saunders v United Kingdom* (1997) 23 EHRR 313, para 68.

The rights are free-standing guarantees – but are also aspects of the over-arching right to a fair trial:

> The court recalls that the guarantees in paragraph 3 of Article 6 are specific aspects of the right to a fair trial set forth in paragraph 1 ... In the circumstances of the case it finds it unnecessary to examine the relevance of paragraph 3(d) to the case since the applicant's allegations, in any event, amount to a complaint that the proceedings have been unfair. It will therefore confine its examination to this point.[18]

The due process rights are therefore discussed in the context of different elements of the criminal trial process in the following sections.

7.2 IS THIS A MATTER THAT TRIGGERS THE CRIMINAL DUE PROCESS RIGHTS?

The initial hurdle for advocates in some cases will be in showing that Art 6(3) has any application at all. The heart of any argument will therefore relate to the issue of the classification of the offence itself.

7.2.1 Autonomous meanings of terms

As has been discussed in Chapter 1, the European Court of Human Rights gives terms an 'autonomous' Convention meaning, rather than accepting at face value the meaning given to a term by the domestic courts. The most important of these autonomous terms is the meaning of 'criminal charge' and 'criminal offence'. However, there are also issues of what will constitute a 'charge' for Strasbourg purposes, and the meaning of the term 'witness'.

In this section we look primarily at the autonomous meaning given to the concept of a 'criminal offence' and at the implications of this Strasbourg categorisation for advocates in the domestic courts. In the final part of this section, we consider briefly the implications arising from the autonomous concept of a 'charge'. The issue of the meaning of 'witness' is dealt with in Chapter 8, where we consider the challenges to evidential matters, which may arise for advocates.

Examples of matters that are defined under domestic law as being civil proceedings would include proceedings that are held before certain Inland Revenue Tribunals, as well as some matters that are classified as civil matters but which are heard by the magistrates' court – albeit in its civil jurisdiction. Strasbourg has long-established that it will not automatically accept the classification which is given to an offence under the domestic law, since to do

---

18 *Edwards v United Kingdom* (1993) 15 EHRR 417, para 33.

so would enable states to evade the Art 6(3) provisions by simply classifying a matter as civil. The leading case is *Engel* where the Strasbourg Court imposed a three-stage test:

> In this connection, it is first necessary to know whether the provision(s) defining the offence charged belong, according to the legal system of the respondent State, to criminal law, disciplinary law or both concurrently. This however provides no more than a starting point. The indications so afforded have only a formal and relative value and must be examined in the light of the common denominator of the respective legislation of the various Contracting States.
>
> The very nature of the offence is a factor of greater import. When a serviceman finds himself accused of an act or omission allegedly contravening a legal rule governing the operation of the armed forces, the State may in principle employ against him disciplinary law rather than criminal law. In this respect, the court expresses its agreement with the government.
>
> However, supervision by the court does not stop there. Such supervision would generally prove to be illusory if it did not also take into consideration the degree of severity of the penalty that the person concerned risks incurring. In a society subscribing to the rule of law, there belong to the 'criminal' sphere deprivations of liberty liable to be imposed as a punishment, except those, which by their nature, duration or manner of execution cannot be appreciably detrimental. The seriousness of what is at stake, the traditions of the Contracting States and the importance attached by the Convention to respect for the physical liberty of the person all require that this should be so ...[19]

The three stages therefore require the court to have regard to: (i) the classification of the offence in domestic law terms; (ii) the 'nature' of the offence; and (iii) the severity of any punishment. Moreover, it will be sufficient if the case falls into any one of the criteria, since they are alternative rather than cumulative – although where there is a continuing ambiguity, the cumulative approach can be used in order to look at the offence in the round.[20]

The key case in the context of United Kingdom law has been *Benham v United Kingdom*,[21] a case concerning allegations of culpable negligence in non-payment of the community charge under the Community Charge (Administration and Enforcement) Regulations 1989. The matter was heard in the magistrates' court but was classified in case law as being a civil matter. Legal aid was therefore not available. The decision of the Strasbourg Court is of value in indicating not merely the application of the *Engel* criteria, but also the relative weight given to each by the court:

---

19 *Engel v Netherlands* (1976) 1 EHRR 706, para 82.
20 See, for example, *Lauko v Slovakia* 4/1998/907/1119, judgment of 2 September 1998.
21 (1996) 22 EHRR 293.

As to the first of these criteria, the court agrees with the government that the weight of the domestic authority indicates that, under English law, the proceedings in question are regarded as civil rather than criminal in nature. However, this factor is of relative weight and serves only as a starting-point ...

The second criterion, the nature of the proceedings, carries more weight. In this connection, the court notes that the law concerning liability to pay the community charge and the procedure upon non-payment was of general application to all citizens, and that the proceedings in question were brought by a public authority under statutory powers of enforcement. In addition, the proceedings had some punitive elements. For example, the magistrates could only exercise their power of committal to prison on a finding of wilful refusal to pay or of culpable neglect.

Finally, it is to be recalled that the applicant faced a relatively severe maximum penalty of three months' imprisonment, and was in fact ordered to be detained for thirty days.[22]

The court therefore concluded that the matter was a criminal matter. However, it was necessary then to go on to consider whether Art 6(3)(c) required the grant of legal aid 'in the interests of justice'. Here the United Kingdom argued that 'it acted within its margin of appreciation in deciding that public funds should be directed elsewhere'[23] – an argument that would now be couched not in terms of the international law doctrine of margin of appreciation, but the domestic law 'discretionary area of judgment' on which the judiciary should defer to the democratically elected bodies. In either event, it was not a successful argument, the court taking the view that 'where deprivation of liberty is at stake, the interests of justice in principle call for legal representation'.[24] This was exacerbated by the relatively complex nature of the provision in issue.

7.2.2 Applying *Engel* in domestic law

7.2.2.1 *Hybrid offences*

Post-Human Rights Act challenges to the classification of matters have been brought in a number of contexts. One particular area of complexity is the growing number of 'hybrid' offences – of which the anti social behaviour order is a prime example. This offence, along with proceedings under the Protection from Harassment Act 1997 and sex offender orders,[25] involves an initial application for an order, which is dealt with by the magistrates court,

---

22 (1996) 22 EHRR 293, para 56.

23 *Ibid*, para 58.

24 *Ibid*, para 61.

25 Under s 2 of the Crime and Disorder Act 1998. For an unsuccessful challenge to the classification of sex offender orders see *B v Chief Constable of Avon and Somerset Constabulary*, Divisional Court [2001] 1 WLR 340.

but which is dealt with on the civil standard of proof, and a subsequent explicitly criminal hearing where there is an allegation to the court that the order has been breached. The issue therefore is whether notwithstanding the domestic classification of the initial hearing as a civil matter, it should be classified as criminal, and thus attract the protections offered by Art 6(2) and (3).

Thus in *M (A Child)*[26] Lord Woolf in the Administrative Court considered the argument that anti social behaviour orders should be classified as criminal offences. The court was impressed by the considerable restriction on liberty that the anti social behaviour order could constitute and the length of time (not less than two years) for which it would be in force but took the view that, looking at the matter in terms of domestic law, the purpose of the restriction was not to punish the individual, but to protect the rights of others. Above all, however, the court took the view that the anti social behaviour order provision fell into two discrete elements – the initial (civil) order, the subsequent, separate (criminal) proceedings for breach.

This finding that the matter proceeded in two separate stages enabled Lord Woolf to distinguish the situation from that dealt with by the Strasbourg Court in its judgments in *Engel* and *Benham. Lauko*[27] was noted, particularly since Strasbourg had found in that case that an offence under the 1990 Minor Offences Act, where one of the potential penalties included a restriction on the person's activities, was a criminal matter. However, *Lauko* was distinguished on the basis that the penalties also included a fine, a clear criminal penalty. There was nothing therefore in the Strasbourg case law that required a different approach to be taken, and the domestic classification of the first hearing as being a civil matter was therefore correct.

The decision was upheld in the Court of Appeal.[28] Lord Phillips MR looked at the range of conduct which could potentially give rise to an anti social behaviour order, and took the view that it was much wider than that which was criminalised by s 4 of the Public Order Act 1986; in consequence it lacked the certainty needed for a criminal offence. Critically, he took the view that the imposition of the order itself – rather than the consequences for breach of that order – could not be seen as amounting to a criminal punishment, drawing an analogy with the imposition of an injunction in civil proceedings.[29] The Court of Appeal took the view that the unique nature of the anti social behaviour order, for which there is 'no precedent', enabled the court to look at the legislative intention of Parliament. This was consistent with the conclusion that the matters were civil matters.

---

26 *R (on the Application of M (A Child)) v Manchester Crown Court* [2001] 1 WLR 358, Admin Court.

27 *Lauko v Slovakia* 4/1998/907/1119, judgment of 2 September 1998.

28 *R (on the Application of M (A Child)) v Manchester Crown Court* [2001] 1 WLR 358 (CA).

29 *Ibid*, paras 38–42.

Applying the Convention test, the Court of Appeal had particular regard to the ruling of the Strasbourg Court in *Steel v United Kingdom*;[30] a case in which Strasbourg held that breach of the peace should be classified as a criminal matter notwithstanding the domestic classification. The Court of Appeal looked at the factors that had led to this conclusion – the duty to keep the peace as a public duty, the power of arrest for breach of the peace, the power to commit to prison those who refuse to be bound over – and applied these to the anti social behaviour order. There was no power to arrest for anti social behaviour; more than mere anti social behaviour was required before an application for an order could be made;[31] moreover, the initial proceedings themselves could not lead to the imposition of a sentence of imprisonment 'or any penalty'. The court concluded that domestic law was in line with Strasbourg in classifying the matter as civil:

> 63 Applications for anti social behaviour orders have the procedural form of civil proceedings under English law. Neither of the other two criminal criteria for which the Strasbourg looks can be satisfactorily demonstrated. Offensive conduct is a prerequisite to proceedings under s 1, but not the only one. The order, while impacting adversely on the defendant, is not imposed as a punishment. In short, anti social behaviour orders are not about crime and punishment, they are about protection of an identified section of the community. I do not consider that, applying the Strasbourg jurisprudence, they are criminal proceedings.[32]

Having accepted this classification, however, the Court of Appeal noted the comments of the Crown Court in its attempt to apply the more stringent civil standard of proof appropriate to such serious matters. In the event, the Crown Court had concluded that:

> ... in reality it is difficult to establish reliable gradations between a heightened civil standard commensurate with seriousness and implications of proving the requirements, and the criminal standard.

Accordingly the court had decided to apply the criminal standard, an approach commended by the Court of Appeal:

> 67 I believe that the course followed by the Crown Court in this case is likely to be appropriate in the majority of cases where an anti social behaviour order is sought and I would commend it.

Thus the position for advocates when faced with such 'hybrid' offences appears to be that, at least so far as the domestic courts are concerned, the initial application and the subsequent proceedings for breach are treated as separate matters. In relation to both anti social behaviour orders and sex

---

30 (1999) 28 EHRR 603.

31 S1 requires that the applicants can show a necessity to protect persons in a particular local government area.

32 *Re M (A Child)* [2001] 1 WLR 358, paras 63 and 64.

offender orders,[33] the initial application has been treated as being a civil matter, both in terms of domestic law and in terms of Strasbourg law. However, it will be appropriate to apply a heightened civil standard of proof, and probably a criminal standard. Since legal aid funding is available under the Criminal Defence Service regime, the most significant implication of the classification is that it will be harder for advocates to raise challenges based on the failure to call witnesses, and the admission of hearsay evidence. If the approach of the higher courts is any indication, however, it is likely that lower courts will at the very least accept that the seriousness of the allegations means that any such evidence must be treated with considerable caution, and that steps must be taken to ensure that the defendants are properly able to reply to the case against them.

7.2.2.2 Disciplinary and regulatory hearings

Arguments have also been advanced in the context of disciplinary proceedings under the Financial Services Act 1986 that in view of the stringent penalties that can be imposed, such proceedings may fall to be categorised as criminal. This argument was rejected in the *Fleurose* case.[34] The court's approach is of value since it so clearly mirrors the form of classificatory analysis envisaged by *Engel*:

50　It seems to me that the principles enunciated by the court give the answer to the question at issue. In Convention jurisprudence the disciplinary proceedings are to be classified as civil rather than criminal. They are categorised under domestic law as civil. The nature of the proceedings leads to the same conclusion in Convention law ... I do not think that the penalty, which can be imposed, namely an unlimited fine, leads to a different conclusion when carrying out the balancing exercise. In the field of financial regulation, the size of a fine can, I think, fairly remain open ... The purpose of the fine is plainly both punitive and a deterrent; but that does not tip the scales in favour of a 'criminal' categorisation. By this classification the applicant is not denied a right to a fair hearing, nor to this court's supervisory jurisdiction.

51　Looking at the matter 'in the round' it is my judgment that applying the three stage test these disciplinary proceedings, whilst possessing some features akin to criminal proceedings, are not to be classified as involving a criminal charge. But it does not automatically follow that none of the Article 6(2) and 6(3) rights is inapplicable. As can be seen from *Albert and Le Compte v Belgium*[35] the essence of a fair hearing required by Article 6(1) may embrace certain of the stipulations; for example paragraphs (a), (b) and (d) of Article 6(2). Essentially, these disciplinary proceedings relate to

---

33　For sex offender orders see *B v Chief Constable of Avon and Somerset Constabulary* [2001] 1 All ER 562; [2001] 1 WLR 340.

34　*R (on the Application of Fleurose) v Securities and Futures Authority Ltd* [2001] EWHC Admin 292; [2001] All ER(D) 189 (Apr).

35　[1983] 5 EHRR 533.

what might be called the private rights and obligations owed by and to the applicant arising from his personal decision to become a trader in a regulated environment. But for that decision, the applicant would not have been susceptible to SFA discipline. Having subjected himself to their disciplinary regime, he has what might be described as the normal private rights which such a person enjoys and which are accorded to him by the common law, and which are ultimately subject to the supervision of the courts; in this sort of case, the Administrative Court. Those rights, in a case such as this, include some of those which are accorded to a person charged with a criminal offence, such as (a), (b) and (d) of Article 6(3). In my view, also, a person who is being disciplined should not have to establish his innocence. But the standard of proof will vary according to the circumstances and little, if any, practical difference is likely to be detectable in practice between civil and criminal discipline.

52 The core distinction in the classification process between what might, for shorthand, be called civil and criminal in Convention Law seems to me to rest on the fact that it is a necessary condition for the existence of a 'criminal charge' that what is being alleged is a breach of a person's obligations to the State arising from being a citizen, through laws which have universal application or whose application is not dependent upon an individual's choice. Whereas, disciplinary cases involving a breach of obligations imposed on a class or group of individuals through their voluntary participation, do not fulfil the condition. But after the distinction is drawn, there may be some disciplinary procedures whose characteristics are so akin to criminal proceedings that the concept of fairness requires more or less the same protections in both. But it is simplistic and wrong to say that because there is an overlap between the two, it is not necessary to make the classification. Those who drafted the Convention have taken pains to confer rights differentially according to a classification process.

Fleurose will be of use to advocates, notwithstanding the rejection of criminal classification, because of the recognition that even matters categorised as civil may give rise to Art 6(3) rights as a component of the general right to a fair trial under Art 6(1). Moreover, the practical significance of the decision in the specific field of financial regulation is diminished with the introduction of the overarching regulatory regime introduced by the Financial Services and Markets Act 2000, which as a result of concentrated lobbying by commercial organisations introduces a right to legal assistance where allegations are raised of market abuse offences, albeit that that the costs of such assistance are to be recovered by the Lord Chancellor from the Financial Services Authority.[36]

---

36 For a fuller discussion of the implications of the Financial Services and Markets Act 2000, and of the lobbying that took place during its parliamentary progress, see Smyth, *Business and the Human Rights Act 1998* (London: Jordans, 2000).

7.2.2.3 Fiscal penalties

Fleurose should not be treated as showing that applications for all 'commercial' or fiscal matters to be categorised as criminal will be unsuccessful. A number of challenges have been raised successfully in the context of Inland Revenue tribunals.[37] In the *Han & Yau* case the Tribunal considered the imposition of civil evasion penalties under s 60 of the Value Added Tax Act 1994, and stated:

16 Here the penalties imposed under both s 60 VAT Act and s 8 Finance Act 1994 are part of the civil code. They give rise to no criminal record and there is no possibility of loss of liberty. But they are penal and not, as I have already observed, compensatory. Moreover, the evident design of the penalty provisions is to deter re-offending. Applying the first *Engel* criteria [sic] the present penalties could be classed as either civil or criminal.

17 The second *Engel* criterion, the nature of the offence, point, I think towards the penalties ranking as criminal charges despite their place in the civil penalty code. The offence in each case involves dishonesty. While dishonesty as such does not give rise to a criminal offence, the dishonesty factor in the behaviour of the person in question gives rise to a s 60 or a s 8 penalty where it is directed at unlawful tax evasion ... The behaviour of the Appellant giving rise to the penalty will typically, as I have observed, have been well within, and sometimes be high on, the scale of criminality.

18 The third *Engel* criterion, the severity of the penalty [is considered in Strasbourg case law] ... Turning to the present cases, the s 60 and s 8 penalties are sufficiently burdensome to fall on the criminal side of the line, applying the third *Engel* criterion.[38]

As can be seen, it is crucial for advocates to provide the court with a satisfactory account of how each stage of the *Engel's* test is made out in relation to any given offence. Applications are more likely to succeed where the court can be taken to the wording of the Strasbourg decision and shown how each stage in the test applies to the matter before the court. In the drive to remove minor matters from the purview of the criminal courts, it is likely that there will be an increasing range of 'administrative offences', where it is argued that any fixed penalty does not amount to a criminal penalty. While many of these matters are likely to be minor charges, such as minor Road

37 See *Han & Yau, Martins & Martins, Morris v Commissioners of Customs and Excise* (VADT, 5 December 2000, Lawtel 28/2/2001), *Murrell v Customs and Excise*, VADT, decision of 13 October 2000, Lawtel 3/1/2001). For a successful argument that penalty determinations against defaulting tax payers were criminal matters, see *King v Walden (Inspector of Taxes)* [2001] STC 822.

38 The VADT decision in *Han & Yau, Martins & Martins, Morris v Commissioners of Customs and Excise* was upheld on appeal [2001] EWCA Civ 1048; [2001] STC 1188, Sir Martin Nourse dissenting. In the higher court the fact that the civil evasion penalty regime decriminalised certain dishonesty offences was seen as being to the clear advantage of the taxpayer. The court was therefore reluctant to categorise the matter as criminal, but did so on the basis that it had replaced prior criminal penalties, that it involved dishonesty and that the amount of the penalty imposed was substantial.

Traffic Act 1988 offences, which would not normally attract legal aid even when classified as criminal matters, advocates may still wish to argue for recognition of the fundamental nature of the offence as a criminal matter in order to ensure that the accused has the advantage of the presumption of innocence accorded by Art 6(2) and the other due process guarantees under Art 6(3).[38a]

Issues for advocates: arguments on the classification of the offence

1   Is there a Strasbourg right in play: which elements of Art 6(2) or (3) are in issue?

Criminal proceedings are given an autonomous meaning at Strasbourg and the court is required to have regard to the Strasbourg case law in determining an issue where a Convention right is in issue.

2   What is the classification of the matter in domestic law?

- If the case is classified as civil in domestic law: is this a case which has such a significant impact on the individual, perhaps because it affects the right to liberty or because of the severity of the consequences that the domestic law would see the Art 6(2) or (3) rights as appropriate notwithstanding the civil nature of the matter?

3   What is the nature of the matter?

- Is it purely disciplinary?
- Does it affect the population at large or only a small (self-selecting?) element of the population?
- How is the matter classified in other countries?
- What is the potential penalty?
- How severe is the potential penalty?
- What form does the penalty take – could it involve loss of liberty or a very substantial fine?
- If the penalty takes monetary form does it involve compensation or reparation or is it purely retributive?
- What consequences flow from categorisation as a criminal offence?

7.2.3   The autonomous meaning of a criminal charge

The rights under Art 6(1) are triggered when a person is subject to a 'criminal charge', and under Art 6(2) and Art 6(3) where a person is 'charged' with a

---

38a Note the rejection of arguments that proceedings under s 4 of the Criminal Procedure (Insanity) Act 1964 were to be classed as crucial on the basis that there would be no finding of guilt, only the finding that the defendant had committed an act: *R v M, R, v Kerr, R v H* [2001] All ER(D) 67, CA.

criminal offence. The issue of whether a person is subject to a charge will therefore have important implications for issues such as the right to a trial within a reasonable time, but also specific criminal due process rights, such as access to a lawyer.

The approach of the European Court has been to take a broad view of 'charge' so as to ensure that the Art 6 protections are as extensive as can be. It is clear that, for Strasbourg purposes, a 'charge' can arise well before a suspect is formally 'charged' as the term would be understood under domestic law.

In *Eckle v Germany*[39] the court held:

> In criminal matters, the 'reasonable time' referred to in Article 6 para 1 begins to run as soon as a person is 'charged'; this may occur on a date prior to the case coming before the trial court ... such as the date of arrest, the date when the person concerned was officially notified that he would be prosecuted or the date when preliminary investigations were opened ... 'Charge', for the purposes of Article 6 para 1, may be defined as 'the official notification given to an individual by the competent authority of an allegation that he has committed a criminal offence', a definition that also corresponds to the test whether 'the situation of the [suspect] has been substantially affected' ...[40]

In *Murray (John) v United Kingdom*,[41] where one of the issues arising was whether inferences could arise from silence under police questioning, the European Court of Human Rights was prepared to extend the right of access to legal advice to the questioning stage where a lack of access would otherwise impact upon the fairness of a subsequent trial. The decision does not make entirely clear whether this indicates that the questioning amounted to a 'charge':

> 62 The court observes that it has not been disputed by the government that Article 6 applies even at the stage of the preliminary investigation into an offence by the police. In this respect it recalls its finding in the *Imbrioscia v Switzerland* ... that Article 6 – especially paragraph 3 – may be relevant before a case is sent for trial if and so far as the fairness of the trial is likely to be seriously prejudiced by an initial failure to comply with its provisions ... As it pointed out in that judgment, the manner in which Article 6 para 3(c) is to be applied during the preliminary investigation depends on the special features of the proceedings involved and on the circumstances of the case ...

> 63 National laws may attach consequences to the attitude of an accused at the initial stages of police interrogation, which are decisive for the prospects of the defence in any subsequent criminal proceedings. In such circumstances Article 6 will normally require that the accused be allowed to benefit from the assistance of a lawyer already at the initial stages of police interrogation. However, this right, which is not explicitly set out in the Convention, may be subject to restrictions for good cause. The question, in

---

39   (1982) 5 EHRR 1.
40   *Ibid*, para 73.
41   (1996) 22 EHRR 29.

each case, is whether the restriction, in the light of the entirety of the proceedings, has deprived the accused of a fair hearing.[42]

In its decision in *Phillips v United Kingdom*,[43] a case concerning a confiscation order under s 2 of the Drug Trafficking Act 1994, the Strasbourg Court concluded that the confiscation proceedings did not amount to a new charge, attracting a presumption of innocence under Art 6(2), but were part of the sentencing process:

> [T]he purpose of this procedure was not the conviction or acquittal of the applicant for any other drugs-related offence. Although the Crown Court assumed that he had benefited from drug trafficking in the past, this was not, for example, reflected in his criminal record, to which was added only his conviction for the November 1995 offence. In these circumstances, it cannot be said that the applicant was 'charged with a criminal offence'. Instead, the purpose of the procedure under the 1994 Act was to enable the national court to assess the amount at which the confiscation order should properly be fixed. The court considers that this procedure was analogous to the determination by a court of the amount of a fine or the length of a period of imprisonment to impose upon a properly convicted offender.[44]

In *Attorney General's Reference (No 2 of 2001)*[45] the Court of Appeal was considering the issue of remedies for a delay that had arisen where serving prisoners were interviewed in June and July 1998 about a disturbance that had taken place that April, but charges had not been laid until February 2000. The court concluded that the on the facts the interviews could not be said to be charges, and thus that no delay had arisen. The court's reasoning on this point, however, is relatively brusque:

> It was contended before the judge that there had taken place an interrogation of the defendant and it was said that this constituted the charge. We disagree with that view. In the ordinary way an interrogation or an interview of a suspect by itself does not amount to a charging of that suspect for the purpose of the reasonable time requirement in Article 6(1). We do not consider it would be helpful to seek to try and identify all the circumstances where it would be possible to say that a charging has taken place for the purpose of Article 6(1), although there has been no formal charge. We feel that the approach indicated by the authority that we have cited clearly expresses the position and we are content to leave the matter in that way.[46]

---

42 (1996) 22 EHRR 29, at paras 62–63. See also *Averill v United Kingdom* (2001) 31 EHRR 36 and *Magee v United Kingdom* (2001) 31 EHRR 35 and *Gourlay v Her Majesty's Advocate*, High Court of Justiciary, Appeal No: C609/99, Lawtel 15 May 2001. *Murray* is discussed further in relation to inferences from the exercise of the right to silence in Chapter 8, below.

43 Judgment of 5 July 2001.

44 *Ibid*, para 34.

45 [2001] EWCA Crim 1568; (2001) *The Times*, 12 July.

46 *Ibid*, para 13.

It seems that in terms both of domestic and Strasbourg case law, the tendency is to look at the consequences that flow from any particular action (such as the refusal to permit access to a lawyer in the police station) and to determine whether Art 6 is breached. It is therefore hard to pin down a constant definition of 'charge'. It is, however, a matter of considerable significance in the context of applications for matters to be stayed on the basis of delay, and this is considered in more detail in the chapter that follows.

7.3 ARRESTS AND THE HRA

Human rights arguments as to the validity of an arrest as such will be of relevance to criminal advocates who wish to challenge the legality of any detention, and who may wish to argue for the exclusion of evidence obtained as a result of the detention, or to argue that the proceedings should be stayed as an abuse of a process that has its roots in an unlawful arrest. The issues of exclusion of evidence and abuse of process arguments are considered in more detail in the following chapter. In this section we look briefly at the core provisions of Art 5, the right to liberty, and the key principles, which underlie in particular the arrest but also bail, which is then considered in the following section:

1   Everyone has the right to liberty and security of person. No one shall be deprived of his liberty save in the following cases and in accordance with a procedure prescribed by law:

(a) the lawful detention of a person after conviction by a competent court;

(b) the lawful arrest or detention of a person for non-compliance with the lawful order of a court or in order to secure the fulfilment of any obligation prescribed by law;

(c) the lawful arrest or detention of a person effected for the purpose of bringing him before the competent legal authority on reasonable suspicion of having committed an offence or when it is reasonably considered necessary to prevent his committing an offence or fleeing after having done so;

(d) the detention of a minor by lawful order for the purpose of educational supervision or his lawful detention for the purpose of bringing him before the competent legal authority;

(e) the lawful detention of persons for the prevention of the spreading of infectious diseases, of persons of unsound mind, alcoholics or drug addicts or vagrants;

(f)   the lawful arrest or detention of a person to prevent his effecting an unauthorised entry into the country or of a person against whom action is being taken with a view to deportation or extradition.

2   Everyone who is arrested shall be informed promptly, in a language which he understands, of the reasons for his arrest and of any charge against him.

3   Everyone arrested or detained in accordance with the provisions of paragraph 1(c) of this article shall be brought promptly before a judge or other officer authorised by law to exercise judicial power and shall be entitled to trial within a reasonable time or to release pending trial. Release may be conditioned by guarantees to appear for trial.

4   Everyone who is deprived of his liberty by arrest or detention shall be entitled to take proceedings by which the lawfulness of his detention shall be decided speedily by a court and his release ordered if the detention is not lawful.

5   Everyone who has been the victim of arrest or detention in contravention of the provisions of this article shall have an enforceable right to compensation.

7.3.1   Is Art 5 engaged – is there detention?

The right to liberty and security of the person is of particular significance and is given a high degree of protection by the Strasbourg Court. In some circumstances, however, there will be an initial issue as to whether the Art 5 threshold has been crossed, particularly where the alleged detention has been in relation to a relatively brief stop and search or to the exercise of immigration controls.

While Strasbourg decisions purport to draw a distinction between those cases where the authorities seek to deprive a person of their liberty and other situations where the authorities merely seek to investigate a matter, the distinctions are not always clear. Thus, in *X v Austria*, where the police took X to an institution so that a blood test could be carried out in relation to ongoing affiliation proceedings, the Commission found that the intention was to deprive X of his liberty, notwithstanding that the underlying court proceedings were civil in nature. By way of contrast, a brief detention in order to carry out a lawful stop and search in *Hojemeister v Germany* was held not to cross the detention threshold.[47]

7.3.2   Is that detention for a permissible reason?

It will be noted that Art 5 provides for the deprivation of liberty in certain circumstances where that deprivation is 'prescribed by law'. The issue of legitimacy of purpose and the requirement for lawfulness are both discussed in Chapter 1 above. The permissible reasons for detention are to be narrowly

---

47   *X v Austria* (1979) 18 DR 154, *Hojemeister v Germany* (1981) unreported, 6 July, but cited by Starmer at 15.50. Note that voluntary attendance at the police station may also trigger Art 5, depending on the 'reality of the situation' – namely, is it practicable for the applicant to leave, and does he know that he has the right to leave: *Walverens v Belgium* 5 March 1980, again unreported but cited by Starmer at 15.52.

construed,[48] but include lawful arrest or detention of a person on reasonable suspicion of offending, in order to prevent offending or to prevent the person from fleeing (Art 5(1)(c)). Since the protection offered by Art 5 is against 'arbitrary' deprivation of liberty there will inevitably be challenges to the issue of what will constitute reasonable suspicion for the purposes of the Art 5(1) grounds. In *Fox, Campbell and Hartley v United Kingdom* the European Court of Human Rights held that:

> ... a 'reasonable suspicion' presupposes the existence of facts of information which would satisfy an objective observer that the person concerned may have committed the offence in question.[49]

In *O'Hara v Chief Constable RUC*[50] the House of Lords considered the issue of 'reasonable suspicion' in relation to the use of information provided to police officers by senior officers and concluded that the test fell in two parts: first, there must be actual suspicion on the part of the arresting officer; secondly, there must be reasonable grounds (judged objectively, rather than subjectively) for that suspicion. This decision has been applied in the case of *Hough v Chief Constable of Staffordshire Constabulary*,[51] where officers arrested Hough at gunpoint on the basis of wrong information that had been entered on the police computer, which suggested that the car he was in was being driven by a person who might be armed. The court applied *O'Hara*, stating:

> The critical question to be asked in all cases is what is in the mind of the arresting officer: he can never be a 'mere conduit' for someone else. It is for that reason insufficient for an arresting officer to rely solely upon an instruction to carry out the arrest. Conversely, however, where the arresting officer's suspicion is formed on the basis of a police national computer entry, that entry is likely to provide the necessary objective justification.[52]

The European Court of Human Rights in *O'Hara v United Kingdom*[53] found no violation of Art 5(1) in respect of the arrest.

Note that in any event the arrest must be for purpose of bringing suspect before court under Arts 5(3) and 5(4), which thus raise certain procedural safeguards. These are considered in detail in relation to bail in the following section. What then is the position if the suspect is never brought before a

---

48 Although note the rather more generous interpretation given to the Art 5(1)(d) 'educational supervision' provision by the Court of Appeal in an early application of the Human Rights Act to secure accommodation orders in *Re K (A Child) (Secure Accommodation Order: Right to Liberty)* [2001] 2 WLR 1141.

49 (1991) 13 EHRR 157, at para 36. Note that challenges are apparently currently pending in relation to the purported exercise by the Metropolitan Police of powers of stop and search without reasonable suspicion under s 60 of the Criminal Justice and Public Order Act 1994 during the 'May Day' disturbances in London in May 2001.

50 [1997] Crim LR 432.

51 [2001] EWCA Civ 39; (2001) *The Times*, 14 February.

52 *Ibid*.

53 *O'Hara v United Kingdom*, Application Number 3755597, judgment of 16/10/2001.

court? In *Brogan v United Kingdom*[54] Brogan was arrested but was subsequently released without charge.The Strasbourg Court held that the issue was whether it had been intended at the time that he was arrested to bring before him before a court.

7.3.3 Can it be argued that an arrest is disproportionate?

It will be recalled that under traditional domestic law principles the police have a wide discretion in the exercise of their power of arrest: *Castorina v CC Sussex Police*.[55] As has been discussed in Chapter 3 above, the Convention principle of proportionality is likely to arise in consideration of the exercise of any permitted interference with a Convention right. There may therefore be circumstances where it will be possible for the advocate to argue that the arrest was unlawful on the basis that a less intrusive means of proceeding could reasonably have been adopted:[56]

> For example, a shop views CCTV footage and believes that the footage shows a woman shoplifting on Tuesday afternoon. The footage is viewed by a police liaison officer on Wednesday morning and a copy of the video is taken to the local police station where it is viewed by police officers. The woman is identified as Joan Smith. Officers are tasked with investigating the offence. Because of the relative low priority of the matter and because the officers are currently on night shift, they do not call at Ms Smith's house until 6.30 pm on Friday. Ms Smith is a lone parent with young children. The police propose to arrest Ms Smith in order to question her. The children will therefore have to be taken temporarily into the care of the local Social Services Department since there is no other person available to care for them.
>
> The arrest is clearly in accordance with law (theft is an arrestable offence under s 24 Police and Criminal Evidence Act 1984). The arrest is also for a prescribed reason – reasonable suspicion of having committed an offence. However, is the exercise of an arrest power at this point disproportionate? Given how long the matter has been outstanding, there appears to be no great urgency. Why can the arrest not be delayed in order to permit Ms Smith to make child care arrangements?
>
> Moreover, it is of course not simply an issue of considering the arrest in terms of Article 5. It is clear that in this example the arrest will amount to an interference with the family life of both Ms Smith and her children. Accordingly Article 8 is engaged, and while the interference is prescribed by

---

54 (1989) 11 EHRR 117.

55 (1998) 138 NLJ 180.

56 The continuing resistance of domestic courts to challenges to the discretion of the police can be seen in the Court of Appeal decision in *Henderson v Chief Constable of Cleveland* [2001] EWCA Civ 335; [2001] 1 WLR 1103 – a case concerning the police decision to delay execution of a warrant until after finishing questioning Henderson on another matter, with the effect that Henderson was then detained over the weekend until the first available court.

law and for a legitimate reason (the prevention of crime), again the issue of the proportionality of the interference must be considered. It will not simply be a case of considering the situation purely in terms of the interference with Ms Smith's rights; the impact on the children, and the interference with their rights, must also be taken into account.[57]

It is likely that issues arising from an arrest whose legality is challenged will be in relation to the admissibility of evidence or the impact on a fair trial. These issues are considered in more detail in the following chapter.

7.4 HUMAN RIGHTS ACT AND LEGAL REPRESENTATION

The right contained in Art 6(3)(c) is for the defendant:

> ... to defend himself in person or through legal assistance of his own choosing or, if he has not sufficient means to pay for legal assistance, to be given it free when the interests of justice so require.

Note that the issue of access to legal advice will also often engage Art 6(3(b) – 'to have adequate time and facilities for the preparation of [the] defence'. In this context it has been argued that the lack of private consultation facilities at the police station amounts to a breach of the provision. One claimant had to give instructions to his solicitor in a cell with a wicket in the door. Another claimant had to make a telephone call to the solicitor within earshot of the police in the custody area. The Divisional Court took the view that while it was not necessary to show prejudice, the fact that one claimant had had the opportunity to instruct a solicitor, and that the other had had adequate time for the preparation of his defence, meant that there had been no breach of the provisions.[58]

The greater part of this section considers access to state funding in ensuring legal assistance in criminal matters. First, however, it is worth touching on the two prior elements of the Art 6(3)(c) right – the right to defend oneself in person, and the right to legal assistance of one's own choosing. The section then considers the issues arising in relation to the availability of legal aid. Finally the section briefly considers the arguments that advocates will need to advance where arguing that prior legal representation has been so defective as to breach Art 6.

---

57 For additional support, *R (on the Application of Stokes) v Gwent Magistrates Court* [2001] EWHC Admin 569; Lawtel, 10/7/2001, where committal of a single parent with young children for non-payment of fines was held to be a disproportionate interference with the children's Art 8 rights. This decision is discussed in Chapter 8, and while *Stokes* relates to sentencing, there is presumably an even stronger argument that interference with Art 8 may be disproportionate at the arrest stage where there is a presumption of innocence.

58 *R (on the Application of M) v Commissioner of Police of the Metropolis, R (on the Application of La Rose) v Commissioner of Police of the Metropolis* [2001] EWHC Admin 553; [2001] All ER(D) 177 (Jul).

7.4.1 Representation in person or by a lawyer of one's own choosing

7.4.1.1 Limitations on representation in person

It will be recalled that in domestic law the accused is entitled to represent himself. There are, however, restrictions on his ability to cross-examine certain classes of witness. Thus an unrepresented defendant is not permitted cross-examine a child witness when charged with an offence relating to an assault (or threat of an assault) on the child, or relating to child cruelty or to a sexual offence of some kind on the child.[59] Equally there is now a prohibition on an unrepresented defendant cross-examining any complainant where the accused is charged with a sexual offence. There is also a general power to prohibit cross-examination by a defendant where such a prohibition would improve the quality of evidence and would not be contrary to the interests of justice.[60] Where cross-examination in person is prohibited the court will invite the defendant to appoint a legal representative. If the defendant declines to do so, the court may appoint a representative of its own motion. In either event a warning will be given to the jury to ensure that the defendant is not prejudiced.

Under Strasbourg case law, the right to represent oneself is not an absolute right. Requirements for a defendant to be represented by lawyers in certain classes of proceedings have been held to comply with Art 6.[61] While the domestic courts can be invited to undertake a more critical examination of the basis of the restriction – particularly since it sits uneasily alongside the more traditional domestic approach to permitting the accused to represent himself – advocates will note that the courts have made clear that notwithstanding the absolute nature of the right to a fair trial, the issue of what is involved in 'fairness' can legitimately take into account other interests, including the interests of the victim:

> It is well established that the guarantee of a fair trial under Article 6 is absolute: a conviction obtained in breach of it cannot stand. *R v Forbes* [2001] 2 WLR 1, 13, para 24. The only balancing permitted is in respect of what the concept of a fair trial entails: here account may be taken of the familiar triangulation of interests of the accused, the victim and society. In this context proportionality has a role to play.[62]

---

59 See s 32(2) of the Criminal Justice Act 1988.

60 See ss 34–39 of the Youth Justice and Criminal Evidence Act 1999.

61 See *Philis v Greece* (1990) 66 DR 260 and *Croissant v Germany* (1993) 16 EHRR 135: in the latter case the European Court seemed more concerned that the court had appointed three lawyers to represent C who was then liable for increased costs in consequence.

62 *Per* Lord Steyn, *R v A* [2001 UKHL 25; [2001] 2 WLR 1546, para 38.

There is a related issue where the rights of vulnerable witnesses are in play, and that is the restriction on cross-examination of such witnesses, both in relation to matters that can be raised in the cross-examination of victims of sexual offences[63] and in the use of video-taped interviews and the use of video links:[64] these issues are considered in relation to the fairness of the trial process and are dealt with in the chapter that follows.

7.4.1.2   Representation by a lawyer of choice

It is unlikely that any domestic court would be restricting the defendant's right to representation by a lawyer of his choice other than on the basis that either the lawyer concerned lacks the requisite rights of audience or that the interests of justice require that a trial is held at a particular time, and in consequence the defendant's initial 'lawyer of choice' is unavailable.

Rights of audience restrictions *per se* will not normally offend against Art 6 assuming that the state can show some rational basis for the restrictions. This is particularly the case since the Strasbourg Court will be looking to ensure that any representation is 'practical and effective':

> The court recalls that the Convention is intended to guarantee not rights that are theoretical or illusory but rights that are practical and effective; this is particularly so of the rights of the defence in view of the prominent place held in a democratic society by the right to a fair trial, from which they derive ...[65]

Where the state can argue, for example, that rights of audience rules ensure the quality of legal representation in particular courts, and where it can be shown that these rules do not restrict the defendant's access to competent legal representation to such an extent that the right is made meaningless, there is unlikely to be an issue. Where, for example, the court refuses to permit a McKenzie friend to assist the defendant in putting his case, the underlying issue will not be one of lack of representation but lack of access to legal aid. The defendant will be arguing that the case is so complex that he needs assistance in putting his case, so that effectively the court was wrong in refusing legal aid to pay for a lawyer to undertake the work.

On a similar basis, lack of access to a lawyer of choice is unlikely to give rise to successful Art 6 arguments provided that the court has had regard to the interests of justice:

> For example, D was arrested on public order charges following large-scale public disturbances at a demonstration. D was advised at the police station by L, a solicitor who is experienced in public order cases and is representing a large number of those arrested at the demonstration. L also attended the

---

63   For example s 41 of the Youth Justice and Criminal Evidence Act 1999: see 8.1.4.2.
64   See ss 32 and 32A of the Criminal Justice Act 1988.
65   *Artico v Italy* (1981) 3 EHRR 1, para 33.

identification parade with D and advised on the stance to be taken during questioning. L has also undertaken initial preparatory work, tracing and interviewing witnesses. To what extent is the court now permitted to fix a trial date at a time when L is not available?

It is submitted that the traditional approach in domestic law would be to recognise D's right to representation by a lawyer of choice, but to balance this against the need for justice to be done expeditiously. It is unlikely that the court would be justified in traditional domestic law if it fixed a trial date without any regard for L's availability. Similarly, when approaching the matter from a Human Rights Act perspective, it seems unlikely that the court is required to do more than to have regard to the balance between the interests of justice and D's right to effective representation. Only where it could be shown that the effectiveness of legal representation was significantly undermined would an application that the hearing breached Article 6 be likely to succeed.[66]

On these facts, it seems unlikely that L is the only suitably qualified lawyer to deal with a mainstream area of work. Provided any substitute lawyer has sufficient time to prepare the case, and where necessary to take further instructions from D, then the interests of justice may mandate an expeditious hearing of the matter while the recollections of witnesses are still fresh, and having regard to the needs of other defendants who may be jointly charged.

It is clear that the right representation by a state-funded lawyer does not permit an unqualified freedom of choice. In *Croissant v Germany*[67] Strasbourg was prepared to uphold the appointment of a state-appointed lawyer in place of the lawyer chosen by the defendant. The court commented:

> It is true that Article 6 para 3(c) entitles 'everyone charged with a criminal offence' to be defended by counsel of his own choosing ... Nevertheless, and notwithstanding the importance of a relationship of confidence between lawyer and client, this right cannot be considered to be absolute. It is necessarily subject to certain limitations where free legal aid is concerned and also where, as in the present case, it is for the courts to decide whether the interests of justice require that the accused be defended by counsel appointed by them. When appointing defence counsel the national courts must certainly have regard to the defendant's wishes; indeed, German law contemplates such a course ... However, they can override those wishes when there are relevant and sufficient grounds for holding that this is necessary in the interests of justice.[68]

---

66 In relation to the need to look in practical terms at the effect of any interference with the right to legal representation see *S v Switzerland* (1992) 14 EHRR 670. Generally speaking it is not necessary to show prejudice where there has been a breach of an Art 6 provision; however, in order to establish that the court has interfered with the right in a manner that is disproportionate – for example, by giving undue priority to the need for compliance with a Narey timetable – inevitably the applicant will need to be able to point to the impact of that interference on his Convention right.

67 (1993) 16 EHRR 135.

68 *Ibid*, para 29.

The breadth of this proposition must be treated with some caution however. It will be noted that Croissant was himself a lawyer and was being tried in relation to activities while representing members of the Red Army Faction. He had accepted two state-appointed lawyers, but objected to the third on the basis of his membership of a political party to which he was opposed; instead he wished to be represented by one of his own former employees.

In the majority of cases, however, it is clear that access to legal representation *per se* will not be a source of human rights argument. In contrast, however, access to publicly funded representation is likely to give rise to many more arguments.

7.4.2 Arguing for the availability of legal aid

Domestic legislation provides that Criminal Defence Service funding may be granted where the matter is one that involves criminal investigations or criminal proceedings. The provision continues:

In this Part 'criminal proceedings' means–

(a) proceedings before any court for dealing with an individual accused of an offence,

(b) proceedings before any court for dealing with an individual convicted of an offence (including proceedings in respect of a sentence or order),

(c) proceedings for dealing with an individual under s 9 of, or paragraph 6 of Schedule 1 to, the Extradition Act 1989,

(d) proceedings for binding an individual over to keep the peace or to be of good behaviour under s 115 of the Magistrates' Courts Act 1980 and for dealing with an individual who fails to comply with an order under that section,

(e) proceedings on an appeal brought by an individual under s 44A of the Criminal Appeal Act 1968,

(f) proceedings for contempt committed, or alleged to have been committed, by an individual in the face of a court, and

(g) such other proceedings concerning an individual, before any such court or other body, as may be prescribed.[69]

The first stage of the argument will be to establish that a matter of Convention law potentially arises, hence triggering the court's duty to have regard to Strasbourg jurisprudence under s 2 of the HRA. The Convention issue will be whether a refusal to grant legal aid will be in breach of Art 6(3)(c). The court

---

69 Section 12(2) of the Access to Justice Act 1999. Note that reg 3 of the Criminal Defence Service (General) Regulations 2001 goes on to prescribe certain matters as criminal proceedings, including 'civil proceedings in a magistrates' court arising from failure to pay a sum due or to obey an order of that court where such failure carries the risk of imprisonment', along with various matters arising in connection with anti social behaviour orders and parenting orders.

will be aware of its status as a public authority for the purposes of the Human Rights Act (s 6(3)(a)) and the requirement under s 3 of the HRA to interpret the primary legislation in a manner which is Convention-compliant if it is possible to do so. The issue therefore becomes whether Art 6(3) is indeed in play, and this in turn will require the court to be addressed on the issues of whether the matter before the court constitutes a criminal offence for Strasbourg purposes. If the court accepts that a criminal offence in the Strasbourg sense of the phrase is before it, then there will be no difficulty in reading the phrase 'criminal proceedings' from the Access to Justice Act as including all offences, which would be defined as criminal offences under the Convention.

Notwithstanding the substantial recent changes to the funding of criminal cases, the underlying principles relating to access to state funding remain those enshrined in the 'interests of justice' criteria of Sched 3, para 5 of the Access to Justice Act 1999 (which is in identical terms to s 22 of the Legal Aid Act 1988 which preceded it). While the means test in relation to applications for criminal legal aid (now, criminal defence service funding) has been abolished for the majority of magistrates' court cases, the existence of a means test does not itself offend against Art 6(3)(c), which provides only that free legal representation is required where the defendant 'has not sufficient means to pay for legal assistance' if 'the interests of justice so require'.

7.4.2.1 The 'interests of justice' criteria and Convention law

The key argument that advocates will wish to bear in mind, both in addressing the court, and in completing applications for CDS funding for representation, is the issue of equality of arms as an integral element of the fair trial process. While it will not be sufficient to argue that equality is automatically absent where one party, the state, is legally represented and the accused is not, advocates will wish to show the court how the lack of representation will necessarily impact on the ability of the accused to put his case effectively to the court.

The European Court has made clear that while the Contracting States maintain substantial freedom of choice in deciding how to comply with Art 6, the decision taken by the state that it is not in the interests of justice to grant legal aid will nonetheless be susceptible to review by the Strasbourg Court.

In *Quaranta v Switzerland* legal aid was not granted in a drug trafficking case. The Strasbourg Court looked not merely at the actual six-month custodial sentence, but at the fact that a three-year sentence had been a possibility, commenting that 'free legal assistance should have been afforded by reason of the mere fact that so much was at stake'.[70] Additionally the court

---

70 *Quaranta v Switzerland* (1991) Series A No 205, para 33.

looked at the complexity of the case – not in *Quaranta* a factual complexity since the offence had been admitted, but the wide range of sentencing measures that arose, not least since the alleged offence had occurred during the probationary period of another offence and had thus activated a suspended sentence. The court commented:

> Such questions, which are complicated in themselves, were even more so for Mr Quaranta on account of his personal situation: a young adult of foreign origin from an underprivileged background, he had no real occupational training and had a long criminal record. He had taken drugs since 1975, almost daily since 1983, and, at the material time, was living with his family on social security benefit.[71]

It is notable that the court took the view that the later representation of the applicant on appeal could not cure this original breach of Art 6, although this was on the basis that the review by the appellate courts was limited. By contrast it will be argued that a full right of review by a superior court, such as an appeal to the Crown Court from the magistrates' courts, may suffice to rectify any failure to grant legal aid in the lower court.

Many of the long-standing 'interests of justice' criteria look to the underlying equality of arms issues – will the accused be able to follow the proceedings; is there a particularly complex point of law; are there witnesses to be traced, or witnesses with whom expert cross-examination is required? Where these grounds can be made out, legal aid should be available in any event. However, there will be cases where it is hard to make out any one specific criterion, and yet the overall length or complexity of the case means that there is a clear imbalance of ability as between the legally represented prosecution and the unrepresented defendant. In such cases courts must be urged to look to the reality of the situation, rather than to take a narrow view of what is required. Indeed, in *Quaranta* it is notable that the prosecution was not represented at the first instance hearing, so that any equality of arms argument focused less on the status vis à vis the prosecution than with the court, itself of course a public authority for Human Rights Act and Convention purposes.

In this context it will be recalled that the Convention is to be interpreted in a way that ensures that it provides an effective remedy. Strasbourg has made clear that it will look to the reality of the situation. Thus, in *Granger v United Kingdom*,[72] Granger, who was appealing against a five year custodial sentence for perjury, had been refused legal aid for the appeal on the basis that the advice of his own counsel suggested that the appeal was unlikely to succeed. At the appeal hearing Granger was permitted to read out statements prepared by his solicitor in advance, whereas the Crown was represented by senior and

---

71 (1991) Series A No 205, para 35.
72 *Granger v United Kingdom* (1990) 12 EHRR 469, at para 47.

junior counsel. The Strasbourg Court held that it was not its role to look into the merits of the appeal on a narrow basis but to look at the effect of the refusal on the case as a whole:

> [T]he applicant, as was not contested, was not in a position fully to comprehend the pre-prepared speeches he read out ... or the opposing arguments submitted to the court. It is also clear that, had the occasion arisen, he would not have been able to make an effective reply to those arguments or to questions from the bench.

> The foregoing factors are of particular weight in the present case in view of the complexity of one of the issues involved.

Indeed the fact that a complex point of law in fact arose in relation to one of the points of appeal, so that the hearing was adjourned for a transcript to be obtained, made it clear that the appeal raised an issue of 'complexity and importance'. The failure to grant legal aid to deal with this point thus breached Art 6.

There is no particular procedure under domestic law for reviewing the refusal of legal aid where a case is subsequently revealed as being more complex than was initially thought. It will, however, normally be easy enough for advocates to identify the stage in the proceedings where the matter has now become so complex that the original refusal of funding should be reviewed. Where defendants are not represented, however, there will be an onus on the court, itself a public authority and hence under a duty to act in a way that does not contravene the defendant's rights, to review its earlier decision and to make legal aid available. It will often be a necessary corollary of this that the case is adjourned in order for a lawyer to be instructed and for effective preparation to be undertaken. Courts will naturally be averse to doing this, but where a court has failed to review its refusal to fund legal representation where the complexity of the proceedings made such representation necessary, the grounds of appeal will include a breach of Art 6, and we would suggest that any such appeal must succeed.[73]

In this regard, when looking at the 'complexity and importance' of any case, advocates will need to be ready to disclose at the initial hearing any substantive human rights arguments that are likely to arise as part of the trial process. These may be arguments that go to process – such as trial venue, bail and so on – or that go to the evidence or indeed the offence in the case. Courts will be under a duty to grant legal aid both under Art 6 and under the traditional domestic 'interests of justice' criteria where satisfied that the case raises complex areas of law. Human rights arguments will generally fall into exactly this category.

---

73 For a fuller discussion of the implications of a breach of Art 6 for the safety of any conviction, see Chapter 8.

> For example, a person is charged with common assault following the beating of a child, and the court may not be minded to grant legal aid in view of the lack of seriousness of the matter, it will be important to identify with a degree of specificity that there are human rights challenges to the admissibility of evidence which, the defence alleges, has been gathered in breach of the defendant's Article 8 rights, or that the defendant wishes to run Article 6 and Article 7 arguments based on the lack of clarity as to the domestic law on the defence of lawful chastisement.[74]

Courts will be rightly sceptical where an advocate puts forward a bare assertion that 'this is a human rights case' as justification for the granting of legal aid. However, where the human rights issues can be identified, so that the assertion can be justified, it is likely that most courts will take the view that legal representation will enable them to ensure that the points are properly addressed in a way that saves the court's time.

7.4.2.2 Can lack of legal aid be 'cured' on appeal?

The focus of Art 6 is on the fairness of the trial process, rather than on the specific elements of a fair trial. It is therefore possible for some breaches of Art 6 to be rectified by the appellate courts.[75] As will be seen in the following chapter, Strasbourg has held that some breaches of the fair trial provision[76] cannot be rectified at the appellate stage. In relation to a failure to grant legal aid in the magistrates' court, it may therefore be possible for defence advocates to argue that the hearing or the sentencing issues have shown the matter to be of greater complexity than was at first envisaged by the lower court, and that legal aid should therefore be granted for the appeal hearing.[77]

7.4.3 The right to effective representation

The right of the defendant to effective representation arises from the underlying doctrine that the Convention provides effective rights:

---

74 *R v H (Reasonable Chastisement)* [2001] EWCA Crim 1024; [2001] 2 FLR 431 where the Court of Appeal held that a trial judge should, pending a change in the law, adjust the direction to the jury to take account of the decision in *A v United Kingdom*. See Chapter 8 for a fuller discussion.

75 See, for example, *Edwards v United Kingdom* (1993) 15 EHRR 417.

76 For example, a defective jury direction on the issue of inferences from the exercise of the right of silence: *Condron v United Kingdom* (2001) 31 EHRR 1.

77 In relation to less serious offences where there is a significant point of law which is to be challenged by way of the Case Stated procedure, the relative procedural complexity of that procedure, along with the fact that the hearing will be on point of law only in the Divisional Court will in our view generally mean that applications for state-funding will have particular merit. There may, however, be a contrary argument that the overlapping jurisdiction of the Crown Court in its appellate guise provides a less complex but equally appropriate forum for the hearing of unrepresented appeals.

In addition, the object and purpose of the Convention as an instrument for the protection of individual human beings requires that its provisions be interpreted and applied so as to make its safeguards practical and effective ...[78]

The application of this principle to legal representation can be seen in the case of *Artico v Italy*,[79] where the lawyer appointed by the court to represent Artico in his attempt to have his convictions quashed declined to do so. Rather than appointing a replacement the court insisted that the lawyer had no right to refuse, leaving Artico unrepresented:

> The court recalls that the Convention is intended to guarantee not rights that are theoretical or illusory but rights that are practical and effective; this is particularly so of the rights of the defence in view of the prominent place held in a democratic society by the right to a fair trial, from which they derive ... As the Commission's Delegates correctly emphasised, Article 6 para 3(c) speaks of 'assistance' and not of 'nomination'. Again, mere nomination does not ensure effective assistance since the lawyer appointed for legal aid purposes may die, fall seriously ill, be prevented for a protracted period from acting or shirk his duties. If they are notified of the situation, the authorities must either replace him or cause him to fulfil his obligations. Adoption of the government's restrictive interpretation would lead to results that are unreasonable and incompatible with both the wording of sub-paragraph (c) and the structure of Article 6 taken as a whole; in many instances free legal assistance might prove to be worthless.[80]

The court continued:

> Admittedly, a State cannot be held responsible for every shortcoming on the part of a lawyer appointed for legal aid purposes but, in the particular circumstances, it was for the competent Italian authorities to take steps to ensure that the applicant enjoyed effectively the right to which they had recognised he was entitled. Two courses were open to the authorities: either to replace Mr Della Rocca or, if appropriate, to cause him to fulfil his obligations ... They chose a third course – remaining passive – whereas compliance with the Convention called for positive action on their part ...[81]

In a domestic context the failure of a lawyer to provide effective representation may mean that there has not been a fair trial. This was recognised in the case of *Nangle*,[82] where various allegations of incompetence, including a failure to investigate an alibi, were raised on an appeal against conviction. The court considered the traditional 'flagrant incompetence' test and held that the domestic law would need review, although it then declined to rule on the appropriate standard:

---

78 *Loizidou v Turkey (Preliminary Objections)* (1995) 20 EHRR 99, at para 72.
79 (1981) 3 EHRR 1.
80 *Ibid*, para 33.
81 *Ibid*, para 36.
82 *R v Nangle* [2001] Crim LR 506.

It follows that we have not been persuaded that any of the grounds so far argued will entitle the appellant to succeed on this appeal. The case was presented, as one in which there had been 'flagrant incompetence' by the legal advisers ... Although we have found that certain aspects of their conduct of the case were deficient, it would be an abuse of language to describe those failings as approaching, let alone amounting, to 'flagrant incompetence'.

In any event, in the light of the present requirement under the European Convention on Human Rights 'flagrant incompetence' may no longer be the appropriate measure of when this court will quash a conviction. What Article 6 requires in this context is that the hearing of the charges against an accused shall be fair. If the conduct of the legal advisers has been such that this objective is not met, then this court may be compelled to intervene. We would add that since we have not been persuaded that such deficiencies as there may have been resulted in any unfairness to the appellant, nor yet imperilled the safety of his conviction, it is not strictly necessary for us to consider what level of incompetence would have to exist before the court could be satisfied that there had been a relevant breach of the provisions of Article 6(1).[83]

In the case of *R v Joshil Thakrar*[84] the court was faced with solicitors who had by and large delegated the preparation of the criminal case to their unqualified office manager. The Court of Appeal noted that the effect of a breach of Art 6 would mean that the conviction would be unsafe. The court therefore proceeded to analyse in some detail the effects of the breaches:

We have already indicated that we find that the appellant's solicitors did fall below the level of reasonably competent solicitors in the way in which they prepared this case for trial on behalf of the appellant. That however is not enough to determine this appeal against conviction. The mere fact that an appellant's solicitors may have failed to carry out their duties to the appellant in a proper manner does not itself mean that a conviction is automatically unsafe. Nor is a conviction to be quashed as a means of expressing the court's disapproval of the solicitor's failures. The test is whether, in all the circumstances, the conviction is safe. Nonetheless, if such failures have prevented an appellant from having a fair trial, within the meaning of Article 6 of the European Convention on Human Rights, that will normally mean that the conviction is unsafe and should be quashed: *Togher* [2001] CLR 124.

Therefore the first question is whether the appellant received a fair trial or whether such a trial was prevented by the failings in preparation on the part of his solicitors. Such an issue is to be determined by considering the proceeding as a whole, as the jurisprudence of the European Court of Human Rights makes clear, and it follows that one cannot confine one's attention merely to the solicitor's preparations in isolation. As this court said in *Nangle* ... if the conduct of an accused's legal advisors has been such that the objective of a fair trial is not met, then this court may be compelled to intervene.

83 [2001] Crim LR 506, paras 63 and 64.
84 [2001] EWCA Crim 1096.

There are two areas where the solicitors' lack of preparation of the case could potentially have prejudiced a fair trial of the appellant. The first is that of the conflict between the appellant's version in interview by the police and the version, which he gave in evidence at trial, and the second concerns the failure to seek any CCTV evidence. We shall take those two matters in that order.

Having reviewed the evidence, the court concluded that the undoubted incompetence of the solicitors had not deprived the defendant of a fair trial:

> Looking at the matter in the round, we conclude that the shortcomings on the part of the appellant's solicitors, reprehensible though they were, did not prejudice the appellant in the way in which his defence was advanced at his trial, nor did they deprive him of a fair trial. There was a very strong case against him in any event. The mobile phone belonging to the complainant was found on him very shortly after the robbery. He was identified by the complainant within minutes of the robbery. The complainant gave evidence at trial that the appellant took the phone from him, having previously restrained him from getting away from the group as a whole. The explanation proffered by the appellant of why he had the complainant's mobile phone on him when stopped by the police was extremely weak and inherently unlikely to be believed by the jury. In addition the appellant had told a number of lies to the police at the time of his arrest, which inevitably must have undermined his credibility. All that evidence is relevant in determining whether his trial was fair when looked at as a whole and in determining whether his conviction is safe.

The effect of the Human Rights Act has therefore been to clarify the prior test of 'flagrant incompetence', but it appears that it will inevitably be necessary for courts to look at the effect of the lawyers' shortcomings and to identify the prejudice that has arisen for the defendant in order to decide whether there has been a breach of the right to a fair trial. In this context, therefore, advocates will continue to need to analyse what steps reasonably competent lawyers, whether solicitors or advocates, would have taken and to show how the failure to take those steps has impacted on the defendant's case.

Whether Strasbourg will be inclined to accept that the weight of evidence against the defendant is a permissible factor remains to be seen. It could be argued, following from the decision in *Condron* (discussed in the following chapter), that the appellate court is necessarily reduced to speculation as to the effect of the defective legal representation on the defendant's case. If this line were to be adopted, however, it is hard to see how the judgment as to competence is to be made other than by referral to the facts of the case, including all such factors as evidential weight. The effect for advocates may therefore be largely the same.

Issues for advocates: legal aid and legal representation

1 Is this a criminal matter within the autonomous sense of the term? (See Issues for advocates: arguments on the classification of the offence: 7.2 above.)

2 Is the prosecuting authority legally represented? (Even if the prosecuting authority is not legally represented, it is likely that lay prosecutors, for example from the Environment Agency, will have a particular expertise in dealing with prosecutions in their field.)

3 Is there a fundamental issue of equality of arms?

(If so, defence advocates should be prepared to specify exactly how the legal representation of the prosecution advantages the prosecution to the detriment of the defence: does the representation enable access to evidence, and increased ability to deal with complex legal argument, or an improved access to the mechanisms of the court?)

4 Identify why the interests of justice require legal representation:

It is likely that the grounds will all be matters which can appropriately be taken into account within the general Access to Justice Act criteria – but the court should be reminded of the need to ensure that the access to legal assistance is effective – is access to a Duty Solicitor sufficient given the complexity of the case?

• In particular, have regard to the complexity of the matter and the importance of what is at stake.

• These matters should be considered in the light of the circumstances of the particular defendant – not the hypothetical 'capable' defendant: see, for example, *Quaranta*, above.

5 Is this a matter where lack of legal representation at an earlier stage can be 'cured' by representation in a higher court?

7.5 THE HRA AND BAIL APPLICATIONS

Prior to the commencement of the Human Rights Act, the Law Commission produced a report on the compatibility of bail provisions with the requirements of the European Convention, Bail and the Human Rights Act 1998.[85] The report was 150 pages in length, illustrating clearly the sheer scope of potential arguments on the application of Convention jurisprudence to domestic court practice. Among the concerns raised by the reports were the removal of the right to bail under s 26 of the Criminal Justice and Public Order Act 1994[86] (where the accused was already on bail 'in court proceedings' at

---

85 Consultation Paper No 157.
86 Section 2A of Part I of Sched 1 to the Bail Act 1976.

the time of the alleged new indictable offence); the removal of a right to bail in all but exceptional circumstances for those accused of second serious offences under s 25 of the Criminal Justice and Public Order Act; and the apparent removal of any right to bail to those persons arrested under s 7 of the Bail Act for suspected breach of a bail condition. The Commission also expressed concern about the potential failure of courts to give adequate reasons for the refusal of bail, a potential lack of rigour in the refusing bail on the basis that the defendant was likely to commit further offences, as well as refusal on the basis that this was necessary for the defendant's own protection, and the operation of Part IIA of Sched 1 to the Bail Act so that the court need not hear arguments which have already been fully argued on earlier occasions.

It is clear, both in Convention law and in domestic case law, that bail applications fall within the provisions of Art 5 (the right to liberty) rather than Art 6. Article 5 is engaged by the requirement in Art 5(1)(c) that:

> ... the lawful arrest or detention of a person [is] effected for the purpose of bringing him before the competent legal authority ...

This provision is to be read in conjunction with the requirement in Art 5(3) that:

> Everyone arrested or detained in accordance with the provisions of paragraph (1)(c) of this article shall be brought promptly before a judge or other officer authorised by law to exercise judicial power and shall be entitled to trial within a reasonable time or to release pending trial.

This in overlaps with the provisions of Art 5(4), which provides:

> Everyone who is deprived of his liberty by arrest or detention shall be entitled to take proceedings by which the lawfulness of his detention shall be decided speedily by a court and his release ordered if his detention is not lawful.

The involvement of a court requires certain 'fundamental guarantees of procedure',[87] although it is clear that the guarantees do not amount to the importation of the full range of fair trial guarantees from Art 6. The core requirement is 'equality of arms', and this overarching principle has important implications for advocates who wish to argue for a greater level of disclosure at the bail application, or who wish to cross-examine, or indeed call, witnesses.

7.5.1 The Strasbourg position

Although Art 5(3) speaks of a right to trial within a reasonable time or to release pending trial, the Strasbourg Court has held that these are separate rights, so that there will be a right to bail pending trial. Accordingly, the court

---

87 *De Wilde, Ooms and Versyp v Belgium (No 1)* (1971) A 12, 373, para 76.

has held that there must be 'relevant and sufficient' reasons for refusing bail pending trial: *Wemhoff v Germany*.[88]

The grounds on which Strasbourg has recognised that bail can properly be refused are broadly in line with the Sched II provisions of the Bail Act 1976 and include:

The need to prevent the defendant from absconding

The need to prevent the defendant from interfering with course of justice

The need to prevent the defendant from committing further offences

The need to preserve public order

Moreover it is permissible for courts to grant bail subject to conditions such as sureties, residence, or the surrendering of a passport where these are necessary in order to meet a specified risk.

While these grounds therefore seem entirely familiar to lawyers who are used to the Bail Act provisions, it is important to stress that the approach taken in Strasbourg suggests that it may require courts to be more stringent in assessing the actual risk posed by a defendant. Thus, Strasbourg has made clear that the reasons for refusing bail must not be 'stereotyped': *Clooth v Belgium*.[89] When deciding whether there are grounds for refusing bail, the court must look to whether there is actual risk; it may not be acceptable, for example, simply to rely upon the defendant's previous criminal record as indicating that a ground is made out. Equally, where the court denies bail on the basis that there is a risk of interference with witnesses, that risk may diminish once witness statements have been taken, and the court may need to review whether there remains a real risk.

A good example of the more sceptical approach of the Strasbourg Court to matters relating to bail can be seen in the context of *Labita v Italy*[90] where the applicant was challenging his pre-trial detention as a suspected member of the Mafia, which had been based on the evidence of a single informer (*pentito*) who had himself previously been a member of the Mafia:

> 156 In the instant case, the allegations against the applicant came from a single source, a *pentito* who had stated in 1992 that he had learned indirectly that the applicant was the treasurer of a mafia-type organisation ... According to the authorities in question, in May 1992 those statements constituted sufficient evidence to justify keeping the applicant in detention, given the general credibility and trustworthiness of the *pentito* concerned ...

> 157 The court is conscious of the fact that the co-operation of *pentiti* is a very important weapon in the Italian authorities' fight against the Mafia. However, the use of statements by *pentiti* does give rise to difficult problems as, by their very nature, such statements are open to

---

88 (A/7) (1979–80) 1 EHRR 55.

89 (A/225) (1992) 14 EHRR 717.

90 Judgment of 6 April 2000.

manipulation and may be made purely in order to obtain the advantages, which Italian law affords to *pentiti*, or for personal revenge. The sometimes ambiguous nature of such statements and the risk that a person might be accused and arrested on the basis of unverified allegations that are not necessarily disinterested must not, therefore, be underestimated ...

158 For these reasons, as the domestic courts recognise, statements of *pentiti* must be corroborated by other evidence. Furthermore, hearsay must be supported by objective evidence ...

In further emphasis upon this focus on the cogency of any evidence, the court also made clear that the weight to be accorded to evidence would inevitably change with time, requiring a review of the grounds for pre-trial detention:

159 That, in the court's view, is especially true when a decision is being made whether to prolong detention pending trial. While a suspect may validly be detained at the beginning of proceedings on the basis of statements by *pentiti*, such statements necessarily become less relevant with the passage of time, especially where no further evidence is uncovered during the course of the investigation.

The Criminal Justice and Court Services Act 2000 introduces a new power for the police to take samples for testing for the presence of Class A drugs from certain categories of detainee. The Act permits the prosecution to make the results known to the court. It should therefore be the case that there is less reliance by prosecuting authorities on hearsay and opinion when suggesting to the court that a particular defendant has a drug habit. However, defence advocates will also wish to draw to the court's attention the need to have due regard to the actual risk arising from any such misuse of drugs. A mere stereotyped view that an offender who has used controlled drugs will necessarily be unreliable and so will fail to attend, or will necessarily offend while on bail, will clearly offend against Art 5. Prosecuting advocates should seek to adduce evidence – from the defendant's previous bail history, or from his criminal record – to show actual risk.

7.5.1.1 *Refusal of bail for the defendant's own protection*

There is little reliable Strasbourg guidance on whether the refusal of bail on this ground is permissible. The Law Commission concluded that the law should not be reformed as it could be interpreted in a Convention compliant way. In particular, the Law Commission stressed that the circumstances where there could be a basis for refusal on this ground were likely to be exceptional and that they should probably relate to the offence rather than the offender. The conclusions are, however, tentatively expressed.[91] We would suggest that the heightened focus given to the right to liberty under Art 5 principles, along with the need for a considerably greater degree of reasoning

---

91 Law Commission Paper, Chapter 7.

from the courts in support of the refusal of bail, indicates that the courts will need very cogent evidence of harm before refusal of bail on this ground is permissible.

7.5.2 Applying the Convention

The starting point for any argument, whether on behalf of the defence, or in response from the prosecution, must be an acceptance that Art 6 is of itself not directly relevant. In the *Havering Justices*[92] case the Divisional Court was asked to consider the right to bail of persons arrested under s 7 of the Bail Act for alleged breaches of bail conditions. The court rejected arguments that such hearings imported Art 6 due process rights, stating that the purpose of the imposition of conditions was in order to meet specified Bail Act concerns and could not be seen as imposing any form of criminal penalty in their own right:

> It is clearly with this principle [of preventing arbitrary detention] in mind that the court has been prepared to borrow some of the general concepts of fairness in judicial proceedings from Article 6. But that does not mean that the process required for conformity with Article 5 must also be in conformity with Article 6. That would conflate the Convention's control over two separate sets of proceedings, which have different objects. Article 5, in the present context, is concerned to ensure that the detention of an accused person before trial is only justified by proper considerations relating to the risks of absconding, and of interfering with witnesses, or the commission of other crimes. Article 6 is concerned with the process of determining the guilt or otherwise of a person who if found guilty would be subject to criminal penalties. It is in that context that the procedural safeguards required respectively under Article 5 and Article 6 must be viewed.[93]

This is not to say, however, that defence advocates should entirely turn their back on the issue. The court in *Havering Justices* was forced to acknowledge that the Strasbourg case law did seem to indicate higher levels of protection in some cases than mere equality of arms. However, the domestic court took the view that such cases had been to some extent undermined by lesser standards of protection in later cases:

> In particular, it seems to me to be important to note that the *de Wilde* case and the *Winterwerp* case represent the high watermark of the argument that the procedural requirements of Article 6 are to be in some way assimilated to consideration of issues under Article 5. Neither decision does more, in my view, than to underline the fact that where a decision is taken to deprive somebody of his liberty, that should only to be done after he has been given a fair opportunity to answer the basis upon which such an order is sought. It

---

92 *R (on the Application of Director of Public Prosecutions) v Havering Magistrates' Court* and *R (on the Application of Mark McKeown) v Wirral Borough Magistrates' Court* [2001] 2 Cr App R 2, 'Havering Justices'.

93 *Ibid*, para 36.

seems to me that in testing whether or not such an opportunity has been given, it is essential to bear in mind the nature and purpose of the proceedings in question.[94]

Thus the issue of the extent to which Art 6 concerns are subsumed within the Art 5 requirement for effective judicial review of detention remains a live one and defence advocates may be able to rely on the facts of a particular case to show that a higher level of review is required from the court in order to safeguard the rights of the accused. However, it remains the case that the focus is on the right to liberty, rather than the right to a fair hearing in the determination of a criminal matter since no criminal matter is being determined at this interim stage.

7.5.2.1 What are the procedural rights that Art 5 requires?

Following from the conclusion that the key test is one of whether the detention is permitted by Art 5, the court in *Havering Justices* identified the key issues as the extent to which Art 5 required evidence to be called and an opportunity for challenge provided. Lord Justice Latham reviewed the Strasbourg approach in cases such as *Shiesser v Switzerland*,[95] and summarised it in traditional natural justice terms:

> Article 5 therefore requires there to be in place a judicial procedure which not only meets the criterion of being in accordance with law, but which also provides the basic protection for a defendant inherent in the concept of judicial proceedings. Such proceedings must ensure equal treatment of the person liable to be detained and the authorities, it must be truly adversarial, and there must be 'equality of arms' between the parties. These concepts inevitably overlap. In language more familiar to common lawyers, a person liable to detention is entitled to natural justice. He must be treated fairly.[96]

However, this leaves a clear difficulty for both prosecution and defence advocates in identifying not merely the level of proof required, but also the procedures to be employed in adducing such evidence as is required. Here the court in *Havering Justices* purported to do little more than follow the existing domestic authorities, while nonetheless indicating that a more stringent approach to the issue of refusal of bail would be required by virtue of Art 5.

> 41 From the decisions in *R v Liverpool Justices, Re Moles* and *R v Mansfield Justices* ... it is clear that the material upon which a justice is entitled in domestic law to come to his opinion is not restricted to admissible evidence in the strict sense ... I see nothing in either Article 5 itself, or in the authorities to which we have been referred, which suggest that, in

---

94 *Ibid.*
95 (1979) 2 EHRR 417
96 *Havering Justices*, para 27.

itself, reliance on material other than evidence which would be admissible at a criminal trial would be a breach of the protection required by Article 5

...

42   What undoubtedly is necessary is that the justice, when forming his opinion, takes proper account of the quality of the material upon which he is asked to adjudicate. This material is likely to range from mere assertion at the one end of the spectrum, which is unlikely, may not have any probative effect, to documentary proof at the other end of the spectrum. The procedural task of the justice is to ensure that the defendant has a full and fair opportunity to comment on, and answer that material. If that material includes evidence from a witness, who gives oral testimony, clearly the defendant must be given an opportunity to cross-examine. Likewise, if he wishes to give oral evidence he should be entitled to. The ultimate obligation of the justice is to evaluate that material in the light of the serious potential consequences to the defendant, having regard to the matters to which I have referred, and the particular nature of the material, that is to say taking into account, if hearsay is relied upon by either side, the fact that it is hearsay and has not been the subject of cross-examination, and form an honest and rational opinion.[97]

7.5.2.2   Havering Justices: *testing the evidential value of assertions*

The principles in *Havering Justices* make clear therefore that where a prosecutor seeks to establish a significant breach of bail conditions such as to persuade the court that one of the exceptions to the right of bail is made out (and the court in *Havering Justices* made clear that the unhappily drafted provisions in the Bail Act do not amount to a requirement to refuse bail where there has been a s 7 arrest), the prosecutor must be prepared to provide the court with cogent evidence. It is for the court to give that evidence such weight as it sees fit, but defence advocates will wish to point to the lack of credibility of evidence where there has been no live testimony, and no cross-examination, or where the evidence has been largely based on hearsay.

7.5.2.3   Arguing for a right to presence?

The existing case law on the right to be present at a bail hearing under Art 5 is at best confused. In *Winterwerp v Netherlands*,[98] a mental health detention case, Strasbourg indicated that it would only be appropriate to replace the individual's presence with that of his legal representative in exceptional circumstances. By way of contrast, however, in the later *Sanchez-Reisse*[99] case, the breach of Art 5 arose not from the requirement that the applicant's case be put by a lawyer, but from the breach of the principle of equality of arms in

---

97   [2001] 2 Cr App R 2, paras 41 and 42.
98   (1979) 2 EHRR 387.
99   (1986) 9 EHRR 71.

failing to permit the applicant to respond in writing to a written opinion of the state to the court.

Clearly, the presence of the accused will not normally be an issue in the magistrates' courts, but will of course be an issue where bail appeals are being heard in the Crown Court, where the defendant is not normally produced from custody. Where, however, there is a need for the defendant to be present, either because his presence is required in order to enable effective cross-examination of prosecution witnesses, or because he himself is to give evidence in support of his application, as is envisaged by *Havering Justices*, it seems inevitable that the court will have to accede to an application for the defendant to be produced from custody.

Nor is the need for presence confined to those cases where there will be a challenge to the prosecution evidence. There may be cases where it is clear that the grant of bail is likely to be conditional on the availability of a place at a bail hostel. In such cases there may be a need for an interview with the liaison probation officer at the court. Since bail must be granted where a condition would adequately address the concerns of the court, the failure to make available a defendant so that suitability for a bail hostel place can be assessed could amount to a breach of Art 5.

7.5.2.4 Bail and arguments for prosecution disclosure

It is a fundamental aspect of the right to a fair trial that criminal proceedings, including the elements of such proceedings that relate to procedure, should be adversarial and that there should be equality of arms between the prosecution and defence. The right to an adversarial trial means, in a criminal case, that both prosecution and defence must be given the opportunity to have knowledge of and comment on the observations filed and the evidence adduced by the other party ...[100]

The right to disclosure clearly arises as an integral element of the Art 6 right to a fair trial. However, since the right arises from the principle of equality of arms, there is then a clear link with the Art 5 procedural requirements. While *Havering Justices* provides a clear basis for prosecution advocates to argue that a distinction must be drawn between rights that are focused on determinative issues, and hence applicable within Art 6, defence advocates will be able to point out that the recognition of the duty of the court to ensure that 'the defendant has a full and fair opportunity to comment on, and answer' the prosecution assertions will inevitably require a disclosure to be made.

---

100 *Rowe and Davis v United Kingdom* (2000) 30 EHRR 1.

To some extent this is already recognised by the *Attorney General's Guidelines on Disclosure*,[101] picking up on the principles articulated in *R v DPP ex p Lee*,[102] where the Divisional Court had noted that the Criminal Procedure and Investigations Act 1996 regime is silent as to disclosure during the period in between the arrest and the committal (or in summary cases, the arrest and the entering of a Not Guilty plea), which would then trigger disclosure of unused material at a fairly late stage. The court had held that there might be some cases where the prosecutor might need to make earlier disclosure of some of the unused material. This is position is now confirmed by the *AG Guidelines*:

> Prosecutors must always be alive to the need, in the interests of justice and fairness in the particular circumstances of any case to make disclosure of material after the commencement of proceedings but before the prosecutor's duty arises under the Act. For instance, disclosure ought to be made of significant information that might affect a bail decision or that might enable the defence to contest the committal proceedings.[103]

While these Guidelines specifically relate to the disclosure of unused material, it is clearly hard to justify the drawing of a distinction between the provision of used or unused material where that material is of relevance to the defence application.

Where an application to the prosecution for disclosure is not successful, advocates will wish to renew the application at the start of the application for bail. The court should be reminded not simply of the *prima facie* right to bail under domestic law (where the case is not one where that domestic presumption has been displaced), but also the requirement under Art 5 for the court to consider:

> ... all the facts arguing for or against the existence of a genuine requirement of public interest justifying, with due regard to the principle of the presumption of innocence, a departure from the rule of respect for individual liberty ...[104]

The court must clearly have regard to the prevailing domestic legislation, the Bail Act 1976. However, while that Act directs the court that bail may only be refused where certain specified grounds are made out (the most common being the substantial likelihood that the defendant will fail to attend, that he will commit further offences and that that he will interfere with witnesses or the course of justice) there is nothing in the Act to prevent the court from requiring that the prosecution make adequate disclosure in order to ensure

---

101 *Attorney General's Guidelines on Disclosure* (hereafter, the *AG Guidelines*), 29 November 2000. Available at http://www.lslo.gov.uk/pdf/guidelines.pdf.

102 [1999] 2 Cr App R 304.

103 *AG Guidelines*, at para 34. This goes some way to countering the cautious approach of Lord Woolf in *Wildman v DPP* [2001] EWHC Admin 4; [2001] Crim LR 565 that courts 'should approach with caution' Strasbourg decisions that appear to require disclosure for pre-trial procedures since each procedure will differ.

104 *Letellier v France* (1992) 14 EHRR 83, para 35.

that the principle of equality of arms is maintained. Indeed, since the court is required to act in a way which is compatible with the Convention rights of the defendant, advocates will be able to argue that the court will be acting unlawfully where it fails to make an order for disclosure in circumstances where the information is required in order to enable the defendant properly to challenge the assertions of the prosecution. Alternatively, where disclosure is not forthcoming, perhaps because the prosecution advocate at court does not himself have access to the information that is needed, the court will have no alternative but to grant bail to the defendant.

7.5.2.5   Applications for adjournments

Where a prosecutor argues that there has been insufficient time to obtain the information to make a bail decision – and under the Narey system,[105] advocates will often find that accused persons are in court within hours of charge – it is important to draw the court's attention to the need for expeditious decision making. Where information is not available to convince the court of a genuine risk, the court will resolve the matter in favour of the defendant:

> the justice must do his best to come to a fair conclusion on the relevant day; if he cannot do so, he will not be of the opinion that the relevant matters have been made out which could justify detention.[106]

7.5.2.6   The right to reasons

Section 5(3) of the Bail Act provides that:

> the court shall, with a view to enabling him [ie the defendant] to consider making an application in the matter to another court, give reasons for withholding bail.

Reasons are of course of particular importance since in the absence of appropriate reasons it will be impossible to ascertain the basis on which bail has been refused, and hence impossible to tell whether the restriction on liberty has been in accordance with the law.[107] The level of reasons provided by the domestic courts has historically been minimal, often advocates will

---

105 Introduced by the Crime and Disorder Act 1998.

106 *Havering Justices*, para 45 – in relation to the apparent lack of a power to adjourn at all when dealing with matters under s 7(4) of the Bail Act. Note that in *R (on the Application of Hussain) v Derby Magistrates Court* [2001] EWHC Admin 507; (2001) 145 SJLB 168, the court took the view that s 7(5) of the Bail Act permitted a district judge to make a determination to refuse bail where the matter had earlier been stood down by a different Bench. There was, the court said, nothing in the language of the statute to indicate that Parliament had required procedural rigidities appropriate to a more formal hearing which would be conducive to delay.

107 The Law Commission make the point that although there is no 'independent Convention duty on a national court to make an adequate record of its reasons', failure to do so will mean that the state will find it difficult to justify the detention. Consultation Paper, para 4.10.

have little more than a certificate of full argument with tick boxes indicating the ground or grounds that the court has considered are made out. The Law Commission took the view that such 'reliance on statutory reasons alone' might offend against the Strasbourg prohibition on making decisions on 'abstract' or 'stereotyped' grounds.

It is worth noting two of the cases cited by the Law Commission as examples of the Strasbourg Court's more rigorous requirements for the provision of a reasoned decision. In *Muller v France*[108] M had admitted various offences, including armed robbery. He was detained for four years pending trial. Among the reasons put forward for objecting to his release was that:

> The accused is implicated in several armed robberies and he has previous convictions for similar offences, so is a habitual offender. He is unlikely to appear for trial in view of the sentence he faces.[109]

The European Court of Human Rights held that there had been a violation of Art 5:

> Like the Commission, the court notes that it is not apparent from the decisions not to release the applicant that there was a real risk of his absconding. Although such a danger may exist where the sentence faced is a long term of imprisonment, the court points out that the risk of absconding cannot be gauged solely on the basis of the severity of the sentence faced ... As far as the danger of re-offending is concerned, a reference to a person's antecedents cannot suffice to justify refusing release ...[110]

Similarly in *IA v France*,[111] where the allegation was that the defendant had murdered his wife, and the grounds for refusal of bail included concerns that he might abscond and that he might 'repeat his offence', the court stated:

> The need to ensure that the applicant remained at the disposal of the judicial authorities ...

> All the decisions relating to Mr IA's detention on remand cite this ground, since the competent courts considered that there was a risk the applicant might abscond if released. They are based in the main on the applicant's links with Lebanon and, in some cases, his 'conduct' ... and the penalty to which he was liable ...

> These are undoubtedly circumstances, which suggest a danger of flight, and the evidence in the file tends to show their relevance in the instant case. Nevertheless, the court notes the sketchiness of the reasoning given on this point in the decisions in issue. It further notes that, although such a danger necessarily decreases as time passes ... the judicial authorities omitted to state

---

108 1997–II, p 374.
109 *Ibid*, para 23.
110 *Ibid*, paras 43–44.
111 1998–VII, p 2951.

exactly why in the present case there was reason to consider that it persisted for more than five years.

The court notes, like the government, that the decisions in issue referred to the inadequacy of judicial supervision and therefore accepts that the question whether the applicant was capable of providing adequate guarantees that he would appear for trial if released was considered. Here again, however, it can only note the deficient reasoning of the decisions concerned.

The need to prevent repetition of the offence.

This ground appears to be of secondary importance in the light of the circumstances of the case. Besides, the orders, which cite it ... do not mention any consideration capable of substantiating it in those circumstances.[112]

It is likely that many courts will now be providing a greater level of detail. As a minimum advocates should expect to be told the ground or grounds on which the court is refusing bail, the factors to which the court has had regard in relation to each ground, and what evidence the court has taken into account in arriving at its decision. In considering the reasons, advocates will also wish to ensure that it is clear from the face of the record why the matters recorded amount to a sufficient reason for refusing bail.

7.5.2.7 Appeal hearings

Appeals against the refusal of bail in the magistrates' court lie to both the High Court and Crown Court. The lack of legal aid in relation to High Court applications has in the past tended to mean that these were rare. In so far as Criminal Defence Service funding is now available, such applications may become more mainstream.

The Convention does not specify that the defendant must have a right to appeal against a refusal of bail, but the Law Commission suggests that the case law indicates a right to periodic review under certain circumstances. The key issue in terms of domestic law is less the regularity of review than the restriction, which is imposed by paras 2 and 3 of Part IIA of Sched I to the Bail Act:

At the first hearing after that at which the court decided not to grant the defendant bail he may support an application for bail with any argument as to fact or law that he desires (whether or not he has advanced that argument previously).

At subsequent hearings the court need not hear arguments as to fact or law, which it has heard previously.

The concern therefore is that the right of review is unduly restricted by these provisions, and it is suggested that the mere effluxion of time, when taken alongside the requirement that the refusal of bail be on non-stereotyped

---

112 1998–VII, paras 105–07.

grounds, means that defence advocates should now be asking the court to review the basis on which bail was previously refused by indicating how prosecution concerns have now been diminished – perhaps because, for example, statements have been taken from vulnerable witnesses. Prosecution advocates will need to be prepared to provide concrete evidence as to why the concerns continue to be valid.

7.5.2.8 Challenges to the substantive law

Exceptional circumstances and bail

It will be recalled that s 25 of the Criminal Justice and Public Order Act 1994, in its original form, provided that a person charged with a second specified offence could not be granted bail:

25 (1) A person who in any proceedings has been charged with or convicted of an offence to which this section applies and in circumstances to which it applies shall not be granted bail in those proceedings.

(2) This section applies, subject to sub-s 3 below, to the following offences –

(a) murder;

(b) attempted murder;

(c) manslaughter;

(d) rape; and

(e) attempted rape.

(3) This section applies to a person charged with or convicted of any such offence only if he has been previously convicted by or before a court in any part of the United Kingdom of any such offence or of culpable homicide and, in the case of a previous conviction of manslaughter or culpable homicide, if he was then sentenced to imprisonment or, if he was then a child or young person, to long-term detention under any of the relevant enactments.

An amendment was made by the Crime and Disorder Act 1998 and came into force on 30 September 1998. The section now provides that bail can be granted if there are 'exceptional circumstances which justify it'. The amendment was made in anticipation of arguments that the blanket refusal of bail would offend against Art 5, a finding that was duly made in relation to the first version of s 25 in the case of *Caballero v United Kingdom*,[113] where the United Kingdom conceded that a breach had occurred. The court's summary of the Commission's findings in *Caballero*, which can be found in *SBC v United Kingdom*[114] is a useful reminder of the very stringent safeguards, which must be in place, before an accused can be denied bail:

113 *Caballero v United Kingdom* (2000) 30 EHRR 643.
114 Judgment of 19 June 2001.

It noted that judicial control of interference by the executive with an individual's right to liberty was an essential feature of the guarantees embodied in Article 5 s 3, the purpose being to minimise the risk of arbitrariness in the pre-trial detention of accused persons. Certain procedural and substantive guarantees ensure that judicial control: the judge (or other officer) before whom the accused is 'brought promptly' must be seen to be independent of the executive and of the parties to the proceedings; that judge, having heard the accused himself, must examine all the facts arguing for and against the existence of a genuine requirement of public interest justifying, with due regard to the presumption of innocence, a departure from the rule of respect for the accused's liberty, and that judge must have the power to order an accused's release. It not being disputed that Mr Caballero fell within the scope of s 25 of the 1994 Act, the Commission found that the possibility of any consideration by a Magistrate of his pre-trial release on bail had been excluded in advance by the legislature by s 25 of the 1994 Act. This removal of the judicial control of pre-trial detention required by Article 5 s 3 of the Convention was found by the Commission to amount to a violation of that article.[115]

However, *Caballero* and the cases that have followed leave open the issue of whether the amendment to s 25, permitting bail to be granted if exceptional circumstances exist, is sufficient to satisfy Art 5. On the face of it, the provision appears to effectively reverse the onus of proof, so that in place of the right to bail envisaged by Art 5, the defendant must instead show that exceptional circumstances exist. The Law Commission, however, took the view that the test could be viewed as a mere rebuttable presumption[116] under which each court would still 'take account of all relevant circumstances and ... reach its decision in a proper manner'. This the Law Commission argued would mean that the court would merely be giving 'special weight to certain factors identified by Parliament as meriting such weight'. If the provision were read in this way, and the argument would be that the court, by virtue of s 6(3) and its s 3 interpretative obligation, would be required to do so, the Law Commission's 'tentative' view was that the provision might not breach Art 5.

The argument that a more wide-ranging reading down of the provision should be undertaken is, however, given some support in relation to the analogous provision under s 2 of the Crime (Sentences) Act 1997,[117] which requires courts to impose a mandatory life sentence when sentencing for a second serious criminal offence unless 'exceptional circumstances' apply. In *Offen*[118] the Court of Appeal took the view that the Human Rights Act required the legislation to be interpreted in a way that protected against

---

115 *Ibid.*
116 The issue of presumptions is considered in relation to the presumption of innocence and is dealt with in the following chapter.
117 Now s 109 of the Powers of Criminal Courts (Sentencing) Act 2000.
118 *R v Offen and Others* [2001] 2 All ER 154.

arbitrary deprivation of liberty. This could be done, it was stated, by simply having regard to the intention of Parliament:

> The question of whether circumstances are appropriately regarded as exceptional must surely be influenced by the context in which the question is being asked. The policy and intention of Parliament was to protect the public against a person who had committed two serious offences. It therefore can be assumed the section was not intended to apply to someone in relation to whom it was established there would be no need for protection in the future. In other words, if the facts showed the statutory assumption was misplaced, then this, in the statutory context was not the normal situation and in consequence, for the purposes of the section, the position was exceptional.[119]

A similar argument in relation to s 25 would re-cast the provision as a form of 'statutory assumption' that a person who was charged with a second specified offence should not be given bail because of the danger that they would re-offend. Article 5 requires that the courts look to the actual danger of re-offending while on bail – it must be 'plausible'[120] – so that the s 25 exercise amounts to a particularly close scrutiny of whether a 'plausible' danger arises. Adopting the reasoning from *Offen*, it can be argued that if no such danger arises on the facts – perhaps because (as in the *SBC* case)[121] the previous offence had been some 16 years earlier and was of a wholly different nature – then the case will be 'exceptional' since the statutory assumption will be misplaced.

Bail for defendants who are already on bail in respect of a prior offence

Section 26 of the Criminal Justice and Public Order Act 1994 inserted para 2A of Part 1 of Sched I to the Bail Act 1976 which provides that a defendant 'need not' be granted bail where he is charged with an indictable or either way offence and it appears to the court that he was already on bail 'in criminal proceedings' at the date of the instant offence. The Law Commission took the view that although this provision could be 'read down' so as to avoid the breach of Art 5 which would arise were the court to 'mechanically' refuse bail on this basis, a better response was to amend the Bail Act so as to make the fact that a defendant appears to have committed a further offence while on bail a factor to be taken into account when deciding whether one of the substantive grounds for refusal of bail is made out. No such amendment has been made.

Advocates must indicate to the court the limitations of the provision. Because of the need for a 'plausible' danger, the court can at most only treat the fact that the defendant is alleged to have offended while already on bail as

---

119 *Ibid*, para 88.
120 *Clooth v Belgium* (A/225) (1992) 14 EHRR 717, para 40.
121 *SBC v United Kingdom*, judgment of 19 June 2001.

a factor which might indicate that he is likely to re-offend if granted bail, or that it indicates a general lack of respect for the order of the court which suggests that he is unlikely to answer his bail. It is, of course, in the interests of advocates appearing for the prosecution, as much as for defence advocates, that the court approaches this issue in the correct way. Where a court simply proceeds on the basis that s 26 is activated and that there is therefore a loss of the *prima facie* right to bail, a Human Rights Act challenge is likely to succeed.

Issues for advocates: bail applications

1   Article 5 governs bail applications – but this requires consideration of certain due process rights implicit in the right of access to a court.

2   Most significantly there needs to be equality of arms between the parties.

3   Refusal of bail is permissible but the reasons for refusal must not be based on 'stereotyped' factors.

4   Likely to abscond: note that the severity of any sentence cannot of itself justify the refusal of bail; the court must have regard to the full range of factors.

5   Commit further offences: there can be no automatic assumption that because the defendant has a criminal history he will therefore commit further offences if granted bail.

6   If s 26 applies, submissions should urge that this provision be read compatibly with the Art 5 right to liberty (s 3 of the HRA) and that this can be done by treating the allegation that the accused has offended while on bail as being a factor in deciding whether there is a substantial risk that he will re-offend if granted bail.

7   Note the argument, if this is a case where s 25 of the Bail Act applies, that 'exceptional circumstances' must similarly be 'read down' so as to provide that exceptional circumstances will necessarily exist where there is no substantial risk of further offences being committed if bail is granted.

8   Has there been prior disclosure of the basis of the prosecution case?

9   How adequate has this disclosure been?

10 Has there been sufficient time for the defence to prepare the case following disclosure?

11 What is the quality of evidence before the court?

12 Is the evidence mere assertion from the prosecutor?

13 If a police officer has given evidence – to what extent is his or her evidence based on hearsay? Has the officer been cross-examined?

14 What opportunity has the defence been given to rebut the evidence? Has the defendant been permitted to give evidence? Have other witnesses been permitted to be called?

15 If the defendant is not present, has the advocate been able to take full instructions?

16 What reasons has the court given for its refusal of bail?

17 Has the defendant been permitted the right to renew his application for bail at reasonable intervals?

7.6 DISCLOSURE

While Art 6 itself makes no explicit reference to a right to disclosure, the right to disclosure has been treated as part of the key requirement of equality of arms, and a fundamental element of the right to a fair trial. In *Edwards v United Kingdom*[122] the European Court of Human Rights stated that:

> ... it is a requirement of fairness under Article 6(1) that the prosecution authorities disclose to the defence all material evidence for or against the accused ...[123]

The right to access to all relevant materials – and this would include both 'used' and 'unused' materials – is seen by Strasbourg as implicit in the right to a fair trial itself:

> It is a fundamental aspect of the right to a fair trial that criminal proceedings, including the elements of such proceedings that relate to procedure, should be adversarial and that there should be equality of arms between the prosecution and defence. The right to an adversarial trial means, in a criminal case, that both prosecution and defence must be given the opportunity to have knowledge of and comment on the observations filed and the evidence adduced by the other party ... In addition Article 6 s 1 requires, as indeed does English law ... that the prosecution authorities should disclose to the defence all material evidence in their possession for or against the accused ...[124]

In addition to the principle of equality of arms between prosecution and defence, disclosure is required to provide adequate time and facilities for preparing a defence[125] and to ensure that cross-examination takes place under conditions of parity.[126]

Part of the difficulty in applying the Strasbourg decisions on disclosure is that at the time of writing, those decisions have all been in respect of disclosure regimes prior to the commencement of the Criminal Procedure and Investigations Act (CPIA) 1996. There is as yet no guidance from Strasbourg

---

122 (1993) 15 EHRR 417.

123 *Ibid*, at para 36.

124 *Rowe and Davis v United Kingdom* (2000) 30 EHRR 1, para 60.

125 Article 6(3)(b). See *Edwards v United Kingdom* (1993) 15 EHRR 417.

126 Article 6(3)(d). See *ibid*, Commission Report para 50. Although Strasbourg tends to treat these guarantees as separate aspects of the general right to a fair trial under Art 6(1).

on the compatibility of the CPIA regime with the requirements of Art 6, although the decisions in respect of earlier common law procedures gives some indication as to the stance that the Strasbourg Court is likely to take. A further factor is the introduction of *Attorney General Guidelines on Disclosure*, which more clearly seek to take into account the implications of Art 6 for the operation of the statutory disclosure regime, and which start with an explicit recognition of the importance of the right to disclosure:

> Every accused person has a right to a fair trial, a right long embodied in our law and guaranteed under Article 6 of the European Convention on Human Rights. A fair trial is the proper object and expectation of all participants in the trial process. Fair disclosure to an accused is an inseparable part of a fair trial.[127]

7.6.1 What must be disclosed?

It is clear from Strasbourg case law that the Crown must disclose the evidence it seeks to rely upon (that is, used material). The obligation also extends to 'the results of investigations carried out throughout the proceedings', 'access to the prosecution file' and 'all relevant elements that have been or could be collected by the competent authorities' for the purpose of exonerating the accused or obtaining a reduction in sentence.[128] This includes material relating to the credibility of a prosecution witness.[129] This will involve the disclosure of material that does not form part of the Crown's case (that is, unused material).

A matter of some concern has been the apparently restrictive provisions for disclosure in Part 1 of the Criminal Procedure and Investigations Act 1996 whereby the prosecution is initially required to disclose only that which is thought to undermine the case for the prosecution against the defence.[130] Any further disclosure is dependent upon defence disclosure and is limited to material that might support the defence that has been disclosed.[131] A strict adherence to this test would not appear to be in line with the materiality test set out by the European Court.

However, this difficulty may be more apparent than real. The *Attorney General's Guidelines* suggest a relatively flexible and generous interpretation of the provisions. In particular para 20 provides that any doubt ought to be resolved in favour of disclosure and paras 36–38 provide a broad idea of material that might undermine the prosecution case – material potentially

---

127 Paragraph 1, *AG Guidelines*.
128 *Jespers v Belgium* (1981) 27 DR 61 at pp 87–88.
129 *Edwards v United Kingdom* (1993) 15 EHRR 417.
130 Section 3 of the Criminal Procedure and Investigations Act 1996.
131 *Ibid*, ss 5–7.

undermines the prosecution case if it has an 'adverse effect on the strength of the prosecution case':

> In deciding what material might undermine the prosecution case, the prosecution should pay particular attention to material that has potential to weaken the prosecution case or is inconsistent with it. Examples are:
>
> Any material casting doubt upon the accuracy of any prosecution evidence.
>
> Any material that may point to another person, whether charged or not (including a co-accused) having involvement in the commission of the offence.
>
> Any material that may cast doubt upon the reliability of a confession.
>
> Any material that might go to the credibility of a prosecution witness.
>
> Any material that might support a defence that is either raised by the defence or apparent from the prosecution papers. If the material might undermine the prosecution case it should be disclosed at this stage even though it suggests a defence inconsistent with or alternative to one already advanced by the accused or his solicitor.
>
> Any material that may have a bearing on the admissibility of any prosecution evidence.
>
> It should also be borne in mind that while items of material viewed in isolation may not be considered to potentially undermine the prosecution case, several items together could have that effect.[132]

It will be noted that the *Guidelines* also confirm that the value of material to the defence in developing lines of cross-examination or submissions to the court may also undermine the prosecution case. The *Guidelines* indicate that material which might support a defence should be disclosed at the initial stage whether such a defence is disclosed or not. This potentially blurs the distinction between primary and secondary prosecution disclosure and increases the amount of material that ought to be disclosed at the primary stage.

It should be noted that the domestic courts, rather confusingly, have not tended to adopt a literal interpretation of the Criminal Procedure and Investigations Act disclosure rules. Thus in *R v Brushett*[133] the Court of Appeal reviewed the disclosure rules without referring to the Criminal Procedure and Investigation Act test at all. Instead the case proceeded on the assumption that the test for disclosure of prosecution unused material was that set out in the earlier case of *R v Keane*,[134] covering material which was relevant or possibly relevant to an issue in the case, which raised or possibly raised a new issue, or which held out a real prospect of proving a lead on evidence going to such issues. *Prima facie* this is much wider than the duty

---

132 *AG Guidelines*, para 37.
133 [2000] All ER(D) 2432, discussed below.
134 [1994] WLR 746.

under the Criminal Procedure and Investigation Act and is more than enough to comply with the Convention requirements set out above.

7.6.2 Limitations on the right to disclosure

The right to disclosure is not absolute. Despite the central importance of disclosure, the European Court does not suggest that a fair trial can never take place where disclosure is withheld:

> ... the entitlement to disclosure of relevant evidence is not an absolute right. In any criminal proceedings there may be competing interests such as national security, or the need to protect witnesses at risk of reprisals or to keep secret police methods of investigation or crime which must be weighed against the rights of the accused.[135]

It follows that the principle of withholding material in the public interest survives the Human Rights Act. More controversial is the level of protection to be provided to an accused person when decisions are made regarding public interest immunity applications.

7.6.2.1 Public interest immunity arguments

Can there be equality of arms if the defence are excluded from the disclosure process? Under the Criminal Procedure and Investigations Act 1996 regime, it will be recalled that any application for material to be withheld from the defence will be the subject of an application to the trial judge. That application may be on notice or without notice, depending on the sensitivity of the material in issue.[136] Following *Jasper v United Kingdom*[137] and *Fitt v United Kingdom*,[138] the involvement of the trial judge, and the continuing duty of disclosure, suggests that the CPIA regime in respect of public interest immunity (pii) matters is likely to be Convention compliant. In *Jasper* the defence were told of the application by the prosecution to the trial judge for the withholding of information, but were not told of the category of information in issue: they were, however, able to outline their defence for the judge. In *Fitt*, the defence received slightly more information in respect of one of the categories of information, which was being withheld. In both cases, the Strasbourg Court was strongly influenced by the involvement of the trial judge in the review process. The court rejected the argument that the use of special counsel to protect the interests of the defendant was necessary and held that the pii regime was not in breach of Art 6.

---

135 *Rowe and Davis v United Kingdom* (2000) 30 EHRR 1, para 61.
136 Sections 14 and 15 of the Criminal Procedure and Investigations Act 1996.
137 (2000) 30 EHRR 441.
138 (2000) 30 EHRR 480.

However, both decisions must be treated with some caution in the light of the bare 9:8 majority within the Strasbourg Court – the dissenting minority all taking the view that the involvement of special counsel, and potentially even the hearing of the matter by a judge not involved in the trial, were needed in order to ensure a procedure which properly counter-balanced the unfairness to the defence. There is likely to be continuing difficulty for the United Kingdom, with its adversarial process, in justifying a procedure, which lacks this central adversarial element – a point made strongly by the dissenting minority:

> The fact that the judge monitored the need for disclosure throughout the trial ... cannot remedy the unfairness created by the defence's absence from the *ex parte* proceedings. In our view, the requirements ... that any difficulties caused to the defence must be sufficiently counterbalanced by the procedures followed by the judicial authorities are not met by the mere fact that it was a judge who decided that the evidence be withheld ... Our concern is that, in order to be able to fulfil his functions as the judge in a fair trial, the judge should be informed by the opinions of both parties, not solely the prosecution.[139]

Where, however, material has been withheld from the trial judge, as was of course the case in the *Rowe and Davis* case, it will generally follow that Art 6 has been breached. In *Atlan v United Kingdom*[140] the prosecution had denied that there was any unused material and only some four years later, and immediately prior to the Court of Appeal hearing, was it revealed that unused material existed. At this point the prosecution successfully applied for the non-disclosure of the material. The Strasbourg Court followed *Rowe and Davis*, stating:

> It is clear to the Court, and the Government do not seek to dispute, that the repeated denials by the prosecution at first instance of the existence of further undisclosed relevant material, and their failure to inform the trial judge of the true position, were not consistent with the requirements of Article 6 s 1 (see the above-mentioned *Rowe and Davis* judgment, s 63).

> The issue before the court is whether the *ex parte* procedure before the Court of Appeal was sufficient to remedy this unfairness at first instance.[141]

The court took the view that although the nature of the unused material had not been disclosed, there was a very strong suspicion that it related to a possible *agent provocateur*, in relation to whom the defence had specifically requested disclosure of any material. The fact that the trial judge had been unaware of the existence of the material meant that he had been unable to

---

139 *Jasper* (2000) 30 EHRR 441, dissenting opinion.

140 European Court of Human Rights, judgment of 29 May 2001; (2001) *The Times*, 3 July. In *R v Botmeh and Alami*, Lawtel 1/11/2001, the Court of Appeal held an *ex parte* hearing to consider material that had not been placed before the trial judge but concluded that even had there been a breach of Art 6, there was no evidence that the defendants had suffered any injustice, not least because they had not used similar material that had been disclosed.

141 *Ibid*, paras 44–45.

perform the balancing act that was required. Moreover, his summing up to the jury might have been very different had he known of its existence. There had therefore been a breach of Art 6.

7.6.2.2 Does the commencement of the Human Rights Act change the position in domestic law?

In *Brushett*[142] the defendant, B, was charged with a large number of assaults and indecent assaults on children who had been in his care when he had been headmaster of an Approved School between 1974 and 1980. The trial judge was required to consider requests for defence access to large quantities of information regarding the complainants obtained from Social Services files. Some material had been obtained by the prosecution, but other material had been produced as the result of defence summonses. In relation to the latter, the trial judge was therefore faced the decision in *Reading Justices*,[143] which provided that documents would not be 'material' for disclosure purposes if they were merely desired for the purpose of possible cross-examination; such documents must be admissible in themselves. Having reminded himself of the principles to be derived from the Strasbourg case law in *Rowe and Davis*, *Jasper* and *Fitt*, the judge took a more flexible approach, concluding that the core concern was that the defendant received a fair trial. With this in mind he stated that he would disclose documents that indicated that the witness had made false allegations in the past, and also those that suggested that another adult might have engaged in sexual activity with the child. The Court of Appeal strongly approved of this approach, holding that there was no difference in principle between the requirements of Art 6 and those imposed by domestic law. The decision of the Strasbourg Court in *Rowe and Davis* made clear that there must be a sufficient counter-balance by the procedures followed by the court in order to offset the difficulties caused to the defence. The trial judge had achieved this balance.

Brushett is a decision, which is clearly sustainable in the light of *Jasper* and *Fitt*, although the court's robust assertion that domestic law is in harmony with the requirements of Art 6 was sustainable only because the trial judge had effectively read down the relevant domestic case law so as to comply with the Strasbourg requirements. The distinction between material held by the prosecution and that held by third parties has been significantly narrowed. Moreover, it is noticeable that the Court of Appeal felt the need to enquire of the trial judge how much time he had spent reading through the material in question. His estimate that he had spent 4–6 days was clearly significant in enabling the court to find that the defendant's rights had been properly taken into account by a judge who had conscientiously read all the applicable material.

---

142 *R v Brushett* [2000] All ER(D) 2432.
143 *R v Reading Justices ex p Berkshire County Council* [1996] 1 CAR 245.

It is clear that there is considerable residual concern in the magistrates' court that there is no proper mechanism for dealing with potential prejudice arising from without notice applications in a forum where the magistrate will be the finder of fact as well as law. In *R (on the Application of Crown Prosecution Service) v Acton Youth Court*[144] the Divisional Court ruled that it would not normally be necessary for the tribunal to remit the matter to a different bench merely because it had heard an *ex parte* pii application, Lord Woolf stating that no additional issues arose simply because of the implementation of the Human Rights Act. While this decision is a necessary one, so long as it is argued that the tribunal will be taking responsibility for actively reviewing the (non) disclosure decision throughout the course of the trial, it is hard to see how defendants can feel that there has been appropriate equality of arms. It is likely that there will be further challenges on this point.

7.6.2.3 Withholding used material

In *Joe Smith*[145] the appellant had been linked by a DNA test to blood found on a display stand from a jeweller's window which had been the subject of a smash and grab. It was argued that if the police had had no grounds on which to arrest Smith, then the hair sample taken following arrest on which the DNA evidence was based should be excluded. The judge decided there were reasonable grounds for the arrest, relying on evidence which was withheld from the defence following an *ex parte* pii hearing. The Court of Appeal rejected arguments that it amounted to a breach of Art 6, applying not only the decision in *Rowe and Davis* but also the judgment in *Fox, Campbell and Hartley v United Kingdom*[146] where Strasbourg held that the United Kingdom could not be required to disclose the confidential sources of information in support of a decision to arrest a suspected terrorist.

Smith is a significant extension of the decisions in the earlier pii cases – which concerned unused material – in that the material withheld was being used in order to support the admissibility of evidence which was used at the trial, albeit by the trail judge and not by the jury. However, the European Court appears to contemplate the withholding of such material when it speaks of exceptions to the right of access to relevant evidence.

7.6.2.4 Destruction of unused material

In *R (on the Application of Ebrahim) v Feltham Magistrates Court*, and the linked case of *Mouat v Director of Public Prosecutions*,[147] the issue was abuse of process

---

144 [2001] EWHC Admin 402; (2001) 98(26) LSG 43.
145 *R v Smith (Joe)* [2001] 2 Cr App R 1.
146 (1991) 13 EHRR 157.
147 [2001] EWHC Admin 130; [2001] 1 WLR 1293.

arguments arising from the destruction of video material which would have been of use to the defence. The Divisional Court drew a distinction between two categories of abuse of process cases. In Category One are those cases where the court concludes that the defendant cannot receive a fair trial, as opposed to Category Two, where the trial is to be stayed because the behaviour of the prosecution is such that it would be unfair for the defendant to be tried. The test in the latter category is purely based on the conduct of the prosecutor, and it is clear from case law that it will be rare for abuse of process arguments to succeed on this basis. The court therefore focused on the first category – whether a fair trial is possible – noting without further comment the applicability of Art 6, but apparently concluding that no Convention issues arose.

Usefully the court looked not only at the requirements of the CPIA Code of Practice on Disclosure, but also the *AG Guidelines*. Paragraph 3.4 of the Code provides:

> In conducting an investigation, the investigator should pursue all reasonable lines of inquiry, whether these point towards or away from the suspect. What is reasonable in each case will depend on the particular circumstances.

From this the court concluded that 'the duty of investigation should be proportionate with the seriousness of the matter being investigated', a somewhat alarming proposition. Arguably the proposition that what is reasonable will depend on the circumstances of the case should not simply be confined to a consideration of offence seriousness – 'it's a minor offence, we aren't going to spend any money ensuring that you get a fair trial' – but a consideration of the type of material that might be relevant to a particular type of case and other factors such as requests made and information supplied by the accused. In particular the *AG Guidelines*, also cited by the court, provide at para 6:

> In discharging their obligations under the statute, code, common law and any operational instructions, investigators should always err on the side of recording and retaining material where they have any doubt as to whether it may be relevant.

This presumption of retention is only of value where the investigation has fully considered the appropriate lines of enquiry.

The court approved the stringent line taken by the higher courts in cases such as *Stallard*[148] where it was held that the ability to cross-examine the victim and to call the defendant to give evidence meant that the destruction of video evidence could in no way prevent a fair trial. In the *Mouat* case (which related to the destruction of video evidence of speeding) it was not sufficient for the prosecution to say that Mr Mouat's failure to protest at the time that he was stopped meant that it was permissible for the police to destroy the video

---

148 *R v Stallard* (2000) unreported, 13 April (CA).

evidence. The Code of Practice required the material to be preserved at least until the end of the suspended enforcement period.

In the *Feltham* case (which related to destruction of store CCTV tapes of the time prior to an alleged assault) it was still possible, following *Stallard*, for the defendant to put forward his account in evidence. Even if the investigating officer had failed to do all that he could to ensure the retention of material that could assist the defence it was still possible for the accused to receive a fair trial.

7.6.3 Disclosure of used material in summary only cases

One of the long-standing complaints of advocates in the magistrates' courts has been the lack of disclosure of the information on which the prosecution intends to rely. Under the Magistrates' Courts (Advance Information) Rules 1985[149] the Crown is obliged to make disclosure only in either-way offences. In *R v Stratford Justices ex p Imbert*[150] it was argued that the CPIA altered this position in that the accused could give no useful defence disclosure if there had been no advance disclosure of the prosecution statements. The accused would therefore not receive secondary prosecution disclosure and his right to a fair trial would be compromised. The Divisional Court asserted that the CPIA had nothing to do with advance disclosure of statements and moreover, the Convention gave no general right to advance disclosure of witness statements. The court did go on to state that as a matter of good practice disclosure should normally be given.

The court in Imbert rejected Art 6 arguments on the disclosure of used materials in summary only trials, and it's likely that this decision would have needed revisiting in the light of the Human Rights Act. However, in practical terms the issue may no longer be contentious for advocates in the light of the clear statement in the *AG Guidelines* that disclosure is to be made:

> The prosecutor should, in addition to complying with the obligations under the CPIA, provide to the defence all evidence upon which the Crown proposes to rely in a summary trial. Such provision should allow the accused or their legal advisers sufficient time properly to consider the evidence before it is called. Exceptionally, statements may be withheld for the protection of witnesses or to avoid interference with the course of justice.[151]

---

149 SI 1985 No 601, as amended.
150 [1999] 2 Cr App R 276.
151 *AG Guidelines*, para 43.

7.6.4 Disclosure in pre-trial applications

The position in regard to disclosure for the purposes of pre-trial applications, such as bail, has been discussed in the preceding section.

7.6.5 Defence disclosure requirements under the Criminal Procedure and Investigations Act 1996

This section has considered the impact of the Human Rights Act on arguments concerning disclosure of material to the defence. It is, of course, the case that the current disclosure regime under the Criminal Procedure and Investigations Act 1996 governs not only disclosure by the prosecution, but also imposes a limited duty of disclosure upon the defence. There is as yet no Strasbourg ruling on whether the imposition of this duty of defence disclosure is in breach of the presumption of innocence under Art 6(2). Case law on the inferences under ss 34, 36 and 37 of the Criminal Justice and Public Order Act 1994[152] suggests that Strasbourg may be prepared to accept a requirement for the defendant to indicate at least the basic nature of his defence[153] in order to ensure that appropriate disclosure can be made. In this regard, however, it is hard to justify the imposition of inferences. Similarly there appears little logical basis for the distinction drawn between the compulsory service of a defence statement in the Crown Court and the lack of any such compulsion in magistrates' court proceedings.

In relation to the first point, it can be argued that if the purpose of requiring a defence statement to be served is to enable the prosecution to comply with its duty of full disclosure, there is no need for any provision penalising the defence for non-service of the defence statement; the defence will simply be receiving less effective disclosure of relevant prosecution materials than would otherwise be the case. The existence of inferences introduces a degree of compulsion, which suggests that the duty to reveal the defence case is not in order to assist the defence, but to assist the prosecution. Arguably the process then becomes more akin to compelled questioning.

The argument that the purpose of the defence statement is more wide-ranging than simply to ensure appropriate prosecution disclosure is supported by the fact that provision of defence statements is not mandatory in the magistrates' court. While the distinction can be justified on the pragmatic basis that more unrepresented defendants are likely to appear in the magistrates' courts than in the Crown Courts, it is hard to see why this justifies the mandatory service requirement in the Crown Court.

---

152 Considered in more detail in the following chapter.
153 As *per* s 5 of the Criminal Procedure and Investigations Act 1996.

A key issue in relation to the duty of defence disclosure is whether it is a precondition of full prosecution disclosure. In the revealing document, *Points for Prosecutors*, the AG anticipates a challenge to the requirement for defence disclosure, asserting:

> Disclosure of material, which might assist the defence, is not contingent upon a statement being provided – the prosecutor has a continuing duty to under s 9 to keep disclosure under review throughout the trial process.[154]

In the *AG Guidelines*, however, it is made clear that the process, at least pre-trial, is clearly contingent on defence disclosure:

> Prosecutors should be open, alert and promptly responsive to requests for disclosure of material supported by the comprehensive defence statement. Conversely, if no defence statement has been served or if the prosecutor considers that the defence statement is lacking specific [sic] and/or clarity, a letter should be sent to the defence indicating that secondary disclosure will not take place or will be limited (as appropriate), and inviting the defence to specify and/or clarify the accused's case.[155]

The *Guidelines* therefore continue to impose a requirement for a relatively high degree of specificity (or comprehensiveness) in order to trigger full secondary disclosure. There is nothing in the Strasbourg case law, which limits the principle of equality of arms in this way, and this two-tier approach is only likely to be defensible on the basis that some limited form of disclosure of the defence is necessary if the prosecution is to be able to give relevant disclosure. In their current form, however, the *Guidelines* clearly support a more coercive approach to the function of the defence statement. It may be that 'a comprehensive defence statement assists the participants in the trial to ensure that it is fair',[156] but the duty of equality of arms recognises that it is the prosecuting authorities that in reality control access to the information and on whom the onus must be placed to ensure that the defence have equality of access to that material.

---

154 *Points for Prosecutors*, available at www.lslo.gov.uk.
155 *AG Guidelines*, para 39.
156 *Ibid*, para 27.

Issues for advocates: disclosure

1   Disclosure is an essential component of a fair trial. This is recognised in domestic law: see *AG Guidelines*.

2   Disclosure extends to all material evidence. It is also clear, in domestic law as in Strasbourg law that the duty of disclosure on the prosecution extends to the duty to gather evidence that assists the defence.

3   Disclosure is not an absolute right and competing interest may need to be weighed against the right. The involvement of the trial judge is essential in this process, especially where the prosecution has applied *ex parte* to withhold disclosure.

4   Where disclosure has been withheld without the involvement of the court there is likely to be a breach of Art 6.

5   Where disclosure is made very late (for example, at trial) has the defendant been denied a fair trial because of the undermining of effective preparation, and hence loss of equality of arms?

CHAPTER 8

HUMAN RIGHTS ADVOCACY AND THE CRIMINAL TRIAL

This chapter considers the core Human Rights Act issues which are likely to arise in the context of criminal trials. The first section focuses on the principles that the Strasbourg Court has applied to issues of evidence in criminal proceedings, and outlines the arguments that advocates will need to be prepared to deal with. In the sections that follow, we consider the implications of the Human Rights Act for the trial process, including such issues as the independence and impartiality of the court, as well as the vexed issue of the effect of delay on the Art 6 guarantee of trial 'within a reasonable time'. The chapter concludes by looking at some of the issues that advocates will need to address when dealing with sentencing and appeals.

8.1 EVIDENTIAL ISSUES AND HRA ARGUMENTS

In this preliminary section we consider certain core principles of Art 6, and in particular the specific criminal process guarantees in Art 6(2) and 6(3), and the impact of these principles on the domestic rules of evidence. The section addresses:

1 the presumption of innocence, and in particular its implications for:
    * provisions that shift the burden of proof to the defence;
    * provisions which affect the right to silence;
    * the admissibility of evidence which has been obtained by compulsion;
2 the circumstances under which evidence must be excluded in order to ensure a fair trial for the purposes of Art 6;
3 issues arising from evidence obtained by entrapment, and in particular the applicability of the Strasbourg Court's decision in *Teixeira v Portugal*[1] in domestic law;
4 the implications of the right to examine witnesses.

8.1.1 Article 6(2): the presumption of innocence

The presumption has clear application to court proceedings:

Paragraph 2 embodies the principle of the presumption of innocence. It requires, *inter alia*, that when carrying out their duties, the members of a court

---

1   *Teixeira de Castro v Portugal* (1999) 28 EHRR 101.

should not start with the preconceived idea that the accused has committed the offence charged; the burden of proof is on the prosecution, and any doubt should benefit the accused. It also follows that it is for the prosecution to inform the accused of the case that will be made against him, so that he may prepare and present his defence accordingly, and to adduce evidence sufficient to convict him.[2]

The right to silence arises from the presumption of innocence and is closely allied to it:

The Court recalls that, although not specifically mentioned in Article 6 of the Convention, the right to silence and the right not to incriminate oneself, are generally recognised international standards which lie at the heart of the notion of a fair procedure under Article 6. Their rationale lies, *inter alia*, in the protection of the accused against improper compulsion by the authorities thereby contributing to the avoidance of miscarriages of justice and to the fulfilment of the aims of Article 6. The right not to incriminate oneself, in particular, presupposes that the prosecution in a criminal case seek to prove their case against the accused without resort to evidence obtained through methods of coercion or oppression in defiance of the will of the accused. In this sense the right is closely linked to the presumption of innocence contained in Article 6(2) of the Convention.[3]

Strasbourg case law has clearly indicated the fundamental nature of the right to a presumption of innocence in a criminal context, and while the presumption of innocence is specifically provided for by way of Art 6(2), the related right not to be compelled to incriminate oneself appears to engage both Art 6(1) and 6(2).

Likely areas where advocates will find themselves addressing the court on the human rights implications that arise from the general presumption of innocence are likely to be in the context of:

1 provisions which place all or part of the burden of proof on the defence (reverse onus provisions).

2 provisions which lower the standard of proof required of the prosecution.

3 provisions which interfere with the right to silence by using the failure to answer questions as part of the case against the defendant.

4 provisions which interfere with the right to silence by requiring the defendant to answer questions failing which he will commit an offence (compelled questioning).

8.1.1.1 *Reverse onus arguments*

If Art 6(2) provides for a presumption of innocence, will provisions which reverse the burden of proof, requiring the defence to prove all or part of the

---

2 *Barbera Messegue and Jabardo v Spain* (1988) 11 EHRR 360, para 77.
3 *Saunders v United Kingdom* (1997) 23 EHRR 313, para 68.

element of an offence, offend against this provision? The leading cases in domestic law are *Kebilene*[4] and *Lambert*.[5] The highly detailed discussion of the nature of 'reverse onus' provision by Lord Hope in *Kebilene* indicates the complexity of the issues – and is a valuable warning to advocates that a simple assertion that a provision amounts to a reversal of the burden of proof is unlikely to do justice to the range of different ways in which the burden may be imposed on the defendant.[6]

Classification of the type of burden

Kebilene, it will be recalled, arose from provisions of s 16A of the Prevention of Terrorism (Temporary Provisions) Act 1989. This section provided that once the prosecution had proved that the defendant had been in possession of any article in circumstances that gave rise to a reasonable suspicion that he had the article in his possession for a terrorist purpose the defendant would be guilty of an offence unless he could prove that he did not have it in his possession for such a purpose.

Lord Hope suggested that the starting point for arguments must be the identification of the type of burden that was being placed on the defence. Where the burden was simply to raise a matter, which it would then be for the prosecution to disprove – the 'evidential burden' – this would not offend against Art 6. Here, however, it was accepted that s 16A placed a 'persuasive' burden on the defence in the sense that it required the defence to prove a matter, albeit on the balance of probabilities. Such persuasive burdens might impose a mandatory presumption on the court where a fact is established; this would be 'inconsistent with the presumption of innocence'. Alternatively, the presumption might be discretionary in the sense that the court could in practice decide what weight it was appropriate to give to the evidence; the compatibility of such a presumption could only be assessed in the light of the trial as a whole.[7] Finally, the presumption might relate to 'exemptions or provisos' – for example where a statute prohibited an act save by licensed individuals, and where the burden of proof of showing that the defendant

---

4   *R v DPP ex p Kebilene and Others* [2000] 2 AC 326.

5   *R v Lambert* (House of Lords) [2001] UKHL 37; [2001] All ER(D) 69 (Jul).

6   While Lord Hope's analysis is technically *obiter* since the case was disposed of on the basis that an attempted judicial review of the decision of the Director of Public Prosecutions to prosecute under a provision with a reverse onus element to it amounted to an impermissible collateral challenge to the substantive litigation, it was nonetheless followed, with some variations in the later *Lambert* decision.

7   There was an additional provision by virtue of which the defendant was taken to be in possession of an item if it was found at premises of which he was the occupier or habitual user. Again it was for the defendant to prove either that he had no knowledge of the item or that he had no control over it. However, since this provision only gave rise to a discretionary presumption of possession, the defence conceded that this was a matter that could only be dealt with after the trial judge had decided whether such a presumption should be drawn.

possessed such a license would be on the defence, but where it would be for the prosecution to prove beyond reasonable doubt that the act had taken place. In Lord Hope's view, such exemptions or provisos might or might not offend against the presumption of innocence.

The underlying Strasbourg principles

As with the right to silence provisions, however, Strasbourg's own case law on reversal of burden of proof provisions is surprisingly unhelpful. The leading case is that of *Salabiaku v France*,[8] where French customs law imposed liability for possession of goods brought into the county without declaration to customs subject only to a defence of *force majeure*:

> Presumptions of fact or of law operate in every legal system. Clearly, the Convention does not prohibit such presumptions in principle. It does, however, require the Contracting States to remain within certain limits in this respect as regards criminal law ... Article 6 para 2 does not therefore regard presumptions of fact or of law provided for in the criminal law with indifference. It requires States to confine them within reasonable limits, which take into account the importance of what is at stake and maintain the rights of the defence.[9]

As Lord Hope noted, the European Court of Human Rights in *Salabiaku* had taken account of the fact that notwithstanding the apparently irrefutable nature of the presumption (which did not expressly provide for any defence) the national courts were in practice not applying the presumption automatically but were assessing its appropriateness in the light of all the evidence. Reviewing the case law, Lord Hope's conclusion was that:

> The cases show that, although Article 6(2) is in absolute terms, it is not regarded as imposing an absolute prohibition on reverse onus clauses, whether they were evidential (presumptions of fact) or persuasive (presumptions of law). In each case the question will be whether the presumption is within reasonable limits.[10]

How to identify a 'reasonable limits' test

At the heart of the issue was the need to balance the rights of the individual with the permissible inroads into those rights required by the interests of society as a whole. Lord Hope accepted the suggestion that the test for finding whether the correct balance had been drawn – and thus in *Salabiaku* terms, whether the presumption was confined within reasonable limits – could be broken down into three stages:

---

8   *Salabiaku v France* (1988) 13 EHRR 379.

9   *Ibid*, para 28.

10   *R v DPP ex p Kebilene and Others* [2000] 2 AC 326, p 385.

(1) what does the prosecution have to prove in order to transfer the onus to the defence? (2) what is the burden on the accused – does it relate to something, which is likely to be difficult for him to prove, or does it relate to something which is likely to be within his knowledge or (I would add) to which he readily has access? (3) what is the nature of the threat faced by society that the provision is designed to combat?[11]

Applying the three-stage test to s 16A, Lord Hope concluded that the prosecution would potentially face a fairly onerous task at trial in order to prove reasonable suspicion. As to the burden on the accused, where the accused could show lack of knowledge of the item, he would not be in possession of it. Thus the burden of proof to show innocent possession would only arise if he was in possession of the item and the prosecution could show the court that there were circumstances that would give rise to reasonable suspicion. Would this persuasive burden then be in breach of Art 6?:

A sound judgment as to whether the burden, which he has to discharge, is an unreasonable one is unlikely to be possible until the facts are known. It is not immediately obvious that it would be imposing an unreasonable burden on an accused who was in possession of articles from which an inference of involvement in terrorism could be drawn to provide an explanation for his possession of them which would displace that inference. Account would have to be taken of the nature of the incriminating circumstances and the facilities, which were available to the accused, to obtain the necessary evidence. It would be one thing if there was good reason to think that the accused had easy access to the facts, quite another if access to them was very difficult.[12]

As to the final question, it was a matter to be taken into account that this provision was aimed at terrorist violence, where there would be strong arguments that the general interests of society in protecting the public from acts of terror, might justify the imposition of a limited burden.

Applying the Kebilene principles

The Court of Appeal in *Lambert*[13] considered the reverse onus provisions in the context both of the defence of diminished responsibility and of the onus on the defence to prove innocent possession under the Misuse of Drugs legislation. It will be noted that the two provisions in issue, have not only different effect, but also a different rationale for the imposition of the burden on the defence. Thus, a successful defence of diminished responsibility will reduce criminal culpability from murder to manslaughter but will not extinguish it; whereas where a defendant successfully shows that he is in innocent possession of a controlled drug this will amount to a complete defence to a charge under the legislation.

---

11   [2000] 2 AC 326, p 386.

12   *Ibid*, p 387.

13   *R v Lambert, R v Ali, R v Jordan* (Court of Appeal) [2001] 1 All ER 1014.

The response of the Court of Appeal to the argument regarding diminished responsibility was brusque:

> The change in the law brought about by section 2 was of benefit to defendants who were in a position to take advantage of it. It does not matter whether it is treated as creating a defence to a charge to murder or an exception or as dealing with the capacity to commit the offence of murder. Section 2 still does not contravene Article 6. We find ample support for our view in the judgments of the Supreme Court of Canada in *R v Chaulk* [1989] ISCR 369 and in the decisions of the European Commission of Human Rights which decide that arguments of this nature are manifestly ill-founded ...[14]

The case of *Lambert* himself concerned the compatibility of the provisions of s 5(4) of the Misuse of Drugs Act 1971 which provides for a specific 'knowledge' defence where a person is charged with possession of drugs, but provides that it is for the accused to prove lack of knowledge. The Court of Appeal reasoning was short:

> It has been imposed by the legislature deliberately for policy reasons it considered justified. Since 1971 that justification has increased ... There is an objective justification in the case of drugs for the choice and it is not disproportionate. It is important in considering the validity of the offences that the defendant will only be punished for the offence he has been proved to have committed if he fails in his attempt to rely on the statutory defences. We do not consider the offences contravene Article 6.[15]

Lambert *in the House of Lords*

The difficulty for advocates in dealing with the House of Lords decision in *Lambert*[16] is that there is as much disagreement as agreement between Their Lordships, all of whom gave full decisions. The decisions deal not only with the reverse onus provision, but also with the general issues of retrospectivity and the interpretative obligation imposed by s 3 of the HRA.[17] These two latter points have already been discussed in Chapters 2 and 4 respectively. However, in respect of the reverse onus provision, there was agreement between all five judges that s 28 of the Misuse of Drugs Act 1971 imposed a probative burden on the defendant. Four of the judges, Lord Hutton dissenting, took the view that the interference with the presumption of innocence was disproportionate and could not be justified. All took the view that it was possible to 'read down' the provision under s 3.

It is worth noting the variations in approach even within those judgments that agreed that the measure was contrary to Art 6(2). Lord Steyn was satisfied that there was objective justification for the measure – namely the need that

---

14 [2001] 1 All ER 1014, para 19.

15 *Ibid*, paras 24–26.

16 *R v Lambert* [2001] UKHL 37 (HL).

17 *Lambert* is also a decision of some importance in relation to the issue of appeals against conviction following alleged breaches of Art 6: this is discussed later in this chapter.

drugs are commonly secreted in 'some container', so that the person in possession will invariably deny knowledge of the contents. However, he looked to the effect of the provision:

> [A]lthough the prosecution must establish that prohibited drugs were in the possession of the defendant, and that he or she knew that the package contained something, the accused must prove on the balance of probabilities that he did not know that the package contained controlled drugs. If the jury is in doubt on this issue, they must convict him. This may occur when an accused adduces sufficient evidence to raise a doubt about his guilt but the jury is not convinced on a balance of probabilities that his account is true. *Indeed it obliges the court to convict if the version of the accused is as likely to be true as not.* This is a far reaching consequence: a guilty verdict may be returned in respect of an offence punishable by life imprisonment even though the jury may consider that it is reasonably possible that the accused had been duped. It would be unprincipled to brush aside such possibilities as unlikely to happen in practice.[18] [Emphasis in the original.]

He considered that the reality of the situation is that possession of the container would inevitably amount to powerful circumstantial evidence against the possessor, who would then need to raise evidence to rebut that inference. There would also potentially be inferences arising from s 34 (and, one might add, s 36) of the Criminal Justice and Public Order Act 1994 from failure to put forward defence facts as to the possession. Moreover, case law in other jurisdictions suggested that a probative burden would offend against constitutional provisions that provided for a presumption of innocence.

Lord Hope too started from the premise that the presumption of innocence is not unqualified – an unsuccessful attempt having been made by the appellant to argue that the Strasbourg Court's decision in *Salabiaku* should not be applied to serious criminal offences:

> [A]s the Article 6(2) right is not absolute and unqualified, the test to be applied is whether the modification or limitation of that right pursues a legitimate aim and whether it satisfies the principle of proportionality ... It is now well settled that the principle, which is to be applied, requires a balance to be struck between the general interest of the community and the protection of the fundamental rights of the individual. This will not be achieved if the reverse onus provision goes beyond what is necessary to accomplish the objective of the statute.[19]

The issue therefore was essentially one of proportionality. Since the Misuse of Drugs Act makes clear that it is not intended that those who neither knew nor had reason to suspect that they were in possession of a controlled drug should be penalised, 'it is hard to see why a person who is accused of the offence of possessing a controlled drug and who wishes to raise this defence should be

---

18 *Ibid*, para 38.
19 *Ibid*, para 88.

deprived of the full benefit of the presumption of innocence'.[20] His Lordship then considered the effect of 'reading down' the burden of proof so as to provide for an evidential burden only on the defence. This would itself often be a substantial burden:

> What the accused must do is put evidence before the court, which, if believed, could be taken by a reasonable jury to support his defence.[21]

In short, the issue becomes less one of what the defendant has to prove, and more an issue of the 'state of mind of the judge or jury when they are evaluating the evidence'.[22] His Lordship noted that the imposition of an evidential burden only had been adopted in both the Terrorism Act 2000 and the Regulation of Investigatory Powers Act 2000, suggesting that Parliament might well have chosen to impose a mere evidential burden had the Misuse of Drugs Act been a more recent enactment.

Notwithstanding these differing approaches to the rationale for the finding that the reverse onus provision offended against Art 6(2) the decision makes clear that advocates in domestic courts will have to accept, at least as a matter of domestic law, that provisions which offend against the presumption of innocence may be permissible if the prosecution can show that the interference with the right is appropriately limited.

A number of propositions are possible:

1　The European Court of Human Rights itself has indicated that presumptions will not necessarily offend against Art 6(2) if kept within proper limits: *Salabiaku*.

2　It may be easier to argue that the presumption has been kept within proper limits if there is evidence that the court has not relied purely on any presumption, but has looked for evidence in support: *Salabiaku*.[23]

3　It may be significant that the domestic courts have been prepared to permit inroads into the presumption of innocence in less important matters (see below the approval of compelled questioning under the Road Traffic Act regime: *Brown v Stott*); in contrast, a number of the judgments in *Lambert* adverted to the potentially severe custodial penalties faced by the defendant.[23a]

20　*Ibid*, para 89.

21　*Ibid*, para 90.

22　*Ibid*.

23　And note the analogous reasoning of the Strasbourg Court in relation to the statutory assumptions underpinning the confiscation regime under the Drug Trafficking Act 1994: see *Phillips v United Kingdom*, European Court of Human Rights, judgment of 5 July 2001.

23a　Note however the comment of Pill LJ in *Lynch v DPP*, Lawtel 9/11/2001, DC, rejecting an argument that the burden of proof on the defendant to show a good reason for possession of a bladed article contrary to s 139 of the Criminal Justice Act 1988 was in breach of Art 6. Pill LJ stated that the more restrictive power of sentence under s 139 should be given 'some, though limited, weight' in striking the balance.

4   It appears common ground that the imposition of a mere evidential burden on the defendant is unlikely to offend against Art 6(2).

5   It appeared to be accepted without argument by the majority in *Lambert* that provisions which require the defendant to prove he falls within some exception to the general prohibition, (as *per R v Edwards*)[24] will not offend against Art 6(2). Note, however, that Lord Hope was not prepared to rule out the possibility that these provisions might be open to challenge.[25] This presumably leaves open the issue of the compatibility of s 101 of the Magistrates' Courts Act 1980.

Issues for advocates: provisions which shift the burden of proof

1   Start by identifying the nature of the provision: does it merely impose an evidential burden (unlikely to offend against Art 6) or does it impose a 'persuasive' burden?

2   If a persuasive burden is imposed, does it create a mandatory presumption, a discretionary presumption or does it relate to an 'exemption or proviso'?

3   Where a provision appears to permit a mandatory presumption, how is this presumption in fact treated by the court? Is this a case where, as in *Salabiaku*, the court will nonetheless assess the weight of evidence against the defendant?

4   In deciding whether a presumption is within reasonable limits, consider:

    •   What does the prosecution have to prove in order to shift the burden of proof to the defence?

    •   What is the nature of the burden on the defence? Is this a matter that the defence is uniquely well placed to prove, or is the burden of proof particularly onerous?

    •   What is the context of the presumption? Is this an area of law where there is a particular need for such a provision? (Note: in this context arguments will undoubtedly arise as to the discretionary area of judgment accorded to the democratically elected body – for which see the discussion in Chapter 3.)

    •   What is the nature of the penalty which the defendant faces?

5   If the court is of the view that the provision offends against Art 6(2), identify the words that are incompatible with the Convention right. How can these words be read in order to ensure Convention compliance? (The decision in *Lambert* indicates that the imposition of a mere evidential burden will often be the appropriate response.)

---

24   [1975] QB 27.
25   'I would not wish to be taken as accepting that exceptions of that kind are always immune from challenge on Convention grounds.' *Lambert*, para 75.

6   Only if the court concludes that the words cannot be read down under s 3, should the court apply the legislation. On appeal to the appellate court (the High Court if in the magistrates' court, the Court of Appeal if a trial on indictment) a declaration of incompatibility can be made if necessary.

8.1.1.2   Provisions which impose a lower standard of proof on the prosecution

The traditional approach of British law has been to require the prosecution to prove its case beyond reasonable doubt. There are, however, a number of provisions where the law permits the prosecution to prove its case to the civil standard of proof. Strasbourg case law is not explicit on the standard of proof required in criminal proceedings, although Starmer suggests, relying in part upon *dicta* in *Goodman v Ireland*,[26] that the court assumes that the accused will be given the benefit of any doubt.[27]

The most significant English provisions where the civil standard of proof is imposed arise in connection with hybrid offences, where there is generally a two stage process, the first of which is dealt with on a civil standard of proof (such as anti social behaviour order provisions), and in relation to other matters categorised in domestic law as civil rather than criminal (particularly fiscal offences). These categories of case, and the domestic case law on their status, have been discussed in Chapter 7 above.

8.1.1.3   The right to silence and inferences

Undoubtedly there is an overlap in the approach to be taken in relation to the issue of the presumptions of guilt and the right to silence, since the effect of the imposition of a presumption is to require the defence to prove an element of the case, effectively removing the general right of the defence to remain silent and to require that the prosecution proves its case.

Article 6, it will be noted, says nothing about the right of silence. However this right has been read into the presumption of innocence in Art 6(2). In the case of *Funke v France*,[28] where the state attempted to argue that customs law gave rise to a particular need to obtain information from the defendant, the court rejected the argument:

> The court notes that the customs secured Mr Funke's conviction in order to obtain certain documents, which they believed, must exist, although they were

---

26   (1993) 16 EHRR CD 26.
27   See Starmer, paras 8.48–49.
28   (1993) 16 EHRR 297.

not certain of the fact. Being unable or unwilling to procure them by some other means, they attempted to compel the applicant himself to provide the evidence of offences he had allegedly committed. The special features of customs law ... cannot justify such an infringement of the right of anyone 'charged with a criminal offence', within the autonomous meaning of this expression in Article 6 to remain silent and not to contribute to incriminating himself.[29]

However, the Court has held that it is possible to draw inferences from exercise of the right of silence. In *Murray (John) v United Kingdom*[30] the court upheld inferences drawn under the Northern Ireland legislation, which predated the English Criminal Justice and Public Order Act 1994 provisions. The court began by reiterating the *Funke* principle that the right to silence was integral to the presumption of innocence:

Although not specifically mentioned in Article 6 of the Convention, there can be no doubt that the right to remain silent under police questioning and the privilege against self-incrimination are generally recognised international standards which lie at the heart of the notion of a fair procedure under Article 6.[31]

However, the court went on to hold that so long as the right to silence was maintained, it would not necessarily amount to a breach of that right for a judge to draw inferences from the exercise of that right as part of the decision as to guilt or innocence:

On the one hand, it is self-evident that it is incompatible with the immunities under consideration to base a conviction solely or mainly on the accused's silence or on a refusal to answer questions or to give evidence himself. On the other hand, the court deems it equally obvious that these immunities cannot and should not prevent that the accused's silence, in situations which clearly call for an explanation from him, be taken into account in assessing the persuasiveness of the evidence adduced by the prosecution.[32]

Murray is not an easy decision to reconcile with the presumption of innocence, and it was thought that the particular composition of judge-only courts in the Northern Ireland context of the case, which permitted the finder of fact to indicate the extent and the weight given to any inference, would mean that the corresponding UK regime under the Criminal Justice and Public Order Act 1994, where inferences would be drawn by magistrates or juries, would breach Art 6(2). However, in the leading case of *Condron v United Kingdom*,[33] the Strasbourg Court ruled that inferences were permissible in jury trials:

---

29   (1993) 16 EHRR 297, para 44.
30   (1996) 22 EHRR 29.
31   *Ibid*, para 45.
32   *Ibid*, para 47.
33   (2001) 31 EHRR 1.

... the fact that the issue of the applicants' silence was left to a jury cannot of itself be considered incompatible with the requirements of a fair trial. It is, rather, another relevant consideration to be weighed in the balance when assessing whether or not it was fair to do so in the circumstances.[34]

However, what the Court made clear in *Condron* was that where a jury was invited to draw an inference, the particular significance of the right to silence made it essential that the jury was properly directed on the nature and extent of the inference. A failure to do so could not be corrected on appeal since the appellate court would inevitably be speculating about the basis of the jury's decision.

The principles set out in *Condron* have been conveniently summarised by the Court of Appeal in *R v Milford*:

(i) the court confines its attention to the facts of the individual case in considering whether the drawing of inferences against the appellant under s 34 of the 1994 Act has rendered the defendant's trial unfair (para 55);

(ii) the right to silence is not an absolute right and the question of whether the drawing of adverse differences from a defendant's silence infringes Art 6, must be determined in the light of all the circumstances of the case (para 56);

(iii) it would be incompatible with the right to silence to base a conviction 'solely or mainly' on the defendant's silence or refusal to answer questions; however the right to silence cannot and should not prevent the defendant's silence, in situations which clearly call for an explanation from him, being taken into account in assessing the persuasiveness of the prosecution evidence (para 56);

(iv) the fact that the issue of the defendant's silence is left to a jury cannot, of itself, be incompatible with the requirements of a fair trial (para 57), but the fact that it is left to the jury heightens the importance of a proper direction from the judge in circumstances where the potential unfairness inherent in an imperfect direction cannot be remedied by the Court of Appeal, which is in no position to assess properly the degree to which the defendant's silence played a significant role in the jury's decision to convict (paras 63 and 66);

(v) in so far as the defendant asserts that he was silent on the advice of his solicitor, the very fact that a defendant is advised by his lawyer to maintain his silence must be given 'appropriate weight' by the court (para 60);

(vi) if a direction is in such terms that the jury, acting in accordance with it, would be at liberty to draw an adverse inference notwithstanding that they were satisfied as to the plausibility of the explanation, then the trial will be unfair (para 61).[35]

A number of issues remain of particular relevance in the domestic courts.

---

34   (2001) 31 EHRR 1, para 57.

35   *R v Milford (David John)* [2001] Crim LR 330, para 54.

A case to answer?

In *Murray* the Strasbourg Court made clear that inferences were permissible because they were merely 'common-sense' inferences from a failure to respond to a case that called for an answer. The importance of there being a case that calls for an answer was underlined by the Strasbourg Court in the case of *Telfner v Austria*[36] where the defendant was convicted of a motoring offence on little more basis than that he was known to be a habitual user of one of the cars involved and he had refused to account for his whereabouts at the time in question:

> In the present case, both the District Court and the Regional Court relied in essence on a report of the local police station that the applicant was the main user of the car and had not been home on the night of the accident. However, the Court cannot find that these elements of evidence, which were moreover not corroborated by evidence taken at the trial in an adversarial manner, constituted a case against the applicant, which would have called for an explanation from his part. In this context, the court notes, in particular, that the victim of the accident had not been able to identify the driver, nor even to say whether the driver had been male or female, and that the Regional Court, after supplementing the proceedings, found that the car in question was also used by the applicant's sister. In requiring the applicant to provide an explanation although they had not been able to establish a convincing *prima facie* case against him, the courts shifted the burden of proof from the prosecution to the defence.[37]

The exact question of how this is translated into domestic law is not easy to pin down. In *R v Doldur*[38] the Court of Appeal stated:

> Acceptance of the truth and accuracy of all or part of the prosecution evidence may or may not amount to sureness of guilt. Something more may be required, which may be provided by an adverse inference from silence if they think it proper to draw one. What is plain is that it is not for the jury to repeat the threshold test of the judge in ruling whether there is a case to answer on the prosecution evidence if accepted by them.

This principle was interpreted by the United Kingdom in the Strasbourg Court in *Condron v United Kingdom* as 'authority for the proposition that the jury must be satisfied that the prosecution have established a *prima facie* case'. The position may be about to be clarified by an amended Judicial Studies Board direction which will expressly state that 'a conviction cannot be based wholly or mainly on the failure of a defendant to speak in interview'.[39] This still arguably leaves open the issue of whether a *prima facie* case is required before an inference can arise. Defence advocates will wish to argue that this is

---

36 European Court of Human Rights, judgment of 20 March 2001.

37 *Ibid*, para 18.

38 *Sub nom R v D (Ilhan) (A Juvenile)* [2000] Crim LR 178.

39 *R v Everson (Louis)* [2001] EWCA Crim 896.

the meaning of 'a case to answer'. The prosecution may, however, suggest that there is nothing in either *Condron* or *Murray* which states in terms that there must be a *prima facie* case, and that the new judicial direction ensures that there is a 'case to answer' sufficient for Art 6 purposes.

Access to legal advice

The issue of access to legal advice has already been discussed in Chapter 7 in relation to the autonomous Strasbourg concept of a charge.

It is clear that the particular significance of inroads into the unqualified right to silence means that Strasbourg expects the defendant's position to be protected by access to legal advice. This is discussed in more detail below: see 8.1.2.2:

> It must also be observed that the applicants' solicitor was present throughout the whole of their interviews and was able to advise them not to volunteer any answers to the questions put to them. The fact that an accused person who is questioned under caution is assured access to legal advice, and in the applicants' case the physical presence of a solicitor during police interview, must be considered a particularly important safeguard for dispelling any compulsion to speak which may be inherent in the terms of the caution.[40]

Silence on legal advice

In *Condron v United Kingdom* the Strasbourg Court made clear that 'appropriate weight' must be given to the fact that a suspect is silence on legal advice. Arguably this is recognised in the principles set out in *R v Argent*:[41]

> ... matters such as time of day, the defendant's age, experience, mental capacity, state of health, sobriety, tiredness, knowledge, personality and legal advice are all part of the relevant circumstances; and these are only examples of what may be relevant.
>
> ....
>
> Like so many other questions in criminal trials this is a question to be resolved by the jury in the exercise of their collective common sense, experience and understanding of human nature. Sometimes they may conclude that it was reasonable for the defendant to have held his peace for a host of reasons, such as that he was tired, ill, frightened, drunk, drugged, unable to understand what was going on, suspicious of the police, afraid that his answer would not be fairly recorded, worried at committing himself without legal advice, acting on legal advice, or some other reason accepted by the jury.[42]

In *R v Betts*[43] the Court of Appeal put it as follows:

---

40 *Condron v United Kingdom* (2001) 31 EHRR 1.
41 [1997] 2 Cr App R 27.
42 *Ibid*, p 33.
43 [2001] 3 Archbold News (CA).

In the light of the judgment in *Condron v United Kingdom* it is not the quality of the decision but the genuineness of the decision that matters. If it is a plausible explanation that the reason for not mentioning facts is that the particular appellant acted on the advice of his solicitor and not because he had no or no satisfactory answer to give then no inference can be drawn.

That conclusion does not give a licence to a guilty person to shield behind the advice of his solicitor. The adequacy of the explanation advanced may well be relevant as to whether or not the advice was truly the reason for not mentioning the facts. A person, who is anxious not to answer questions because he has no or no adequate explanation to offer, gains no protection from his lawyer's advice because that advice is no more than a convenient way of disguising his true motivation for not mentioning facts.[44]

One particular problem is that it will necessary to reveal the basis of legal advice in order to fully counter any inference. Generally this will amount to a waiver of privilege.[45] It was argued at the Strasbourg Court that this amounted to a breach of Art 6, since it interfered with lawyer client confidentiality. This argument was rejected without much explanation by the Strasbourg Court:

The Court would observe at this juncture that the fact that the applicants were subjected to cross-examination on the content of their solicitor's advice cannot be said to raise an issue of fairness under Article 6 of the Convention. They were under no compulsion to disclose the advice given, other than the indirect compulsion to avoid the reason for their silence remaining at the level of a bare explanation. The applicants chose to make the content of their solicitor's advice a live issue as part of their defence. For that reason they cannot complain that the scheme of section 34 of the 1994 Act is such as to override the confidentiality of their discussions with their solicitor.[46]

Effect of a defective jury direction

In *Condron v United Kingdom* the Strasbourg Court rejected the government's submissions that any breach of Art 6 at the trial had been rectified by the appeal proceedings on the basis that 'the Court of Appeal had no means of ascertaining whether or not the applicants' silence played a significant role in the jury's decision to convict'.[47] Trying to assess the impact of the misdirection on the jury would be:

... a speculative exercise which only reinforces the crucial nature of the defect in the trial judge's direction and its implications for review of the case on appeal.

---

44 [2001] 3 Archbold News (CA), paras 53 and 54.

45 *R v Condron* [1997] 1 Cr App R 185. A waiver will not take place where it simply a rebuttal of an allegation that the defendant has recently fabricated his account.

46 *Condron v United Kingdom* (2001) 31 EHRR 1, para 60.

47 *Ibid*, para 63.

> [I]n the case at issue it was the function of the jury, properly directed, to decide whether or not to draw an adverse inference from the applicants' silence. Section 34 of the 1994 Act specifically entrusted this task to the jury as part of a legislative scheme designed to confine the use, which can be made of an accused's silence at his trial. In the circumstances the jury was not properly directed and the imperfection in the direction could not be remedied on appeal. Any other conclusion would be at variance with the fundamental importance of the right to silence, a right, which, as observed earlier, lies at the heart of the notion of a fair procedure guaranteed by Article 6. On that account the Court concludes that the applicants did not receive a fair hearing within the meaning of Article 6 para 1 of the Convention.[48]

This is an aspect of the decision, which is giving rise to continuing problems for the domestic courts who are clearly reluctant to overturn convictions on what would traditionally be seen as minor defects in the jury direction. The issue is discussed more fully at 8.5.2 below.

Inferences from failure to testify

In the *Murray (John)* judgment the European Court of Human Rights found no breach of Art 6 from the drawing of inferences from the defendant's failure to testify. In domestic law the matter is governed by the Court of Appeal decision in *R v Cowan and Others*,[49] which laid down a number of conditions before inferences could properly be drawn under s 35 of the Criminal Justice and Public Order Act. The conditions include a requirement that there must be a *prima facie* case to answer. It seems that inferences under s 35 will not offend against Art 6 provided there has been access to legal advice and the correct directions are given.

Inferences from failure to account for objects and presence

As yet there has been no decision from the European Court of Human Rights on the status of inferences under ss 36 and 37 of the Criminal Justice and Public Order Act 1994, and indeed there has been very little case law in the domestic courts on these provisions. One distinction between these inferences and the inferences that may be drawn under s 34 from failure to mention defence facts when questioned under caution, is that the ss 36 and 37 inferences are part of the prosecution case. It appears that it is not therefore necessary for there to be a *prima facie* case before such inferences can arise. Moreover, while a jury cannot convict on the basis of one inference alone, there is nothing to stop a jury from convicting on the basis of two or more separate inferences. This would appear to offend against the principle that there must be 'a case to answer' and that the conviction must not rest solely or mainly on a person's silence.

---

48 (2001) 31 EHRR 1, paras 64–66.
49 [1996] 1 Cr App R 1.

Issues for advocates: inferences from silence

1 The right to silence is at the heart of the notion of a fair trial for Art 6 purposes: *Murray (John)*.

2 A conviction cannot therefore be based solely or mainly on a person's silence.

3 However, there may be situations which clearly call for an answer, and where the suspect's silence can be taken into account in assessing how persuasive the prosecution case is.

   • Note that it is not entirely clear whether there is a distinction between 'a case that calls for an answer', not drawing inferences where the case is based 'mainly' on silence and the need for a *prima facie* case. The first two are clearly laid down by the European Court of Human Rights; the latter was argued as being a requirement by the United Kingdom in the *Condron* case.

4 Because of the particular importance of the right to silence, an inference cannot be drawn unless there has been an opportunity to have access to legal advice: *Murray (John)*.

5 The fact that the suspect has been silent on legal advice is relevant and must be given 'appropriate weight'.

6 Such inferences are permissible in the context of jury trials, although the fact that it was a jury trial is a further 'relevant consideration' in deciding whether it is appropriate to draw an inference.

7 The jury must be correctly directed on the law, and an imperfect direction will not be remediable by the appellate court. (Cf a non-direction: *Francom*.)[50]

8.1.1.4 Compelled evidence

The leading case in this context is *Saunders v United Kingdom*,[51] although there is a degree of overlap between the issues in relation to compelled answers to questions, and inferences from the exercise of a right not to answer such questions.

The Strasbourg approach to compelled answers has been that they offend against Art 6(1) and (2):[52]

> The right not to incriminate oneself is primarily concerned, however, with respecting the will of an accused person to remain silent.[53]

---

50 [2001] 1 Cr App R 17.
51 (1997) 23 EHRR 313.
52 The Strasbourg decisions are not always clear as to whether a breach has arisen in relation to Art 6(1), 6(2) or both, nor is the distinction necessarily of significance in a criminal context.
53 *Ibid*, para 69.

It is here that the approach of the domestic courts seems most clearly to diverge from Strasbourg case law, indicating the problem that advocates will face in seeking to exclude evidence, which has been obtained as the result of an answer under compulsion. The Youth Justice and Criminal Evidence Act 1999 provisions have made clear that answers obtained under compulsion under various pieces of commercial legislation (such as the Companies Act 1985, the Insolvency Act 1986 and the Company Directors Disqualification Act 1986)[54] will not be admissible in subsequent criminal proceedings. Compelled questions still remain in other contexts, however, and challenges have been brought, most notably in the context of s 71 of the Environmental Protection Act 1990 (the *Hertfordshire CC* case)[55] and in relation to s 172 of the Road Traffic Act 1988 (*Brown v Stott*).[56]

In these two decisions advocates have guidance from the House of Lords and the Privy Council respectively, and the approach taken by those courts shows the problems that defence advocates are likely to face when running arguments in domestic courts based on the exclusion of evidence obtained by compulsion.

In the *Hertfordshire CC* case, the defendant was required under s 71(2) of the Environmental Protection Act 1990 to account for the presence of 100 tons of clinical waste on its site. It is an offence under s 71(3) to fail to provide an answer. The defendant argued, however, that to require an answer would be to breach his Art 6(2) right not to incriminate himself (and it will be noted at this point that the rights under Art 6 extend equally to the corporate entity as to the living person). The House of Lords, however, held that the conviction for failing to provide the information should be upheld. Lord Cooke stated:

> He was bound to comply, but could successfully contend in any subsequent prosecution that his answers could not be put in evidence against him.[57]

In the *Brown* case, Mrs Brown was arrested on suspicion of shoplifting at her local supermarket. In the car park of the supermarket the police officers asked her to identify her car and then, suspecting that she was over the blood alcohol limit, required to state who had driven the car to the supermarket under s 172 of the Road Traffic Act 1988. At trial Mrs Brown's advocate raised the *Saunders* decision in order to argue that the provision offended against Art 6(2).

The Court of Justiciary upheld the exclusion of the evidence obtained by the questioning, following a thorough review of both the Strasbourg jurisprudence (and in particular the *Saunders* decision) and the jurisprudence

---

54 Schedule 3 to the Youth Justice and Criminal Evidence Act 1999.

55 *R v Hertfordshire CC ex p Green Environmental Industries Ltd* [2000] 2 AC 412.

56 [2001] 2 WLR 817.

57 [2000] 2 AC 412, p 426. *Quaere* whether this is now the case following the decision in *Brown v Stott*: does that permissive principle extend to compelled questioning under the Environmental Protection Act 1990?

of other countries, including the courts in New Zealand, Canada and the United States. The Court held that while the question could be asked under s 172, the Human Rights Act then required that the provision be read in such a way as to prevent any breach of Art 6, and that this could be achieved by ruling that the evidence of any compelled answer could not then be used at any subsequent trial – 'use immunity'.

The Privy Council overturned this decision. The two leading judgments are those of Lord Bingham and Lord Steyn. Lord Bingham looked to the wider role of the European Convention of Human Rights in balancing the rights of the individual and society as a whole. As part of the balancing act, Lord Bingham highlighted what he saw as the limited nature of the inroad into the presumption of innocence – a single question:

> Section 172 provides for the putting of a single, simple question. The answer cannot of itself incriminate the suspect, since it is not without more an offence to drive a car. An admission of driving may, of course, as here, provide proof of a fact necessary to convict, but the section does not sanction prolonged questioning about the facts alleged to give rise to criminal offences such as was understandably held to be objectionable in *Saunders*, and the penalty for declining to answer under the section is moderate and non-custodial. There is in the present case no suggestion of improper coercion or oppression such as might give rise to unreliable admissions and so contribute to a miscarriage of justice, and if there were evidence of such conduct the trial judge would have ample power to exclude evidence of the admission.[58]

For Lord Steyn the issues were similar:

> [S]ection 172(2) addresses a pressing social problem, namely the difficulty of law enforcement in the face of statistics revealing a high accident rate resulting in death and serious injuries. The legislature was entitled to regard the figures of serious accidents as unacceptably high. It would also have been entitled to take into account that it was necessary to protect other Convention rights, viz the right to life of members of the public exposed to the danger of accidents: see Article 2(1). On this aspect the legislature was in as good a position as a court to assess the gravity of the problem and the public interest in addressing it. It really then boils down to the question whether in adopting the procedure enshrined in section 172(2), rather than a reverse burden technique, it took more drastic action than was justified. While this is ultimately a question for the court, it is not unreasonable to regard both techniques as permissible in the field of the driving of vehicles. After all, the subject invites special regulation; objectively the interference is narrowly circumscribed; and it is qualitatively not very different from requiring, for example, a breath specimen from a driver.[59]

---

58   *Brown v Stott* [2001] 2 WLR 817, para 44.
59   *Ibid*, para 59.

This approach to the status of Art 6 is echoed in the House of Lords in *R v A*[60] (prohibition on cross-examination of rape victims on previous sexual contact with the defendant) where some reference is made to the qualified nature of the component elements of Art 6, albeit within the unqualified right to a fair trial:

> But Article 6 does not give the accused an absolute and unqualified right to put whatever questions he chooses to the witnesses. As this is not one of the rights which are set out in absolute terms in the article it is open, in principle, to modification or restriction so long as this is not incompatible with the absolute right to a fair trial in Article 6(1). The test of compatibility which is to be applied where it is contended that those rights which are not absolute should be restricted or modified will not be satisfied if the modification or limitation does not pursue a legitimate aim and if there is not reasonable proportionality between the means employed and the aim sought to be achieved.[61]

Proportionality is mentioned in a number of the judgments:

> The only balancing permitted is in respect of what the concept of a fair trial entails: here account may be taken of the familiar triangulation of interests of the accused, the victim and society. In this context proportionality has a role to play.[62]

> It seems to me that the critical question, so far as the accused's right to a fair trial is concerned, is that of proportionality.[63]

For advocates seeking to rely upon any of the elements of Art 6, the problem then becomes the extent to which a fair trial is possible in the face of allegedly proportionate interference with some component element – such as the presumption of innocence (Art 6(2) – *Brown*) or the right to cross-examine witnesses (Art 6(3)(d) – *R v A*). In *Brown* Lord Bingham considered the Strasbourg jurisprudence and stated:

> The case law shows that the Court has paid very close attention to the facts of particular cases coming before it, giving effect to factual differences and recognising differences of degree. *Ex facto oritur jus.*

As one eminent practitioner has commented:

> This passage implies a degree of relativism, which almost suggests that the Strasbourg case law is devoid of principle. Whilst an emphasis on flexibility is understandable for a national court applying the Convention to a difficult and controversial case, it is a disappointingly bleak assessment of the Strasbourg legacy.[64]

---

60 *R v A* [2001] UKHL 25; [2001] 2 WLR 1546.
61 *Ibid, per* Lord Hope, para 91.
62 *Per* Lord Steyn, para 38.
63 *Ibid, per* Lord Hope, para 93.
64 The Convention and the Criminal Courts: Recent developments in UK human rights law, Ben Emmerson QC, Criminal Bar Association Lecture, 13 March 2001.

This heavily qualified approach to Art 6 by the domestic courts makes it all the more important that advocates are prepared to apply relevant Strasbourg case law, rather than simply appealing in general terms to an unspecified 'right to a fair trial'. The starting point for argument must be any existing Strasbourg jurisprudence, since a case directly on point is likely in most cases to provide a relatively definitive answer.[65] Where those prosecuting seek to curtail in some way one of the elements of Art 6, the onus will then be on them to demonstrate some pressing reason why the right should be restricted at all. Only where the court accepts that there is an overriding need to limit the right in issue, will the issue of proportionality arise.

The difficulty for advocates in domestic courts in responding to arguments on this basis is the apparent conflict between domestic case law and the *dicta* of the Strasbourg Court. Note the justification put forward by Lord Bingham for the 'limited' interference with the Art 6(2) presumption of innocence in *Brown*:

> The high incidence of death and injury on the roads caused by the misuse of motor vehicles is a very serious problem common to almost all developed societies. The need to address it in an effective way, for the benefit of the public, cannot be doubted. Among other ways in which democratic governments have sought to address it is by subjecting the use of motor vehicles to a regime of regulation and making provision for enforcement by identifying, prosecuting and punishing offending drivers ... There being a clear public interest in enforcement of road traffic legislation the crucial question in the present case is whether section 172 represents a disproportionate response, or one that undermines a defendant's right to a fair trial, if an admission of being the driver is relied on at trial.[66]

This should be contrasted with the Strasbourg Court's rejection of the United Kingdom's similar public interest argument in *Saunders*:

> [The Court] does not accept the Government's argument that the complexity of corporate fraud and the vital public interest in the investigation of such fraud and the punishment of those responsible could justify such a marked departure as that which occurred in the present case from one of the basic principles of a fair procedure. Like the Commission, it considers that the general requirements of fairness contained in Article 6, including the right not to incriminate oneself, apply to criminal proceedings in respect of all types of criminal offences without distinction, from the most simple to the most complex.[67]

Indeed, in their decision in *Lambert*, where the *Brown* case was cited with clear approval by Their Lordships, Lord Steyn set out what he referred to as the

---

65 Although note the apparent rejection of the *ratio* of *Saunders* in some of the judgments in *Brown*.

66 *Brown v Stott* [2001] 2 WLR 817, para 43.

67 (1997) 23 EHRR 313, para 74.

'eloquent explanation by Sachs J of the significance of the presumption of innocence':[68]

> There is a paradox at the heart of all criminal procedure in that the more serious the crime and the greater the public interest in securing convictions of the guilty, the more important do constitutional protections of the accused become. The starting point of any balancing enquiry where constitutional rights are concerned must be that the public interest in ensuring that innocent people are not convicted and subjected to ignominy and heavy sentences massively outweighs the public interest in ensuring that a particular criminal is brought to book ... Hence the presumption of innocence, which serves not only to protect a particular individual on trial, but to maintain public confidence in the enduring integrity and security of the legal system. Reference to the prevalence and severity of a certain crime therefore does not add anything new or special to the balancing exercise. The perniciousness of the offence is one of the givens, against which the presumption of innocence is pitted from the beginning, not a new element to be put into the scales as part of the justificatory balancing exercise.[69]

But Lord Steyn, having quoted this lengthy passage with approval, then continues:

> The logic of this reasoning is inescapable. It is nevertheless right to say that in a constitutional democracy limited inroads on the presumption of innocence may be justified.[70]

The status of the Saunders decision

Given the conflict between domestic law and the case law of the European Court of Human Rights, can it be argued that the decision of the Strasbourg Court in *Saunders* is no longer good law, and that Strasbourg would be unlikely to follow that judgment if the case were to be before it again?

The answer suggested by the judgments of the European Court of Human Rights in *Heaney and McGuinness v Ireland and Quinn v Ireland*[71] is that *Saunders* remains good law.

Both *Heaney* and *Quinn* concerned the application of s 52 of the Offences Against the State Act 1939, which made refusal to answer certain questions as to presence a criminal offence. It is notable in *Heaney* that although Heaney was charged with both a substantive terrorist offence, and the s 52 offence, he was acquitted of the former, so that the Irish Government was arguing not simply that the two provisions were separate, but that the s 52 offence could

---

68   *Lambert* [2001] UKHL 37; [2001] All ER(D) 69 (Jul), para 34.

69   *State v Coetzee* [1997] 2 LRC 593, at 677, quoted by Lord Steyn in *Lambert, ibid*.

70   *Lambert* [2001] UKHL 37; [2001] All ER(D) 69 (Jul), para 34.

71   *Heaney v Ireland* [2001] Crim LR 481. *Quinn v Ireland* (2000) unreported. Both decisions of the European Court of Human Rights on 21 December 2000, a few weeks after the Privy Council's decision in *Brown v Stott*.

not offend against Art 6(2) on the facts of the case since *Heaney* had been acquitted of the substantive offence. The Strasbourg Court rejected this argument, quoting its mantra that the rights in the Convention had to be 'practical and effective as opposed to theoretical and illusory':

> Applying this approach to the present case, the Court observes that, if the applicants are unable to invoke Article 6, their acquittal in the substantive proceedings would exclude any consideration under Article 6 of their complaints that they had been, nevertheless, already punished prior to that acquittal for having defended what they considered to be their rights guaranteed by Article 6 of the Convention.[72]

More significantly, in view of the domestic decisions, which impose a principle of proportionality in relation to inroads into the right to silence, and particularly in view of the focus in *Brown* on the particular nature of the offence, the Strasbourg Court appears to have emphatically rejected proportionality as a principle that is applicable:

> The Government contended that section 52 of the 1939 Act is, nevertheless, a proportionate response to the subsisting terrorist and security threat given the need to ensure the proper administration of justice and the maintenance of public order and peace.

> The Court has taken judicial notice of the security and public order concerns detailed by the Government.

> However, it recalls that in the *Saunders* case (at s 74) the Court found that the argument of the United Kingdom Government that the complexity of corporate fraud and the vital public interest in the investigation of such fraud and the punishment of those responsible could not justify such a marked departure in that case from one of the basic principles of a fair procedure. It considered that the general requirements of fairness contained in Article 6, including the right not to incriminate oneself, 'apply to criminal proceedings in respect of all types of criminal offences without distinction from the most simple to the most complex'. It concluded that the public interest could not be invoked to justify the use of answers compulsorily obtained in a non-judicial investigation to incriminate the accused during the trial proceedings.

> Moreover, the Court also recalls that the *Brogan* case ... concerned the arrest and detention, by virtue of powers granted under special legislation, of persons suspected of involvement in terrorism in Northern Ireland. The United Kingdom Government had relied on the special security context of Northern Ireland to justify the length of the impugned detention periods under Article 5 s 3. The Court found that even the shortest periods of detention at issue in that case would have entailed consequences impairing the very essence of the relevant right protected by Article 5 s 3. It concluded that the fact that the arrest and detention of the applicants were inspired by the legitimate aim of protecting the community as a whole from terrorism was not, on its own, sufficient to ensure compliance with the specific requirements of Article 5 s 3 of the Convention.

---

72 *Heaney v Ireland* [2001] Crim LR 481, para 45.

> The Court, accordingly, finds that the security and public order concerns of the government cannot justify a provision, which extinguishes the very essence of the applicants' rights to silence and against self-incrimination guaranteed by Article 6 s 1 of the Convention.
>
> Moreover, given the close link, in this context, between those rights guaranteed by Article 6 s 1 and the presumption of innocence guaranteed by Article 6 s 2 of the Convention (see paragraph 40 above), the Court also concludes that there has been a violation of the latter provision.[73]

One argument that seeks to reconcile the decisions in *Brown* and *Heaney* is to take the point that the Strasbourg Court in the latter case clearly took the view that the provision 'extinguishes the very essence' of the right to silence. By way of contrast, the Privy Council sought to argue in *Brown* that the Road Traffic Act provision provided for a single, simple question – although it can be said that the issue of who was driving the car is such a central element in the case that that too must surely extinguish the very essence of the right to silence.

Another, related, factor which might reconcile the two decisions is the issue of the punishment that could be imposed. The financial penalty for failure to respond to the Road Traffic Act question is substantially less onerous than the custodial penalty that could be imposed for a failure to answer the Offences Against the State Act question. However, to assess whether a provision extinguishes the 'very essence' of a right simply by reference to the punishment that can be imposed for refusing to comply with the provision lacks any real logic.

In our view, this is an area of law where the English approach is unlikely to be compatible with what Strasbourg considers to be required. At present it would be unrealistic for advocates to argue that as a matter of domestic law the rights under Art 6 are unqualified. Where more recent Strasbourg authority throws some doubt on the approach taken by the domestic courts, this must be pointed out to the court, but the justification, the nature and the extent of the interference with the right to a fair trial must all be taken into account, as must the proposition that whatever interference is permitted, the substantive right to a fair trial must be preserved.

Does the rule against compelled questioning extend to other forms of compelled evidence?

Defence advocates may wish to challenge the admissibility of various forms of evidence – whether breath tests, blood samples or other physical samples, or documentary evidence – which have been obtained from the defendant under compulsion. In *Saunders* the European Court of Human Rights drew a distinction between physical evidence and compelled questioning:

---

73 *Heaney v Ireland* [2001] Crim LR 481, paras 57–59.

The right not to incriminate oneself is primarily concerned, however, with respecting the will of an accused person to remain silent. As commonly understood in the legal systems of the Contracting Parties to the Convention and elsewhere, it does not extend to the use in criminal proceedings of material which may be obtained from the accused through the use of compulsory powers but which has an existence independent of the will of the suspect such as, *inter alia*, documents acquired pursuant to a warrant, breath, blood and urine samples and bodily tissue for the purpose of DNA testing.[74]

In *Attorney General's Reference (No 7 of 2000)*[75] the Court of Appeal took the view that the use by the prosecution of documents which had been obtained by the Official Receiver under compulsory provisions in the Insolvency Act did not offend against Art 6. This decision must, however, be contrasted with the decision of the European Court, handed down the following month, in *JB v Switzerland*,[76] which concerned the imposition of a series of 'disciplinary fines' on the applicant by the Swiss tax authorities for his failure to submit certain documents. The Court first concluded that the matter was within Art 6(2) since the size and the punitive nature of the penalties suggested a criminal rather than civil matter. Applying the principles from *Funke*,[77] there had therefore been a breach of Art 6(1):

> The right not to incriminate oneself in particular presupposes that the authorities seek to prove their case without resort to evidence obtained through methods of coercion or oppression in defiance of the will of the 'person charged'.
>
> ...
>
> [I]t appears that the authorities were attempting to compel the applicant to submit documents, which would have provided information as to his income in view of the assessment of his taxes.
>
> ...
>
> The Court notes that in its judgment ... the Federal Court referred to various obligations in criminal law obliging a person to act in a particular way in order to be able to obtain his conviction, for instance by means of a tachograph installed in lorries, or by being obliged to submit to a blood or a urine test. In the Court's opinion, however, the present case differs from such material, which, as the Court found in the *Saunders* case, had an existence independent of the person concerned and was not, therefore, obtained by means of coercion and in defiance of the will of that person.[78]

It is hard to establish quite why documents should be said not to have an existence independent of the will of the accused. Arguably there is a far

---

74   *Saunders* (1997) 23 EHRR 313, para 69.
75   [2001] EWCA Crim 888; (2001) 98(22) LSG 35.
76   European Court of Human Rights, judgment of 3 May 2001.
77   (1993) 16 EHRR 297.
78   *Ibid*, paras 64–68.

greater coercion of the will in the requirement to give blood or urine or breath samples. Moreover, it could still be argued that, in its particular context, the decision in *Attorney General's Reference (No 7 of 2000)* is valid, on the basis that the procurer of the evidence (the Official Receiver), was not acting with a view to prosecuting the individual. This is a slightly unattractive argument, since it enables the prosecuting public authority (one arm of the state) to rely upon evidence obtained under compulsion by a different public authority (another arm of the state) in a manner that is arguably akin to the obtaining of the compelled testimony by DTI inspectors in the *Saunders* case, and its subsequent use by the prosecution in the criminal matter that followed.

Advocates, both for the prosecution and the defence, need to be aware of the domestic case law, but also the fact that it was a decision taken prior to an apparently contradictory Strasbourg decision on point. It is therefore arguably a good example of a case where the s 2 of the Human Rights Act duty to take account of Strasbourg decisions will need to be brought to the attention of the court in inviting them to depart from what would otherwise be recent and authoritative Court of Appeal authority.

8.1.2 Exclusion of evidence

It is common for the European Court of Human Rights, when handing down a decision in a criminal context, to stress that the rules of evidence are a matter for the national courts, the supervisory nature of the international court limiting its role to a review of whether there has been a fair trial looked at as a whole. The classic statement of this principle can be found in the case of *Schenk v Switzerland*.[79] In this case the prosecution case relied upon evidence of conversations with a supposed hit man, which had been secretly recorded in breach of the defendant's right to privacy under national law. The European Court of Human Rights stated:

> According to Article 19 ... of the Convention, the Court's duty is to ensure the observance of the engagements undertaken by the Contracting States in the Convention. In particular, it is not its function to deal with errors of fact or of law allegedly committed by a national court unless and in so far as they may have infringed rights and freedoms protected by the Convention.

> While Article 6 ... of the Convention guarantees the right to a fair trial, it does not lay down any rules on the admissibility of evidence as such, which is therefore primarily a matter for regulation under national law.

> The Court therefore cannot exclude as a matter of principle and in the abstract that unlawfully obtained evidence of the present kind may be admissible. It has only to ascertain whether Mr Schenk's trial as a whole was fair.[80]

---

79 (1991) 13 EHRR 242.
80 *Ibid*, paras 45–46.

The Court took into account the fact that the rights of the defence had been taken into account: the unlawful nature of the material had been conceded by the prosecution and the defence had been given the opportunity to challenge both its admissibility and its authenticity, as well as having been able to examine the informer who had recorded the material, and having had the opportunity to examine the supervising police officer. Moreover, the Court emphasised the taped evidence was not the only evidence in the case. The Court took the view that there had been no breach of Art 8.

In other cases the Strasbourg Court has made clear that its self-denying ordinance in respect of national rules of evidence will not apply where the court takes the view that the admission of the evidence results in unfairness. Thus, for example, in *Condron v United Kingdom*[81] the Court had concluded that while the rules against inferences under s 34 of the Criminal Justice and Public Order Act 1994 did not of themselves offend against Art 6, the defective jury direction meant that there had been a breach of Art 6 that could not be cured on appeal.

It will be recalled that courts and tribunals are clearly public authorities for the purposes of the Human Rights Act. Thus courts will be acting unlawfully if they act in manner that breaches an individual's human rights. While the power to exclude evidence under s 78 of the Police and Criminal Evidence Act 1984 may be couched in discretionary terms, there will be no discretion where courts conclude that to admit evidence will breach the defendant's Art 6 right to a fair trial. This will be of relevance where advocates are seeking to persuade the courts to distinguish earlier, pre-Human Rights Act decisions, where it can be shown that these decisions are not compatible with the position taken by the Strasbourg Court.

8.1.2.1 Exclusion of evidence obtained in breach of Article 8

The European Court of Human Rights *dicta* in *Schenk* meant that there were considerable expectations when *Khan v United Kingdom*[82] eventually arrived before the Strasbourg Court. What was most striking about *Khan* was that it was a case where the issue of illegally obtained evidence was so clear. The police had bugged a house in the hope of obtaining evidence about the occupiers' involvement in drug trafficking. Khan visited the house. He had been stopped entering the country with his cousin some months earlier. The cousin had been in possession of a substantial amount of drugs and had been arrested and charged. Khan had not been implicated. Now however the police obtained evidence on tape of his involvement, and he was arrested and charged. It was conceded by the defence that it was Khan's voice on the tape, and by the prosecution that although the bugging of the premises had been

---

81 (2001) 31 EHRR 1.
82 8 BHRC 310.

authorised by the Chief Constable, it had nonetheless involved a civil trespass. It was clear at trial that the recording was the only significant evidence of Khan's guilt. At *voir dire* the judge declined to exclude the evidence under s 78, and Khan pleaded guilty. On appeal both the Court of Appeal and the House of Lords upheld the decision of the trial judge, Lord Nicholls stating that s 78 and Art 6 'walk hand in hand'.[83]

The European Court of Human Rights concluded that there had been a breach of Art 8 on the basis that the bugging of the premises was not 'in accordance with the law' for Art 8 purposes since there was no statutory framework, neither the Police Act 1997 nor the Regulation of Investigatory Powers Act 2000 then being in force. However, the Court concluded that:

38   The central question in the present case is whether the proceedings as a whole were fair. With specific reference to the admission of the contested tape recording, the Court notes that, as in the *Schenk* case, the applicant had ample opportunity to challenge both the authenticity and the use of the recording. He did not challenge its authenticity, but challenged its use at the *voir dire* and again before the Court of Appeal and the House of Lords. The Court notes that at each level of jurisdiction the domestic courts assessed the effect of admission of the evidence on the fairness of the trial by reference to section 78 of PACE, and the courts discussed, amongst other matters, the non-statutory basis for the surveillance. The fact that the applicant was at each step unsuccessful makes no difference ...

39   The Court would add that it is clear that, had the domestic courts been of the view that the admission of the evidence would have given rise to substantive unfairness, they would have had a discretion to exclude it under section 78 of PACE.

40   In these circumstances, the Court finds that the use at the applicant's trial of the secretly taped material did not conflict with the requirements of fairness guaranteed by Article 6 s 1 of the Convention.

A number of points were taken into account by the Court in assessing the issue of fairness:

1   It is clear that the Court took the view that the breach of Art 8 was, in nature, a largely technical one. The bugging had not been unlawful as a matter of domestic law.

2   The police had followed existing domestic law guidelines in undertaking the operation.

3   There had been no element of entrapment of the defendant. His recorded comments had been entirely voluntary.

4   Additionally (see extract above), this was a case where the defendant did not challenge the authenticity of the recording.

---

83   *R v Khan* [1996] 3 WLR 162.

5 It was a case where the defendant had had the opportunity at each stage in the trial and appeals process to argue for the exclusion of the evidence.

6 It was also a case where the defendant had pleaded guilty following the judge's ruling.

It can be argued that all of these factors leave open the issue of whether there is a general principle in *Khan* that breaches of Art 8 will not require the exclusion of evidence obtained as a result. In more marginal cases, where there are disputes as to the reliability of the recording or its authenticity, for example, the Strasbourg Court might be more swayed by the argument that a trial, which rests solely upon such evidence, cannot be fair. However, the decision in *Khan* certainly provides prosecuting advocates with a strong precedent on which to base arguments that the more technical breaches of, for example, Art 8 will not of themselves require the exclusion of evidence.

This certainly appears to be the stance that has been adopted post-*Khan* in the domestic courts.[84] Of a number of cases that have followed *Khan*, the most striking is *R v Loveridge*,[85] where the police covertly filmed the defendants in the magistrates' court, in order to obtain material for use for comparisons with evidence from video cameras at the sites of the various robberies. The covert filming in court was in breach of the restrictions in s 41 of the Criminal Justice Act 1925, as well as being in breach of the Police and Criminal Evidence Act provisions. Moreover, the court rejected the prosecution's arguments that the defendants could have no right to privacy for Art 8 purposes in a public place, such as the court. Notwithstanding these rulings, however, the court went on to find that the evidence had properly been admitted:

> However, so far as the outcome of this appeal is concerned, the breach of Art 8 is only relevant if it interferes with the right of the applicants to a fair hearing. Giving full weight to the breach of the Convention, we are satisfied that the contravention of Art 8 did not interfere with the fairness of the hearing. The judge was entitled to rule as he did. The position is the same so far as s 78 of the Police and Criminal Evidence Act 1984 is concerned.[86]

The domestic courts seem to be treating the decision in *Khan* as applicable to the range of situations where there are allegations of breaches of Art 8, even in circumstances such as *Loveridge* where the court finds that there have been breaches of the domestic law. The brevity of the reasoning in *Loveridge* gives little guidance as to the approach of the court. *Khan* seems to be being treated

---

84 For cases on legally obtained evidence and Art 8 issues, see *R v P* [2001] 2 WLR 463, HL, a case concerning the use of telephone intercepts outside the UK, and which were therefore outside the terms of the Interception of Communications Act regime, where the House of Lords took the view that there had been no breach of Art 8 and that the criteria to be applied under Art 6 were the same as under s 78 of PACE. The case was followed in *R v Wright* [2001] All ER(D) 129 (Jun) which concerned intercepts from a private telephone system, which were also therefore outside the provisions of the IOCA.

85 *R v Loveridge* [2001] EWCA Crim 973; (2001) 98(23) LSG 36.

86 *Ibid*, para 33.

as a message that Art 6 in some way 'trumps' Art 8. Clearly, this is not the case – but advocates who couch arguments solely in terms that a breach of Art 8 requires the exclusion of evidence will not get far. A breach of Art 8 may help to found an application for exclusion of evidence under s 78, but it seems likely that applications are more likely to succeed where the evidence obtained in breach of the article is of poor quality or is unreliable for some other reason. Where the reliability of the evidence is in dispute the circumstances under which it has been obtained may influence the court. In so far as this has traditionally been the approach under domestic law,[87] the current position under *Khan* seems to add little.[88]

8.1.2.2 Breaches of other Convention articles and the exclusion of evidence

Evidence obtained as a result of torture, inhuman or degrading treatment

Strasbourg has increasingly indicated the positive responsibility of the state in respect of Art 3. In particular the use of force on those in custody is likely to amount to a breach of Art 3 unless there is justification for it:

> The Court emphasises that, in respect of a person deprived of his liberty, any recourse to physical force which has not been made strictly necessary by his own conduct diminishes human dignity and is in principle an infringement of the right set forth in Article 3 ... of the Convention. It reiterates that the requirements of an investigation and the undeniable difficulties inherent in the fight against crime cannot justify placing limits on the protection to be afforded in respect of the physical integrity of individuals.[89]

It is clear that the admission of evidence, which has been obtained in breach of Art 3, will breach the fair trial provisions of Art 6.[90] In domestic law s 76(2)(a) of the Police and Criminal Evidence Act 1984 of course requires the exclusion of confession evidence unless the prosecution can satisfy the court beyond reasonable doubt that it was not obtained by oppression, while the broader terms of s 76(2)(b) (things said or done likely to render the confession unreliable) will catch conduct that might fall short of oppression.

In respect of non-confession evidence, however, there is no clear line of authority in respect of the court's discretion to exclude evidence, whether

---

87 See s 78 of the Police and Criminal Evidence Act 1984.

88 See also *R v Bailey, Brewin and Gangji* [2001] EWCA Crim 733; [2001] 5 Archbold News 1, where the Court of Appeal upheld the trial judge's decision to admit evidence recorded by undercover officers who had been invited into the defendants' flat. The officers had set up an operation in a neighbouring flat intended to catch burglars who wished to fence goods, but having been invited into the defendants' flat found that a substantial drug dealing operation was going on, and recorded the defendants' conversation concerning it. The recording was held to be admissible.

89 *Ribitsch v Austria* (1995) 21 EHRR 573, para 38. See also *Tekin v Turkey*, RJD 1998–IV 53.

90 *Austria v Italy* (1963) 6 Yearbook 740. Technically an *obiter* comment but the high degree of importance accorded to Art 3 suggests that this is a fundamental principle from which Strasbourg is unlikely to move.

under common law or under s 78 of the Police and Criminal Evidence Act. Indeed, what authority there is, has traditionally suggested that the fact that evidence has been obtained illegally will not render it inadmissible. Moreover, s 76(4) of the Police and Criminal Evidence Act 1984 provides that the 'fruit of the poisoned tree' doctrine does not apply to evidence obtained as the result of a tainted confession. Arguably in these circumstances, arguments will still arise that if a breach of Art 3 is established, the discretion to exclude evidence under s 78 will have to be exercised so as to exclude the material.

Evidence obtained in breach of Art 5

What is the position in respect of evidence obtained at a time when a person had been unlawfully detained, whether because there were no grounds for his arrest, or the due process provisions of Art 5 had not been complied with? In either event it is likely that there will have been a breach of the provisions of the Police and Criminal Evidence Act 1984, and arguments will be advanced under traditional domestic law principles under s 78 of that Act (and s 76 where confession evidence is involved). In such circumstances, the principles in *Khan* suggest that the consideration of the impact of the admission of the evidence on the fairness of the proceedings under s 78 may well suffice. In this regard, however, it will be noted that the argument for exclusion is in at least one respect stronger than in *Khan*, since the actions will be in breach of national law, in contrast to *Khan*. Where there is no breach of the Police and Criminal Evidence Act 1984, but it is alleged that the deprivation of liberty is nonetheless in breach of Art 5, we would suggest that if the court finds a breach of Art 5[91] it is likely to be appropriate in most cases to proceed by analogy with a breach of the Police and Criminal Evidence Act.

Access to a lawyer

It has been noted that access to legal advice will arise where a person is charged with a criminal offence.[92] Where inferences may arise from a failure to answer questions, the Strasbourg Court has indicated that access to legal advice is likely to be a pre-requisite if the evidence is to be admissible. In *Imbrioscia v Switzerland* the Court held that Art 6(3) might be relevant before a case was sent for trial if the fairness of the trial was 'likely to be seriously prejudiced by an initial failure to comply with its provisions'.[93]

In the *Murray (John) v United Kingdom* decision, in the context of the inferences that could be drawn under the Criminal Evidence (Northern

---

91 For example, if an arrest were to be held to be a disproportionate response in the circumstances: see the discussion at 7.3.3.

92 Both the right to legal advice and the autonomous meaning of charge are discussed in Chapter 7.

93 Series A No 275, p 13, para 36.

Ireland) Order 1988, the Court was emphatic as to the need for access to legal advice because of the potential effects arising from inferences:

> The Court is of the opinion that the scheme contained in the Order is such that it is of paramount importance for the rights of the defence that an accused has access to a lawyer at the initial stages of police interrogation. It observes in this context that, under the Order, at the beginning of police interrogation, an accused is confronted with a fundamental dilemma relating to his defence. If he chooses to remain silent, adverse inferences may be drawn against him in accordance with the provisions of the Order. On the other hand, if the accused opts to break his silence during the course of interrogation, he runs the risk of prejudicing his defence without necessarily removing the possibility of inferences being drawn against him. Under such conditions the concept of fairness enshrined in Article 6 requires that the accused has the benefit of the assistance of a lawyer already at the initial stages of police interrogation. To deny access to a lawyer for the first 48 hours of police questioning, in a situation where the rights of the defence may well be irretrievably prejudiced, is – whatever the justification for such denial – incompatible with the rights of the accused under Article 6.[94]

This principle has been re-stated in the 'inferences' cases that followed *Murray*. In particular in *Averill v United Kingdom*[95] (another Northern Ireland case heard before a judge sitting without a jury), where Averill had been denied access to a lawyer during the first 24 hours of his detention, during which time he was questioned, the Court indicated that the lack of access to a lawyer during this initial period was a relevant consideration when considering the inferences which had been drawn from his silence during the whole period of detention:

> For the Court, considerable caution is required when attaching weight to the fact that a person, arrested, as in this case, in connection with a serious criminal offence and having been denied access to a lawyer during the first 24 hours of his interrogation, does not provide detailed responses when confronted with incriminating evidence against him. Nor is the need for caution removed simply because an accused is eventually allowed to see his solicitor but continues to refuse to answer questions.[96]

It may be argued that s 34 now provides that inferences cannot arise if the suspect has not had access to legal advice. Section 34(2A)[97] is in slightly narrower terms:

> (2A)Where the accused was at an authorised place of detention at the time of the failure, sub-sections (1) and (2) above do not apply if he had not been

---

94   *Murray (John) v United Kingdom* (1996) 22 EHRR 29, para 66.
95   *Averill v United Kingdom* (2001) 31 EHRR 36.
96   *Ibid*, para 48.
97   Similar provisions exist in relation to the inferences under s 36 and s 37 of the Criminal Justice and Public Order Act 1994.

allowed an opportunity to consult a solicitor prior to being questioned, charged or informed as mentioned in sub-section (1) above.

Since the provision only arises where the suspect is at 'an authorised place of detention', there remains some scope for prosecution arguments that inferences are possible in those narrow circumstances where questioning is permitted prior to arrival at the police station.[98] We would argue that in the unlikely event that the prosecution sought to rely upon inferences from silence arising prior to the opportunity to take legal advice the principles set out in the Strasbourg decisions suggest that to draw inferences in such circumstances would be in breach of Art 6.

Issues for advocates: arguments for the exclusion of evidence

1 Identifying the breach:

*   In particular, there will be a need for precision in identifying the relevant aspects of the Convention right, which are said to be in issue. A general appeal to 'my client's Art 8 right' is unlikely to be well received. The onus will be on the defence advocate to show which element of Art 8 is engaged, and prosecution advocates will need to be able to show that the interference, if admitted, is for a prescribed reason, is in accordance with law and is necessary in a democratic society.

2 The effect of a breach:

*   Can it be said that the breach goes to the 'very essence' of the right – note the principles in relation to evidence obtained by compelled questioning in breach of Art 6 in *Heaney v Ireland*.

*   It cannot, however, be said that there is any principle which requires the exclusion of evidence merely because it has been obtained in breach of any Convention right. In relation to absolute rights, such as Art 3, however, it is unlikely that evidence obtained in breach of such a right could be admitted without being in breach of Art 6. Contrast, however, breaches of qualified rights, such as Art 8.

3 Reliability: there are clear suggestions in the case law of the Strasbourg Court that there may be more of a case for arguing that the admissibility of evidence would be in breach of Art 6 where the reliability of the evidence is in issue. Note that in the *Khan* case the fact that the reliability of the evidence was not in dispute seemed to outweigh the fact that it was the sole significant evidence of the defendant's guilt.

4 Other evidence: the clear suggestion in *Schenk* that it was important that there was other evidence in the case seems to have been undermined by

---

98 Normally questioning post-arrest will amount to an interview for the purposes of PACE Code C11.1A and C11.1. There are certain prescribed circumstances where interviewing is permitted prior to arrival at the police station where a specified risk arises.

the later decision in *Khan*. Nonetheless, where prosecution advocates can point to other evidence of guilt, it seems that the likelihood of a breach of Art 6 in relation to the admissibility of the impugned evidence will be lessened.

5 The court as public authority: note that the court as public authority will take issue with evidence which may raise Convention issues of its own motion.

6 The prosecutor as public authority: similarly, there is a strong argument that the prosecuting agencies, as public authorities, will act unlawfully where they seek to progress a prosecution based on evidence whose admissibility would be in breach of Art 6. On its face, this proposition appears to lend little to the domestic law principle that the prosecutor is a minister of justice. However, it creates a particular problem for prosecutors who are faced with an apparent conflict between domestic law and the case law of the Strasbourg Court.

8.1.3 Entrapment

The leading recent Strasbourg decision on entrapment is *Teixeira v Portugal*[99] where, notwithstanding its stance that evidential matters were *per se* matters for domestic courts, the Strasbourg Court took the view that the use of the evidence of undercover police officers, who had in the Court's view acted as *agents provocateurs*, meant that there had been a breach of the right to a fair trial:

> The use of undercover agents must be restricted and safeguards put in place even in cases concerning the fight against drug trafficking. While the rise in organised crime undoubtedly requires that appropriate measures be taken, the right to a fair administration of justice nevertheless holds such a prominent place ... that it cannot be sacrificed for the sake of expedience. The general requirements of fairness embodied in Article 6 apply to proceedings concerning all types of criminal offence, from the most straightforward to the most complex. The public interest cannot justify the use of evidence obtained as a result of police incitement.[100]

The Court's decision is not easy to translate into a domestic law context. It can be argued that a significant element of the Court's concern was the lack of judicial supervision in the police operation, an issue that is not applicable to domestic law – although compliance with the new Regulation of Investigatory Powers Act 2000 regime would doubtless be a pre-requisite. Equally, it can be argued that the focus of the Strasbourg Court's decision is the alleged

---

99 (1999) 28 EHRR 101.
100 *Ibid*, para 36.

'incitement' by the police officers, so that the issue is less the use of undercover officers *per se* and rather the issue of whether the defendant was already pre-disposed to commit the offence – a distinction which can already be found in domestic case law. In particular the Strasbourg Court clearly took the view that there was initially no evidence that Mr Teixeira was involved in the supply of hard drugs (he was not the original target of the operation), nor that he had ready access to such drugs (he had to contact others to obtain the supply), and thus no evidence that this was an offence which he would have committed but for the involvement of the officers.

8.1.3.1 The application of Teixeira in domestic law

The difficulties of imposing a 'pre-disposition' test, where the judgment has to be made with the benefit of hindsight, are well illustrated by the case of *Nottingham City Council v Amin*.[101] Amin, an off duty minicab driver, who was not licensed to ply for hire in Nottingham, was hailed in the Nottingham area by two plain clothes special constables even though his For Hire light was not on. He responded to their hail by stopping, taking them to a destination and accepting a fare. At his trial in the magistrates' court, he successfully argued that the evidence had been obtained by incitement within the meaning of *Teixeira* since the officers had not confined themselves to 'investigating [the defendant's] criminal activities in an essentially passive manner but exercised an influence such as to incite the commission of the offence'.[102]

The Divisional Court allowed the prosecutor's appeal and remitted the matter back to the magistrate, Lord Bingham distinguishing the *Teixeira* decision on the basis that:

> It seems to me that that conclusion has to be understood in the context of the whole argument before the court on that occasion and on the special facts of the case. It is true that in the present case the criminal activity alleged was more minor. It is also true that the facts are much simpler and that they simply cannot lend themselves to the construction that this defendant was in any way prevailed upon or overborne or persuaded or pressured or instigated or incited to commit the offence. The question for the stipendiary magistrate was whether, on the facts which he found, the admission of this evidence had such an adverse effect on the fairness of the proceedings that he should exclude it, or whether (to put the test in a different way) the effect of admitting it was to deny the defendant a fair trial.[103]

Thus, the focus of the test remained the s 78 issue of overall fairness, and the argument that officers' conduct had gone beyond a 'merely passive investigation' was sidestepped in favour of a general test of incitement.

---

101 [2000] 1 Cr App R 426.
102 (1999) 28 EHRR 101, para 38.
103 [2000] 1 Cr App R 426, p 427.

In *R v Loosely*,[104] the decision in *Amin* was referred to approvingly by the House of Lords, albeit that their Lordships applied different analyses to the appropriate approach to issues of entrapment. The starting point in all their Lordships' judgments is the principle that the court has an inherent power and duty to prevent the abuse of its process. This principle ensures that the agents of the state do not misuse the law enforcement function of the court to oppress the citizen. Whether this amounts to the same test as 'a fair trial' is not wholly clear, but the clear suggestion from the judgments is that the effect will be the same since the focus is the protection of the citizen from the power of the court.

For Lord Nicholls, the factors to be taken into account in identifying the limits on police conduct include:

(1) Was this an 'unexceptional opportunity' to commit an offence?

(2) How proportionate was the conduct?

(3) Is the conduct of the law enforcer such that it would bring the administration of justice into disrepute? In particular:

(a) What is the nature of the offence? Does it require the techniques employed?

(b) What was the reason for the operation? How reasonable was any suspicion?

(c) What was the nature and extent of police participation in the crime? The greater the inducement or persuasion the more likely it is that the police will have 'overstepped the boundary'.

(d) The criminal record of any defendant is unlikely to be relevant unless it can be linked to other factors that show the defendant is currently engaged in criminal activity.

Lord Hoffman's approach similarly accepts the distinction between circumstances where there could be said to have the causing of the commission of an offence rather than the simple provision of an opportunity for it to be committed. Lord Hoffman, however, notes that while 'the test of whether the law enforcement officer behaved like an ordinary member of the public works well and is likely to be decisive in many cases of regulatory offences', this test might not always be appropriate:

> But ordinary members of the public do not become involved in large scale drug dealing, conspiracy to rob (*R v Mealey and Sheridan* (1974) 60 Cr App R 59) or hiring assassins (*R v Gill* [1989] Crim LR 358; *R v Smurthwaite* [1994] All ER 898). The appropriate standards of behaviour are in such cases rather more problematic. And even in the case of offences committed with ordinary members of the public, other factors may require a purely causal test to be modified.[105]

---

104 *R v Loosely; Attorney General's Reference No 3 of 2000* [2001] UKHL 53, judgment of 25 October.

105 *Ibid*, para 55.

The other factors that Lord Hoffman proposes include the extent to which there is existing suspicion of a person, while stressing that pre-disposition itself is an irrelevance:

> Since the English doctrine assumes the defendant's guilt and is concerned with the standards of behaviour of the law enforcement officers, predisposition is irrelevant to whether a stay be granted or not. The facts which lead the police to suspect that crimes are being committed and justify the use of an undercover officer or test purchaser may also point to the accused and show predisposition.[106]

In cases of pure 'honesty testing' such as test purchases, where there might be no pre-existing suspicion, applicable codes of practice ensured that the operations must be subject to the supervision and authorisation of senior officers who would only approve such operations where there was reasonable suspicion that offences were being committed. In this context, however, a pure 'active or passive' approach is inadequate:

> In cases in which the offence involves a purchase of goods or services, like liquor or videotapes or a taxi ride, it would be absurd to expect the test purchaser to wait silently for an offer. He will do what an ordinary purchaser would do. Drug dealers can be expected to show some wariness about dealing with a stranger who might be a policeman or informer and therefore some protective colour in dress or manner as well as a certain degree of persistence may be necessary to achieve the objective ... A good deal of active behaviour in the course of an authorised operation may therefore be acceptable without crossing the boundary between causing the offence to be committed and providing an opportunity for the defendant to commit it.[107]

The 'unexceptional opportunity' posited by Lord Nicholls seems effectively to be a variable factor: what will be 'unexceptional' will depend on the nature and seriousness of the offence.

To these factors, Lord Hutton adds the issues of whether the defendant already had the intention of committing the offence or a similar offence, and whether there was 'persistent importunity, threats, deceit, offers of rewards or other inducements that would not ordinarily be associated with the commission of the offence or a similar offence'.[108]

Applying these somewhat disparate general principles to the facts of the two cases, the House of Lords was in agreement. In the first of the two cases, Loosely's name had been given to an undercover officer who was investigating illegal drug use at a public house by a man in the public house. The officer had rung Loosely and had asked him to 'sort us out a couple of bags'. Loosely had directed the officer to his flat and supplied the heroin. Heroin was supplied in a similar fashion on two subsequent occasions. The

---

106 *Ibid*, para 68.

107 *Ibid*, para 69.

108 *Ibid*, para 100, quoting the dissenting judgment from *Ridgeway v The Queen* (1995) 184 CLR 19.

House of Lords was unanimous in concluding that the trial judge had been entirely correct to reject the application of exclusion of the evidence under s 78 and that there had no breach of Art 6. Equally, the House of Lords was unanimous in overturning the Court of Appeal's decision in *Attorney General's Reference (No 3 of 2000)*, and upholding the decision of the trial judge that that defendant had never dealt in heroin, had been induced to procure heroin by the prospect, held out by the undercover officers, of a profitable trade in smuggled cigarettes and that the police had therefore caused him to commit an offence which he would not otherwise have committed.

Does the approach of the House of Lords in *Loosely* comply with the requirements of the European Court of Human Rights in *Teixeira*? The first point is that while the approaches of their Lordships clearly differ, their Lordships all assert that the underlying principles are the same, and that these principles, focusing as they do on the protection of the individual from the arbitrary and intrusive power of the law enforcement agencies, are sufficient to ensure compliance with Art 6, and indeed are in agreement with the approach taken by the Strasbourg Court in *Teixeira*.[109] However, for advocates, there is a continuing difficulty in establishing whether the different approaches adopted by the two courts amount to a difference of principle, or whether, as the House of Lords asserts, they offer an identical protection. Lord Hoffman's emphasis on the degree of supervision exercised by the authorities is undoubtedly significant in seeking to ensure protection against arbitrary incitement by law enforcement agencies, and is arguably an appropriate domestic parallel to the supervisory role of the investigating judge which the Strasbourg Court saw as lacking in the Portuguese case.

Similarly, Lord Nicholls' list of factors which assess the rationale of any undercover operation and the proportionality of any interference are clearly important safeguards. However, if Strasbourg stands by its distinction between active and passive operations, as proposed in *Teixeira*, it seems unlikely that these factors are sufficiently stringent; indeed there is a clear rejection by Lord Hoffman of the viability of a pure active/passive approach. Finally, it is interesting to note the general agreement in the domestic court of the limited relevance of previous convictions and of evidence of pre-disposition. Arguably, this goes further than *Teixeira* and is a statement of principle which is clearly to be welcomed.

8.1.3.2 *If evidence has been obtained in breach of Art 6 what steps should the court take?*

The Strasbourg Court in *Teixeira* held that the evidence had been obtained by entrapment and thus to admit it would be in breach of Art 6. Logically,

---

109 This contrasts with the approach of the Court of Appeal in *Attorney General's Reference (No 3 of 2000)* [2001] EWCA Crim 1214; (2001) *The Times*, 27 June, where *Teixeira* was described as being 'on its own facts'. Indeed, the Attorney General's Reference in that case is one of two cases considered in *Loosely*, where it was overturned.

therefore, the argument would follow that since a court is a public authority for the purposes of s 6 of the Human Rights Act, it would act unlawfully if it admitted evidence which would breach the defendant's right to a fair trial.[110] Some doubt about this proposition may exist, however, as a result of the decision in *Attorney General's Reference (No 2 of 2001)*,[111] which suggests, in the context of a breach of the right to trial within a reasonable time, that the court will not be in breach of s 6 where it remedies that breach of Art 6 by, for example, reducing sentence or compensating the victim. The decision in that case, as is discussed below, is far from easy to follow, and in any event it is hard to see what remedies other than excluding the evidence the court could take once it has concluded that it has been obtained in circumstances that breach Art 6.

Issues for advocates: arguments for the exclusion of entrapment evidence

1 Has there been entrapment?

- Strasbourg test: have the officers 'confined themselves to investigating applicant's criminal activity in an essentially passive manner' or have they 'exercised an influence such as to incite commission of offence'?

- English test: has the evidence been obtained in a manner which is an affront to the court? Factors will include (*per* Lord Nicholls): was this an 'unexceptional opportunity to offend'; how proportionate was any interference; what was the nature of the offence; what was the reason for the operation; what was the nature and extent of police participation; (*per* Lord Hoffman) what was the extent of any supervision; (*per* Lord Hutton) how persistent were any threats, inducements and the like?

2 Reliability

- Is the veracity of the evidence disputed?

- Is this a case where undercover officers have been used to circumvent PACE?

- Have the requirements of the Regulation of Investigatory Powers Act 2000 been complied with?

3 Other evidence

- Is this a case that depends solely upon evidence obtained by undercover operations?

4 The court as public authority

- There will be no discretion. If there has been entrapment, the evidence will breach Art 6 and must be excluded.

---

110 This is, of course, in contrast to the position in *Khan*, where the breach was of Art 8, but it was held that the admission of the evidence was not in breach of Art 6.

111 [2001] EWCA Crim 1568; (2001) *The Times*, 12 July: discussed below in the context of delay (see 8.3.6).

- Domestic law would in any event require its exclusion under s 78 of PACE if it were found to have been obtained in breach of the 'English test'.

5 The prosecutor as public authority: similar arguments will apply to the prosecutor in seeking to adduce the evidence. The counter-argument is that it must be for the court to decide whether there has been a breach of Art 6 in all but the most obvious cases of entrapment. In any event, it appears that the appropriate procedure is to challenge the admission of evidence during or at the start of the trial process: *Kebilene*.

8.1.4 The right to examine witnesses

Article 6(3)(d) provides that everyone charged with a criminal offence has the right:

> to examine or have examined witnesses against him and to obtain the attendance and examination of witnesses on his behalf under the same conditions as witnesses against him.

'Witness' has an autonomous meaning for Strasbourg purposes, seemingly comprising any form of evidence from a person, which is taken into account by the court:

> In principle, all the evidence must be produced in the presence of the accused at a public hearing with a view to adversarial argument ... This does not mean, however, that in order to be used as evidence statements of witnesses should always be made at a public hearing in court: to use as evidence such statements obtained at the pre-trial stage is not in itself inconsistent with paragraphs 3(d) and 1 of Article 6 provided the rights of the defence have been respected.

> As a rule, these rights require that an accused should be given an adequate and proper opportunity to challenge and question a witness against him, either at the time the witness was making his statement or at some later stage of the proceedings ...[112]

A number of potential issues arise, the most prominent of which is the admissibility of hearsay evidence, but which also potentially include challenges to the admissibility of evidence where a video link or any other form of shielding of the witness is employed.

---

112 *Kostovski v Netherlands* (1990) 12 EHRR 434, para 41.

8.1.4.1 Hearsay evidence

The most common route for obtaining the admission of hearsay evidence in criminal proceedings in the domestic courts is the Criminal Justice Act 1988.[113] These provisions will be familiar to advocates. Section 23 permits the use of first hand hearsay in certain circumstances where there is a specified reason (such as death, illness, presence abroad) why the witness cannot be called. Section 24 is a wider provision permitting the use of documentary hearsay where the document has been made in the course of various forms of business activity. Where the document was prepared as part of a criminal investigation or with criminal proceedings in mind, it will normally be necessary to show that there is a s 23 reason why the witness cannot be called. The court has a general discretion to exclude evidence in the interests of justice (s 25), and where the evidence has been prepared as part of a criminal investigation or with the criminal proceedings in mind, the court must exclude the evidence unless satisfied that it is in the interests of justice to admit it (s 26). Section 28 of the Act permits the defence to challenge the credibility of the evidence in any way that they would have had the witness been called.

The general structure of the Criminal Justice Act provisions, and in particular the maintenance of the exclusionary discretion, was held to be compatible with Art 6 by the European Commission in the case of *Trivedi v United Kingdom*,[114] where the evidence of the main witness (Mr C) was admitted on the basis that he was elderly and was no longer in a fit state to give evidence:

> In the present case the Commission notes that before deciding to admit the statements of Mr C into evidence the trial judge conducted a detailed inquiry into Mr C's condition, including his memory at the material time. After hearing oral evidence as well as submissions by both sides in the absence of the jury, the judge concluded that there was nothing about the quality of the statements of Mr C which gave such concern as would lead the court to exercise its discretion to exclude them from evidence.

> The Commission further observes that Mr C's statements were not the only evidence in the case to show that the applicant had claimed for visits to Mr C, which had not occurred. In particular, strong support for the prosecution case was provided by the prescription forms made out by the applicant for Mr C which were subjected to forensic examination and which were shown to have been written in three groups in reverse order of date. Moreover, as the trial judge noted, in the absence of oral evidence from Mr C, the applicant had the

---

113 Schedule 2 to the Criminal Procedure and Investigations Act 1996 contains a very wide power that permits committal evidence to be used at trial. The extent of this little-noticed power has caused some concerns, but in practice we are not aware of the power having been used, and the draft bill accompanying the Law Commission's Report No 245 (*Evidence in Criminal Proceedings: Hearsay and Related Topics*) contains a provision for its abolition. It seems unlikely to be of relevance therefore.

114 [1997] EHRLR 521.

opportunity to give uncontroverted evidence about the reason for preparing the prescriptions in that form.

The Commission further notes that not only was counsel for the applicant given a full opportunity to comment on the statements of Mr C to the jury with a view to casting doubt on his credibility or reliability, but in his summing-up the trial judge expressly warned members of the jury that they should attach less weight to the statements of Mr C, which had not been tested in cross-examination, than to the evidence of witnesses who had been heard orally before the court.

Having regard to the above the Commission is of the opinion that the admission in evidence of Mr C's statements did not fail to respect the rights of the defence and that the proceedings considered as a whole were fair within the meaning of Article 6 of the Convention.

It seems clear, therefore, that provided the s 25/26 discretion is applied rigorously by the trial judge, the Criminal Justice Act regime is likely to be Convention compatible:

In our opinion, the narrow ground which the trial judge has to be sure exists before he can allow a statement to be read to the jury coupled with the balancing exercise that he has to perform and the requirement that having performed that exercise he should be of the opinion that it is in the interest of justice to admit the statement having paid due regard to the risk of unfairness to the accused means that the provisions of sections 23 to 26 of the 1988 Act are not in themselves contrary to Article 6 of the Convention.[115]

Concerns arise, however, because it is not infrequently the case in the lower courts that hearsay evidence is admitted without a rigorous examination of whether the s 23 reason can properly be said to be made out,[116] and without properly considering the impact of the admission of that evidence on the fairness of the trial proceedings. There are increasing indications that the appellate courts are seeking to ensure that the prosecution has demonstrated that all proper steps have been taken to ensure that the defence are not disadvantaged by the production of evidence in this form, and that the judge has properly taken into account the prejudice to the defence.[117]

---

115 *R v Thomas and Flannagan* [1998] Crim LR 887. The Court of Appeal took into account the fact that neither conviction was based solely on the hearsay evidence, that the statement was taken at committal and the witness had therefore been subject to some scrutiny and limited cross-examination, and that a strong direction had been given to the jury as to the hearsay nature of the evidence and the bad character of the absent witness.

116 See, for example, *R v Coughlan*, CA, unreported, judgment of 2 March 1999, where the witness was said to be in Africa, but was later found by the defence, with a minimum of effort, to be living in the area.

117 See *R v Radak, Adjei, Butler-Rees and Meghjee* [1999] 1 Cr App R 187, where the Court of Appeal took the view that the prosecution should have obtained the evidence of a major prosecution witness by utilising the Criminal Justice (International Co-operation) Act 1990 provisions which would have enabled the defence to cross-examine this central witness. To a similar effect, see *Luca v Italy* [2001] Crim LR 747, where a conviction is based to a decisive degree on depositions from a witness who the defence have never had the opportunity to cross-examine, whether a trial or the taking of the deposition, the rights of the defence would be restricted to a degree incompatible with Art 6.

Clearly challenges to hearsay evidence are likely to be more successful where the defence can show substantial prejudice. This will be the case where the reliability of the evidence is in issue, and even more so where the case rests to a large extent on the hearsay evidence. Arguably, however, this is an approach which is already adopted in domestic law, but advocates may wish to point to Art 6(3)(d) as emphasising the importance of this principle.

8.1.4.2 Witness protection measures

Witness protection measures are increasingly common in the domestic courts. These include such measures as the provision of screens, the giving of evidence by video link, or on video, and prohibitions on the cross-examination of rape victims by the defendant and on any issue going to prior sexual contact with the defendant, except under certain narrow exceptions.

The Strasbourg case law makes clear that restrictions may be permitted, provided that there is a satisfactory reason for the restriction and provided that the rights of the defence are properly safeguarded. In the *Van Mechelen*[118] case, the European Court was not satisfied that it was necessary for a large number of police officers to give evidence anonymously. It was part of the duty of police officers to give evidence in public, and the status of the police as an arm of the state made this an important safeguard:

> 56 In the Court's opinion, the balancing of the interests of the defence against arguments in favour of maintaining the anonymity of witnesses raises special problems if the witnesses in question are members of the police force of the State. Although their interests – and indeed those of their families – also deserve protection under the Convention, it must be recognised that their position is to some extent different from that of a disinterested witness or a victim. They owe a general duty of obedience to the State's executive authorities and usually have links with the prosecution; for these reasons alone their use as anonymous witnesses should be resorted to only in exceptional circumstances. In addition, it is in the nature of things that their duties, particularly in the case of arresting officers, may involve giving evidence in open court.
>
> 57 On the other hand, the Court has recognised in principle that, provided that the rights of the defence are respected, it may be legitimate for the police authorities to wish to preserve the anonymity of an agent deployed in undercover activities, for his own or his family's protection and so as not to impair his usefulness for future operations ...
>
> 58 Having regard to the place that the right to a fair administration of justice holds in a democratic society, any measures restricting the rights of the defence should be strictly necessary. If a less restrictive measure can suffice then that measure should be applied.

---

118 *Van Mechelen v Netherlands* (1997) 25 EHRR 647.

59 In the present case, the police officers in question were in a separate room with the investigating judge, from which the accused and even their counsel were excluded. All communication was via a sound link. The defence was thus not only unaware of the identity of the police witnesses but were also prevented from observing their demeanour under direct questioning, and thus from testing their reliability ...

60 It has not been explained to the Court's satisfaction why it was necessary to resort to such extreme limitations on the right of the accused to have the evidence against them given in their presence, or why less far-reaching measures were not considered.[119]

By contrast, in the *Doorson* case[120] the court was prepared to accept that the witnesses, who were drug addicts who were giving evidence against an alleged dealer, had a justifiable fear of reprisals. In that case the defence had been able to put questions to the anonymous witnesses via the examining magistrates, and the Strasbourg Court took the view that there had been an adequate protection of the rights of the defendant.

In *R (on the Application of DPP) v Redbridge Youth Court; R (on the Application of 'L') v Bicester Youth Court*[121] challenges were brought to the use of video evidence and a video link under s 32A and s 32 of the Criminal Justice Act 1998. The Divisional Court held that the it was appropriate to provide protection to certain classes of witness, of whom the child witnesses in the cases were one, and that the rights of the defence were safeguarded:

[T]he general legislative purpose of both sections is the same, namely to provide, in relation to a child, conditions which are most conducive to ensuring that a child is able to give as full an account as possible of the events in question. The procedures are intended to provide a mechanism whereby a child witness who might otherwise be upset, intimidated or traumatised by appearing in court is not as a result inhibited from giving a full and proper account of the events of which he or she was a witness: see *R v McAndrew Bingham* [1991] 1 WLR 1897. It follows that orders under either section are appropriate where there is a real risk that the quality of the evidence given by that child would be so affected or that it might even be impossible to obtain any evidence from that child. Fairness to the defendant is achieved by enabling the defendant to see the witness giving evidence in interview, or by a television link, and having a full opportunity to cross examine by way of the television link.

...

Article 6 of the European Convention on Human Rights does not, in my judgment, provide any further assistance in resolving the difficult question

---

119 (1997) 25 EHRR 647, paras 56–60.
120 *Doorson v Netherlands* (1996) 22 EHRR 330.
121 [2001] EWHC Admin 209; [2001] Crim LR 473. Note that the Criminal Justice Act provisions are due to be replaced by special measures provisions under the Youth Justice and Criminal Evidence Act 1999. The considerations set out in *Redbridge* should remain applicable although the different wording of the Youth Justice and Criminal Evidence Act will require that the provisions are looked at afresh.

which the court has to answer under either section. As the European Court of Human Rights recognised in *Doorson v The Netherlands* it is appropriate to provide protection to certain classes of witness. It seems to me to be clear that child witnesses fall into a category of witness, which is entitled to such protection. Provided that a decision of a court is based on the purpose for which such protection is provided, steps taken to provide that protection cannot result in unfairness to a defendant provided always that the defendant is given a fair opportunity both to test that evidence and to answer it. The procedures under s 32 and 32A of the Act provide that opportunity.[122]

Limitations on the right to cross-examine certain witnesses

There are increasing restrictions on the right of the defendant to conduct his own cross-examination of certain classes of witness, even where he is choosing to conduct his own trial. Thus for example an accused charged with a sexual offence is not permitted to cross-examine in person the complainant: s 34 of the Youth Justice and Criminal Evidence Act 1999. Where there is a prohibition on cross-examination by the defendant the court will invite the defendant to appoint a lawyer, and if he fails to do so, the court may appoint one for him: s 38 of the Youth Justice and Criminal Evidence Act 1999. The wording of Art 6(3)(d) ('to have examined') makes clear that there is unlikely to be a right to cross-examine a witness in person provided that it is possible for the witness to be examined on behalf of the defence.

More problematic is – or was – the prohibition on the subject matter of cross-examination contained in s 41 of the Youth Justice and Criminal Evidence Act 1999. The provision has been concisely summarised by Lord Slynn:

> Section 41 of the Youth Justice and Criminal Evidence Act 1999 prohibits the giving of evidence and cross-examination about any sexual behaviour of the complainant except with leave of the court. Leave may be given where (a) consent is an issue and where the sexual behaviour of the complainant is alleged to have taken place 'at or about the same time as the event which is the subject-matter of the charge against the accused' (section 41(3)(b)) and (b) where the sexual behaviour of the complainant to which the question or evidence relates is alleged to have been 'in any respect, so similar' to the sexual behaviour which is shown by evidence to have taken place as part of the event which is the subject-matter of the charge or to any other sexual behaviour of the complainant which took place at or about the same time as that event 'that the similarity cannot reasonably be explained as a coincidence' (section 41(3)(c)).

> Such questions are not to be allowed if their purpose is to establish material to impugn the credibility of the complainant as a witness. Leave may also be given if the evidence of the complainant's sexual behaviour goes no further than to rebut prosecution evidence.[123]

---

122 *Ibid.*
123 *R v A* [2001] UKHL 25; [2001] 2 WLR 1546, paras 7–8.

Notwithstanding some doubts from Lord Hope as to whether it was necessary at this point to 'read down' the provision under s 3 of the Human Rights Act,[124] Their Lordships took the view that the wide reach of the provision could lead to an unfair trial and that a residual discretion had to be left to the trial judge to assess the circumstances under which such cross-examination could properly be permitted:

> After all, it is realistic to proceed on the basis that the legislature would not, if alerted to the problem, have wished to deny the right to an accused to put forward a full and complete defence by advancing truly probative material. It is therefore possible under section 3 to read section 41, and in particular section 41(3)(c), as subject to the implied provision that evidence or questioning which is required to ensure a fair trial under Article 6 of the Convention should not be treated as inadmissible. The result of such a reading would be that sometimes logically relevant sexual experiences between a complainant and an accused may be admitted under section 41(3)(c). On the other hand, there will be cases where previous sexual experience between a complainant and an accused will be irrelevant, eg an isolated episode distant in time and circumstances. Where the line is to be drawn must be left to the judgment of trial judges. On this basis a declaration of incompatibility can be avoided. If this approach is adopted, section 41 will have achieved a major part of its objective but its excessive reach will have been attenuated in accordance with the will of Parliament as reflected in section 3 of the 1998 Act. That is the approach that I would adopt.[125]

It is clear, both from the tenor of the judgment in *A* and from the Strasbourg case law, that defence advocates are unlikely to succeed simply by asserting that a defence right has been encroached upon, so long as the prosecution are able to show that there are competing rights (the rights of society, and often the rights of the witness himself or herself) which must be taken into account:

> The only balancing permitted is in respect of what the concept of a fair trial entails: here account may be taken of the familiar triangulation of interests of the accused, the victim and society.[126]

This is not an untrammelled right to interfere with a fair trial. There will come a point where the interference is so great that a fair trial will not be possible, and either the rights of the witness must be limited or the trial must be discontinued. The case law suggests, however, that this will not arise frequently.

---

124 [2001] UKHL 25; [2001] 2 WLR 1546, para 106.
125 *Ibid, per* Lord Steyn, para 45.
126 *Ibid, per* Lord Steyn, para 38.

8.2 CHALLENGES TO SUBSTANTIVE CRIMINAL OFFENCES

While the focus of Art 6 is on the fairness of the trial process, it may be the case that substantive provisions of criminal law themselves offend against Convention rights.

Thus, in *ADT v United Kingdom*,[127] the defendant was convicted of gross indecency contrary to s 13 of the Sexual Offences Act 1956 on the basis that the consensual sexual acts which he had engaged in with other men were not within the exception in s 1(2) of the Sexual Offences Act 1967, decriminalising homosexual activity done in private, since they involved more than two men. The European Court of Human Rights found that the provision breached the defendant's Art 8 right to private life:

> Given the narrow margin of appreciation afforded to the national authorities in the case, the absence of any public health considerations and the purely private nature of the behaviour in the present case, the Court finds that the reasons submitted for the maintenance in force of legislation criminalising homosexual acts between men in private, and *a fortiori* the prosecution and conviction in the present case, are not sufficient to justify the legislation and the prosecution.[128]

Similarly, in *Sutherland v United Kingdom*[129] the Commission agreed that the fixing of the age for consent to homosexual acts at 18, as opposed to 16 for heterosexual acts, was in breach of Arts 8 and 14.

If a person were therefore to be charged with gross indecency, contrary to the Sexual Offences Acts, the defence would presumably raise the fact that the provisions are demonstrably in breach of Art 8, as demonstrated by the *ADT* judgment, and would argue that the provision must therefore be 'read down' so as to be Convention-compliant. There have also been suggestions that it may be possible for the defence to raise the Convention right as a defence *simpliciter* by way of s 7 of the Human Rights Act:

> 7(1) A person who claims that a public authority has acted (or proposes to act) in a way which is made unlawful by section 6(1) may
>
> ...
>
> (b) rely on the Convention right or rights concerned in any legal proceedings ...

8.2.1 Substantive law and the protection of third party rights

It is implicit in almost all criminal offences that the law exists to protect the interests of society as a whole, and often to protect the specific rights of the

---

127 [2000] 2 FLR 697.
128 *Ibid*, para 38.
129 [1998] EHRLR 117.

victim. Thus, in *R v H (Reasonable Chastisement)*[130] the trial judge was concerned that if he were to give the traditional direction on the common law defence of lawful chastisement he would be acting unlawfully in failing to give adequate protection to the victim's rights under Art 3, in the light of the Strasbourg Court's judgment in *A v United Kingdom*,[131] which had held that the scope of the defence was too wide to provide adequate protection of the victim's rights. The Court of Appeal held that the judge could direct the jury in accordance with the factors as the reasonableness of any chastisement, which had been identified by the Strasbourg authority, thereby protecting the victim's rights. The common law defence had clearly developed in the light of the decision in *A v United Kingdom* and subsequent statements of intention by the state.[132]

8.2.2 Freedom of speech cases

There are likely to be situations where challenges arise in relation in particular to Art 10 issues of freedom of speech. The rights under Art 10 are, of course, qualified, and interference is permitted, *inter alia*, in order to protect the rights and freedoms of others. In addition, the provisions of s 12 of the Human Rights Act which require special consideration of the importance of free expression are are not applicable in criminal proceedings. Nonetheless, the high degree of protection which freedom of speech attracts makes the issue of whether any interference is 'necessary in a democratic society' a stringent test to meet. The matter is further complicated by the positive duty on the state to protect the Art 10 rights of any individual. In many cases where there is protest and counter-protest, a number of conflicting rights are likely to be engaged.

Steel and Others v United Kingdom[133] illustrates the range and complexity of the issues. Of the five applicants, all were arrested for breach of the peace, although additional charges were also originally brought against Steel herself. Steel was arrested at a protest against a grouse shoot. Lush was arrested in a protest against a motorway extension. Needham, Polden and Cole were arrested as they handed out leaflets critical of arms sales outside a 'Fighter Helicopter' conference, although the charges of breach of the peace were subsequently dropped. The European Court of Human Rights ruled that breach of the peace was sufficiently certain to comply with Art 5 and upheld the arrest and detention of Steel and Lush, going on to hold that the

---

130 *R v H (Reasonable Chastisement)* [2001] EWCA Crim 1024; [2001] 2 FLR 431.
131 (1999) 27 EHRR 611.
132 The court relied upon the decision in *SW v United Kingdom* (1995) 21 EHRR 363, a case concerning the removal of the marital rape exception, as making clear that the development of the common law would not offend against Art 7.
133 (1999) 28 EHRR 603.

interference with their Art 10 right to freedom of expression had been prescribed by law and proportionate. By contrast, however, the Court found that since the allegations of breach of the peace were never proceeded with against Needham, Polden and Lush, it was necessary for the Court to consider the allegations itself. The Court concluded that there had been no basis for the arrests in domestic law since the behaviour could not have amounted to a breach of the peace, and thus that the arrest and initial detention were unlawful, and hence the interference with the Art 10 rights could not have been 'prescribed by law'.[134]

While the primary challenges in *Steel* were to the issue of whether breach of the peace was sufficiently certain to comply with Strasbourg requirements, the proportionality of the interference with the right to freedom of expression was also in issue. The court was clearly influenced by recent decisions that suggested that the common law had developed so that breach of the peace required an element of prospective violence. While Public Order Act provisions have the advantage of being in statutory form, and hence have a greater clarity of content than breach of the peace, defence advocates will want to ensure that the provisions are not being used to criminalise conduct which is more appropriately treated as being the lawful exercise of an Art 10 right.

Thus, in *Redmond-Bate v Director of Public Prosecutions*,[135] where three women preaching on the steps of Wakefield Cathedral were arrested for breach of the peace on the basis that their conduct had caused a crowd to gather, some of whom were hostile to the speakers, Sedley LJ, allowing the appeal of Redmond-Bate against conviction for obstructing a police officer, stated:

> [The prosecution] was prepared to accept that blame could not attach for a breach of the peace to a speaker so long as what she said was inoffensive. This will not do. Free speech includes not only the inoffensive but also the irritating, the contentious, the eccentric, the heretical, the unwelcome and the provocative provided it does not tend to provoke violence. Freedom only to speak inoffensively is not worth having.

It is a principle that may need to be raised by defence advocates faced with courts whose instinct can be appear to be to penalise those who disrupt the status quo.

Note that where a challenge is to be mounted to a criminal offence on the basis that the Convention provides a defence, or that the proceedings themselves thereby involve an interference with the defendant's Convention

---

134 'One may venture the comment that the proportionality decision was no more than another way of saying that in the absence of any ground to anticipate violent or provocative behaviour from the three applicants, there was nothing by which the appropriateness of intervention in the interests of public order could be gauged.' *Per* Sedley LJ in *Redmond-Bate*; see below.

135 [2000] HRLR 249.

right, the *Kebilene* decision makes clear that the challenge should normally be mounted by way of an abuse of process argument at the start of the trial, or in a pre-trial hearing, rather than by way of collateral litigation.

8.3 TRIAL PROCESS

Many of the issues implicit in the trial process – such as access to a lawyer, disclosure of material, burden of proof – have been considered in the previous chapter, or earlier in this chapter. This section considers some of the remaining issues which relate specifically to the conduct of the trial – such as the independence and impartiality of the court, the right to a reasoned judgment, the potentially problematic status of Clerks to the Justices, the right of the defendant to be present at trial, and issues of arising from delay.

8.3.1 The independence and impartiality of the court

Article 6(1) provides that:

> In the determination of his civil rights and obligations or of any criminal charge against him everyone is entitled to a fair and public hearing within a reasonable time by an independent and impartial tribunal established by law.

It is clear that the rights to an independent and to an impartial tribunal are separate but related. In relation to independence, the Strasbourg Court has held:

> In determining whether a body can be considered to be 'independent' – notably of the executive and of the parties to the case … the Court has had regard to the manner of appointment of its members and the duration of their term of office … the existence of guarantees against outside pressures … and the question whether the body presents an appearance of independence …[136]

Impartiality similarly depends to some extent on the appearance of the body:

> The personal impartiality of members of a body covered by Article 6 is to be presumed until there is proof to the contrary … In the present case, the applicant has adduced no evidence to give the Court any cause for doubt on this score.

> However, it is not possible to confine oneself to a purely subjective test: in this area, appearances may be of a certain importance and account must be taken of questions of internal organisation …[137]

In *Campbell and Fell* the Court was considering the status of the Board of Visitors in a prison disciplinary context, but an early Human Rights Act

---

136 *Campbell and Fell v United Kingdom* (1984) 7 EHRR 165, at para 78.
137 *Ibid*, paras 84 and 85.

challenge in Scotland indicated that challenges to the more traditional criminal courts were likely.

8.3.1.1 Lack of independence: the part-time judiciary

In the Scottish case of *Starrs v Ruxton*[138] the High Court of Justiciary considered whether temporary sheriffs in Scotland were independent and impartial as required by Art 6. The court unanimously found that they were not. The decision led to the suspension of all 129 temporary sheriffs in Scotland and has ultimately led to the reform of the Scottish judicial appointments system in the Bail, Judicial Appointments Etc (Scotland) Act 2000.

This case was a challenge to the lawfulness of a prosecution in front of a temporary sheriff. Temporary sheriffs were appointed by the Scottish Executive on the recommendation of the Lord Advocate. The Lord Advocate was a member of the Executive and was also nominally responsible for all criminal prosecutions in Scotland. Temporary sheriffs were appointed on a one-yearly renewable basis. At any time during the year they could be recalled without reason or at the end of the period their appointment might not be renewed, again no reason being required. There were no statutory provisions regulating the criteria for appointment, removal or non-renewal. For many temporary sheriffs, the office was a stepping-stone to a post as a permanent sheriff. The office was a paid judicial office, the equivalent of an assistant recorder in England.

The court had regard in particular to the reasoning of the Strasbourg Court in *Campbell and Fell* and concluded that while the initial appointment by the executive was not inherently improper, problems arose from the temporary nature of the position and the lack of clarity about the grounds on which it might be terminated:

> A short term of office is not, in my opinion, necessarily objectionable ... Temporary appointments are however, apt to create particular problems from the point of view of independence, particularly where the duration of the appointment is not fixed so as to expire upon the completion of a particular task or upon the cessation of a particular state of affairs (such as some emergency or exigency).[139]

In this context the problem was the fact that the temporary sheriffs might well be candidates for a permanent appointment:

> Given that temporary sheriffs are very often persons who are hoping for graduation to a permanent appointment, and at the least for the renewal of their temporary appointment, the system of short renewable appointments creates a situation in which the temporary sheriff is liable to have hopes and

138 2000 SLT 42.
139 *Ibid*, para 22.

fears in respect of his treatment by the executive when his appointment comes up for renewal: in short a relationship of dependency. This is in my opinion a factor pointing strongly away from 'independence' within the meaning of Article 6.[140]

Because of this hope of preferment, and the possibility of a purely informal 'sidelining' of the temporary sheriff were he to fall foul of the executive, there was a lack of independence. Or as Lord Reid put it:

> Judicial independence can be threatened not only by interference by the Executive, but also be a judge's being influenced, consciously or unconsciously, by his hopes and fears as to his possible treatment by the Executive. It is for that reason that a judge must not be dependent on the Executive, however well the Executive may behave: 'independence' connotes the absence of dependence.[141]

In consequence of the *Starrs* decision, the government acted so as to provide security of tenure for all assistant recorders in the English jurisdiction.[141a]

8.3.1.2 Arguments about the independence of the lay magistracy

Lay justices are appointed by the Lord Chancellor and may be removed by him, by virtue of s 5 of the Justices of the Peace Act 1997. While the statute appears to give the Lord Chancellor an unfettered discretion, in fact people are nominated by local Advisory Committees. In addition to the statutory geographical residence requirement,[142] the Lord Chancellor applies various extra-statutory criteria, which are set out on in unpublished guidelines[143] – these include health, age and local knowledge criteria. The guidelines also provide detailed information as to the circumstances, which may lead to a magistrate being removed from office.

Can it then be argued that the lay magistracy lacks the independence required by Art 6? Here the key provision again seems to arise from the *Campbell and Fell* case, where the European Court of Human Rights stated:

> Members of Boards hold office for a term of three years or such less period as the Home Secretary may appoint ... The term of office is admittedly relatively short but the Court notes that there is a very understandable reason: the members are unpaid ... and it might well prove difficult to find individuals willing and suitable to undertake the onerous and important tasks involved if the period were longer. The Court notes that the Rules contain neither any regulation governing the removal of members of a Board nor any guarantee for their irremovability. Although it appears that the Home Secretary could require the resignation of a member, this would be done only in the most

---

140 *Ibid*, para 23.

141 *Ibid*, para 39.

141a See too *Husain v Asylum Support Adjudicator*, Lawtel 12/10/2001, where the security of tenure was sufficient to ensure independence.

142 Section 6 of the Justices of the Peace Act 1997.

143 *Guidelines for Advisory Committees*; to be found at www.lcd.gov.uk.

exceptional circumstances and the existence of this possibility cannot be regarded as threatening in any respect the independence of the members of a Board in the performance of their judicial function. It is true that the irremovability of judges by the executive during their term of office must in general be considered as a corollary of their independence and thus included in the guarantees of Article 6 para 1 ... However, the absence of a formal recognition of this irremovability in the law does not in itself imply lack of independence provided that it is recognised in fact and that the other necessary guarantees are present ...[144]

Moreover, applying the reasoning from *Starrs* that the crux of the lack of independence of deputy sheriffs is the hope of future paid permanent appointment, the lay nature of the magistracy, which gives rise to no possibility of future paid appointment, suggests that there is not the 'dependence' on the state which precludes 'independence' for the purposes of Art 6.

8.3.1.3 Courts and impartiality

The Strasbourg test for assessing the impartiality of the court is based upon an objective assessment:

Under the objective test, it must be determined whether, quite apart from the judge's personal conduct, there are ascertainable facts which may raise doubts as to his impartiality. In this respect even appearances may be of a certain importance. What is at stake is the confidence which the courts in a democratic society must inspire in the public and above all, as far as criminal proceedings are concerned, in the accused. Accordingly, any judge in respect of whom there is a legitimate reason to fear a lack of impartiality must withdraw ...

This implies that in deciding whether in a given case there is a legitimate fear that a particular judge lacks impartiality, the standpoint of the accused is important but not decisive. What is decisive is whether this fear can be held objectively justified.[145]

The principle was applied in *Hoekstra and Others v Her Majesty's Advocate*[146] where the court concluded that a newspaper article by Lord McCluskey, who had been hearing the appeal of the defendants, which referred to the incorporation of the European Convention as 'devastating' and as 'a field day for crackpots', meant that he could not be regarded as objectively impartial.[147]

---

144 *Campbell and Fell v United Kingdom* (1984) 7 EHRR 165, para 80.

145 *Hauschildt v Denmark*, Series A No 154 (1990) 12 EHRR 266, para 48.

146 *Hoekstra v HM Advocate (No 3)* [2000] HRLR 410.

147 The court made clear that it was the way that the judge set out to make clear in the popular press that his hostility to the Convention was 'long-standing and deep-seated' which gave rise to the perception. It would be otherwise in relation to articles in moderate language in legal journals.

There had been criticisms of the English test for bias, as set out in *R v Gough*,[148] on the basis that it did not properly take account of the objective test of bias. This was considered in the case of *Re Medicaments and Related Classes of Goods (No 2)*[149] where the *Gough* test was subjected to a 'modest adjustment' intended to bring it into line with the Strasbourg test:

> 84 ... The difference is that, when the Strasbourg Court considers whether the material circumstances give rise to a reasonable apprehension of bias, it makes it plain that it is applying an objective test to the circumstances, not passing judgment on the likelihood that the particular tribunal under review was in fact biased.

> 85 When the Strasbourg jurisprudence is taken into account, we believe that a modest adjustment of the test in *R v Gough* is called for, which makes it plain that it is, in effect, no different from the test applied in most of the Commonwealth and in Scotland. The court must first ascertain all the circumstances, which have a bearing on the suggestion that the judge was biased. It must then ask whether those circumstances would lead a fair-minded and informed observer to conclude that there was a real possibility, or a real danger, the two being the same, that the tribunal was biased.

> 86 The material circumstances will include any explanation given by the judge under review as to his knowledge or appreciation of those circumstances. Where that explanation is accepted by the applicant for review it can be treated as accurate. Where it is not accepted, it becomes one further matter to be considered from the viewpoint of the fair-minded observer. The court does not have to rule whether the explanation should be accepted or rejected. Rather it has to decide whether or not the fair-minded observer would consider that there was a real danger of bias notwithstanding the explanation advanced.[150]

The decision appears to bring domestic law into line with Convention case law.

Interference with the defence case by the judge

At time of writing the case of *CG v United Kingdom*[151] is awaiting judgment before the Strasbourg Court. The applicant alleges breaches of Art 6 based on the behaviour of the trial judge, and in particular his frequent interruptions when her advocate was conducting the cross-examination of prosecution witnesses and his examination of the applicant. According to the Strasbourg record:

> In particular, it was submitted that during the defence counsel's cross-examination of the main prosecution witness, S, the judge intervened so

---

148 [1993] AC 646.
149 [2001] 1 WLR 700. Also reported as *Director General of Fair Trading v Proprietary Association of Great Britain and Another*.
150 *Ibid*, para 84–86.
151 Application No 43373/98. Heard on 26 June 2001.

frequently that the defence counsel was prevented from testing the accuracy of a schedule of banking payments prepared by S which was the basis of the prosecution case, or from developing possible lines of defence, such as that the loss had occurred prior to the commencement of the schedule. In addition, the applicant complained that the judge had constantly interrupted her examination-in-chief, making it impossible for her to give her evidence in a coherent manner, and had hectored her counsel to such an extent that he had felt unable to continue and had curtailed the examination. The grounds of appeal referred to the transcript of the trial which showed interventions by the judge on almost every page of S's cross-examination on twenty-two of the thirty-one pages dealing with the applicant's examination-in-chief.[152]

The Court of Appeal had dismissed the appeal against conviction on the basis that the conviction was safe, albeit that it recognised some force in the defendant's contentions, stating:

> It does seem to us that on occasions this very experienced and highly regarded circuit judge (now retired) did enter the arena, sometimes for legitimate reasons and at other times perhaps without justification. It does seem to us also that counsel found himself incommoded and disconcerted by those interventions and interruptions. Counsels have to possess (and if they do not have them they have to grow) rather thick skins. There was never an occasion where the learned judge in the course of trial, so it appears to us, made a ruling to the effect that Mr Engel [the defence barrister] should not continue with the line of defence that he was attempting to develop either in cross-examination or through his own witness. It appears to us that perhaps Mr Engel was on this occasion a trifle oversensitive. That does not, of course, detract from the validity of the criticisms – some well founded, some not – in the round.

The issues before the court concern the interference with the Art 6(3)(d) right to examine witnesses, but more generally the right to a fair trial. The underlying issue, however, must also be a lack of impartiality, an appearance on the part of the judge to side with the prosecution. Regardless of the outcome, the case is a useful reminder for advocates that issues of bias are likely to continue to arise.

8.3.2 Reasons

8.3.2.1 Is there a duty to give reasons?

The European Court of Human Rights has made clear that Art 6 will generally require that reasons are given for judicial decisions as an integral element of the right to a fair trial. In part the duty to give reason arises under the general terms of Art 6(1), so that it is possible for the parties and the public to know on what basis a decision has been arrived at:

---

152 *Ibid.*

> The Court notes in this context that while Article 6 para 1 obliges the courts to give reasons for their judgments, it cannot be understood as requiring a detailed answer to every argument adduced by a litigant. The extent to which the duty to give reasons applies may vary according to the nature of the decision at issue.

> ... the Court would emphasise that the notion of a fair procedure requires that a national court which has given sparse reasons for its decisions, whether by incorporating the reasons of a lower court or otherwise, did in fact address the essential issues which were submitted to its jurisdiction and did not merely endorse without further ado the findings reached by a lower court.[153]

The duty to give reasons also arises from the Art 6(3)(b) right, in that it enables the defendant to decide whether to appeal against a decision:

> The Contracting States enjoy considerable freedom in the choice of the appropriate means to ensure that their judicial systems comply with the requirements of Article 6 ... The national courts must, however, indicate with sufficient clarity the grounds on which they based their decision. It is this, *inter alia*, which makes it possible for the accused to exercise usefully the rights of appeal available to him. The Court's task is to consider whether the method adopted in this respect has led in a given case to results, which are compatible with the Convention.[154]

8.3.2.2 *What level of reasoning is required?*

It is clear that the level of reasoning required will vary from case to case. In *Zoon v Netherlands*[155] the Commission found that the first instance court had failed to make available the full reasons for its decision until after the deadline for appeals. The European Court of Human Rights, however, held that the decision had been available on written application, and that the fact that it was an abridged decision did not, on the facts, substantially affect the applicant's ability to appeal:

> 46 The applicant's defences concerned the validity of the summons, the admissibility of the prosecution case, the lawfulness of the way in which evidence had been obtained, the qualification in law of the acts charged and mitigating circumstances ... These issues were addressed in the judgment in its abridged form ... The applicant does not deny this.

> 47 It is true that the items of evidence on which the actual conviction was based are not enumerated in the judgment. However, the applicant never denied having committed the acts charged and never challenged the evidence against him as such. Moreover, the applicant has not claimed, nor does it appear, that his conviction was based on evidence that was neither contained in the case-file nor presented at the hearing of the Regional Court.

---

153 *Helle v Finland* (1997) 26 EHRR 159, paras 55 and 60.
154 *Hadjianastassiou v Greece* (1993) 16 EHRR 219, para 33.
155 Judgment of 7 December 2000.

48 It is further noted that in Dutch criminal procedure an appeal is not directed against the judgment of the first-instance court but against the charge brought against the accused. An appeal procedure thus involves a completely new establishment of the facts and a reassessment of the applicable law. It follows, in the Court's opinion, that the applicant and his counsel would have been able to make an informed assessment of the possible outcome of any appeal in light of the judgment in abridged form and of the evidence contained in the case-file.[156]

What the case makes clear is that advocates will need to be ready to show with some degree of precision exactly how the failure to provide reasons has prejudiced the defendant's ability to conduct his case.

8.3.2.3   How does the duty to give reasons impact upon domestic criminal procedures?

It has been accepted that it is in the nature of the jury system that juries cannot be required to give reasons:

The absence of reasons in the High Court's judgment was due to the fact that the applicant's guilt was determined by a jury, something which that cannot in itself be considered contrary to the Convention ... Thus, the Court considers that nothing in the case suggests that the conviction of the applicant was arbitrary.[157]

However, the lack of reasons can then place restrictions on the ability of appellate courts to correct misdirections to the jury:

It cannot be excluded that the jury accepted Mr Curtis' explanation for his silence and did not therefore draw an adverse inference against him; it cannot be excluded either that the jury may have accepted the applicants' defence to the charges, for example their claim that the police had planted incriminating evidence in their flat ... and that the evidence against them was not as overwhelming as the Court of Appeal considered. In any event, it is a speculative exercise, which only reinforces the crucial nature of the defect in the trial judge's direction and its implications for review of the case on appeal.[158]

---

156 *Ibid.*

157 *Saric v Denmark*, European Court of Human Rights, App No 31913/96, admissibility decision of 2 February 1999.

158 *Condron v United Kingdom* (2001) 31 EHRR 1, para 64. However, see also *R v Denton* [2001] 1 Cr App R 16, where the Court of Appeal felt able to make good the failure of the trial judge to give adequate reasons for exercising his discretion under s 26 of the Criminal Justice Act 1988 in admitting evidence from a witness who was in fear. However, the court did stress the importance of providing such reasons: 'In our judgment, on this aspect of the matter, the judge plainly did not give reasons for admitting the statements. It is clear that he should have done so. It is clear that the reasons for exercising the discretion under s 26, like ... the reasons for exercising any other discretion, ought to be given by the trial judge, however briefly. That has been the position in English law for many years and it is a matter to which Art 6 of the European Convention gives added emphasis.' (Paragraph 35.)

In domestic law the traditional stance that magistrates are not required to give reasons has been subject to considerable erosion.[159] Some attempt has been made to argue by analogy with cases on Art 5, that there is now a duty on magistrates to give reasons, but the analogy is not wholly satisfactory, since the issues in relation to Arts 5 and 6 are clearly different. In *Pullum v Crown Prosecution Service*[160] the matter was a straightforward dispute between the defendant and the alleged victim as to who had been the aggressor in a minor assault that had followed a road traffic accident. The Divisional Court was asked to consider the reasons given by the Crown Court for rejecting the defendant's appeal against conviction Lord Bingham stated:

> Nonetheless, by saying that the appeal was dismissed, as was said in the present case, it seems plain that the Recorder was announcing the result and not giving a reason for its decision. In saying 'We find there was an assault' the Recorder was again saying no more than that the case was found to be proved. That would of course follow from the dismissal of the appeal. There was, as I conclude, in those two sentences no reasoning at all. It is true that the case was a simple one. The court was entitled to decide it in favour of the prosecution and against the appellant if it was satisfied that Mr Doherty [the alleged victim]'s evidence was essentially correct. In deciding whether there had or had not been an assault it was entitled to discount the evidence about how the incident originated or in any event it was entitled to make no finding on those points. Nor was it essential to reach a concluded view as to what had happened afterwards. It would, however, seem to me that the minimum which the appellant was entitled to expect was a clear statement as to what evidence the court had accepted; a clear statement that it did, as was stated in the case stated, base itself specifically on Mr Doherty's evidence of what had occurred at the assault stage; a clear statement that no question of self-defence or accident arose; and that any evidence of provocation was immaterial. Had the court announced its decision in approximately the terms of the case stated the appellant would in my view have had no possible grounds for complaint.[161]

This decision was in relation to the Crown Court in its appellate capacity. It can however be argued that similar principles should apply to the magistrates' court, and indeed the *Practice Note* provides that:

> In addition to advising the justices it shall be the legal adviser's responsibility to assist the court, where appropriate, as to the formulation of reasons and the recording of those reasons.[162]

---

159 Among the many areas where there is pre-existing duty to give reasons in domestic law are in relation to the refusal of bail (and in some circumstances the granting of it), when imposing a custodial sentence or suspending such a sentence, when granting or refusing legal aid, and when making a finding of 'special reasons' or 'exceptional hardship' in Road Traffic Act cases.

160 [2000] COD 206

161 *Ibid*, at para 20.

162 *Practice Note 2 October 2000 (Justices: Clerk to the Court)* [2000] 1 WLR 1886, para 3.

8.3.3 Clerks to the justices

8.3.3.1 Arguments as to the status of the justices' clerk

A number of issues underpin the concerns that the role of the justices' clerk may offend against Art 6, particularly where it has been the practice of the clerk to retire to give advice to lay justices. It may be argued that the provision offends against the right to a public hearing, that the retirement of the clerk gives rise to a loss of equality of arms (since the clerk is an employee of the state, which will generally be the prosecutor), and indeed that the practice means that the court lacks independence since the clerk lacks security of tenure.

In relation to the argument that the clerk lacks independence – as *per Starrs* (for which see above) – the conclusion of the High Court of Justiciary in *Procurator Fiscal, Kirkcaldy v Kelly*,[163] where the issue was the status of a clerk in the district court, was that the clerk was not a member of the court. No breach of Art 6 therefore arose from the retirement of the clerk to give advice to the justices:

> In our opinion, the clerk's role as legal adviser is clearly confined to that of adviser on the law. It is to provide the justice or justices with such information as to the law as is necessary to equip them to fulfil the role of decision-maker or decision-makers, which is exclusively their role.

8.3.3.2 The right to a public hearing

However, even if the clerk is not a member of the court, can it be argued that the retirement of the clerk with the justices offends against the Art 6(1) right to a public hearing?

In practice the issue is now addressed by the *Practice Note (Justices: Clerks to the Court)*,[164] which makes clear the importance of ensuring that justice is seen to be done. Thus where the clerk is to give advice as to evidence, the *Practice Note* provides:

> At any time, justices are entitled to receive advice to assist them in discharging their responsibilities. If they are in any doubt as to the evidence that has been given, they should seek the aid of their legal adviser, referring to his/her notes as appropriate. This should ordinarily be done in open court.[165]

Similarly where the issue is one of law, the *Practice Note*, emphasising the principle of open justice, continues:

> Where the justices request their adviser to join them in the retiring room, this request should be made in the presence of the parties in court. Any legal

---

163 *Sub nom Clark v Kelly* 2000 SLT 1038.
164 [2000] 1 WLR 1886.
165 *Ibid*, para 8.

advice given to the justices other than in open court should be clearly stated to be provisional and the adviser should subsequently repeat the substance of the advice in open court and give the parties an opportunity to make any representations they wish on that provisional advice. The legal adviser should then state in open court whether the provisional advice is confirmed or if it is varied the nature of the variation.[166]

Interestingly, in the *Kelly* case, the Scottish court considered Strasbourg jurisprudence and found that one case at least suggested that retirement of the clerk was unlikely to offend against Art 6. The court noted that in the case of *Delcourt v Belgium*, where there had been (at the very least) a connection between the adviser who had withdrawn with the judges and the prosecuting agency (same department, different sections), so that there was an argument that the prosecution had had the opportunity to advance its case in private, the Strasbourg Court had nevertheless found no breach of Art 6.[167]

In the light of the *Practice Note*, however, advocates will clearly be able to rely upon domestic law, rather than needing to resort to the Convention, where any argument arises over the continuing giving of advice in private.

8.3.4 The role of the clerk at a means enquiry

There are clear difficulties of perception that arise from the interrogatory role of the clerk at means enquiries. In *R v Corby Justices ex p Mort*[168] the Divisional Court rejected arguments that this gave rise to a breach of Art 6, stating:

It would undoubtedly be contrary to ordinary standards of fairness, and also to established practice, if the clerk were to assume an adversarial or partisan role in the conduct of any proceedings, including a means inquiry. There should be no question of his setting out to establish wilful refusal or culpable neglect, and there should be no question of his advising the justices on the facts or communicating his personal opinion of the facts to them. So much is clear beyond argument. But there is in our opinion no objection to a clerk, at the express or implied request of the justices, asking questions of a debtor relevant to his or her means for purposes of a means inquiry.

The *Practice Note* echoes this and now provides:

The role of legal advisers in fine default proceedings or any other proceedings for the enforcement of financial orders, obligations or penalties is to assist the

---

166 *Ibid.*

167 *Delcourt v Belgium* (1979) 1 EHRR 355. The authors of *Criminal Justice, Police Powers and Human Rights*, Starmer *et al*, 2001, Blackstone, cite in particular the decision of the Strasbourg Court in *Krcmar v Czech Republic*, judgment of 3 March 2000, where the court held that the concept of a fair hearing also required that parties have the opportunity to 'have knowledge of and comment on, all evidence adduced or observations filed, with a view to influencing the courts' decision'. Arguably the requirement in the *Practice Note* that any advice given in private be provisional should ensure that all parties have access to those observations.

168 (1998) 162 JPN 321.

court. They must not act in an adversarial or partisan manner. With the agreement of the justices a legal adviser may ask questions of the defaulter to elicit information which the justices will require to make an adjudication, for example to facilitate his or her explanation for the default. A legal adviser may also advise the justices in the normal way as to the options open to them in dealing with the case. It would be inappropriate for the legal adviser to set out to establish wilful refusal or neglect or any other type of culpable behaviour, to offer an opinion on the facts, or to urge a particular course of action upon the justices. The duty of impartiality is the paramount consideration for the legal adviser at all times, and this takes precedence over any role he or she may have as a collecting officer.[169]

Whether this is adequate, especially in the light of the acknowledgement that the test for bias is now an objective one[170] is open to question. *Mort* is currently awaiting hearing at Strasbourg and further developments in this area seem likely.

8.3.5 The right to be present at trial

Although this is not expressly mentioned in paragraph 1 of Article 6, the object and purpose of the article taken as a whole show that a person 'charged with a criminal offence' is entitled to take part in the hearing. Moreover, sub-paragraphs (c), (d) and (e) of paragraph 3 guarantee to 'everyone charged with a criminal offence' the right 'to defend himself in person', 'to examine or have examined witnesses' and 'to have the free assistance of an interpreter if he cannot understand or speak the language used in court', and it is difficult to see how he could exercise these rights without being present.[171]

It is clear that the reverse of the proposition does not apply: the state cannot refuse to hear the defence of an accused person who is absent from a hearing where he is represented by a lawyer.[172]

It is also clear under domestic law that the defendant will normally have a right to be present at his trial. The removal of an unruly defendant is a comparatively rare step and will not offend against Art 6 where it can be shown that the interests of justice require such a step. In *Colozza*, the European Court made clear that trial *in absentia* would not necessarily offend against Art 6 provided the defendant had been given clear notification of the hearing. In that case, however, the court was not satisfied that there was any satisfactory basis for the presumption of notification:

---

169 [2000] 1 WLR 1886, para 11.

170 See the discussion of *Re Medicaments* at 8.3.1.3 above.

171 *Colozza v Italy* (1985) 7 EHRR 516, at para 27.

172 *Krombach v Bamberski*, European Court of Justice (2000) *The Times*, 30 March: 'the refusal to hear the defence of an accused person who is not present at the hearing constitutes a manifest breach of a fundamental right' (para 40). Note that this is a case of the ECJ interpreting the Convention, rather than a decision of the Strasbourg Court.

> In the instant case, the Court does not have to determine whether and under what conditions an accused can waive exercise of his right to appear at the hearing since in any event, according to the Court's established case law, waiver of the exercise of a right guaranteed by the Convention must be established in an unequivocal manner ....
>
> In fact, the Court is not here concerned with an accused who had been notified in person and who, having thus been made aware of the reasons for the charge, had expressly waived exercise of his right to appear and to defend himself. The Italian authorities, relying on no more than a presumption ... inferred from the status of *'latitante'* which they attributed to Mr Colozza that there had been such a waiver.[173]

In domestic law there is provision for the re-hearing of a matter heard *in absentia* in the magistrates' court where the defendant makes a statutory declaration that he did not know of the summons or of the proceedings,[174] and it seems likely that this will be sufficient to comply with Art 6.

In *R v Haywood; R v Jones; R v Purvis*[175] the Court of Appeal confirmed that there is a presumption against a trial taking place *in absentia*:

> The trial judge has a discretion as to whether a trial should take place or continue in the absence of a defendant and/or his legal representatives.
>
> That discretion must be exercised with great care and it is only in rare and exceptional circumstances that it should be exercised in favour of a trial taking place or continuing, particularly if the defendant is unrepresented.[176]

The court set out a lengthy list of factors to be taken into account – including the circumstances that have led to the defendant's absence, the nature and effect of any adjournment, the effect on the ability of the defendant's representatives to conduct his case, and the general public interest in a timely trial, including the interests of victims and witnesses. The judgment includes a detailed consideration of the relevant Strasbourg case law, and will now constitute the leading authority on trial *in absentia*. While the decision is specifically in respect of trials on indictment, the underlying principles seem equally applicable to the magistrates' court.[177]

---

173 (1985) 7 EHRR 516, para 28.
174 Section 14 of the Magistrates' Courts Act 1980.
175 [2001] 3 WLR 125.
176 *Ibid*, para 18 at points 3 and 4.
177 Note that the petition of Jones to appeal has been allowed: 27 June 2001.

8.3.5.1 A right to effective participation

The defendant also has a right to participate effectively in the trial process.[178] In *Stanford v United Kingdom*[179] the defendant was in a glass-fronted dock and complained that he could not hear the evidence of some of the witnesses because of poor acoustics. His barrister and solicitor knew of his concerns but took the view that were he to be moved closer to the child victim this could be seen as an attempt to intimidate her, and that they could adequately take his instructions. The Strasbourg Court took the view that this was a matter where the state could not be liable for the decisions of the defendant's lawyers but added that poor acoustics could potentially engage Art 6:

> The applicant further maintained that the Government bore responsibility for the poor acoustics of the courtroom. While this is undoubtedly a matter which could give rise to an issue under Article 6 of the Convention, the expert reports which were carried out both before and after the applicant's complaint indicated that, apart from a minimal loss of sound due to the glass screen, the acoustic levels in the courtroom were satisfactory ...[180]

The principle of effective participation remains an important one, however, and may continue to arise in circumstances where court layout, overcrowding or other factors substantially affect the defendant's ability to participate in the trial process.[181] In this respect the handcuffing of prisoners may impact upon their ability to participate effectively, whether because of discomfort, the ability to write or handle papers properly or the distraction arising from being handcuffed, and defence advocates should be prepared to raise any concerns that are mentioned by their clients arising from this.[182]

8.3.6 The right to a hearing within a reasonable time

There are a number of key issues when considering a potential breach of the provision that a hearing must take place within a reasonable time. In criminal matters it is necessary to decide at what point the defendant should be treated as subject to a 'charge' – and the implications of the autonomous meaning of

---

178 See most notably the decision in *T v United Kingdom* (1999) 30 EHRR 121 concerning the inability of the juvenile defendants to participate effectively in the Crown Court proceedings. See *R v Brown and Others* [2001] All ER(D) 392 (Jul), CA, where psychiatric evidence that the defendant was not fit to represent himself was adduced. However, evidence also made clear that the defendant was well enough to instruct a lawyer. Since it had been his choice not use a lawyer to conduct his case, there was no breach of Art 6.

179 (1994) *The Times*, 8 March. See also *Prinz v Austria* (2001) 31 EHRR 12.

180 *Ibid*, para 29.

181 See also *R (on the Application of King) v Isleworth Crown Court* [2001] EHLR 14 where the Administrative Court held that the Crown Court, hearing an appeal against conviction from an appellant in person who had impaired health arising from previous strokes, had failed to take adequate account of the appellant's condition and should have permitted an adjournment, having particular regard to Art 6.

182 For the argument that handcuffs may amount to a breach of Art 3, see *Raninen v Finland* (1997) 26 EHRR 563.

this term have been discussed in Chapter 7. There is also an issue as to whether it is necessary to show prejudice in order to establish a breach of the provision, and whether the breach of the provision itself will mean that there has not been a fair trial. In domestic law it is then necessary to go further and to consider what the implications are of a finding that there has not been a fair trial.

A number of factors will be taken into account in determining whether there has been a delay. The approach of the Strasbourg Court has been to look both at the overall period taken but also to break down the period into its constituent elements, and to look for justification for each element of the time taken to progress a case.[183] The complexity of the matter, the conduct of the parties, and the interdependence with other matters are all relevant considerations. The importance of what is at stake for the defendant is a relevant consideration,[184] although doubt was expressed in *Her Majesty's Advocate v McGlinchey*[185] at the proposition that the more serious the charge, the more important it was that the prosecution 'get it right' and hence the longer the period allowed.

8.3.6.1 Is it necessary to show prejudice to the defence?

It is clearly established in domestic law, prior to the commencement of the Human Rights Act, that delay was relevant to an application for a stay of proceedings only where the defendant was able to show that he would suffer 'serious prejudice to the extent that no fair trial can be held ...'[186]

Is the position the same under Art 6? The answer depends on whether the Art 6(1) provisions, which entitle a defendant to a fair trial by an impartial and independent tribunal within a reasonable time, are treated as three separate guarantees or a single overarching guarantee of a fair trial, of which the three elements are components. Because Strasbourg case law treats each case on delay on its own particular facts, there is no specific statement that it is necessary to show prejudice. Indeed, in many cases the Strasbourg Court has been prepared to find that periods of delay have been in breach of Art 6

---

183 Recent rulings on delay involving the United Kingdom include *IJL and Others v UK* (2000) 9 BHRC 222, where the court found no breach of Art 6 where there had been a four year period from the commencement of the prosecution until end of appeal as it was a complex fraud case. In *Howarth v United Kingdom* (2000) 9 BHRC 253, where there was a delay of two years between sentence and the hearing of the appeal against conviction (along with a simultaneous *Attorney General's Reference* on sentence) the court found a breach of Art 6 as no adequate reason for delay had been provided.

184 See *FE v France* (1998) 27 EHRR 667, para 53: 'The Court reiterates that the reasonableness of the length of proceedings is to be assessed in the light of the circumstances of the case and having regard to the criteria laid down in the Court's case law, in particular the complexity of the case and the conduct of the applicant and of the relevant authorities. On the latter point, what is at stake for the applicant in the proceedings has to be taken into account ...'

185 *HM Advocate v McGlinchey* 2000 SLT 995.

186 *Attorney General's Reference (No 1 of 1990)* [1992] QB 630, 644.

without specifically considering the prejudice to the defendant. Thus in *Majaric v Slovenia*,[187] where part of the state's answer to the allegations was the pressure on the national courts, the European Court of Human Rights stated:

> As to the reference by the government to the heavy workload of the domestic courts resulting from the economic and legislative reforms in Slovenia, it is recalled that Article 6 s 1 imposes on Contracting States the duty to organise their judicial system in such a way that their courts can meet each of its requirements ... The Court has before it no information, which would indicate that the difficulties encountered in Slovenia during the relevant period were such as to deprive the applicant of his entitlement to a judicial determination within 'a reasonable time'. Furthermore, the respondent State has not indicated any measures it has taken to reduce the workload of the courts ...
>
> There has accordingly been a breach of Article 6 s 1 of the Convention.[188]

The difficulty is that the idea of prejudice is, of course, implicit in the concept of an unreasonable delay. One of the factors that will show that the delay is unreasonable is the impact that it has had on the defendant. In *Stogmuller v Austria*[189] the European Court of Human Rights stated that:

> The [Article 6(1)] provision applies to all parties to court proceedings; in criminal matters, especially, it is designed to avoid that a person charged should remain too long in a state of uncertainty about his fate.[190]

The clear indication therefore is that the right to a prompt trial is a free standing right, and this is the approach that has been adopted by the Scottish courts.[191] In *Crummock*, the Appeal Court of the High Court of Justiciary stated:

> In order to justify a plea of delay under Article 6(1) it is not necessary for an accused to show that prejudice has been, or is likely be, caused as a result of the delay.[192]

Privy Council case law

The approach of the Privy Council is conflicting. In *Darmalingum v State*,[193] an appeal from the Supreme Court of Mauritius, the Privy Council was asked to consider a delay of eight years between arrest and conviction, and a further five years between conviction and the disposal of the appeal. The Mauritius Bill of Rights had a fair hearing provision (s 10) modelled closely upon Art 6 of the European Convention. Lord Steyn, giving the decision of the Privy Council, stated:

---

187 Judgment of 8 February 2000.
188 *Ibid*, paras 39–40.
189 (1969) 1 EHRR 155.
190 *Ibid*, para 5.
191 See, for example, *McGlinchey* 2000 SLT 995.
192 *Crummock (Scotland) Ltd v HM Advocate* 2000 SLT 677, para 6.
193 *Darmalingum v Mauritius* [2000] 2 Cr App R 445.

It will be observed that section 10(1) contains three separate guarantees, namely (1) a right to a fair hearing; (2) within a reasonable time; (3) by an independent and impartial court established by law. Hence, if a defendant is convicted after a fair hearing by a proper court, this is no answer to a complaint that there was a breach of the guarantee of a disposal within a reasonable time. And, even if his guilt is manifest, this factor cannot justify or excuse a breach of the guarantee of a disposal within a reasonable time. Moreover, the independence of the 'reasonable time' guarantee is relevant to its reach. It may, of course, be applicable where by reason of inordinate delay a defendant is prejudiced in the deployment of his defence. But its reach is wider. It may be applicable in any case where the delay has been inordinate and oppressive. Furthermore, the position must be distinguished from cases where there is no such constitutional guarantee but the question arises whether under the ordinary law a prosecution should be stayed on the grounds of inordinate delay. It is a matter of fundamental importance that the rights contained in section 10(1) were considered important enough by the people of Mauritius, through their representatives, to be enshrined in their constitution. The stamp of constitutionality is an indication of the higher normative force, which is attached to the relevant rights ...[194]

However, in *Flowers v The Queen*[195] a differently constituted Privy Council distinguished the *Darmalingum* decision:

The judgment of the Board does not refer to the passage in the judgment of the Board in *Bell v The Director of Public Prosecutions* which recognises that the right given by section 20 of the Constitution of Jamaica must be balanced against the public interest in the attainment of justice or to the passage which states that the right to a trail within a reasonable time is not a separate guarantee but, rather, that the three elements of section 20(1) form part of one embracing form of protection afforded to the individual.

Therefore in deciding whether the appellant's conviction should be quashed because of the lengthy period of delay their Lordships are of the opinion that they are entitled to take into account the considerations that he has been proved on strong evidence to be guilty of a murder in the course of an armed robbery, that this type of offence is very prevalent in Jamaica and that it poses a serious threat to the lives of innocent persons.[196]

The decision in *Flowers* has been the subject of considerable criticism,[197] but clearly has the potential to undermine the clear approach taken in the Scottish cases, as well as in *Darmalingum*.

---

194 [2000] 2 Cr App R 445, p 451.

195 [2000] 1 WLR 2396.

196 *Ibid*, pp 2414–15.

197 'The function of the judiciary should be to give effect to fundamental rights. A right which may be overridden in the public interest at the discretion of the judiciary becomes a right of little value. And far from the seriousness of the offence and clear evidence of guilt being matters to weigh against the defendant, they should be left out of account altogether. It is in the case of the most heinous crimes that there is the need for greatest vigilance.' James Richardson, 'Commentary on *Flowers*' in Criminal Law Week, CLW/00/42/02.

Delay and domestic law

The decision in *Attorney General's Reference (No 2 of 2001)*[198] on the issue of prejudice is hard to follow. The difficulty is that the Attorney General's first question conflates the issue of whether prejudice is necessary with the issue of the remedy for breach of the reasonable time provision:

> Whether criminal proceedings must be stayed on the ground that there has been a violation of the reasonable time requirement … In circumstances where the accused cannot demonstrate any prejudice arising from the delay.

On this point the court states:

> We consider that in normal circumstances a negative answer will be appropriate. But we are not prepared to say that there cannot be circumstances (which at the present time we are unable to identify) where, notwithstanding the absence of prejudice, it can be said that it would be appropriate for a trial to take place.[199]

The court seems to avoid the issue of prejudice, and indeed to side-step the issue of whether the right to a trial within a reasonable time is a free-standing right, by focusing instead on the remedies that should arise from an assumed breach of the right. Although the decisions in *Flowers* and *Darmalingum* are discussed, although there is no reference to the developing Scottish case law, they are considered in relation to the issue of remedy. The decision is therefore discussed in the following section.

8.3.6.2 *What is the effect of a breach of the provision?*

> [I]f there has been prejudice caused to a defendant, which interferes with his right to a fair trial in a way which cannot otherwise be remedied, and then of course a stay is the appropriate remedy. But in the absence of prejudice of that sort, there is normally no justification for granting a stay.[200]

In *Attorney General's Reference (No 2 of 2001)* the defendant's argument, as restated by the court, was that the breach of Art 6 arising from the delay meant that the court, as a public authority for the purposes of s 6 of the Human Rights Act, would be acting unlawfully if it were to permit the proceedings to continue. A stay is therefore the only appropriate remedy. The court dismisses this. In a civil case, the court states, if a complaint of breach of time must then lead to a stay, this could amount to unfairness to the other party and a breach of his or her right to a fair trial. In criminal proceedings, an automatic stay would infringe the rights of the victim and the public at large in the detection and punishment of crime.

These arguments, we respectfully suggest, are not convincing. The primary focus in a criminal matter must be on the rights of the defendant,

---

198 [2001] EWCA Crim 1568; (2001) *The Times*, 12 July, previously discussed in Chapter 7.
199 *Ibid*, para 24.
200 *Ibid*, para 23.

who is after all being prosecuted by the state and who is at risk of punishment by the State; the argument that the wider public interest can justify significant interference with Art 6 rights was rejected by the Strasbourg Court in cases such as *Saunders*.[201]

If, as the court suggests, a stay will not (or will not normally) be the appropriate remedy, absent prejudice, what then are the appropriate steps where a breach of the timely trial provisions is found, but which falls short of the degree of the prejudice which is required to be shown under the principles in *Attorney General's Reference (No 1 of 1990)*?:

> 20 It seems to us in general that the approach that previously existed as to the provision of the remedy of staying the proceedings should be confined, as it was prior to the Convention becoming part of our domestic law, to situations, which in general terms can be described as amounting to an abuse of the process of the courts. But there are many other actions, which the court can take which avoid the need for such action. In particular, if the court comes to the conclusion that this would provide the appropriate remedy, the court can mark the fact that the way the prosecution has been conducted does contravene the reasonable time requirement in Article 6(1) and acknowledge the rights of the defendant by so doing. In many cases the court will come to the conclusion that that is not a sufficient recognition of the defendant's rights. If that were so, then the court can take other action. It can, for example, take account of the failure to proceed with the case with due expedition in the sentence which the court imposes. It has always been the practice for the courts in this jurisdiction to take into account delays of the sort to which we have referred when sentencing a defendant. It does so, recognising that it is inevitably a disadvantage to a defendant to have a charge hanging over his or her head longer than is reasonably required. The criminal process inevitably subjects an individual to distress. Albeit that they are acquitted at the end of the process, they still have been subjected to unnecessary distress. The difference, which the Human Rights Act 1998 makes, is that the remedies available to a court can be greater than they were hitherto. In particular, it is now in appropriate circumstances open to the courts to make awards of compensation. This court accepts that where a person is acquitted at a subsequent trial, it could be appropriate for there to be compensation if there has been delay which contravenes the reasonable time requirement in Article 6(1) of the Convention. It depends on all the circumstances whether compensation is appropriate.[202]

---

201 Nor is the argument any more convincing in a civil matter. If the defendant successfully applies for a matter to be stayed on the basis that there has been a breach of his right to a timely trial, the claimant will have an action against the Lord Chancellor's Department, a public authority, for failing to make adequate provision so as to protect his Art 6 rights if the delay arises through the fault of the court service.

202 Note that the Crown Court has no power to award damages under the Human Rights Act. It is not therefore clear if the court is proposing that a separate civil action would be commenced in the civil courts for damages for breach of Art 6. As the Court of Appeal is a unitary court, it will have power to award damages, even in the Criminal Division, because of its power to award damages in civil proceedings.

21 There is a certain amount of authority on this subject. However, there is no authority which supports the conclusion that a stay is the appropriate remedy, except in limited circumstances where it is no longer possible for a defendant to have a fair trial, bearing in mind the ability of the court to exclude evidence or to take other action to achieve a fair trial. If a fair trial is not possible, then a stay would have to be imposed. Equally, it would be appropriate to stay proceedings if the situation is one where it could be said that to try the accused would in itself be unfair.

The Privy Council's decision in *Darmalingum* is noted and distinguished on the basis that:

> Although the opening words of Lord Steyn are of a general nature, they would not be applicable here because they are inconsistent with the jurisprudence of the Strasbourg Court, which recognises, for example, that a reduction of sentence is an appropriate remedy for a breach of Article 6(1).

Although no reference is given the basis for this proposition appears to the decision of the Strasbourg Court in *Eckle v Germany*,[202a] itself recently re-iterated in the decision of *Beck v Norway*,[202b] where the defendant in a complex fraudulent pyramid scheme was held to have faced a delay of two years from the issue of the indictment to the institution of proceedings. The state argued that any delay had been dealt with by a substantial reduction in sentence so that the applicant could not be treated as a victim for Strasbourg purposes. The European Court held that:

> the mitigation of a sentence on the ground of the excessive length of proceedings does not in principle deprive the individual concerned of his status as a victim within the meaning of Article 34 of the Convention. However, this general rule is subject to an exception when the national authorities have acknowledged in a sufficiently clear way the failure to observe the reasonable time requirement and have afforded redress by reducing the sentence in an express and measurable manner.[202c]

Here the Court was satisfied that the national courts had accepted that there had been a breach of Art 6(1) because of the delay and that there had been a specific and identifiable discount on sentence to take account of this.

There seems therefore to be a clear conflict between the approach of the Privy Council and the Strasbourg approach. There is, of course, nothing to prevent the domestic courts from adopting a higher standard of protection than that offered by the European Convention. It seems inevitable that prosecution advocates will rely upon the decision in the *Attorney General's Reference (No 2 of 2001)* and the decision in *Flowers* to resist applications for stays. It is clearly equally inevitable that defence advocates will continue to rely upon the decision in *Darmalingum*, and possibly more convincingly on the

---

202a (1982) 5 EHRR 1.
202b European Court of Human Rights, judgment of 26 June 2001, Application No 26390/95.
202c *Ibid*, para 27.

Scottish authorities which fully discuss the requirements of Art 6, in arguing that the right to a timely trial is a free-standing right, the remedy for which must be a stay. It is a matter which is clearly in urgent need of resolution by the House of Lords.

8.3.6.3 Delay in cases involving children

In cases which involve children as defendants, it is arguable that there is a clear line of authority which arises from the particularly vulnerable nature of child defendants, and which mean that a stay will be the appropriate remedy, notwithstanding the comments in *Attorney General's Reference (No 2 of 2001)*. The basis for this is Art 6, but viewed in conjunction with other international law documents, such as the Beijing Rules. In *HM Advocate v P*,[203] the arguments were put as follows:

> [11] So far as proceedings against children are concerned, it is recognised by Crown Office, as the Advocate Depute explained, that such proceedings call for particular expedition, whether the child is an accused or a complainer or, as in this case, both. That approach is in my opinion in accordance with the requirements imposed in this particular context by Article 6(1). Such an approach is also in accordance with the requirements of the UN Convention on the Rights of the Child and the Beijing Rules, each of which the European Court of Human Rights has used as a source of guidance as to the requirements imposed by the European Convention in relation to proceedings involving juvenile offenders: see in particular *V v The United Kingdom* ... Article 40(2)(b) of the UN Convention provides:
>
>> Every child alleged as or accused of having infringed the penal law has at least the following guarantees:
>>
>> ...
>>
>> (ii) to have the matter determined without delay ...
>
> Rule 20 of the Beijing Rules provides: 'Each case shall from the outset be handled expeditiously, without any unnecessary delay.'
>
> These requirements reflect the general approach adopted in the UN Convention and the Beijing Rules, that children accused of committing crimes should be treated in a manner which takes into account the child's age and the desirability of promoting the child's reintegration and the child's assuming a constructive role in society.

In *HM Advocate v P* the defendants were charged with rape. At the time of the alleged offence they were 13 and 14 years old respectively. The court considered the particular issues that arose in relation to delay when dealing with such defendants:

> [12] Where a child of 13 is accused of committing a serious offence, it is plainly desirable that the child should be brought to trial (if criminal proceedings are considered appropriate) as quickly as is consistent with the proper

---

203 2001 SLT 924.

preparation and consideration of the case. For a period of two years to elapse between the child's being charged with the offence and the child's being placed on trial has a number of undesirable consequences. Without attempting to list them exhaustively, the following may be mentioned. A child of 13 may be very different from the same child when he or she is 15 years old, both in terms of physical development and in terms of maturity and understanding. If the trial is to be held before a jury, as in the present case, the jury may have a very different impression if a 15 year old boy is in the dock, from the impression which they would have had if they had seen the same individual when he was 13. It may be much more difficult to assess the state of a child's understanding, when he was 13, of sexual matters and sexual relationships, if the child is not placed on trial, and is not able to give evidence, until he is two years older. For the child himself (or herself), a period of two years awaiting trial will form a significant part of childhood, and more particularly of the period of secondary schooling, which cannot be compared with the significance of a two year period to an adult. If the 13 year old child is in fact guilty of an offence, and requires the sort of reformative measures, which disposals in respect of child offenders are intended to include, then again it is undesirable that the initiation of such measures should be delayed by a period of years. Reverting to the aims of the 'reasonable time' requirement, for a period of two years to elapse before justice is rendered in a case involving a child of 13 is for these reasons liable to jeopardise its effectiveness and credibility; and for the child to remain for that period in a state of uncertainty about his fate may have especially harmful consequences. I have mentioned matters which relate to the child accused, because such matters are particularly relevant in the context of Article 6(1); it is scarcely necessary to add that prolonged delay in bringing a case to trial may also have seriously harmful effects upon a child complainer, especially (as in the present case) in a case of alleged rape.

The court considered that the period of two years between charge and trial was a breach of the reasonable time provision, and the indictment was dismissed.

A very similar approach was taken in *Kane v HM Advocate*,[204] where the defendant was charged when he was 13 with various sexual offences committed on younger children. The court therefore took into account both the defendant's particular needs, but also the needs of the child witnesses. The court was not satisfied that there had been due expedition at every stage of the proceedings, and concluded that the overall period of delay had been unreasonable. The remedy was for the dismissal of the indictment.

The new time limits in the Youth Courts are likely to mean that there will now be far fewer cases which proceed to trial where there has been significant delay since formal charge, but it will be recalled that since 'charge' has an

---

204 Appeal No 3296/01, Appeal Court, High Court of Justiciary, opinion of 4 May 2001.

autonomous meaning, there may be situations where it can be argued that the defendant has been subject to a 'charge' prior to the formal time limits commencing. In such cases the Scottish authorities are likely to be relevant. Prosecuting advocates will argue that these cases have effectively been supplanted by *Attorney General's Reference (No 2 of 2001)*. Defence advocates will in this context be able to point to the Beijing Rules and to argue that the *Attorney General's Reference* can properly be distinguished in that it does not consider the particular issues arising in relation to child defendants.

8.3.6.4 Systemic delay

It is sometimes argued that systemic delay will not engage the responsibility of the state. To some extent all delays arising in the context of State prosecutions could be classed as systemic, having their causes in an underlying inadequacy in the justice systems. The principle is said to arise from the decision of the court in *Buchholz v Germany*,[205] where the European Court was considering delays, which had arisen in the mid-1970s in the context of German Labour courts. The court stated:

> The court points out that the Convention places a duty on the Contracting States to organise their legal systems so as to allow the courts to comply with the requirements of Article para 1 ... including that of trial within a 'reasonable time'. Nonetheless, a temporary backlog of business does not involve liability on the part of the Contracting States provided that they have taken reasonably prompt remedial action to deal with an exceptional situation of this kind.

It must be stressed that in arriving at this decision, the Court accepted that an economic recession had resulted in an abnormally heavy burden of business on the courts that dealt with employment matters. It is not a decision which would be applicable to a situation where there was an ongoing or chronic failure in the system. In *O'Brien and Ryan v HM Advocate*,[206] the court accepted, with some hesitation, that the ten month delay at the forensic laboratory in analysing blood stains, and delays in the production of transcripts by the police, fell within the *Buchholz* principle:

> Is this such a case, in relation to ... the delays in question? And is the overall result a breach of the appellants' rights under Article 6(1)? We have not found it easy to answer these questions. If the situation at the forensic laboratory, which is revealed by this case, has been or is being left untouched, with no attempt to achieve substantial improvement in clearing the work-load, there would in our opinion be a systemic unreasonableness in the resultant delays. And we are likewise persuaded that the delay revealed in this case in the production of transcripts by the police would be unreasonable if the situation has been or is being left in that state. In the light of what has been revealed in this case, prompt remedial action is in our opinion clearly called for, and if not taken could properly be regarded as a systemic and unreasonable failure, if

---

205 (1981) 3 EHRR 597.

206 Appeal Court, High Court of Justiciary, opinion of 7 June 2001.

comparable delays occurred in future cases. In relation to the present case, however, we have come with some hesitation to the conclusion that it has not been shown, on either matter, that the defects had passed from being temporary into being inherent and uncured elements in the system. And that being so, we are not persuaded that either of these delays is to be seen as demonstrating a persistent under-funding of the system by Government that had become unreasonable.[207]

It is important, however, that the principle is kept within its appropriate bounds. It relates to temporary and short-term delays, which arise from a sudden, and arguably, unpredictable increase in the workload of an organisation. The duty on the state under Art 6, and therefore upon all public authorities under s 6 of the Human Rights Act, is to provide the defendant with a trial within a reasonable time. The cause of delays will be relevant. In exceptional circumstances, *Buchholz* suggests that they may permissible. But the right to trial within a reasonable period remains the underlying principle.

Issues for advocates: arguments on delay

1   Identifying the Art 6 right.

2   The court as public authority.

3   Has there been a delay?
   - Overall time.
   - Explanation for each period of delay in progressing the matter.
   - Complexity of the case.
   - Conduct of the parties and potentially of third parties.
   - Is this a case of short-term systemic delay? *Buchholz*?
   - Is this a case involving a child defendant?
   - Importance of the matter for the defendant.

4   Is the right to trial within a reasonable time a free-standing right – or is it necessary to show that there has been an interference with the right to a fair trial?
   - Conflict of authorities between *Darmalingum* and *Flowers*.
   - Scottish authorities, especially *Crummock*, which suggest it is not necessary to show prejudice.
   - Decision of the Court of Appeal in *Attorney General's Reference (No 2 of 2001)*: it is not a free-standing right.

---

207 *Ibid*, para 12.

5 Remedy for delay:
  - *Attorney General's Reference (No 2 of 2001)*: old case law on prejudice remains valid. Consider reductions in sentence or compensation (if acquitted). See also *Beck v Norway*.
  - Cf *Darmalingum* and Scottish cases which suggest that the conviction must be quashed.

8.4 SENTENCING ARGUMENTS

There is no express provision in the Convention, which deals with sentencing issues. It is no doubt for this reason that few cases have arisen in relation to mainstream sentences of the court, and that challenges have tended to arise in respect of life sentences, and matters ancillary to sentencing, such as confiscation orders. Challenges will frequently be couched in terms of breaches of Convention rights other than Art 6, and it is therefore necessary to look briefly at the range of potential avenues of challenge to sentencing decisions.

8.4.1 Punishments that may engage Art 3

It is clear that Art 3 may be engaged by sentences of the court, but Strasbourg has stated that the threshold is high:

> [O]nly in exceptional circumstances could the length of a sentence be relevant under Article 3.[208]

In *Costello-Roberts v United Kingdom*,[209] a case that concerned the beating of a child in a private school, the European Court stated:

> In order for punishment to be 'degrading' and in breach of Article 3, the humiliation or debasement involved must attain a particular level of severity and must in any event be other than that usual element of humiliation inherent in any punishment. Indeed Article 3, by expressly prohibiting 'inhuman' and 'degrading' punishment, implies that there is a distinction between such punishment and punishment more generally.

> The assessment of this minimal level of severity depends on all the circumstances of the case. Factors such as the nature and context of the punishment, the manner and method of its execution, its duration, its physical and mental effects and, in some cases, the sex, age and state of health of the victim must all be taken into account. [210]

---

208 *C v Germany* (1986) 46 DR 179.

209 (1993) 19 EHRR 112. See also *Tyrer v United Kingdom* (1978) 2 EHRR 1: breach of Art 3 arising from birching in the Isle of Man.

210 *Ibid*, para 30.

8.4.1.1 Article 3 and arbitrary detention

In *V v United Kingdom*[211] one of the arguments was that the indeterminate detention of juveniles during Her Majesty's Pleasure offended against Art 3. The Strasbourg Court rejected this:

> The Court recalls that States have a duty under the Convention to take measures for the protection of the public from violent crime ... It does not consider that the punitive element inherent in the tariff approach itself gives rise to a breach of Article 3, or that the Convention prohibits States from subjecting a child or young person convicted of a serious crime to an indeterminate sentence allowing for the offender's continued detention or recall to detention following release where necessary for the protection of the public ...[212]

Article 3 issues are most likely to arise where offenders with mental health problems are sentenced in a way which does not acknowledge the effect of their illness. Where the treatment of the offender can be shown to be in accordance with medical principle, it is unlikely that a breach will be found:

> The established principles of medicine are admittedly in principle decisive in such cases; as a general rule, a measure, which is a therapeutic necessity, cannot be regarded as inhuman or degrading. The Court must nevertheless satisfy itself that the medical necessity has been convincingly shown to exist.[213]

In *Keenan v United Kingdom*,[214] a prisoner with mental health problems, possibly exacerbated by a change in his medication while in prison, was punished for an assault on prison staff by being given seven days' segregation in the punishment block and an additional 28 days on his time to be served. He hanged himself while in the punishment block. While the European Court of Human Rights found no breach of Art 2 (the right to life), it considered his long history of disturbed behaviour and the strong evidence of Keenan being a suicide risk, and concluded that the lack of care, of which the punishment was part, amounted to a breach of Art 3:

> The lack of effective monitoring of Mark Keenan's condition and the lack of informed psychiatric input into his assessment and treatment disclosed significant defects in the medical care provided to a mentally ill person known to be a suicide risk. The belated imposition on him in those circumstances of a serious disciplinary punishment – seven days' segregation in the punishment block and an additional 28 days to his sentence imposed two weeks after the event and only nine days before his expected date of release – which may well have threatened his physical and moral resistance, is not compatible with the standard of treatment required in respect of a mentally ill person. It must be

---

211 (1999) 30 EHRR 121.
212 *Ibid*, para 97.
213 *Herczegfalvy v Austria* (1992) 15 EHRR 437, at para 82.
214 10 BHRC 319; (2001) *The Times*, 18 April.

regarded as constituting inhuman and degrading treatment and punishment within the meaning of Article 3 of the Convention.[215]

Article 3 arguments have also been raised in relation to the mandatory life sentence provisions for murder. In *Lichniak*,[216] Counsel for the applicant argued that the mandatory life sentence for murder was itself in breach of both Art 3 and Art 5. The court summarised the applicant's argument on the Art 3 point in the following terms:

> [Counsel] submits that the mandatory life sentence is inhuman and degrading by reason of its disproportionality, in that it orders lifelong detention, is imposed irrespective of the individual circumstances of the offender or of the crime, is imposed on offenders of widely differing culpability, imposes a far greater punishment on those convicted of murder even in circumstances where the borderline between murder and manslaughter has only just been passed, and serves no useful penological purpose.

Both Art 3 and Art 5 arguments were unsuccessful, with the Court of Appeal referring to the weight of relatively recent Strasbourg authority. The court continued:

> 41 The only other decision to which we need refer in relation to Article 3 is the decision on admissibility of the European Commission in Bromfield on 1 July 1998 ... There the applicant, aged 20, had been sentenced to custody for life after being convicted of murder. Dealing with his complaint in relation to Article 3 paragraph 2 of the decision states:
>
> The Commission recalls that there is no incompatibility with the Convention in the imposition of a life sentence as a security or retributive measure in a particular case or in a decision to keep a recidivist or habitual offender at the disposal of the government (*Weeks v United Kingdom*). While in the cases concerning detention during Her Majesty's pleasure, the Court commented that a sentence pursuant to which young persons forfeited their liberty for the rest of their lives might raise issues under Article 3 of the Convention (see Hussain), the Commission considers that these remarks apply to sentences of life imprisonment imposed on children under the age of 18 to whom special considerations apply. It does not find that the imposition of a mandatory sentence of life imprisonment in respect of the offence of murder committed by young adults between the ages of 18 and 21 discloses treatment or punishment prohibited by Article 3 of the Convention.
>
> 42 In our judgment the weight of the jurisprudence is overwhelming. Whatever one may think about the desirability of a change of policy it cannot be accepted that a mandatory sentence of life imprisonment for murder is incompatible with Article 3.[217]

---

215 *Ibid*, para 115.
216 *R (on the Application of Lichniak) v Secretary of State for the Home Department; R v Lichniak and Another* [2001] EWHC Admin 294; [2001] All ER(D) 22 (May)
217 *Ibid*, paras 41–42.

The argument has been run with more success in relation to the mandatory life sentence provisions in s 2 of the Crime (Sentences) Act 1997,[218] where one of the arguments put to the Court of Appeal in *R v Offen*[219] was that the provisions were arbitrary, and thus disproportionate, nature could offend against Art 3 and Art 5. The court agreed:

> [W]e recognise that there have been, and will be, cases where section 2 of the 1997 Act has, and will, operate in a proportionate manner. However, as the section has hitherto been interpreted, it can clearly operate in a disproportionate manner. It is easy to find examples of situations where two offences could be committed which were categorised as serious by the section but where it would be wholly disproportionate to impose a life sentence to protect the public. Whenever a person is convicted of an offence, there is always some risk that he or she may offend again. Equally, there are a number of significant cases in which two serious offences will have been committed where the risk is not a degree, which can justify a life sentence. We refer again to the very wide span of manslaughter, which is a serious offence within the Act. An unjustified push can result in someone falling, hitting his head and suffering fatal injuries. The offence is manslaughter. The offender may have committed another serious offence when a young man. A life sentence in such circumstances may well be arbitrary and disproportionate and contravene Article 5. It could also be a punishment, which contravenes Article 3.[220]

The court's approach was therefore to read down the provision (or, as the court also suggested, simply to give effect to what the court felt had been Parliament's original intention) by treating the 'exceptional circumstances' proviso, under which a mandatory life sentence need to be applied, as being applicable wherever it could be shown that the statutory 'presumption' (namely, that a person convicted of two serious offences was a danger or risk to the public) was misplaced.

Fixed penalties remain the exception rather than the rule, so that in the normal run of cases there will have been judicial consideration of the penalty to be applied. Under these circumstances it is unlikely that the high test required to show a breach of Art 3 will add anything to arguments in normal domestic law that a sentence is wrong in law.

8.4.2 Article 5 and the prohibition on arbitrary detention

Article 5 issues arise primarily in relation to challenges to life sentences.

Historically Strasbourg has drawn a distinction between mandatory and discretionary life sentences. The former, somewhat artificially, are treated as being wholly punitive, while discretionary life sentences are seen as having an

---

218 Now s 109 of the Powers of Criminal Courts (Sentencing) Act 2000.
219 *R v Offen, McGilliard, McKeown, Okwuegbunam* [2001] 2 All ER 154.
220 [2001] 2 All ER 154, para 107.

element of punitive sentencing and of preventative sentencing. The division of the discretionary life sentence into separate punitive and protective elements means that regular review is required once the punitive element was served in order to ensure that the need for continuing preventative detention continues to arise.[221] In *Hirst v United Kingdom*[222] the Strasbourg Court found a breach of Art 5 because of a lack of frequency in the review process.

The arbitrary nature of detention under the s 2 of the Crime (Sentences) Act 1997 provision has been discussed in the previous section. Arguments that the mandatory life sentence for murder is also incompatible with Art 5 were also advanced in the *Lichniak* case.[223] These were unsuccessful in the light of Strasbourg case law such as *Wynne*:

> A clear distinction was drawn between the discretionary life sentence, which was considered to have a protective purpose, and a mandatory life sentence, which was viewed as essentially punitive in nature.[224]

The argument that the punishment was arbitrary was rejected:

> [A]s regards mandatory life sentences, the guarantee of Article 5(4) was satisfied by the original trial and appeal proceedings and confers no additional right to challenge the lawfulness of continuing detention or re-detention following revocation of the life sentence.[225]

Moreover, to the extent that the applicant's argument in *Lichniak* was that the sentence imposed was not appropriate, the court appeared to accept the Secretary of State's argument that the appropriateness of any penalty felt outside Art 5, which was concerned merely with the lawfulness of detention. Given the widespread acceptance that the current distinctions between the mandatory and discretionary life sentence regime lack logic, it is likely that challenges will continue.

8.4.3 Article 6 and sentencing

It is clear that Art 6 extends to the sentencing stage, although the presumption of innocence in Art 6(2) will clearly no longer be applicable:

> Once an accused has properly been proved guilty of that offence, Article 6 s 2 can have no application in relation to allegations made about the accused's character and conduct as part of the sentencing process, unless such accusations are of such a nature and degree as to amount to the bringing of a new 'charge' within the autonomous Convention meaning ...[226]

---

221 *Thynne, Wilson and Gunnell v United Kingdom* (1991) 13 EHRR 666.

222 (2001) *The Times*, 3 August (ECHR).

223 See preceding section.

224 *Wynne v United Kingdom* (1994) 19 EHRR 353, para 33.

225 *Ibid*, para 36.

226 *Phillips v United Kingdom*, European Court of Human Rights, judgment of 5 July 2001, para 35.

In *Phillips v United Kingdom*,[227] however, the European Court of Human Rights concluded that confiscation orders under Drug Trafficking Act 1994 could engage Art 6(1), on the basis that the right to be presumed innocent and to place the burden of proof upon the prosecution arose in the context of the general Art 6(1) right to a fair trial, notwithstanding that Art 6(2) did not apply. However the court concluded that even though the penalty for non-payment of the confiscation order was a potential two-year addition to his sentence, the measure did not amount to an additional conviction. The court also stated that the provision contained full due process safeguards, such as a public hearing, advance disclosure and the production of evidence. Moreover, although there was a statutory assumption as to property being the benefits of drug trafficking, the judge nevertheless sought further information as to ownership. Under the circumstances the presumption was 'confined within reasonable limits' and the measure, as a whole, did not offend against Art 6.[228]

Article 6 arguments have also been raised in relation to the power of the Home Secretary to fix the tariff element of mandatory life sentences for murder. An attempt was made to argue by analogy with the decision in *V v United Kingdom*[229] where Strasbourg had held that the sentence of detention during Her Majesty's pleasure attracted Art 6 protection. In *Anderson*,[230] however, the Divisional Court rejected the applications, upholding the traditional distinction drawn by the Strasbourg Court between discretionary and mandatory life sentences.

8.4.4 Sentencing and other Convention issues

8.4.4.1 Article 7 arguments

Article 7 proscribes retrospective criminalisation of conduct. This provision will therefore catch provisions, which seek to impose a more substantial penalty than was available at the time that the offence was committed.[231]

---

227 *Ibid.*

228 Inevitably, in view of the finding on Art 6, a similar argument under Art 1, Protocol 1 was also unsuccessful. Similar arguments have been raised in *HM Advocate v McIntosh (Sentencing)* [2001] UKPC D1; [2001] 3 WLR 107, where the Privy Council held that confiscation under s 3(2) of the Proceeds of Crime (Scotland) Act 1995 did not engage Art 6(2), overturning the decision of the High Court of Justiciary. An appeal to the House of Lords is pending against the decision of the English Court of Appeal in *R v Benjafield and Other Appeals* [2001] 2 All ER 609, in which the Court of Appeal held that there was no breach of Art 6 as a whole in the making of a drug confiscation order.

229 (1999) 30 EHRR 121.

230 *R (on the Application of Anderson) v Secretary of State for the Home Department* [2001] EWHC Admin 181, [2001] HRLR 33.

231 *Welch v United Kingdom* (1995) 20 EHRR 247: confiscation order under the Drug Trafficking Act, which had not been in force at the time of the commission of the offences was in breach of Art 7.

As has been noted already in the context of the 'lawful chastisement' defence in *R v H*,[232] the development of the common law has been held not to offend against Art 7. The *R v H* decision drew heavily upon the Strasbourg judgment in *SW v United Kingdom*,[233] which itself turned on the issue of the foreseeability of the development of the common law in the removal of the marital rape immunity:

> The decisions of the Court of Appeal and then the House of Lords did no more than continue a perceptible line of case law development dismantling the immunity of a husband from prosecution for rape upon his wife ... There was no doubt under the law as it stood on 18 September 1990 that a husband who forcibly had sexual intercourse with his wife could, in various circumstances, be found guilty of rape. Moreover, there was an evident evolution, which was consistent with the very essence of the offence, of the criminal law through judicial interpretation towards treating such conduct generally as within the scope of the offence of rape. This evolution had reached a stage where judicial recognition of the absence of immunity had become a reasonably foreseeable development of the law ...

> 44 The essentially debasing character of rape is so manifest that the result of the decisions of the Court of Appeal and the House of Lords - that the applicant could be convicted of attempted rape, irrespective of his relationship with the victim – cannot be said to be at variance with the object and purpose of Article 7 ... of the Convention, namely to ensure that no one should be subjected to arbitrary prosecution, conviction or punishment ... What is more, the abandonment of the unacceptable idea of a husband being immune against prosecution for rape of his wife was in conformity not only with a civilised concept of marriage but also, and above all, with the fundamental objectives of the Convention, the very essence of which is respect for human dignity and human freedom.

> 45 Consequently, by following the Court of Appeal's ruling in *R v R* in the applicant's case, Mr Justice Rose did not render a decision permitting a finding of guilt incompatible with Article 7 of the Convention.

The Strasbourg decision makes clear that a substantial element in its reasoning is that the prior immunity was itself objectionable. Indeed, there is presumably an argument that the victim could properly have alleged that the existence of the immunity was in breach of the state's positive duty under Art 3 to protect her from degrading treatment.

The *SW* decision has been re-visited in the domestic courts in *R v Alden*,[234] where the defendant alleged that his sentence for various sexual offences against men and boys while he was employed at an approved school were in breach of Art 7. The offences had been committed between the late 1960s and the mid-1980s and the basis of the objection was that sentencing levels had

---

232 Discussed above.
233 (1995) 21 EHRR 363.
234 [2001] EWCA Crim 296; *Sub nom R v A (Barrie Owen)* [2001] HRLR 32.

increased since that time. This was rejected by the Court of Appeal who found that:

> The schedule [of sentences provided by the defence in support of the argument that there had been an increase in the 'tariff'] does not in our view demonstrate that any sea change in sentencing guidelines has occurred. On the contrary the repeated reference to *Willis* [the long-standing guideline case] by this Court establishes that [the] same guidelines have been consistently applied over the decades. Any apparent variation is due to the gravity of offences coming before the Court.[235]

Moreover, the court concluded that Art 7 focused only on the maximum penalty prescribed for the offence, and not on the actual sentencing levels.[236] Thus, even had there been a re-evaluation and subsequent increase in the 'tariff', so long as there had been no retrospective change in the available maximum, the court suggests that no Art 7 issue will arise. Whether Art 7 is limited to consideration of the maximum sentence as *Alden* suggests, is far from clear however.

8.4.4.2 Article 8 issues

In *Laskey v United Kingdom*,[237] where the criminalisation of consensual sadomasochistic activity was upheld by the Strasbourg Court on the narrow basis that the interference with Art 8 was justified in order to protect public health, there was some suggestion that had the substantial custodial penalty originally imposed not been reduced by the domestic appellate courts, the penalty would have been disproportionate and in breach of Art 8. A similar argument would presumably arise in relation to punishments where the prosecution interferes with an Art 10 right, and where the courts must therefore ensure that any punishment is not so disproportionate as to step outside what amounts to a permitted interference.

The issue the proportionality of interference with Art 8 has arisen in domestic courts in a different context, focusing on the Art 8 rights of others, and in particular children of the family. In *R (on the Application of Stokes) v Gwent Magistrates Court*[238] the Divisional Court ruled that the imposition of a suspended committal order on a lone parent of four in respect of outstanding fines and compensation orders (some of which were in respect of offences committed by the children) offended against Art 8. The court considered a pre-Human Rights Act decision[239] in respect of committal in these circumstances and commented:

---

235 *Ibid,* para 45. *Alden* has been followed in *R v Cathra* [2001] All ER(D) 88, CA.
236 *Ibid,* see para 54.
237 *Laskey, Jaggard and Brown v United Kingdom* (1997) 24 EHRR 39.
238 [2001] EWCA Admin 569; Lawtel 10/7/2001.
239 *R v Northampton Justices ex p Kerry Ferguson* (1999) QBD, 2 December.

If a matter of this kind were brought before a court today, the justices would have the provisions of Article 8 of the European Convention of Human Rights ringing in their ears. They were being invited to commit to prison a mother of four children, aged 16, 15, 6 and at that time less than one year old, and each of those children has a right to respect for their family life recognised by the Convention.[240]

The court considered the decision in *W and B (Children: Care Plan)*[241] and continued:

In cases of this kind decided today, when a court concerned with fines enforcement is contemplating making an order which would separate completely a mother from her young children and send her to prison for a period of time with unknown consequences of the effect of that order on her young children, it must take into account the need for proportionality and must ask itself, given the seriousness of the intervention it is minded to make in terms of taking a mother away from her young children and imprisoning her: Is this proposed interference with the children's right to respect for their family life proportionate to the need which makes it legitimate?

No court would say for one moment that there might not be a case (so long as the power of committal to prison as a power of last resort in relation to the enforcement of fines and compensation orders remains on the statute book) in which the pursuit of the aim to make a mother comply with her legal obligations overrode the rights of her children to have the benefit of her care at home, however much damage the interference might cause to the children and their enjoyment of their rights. But there is no doubt in my judgment that the implications of Article 8 are now a matter which a court must take seriously into account when making a decision of this kind: see section 6(1) of the Human Rights Act 1998, which reinforces the strong message which has been coming from this court in recent years that committal must be a remedy of final resort if all else has failed.[242]

Stokes is a decision of potentially wide application. Clearly it can be argued that there is a particular concern that imprisonment is not appropriate where the original sentence was only a fine – and on this basis it can be argued that *Stokes* is of less relevance where the court is considering imposing a custodial penalty on the basis of offence seriousness. As against this, it can be pointed out that the requirement for proportionality in the interference with Art 8 is not limited in this way, and while *Stokes* is of particular relevance to non-payment of fines, and presumably non-compliance with community sentences of different types, it remains applicable to the full range of sentencing issues.

---

240 [2001] EWCA Admin 569; Lawtel 10/7/2001, para 34.
241 *W and B (Children: Care Plan)* [2001] EWCA Civ 757; [2001] FCR 450.
242 [2001] EWCA Admin 569; Lawtel 10/7/2001, paras 36–37.

8.4.5 Ancillary sentencing issues

8.4.5.1 Costs

Strasbourg has made clear that Art 6(2) can apply to the issue of the refusal of costs following an acquittal on the basis that the matter is inextricably linked with the preceding criminal proceedings:

> The Court recalls that the applicant can rely on Article 6 s 2 of the Convention, irrespective of the fact that the contested decision was given after his acquittal had become final, as Austrian legislation and practice link the two questions – the criminal responsibility of the accused and the right to compensation – to such a degree that the decisions on the latter issue can be regarded as a consequence and, to some extent, the concomitant of the decision on the former.[243]

Thus, the refusal of costs on the basis that lingering suspicions as to the defendant's guilt remain will offend against Art 6:

> The Court, thus, considers that once an acquittal has become final – be it an acquittal giving the accused the benefit of the doubt in accordance with Article 6 s 2 – the voicing of any suspicions of guilt, including those expressed in the reasons for the acquittal, is incompatible with the presumption of innocence.[244]

The old practice direction, which enabled courts to deny costs to a successful defendant on the basis that he had been acquitted on a technicality only, was amended by the *Practice Direction (Crime: Costs in Criminal Proceedings) (No 2)*[245] because it was likely to be in breach of the European Convention on Human Rights. While the justices do not have to hold an oral hearing in deciding whether the defendant has been the author of his own prosecution, there must some independent evidence.[246] It is still therefore the case in domestic law that costs can be refused following an acquittal where it said that it is the defendant's conduct that brought suspicion upon him or which led the prosecution to think that the case against him was stronger than it was.[247] This leaves open therefore the possibility that costs might be refused in the Crown Court in circumstances which were incompatible with the presumption of innocence, but that there would be no remedy under the Human Rights Act.

---

243 *Rushiti v Austria*, European Court of Human Rights, judgment of 21 March 2000, para 27.

244 *Ibid*, para 31.

245 [1999] 1 WLR 1832.

246 *Mooney v Cardiff Justices* (1999) *The Times*, 17 November.

247 See the discussion of *R (on the Application of Regentford Ltd) v Crown Court at Canterbury* [2001] HRLR 18 in Chapter 2, above.

8.4.5.2 Ancillary orders

The general pattern in domestic law seems to be for the categorisation of many of the restrictive orders, which now accompany 'traditional' criminal sentences as civil matters. Both anti social behaviour orders and sex offender orders have been classified by the domestic courts as civil proceedings.[248] In *Gough*[249] football banning orders under ss 14A and 14B of the Football Spectators Act 1989 (as amended by the Football (Disorder) Act 2000) were held not to be criminal penalties, so that no issues of retrospective criminalisation contrary to Art 7 arose.[250]

This is not to say that 'sentencing' issues of a type do not arise. Indeed, in *Jones v Greater Manchester Police Authority*[251] where the Divisional Court was asked to consider a sex offender order which provided that a 63 year old offender:

> should not enter any public park, children's playground or public swimming bath in England and Wales at any time; he was not to entice, approach, communicate or be in the company of any person under the age of 18 years; and he was not to leave England and Wales or to apply for international travel documents without first notifying the police and without the permission of the court.[252]

The order was for life. The court upheld the order but noted that both Art 6 and Art 8 were still relevant:

> Clearly, however, the proceedings must be fair, pursuant to Art 6(1); and because the consequence of an order under either s 1 or s 2 of the 1998 Act is the restriction of liberty inherent in the type of order envisaged by those sections, there is an interference with the private life of the defendant, which attracts the protection of Art 8. Accordingly, the interference must be in accordance with law and such as is necessary in a democratic society in the interests of national security, public safety or the economic well-being of the country or for the protection of the public from disorder or crime, for the protection of health or morals or for the protection of rights and freedoms of others.[253]

---

248 See *R (on the Application of M (A Child)) v Manchester Crown Court* (Admin Court) [2001] 1 WLR 358, (Court of Appeal) [2001] EWCA Civ 281; [2001] 1 WLR 1085 and *B v Chief Constable of Avon and Somerset Constabulary* [2001] 1 WLR 340, both discussed in Chapter 7.

249 *Gough and Another v Chief Constable of Derbyshire; R (on the Application of Miller) v Leeds Magistrates' Court; Lilley v Director of Public Prosecutions* [2001] EWHC Admin 554; (2001) *The Times*, 19 July.

250 For an argument that the decision is incorrect in respect of s 14A orders, see James Richardson's commentary at Criminal Law Week (criminal-law.co.uk) 01/28/14.

251 [2001] EWHC Admin 189.

252 *Ibid*, para 3.

253 *Ibid*, para 16. It should be noted that the facts of the case were extreme, with the offender having over 30 previous convictions, and having been described as 'a fixated paedophile with no insight into his offending and no inclination to seek treatment which would reduce the risk' so that there was a high risk of re-offending. For a consideration of the proportionality of restrictions on a life licence, see *R (on the Application of Craven) v Secretary of State for the Home Department* [2001] EWHC Admin 850; [2001] All ER(D) 74.

A similar need for scrutiny will arise in many of these contexts. The issue will not simply be the width – and thus proportionality – of the proposed restrictions. Advocates for both sides will need to ensure that the order of the court expresses any order in terms that are sufficiently clear for the defendant to know what is required of him or her. It is clear from Strasbourg case law that bind-overs are criminal offences,[254] but in *Hashman and Harrap v United Kingdom*[255] the order that the applicants be bound over not to behave *contra bonos mores* lacked certainty and thus did not comply with the requirement under Art 10(2) that it be 'prescribed by law'.

It will be recalled that in *Phillips v United Kingdom*[256] the European Court of Human Rights has concluded that confiscation orders under the Drug Trafficking Act 1994 do not amount to a separate criminal charge, but still attract generic Art 6 protections.

8.5 APPEALS: SAFETY AND UNFAIRNESS

8.5.1 Applicability of Art 6 to appeals

Although Art 6 applies to the appeal stage,[257] not all the rights will be applicable. Strasbourg case law suggests in particular that where appeals are on point of law only the right of the appellant to be present and the right to an oral hearing may not always arise. However, underlying principles, such as equality of arms, may require a greater degree of protection in some circumstances. Thus, in *Belziuk v Poland*[258] the appellant was denied the right to be present at his appeal against a conviction for theft, for which he had been sentenced to three years' custody. He would have had the opportunity of giving evidence at the hearing, and the prosecution were present to make submissions against his appeal. The Strasbourg Court looked in some detail at the disadvantage that had arisen in consequence:

> Had he been present at the appeal hearing, he would have had an opportunity to challenge his conviction and the submissions of the public prosecutor and to present evidence in support of his appeal. It is also to be noted that the applicant's interests were not in fact represented at the appeal since there was no counsel present on his behalf. It is immaterial that he chose not to be legally represented, as the Government have maintained ... Under Article 6 ss 1 and 3(c) of the Convention taken together he had the right in the circumstances

---

254 See, for example, *Steel and Others v United Kingdom*, discussed above.
255 *Hashman and Harrap v United Kingdom* [2000] Crim LR 185.
256 See above.
257 *Delcourt v Belgium* (1979) 1 EHRR 355.
258 (2000) 30 EHRR 614.

to be present at his appeal and to defend himself in person. It follows that the applicant's right to a hearing in his presence has been violated.

39   The Court recalls that the Government maintained that the public prosecutor, who had not appealed against the judgment of the trial court, was present at the appellate hearing not in the capacity of prosecuting authority but as the guardian of the public interest ... However, the prosecutor's submissions before the Tarnów Regional Court were directed at having the applicant's appeal dismissed and his conviction upheld. In so doing his role was that of a prosecuting authority in the traditional sense ... Respect for the principle of equality of arms and the right to adversarial proceedings therefore required that the applicant be allowed to attend the hearing and to contest the submissions of the public prosecutor. Nor can it be maintained in the circumstances that the resulting inequality could have been redressed had the applicant availed himself of the opportunity to forward written submissions to the Regional Court ... having regard both to the presence of the public prosecutor in the courtroom and to the forcefulness of his oral statements.[259]

A breach of Art 6 therefore arose.

8.5.1.1   A right to appeal where the defendant has absconded?

The traditional principle in domestic law has been that where a defendant has absconded prior to conviction or sentencing as the case might be, the appellate courts will conclude that the solicitors will normally lack authority in respect of the appeal: see *R v Jones*.[260] Moreover, it will only be in exceptional circumstances that a late appeal is permitted in such circumstances.

However, in *Omar v France*[261] a French rule, which required the defendant to surrender to custody as a prerequisite for any appeal, was held to be disproportionate. The implications of the *Omar* decision were considered by the Court of Appeal in *R v Charles (Jerome); R v Tucker (Lee)*,[262] where it was concluded that domestic policy could amount to a breach of Art 6:

Having considered the matter carefully, we do not share the view expressed in *Jones (No 1)* that where a defendant has, by absconding, put it out of his power to give instructions, his solicitors have not been duly authorised to prosecute appeal proceedings on his behalf. We derive some comfort from the case of *Gooch* in reaching this conclusion. Whilst accepting the remote risk that the absconder does not want to appeal, we take the view that a single judge or the Full Court is entitled (but not bound), to conclude that the legal representatives submitting the application for permission have the actual or implied authority so to do. The applicant might have wished grounds to be advanced further to

---

259 (2000) 30 EHRR 614, paras 38–39.
260 (1971) 55 Cr App R 321
261 (1998) 29 EHRR 210.
262 [2001] EWCA Crim 129; (2001) *Daily Telegraph*, 7 February.

those, which his legal representative decides to advance. That must be a risk, which he takes. Nor do we think that it is appropriate for the Registrar in future to treat an application in these circumstances as ineffective. Applications should be put before the single judge.[263]

It seems likely that this change in domestic procedures is sufficient to comply with Art 6.

8.5.2 Are appeals curative?

It will be recalled that the Art 6 guarantee extends from 'charge' to the end of the proceedings. It therefore includes the appeal process, with the effect that in some circumstances it will be possible for the appeal process to ratify what would otherwise be breaches of Art 6 in the context of the original trial.

In *Edwards v United Kingdom*[264] facts which went to the credibility of police officers had not been disclosed to the defence at the trial. The Strasbourg Court considered the impact of the disclosure of this information during the appeal process:

36 The Court considers that it is a requirement of fairness under paragraph 1 of Article 6 ... indeed one which is recognised under English law, that the prosecution authorities disclose to the defence all material evidence for or against the accused and that the failure to do so in the present case gave rise to a defect in the trial proceedings. However, when this was discovered, the Secretary of State, following an independent police investigation, referred the case to the Court of Appeal which examined the transcript of the trial including the applicant's alleged confession and considered in detail the impact of the new information on the conviction ...

37 In the proceedings before the Court of Appeal the applicant was represented by senior and junior counsel who had every opportunity to seek to persuade the court that the conviction should not stand in view of the evidence of non-disclosure. Admittedly the police officers who had given evidence at the trial were not heard by the Court of Appeal. It was, none the less, open to counsel for the applicant to make an application to the Court – which they chose not to do – that the police officers be called as witnesses ...

38 In the course of the hearing before the European Court the applicant claimed, for the first time, that without the disclosure of the Carmichael report to the applicant or to the Court of Appeal the proceedings, considered as a whole, could not be fair ... However it is not disputed that he could have applied to the Court of Appeal for the production of this report but did not do so. It is no answer to the failure to make such an application that the Crown might have resisted by claiming public interest immunity since such a claim would have been for the court to determine ...

---

263 *Ibid*, para 53.
264 (1993) 15 EHRR 417.

39 Having regard to the above, the Court concludes that the defects of the original trial were remedied by the subsequent procedure before the Court of Appeal ... Moreover, there is no indication that the proceedings before the Court of Appeal were in any respect unfair.[265]

It will be recalled that in *Condron v United Kingdom*,[266] in the context of a misdirection to the jury on inferences from the right of silence, that the European Court of Human Rights concluded that the breach of Art 6 at the trial stage could not be rectified on appeal. It is not yet clear how widely the *Condron* principle can be extended. Is it simply confined to right to silence cases – and other cases where the interference is with a fundamental right? Or does it extend to all cases where the appellate court is left to speculate on the effect of the breach on the jury? This has led to some less than convincing decisions, even in the context of the right to silence, in which *Condron* has been distinguished. In *R v Francom*,[267] for example, where the issue was a failure to direct the jury that no inference could arise from a period of silence, the Court of Appeal held that this was a non-direction rather than a mis-direction, and on this basis that the conviction need not be disturbed.

In arguing that there has been a breach of Art 6, therefore, it is necessary to look to the appeal process to see if it can be argued that the appeal has rectified the earlier breach, and also to consider whether the breach is of a type that cannot be rectified.

But if there is an admitted breach of Art 6, what is the implication of this breach for the appellate court process, and in particular for the domestic test contained in s 2 of the Criminal Appeals Act 1968 that a conviction will be overturned if it is unsafe.

8.5.3 Does unfair mean unsafe?

There is evidence of a fundamental disagreement within the domestic courts as to whether the fact that a trial has been unfair within the meaning of Art 6 leads to the inevitable finding that the conviction is unsafe for the purposes of s 2 of the Criminal Appeal Act 1968.[268]

There have been a number of comments from the House of Lords to indicate that the answer to this is that an unfair trial must lead to an unsafe conviction.

Thus, in *R v Forbes*, Lord Bingham delivering the judgment of the court stated:

---

265 *Ibid*, paras 36–39.

266 (2001) 31 EHRR 1.

267 [2001] 1 Cr App R 17.

268 The issue has, of course, also arisen in the context of delay, and in particular in the Privy Council decision in *Darmalingum*, and the Court of Appeal decision in *Attorney General's Reference (No 2 of 2001)*, both discussed above.

Reference was made in argument to the right to a fair trial guaranteed by Article 6 of the European Convention on Human Rights. That is an absolute right. But, as the Judicial Committee of the Privy Council has very recently held in *Stott v Brown* ... the subsidiary rights comprised within that article are not absolute, and it is always necessary to consider all the facts and the whole history of the proceedings in a particular case to judge whether a defendant's right to a fair trial has been infringed or not. If on such consideration it is concluded that a defendant's right to a fair trial has been infringed, a conviction will be held to be unsafe within the meaning of section 2 of the Criminal Appeal Act 1968. We would endorse the recent judgment of the Court of Appeal (Lord Woolf CJ, Steel and Butterfield JJ) in *R v Togher* ...[269]

Similarly, in *R v A* Lord Steyn said:

It is well established that the guarantee of a fair trial under Article 6 is absolute: a conviction obtained in breach of it cannot stand.[270]

In the light of these comments it might seem as if the matter is settled. It is true that in the Court of Appeal re-hearing in *R v Davies, Rowe and Johnson*,[271] where the court was faced with a finding from the Strasbourg Court that there had been a breach of Art 6, the domestic court held that it did not automatically follow that the conviction was unsafe:

The duty of the ECHR is to determine whether or not there has been a violation of the European Convention or in this case, more particularly, of Article 6(1). It is not within the remit of ECHR to comment upon the nature and quality of any breach or upon the impact such a breach might have had upon the safety of the conviction.

...

We are satisfied that the two questions must be kept separate and apart. The ECHR is charged with inquiring into whether there has been a breach of a convention right. This court is concerned with the safety of the conviction. That the first question may intrude upon the second is obvious. To what extent it does so will depend upon the circumstances of the particular case. We reject, therefore, [the appellant's] contention that a finding of a breach of Article 6(1) by the ECHR leads inexorably to the quashing of the conviction. Nor do we think it helpful to deal in presumptions. The effect of any unfairness upon the safety of the conviction will vary according to its nature and degree. At one end of the spectrum [the Crown] cites the example of an appropriate sentence following a plea of guilty passed by a judge who for some undisclosed reason did not constitute an impartial tribunal. At the other extreme there may be a case where a defendant is denied the opportunity to give evidence in his own behalf. In both cases there might well be a violation of Article 6. Is each to be treated in the same way? Not in the opinion of this court.[272]

---

269 [2001] 2 WLR 1 at para 24. *R v Togher* [2001] 1 Cr App R 33.
270 *R v A* [2001] UKHL 25, [2001] 2 WLR 1546, para 38.
271 [2001] 1 Cr App R 8.
272 *Ibid*, paras 64–65.

In the face of such clear (if brief) contrary statements from the House of Lords in the later cases of *Forbes* and *R v A*, we would suggest that the decision in *Davies* should not be followed. There are two difficulties with this, however.

First, the comments in *Forbes* and *R v A* are arguably *obiter*, and they do not explicitly overrule the Court of Appeal's comments in *Davies*.[273]

More worryingly, however, in their Lordships' speeches in *Lambert* there are clear suggestions that the conviction would have been treated as safe even had their Lordships concluded that the Human Rights Act had had retrospective effect. Again, because the majority of their Lordships concluded that no breach of Art 6 had arisen because the trial had taken place prior to October 2000, the comments are arguably *obiter*. However, Lord Steyn, the only judge to conclude that the Human Rights Act was retrospective commented:

> My Lords, this is a case of an accused found in possession of two kilograms of cocaine worth over £140,000. It must be comparatively rare for a drug dealer to entrust such a valuable parcel of drugs to an innocent. In any event the appellant's detailed story stretches judicial credibility beyond breaking-point. Even if the judge had directed the jury in accordance with law as I have held it to be the appellant's conviction would have been a foregone conclusion. I would dismiss the appeal.[274]

Similarly, Lord Hope stated:

> Had it been necessary to do so, I would have held that his conviction was not unsafe on the ground that the jury would have reached the same result if a direction had been given to them, which was compatible with the Convention right. I would dismiss the appeal.[275]

The position for advocates therefore remains regrettably unclear. We would suggest that a finding that the defendant has had an unfair trial, whatever the cause of that unfairness, must as a matter of principle give rise to a finding that the conviction is unsafe. However, it is clear that this is not yet a position, which has the full support of the senior judiciary.

---

273 For a middle view seeking to reconcile the two approaches see *R v Milford* [2001] Crim LR 330, para 58: 'It follows, that if, in all the circumstances of the case, the act or omission complained of amounts to a substantial or significant departure from the norms of fairness recognised by the ECHR, then it will be treated as rendering the verdict unsafe, whereas some act or omission which in all the circumstances amounts to no more than a technical or insubstantial departure will not necessarily be so regarded.'

274 *R v Lambert* [2001] UKHL 37 (HL), para 43.

275 *Ibid*, para 119.

CHAPTER 9

CIVIL COURTS AND TRIBUNALS

9.1 INTRODUCTION

The HRA has a major impact on civil litigation in courts and tribunals. The HRA contains a new mechanism for the resolution of disputes about Convention rights, permitting either a free-standing claim by the alleged victim or allowing him or her to rely on the alleged breach in any other legal proceedings. Although the Act does not create a new series of private law rights, it does create a new cause of action against public authorities for breach of statutory duty and influences statutory interpretation and the development of the common law even in disputes between wholly private parties. This, coupled with the ability of the courts to provide remedies against public authorities for breach or anticipated breach of Convention rights, creates a new framework for the determination human rights litigation.

Moreover, the inclusion of the courts and tribunals in the definition of public authority means that they have a direct duty under Art 6 of the Convention to provide litigants with a fair trial whenever they determine civil rights and obligations. This includes a series of implicit and explicit procedural guarantees. This chapter provides an overview of the relevant law and explores the practical consequences for advocates.

Issues for advocates: preliminary considerations

Advocates are faced with a number of important challenges and opportunities. Among these are the following:

- Applying the appropriate Convention law whenever Convention rights are in dispute in civil proceedings.
- Assessing whether the procedure in question determines a civil right or obligation so as to trigger the procedural guarantees in Art 6.
- Assisting the court or tribunal to decide whether and to what extent the Convention rights affect the scope and content of existing civil rights.
- Understanding and explaining the impact the procedural guarantees should have in a given case.
- Applying the HRA provisions on remedies in cases where a Convention violation is found.

9.2 THE HUMAN RIGHTS ACT IN CIVIL PROCEEDINGS

The Human Rights Act procedures can be relied upon to invoke Convention rights across all areas of civil litigation. The mechanism for their introduction is either the s 7(1)(a) free-standing claim or the s 7(1)(b) reliance on Convention rights. In respect of the former, a claim includes a counterclaim. It also includes an appeal against the decision of a court or tribunal and judicial review proceedings.[1] In respect of the latter, this enables Convention rights to be added as a further dimension to existing common law and equitable causes of action and also in defences to such proceedings.[2]

The Act does not specify whether the unlawful act in s 6 is unlawful in terms of public law or private law. The Act clearly contemplates proceedings being brought by way of public law judicial review or private law civil suit,[3] although one court has ruled that if an action otherwise falls within the definition of judicial review in Pt 54 of the CPR, then it should be brought under that procedure even if it raises Human Rights Act points.[4]

The role of the advocate when introducing or responding to Convention rights points in civil litigation is to ensure that the court is clear as to the relevance of the point to the matter before it. For example, the Convention might be used in an attempt to limit a statutory or common law defence advanced by a public authority.[5] Alternatively it might be raised in an attempt to broaden the scope of an existing tort[6] and for a variety of other purposes. The advocate should also have in mind the obligations on the court when human rights arguments are raised. In *Lambert*[7] Lord Hope made clear that the court's duty under s 6 went beyond a simple procedural duty and affected matters of substance in the law:

> I would be inclined to give the word 'act' a broad and purposive meaning … It seems to me that, it is not only the manner of the decision-taking exercise that is brought under scrutiny … The court is prohibited from carrying out the 'act' of statutory construction otherwise than in accordance with that obligation. A decision which is based on the application and development of the common law also is an act by the court, so I think that it must follow that this too is subject to the prohibition in s 6(1). Thus it is unlawful for a court to conduct a hearing in a way, which is incompatible with a person's Article 6 Convention rights. But the prohibition in s 6(1) also affects matters of substance. So it will

---

1   See Chapter 2, para 2.3.1.
2   See Chapter 2, para 2.3.2.
3   Section 7(2) and CPR, r 7.11.
4   *Rushbridger v Attorney General* [2001] EWHC Admin 529; see para 2.6, above.
5   Article 2 or 3 might be used in order to try to limit the defence of the reasonable force defence in claims of trespass to the person. See Wadham, paras 8.2.3 and 8.3.1.
6   See *Douglas v Hello!* [2001] 2 WLR 992.
7   [2001] UKHL 37; [2001] All ER(D) 69 (Jul).

be unlawful within the meaning of s 6(1) for a court to determine a criminal charge on an interpretation of a statute, which ignores the interpretative obligation in s 3(1), or on a proposition of law which is incompatible with a Convention right.[8]

Although this was a criminal case, the reasoning is equally applicable in the civil context. It means that whenever the court is faced with a decision as to the construction of the common law or the exercise of discretion, it is obliged to seek a result that is compatible with the Convention rights of the parties appearing before it. This is the case whether or not the Convention right was recognised as a right in previous domestic law. These issues have been examined in earlier chapters. Although Convention rights are distinct from civil rights, the former will clearly have an effect on the scope of the latter. However whenever the courts accept that civil rights or obligations are at stake, Art 6 provides special procedural protection for a fair trial as a discrete right. This applies whether or not any other Convention rights are involved. The rest of this chapter focuses on when the fair trial provisions of Art 6 will apply and what advocates can expect from a fair hearing in a civil trial.

9.3 TRIGGERING ART 6 PROTECTION

In the context of civil litigation, Art 6 applies to a person's case, 'whenever there is the determination of his civil rights and obligations'.[9] Thus, it is not all disputes in the courts that will give rise to the Convention requirement to a fair trial. The case must have a number of minimum characteristics.

Issues for advocates: cumulative triggers for the operation of Art 6

Each of the following features must be satisfied before the Convention will require the Art 6 fair trial guarantees to be secured:

- The right or obligation concerned must be civil or 'private' in nature.
- The right or obligation must be recognised or have a basis in domestic law.
- There must be a real dispute or 'contestation' over the right or obligation.
- The procedure concerned must 'determine' the right or obligation concerned.

The next section will briefly consider each of these points in turn.

---

8   [2001] UKHL 37; [2001] All ER(D) 69 (Jul), at para 114.
9   Article 6(1).

9.3.1 Is the right or obligation civil in nature?

The main distinction in this context is between public rights and obligations on the one hand and private rights and obligations on the other. The former do not attract the protection of Art 6 whereas the latter do. As previously noted, the phrase 'civil rights or obligations' is an autonomous Convention concept. This means that the courts will decide whether Art 6 applies on the basis of its substantive character and will not necessarily be bound by the classification by the domestic law of the proceedings as public or private.

The European Court put it as follows:

> 94 For Article 6, paragraph (1) (Art 6–1), to be applicable to a case ('*contestation*') it is not necessary that both parties to the proceedings should be private persons ... The wording of Article 6, paragraph (1) (Art 6–1), is far wider; the French expression *contestations sur (des) droits et obligations de caractère civil*, covers all proceedings the result of which is decisive for private rights and obligations. The English text 'determination of ... civil rights and obligations', confirms this interpretation. The character of the legislation which governs how the matter is to be determined (civil, commercial, administrative law, etc) and that of the authority which is invested with jurisdiction in the matter (ordinary court, administrative body, etc) are therefore of little consequence.[10]

The courts will look for the following characteristics when deciding whether a particular right is civil in nature:

1   Economic or pecuniary interests. In *Editions Periscope v France*[11] the court held that:

    > ... the subject matter of the applicant company's action was 'pecuniary' in nature and that the action was founded on an alleged infringement of rights which were likewise pecuniary rights. The right in question was therefore a 'civil right', notwithstanding the origin of the dispute and the fact that the administrative courts had jurisdiction.[12]

2   Personal or private interests. It is not only economic interests that trigger civil rights. If the courts are satisfied that personal interests are concerned they will be likely to find that Art 6 is applicable. For example, in *W v United Kingdom*[13] the court held that care proceedings involving the termination of a parent's right of access to his child in care involved a civil right.

---

10   *Ringeisen v Austria* (1971) 1 EHRR 455 at para 94.
11   (1992) 14 EHRR 597.
12   *Ibid*, at para 40.
13   (1987) 10 EHRR 29.

Issues for advocates: decisions relating to civil rights and obligations

Advocates need to be able to judge whether a dispute involves a civil right or obligation or whether it is purely public in character so as not to give rise to Art 6 considerations. The following list provides illustrations of previous decisions where the courts have addressed whether a dispute is of a civil character so as to satisfy the first trigger for the application of Art 6.

Situations determining civil rights or obligations

- Disputes regarding property will generally be found to relate to civil rights or obligations. This includes real property,[14] contractual disputes,[15] and licensing decisions affecting the ability to engage in commercial activity.[16]

- Disputes over welfare benefits have also generally been seen as relating to civil rights. This is more obviously the case in respect of contributory schemes,[17] but also applies in respect of needs-based social security entitlements.[18]

---

14   See, for example, *Gillow v United Kingdom* (1989) 11 EHRR 335 where residence requirements in Guernsey prevented the applicants from living in their house on the island. In *R (on the Application of Johns) v Bracknell Forest DC* (2001) 33 HLR 45 the Administrative Court held that the review by a local authority of its decision to terminate an introductory tenancy amounted to the determination of a civil right. Longmore J said that the dispute was about 'the conditions under which such rights as remain for public housing tenants in their first year can be terminated'. Given the statutory right to request a review the council was not simply exercising a power.

15   In *Wilson v First County Trust* [2001] EWCA Civ 633; [2001] 3 WLR 42 the Court of Appeal rejected an argument that because the creditor had parted with monies in circumstances where it would not be entitled to have them repaid, it ought to be seen as a voluntary disposition or gift and thus not engage Art 6 at all. The court held that statutory restrictions on enforcement of a credit agreement engaged Art 6 as they could have the effect of preventing the bargain entered into by the creditor and debtor from being carried out (see paras 26–28). In *McLellan v Bracknell Forest BC* [2001] EWCA 510, the Court of Appeal held that eviction from an introductory tenancy determined a civil right despite the lack of security of tenure.

16   For example, *Pudas v Sweden* (1988) 10 EHRR 380 which involved the revocation of a licence to run a taxi service. There seems to be little scope for a difference of approach in respect of the granting of licences and the renewal or revocation thereof. In *Benthem v Netherlands* (1985) 8 EHRR 1 the European Court said at para 36: 'The grant of the licence to which the applicant claimed to be entitled was one of the conditions for the exercise of part of his activities as a businessman. It was closely associated with the right to use one's possessions in conformity with the law's requirements. In addition, a licence of this kind has a proprietary character, as is shown, *inter alia*, by the fact that it can be assigned to third parties.'

17   *Feldebrugge Netherlands* (1986) 8 EHRR 425.

18   *Salesi v Italy* (1998) 26 EHRR 187. In *Husain v Asylum Support Adjudicator* [2001] EWHC Admin 852, the court held that although support under the Immigration and Asylum Act 1999 was discretionary, the reality was that eligible asylum seekers had a right to have decisions reviewed by an independent tribunal because the regulations supplementing the Act indicated that there were mandatory duties regarding those already in receipt of support. Interestingly, this position was supported by the court's view that withdrawal of support from a destitute asylum seeker would violate Art 3.

- Professional discipline cases generally give rise to Art 6 protection due to their effect on future prospects of employment in a particular profession.[19] Advocates should not, however, make the mistake of thinking that Art 6 must apply in respect of all disciplinary proceedings taken within organisation, even a public authority. Public authority employers, although bound by Human Rights Act even in their private functions, are not determining the private law right. There is no 'dispute' or 'contestation' at this stage. This arises when the individual employee challenges the decision in the court or tribunal. This is different from the disciplinary measures of a professional body, which can affect the ability of the individual to practice in his or her profession at all. The Consultancy Service Index does not determine civil rights,[20] although the distinction between a rule preventing a person from working in a field and one that merely informs every potential employer that the government considers him or her unsuitable for such work is perhaps theoretical only.[21]

- Family disputes give rise to the determination of civil rights and obligations. Clearly this is the case in respect of private family law disputes such as divorce, ancillary relief and disputes over children.[22] However, it also extends to public child-care proceedings.[23] It may also apply at an earlier stage when the case is being dealt with only by the social services department.[24]

- In respect of deprivation of liberty, the relevant article (or *lex specialis*) is normally seen as Art 5, not Art 6.[25] Although Art 5(4) contains its own procedural guarantees,[26] they are not equivalent to Art 6. Nevertheless,

---

19 In *Ghosh v General Medical Council Privy Council* [2001] UKPC 29; (2001) *The Times,* 25 June the Privy Council accepted without hesitation that the de-registration of a doctor by the GMC professional conduct committee amounted to a determination of her civil right and thus attracted the protection of Art 6. In *Tehrani v United Kingdom Central Council for Nursing Midwifery and Health Visiting* [2001] IRLR 208 there was again no doubt that the removal of the petitioner's name from the nursing register would determine her civil rights. The reason was that the step would exclude her from certain nursing posts either as a matter of law or as the result of the application of criteria imposed by prospective employers.

20 *R v Secretary of State for Health ex p C* [2000] 1 FLR 627 (CA).

21 The test applied in *Tehrani,* above, which included the criteria imposed by prospective employers, would suggest that the reality is that inclusion on the index effectively precludes the person from certain forms of employment.

22 *Glaser v The United Kingdom* [2001] 1 FLR 153; *P v P (Removal of Child to New Zealand)* [2001] EWCA Civ 166; [2001] 2 WLR 1826.

23 *Olsson v Sweden* (1989) 11 EHRR 259.

24 *W v United Kingdom* (1987) 10 EHRR 29.

25 See *R (on the Application of the DPP) v Havering Magistrates Court, R (on the Application of McKeown) v Wirral Borough Magistrates' Court* [2001] 2 Cr App R 2 where the Administrative Court ruled that decisions to revoke bail were not determinative of civil or criminal rights.

26 *Winterwerp v Netherlands* (1979) 2 EHRR 387.

in *Aerts v Belgium*,[27] the European Court stated that a challenge to the lawfulness of the applicant's detention was indeed a determination of a civil right – the right to liberty. The court gave no reasons for its conclusion but if it is followed by the domestic courts it will produce a major overlap between the two articles. In *Greenfield v Secretary of State for the Home Department*[28] the Divisional Court held that an additional period of detention under a prison sentence following a positive test for drugs in prison did not determine either criminal or civil rights. The matter was purely disciplinary and the detention was already authorised by the original court proceedings so there was no separate determination of his rights.[29] The court did acknowledge that, following *Aerts*, claims for deprivation of liberty could potentially be brought under Art 6 but this did not assist the applicant as he was not unlawfully detained.

- Claims for compensation made where there is a clear right to obtain the compensation if a specific test is satisfied amount to civil rights.[30] This would cover areas such as compensation for breach of employment rights, compensation for unlawful discrimination, compensation for compulsory purchase and compensation for imprisonment following a miscarriage of justice.[31] It would not apply where the payment of compensation was discretionary only.[32] It might be thought that a claim for damages under s 7 of the Human Rights Act against a public authority would amount to a civil right under this category, but it should be recalled that there is no right to compensation under s 8 of the Act – it is purely discretionary.

Situations not relating to civil rights or obligations

- Decisions relating to immigration and asylum status have not yet been held to determine civil rights under the Convention.[33] The position is

---

27 (2000) 29 EHRR 50.
28 [2001] EWHC Admin 129 [2001] HRLR 35. Note that the decision was upheld by the Court of Appeal: *R (on the Application of Carroll) v Secretary of State for the Home Department* [2001] EWCA Civ 1224.
29 See also *R (on the Application of Sunder (Manjit Singh)) v Secretary of State for the Home Department* [2001] EWHC Admin 252 where a decision to re-categorise a prisoner as category A with a high escape risk did not involve the determination of his civil rights. Although he had been deprived of his civil rights, this was a result of his conviction, not of any decision of the category A committee.
30 *Tinnelly v United Kingdom* (1999) 27 EHRR 249.
31 Section 133 of the Criminal Justice Act 1988 obliges the Home Secretary to pay compensation to a person who can show beyond reasonable doubt that s/he has been the victim of a miscarriage of justice. There is also an *ex gratia* scheme operated by the Home Office which would not give rise to rights under Art 6.
32 In *Masson v Netherlands* (1996) 22 EHRR 491 the fact that the court had a discretion whether to award compensation to people acquitted following criminal proceedings indicated that no right to compensation existed.
33 See, for example, *Agee v United Kingdom* (1976) 7 DR 164.

that those who do not have citizenship have no private right to remain in the country. The decision-making process thus operates purely in public law.

- The right to education in Art 2 of Protocol 1 is not in the nature of a civil right or obligation. In *R (on the Application of B (A Child)) v Head Teacher and Governing Body of Alperton Community School*[34] the court found that an independent appeals panel set up under the School Standards and Framework Act 1998 did not have to comply with the requirements for independence and impartiality in Art 6. This reflected the following view of the European Commission in *Simpson v UK*:[35]

  > Although the notion of a civil right under this provision is autonomous of any domestic law definitions, the Commission considers that for the purposes of the domestic law in question and the Convention, the right not to be denied elementary education falls, in the circumstances of the present case, squarely within the domain of public law, having no private law analogy and no repercussions on private rights or obligations.

- Taxation disputes do not involve the determination of civil rights. They are said to have their origin in the 'specific provisions of public law supporting an economic policy'.[36]

It should be recalled that the purpose of assessing whether a civil right is at stake is in order to anticipate whether the procedural protection offered in Art 6 will be applicable. The content of that protection is examined below.

9.3.2 Is the right recognised in domestic law?

Article 6 is about giving citizens a fair hearing when civil rights are decided. It does not require the state to create any specific civil rights. Nor does it dictate the content of existing rights – it applies to the procedure to be adopted in disputes over the civil rights that already exist. It is often said that it does not affect the substantive law. In *James v United Kingdom*,[37] which concerned the inability of a landlord to challenge applications by his tenants to purchase the freehold of their premises, the European Court stated as follows:

> Article 6 para 1 (Art 6–1) extends only to 'contestations' (disputes) over (civil) 'rights and obligations' which can be said, at least on arguable grounds, to be recognised under domestic law; it does not in itself guarantee any particular content for (civil) 'rights and obligations' in the substantive law of the Contracting States. Confirmation of this analysis is to be found in the act that

34 [2001] EWHC Admin 229; (2001) *The Times*, 8 June.
35 (1989) 64 DR 188.
36 *X v Austria* (1980) 21 DR 246.
37 (1986) 8 EHRR 123.

Article 6 para 1 (Art 6–1) does not require that there be a national court with competence to invalidate or override national law. In the present case, the immediate consequence of the British legislation in issue is that the landlord cannot challenge the tenant's entitlement to acquire the property compulsorily in so far as the acquisition is in conformity with the legislation.[38]

Article 6 will also apply to 'disputes of a "genuine and serious nature" concerning the actual existence of the right as well as to the scope or manner in which it is exercised'.[39] However, once the scope and content of a right has been determined by the courts Art 6 will not insist on any specific content. In *Z v United Kingdom*[40] the European Court altered its previous approach in *Osman v United Kingdom*.[41] In *Osman* the Court held that a rule of common law, which excluded liability for the police in negligence, denied the applicants access to a court. The reason was that the immunity was blanket in nature. In Z, however, the Court decided that the immunity in domestic law (in that case for social services departments) was actually part of the definition of the tort itself, not some extraneous limitation on the right to bring a claim.

In the present case, the court is led to the conclusion that the inability of the applicants to sue the local authority flowed not from immunity but from the applicable principles governing the substantive right of action in domestic law. There was no restriction on access to court ... The applicants may not therefore claim that they were deprived of any right to a determination on the merits of their negligence claims. Their claims were properly and fairly examined in light of the applicable domestic legal principles concerning the tort of negligence ... It is nonetheless the case that the interpretation of domestic law by the House of Lords resulted in the applicants' case being struck out. The tort of negligence was held not to impose a duty of care on the local authority in the exercise of its statutory powers. [The applicant's] experiences were described as 'horrific' by a psychiatrist ... and the court has found that they were victims of a violation of Article 3 ... The applicants are correct in their assertions that the gap they have identified in domestic law is one that gives rise to an issue under the Convention, but in the court's view it is an issue under Article 13, not Article 6 s 1.[42]

It follows that common law privileges, immunities, etc, are permissible under the Human Rights Act in so far as Art 6 is concerned. The Z case did find a violation of Art 13 as a consequence of the immunity but this was due to the fact that there were serious breaches of other articles of the Convention in that case (principally Art 3) that could not be tested in court. The upshot is that it is permissible to provide immunity within the normal civil law so long as there is scope for compensating breach of Convention rights.

---

38   (1986) 8 EHRR 123, at para 81.
39   *Z v United Kingdom* [2001] 2 FCR 246, at para 87.
40   *Ibid.*
41   (2000) 29 EHRR 245.
42   [2001] 2 FCR 246, at paras 99–102.

9.3.3   Is there a real dispute that is being determined?

Article 6 does not apply simply because a party claims that the case involves a determination of a civil right or obligation. As we have seen there must be a dispute (or in the French, *'contestation'*) before Art 6 can be said to be in play. In *Z v United Kingdom*,[43] having re-iterated the requirement for there to be a dispute or *'contestation'* the court went on:

> It will however apply to disputes of a 'genuine and serious nature' concerning the actual existence of the right as well as to the scope or manner in which it is exercised ... In the present case, the applicants were claiming damages on the basis of alleged negligence, a tort in English law which is largely developed through the case law of the domestic courts ... It was in the applicants' case that the domestic courts were called on to rule whether this situation fell within one of the existing categories of negligence liability, or whether any of the categories should be extended to this situation ... The court is satisfied that at the outset of the proceedings there was a serious and genuine dispute about the existence of the right asserted by the applicants under the domestic law of negligence, as shown *inter alia* by the grant of legal aid to the applicants and the decision of the Court of Appeal that their claims merited leave to appeal to the House of Lords. The government's submission that there was no arguable (civil) 'right' for the purposes of Article 6 once the House of Lords had ruled that no duty of care arose has relevance rather to any claims which were lodged or pursued subsequently by other plaintiffs. The House of Lords' decision did not remove, retrospectively, the arguability of the applicants' claims ... In such circumstances, the court finds that the applicants had, on at least arguable grounds, a claim under domestic law.[44]

The court thus went on to address whether Art 6 had been satisfied in the House of Lords proceedings and found that it had. The House of Lords decision clearly establishes for all future cases that there is no civil right at stake and thus prevents future grievances from taking advantage of the Art 6 protection.

Article 6 does not apply in all situations where a civil right is being considered. It only applies if the procedure concerned is 'decisive' for the right or obligation concerned, that is, there must be a determination of the right or obligation. This was explained in a recent case in relation to introductory tenancies:

> So where, as in the case of introductory tenancies, almost the only inhibition on the local authority obtaining a court order is that it must, if requested, have conducted a review in accordance with the terms of the statute, whereupon the court is bound to grant a possession order, it seems to me that the review conducted by the local authority is 'directly decisive' for the right of the local

---

43   [2001] 2 FCR 246.
44   *Ibid*, at paras 87–89.

authority to obtain a possession order and the obligation of the tenant to yield up his or her tenancy. I therefore conclude that Article 6 is engaged.[45]

The requirement for a determination is the reason why not all decisions regarding civil rights or obligations trigger Art 6. A preliminary procedure for the resolution between the parties of their positions in respect of the civil right or obligation will not give rise to Art 6 safeguards even if one of the parties is a public authority. Thus, internal disciplinary procedures in a contract of employment will not engage Art 6. Similarly, university academic investigation panels do not determine the student's civil rights under his or her contract with the institution. In *Fayed v United Kingdom*[46] the European Court held an official investigation into the applicant's business practices did not determine his civil right to a reputation despite the fact that it made findings of dishonesty on his part. There was an important distinction between an investigation, which did not determine civil rights, and an adjudication, which did. This fell into the former category. Even where the public authority terminates its contract with an individual (for example, through termination of employment) Art 6 is not triggered. This is because there is at that stage no dispute or 'contestation' for the Art 6 right to fix upon. When proceedings are issued in a court or tribunal then the right to a fair trial will commence. This is not always the case. We have already seen that civil rights can be at stake in professional disciplinary procedures. This is because although the immediate question that is answered is the charge of indiscipline, the decision may in fact be determinative of the person's right to work in a particular profession.

The requirement for a 'determination' might call into question whether those stages of civil litigation not relating to the central issues of liability and quantum would be covered by the requirement for fairness. Indeed a series of Commission decisions suggested that interlocutory applications and post-judgment enforcement matters are not covered by Art 6.[47] However, the European Court seems to take a more expansive view as to what falls within the concept of 'determination'. For example, in respect of enforcement proceedings the court has stated:

> The court accordingly takes the view ... that the 'enforcement' proceedings were not intended solely to enforce an obligation to pay a fixed amount; they also served to determine important elements of the debt itself ... Those proceedings must therefore be regarded as the second stage of the proceedings

---

45 *R (on the Application of Johns) v Bracknell Forest DC* (2001) 33 HLR 45, *per* Longmore J. He rejected any notion that the court's final order would be the determinative step. The court had no power to second guess the council so to describe that stage, as the decisive step would be artificial. The decision was upheld on appeal: see *McLellan v Bracknell Forest BC* [2001] EWCA 510.

46 (1994) 18 EHRR 393.

47 *X v UK* (1981) 24 DR 57 (interim relief); *Jensen v Denmark* (1991) 68 DR 177 (enforcement of judgments); *Alsterland v Sweden* (1988) 56 DR 229 (award of costs); and *Porter v United Kingdom* (1987) 54 DR 207 (leave to appeal).

> ... It follows that the dispute (contestation) over the applicant's right to damages would only have been resolved by the final decision in the enforcement.[48]

And in respect of costs:

> The Commission in its report found that the costs proceedings were not in any way linked to the substantive dispute between the applicants and their neighbours since the dispute over costs arose after the substantive dispute had been resolved and had no relevance to it ... The court recalls that Article 6 s 1 of the Convention requires that all stages of legal proceedings for the determination of ... civil rights and obligations not excluding stages subsequent to judgment on the merits, be resolved within a reasonable time ... The court observes that the legal costs which formed the subject matter of the proceedings in question were incurred during the resolution of a dispute between neighbours, which undoubtedly involved in the determination of civil rights and obligations.[49]

Early decisions under the Human Rights Act suggest that a similarly broad view of 'determination' will apply in the domestic courts.[50]

9.3.4 Determination of civil rights outside of the court and tribunal system

There is a wide range of situations where officials or administrative bodies determine civil rights. Examples include Housing Benefit Review Boards,[51] reviews of introductory tenancies,[52] licensing decisions[53] and planning determinations.[54] There will be obvious difficulties in such bodies complying with all of the requirements of a fair hearing. For example, many decisions of this nature are internal reviews of executive decisions. They cannot hope to comply with the requirement for independence and impartiality. However, this is not to say that such decisions must therefore amount to a breach of the right to a fair hearing. The Convention is flexible enough to accommodate administrative decisions being taken that affect citizens' civil rights while at the same time requiring conformity with the rule of law. The approach adopted is that either the body itself must comply with Art 6, or there must be

---

48   *Silva Pontes v Portugal* (1994) 18 EHRR 156.

49   *Robins v United Kingdom* (1998) 26 EHRR 527.

50   *Re SK & AK (Children) sub nom Kensington and Chelsea Royal Borough Council v (1) NK (2) SK (3) AK*, Family Division, 20/10/2000.

51   See *R (on the Application of Bewry) v Norwich City Council* [2001] All ER(D) 461 (Jul).

52   See *R (on the Application of Johns) v Bracknell Forest DC* (2001) 33 HLR 45.

53   See *Kingsley v United Kingdom* (2001) *The Times*, 9 January.

54   *Bryan v United Kingdom* (1995) 21 EHRR 342; cf *R v Secretary of State for the Environment, Transport and the Regions ex p Holding and Barnes and Others ('Alconbury')* [2001] EWHL 23; [2001] 2 WLR 1389.

a right of appeal or review to a court or tribunal that complies with Art 6. The court or tribunal must have 'full jurisdiction' in the sense that it can fully review the decision under scrutiny. In one sense these questions might seem to be outside of the confines of this book, given its focus on use of the Convention in the courts. The whole point in issue here is the fact that the determination takes place outside of the court or tribunal. Nevertheless, we deal with it briefly below because advocates often find themselves representing clients before diverse administrative bodies. Secondly, it is bound to affect the advice given to clients whose civil rights are affected or to public authority clients who seek to make their procedures Convention compliant.

There is some uncertainty as to what is required for a court to be of full jurisdiction. In *W v United Kingdom*[55] the European Court found that judicial review was insufficient as the court could not review the merits of a decision but would confine itself to ensuring that the council had not acted illegally, unreasonably or unfairly. In the later case of *Bryan v United Kingdom*[56] the European Court found that where there was no dispute as to the facts found by a planning inspector and the applicant's challenge was addressed point by point on a statutory appeal, albeit that the appeal was not on the merits of the case, there was sufficient fairness to comply with Art 6. *Bryan* was followed in *Stefan v United Kingdom*[57] where the Commission held that the determination by a regulatory body that the applicant was not a fit and proper person to be registered medical practitioner was subject to a court of full jurisdiction on an appeal on a point of law. It was also followed in *X v United Kingdom*[58] where the Commission held that the availability of judicial review of a decision that the applicant was not a fit and proper person to be an executive officer of an insurance company satisfied the requirement for a court of full jurisdiction. *Bryan* was distinguished in *Kingsley v United Kingdom*[59] where the European Court held that if bias were alleged against the decision-maker (the Gaming Board) judicial review was insufficient as the only remedy would be to send the case back to the same body, perpetuating the problem that led to the dispute in the first place.

Post-HRA decisions have tended to emphasise the *Bryan v United Kingdom* approach so that administrative decisions, so long as they satisfy the fairness standards applied on a judicial review, will not violate Art 6 even though they determine civil rights. In *R (on the Application of Johns) v Bracknell Forest DC*[60] the Divisional Court held that the availability of judicial review of a council

---

55 (1987) 10 EHRR 29.
56 (1995) 21 EHRR 342.
57 (1997) 25 EHRR CD 130.
58 (1998) 25 EHRR CD 88.
59 (2001) *The Times*, 9 January.
60 (2001) 33 HLR 45.

review relating to termination of an introductory tenancy was Convention-compliant. Longmore J said that the fact the court could not take the decision for itself was not fatal:

> In an appropriate case, the court could order that the fresh review be conducted by a different reviewing officer from the officer who conducted the first review and, if necessary, an officer senior to the first officer. [The *Kingsley* principle] can only apply in cases where the court concludes that there has been an actual lack of impartiality as opposed to merely the appearance of it.[61]

In *Alconbury*[62] the House of Lords had to deal with challenges to the call in procedure adopted by the government in planning matters. The House decided that the procedure was compatible with Art 6 despite no appeal to a court on the merits of the decision taken. Judicial review was said to be sufficient to amount to review by a court of 'full jurisdiction'.

Lord Hoffman said as follows:

> The reference to 'full jurisdiction' has been frequently cited in subsequent cases and sometimes relied upon in argument as if it were authority for saying that a policy decision affecting civil rights by an administrator who does not comply with Article 6(1) has to be reviewable on its merits by an independent and impartial tribunal. It was certainly so relied upon by counsel for the respondents in these appeals. But subsequent European authority shows that 'full jurisdiction' does not mean full decision-making power. It means full jurisdiction to deal with the case, as the nature of the decision requires.[63]

His Lordship said that the Divisional Court had seriously misunderstood the *Bryan* decision when if found a breach of Art 6. He emphasised the fact that the court in *Bryan* looked at the nature of the administrative procedure in deciding whether a subsequent review by a court on a point of law amounted to full jurisdiction:

> ... in assessing the sufficiency of the review available to Mr Bryan on appeal to the High Court, it is necessary to have regard to matters such as the subject matter of the decision appealed against, the manner in which that decision was arrived at, and the content of the dispute, including the desired and actual grounds of appeal.[64]

It followed, according to Lord Hoffman, that the safeguards available on the planning procedure in question were highly relevant in determining whether limited review by the courts was adequate to amount to full jurisdiction. All the Law Lords agreed that it was.

---

61 (2001) 33 HLR 45, para 36. This was followed, post-*Alconbury*, on appeal: *McLellan v Bracknell Forest BC* [2001] EWCA 510.
62 [2001] EWHL 23; [2001] 2 WLR 1389.
63 *Ibid*, at para 87.
64 (1995) 21 EHRR 342, at para 44.

9.4 WHAT CONSTITUTES A FAIR CIVIL TRIAL?

Article 6(1) provides, where relevant, as follows:

> In the determination of his civil rights and obligations ... everyone is entitled to a fair and public hearing within a reasonable time by an independent and impartial tribunal established by law.

9.4.1 Right to bring proceedings and restrictions thereon

The right of access to a court is not explicit in Art 6 but is an implied right. The crucial question was expressed as follows in *Golder v United Kingdom*:[65]

> Is Article 6 para 1 limited to guaranteeing in substance the right to a fair trial in legal proceedings, which are already pending, or does it in addition secure a right of access to the courts for every person wishing to commence an action in order to have his civil rights and obligations determined?

The court answered this by emphatically supporting the need for a right of access to the courts:

> Were Article 6 para 1 to be understood as concerning exclusively the conduct of an action, which had already been initiated before a court, a Contracting State could, without acting in breach of that text, do away with its courts, or take away their jurisdiction to determine certain classes of civil actions and entrust it to organs dependent on the government. Such assumptions, indissociable from a danger of arbitrary power, would have serious consequences, which are repugnant to the aforementioned principles, and which the court cannot overlook ... It would be inconceivable, in the opinion of the court, that Article 6 para 1 should describe in detail the procedural guarantees afforded to parties in a pending lawsuit and should not first protect that which alone makes it in fact possible to benefit from such guarantees, that is, access to a court. The fair, public and expeditious characteristics of judicial proceedings are of no value at all if there are no judicial proceedings.[66]

The right of access to the court is not an absolute right, however. It may be subject to restrictions that are proportionate and serve a legitimate aim. The court in *Golder* accepted that the right, being implied, could also be subject to implied limitations. It follows that restrictions on bringing or defending proceedings are not in principle in violation of the right of access to a court. The following examples illustrative the approach of the courts but there are others.[67]

---

65 (1975) 1 EHRR 524.
66 *Ibid*, at para 35.
67 For example, restrictions on proceedings by bankrupts.

9.4.1.1 Vexatious litigants

In *Ebert v Official Receiver*[68] the Court of Appeal said that the procedures in s 42 of the Supreme Court Act 1981 for obtaining civil procedure orders restricting the ability of vexatious litigants to bring proceedings were detailed and elaborate and respected the important Convention principle that procedures concerning the assertion of rights should be under judicial rather than administrative control. They also satisfied the notion that any order inhibiting a citizen's freedoms should not be made without detailed enquiry and that the citizen should be able to seek review of the issues in the context of new facts and of new complaints that he wished to make. Their Lordships found that domestic practice had been approved by the Commission in *H v United Kingdom*[69] and was wholly consistent with the right of access to a court explained in *Golder v United Kingdom*. The courts were a finite resource and the orders were a proportionate response in order to ensure they were not monopolised by a few people to the detriment of the public.[70]

9.4.1.2 Security for costs

In *Tolstoy Miloslavsky v United Kingdom*[71] the European Court considered whether an order that the appellant pay into court a sum of £125,000 as security for costs of a libel appeal was a permissible restriction on the right of access to the courts. It decided that the amount was proportionate given the need to preserve the position of the respondent, should the appeal fail, the fact that there was no evidence he could not have secured the amount, given time and that the Court of Appeal had carefully considered whether the sum would deny him justice and whether he had any reasonable prospects of success.

In *Nasser v United Bank of Kuwait*[72] the Court of Appeal said that the courts' decisions in respect of security for costs would have to be revisited in light of the Convention principles. The importance of access to the courts, including appeal courts, meant that a genuine claim, at least one with apparent prospects, should not be stifled by a requirement to put up security that an appellant could not provide. In addition, the courts should be careful not to discriminate against litigants on the basis that they reside outside of the court's jurisdiction and the enforcement mechanisms of international agreements. To do so would be to breach their right of access to a court in conjunction with Art 14. The case indicates a greater sensitivity to the

---

68 [2001] EWCA Civ 340; (2001) *The Independent*, 21 March.
69 (1985) 45 D & R 281.
70 Their Lordships also approved the decision of the Divisional Court in *HM Attorney General v Covey* (2001) *The Times*, 2 March.
71 (1995) 20 EHRR 442.
72 [2001] EWCA Civ 556.

potentially stifling effect of a significant order of security for costs and the need to be careful to achieve an amount within the reach of the litigant, if this is consistent with adequate security.

9.4.1.3 Limitation periods and qualifying periods

The purpose of limitation periods is to ensure legal certainty and finality and to protect defendants from stale claims.[73] They are in principle acceptable under Art 6 so long as they operate in a proportionate manner. A qualifying period, such as that for unfair dismissal, protects potential defendants from claims until employees have satisfied a certain period of time within the workplace and the relationship can reasonably be seen to be a long-term one.

In *Family Housing Association v Donellan*[74] the High Court was faced with an attack on the real property limitation period in ss 15 and 17 of the Limitation Act 1980. It held that where the law prescribed limitation rules that were proportionate and not so restrictive as to impair the very essence of the right to bring his case to court, it did not infringe the right to a fair trial. The 1980 Act period of 12 years clearly gave the title holder a reasonable opportunity to bring a claim asserting his ownership and stop the period of adverse possession running.[75]

In *Cachia v Faluyi*[76] the Court of Appeal decided that the apparent limitation in the Fatal Accidents Act 1976 would be re-interpreted under s 3 of the Human Rights Act so that it presented no artificial bar to a claim where a writ had been issued but not served, and a second writ was issued within the primary limitation period. To do otherwise would be to violate the rights of children of a deceased victim of a road traffic accident of access to the court.

9.4.2 Legal aid

There is no explicit right to legal aid in Art 6 except where the proceedings involve the determination of a criminal charge. Thus, if there is to be a right to legal aid it must be implied into the article. The only circumstances in which this might be done are where without representation the litigant cannot secure effective access to the court. In *Airey v Ireland*[77] the European Court stated that the right of access must be practical and effective not illusory. The question was whether the applicant could have presented her case 'properly and satisfactorily without representation. In the circumstances of the case – judicial

---

73 See *Stubbings v United Kingdom* (1996) 23 EHRR 213.
74 [2001] All ER(D) 156 (Jul).
75 See also *Pye v Graham* [2001] EWCA Civ 117; [2001] HRLR 27.
76 [2001] EWCA Civ 998; [2001] All ER(D) 299 (Jun).
77 (1979) 2 EHRR 305.

separation proceedings that were no uncomplicated, her emotional involvement and the complex factual disputes it decided that without legal representation her right of access to the court was not effective.

However, it said that this conclusion:

> ... does not hold good for all cases concerning 'civil rights and obligations' or for everyone involved therein. In certain eventualities, the possibility of appearing before a court in person, even without a lawyer's assistance, will meet the requirements of Article 6 ... much must depend on the particular circumstances. In addition, whilst Article 6 para 1 guarantees to litigants an effective right of access to the courts for the determination of their 'civil rights and obligations', it leaves to the State a free choice of the means to be used towards this end. The institution of a legal aid scheme ... constitutes one of those means but there are others such as, for example, a simplification of procedure.[78]

It follows that conditional fee arrangements and legal insurance may well satisfy the requirements of Art 6 for effective access. The Legal Services Commission Funding Code permits funding of representation in the courts but generally not in tribunals.[79] It is, though, possible for the Lord Chancellor to authorise the funding of particular cases in exceptional circumstances under s 6(8)(b) of the Access to Justice Act 1999.

The Legal Services Commission Funding Code Guidance states as follows:

> Article 6 is directly relevant to decision-making under the Funding Code. Indeed it is an aim of the Access to Justice Act 1999, and the rules of the Funding Code in particular, to ensure that individuals have the opportunity of a fair hearing in the determination of their civil rights. The Funding Code Criteria seek to achieve this for cases which have sufficient merit to justify public funding ... where the Commission has a discretion, for example whether funding should be requested for a case under s 6(8)(b) of the 1999 Act, the Commission will take into account the Article 6 implications for the individual client. It is therefore material to consider when exercising any discretion whether, without public funding, the individual would be deprived of a fair hearing.[80]

Cases that raise 'significant human rights issues' are priority area under the Code. Such cases may be funded even if prospects of success are only borderline. To be significant, the ECHR issues must be an important part of the case, which are likely to make a difference to its outcome. It is not necessary to show that, without the human rights arguments, the case would

---

78 (1979) 2 EHRR 305, at para 26.

79 There are exceptions for the Protection of Children Tribunal, the Special Commissioners of Income Tax, the VAT and Duties Tribunal and the Proscribed Organisations Appeal Commission – see Lord Chancellor's Direction under s 6(8) of the Access to Justice Act 1999, 2 April 2001.

80 LSC Funding Code Guidance, para 6.5(1)(a). Available on the Commission's website: www.legalservices.gov.uk.

fail. However, a case will not raise significant human rights issues if are included as an afterthought to bolster the claim or are unlikely to carry weight with the court. The Commission also takes into account the prospects of success of the argument that there has been a breach of human rights. There must be a reasonable case (at least borderline) that human rights have been breached.[81]

9.4.3 Right to a public hearing

In addition to the general requirement that a hearing be in public, Art 6(1) goes on to provide that:

> ... judgment shall be pronounced publicly but the press and public may by excluded from all or part of the trial in the interests of morals, public order or national security in a democratic society, where the interests of juveniles or the protection of the private life of the parties so require, or to the extent strictly necessary in the opinion of the court in special circumstances where publicity would prejudice the interests of justice.

The right to a public hearing is thus expressly qualified but the holding of proceedings in private is not something that should be countenanced lightly. It must be a proportionate response to one of the justifications specified. In *Scarth v United Kingdom*[82] the holding of a small claim 'arbitration' in the county court in private was found to violate the applicant's right to trial in public. The Civil Procedure Rules took account of this decision in creating a presumption that all claims, including small claims track cases are held in public. In *Diennet v France*[83] the court suggested that a court or tribunal should sit in public until a matter arises that requires confidentiality. It deprecated private hearings being used as an administrative convenience.

In *Secretary of State for Defence v Times Newspapers Ltd and Another*[84] the High Court was faced with a conflict between the principle of open justice on the one hand and a risk to life and limb on the other. *The Times* argued that the holding of a civil case against a former soldier in private was a violation of Art 6. In fact there was no public record of the case at all and all of the documentation was lodged with the Treasury Solicitor. The paper sought orders to provide for a date when the material could become public or a date on which the Secretary of State should have to justify the continuance of the secrecy. It also sought a declaration that the practice of holding such secret hearings was contrary to s 6 of the Human Rights Act 1998. The court held that open justice was an overriding principle but that it had to give way to the

---

81   *Ibid*, at para 6.6.
82   [1999] EHRLR 66.
83   (1995) 21 EHRR 554.
84   QBD, Lawtel 29/3/2001.

interests of national security, the right to life and the right to be protected against torture and/or inhuman or degrading treatment. Nevertheless, the proceedings ought to have commenced in open court. Any redactions of documents should be approved by the judge. The court should be particularly careful to ensure that the wording of the orders was no wider than was necessary and proportionate. Orders departing from the principle of open justice should not usually be open-ended but were justified in this particular case.

9.4.4 Right to trial within a reasonable time

In civil proceedings time generally runs from the date of commencement of proceedings to the date of final determination, which will include enforcement.

In *Glaser v United Kingdom*[85] the European Court dealt with an allegation that the enforcement of a contact order relating to his children was unreasonably long (four years) so as to breach his right to trial within a reasonable time. The court stated as follows:

> The reasonableness of the length of proceedings is to be considered in the light of the criteria laid down in the court's case law, in particular the complexity of the case, the conduct of the applicant and that of the relevant authorities. On the latter point, the importance of what is at stake for the applicant in the litigation has also to be taken into account. It is, in particular, essential that custody and contact cases be dealt with speedily.[86]

In the circumstances the court thought that the matter was complicated by the fact that an English order was sought to be enforced in a Scottish court, that although there had been some delay on the part of the authorities, they had generally acted with due diligence and the fact that the applicant himself had contributed to some of the delay through failing to request hearings promptly, agreeing to lengthy adjournments and asking for inappropriate orders.

Issues for advocates: criteria for assessing delay

The case of *Glaser* neatly illustrates the criteria that will be addressed by the courts in considering delay. They may be summarised as follows:

The nature of the right in issue. The courts will consider what is at stake for the litigant and certain interests will require a speedier resolution than others. Custody and contact issues relating to children are by their nature

---

85 *Glaser v United Kingdom* [2001] 1 FLR 153.
86 *Ibid*, at para 93.

matters that ought to be dealt with quickly as delay can result in the *de facto* determination of the issue prior to the hearing.[87]

The complexity of the case in terms of factual disputes, legal difficulty and any procedural obstacles, such as the cross-border enforcement problems encountered in *Glaser*.

The conduct of the courts and other public authorities. Unexplained delay on the part of the court, court staff, and those responsible for enforcing judgments will count against the authorities. Justifications for delay will obviously be viewed in light of the complexity mentioned in the previous paragraph.

The conduct of the alleged victim. This will include his or her legal representatives. If he or she is found to be responsible for any of the delay this will be a factor suggesting that there is no unreasonable delay. The court does not appear to approach the situation by simply deducting the time that the alleged victim is responsible for from the overall period but rather permits such conduct to be viewed in the round in deciding whether delay in achieving a final determination is unreasonable.

9.4.5 Independence and impartiality

The requirements of independence and impartiality are the same in respect of civil and criminal proceedings. Detailed consideration has been given to its implication for criminal trials in Chapter 8. Here we examine the general principles underlying the right. The requirements of the Convention were summarised by the European Court in *Findlay v United Kingdom*[88] as follows:

> The court recalls that in order to establish whether a tribunal can be considered as 'independent', regard must be had *inter alia* to the manner of appointment of its members and their term of office, the existence of guarantees against outside pressures and the question whether the body presents an appearance of independence.

> As to the question of 'impartiality', there are two aspects to this requirement. First, the tribunal must be subjectively free of personal prejudice or bias. Secondly, it must also be impartial from an objective viewpoint, that is, it must offer sufficient guarantees to exclude any legitimate doubt in this respect.[89]

In *Locabail (UK) Ltd v Bayfield Properties Ltd*[90] the Court of Appeal explained in more detail the importance of the Convention right to an impartial tribunal:

---

87 In *H v United Kingdom* (1988) 10 EHRR 95 the court found a violation in respect of child care proceedings lasting for over two and a half years.

88 (1997) 24 EHRR 221.

89 *Ibid*, at para 73.

90 [2000] QB 451.

In determination of their rights and liabilities, civil or criminal, everyone is entitled to a fair hearing by an impartial tribunal. That right, guaranteed by the European Convention for the Protection of Human Rights and Fundamental Freedoms, is properly described as fundamental. The reason is obvious. All legal arbiters are bound to apply the law, as they understand it to the facts of individual cases as they find them. They must do so without fear or favour, affection or ill will, that is, without partiality or prejudice. Justice is portrayed as blind not because she ignores the facts and circumstances of individual cases but because she shuts her eyes to all considerations extraneous to the particular case.

Any judge (for convenience, we shall in this judgment use the term 'judge' to embrace every judicial decision-maker, whether judge, lay justice or juror) who allows any judicial decision to be influenced by partiality or prejudice deprives the litigant of the important right to which we have referred and violates one of the most fundamental principles underlying the administration of justice. Where in any particular case the existence of such partiality or prejudice is actually shown, the litigant has irresistible grounds for objecting to the trial of the case by that judge (if the objection is made before the hearing) or for applying to set aside any judgment given. Such objections and applications based on what, in the case law, is called 'actual bias' are very rare, partly (as we trust) because the existence of actual bias is very rare, but partly for other reasons also. The proof of actual bias is very difficult, because the law does not countenance the questioning of a judge about extraneous influences affecting his mind; and the policy of the common law is to protect litigants who can discharge the lesser burden of showing a real danger of bias without requiring them to show that such bias actually exists.[91]

This was said by the Privy Council in *Millar v Procurator Fiscal, Elgin*[92] to apply equally to the requirement for independence and to justify the view that unless the right was waived it could not be compromised or eroded. Lord Bingham put it in the following terms:

There are few, if any, convention rights of more practical importance to the citizen than the right to a fair trial. The conduct of trials at all stages by an independent and impartial tribunal is in my view recognised by the convention and the authorities, subject to waiver where that is permissible, as a necessary although not a sufficient safeguard of the citizen's right to a fair trial. It is a safeguard, which should not, least of all in the criminal field, be weakened or diluted, whatever the administrative consequences.[93]

Thus the right to an independent and impartial tribunal is a pre-condition of a fair trial. Unlike many other aspects of the Art 6 guarantee, it cannot be balanced against any countervailing public interest.

---

91 *Ibid*, at pp 471–72.
92 [2001] UKPC D4; (2001) *The Times*, 27 July.
93 *Ibid*, at para 26.

9.4.6 The right to participate effectively at a hearing

This generic heading identifies a bundle of rights that have been implied into Art 6 in the civil context including equality of arms, the right to an adversarial hearing, and disclosure of relevant material.

9.4.6.1 Equality of arms

Central to the notion of a fair trial is the idea that each party will have an equal opportunity to present his or her case. No party ought to be permitted to dominate the proceedings at the expense of others. The principle is termed 'equality of arms' and has been recognised on numerous occasions. In *Dombo Beheer BV v Netherlands*[94] the European Court dealt with a case where the applicant company's representative at a meeting with a bank was not permitted to give evidence because he was 'identified with the applicant company' whereas the bank's representative was permitted to give evidence. The court said:

> ... certain principles concerning the notion of a 'fair hearing' in cases concerning civil rights and obligations emerge from the court's case law. Most significantly for the present case, it is clear that the requirement of 'equality of arms', in the sense of a 'fair balance' between the parties, applies in principle to such cases as well as to criminal cases ... The court agrees with the Commission that as regards litigation involving opposing private interests, 'equality of arms' implies that each party must be afforded a reasonable opportunity to present his case – including his evidence – under conditions that do not place him at a substantial disadvantage vis à vis his opponent. It is left to the national authorities to ensure in each individual case that the requirements of a 'fair hearing' are met.

The inequality inherent in the proceedings meant that there had been a breach of Art 6. The principle is a simple one and is applicable across a wide range of situations requiring equal treatment between the parties. It has also led the court to import more specific guarantees into Art 6.

R (on the Application of King) v Isleworth Crown Court[95] is a criminal case but the lesson it offers to courts is relevant to civil litigation too. The claimant was seeking a judicial review of the refusal of the Crown Court to quash his conviction for minor offences under the Housing Act 1985. He had a reduced mental capacity due to a stroke. Including less ability with concentration, short-term memory, ability to assimilate thoughts and to express himself succinctly and accurately. Having waited all day, he informed the judge of his medical condition, and asked for an adjournment. He alleged that he was pressurised by the judge to avoid going over matters that he thought were

---

94   (1994) 18 EHRR 213.
95   [2001] EHLR 14.

relevant. He submitted that he had been prevented from presenting his appeal effectively.

The High Court held that the hearing had amounted to a breach of the appellant's right to a fair trial. It acknowledged the need to conduct business economically and efficiently, but said that it was very important that court proceedings should not only be fair, but should also be seen to be fair. Courts had to be seen to be sensitive to difficulties endured by some court users. The case illustrates the need for judges to be aware of the need to recognise and accommodate special needs where possible. This need is particularly acute in cases like this one where the vulnerable person is representing him or herself. There is now an *Equal Treatment Bench Book* that may be referred to in appropriate circumstances.

The Court of Appeal recently held that there was no right to withhold a defence in civil proceedings on the basis that the answer may incriminate the civil defendant.[95a] In deciding whether the defence would be thereby constrained from putting forward a defence, the court said that the following considerations were relevant:

(i) there was no right to silence in civil proceedings;

(ii) the defence was unlikely to prejudice the criminal proceedings given the need for early defence disclosure in criminal cases; and

(iii) a positive defence was likely to exculpate rather than incriminate.

9.4.6.2 *The right to an adversarial hearing*

This is a specific aspect of equality of arms. It requires that each party must be allowed to know and comment on all the evidence and legal submissions adduced by the other parties so as to try to influence the court's decision. The principle applies similarly if submissions are made to the court by non-parties such as clerks, lower courts, those seeking to intervene or make legal points as interested parties. The principal duty will be on the court to ensure that each party has copies of any documents or other submissions received that seek to influence the decision of the court but advocates will in appropriate cases wish to request copies of such documents or confirmation that none exist.

As part of this right, each party ought to be given a fair opportunity to address the court. In *Attorney General v Covey*[96] the Court of Appeal said that although Art 6 demanded a fair and reasonable opportunity to address the court, it did not involve an unlimited and uncontrolled opportunity. The appellant's opportunity to address the court had been restricted by the trial judge in an application for a civil proceedings order preventing him from instituting proceedings as a vexatious litigant. Nevertheless, he had ample opportunity to make points in his favour.

95a *V v C*, Lawtel 16/10/2001.
96 (2001) *The Times*, 2 March.

408

A fair civil trial does not necessarily require that litigants be given an opportunity to cross-examine witnesses. This should be permitted if the witness is actually called to give evidence, but there is no requirement equivalent to Art 6(3)(d) restricting the possibility of hearsay evidence. In *Clingham v Kensington and Chelsea RLBC*[97] the court was dealing with anti-social behaviour proceedings. The appellant appealed against the decision of a magistrate to admit evidence from police officers as to complaints received about the appellant from neighbours and others living in his community about anti-social behaviour on his part. The court proceeded on the basis that the proceedings were civil in nature.[98] It held that there was nothing in Art 6 to require the automatic exclusion of hearsay in civil proceedings. The fact that there was no possibility of cross-examination did not automatically result in an unfair trial. It was a matter that could properly be taken into account by the court in weighing the evidence.

9.4.6.3 The right to disclosure

Without adequate disclosure in advance of a hearing the effective participation of parties is prejudiced. The European Court has accepted that disclosure of relevant information is essential for the equality of arms principle to be satisfied. For example, in *McMichael v United Kingdom*[99] the court considered an allegation that there had been a breach of Art 6 by reason of the failure to disclose social reports updating the information on the applicant's child, reviewing the history of the case and making recommendations. The court found that despite the fact that the chairman of the hearing did inform her of the substance of the documents the actual documents ought to have been disclosed:

> ... notwithstanding the special characteristics of the adjudication to be made, as a matter of general principle the right to a fair – adversarial – trial 'means the opportunity to have knowledge of and comment on the observations filed or evidence adduced by the other party' ... In the context of the present case, the lack of disclosure of such vital documents as social reports is capable of affecting the ability of participating parents not only to influence the outcome of the children's hearing in question but also to assess their prospects of making an appeal to the Sheriff Court.

It is clear that disclosure of sensitive material may be withheld in the civil courts in the public interest in the same way as it may be in the criminal courts, but in the absence of such considerations disclosure should always be made. The s 6 duty also affects the court's exercise of its powers to order disclosure in civil proceedings. Failure to order disclosure of material that is required in order to ensure a fair trial will amount to an unlawful act under s 6.

---

97 [2001] EWHC Admin 1; (2001) 165 JP 322.
98 See Chapter 7, para 7.2.2.1 and the discussion of *R (on the Application of M (A Child)) v Manchester Crown Court (Court of Appeal)* [2001] EWCA Civ 281; [2001] 1 WLR 1085.
99 (1995) 20 EHRR 205.

9.4.7 A right to reasons

In *Hiro Balani v Spain*[100] the court stated as follows:

> The court reiterates that Article 6 para 1 (Art 6–1) obliges the courts to give reasons for their judgments, but cannot be understood as requiring a detailed answer to every argument ... The extent to which this duty to give reasons applies may vary according to the nature of the decision. It is moreover necessary to take into account, *inter alia*, the diversity of the submissions that a litigant may bring before the courts and the differences existing in the Contracting States with regard to statutory provisions, customary rules, legal opinion and the presentation and drafting of judgments. That is why the question whether a court has failed to fulfil the obligation to state reasons, deriving from Article 6 (Art 6) of the Convention, can only be determined in the light of the circumstances of the case.

This amounts to a general right to have a reasoned decision from the court or tribunal dealing with the case. Advocates who intend to appeal, should a case be decided adverse to their client's interests, will be likely seek a reasoned decision from the court and will raise any contentious points in some detail in order to encourage the court to provide detailed reasons. The failure of a court or tribunal to deal with an important part of a submission is likely to breach Art 6.[101]

9.5 SPECIFIC ISSUES RELATING TO TRIBUNALS

Some tribunals clearly determine civil rights and obligations, for example the employment tribunal. Some do not, for example, the Immigration Appeal Tribunal and the Mental Health Review Tribunal but are subject to their own rules of procedural fairness and to natural justice. Some tribunals are less clear cut, for example, the Social Security Commissioners, tax commissioners and the VAT and Duties Tribunal. In any event, the tribunals are not immune from determining Convention points as any litigant can rely on the Convention rights in any legal proceedings. This includes proceedings before a tribunal. Some tribunals have anticipated this with guidance to Chairs and to advocates.[102]

---

100 (1995) 19 EHRR 566.

101 It should be recalled that the remedy for such a breach is an appeal or judicial review. There is no right to damages against a judicial act done in good faith, apart from to compensate where required by Art 5(5): s 9(3).

102 For example, the Mental Health Review Tribunals, *Human Rights Law – Guidance for Mental Health Review Tribunals*, September 2000; Appeals Service President's Protocol No 6, 14 July 2000; *Practice Direction issued by the President of the VAT and Duties Tribunals and the Presiding Special Commissioner* – October 2000.

9.5.1 Is the tribunal bound by the Convention?

A basic reading of the Human Rights Act reveals that tribunals are bound by the provisions of the Act in exactly the same way as courts. The following summary may be of some assistance:

- Tribunals are subject to the requirement to take into account Strasbourg case law under s 2.

- Section 3 specifies neither courts nor tribunals but simply requires all legislation to be read and given effect compatibly with the Convention if possible. It clearly applies to tribunals.

- Tribunals are not able to make declarations of incompatibility under s 4.

- Tribunals are public authorities for the purpose of s 6(3)(a). They are therefore bound by the s 6 duty to act compatibly with Convention rights.

- In s 7, victims can rely on Convention rights in legal proceedings. 'Legal proceedings' includes proceedings brought by or at the instigation of a public authority and an appeal against the decision of a court or tribunal.[102a]

- In s 8 all references to a court include a tribunal. A tribunal may therefore grant any remedy for breach of Convention rights within its powers if it considers it to be just and equitable. It may only grant damages if it is empowered to grant compensation in civil proceedings.

- In s 9, all references to a court include a tribunal. Thus the protection for judicial acts applies to the judicial act of a tribunal and includes an act done by or on behalf of a tribunal member.

- In s 11, a person's right to make any claim or bring any proceedings, which could be brought apart from, ss 7 to 9 include tribunal proceedings.

- The special provisions in relation to freedom of expression and freedom of religion in ss 12 and 13 apply equally to tribunals as they do to courts.

9.5.2 Delay in tribunals

Tribunals are subject to the same requirements to hold a hearing within a reasonable time as any other court under Art 6. However, there is one situation where a tribunal is subject to a more rigorous requirement than that required under Art 6. The Mental Health Review Tribunal determines whether detained patients can be discharged from hospital. The Court of Appeal has recently reviewed policies relating to listing hearings and found them to be wanting. In *R (on the Application of C) v Mental Health Review*

102a The Employment Appeal Tribunal has recently ruled that the informality at tribunal hearings was geared towards assisting and encouraging litigants in person. It followed that the lack of representation could not of itself lead to inequality of arms: *Dr Uruakpa v Royal College of Veterinary Surgeons*, Lawtel 26/10/2001.

Tribunal[103] the policy of listing restricted patients' applications for discharge eight weeks following the application was unlawful. It was borne of administrative convenience rather than necessity and would undoubtedly lead to breaches of the requirement in Art 5(4) to review the lawfulness of detention 'speedily'.

9.5.3 Need for advance notification despite non-applicability of CPR requirements

If an advocate is going to raise Convention arguments and case law at a tribunal hearing it makes sense to follow the Practice Direction to CPR Pt 39 regarding exchange of authorities.[104] A number of tribunals already request such exchange and some have formally adopted the CPR approach but in any event it reflects good practice and is more likely to lead to a well-informed hearing. The relevant extract is set out here for convenience:

> **Practice Direction: (CPR PD 39): (Miscellaneous Provisions Relating to Hearings)**
>
> …
>
> 8.1 If it is necessary for a party to give evidence at a hearing of an authority referred to in s 2 of the Human Rights Act 1998
>
> > (1) the authority to be cited should be an authoritative and complete report; and
> >
> > (2) the party must give to the court and any other party a list of the authorities he intends to cite and copies of the reports not less than three days before the hearing.

9.5.4 Reacting to decisions in higher courts

In *R (on the Application of H) v Mental Health Review Tribunal North and East London Region*[105] the Court of Appeal held that provisions of the Mental Health Act were incompatible with the patient's right to liberty under Art 5 in that the burden of proof was, according to the statutory test, placed upon the patient as opposed to the state. A declaration of incompatibility was granted and tribunals were left having to enforce a law that was not compatible with the Convention. However, this did not mean that all decisions under s 72/73 amounted to a violation. As the Court of Appeal pointed out, common practice was for tribunals to make positive findings that the criteria for

---

103 [2001] EWCA Civ 1110; [2001] All ER(D) 24 (Jul).

104 See Chapter 2, para 2.10.2.

105 [2001] EWCA Civ 415; [2001] HRLR 36.

detention still applied and to record their decision in accordance with those findings. If they did this they would not, despite the incompatibility of the statutory test, breach the patient's Convention right to liberty. They would effectively be finding that the state had satisfied the burden of proof that the Convention requires. Thus guidance has been issued to tribunals seeking to ensure a uniform approach to discharge decisions.[106]

9.5.5   Limitations regarding remedies

The case of *Younas v Chief Constable Thames Valley Police*[107] in the Employment Appeal Tribunal illustrates the limitation on the powers of the Employment Tribunal and informs advocates about the appropriate strategy to adopt when seeking to challenge defects in the law in tribunals. The applicant police officer was prevented by the Employment Rights Act 1996 from bringing a claim for unfair dismissal. He sought an indefinite adjournment from the tribunal on the basis that the provision may be amended at some point in the future so that he would then be able to pursue his claim. The EAT pointed out that the tribunal had no power to make any declaration of incompatibility and must apply the law as it stands currently, including the exclusion on police officers. The appropriate strategy in such a case would seem to be to ask the tribunal to go through the motions of rejecting the claim so that an application for a declaration of incompatibility may be made. Note that the EAT does not have the power to make such a declaration either and so the preferred route would be an application for judicial review of the tribunal decision.

---

106 Department of Health, *Guidance to Chairmen of Mental Health Review Tribunals*, 5 April 2001, discussed further in Chapter 5, para 5.5.2.
107 [2001] All ER(D) 14 (Jul).

INDEX

Index